To Ian   With best wishes

CW00701536

From one Local Historian, ... survivor of
Southampton Institute, to another.
            RESPECT!

July 2008

Aristocrat
And
Regicide

The Life And Times Of
Thomas, Lord Grey Of Groby
The Ermine Unicorn
(1623 - 1657)

By

Jeff Richards

New Millennium
192 Kennington Road, London SE11 4LD

Copyright © 2000 Jeff Richards

All rights reserved. No part of this publication may be
reproduced in any form, except for the purposes
of review, without prior written permission
from the copyright owner.

The moral right of Jeff Richards to be indentified as the
author of this work, except where otherwise acknowledged,
has been asserted by him in accordance with the
Copyright, Designs and Patents Act 1988.

British Library Cataloguing in Publication Data.
A catalogue record for this book is available
from the British Library.

Printed by
Morgan Technical Books Ltd., Wotton-under-Edge, Glos.
Issued by New Millennium*
ISBN 1 85845 270 8
*An imprint of The Professional Authors' & Publishers' Association

DEDICATION

This book is dedicated to my parents, Clarence and Alice Richards,
who first awoke my interest in the
Greys of Groby and Bradgate.

ACKNOWLEDGEMENTS

This book owes much to the advice, assistance and support of others. In particular, I am indebted to the following people :-

Martyn Bennett
David Fleming
The Denbighs of Newnham Paddox, Warwickshire
The Spencers of Althorp, Northamptonshire

and to the following organisations :-

Ashmolean Museum Oxford
Courtauld Institute of Art University of London
Leicester Museum Service
Leicester Reference Library
Leicestershire County Record Office
National Portrait Gallery
National Trust (Durham Massey Collection)
Warwickshire County Record Office

In particular I should like to thank Alastair Laing, Adviser on Pictures and Sculpture to the National Trust, for his help regarding the portraits of members of the Grey family.

I would also like to record my appreciation to Sandy Harlow, Carol Ennew and Sue Fricker for word processing the text, and finally I must thank my wife Janet, for her on-going support and encouragement over the many years it has taken to produce this work.

CONTENTS

DEDICATION iii

ACKNOWLEDGEMENTS v

CONTENTS vii

LIST OF ILLUSTRATIONS ix

INTRODUCTION xi

NOTES TO INTRODUCTION... xv

CHAPTER ONE   THE GREYS OF GROBY, BRADGATE AND
                LEICESTERSHIRE 1

CHAPTER TWO   INTO THE STORM: FROM YOUNG MP
                TO EDGEHILL FIELD (1640 - 1642) 43

CHAPTER THREE   THE MILITARY COMMANDER (1642-1643)
                "A YOUNG MAN OF NO EMINENT PARTS?" 81

CHAPTER FOUR   THE MILITARY COMMANDER (1643)
                A HERO OF GLOUCESTER AND NEWBURY........... 121

CHAPTER FIVE   THE MILITARY COMMANDER (1644)
                "POORE LEICESTERSHIRE !" 139

CHAPTER SIX   THE 'SELF-DENYING' MP AND THE KING'S
                'LEICESTER MARCH': SIEGE, STORM
                AND REDEMPTION (1645) 185

CHAPTER SEVEN   THE RISING POLITICIAN (1646 - 1647)
                EMERGENCE OF A RADICAL 233

CHAPTER EIGHT   THE RISING POLITICIAN (1647 - 1648) ARMY
                RADICALS AND THE SECOND CIVIL WAR 255

CHAPTER NINE   THE ARISTOCRATIC REGICIDE (1648 - 1649)..... 283

CHAPTER TEN   THE COUNCILLOR OF STATE (1649)
                "IN THE FIRST YEAR OF FREEDOM, BY
                GOD'S BLESSING RESTORED". 329

CHAPTER ELEVEN   THE COUNCILLOR OF STATE (1649-1653)

"IN HIS MERIDIAN GLORY" 361

CHAPTER TWELVE   DECLINE AND FALL (1653 - 1657) 399

CHAPTER THIRTEEN EPILOGUE (1657 - 1667) 437

CHAPTER FOURTEEN ASSESSMENT: THOMAS, LORD GREY OF GROBY 467

POSTSCRIPT 481

DETAILS OF ILLUSTRATIONS 493

BIBLIOGRAPHY 507

INDEX OF PEOPLE 517

INDEX OF PLACES 539

LIST OF ILLUSTRATIONS

Thomas Grey, Baron Groby (1623-1657) xxiii

Family Tree – The Greys of Bradgate and Groby xxiv

Map of 17th Century Leicestershire 35

Lady Jane Grey (1537-1554) 36

Family tomb of the Greys in the Chapel at Bradgate House 37

Lady Anne Cecil (1603-1676) 38

Henry Grey, First Earl of Stamford, Baron Grey of Groby,
Bonvile & Harrington (1599-1673) 39

Lady Anne Grey (nee Cecil) Countess Stamford (1603-1676) 40

Henry Grey, Earl of Stamford (1599-1673) 41

Seventeenth century view of Bradgate 42

King Charles I 78

Robert Devereux, Earl of Essex 79

Civil War Armies 80

Oliver Cromwell 117

Colonel John Hutchinson 118

Lucy Hutchinson 119

Sir John Meldrum 120

The Earl of Essex – A Hero of Newbury and Gloucester 138

Map: West Goscote Hundred, Leicestershire 181

Map: The civil war in the East Midlands 182

Four military colours 183

Cavalry Combat 184

An aspect of the town of Leicester during the civil war (1642-5) 228

Prince Rupert, Count of the Rhineland Palatine 229

Prince Rupert summoning the garrison of Leicester
to surrender 30th May 1645 230

Sir Thomas Fairfax 231

Map: The campaign of the King's 'Leicester March', 1645 232

Basil Fielding, Earl of Denbigh 252

Sir George Booth, Lord Delamere 253

Elizabeth Booth (nee Grey), Baroness Delamere 254
Henry Ireton 280
Oliver Cromwell 281
James, Duke of Hamilton 282
King Charles I in armour 324
The trial of King Charles I by the High Court of Justice 325
An account of the trial of King Charles I 326
The death warrant of King Charles I 327
The execution of King Charles I 328
Sir Arthur Heselrige 358
Henry Marten 359
Algernon Sidney 360
Edward Massey 392
Thomas, Lord Grey of Groby, with page 393
Anchitel Grey 394
Unknown subject – probably John Grey 395
Leonard Grey 396
Diana Bruce (nee Grey) Countess Ailesbury 397
Mary Grey 398
Cromwell's dissolution of the Rump of the Long Parliament,
20th April 1653 434
Lord Protector Oliver I 435
Edmund Ludlow 436
Colonel Francis Hacker 463
Peter Temple 464
Henry Grey, Earl of Stamford (1599-1673) 465
Robert Bruce, Earl of Ailesbury 466
Thomas, Lord Grey of Groby (1623-1657) 'The Ermine Unicorn' . 479
Unknown Lady of the Bourchier family 480
Elizabeth, Countess Stamford (nee Harvey) 489
Thomas Grey, Second Earl of Stamford (1653-1720) 490
Mary, Countess Stamford (nee Maynard) 491
Ruins of Bradgate House – past and present 492

INTRODUCTION

"History without political science has no fruits; political science without history has no roots."
(John Seeley - 'Introduction to Political Science')

The purpose of this book is to present as full a picture as possible of a major yet hitherto neglected character who is a good example of those shadowy figures usually eclipsed by Oliver Cromwell and a few other grandees in most studies of the English Civil War and Commonwealth periods. It is not a book on local history, nor a book on military history; though hopefully it includes sufficient elements of these to be of interest to local and military historians, laymen and professionals. It is primarily a historical biography which seeks to set Thomas, Lord Grey of Groby in his place and time, both locally and nationally, in war and in peace.

He is perhaps best known to history, unfortunately, through Clarendon's description of him as 'a young man of no eminent parts'. This has been a biased and too often damning epitaph which requires examination and refutation. It has formed the main basis for the assessments of later historians and biographers of other subjects who almost all cite this reference. Grey of Groby was also criticised by a certain Oliver Cromwell for his unwillingness to move with his forces very far from the Leicestershire area in the early part of the civil war - a caution which I will argue was well justified by subsequent events. Thomas, Lord Grey of Groby presents an intriguing character, given his youthful age at the time of the outbreak of the English Civil War, his largely ignored yet prominent military role as a regional commander of the parliamentarian forces in the hostilities, his manoeuvrings as a member of the Long and Rump Parliaments, and his radical political views and ambitions during the period of the Commonwealth. His involvement in such momentous events as Pride's Purge, the trial and sentencing of King Charles I, and his membership of the Council of State during the English Commonwealth all merit further attention. By examining Lord Grey as a man of his times; a military commander, a politician, and a member of the aristocracy - on both the local and national stages - it is hoped that our knowledge of the people and the events which comprised the era of the Great Rebellion will be added to. It is also time that the role played by this illustrious son of Leicestershire was brought to the attention of a wider public both within and beyond the confines of that county.

The shape of any biography is determined by the nature of the source materials available, both primary and secondary. In the case of primary sources the research is subject to the ravages of time and decay and the vagaries of fortune. These tend to be arbitrary. In some cases household accounts may survive, in others they may not. The same is true of contemporary correspondence which may, if it does still exist, be found to cover some years but not others, or to be from one party but not from the other. Some of these do survive in the case of Lord Grey of Groby and they are included in this book . The Grey Family papers, however, now part of the Durham Massey National Trust Archives in the John Rylands Research Institute at the University of Manchester, contain nothing of real significance for this particular story. State papers do have a high survival record, as do legal documents, but at the local level records as with private correspondence are less well preserved and often more difficult to locate. Another problem of working in this historical period is that of deciphering some of the manuscripts whether written in English or in Latin. For example, I spent over two hours in the Public Record Office, Chancery Lane, London studying Grey of Groby's last will and testament and still had difficulty in making out all the words in it clearly. This is at the same time exciting, frustrating, interesting, and depressing. Depression is not the least of the afflictions with which the historical researcher of a biography has to contend as I discovered. Yet there is something very moving about working with original documents which bring back to life the thoughts, emotions, day to day concerns and lives of their authors, and those of their relatives and contemporaries. Then there are the commentaries and/or memorials of the time written at, or shortly after, the events concerned. In addition, there are secondary sources which can shed their own light on the subject area. These can be of invaluable use but the researcher should tread warily as they almost invariably, in the nature of things, give partial and/or prejudicial views too; in some cases compounding earlier interpretations of the past which may be erroneous, and sometimes conflicting with them thus raising more uncertainty.

One of the major problems and frustrations in the writing of historical biography is that of uneven information spread or 'gaps'. John Adair, in his work on the life of John Hampden(1) refers to the "irritating obscurity" surrounding certain key details of the subject's life. I encountered similar problems with Thomas Grey over the exact details of his place and time of birth. These were partially worked out by the analysis of other information - the year of his birth being ascertained by reference to his recorded age at the time of his marriage, the location by a more lengthy process of investigation. It would have been much easier and more satisfying in terms of certainty if the parish records for the correct year or the appropriate bishop's transcripts had survived to confirm my calculations. Sometimes, too, there is hectic activity everywhere; at other times nothing of great moment appears to be happening. Yet this goes back to the very nature of biographical work which is that of life itself. It is not neatly packaged with all the answers readily available and an even distribution of action. Herein lies its attraction as well as its frustration. The writer in the preface to the

'Memorials' of Edmund Ludlow, a contemporary and comrade of Thomas Grey, makes this point with seventeenth century eloquence.

> *"Yet is not this portion of time altogether of a piece; every day brings forth not a petition of right, nor an Edge-hill battle; there are intervals, there are flats where fortune drives swimmingly without rattle or disturbance, as well as ups and downs and precipices, where she jolts and tumbles, and overturns everything in the way.*
> *Hence it is that the course of some years scarce affords matter for a diary; and again, some days yield sinews and substance, and business proportionable, to fulfil the measure of a complete history."(2)*

Another problem which arises from the use of the source material is that of confusion over names. In particular in the case of this work I have encountered a plethora of Greys and several instances of mistaken identity on the part of writers past and present. It is my profound hope that I have detected all of these cases where they occur in respect of Thomas Grey of Groby and that I have not made the same mistake. It is not easy to avoid. For one thing there appears to have been a large number of Greys in seventeenth century Leicestershire. To confuse things even more, the contemporary spelling can, and frequently does, vary from Grey to Gray to Greye. Henry Grey, first Earl of Stamford, often referred to himself by his original title (and that inherited by his eldest son Thomas) as Lord Grey. In order to reduce the confusion I shall refer to the father as 'Stamford' and the son as 'Grey of Groby' throughout this work(3). Also in Leicestershire, as well as Thomas's brothers Anchitel, John and Leonard there were their relatives the Greys of Ruthin at Burbage. The most prominent of these were Henry Grey, Earl of Kent, and his brother, Theophilus Grey, who at one time commanded the Leicester garrison under Lord Grey of Groby's authority. Still in the same county there are references to Captain (later Colonel) Henry Grey and Edward Grey who were both officers in Lord Grey of Groby's Regiment and others of the same name who were not of the aristocratic family. This coincidence of names has sometimes led to a confusion over signatures as in the case of a military pass issued by the acting Governor of Leicester in April 1644 being incorrectly attributed to the Earl of Stamford rather than to Colonel Henry Grey(4). Leicestershire at this time seems to have been something of a 'grey area'! To complicate matters still further there were on the Parliamentary side nationally Lord

Grey of Wark(5), and Lord Gray, a Scottish peer, both of whom are sometimes confused by writers with Lord Grey of Groby(6).

Within the general problem of historiography, with its limitations of partial information, relative obscurity, confusion over individuals, uneven coverage of times and events, is the question of subjectivity and prejudice. It is equally misleading yet it can be more insidious and pernicious than the others if presented in a subtle form. Many of the past assessments of Lord Grey of Groby have been based on the judgements of hostile commentators such as Edward Hyde (Lord Clarendon) and Clement Walker, and further by later chroniclers who rely unduly upon them. As an example I would instance how John Nichols, the Leicestershire historian of the early nineteenth century, draws almost verbatim, but without clear acknowledgement, from the pen of the arch-royalist cleric the Reverend Mark Noble and his *History of the English Regicides* which is in turn based on cavalier caricatures and lampoons of the leading parliamentarians(7). I have attempted to determine the stance adopted by all commentators wherever possible and, whilst not seeking to idolise or to idealise my subject, to develop and present a rounded picture of Thomas, Lord Grey of Groby from the views of friends and enemies alike; to borrow from Cromwell, a portrait which will show him "warts and all".

Throughout this work I have attempted to be consistent in the style of presentation adopted in relation to the use of quotations, dates, and references. Where quotations from contemporary seventeenth century sources are used the spelling has usually been left in the original form. Such quotations are delivered in italic script and usually in bold type face. In all dates given the year has been taken to begin on 1 January, as it does now, and not on 25 March which was the practice in the early seventeenth century. Asterisks marked thus (*) in the end of chapter references to Nichols' *History and Antiquities of Leicestershire* are part of the original pagination used by Nichols and denote inserted pages.

C. V. Wedgwood, a highly respected historian who has written widely on topics during the reign of Charles I and the Interregnum, has defined history as, "the fragmentary record of the often inexplicable actions of innumerable bewildered human beings, set down and interpreted according to their own limitations by other human beings, equally bewildered"(8).

This illustrates, once again, the fascination and difficulty of attempting to produce an accurate account of events and the causal factors behind them.

Finally, as a justification for the approach I have adopted with this book I would echo Thomas Carlyle's dictum that history is the essence of innumerable biographies. I have been sustained throughout by the belief that the proper study of history is humanity - not laws, treaties, elections or eras - but people who loved, hated, fought, achieved sometimes and sometimes failed - just like Thomas, Lord Grey of Groby.

NOTES TO INTRODUCTION

1.   John Adair *A Life of John Hampden - The Patriot* (1594-1643) (Macdonald and Jane's, London 1976)
2.   Edmund Ludlow *Memorials* (First edition p.vi)
3.   A family tree of the Greys of Groby and Bradgate appears on page xxiv.
4.   *Bloodie Rebellion - Leicestershire & Rutland in the Civil War* Leicestershire Museums Service - Archive Teaching Unit No.1 Item 7, 1979.
5.   Adair, op. cit. p.221 He confuses Grey of Wark with Grey of Groby here.
6.   In order to further reduce potential confusion a list of key members of the Grey family (together with other Greys, and their local rivals the Hastings families) with many of their life span dates is given on pages xvii, xix, and xxi.
7.   John Nichols *The History and Antiquities of the County of Leicester* Vol III Part II. (West Goscote) pp. 678 & 679, drawn from Reverend Mark Noble *Lives of the English Regicides* Vol. I pp. 260-276. (London, 1798)
8.   C. V. Wedgwood *The Historian and the World* (1942) republished in *History and Hope* - C.V.Wedgwood's collected essays. (Fontana, August 1989)

GREYS OF GROBY AND BRADGATE
IN CHRONOLOGICAL ORDER

Greys of Groby and Bradgate, Earls of Stamford (general)

Sir John Grey, Lord Ferrers of Groby (1432-1461)

Sir Thomas Grey, 1st Marquis of Dorset (1451-1501)

Thomas Grey 2nd Marquis of Dorset (1477-1530)

Henry Grey 3rd Marquis of Dorset, Duke of Suffolk [Lady Jane Grey's father – beheaded 1554]

Frances Grey (nee Brandon), Duchess of Suffolk (died 1559)

Jane Grey, Lady ('The Nine Day's Queen') (1537-1554)

Sir John Grey of Pirgo, Essex (died 1564)

Sir Henry Grey, 1st Baron/Lord Grey of Groby (died 1614)

John Grey (died 1611)

HENRY GREY, 2nd **Lord Grey of Groby**, 1ST EARL OF STAMFORD **(1599-1673)**

ANNE GREY (NEE CECIL), 1ST COUNTESS OF STAMFORD **(1603-1676)**

THOMAS GREY, 3rd LORD GREY OF GROBY (son of 1st Earl of Stamford) **(1623-1657)**

Dorothy Grey (nee Bourchier), 3rd Lady Grey of Groby (born 1627)

Anchitel Grey (son of 1st Earl of Stamford) (1642-1702)

John Grey (son of 1st Earl of Stamford)

Leonard Grey (son of 1st Earl of Stamford)

Elizabeth Grey (daughter of 1st Earl of Stamford), later Elizabeth Booth, Countess Delamere

Diana Grey (daughter of 1st Earl of Stamford), later Diana Bruce, Countess Ailesbury

Mary Grey (daughter of 1st Earl of Stamford), later Mary Sulyarde

Anne Grey (daughter of 1st Earl of Stamford)

Jane Grey (daughter of 1st Earl of Stamford)

Elizabeth Grey (daughter of 3rd Lord Grey of Groby) later Elizabeth Benson

Anne Grey (daughter of 3rd Lord Grey of Groby) later Anne Grove

THOMAS GREY (son of 3rd Lord Grey); 4th **Lord Grey of Groby**, 2ND EARL OF STAMFORD **(1654-1720)**

Elizabeth Grey (nee Harvey), 2nd Countess Stamford

Mary Grey (nee Maynard), 3rd Countess Stamford

Diana Grey (daughter of 2nd Earl of Stamford) – died whilst a child

OTHER GREYS – NOT OF THE PREVIOUS FAMILY

Grey of Burbage, Lords of Ruthin (distantly related to the Greys of Groby and Bradgate) including :- Henry Grey, Lord Ruthin, later Earl of Kent.
Theophilus Grey, brother of the Earl of Kent

Henry Grey, Colonel
Edward Grey, Captain } Officers in the Leicester garrison

Lord Grey of Wark, (in East Anglia)
Lord Gray,   (a Scottish peer)

Hastings of Ashby-de-la-Zouch and Castle Donnington
In Chronological order

Hastings of Ashby Castle and Castle Donington (general)
Hastings, Lord (medieval – War of the Roses)
Hastings, Earls of Huntingdon (general)
Hastings, Henry 3rd Earl of Huntingdon ('The Puritan Earl')
Hastings, Henry 4th Earl of Huntingdon (Lady Jane Grey period)
Hastings, Henry 5th Earl of Huntingdon (Father to Ferdinando and Henry, below)
Hastings Ferdinando, Lord hastings, later 6th Earl of Huntingdon
Hastings, Henry, later Lord Loughborough (sometimes called Colonel Hastings)

Other Hastings Family Branches

Hastings of Braunstone
Hastings of Glenfield
Hastings, Edward, of Loughborough
Hastings of Humberstone

"The Ermine Unicorn"

"Hast thou given the horse his might?

Has thou clothed his neck with the quivering mane?

Hast thou made him to leap as a locust?

The glory of his snorting is terrible.

He paweth in the valley and rejoiceth in his strength:

He goeth out to meet the armed men.

He mocketh at fear, and is not dismayed;

neither turneth he back from the sword.

The quiver rattleth against him,

The flashing spear and the javelin.

He swalloweth the ground with fierceness and rage;

Neither daunted is he by the voice of the trumpet.

He saith among the trumpets, Aha!;

and he smelleth the battle afar off,

the thunder of the captains and the shouting."

(Book of Job   Chapt. 39 vs. 19-25)

Per Bellum Ad Pacem

Thomas Grey, Baron Groby (1623-1657)

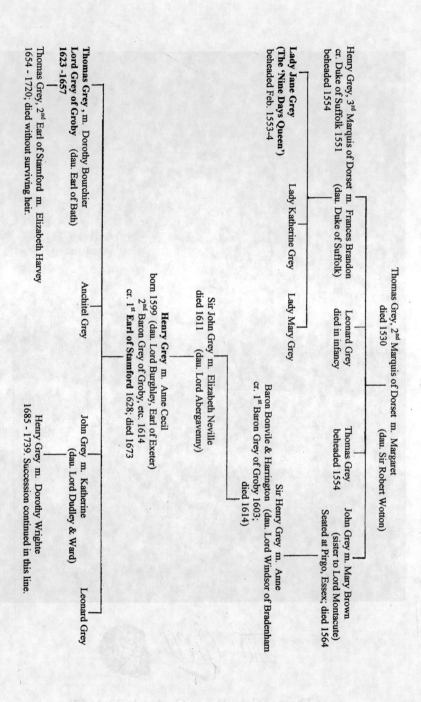

Family Tree – The Greys of Bradgate and Groby

Thomas Grey, 2nd Marquis of Dorset m. Margaret
died 1530   (dau. Sir Robert Wotton)

Henry Grey, 3rd Marquis of Dorset m. Frances Brandon
cr. Duke of Suffolk 1551   (dau. Duke of Suffolk)
beheaded 1554

Leonard Grey
died in infancy

Thomas Grey
beheaded 1554

John Grey m. Mary Brown
(sister to Lord Montacute)
Seated at Pirgo, Essex; died 1564

Lady Jane Grey
(The 'Nine Days Queen')
beheaded Feb. 1553-4

Lady Katherine Grey

Lady Mary Grey

Sir John Grey m. Elizabeth Neville
died 1611   (dau. Lord Abergavenny)

Baron Bonvile & Harrington
cr. 1st Baron Grey of Groby 1603;
died 1614

Sir Henry Grey m. Anne
(dau. Lord Windsor of Bradenham
died 1614)

Henry Grey m. Anne Cecil
born 1599 (dau. Lord Burghley, Earl of Exeter)
2nd Baron Grey of Groby, etc. 1614
cr. 1st **Earl of Stamford** 1628; died 1673

Thomas Grey, m. Dorothy Bourchier
Lord Grey of Groby (dau. Earl of Bath)
1623 -1657

Anchitel Grey

John Grey m. Katherine
(dau. Lord Dudley & Ward)

Leonard Grey

Thomas Grey, 2nd Earl of Stamford m. Elizabeth Harvey
1654 - 1720; died without surviving heir.

Henry Grey m. Dorothy Wrighte
1685 - 1739. Succession continued in this line.

xxiv

CHAPTER ONE
THE GREYS OF GROBY, BRADGATE AND LEICESTERSHIRE

A MA PUISSANCE (By My Power)
(Family Motto of the Greys)

The Greys of Groby and Bradgate were successors to a family of high rank and influential connections in the aristocracy of England. They claimed descent from one Anchitel De Grey who was a supporter of William the Conqueror and took part in the Norman invasion of 1066. By the time of the outbreak of the Great Rebellion of 1642 the Greys of Groby had been entangled through conspiracy, feud and marriage with many of the other great families of the land. They had risen from relative obscurity in the fifteenth century to the point where one member of the family was actually crowned as Queen of England, if only for nine days - just seventy years before the birth of the subject of this book.

This study of the life and times of Thomas Grey, Third Baron Grey of Groby, begins by tracing briefly the history of his family and their connection with the Leicestershire manor whose name appears in their title.

The village of Groby (spelt Grooby in the seventeenth century as it is still pronounced locally in the twenty-first century) is located some five miles to the north west of Leicester on the edge of the Charnwood Forest. It lies on the road which leads from the county town in the direction of Ashby-de-la-Zouch and Burton-upon-Trent.

The Manor of Groby, from which the Greys derived their title, is listed in the Domesday Book.[1] In Edward the Confessor's reign, together with its sister manor of Ratby a mile further west, it was held by a local English landowner named Ulf. According to the 1086 Domesday Survey, Ulf possessed these two lands with full jurisdiction ("cum saca et soca"). He probably gave his name to nearby Ulverscroft in the Charnwood Forest which became the site of an Augustinian Priory in 1130, but nothing more is known of this first recorded Lord of Groby. The Domesday recorder lists Groby (entered as Grobi) as being equal in size to six ploughlands less three oxgangs. There were ten villagers (villeins), one freeman (socman), and five smallholders (bordars) with three ploughs. In addition, there were two ploughs in the lordship of the manor although it is implied that the land under cultivation was only equal in capacity to four ploughs. There was woodland in the manor recorded as being two leagues long and half a league wide (640 acres). In the case of Ratby (listed as Rotebi) there was land to the extent of six ploughlands less three oxgangs again but this was capable of cultivation by six ploughs as the manor stretched beyond the village proper and included neighbouring hamlets. In the lord's desmense were two ploughs and a slave. There were ten villagers (villeins), a priest (and one may assume, therefore, a church of some sort), and five smallholders (bordars) having three ploughs. In all these records, of course, the women and children of the villages went unrecorded. Ratby also had a mill although there is no mention of a person designated specifically as a miller. The two manors had both been valued at twenty shillings a year before the Norman Conquest and were valued at sixty shillings each in the Domesday Survey. Such appears to have been the rate of early Norman period inflation or increase in value - a threefold increase in the space of twenty years!

Following the events of 1066 the lands of these manors, along with many others in this part of the country, were awarded to Hugo de Grentesmainell, a Norman lord, as part of his extensive rewards for service to William the Conqueror. He was created baron of Hinckley and High Steward of England by William Rufus. He was also probably responsible for the building of the stone church on the hill in the centre of Ratby which dominates the village from a distance to this day. The twin manors then passed through the marriage of one of de Grentesmainell's daughters to the Beaumonts, Earls of Leicester. In turn they passed on by marriage through the female line to the de Quincy family who subsequently succeeded to the Earldom.

The lands were eventually inherited by a grandson of Roger de Quincy - a William de Ferrers who was afterwards created Lord Ferrers of Groby. The lordship of Groby was listed in the Itinerary of 1280 as comprising Groby, Ratby, Markfield and Whittington Grange collectively as one vill. It also included a hunting park for the lord of the manor at Bradgate (sometimes referred to as Broadgate) a mile and a half north east of Groby village and on the other side of the large expanse of water known as Groby Pool. The name 'Bradgate' is derived from the term 'Broadgate' - the Broad Way or Causeway - an ancient route way which still exists on the south side of Cropston reservoir and used to traverse a large part of north-central Leicestershire in an east-west direction. The park provided sport, sustenance, and revenue for the lord and his family and fuel for his humble tenants from the 'coppice' shrubs and undergrowth beneath the large standard trees. The centre of the desmense was the manor house which still stands in the middle of Groby village today opposite the Ratby Lane. There was, however, no church in Groby and, although the lord had his domestic chaplain, the Norman church in Ratby formed the ecclesiastical heart of the holdings. In the period 1140 to 1200AD there are written references to the villages as Groubi and Rotebi respectively.

William de Ferrers, first baron of Groby, took the coat of arms of the de Quincy family until the male line of the elder house (the Ferrers of Chartley, in Staffordshire) became extinct. The manor of Groby, including its deer park at Bradgate, remained in the hands of the Ferrers family until 1445 when Elizabeth, the only surviving daughter of Henry de Ferrers, succeeded her grandfather William on his death. Elizabeth, who was aged 26 at the time, was married to a Sir Edward Grey. This began the association of the Grey family with Groby and Bradgate. It also marked the connection between the families of Grey and Ferrers which was to have a role to play later in the seventeenth century.

An early product of the union of the families of Grey and Ferrers was their son, John, who at the age of 25 inherited the manor upon his father's death in December 1456. In the following year as Sir John Grey, Lord Ferrers of Groby, he married the Lady Elizabeth Woodville. Elizabeth Woodville was renowned for her beauty and this union was to mark the rise of the Grey family of Groby to national fame, if not fortune.

Sir John Grey fought on the Lancastrian side in the so-called 'Wars of the Roses' and was killed at the second battle of St. Albans. When the Yorkist Edward IV was proclaimed King, the Greys, having been on the 'wrong' side, had their estates confiscated. William Shakespeare[2] has made us familiar with the story of how the beautiful widowed Lady Grey so impressed the king that he married her secretly on 1 May 1464, and in doing so earned the enmity of Warwick the Kingmaker and the King of France. With this royal marriage Elizabeth had the Grey estates restored and her sons became step-sons of the king. The elder son, Thomas, was created Marquis of Dorset. The younger son was knighted as Sir Richard Grey. Just before Edward IV died he tried to end the enmity that already existed between the Greys and the leading Leicestershire Yorkist, Lord Hastings - one of his main supporters. Hastings, of Ashby-de-la-Zouch, at the time had just commenced the construction of Kirby Muxloe Castle a mile to the south of Ratby. In front of Edward IV Dorset and Hastings joined hands and promised to be reconciled, but their promises scarcely outlived the king and the feud between the Hastings and the Grey families ran on for at least the next two centuries, reaching its most open and violent form during the Civil War.

When Edward IV died the Greys and the Woodvilles planned an early coronation for Elizabeth's young son Edward V, but his uncle, Richard, Duke of Gloucester, outmanoeuvred them. He gained custody of the young king and his brother, and set about eliminating his opponents in the Woodville faction, including Sir Richard Grey who was beheaded. On the day that Edward V should have been crowned, Richard instructed the London preachers to proclaim from their pulpits that Edward IV was illegitimate, so his sons were not heirs to the crown, and that in any case the marriage to Elizabeth Woodville was not valid. Richard of Gloucester then graciously, and with a proper show of reluctance, accepted the crown for himself as Richard III.

Within a couple of months rumours were beginning to spread about the two young princes in the Tower of London, who had not been seen since the coronation of their uncle. When the Greys realised that their stake in the crown was thwarted they turned away from the House of York and switched their support once more to the Lancastrians and their claimant, Henry Tudor. Thomas Grey, Marquis of Dorset, with a price on his head, escaped to Brittany and joined Tudor. After his victory at Bosworth Field in Leicestershire in 1485 Henry Tudor, now as Henry VII, married Elizabeth Woodville's daughter, Elizabeth of York, half sister to Dorset. The Greys still had influence and relations in high places.

After spending some time on military missions in France, Dorset turned his attention to his Leicestershire estates. He found the old manor house at Groby too small and out-dated for his life style and position in national politics. To begin with he began to alter and enlarge the manor house. Eventually, in 1490, he commenced the construction of a much larger and splendid country house in the hunting park at Bradgate. When he died in 1501 his new residence was still unfinished. The work was continued by his son, also Thomas, Marquis of Dorset, who was unpopular with Henry VII but a favourite of the young Henry VIII. As the new king matured he recruited new advisers and Dorset spent a lot more of his time at Bradgate. He died in 1530 and was succeeded by his son Henry who managed to free himself of his first wife and then married Frances, daughter of Princess Mary (Henry VIII's sister) and Charles Brandon, Duke of Suffolk. This marriage advanced Henry Grey's position at court under Henry VIII and Edward VI. He inherited from his second wife's family the title of Duke of Suffolk. He had three daughters - the eldest of whom was born in 1537 and was christened Jane. She was to become known to national history as Lady Jane Grey - the Nine Days Queen.

John Leland, the king's antiquary, visited Bradgate about the year 1540 and described it as follows:

"From Brodegate to Groby a mile and a half much by wodden lande. There remayne few tokens of the old castelle more than yet is, the hille that the kepe of the castelle stoode on, very notable, but there is now no stone work upon it; and the late Thomas marquesh filled up the diche of it with earth, entending to make an herbare there. The ould parte of the worke that now is at Groby was made by the Ferrares. But newer workes and buildinges there were erectid by the Lord Thomas first marquise of Dorset; among the which workes he began and erectid the

4

fundation and waulles of a great gate-house of brike, and a tour; but that was lefte half onfinished of hym, and so it standeth yet. This Lord Thomas erectid also and almost finishid, ii toures of brike in the fronte of the house, as respondent on eche side to the gate-house. There is a faire large parke by the place a vi (6) miles in cumpase. There is also a poore village by the place" (Newtown Linford) *"and a little broke by it; and a quarter of a mile from the place, in the bottom, there is as faire a large pole"* (Groby Pool) *"as lightely is in Leyrcestreshire. There iss with a broket out of this lake that after cummith by Groby, and there dryvith a mylle, and after resortith to Sore river."*[(3)]

Leland was the first contemporary writer known to have recorded that there was at Bradgate *"a lodge lately builded there by the lorde Thomas Gray, marquise of Dorset, father to Henry that is now marquise."*[(4)] Another source from the same period records that in 1564 the village of Groby contained twenty seven families.

The tragic story of Lady Jane Grey has been too well rehearsed elsewhere to be covered here in detail, yet it was of great significance to the family and the locality and its legacy was to have implications in the following century and therefore it requires some mention. Jane was the child of ambitious parents. Her father Henry, Duke of Suffolk, and John Dudley, Duke of Northumberland, were anxious to prevent Edward VI's succession by his sister, the Roman Catholic Mary Tudor, and to secure the levers of national power for themselves. They married the fifteen year old Lord Guilford Dudley to the sixteen year old Lady Jane. Following the king's death Jane was crowned Queen at the Tower of London on 10th July 1553. Her brief and tragic reign lasted only nine days. When Mary's supporters gained power Northumberland was executed. Jane and Guilford Dudley were first imprisoned and were then executed on 12th February 1554, following Wyatt's abortive rebellion. The Duke of Suffolk went into hiding but was captured in Warwickshire by his arch-rival the Earl of Huntingdon, the head of the Hastings family, who had been sent against him by Queen Mary with a force of three hundred men. Huntingdon had deemed it politic to leave the Suffolk-Northumberland plot, to which he had once been a party, and to return to the Roman Catholic faith. Suffolk was taken to the Tower of London and executed. His widow, Frances, was permitted to retain only the estates of Beaumanor and Groby and the family forfeited all titles of nobility. Upon her death in 1559 Beaumanor and Groby (including the Bradgate residence) passed to her brother-in-law Sir John Grey who lived at Pirgo in Essex. The family went into decline as far as their influence in Leicestershire was concerned and it was not to revive until the reign of James I, the first Stuart monarch of England.

Even from the time of Henry VIII the predominant power locally, and particularly in the town of Leicester, was the Earl of Huntingdon, the head of the Hastings family based at Ashby-de-la-Zouch and Castle Donington. Usually the Earl or a member of his family was also Lord Lieutenant of Leicestershire; High Sheriff of Leicester and Steward of the Honor of Leicester - the latter being a widespread group of lands owing fees to the old Earldom of Leicester, now absorbed in the Crown. The Earl considered it his prerogative to nominate those who should represent the borough and the shire in Parliament. The most dominant figure amongst these magnates was Henry, the third Earl, known as 'the Puritan Earl'[5], who died in 1595. Between 1547 and 1628 seven members of the Hastings family represented Leicester in Parliament. They dominated the county gentry and successfully resisted the attempts of the Greys to challenge their hegemony. In terms of life-style and architectural pretensions **"the new brick manor house at Bradgate was the only one to rival the splendour of the Hastings' stately pile at Ashby."**[6] The Earl of Huntingdon was actually married to the sister of Lady Jane Grey's husband, Guilford Dudley. Huntingdon had paid homage to Jane as Queen but deserted her as soon as he could. It suited the Hastings interest both nationally and locally to switch their support to Mary Tudor and to crush the royal pretensions of the Greys. **"Leicestershire became a Hastings preserve for the rest of the sixteenth century."**[7] The local historians, past and present, seem quite clear on this point. Even on the religious issue where the Hastingses seem to have alternated between Puritanism and Roman Catholicism their position does not seem to have been unduly weakened.

"The Reformation had singularly little effect upon Leicestershire politics; the great families, whatever their differences with each other moved comfortably with the times. Even Edward Hastings of Loughborough, the ardent supporter of Queen Mary (Cardinal Pole, Mary's closest adviser, was a relative of the Hastings family) and her executor, took the Oath of Supremacy after a taste of the Tower and died a Protestant. The upshot of this was to add to the political tranquillity of the county and recusancy never became a problem in Leicestershire."[8]

Thus, contrary to what might have been expected, the accession of Elizabeth I did little to upset the balance of political forces locally. Roman Catholicism was not strong in the county by this time and the main branch of the Hastings family had swung back to its alliance with puritanism. The Greys, therefore, failed to make much political capital out of the religious revolution, although their own protestant credentials were never in doubt. Due mainly to the influence of 'the Puritan Earl' **"the political history of Leicestershire in this reign** (Elizabeth I) **is largely the history of the**

Hastings family."[9] It is argued, moreover, that **"from the Reformation to the Civil War the political life of Leicestershire was dominated by the Earls of Huntingdon; there was no power comparable to theirs, and their relatives and clients represented both county and borough almost continuously in Parliament."**[10]

Following the death of Sir John Grey of Pirgo in 1564 the seat of the Grey family returned from Essex back to Bradgate. The move was made by his son, Sir Henry Grey, a cousin of the ill-fated Lady Jane. When King James VI of Scotland became also James I of England in succession to Queen Elizabeth the Grey family fortunes began a marked revival. The new monarch was always keen to raise money and Sir Henry Grey was able to purchase one of the baronetcies sold to fund the plantation of Ulster and thus to gain the title of Lord Grey of Groby in 1603. It may be thought by some that the Greys were later to prove less than appreciative of this Stuart generosity, but perhaps they felt that after the glories of Duke and Marquis the title 'Lord (Baron) Grey of Groby' was scant restoration. Indeed, this observation has been made by earlier commentators.

> **"It seems this partial restoration of honour very little satisfied the fallen family of Grey ..... Sir Edward Walker, in his `Observations on the Inconveniences that have attended the frequent Promotions to Titles of Honour and Dignity since King James came to the Crown of England', says "For example; had King James either absolutely restored Sir Henry Grey, whom he created lord Grey of Groby, to be marquis of Dorset, or left him a knight as he found him, `tis possible his grandson and great grandchild might not have been able or considerable enough to have acted as they have done."**[11]

In passing, we may note that at the same time the title of Earl of Essex was restored to Robert Devereux - son of the Earl beheaded in 1601 - another nobleman who was to show his gratitude to the House of Stuart in the 1640s by commanding the first armies of the rebellious Parliament against the Crown. In similar vein to the above quotation the Devereux family were referred to by royalist commentators as having *"rebellion in the blood"*.

Sir Henry Grey's eldest son and heir-apparent, Sir John Grey, died before him in 1611 and was buried at the junior Grey residence in Leicestershire at Broughton Astley. At an earlier stage Sir John had attempted rather clumsily and prematurely to recover the power in the county that his family had previously enjoyed. In 1599 he had alienated his potential allies on the Leicester Corporation when he had become engaged in a dispute about the jurisdiction of the borough magistrates as opposed to that of the justices of the shire such as himself. His blustering and threatening behaviour only succeeded in creating opposition in the borough. In 1600, having managed to get himself appointed to a commission for the assessment of tax, he found that the Corporation first got a Hastings added too and then got him displaced altogether.[12] In 1601 he had met with another defeat when, with the help of the Earl of Rutland, he unsuccessfully challenged the Hastings nominees at a Parliamentary election in the county. Sir Henry, as first Lord Grey of Groby, wisely refrained from meddling in either national or local politics. He was not without influence, however, and in August 1611 he wrote to the Earl of Huntingdon advising him to call a general meeting of the gentry of Leicestershire to consider the question of the composition (i.e. the taxation) for the provision for the upkeep of the royal household.[13] Sir Henry finally died in 1614 as peacefully as he had lived. He was succeeded by his grandson, also Henry, on 26th July 1614 and who was at the time aged fifteen.

Henry, second Lord Grey of Groby, was born at Bradgate and was later to be buried there. His mother was Elizabeth, daughter of Edward Nevill, Lord Abergavenny. She seems to have spent much of her time in Ireland, having remarried after Sir John Grey's death a Sir John Bingley, Remembrancer of the Exchequer in 1617. Much later, in early March 1640, King Charles wrote from Westminster to Thomas Wentworth, Earl of Strafford, who was Lieutenant General and Governor-General of Ireland, with a writ to deliver to Dame Elizabeth Bingley, widow of Sir John Bingley, late one of the Privy Council for Ireland, 3,000 acres of land out of the plantation to be made in the province of Munster. This was in consideration of the services of the said Sir John Bingley in discovering the king's right to the lands of Londonderry in Ulster, *"wherein he did not only employ his own labour, but also disbursed divers sums of money"*.[14]

Henry was at Trinity College, Cambridge when his grandfather died - matriculating the following year in Easter 1615 and being awarded an MA in the same year at the age of sixteen on the occasion of a visit to the college by King James I. This new Lord Grey of Groby clearly regarded Bradgate as the centre of the properties and lands to which he now had title. He preserved for posterity the memory of the first Lord Grey of Groby by having built the effigies and tomb for his paternal grandparents in the family chapel at Bradgate. The tomb and the chapel remain intact to this day in the ruins of Bradgate House in Bradgate Park. Another major concern was to consolidate and then strengthen the dynasty. He married in July 1620, at the age of 20/21, one Anne Cecil, youngest daughter and co-heiress of William Cecil, Earl of Exeter. Through this marriage he obtained the castle, borough, and manor of Stamford in Lincolnshire.

It must have been a very short honeymoon because a letter written in French from Prague on 27th July 1620, received in England on 20th August describes how Lord Grey is in command of English troops arriving in Lusatia. *"Les Anglois* [sic] *conduits par le Milor Grey, en nombre de 2,500, sont arrivez en Lusace fort bien et ordre".*[15] These were part of a larger volunteer English expeditionary force campaigning in the early stages of the Thirty Years War in Germany on behalf of Frederick, the calvinist Elector of the Rhineland Palatinate and (briefly) the King of Bohemia ('The Winter King') and his wife, the English princess Elizabeth. In overall command of the English forces in the allied army against the armies of the Imperialist Hapsburgs and the Catholic League was Sir Horace Vere, supported by the Earls of Oxford and Essex and Thomas Wentworth, who was to become the Earl of Strafford. *"Ce que feront aussy* [sic] *les Anglois conduits par le General Vere, ou les Comtes d'Oxford et d'Essex, et le Colonel Wentworth, etc. ont charge".*[16] The second Lord Grey of Groby was to compensate for his absence from Bradgate later by sireing a number of children, nine of whom survived to the age of majority.

In November 1620, he was summoned to Parliament and from then on was to be in Parliament, either as a member of the House of Commons or as a member of the House of Peers, for almost the rest of his life. He resided, however, principally at Bradgate from where he worked hard to restore the position of the Greys in Leicestershire; a position which had been eclipsed by the Hastings family since 1554.

Bradgate House, the centre of the Grey's reviving power, had been regarded at the time of its initial construction by the Marquis of Dorset between 1490 and 1520 as being one of the most imposing buildings in the Midlands. John Leland, writing in approximately 1538, referred to the feeling that *"the fair, large, and beautiful palace built at Broadgate by Thomas Grey marquis of Dorset challengeth the pre-eminence* (of the Stone Tower of the Hastings' at Ashby-de-la-Zouch castle) *above the rest."*[17] The unfortunate young Lady Jane Grey whilst imprisoned in the Tower of London awaiting execution is reputed to have sighed for one last visit to *"fair and lovely Bradgate"*.

The House had the distinction of being one of the earliest unfortified country houses in England. This lack of fortification was characteristic of such houses built during the stable period of early Tudor government. It combined the amenities of a hunting palace with the comforts of a private villa. The original house was built in the shape of an 'E' and was about two hundred feet long from east to west. At each corner of the house stood a high brick octagonal tower, faced at the angles with white freestone to contrast with the red brick, a characteristic feature of Tudor architecture. The symmetry of the plan of the house showed the influence of the Renaissance, but the interior design of the original building had remained basically medieval. Changes in layout and additions to the main structure

9

were made by the Greys after their return in the early seventeenth century as forms of modernisation.

The great hall formed the major part of the central block, being the main feature of any nobleman's residence. The hall at Bradgate was about eighty feet long by thirty feet wide and was lighted by large wainscoted bay windows on the north and south sides. Its height extended from the bottom to the top of the house. The hall was ringed by galleries which had tapestry hangings and elaborately carved chimney-pieces, so that the family motto 'A Ma Puissance', supported by two unicorns, ermined, armed and crested and hooped with gold, confronted the spectator at regular intervals.

A large cellar was required to store the provisions for the substantial household kept by a family of the stature of the Greys. The cellar at Bradgate extended beneath the floor of the great hall and towards the western side of the house. The wine cellar was lined with stone to keep the temperature low and niches were cut into the walls to take lamps or candles.

The kitchen lay in the west wing of the house together with an assortment of domestic offices. These included a bakery, a buttery, a pantry, a brewery, and even a wine press. It is possible that there was an ice-house on the south side of the house, but it seems more likely that this would have been located in the woods beyond the house to ensure the lowest possible temperature, as was the case at nearby Beaumanor. Ashes taken from the kitchen and bakery were deposited in large heaps to the west of the house and which can be seen as grass covered mounds today. The main feature of the kitchen was the vast fireplace, fifteen feet wide, which was used for spit-roasting and was large enough later, during Booth's Rebellion in 1659, to be used to conceal pikes, halberds, and other weapons in the lower part of its chimney. An ash chute led from the kitchen ovens to ash heaps outside the house. Also on this side of the house a further brewery and a dairy were added at the beginning of the seventeenth century following the family's return. A household community such as the Greys of Bradgate lived a largely self-sufficient life in many respects.

A tall square tower in the middle of the western wall provided an external staircase which led to the servants' quarters. These upstairs rooms would have been poorly furnished and during the winter months the servants must have been glad of the warmth radiating from the great fireplace in the kitchen and bakery below them.

The private apartment of the Grey family lay in the east wing of the house. Family apartments normally led off from the great hall, with a parlour in the ground floor and a solar or loft above it. It is likely that in the earlier years at Bradgate the family would have used this main parlour for most of the year and retreated to the south facing parlour during the winter. The small kitchen in this part of the house would have helped to warm the winter parlour. Its main function would have been in the preparation of private meals for the family. The octagonal tower above the kitchen has traditionally been known as 'Lady Jane's Tower'. It has often been assumed that it was to this tower that the gentle, studious and ill-fated girl often retreated when she wished to escape from the attentions of her ambitious parents and to read the Greek and Latin classics. From the higher windows of the tower she would also have enjoyed the magnificent views of the lower reaches of the hunting park.

The winter parlour and the private dining room both had access to the chapel, which is now the only complete building remaining at Bradgate. The interior gallery reserved for the use of the family no longer exists but on the outside of the chapel the remains of the stairs leading up to it can be seen. Lighting was provided by mullion windows on the south and west sides of the building. Inside the chapel is one of the finest alabaster tombs in the country. It is a splendid monument and represents the effigies of Henry Grey, first Lord Grey of Groby, and his wife Ann, who was a daughter of Lord Windsor of Bradenham. This was the man who had re-established the Grey dynasty at Bradgate and begun the rebuilding of their fortunes in Leicestershire. Above the tomb and on top of the elaborately carved pillars, archway and roof stands an elaborate achievement of arms. The shield depicts the arms of the noble families to whom the Greys were related by marriage at the time; including those of Grey itself, Hastings, Valence, Ferrars, Astley, Woodville, Bonvile, and Harrington. Supporting the shield on the left and the right respectively are a lion and a unicorn, both rampant. Strangely, the print reproduced from Nichols on page 37 shows the usual supporters of the Grey family coat of arms - two ermine unicorns rampant. – rather than these 'royal' supporters. Above the helmet and mantle surmounting the shield is the device of a sun in splendour. In the centre of the blazing sun stands the figure of an ermine unicorn. Under the shield and supporters is emblazoned again the family motto "A MA PUISSANCE". Beneath the floor of the chapel is a vault in which lie the remains of several members of the Grey family. In the early seventeenth century the vault already contained the earthly remains of the Marquis of Dorset and his wife, and the two people represented in effigy on the monument.[18]

There were guest apartments which lay to the north of the house and which had been built following the return to Bradgate. These would have been in increasing use as the family's fortunes were being restored. It is believed that King James I visited the house as part of a royal progress in 1617. From their windows the guests would overlook the formal gardens, including the square sunken garden, on the northern side of the house. This area had been used during the Tudor period as a tiltyard. Despite its relatively small area when compared to the size of a tiltyard proper it was built by the first Marquis of Dorset for jousting practice only and was, therefore, quite sufficient. The Marquis had been one of the most noted jousters of his day.

11

At one corner of the former tiltyard stood a mill. The mill wheel was turned by the stream which flowed down from the lake in the northern part of the garden. Water could be released from the lake into the stream by opening three chambers situated behind a grill set in the southern corner. Iron handles were attached to oak bungs set into each of these chambers and when these were pulled out the water poured through into the stream and turned the mill wheel. Another channel fed by the lake also served to flush out the system of drainage tanks in the house. Drinking water was supplied to the house from a spring in Elder Tree Wood within the park by way of a tiled conduit and was fed by gravity to a roof tank. The tank was situated in a tower at the northwest corner of the house. Between the mill and the main house buildings lay a walled garden. The wall beneath the former tiltyard and now sunken garden was supported by enormous buttresses. This wall was constructed in the same local red brickwork as the rest of the house. Part of the walled garden consisted of a kitchen garden providing herbs, fruit and vegetables. The herbs were grown for both culinary and medicinal purposes. An enormous ancient mulberry tree which still survives overhung the wall of the kitchen garden. It is believed locally that this is one of seven mulberry trees brought to England by Sir Walter Raleigh early in the seventeenth century. Certainly a large number of mulberry trees were planted in the gardens at Bradgate during the Stuart period.

Some key changes had been made to the layout of Bradgate House and its grounds at the beginning of the seventeenth century. The main architectural change was the transfer of the main entrance from the south side of the house, where it had been in Tudor times, to the eastern side. The new entrance was built in stone and was approached down an imposing avenue of Spanish chestnut trees. The main gardens on the north side of the house were laid out with spacious lawns fringed with box hedges and rows of trees. Gardens occupied much attention at this time and this growing interest in them illustrates the more general cultivation by the Puritan aristocracy and gentry of their private domestic lives and that of their families. The deer park itself remained in its wild state with its ferns, rocky outcrops, and ancient oaks, although the oak trees were regularly pollarded for firewood. All this is well illustrated in the drawing by Leonard Knyff which appears both on the cover and inside this book.

Writing some 150 odd years later John Nichols was to wax lyrical with the following description of Bradgate's Park even though by this time, *".....the courts of this once magnificent mansion are now occupied by rabbits, and shaded by chestnut trees and mulberries."*

"The approach to Bradgate from Thurcaston is strikingly picturesque; and the view from the keeper's lodge is truly

*enchanting. On the left appears a large grove of venerable trees.
On the right stand the ruins of Bradgate, surmounted by rugged
rocks and aged oaks; the forest hills .....forming the background
of the prospect. The valley, through which the trout stream runs,
extends in front with clumps to shade the deer; and terminates
in a narrow winding glen fringed with `Pan's own umbrage
dark and deep'.*

> *"Not proud Olympus yields a nobler sight,*
> *Tho' Gods assembled grace his tow'ring height,*
> *Than what more humble mountains offer here.*
> *Where in their blessings all those Gods appear".*[19]

This was the splendid setting within which the second Lord Grey of
Groby applied himself to the management of his estates and towards playing
that part upon the stage of county and national affairs for which his family
background, wealth, status, and education had equipped him.

In 1623 Henry and Anne produced their son and heir, Thomas. He was
to be the first of nine children born of their union; four sons (Thomas,
Anchitel, John and Leonard) and five daughters (Elizabeth, Diana, Jane,
Anne, and Mary). The year of Thomas' birth is calculated from his age as
given later on his marriage licence. The exact date and place of birth are
not known for certain but it seems most probably, given his father's
sentimental and economic attachments, that Thomas was born at Bradgate.
He would have been baptised by the family chaplain, the Reverend Thomas
Stirke. Stirke was also the minister of the church in the hamlet of Newtown
Linford which stood at the southwestern edge of the park. This hamlet of
small cottages, taking its name from its location at the ford across the Lin
stream, which darkly glitters as it flows through the park, provided
accommodation for many of those who worked for the Bradgate estate.

Following the death of his father-in-law Henry Grey was created by
letters patent Earl of Stamford in 1628 as part of his wife's inheritance.
Amongst other benefits this brought him increased status, a seat in the
House of Lords, and a list of titles that now included Earl of Stamford, in
addition to his earlier titles of Lord Grey of Groby, Bonville, and Harrington.
Thomas, at the age of five, succeeded to the original title and became the
third Lord Grey of Groby. For reasons of clarity these are the names by
which they will normally be referred to in the following pages : Henry
Grey is Stamford, and his son Thomas is the Lord Grey of Groby.

Little is known about the early life of Thomas, Lord Grey of Groby.
We can, however, speculate with a reasonable degree of accuracy about
the sort of life he was born into from what is known of the life-style of
families such as the Greys of Groby and Bradgate at this time. No details

remain concerning his schooling. He may have gone to grammar school in Leicester or away to London, but is more likely to have been tutored at home at Bradgate, at least to begin with. There is no record of him having gone to university but this is not so unusual. His father, as has been noted, went to Trinity College, Cambridge; his own son, also named Thomas, was later to go up to Christ Church College, Oxford, after the Restoration in 1667. It was, however, not unknown for leading family heads or their heirs in Leicestershire to go on to the Inns of Court, as he did later, without having first gone to university.

Of those who did go to university from Leicestershire aristocratic and gentry families there was a marked preference for Cambridge. As Cambridge and Oxford are equidistant from Leicester the preference for the fenland university, traditionally more radical and Puritan than its more High Church and Laudian rival, rested upon foundations other than geographical expediency. Religion was seen at the time as a significant bond that held society together and could even be regarded as the basis of all political organisation. It was also thought to be natural that the intellectual life of the universities should be closely concerned with issues of Church organisation and theology. The collision of ideas between the Laudians (or Arminians as they were sometimes termed) and the Puritans was not, therefore, a remote and specialised controversy but a conflict on a matter of central importance to English life. Both universities included strong advocates of the two schools of thought in their colleges but Cambridge was predominantly Puritan while Oxford largely supported Archbishop Laud (an ex-rector of Ibstock parish in north-west Leicestershire) and his policies in Church and State. Later, during the first civil war, Oxford was to serve as the king's main headquarters. Important families in Leicestershire who had strong links with Cambridge included, in addition to the Greys of Bradgate, their cousins the Greys of Burbage, the Hastings' of Ashby, the Dixies, the Halfords, the Hartopps, the Manners', the Skeffingtons, and the Skipwiths; so it was not only a numerical superiority of which Cambridge could boast. Most of these families, particularly the leading ones, were of a distinctive Puritan allegiance. Another factor concerning university attendance should also be noted at this point. In English life at this time going to an Oxford or Cambridge college was for the sons of the upper classes almost like going away to grammar or public school in later centuries. The age of entry to university was much lower in the seventeenth century. Edward Hyde, for example, later Lord Clarendon, went up to Oxford at the age of thirteen, and John Milton, the great Puritan writer and poet, went to Cambridge when he had just turned sixteen. We have already noted that Henry Grey had matriculated at Cambridge at the age of sixteen and had been awarded a Master of Arts degree in the same year.

Another major stage in the usual educational pattern for young landed gentlemen at this time was to spend two or three years in legal studies at one of the Inns of Court in London. Going to the Inns of Court to become legally qualified in order to be fitted for the exercise of the customary tasks of government and the administration of justice in the locality was widely regarded as a necessary form of higher education for economic, cultural and legal reasons. A marked preference was shown by the leading Leicestershire families for Gray's Inn over the three other Inns of Court. A survey carried out based on the leading county families in 1640 showed that twenty-six of the forty-four men who attended an Inn of Court during this period were at Gray's. The predominance of Gray's Inn among family heads and heirs was even greater, with twenty-two of the thirty-two with legal training having acquired it there.[20] Gray's was the Inn favoured by those who simply desired a thorough knowledge of the law, and nine family heads went there without previously having been to university. Gray's Inn, rather appropriately, was attended by both Henry Grey and his son Thomas. In 1632, at the age of thirty-three, the Earl of Stamford was admitted to Gray's Inn. His son was to be admitted in March 1641, aged eighteen, whilst already in London as an elected member of the House of Commons for the Borough of Leicester. He was then to be caught up in the political storms leading to the civil war and the subsequent military activities at both local and national level which brought him to the centre of state affairs and away from parochial matters. This lay well ahead in the 1630s, however, and in the case of most of his county contemporaries their concerns would remain close to home. Despite the fact that many gentry attended the universities and some of the wealthier families spent part of the year in London, the vast majority of the county gentry passed most of their lives within a few miles of their own estates. The brief years at university or one of the Inns of Court were no more than an interlude, principally designed to equip them to carry out their functions as justices, squires, and landlords in their own county. After the time spent at Oxford or Cambridge or in London, most of them settled back into the routine of country life.

There were factors other than the time spent at university or the Inns of Court which could influence the wider education of a young member of the upper classes such as Thomas, Lord Grey of Groby. The advantages of travel, especially on the continent of Europe, and a wider cultivation of cultural appreciation in arts, literature and forms of recreation were also recognized and often recommended. The following advice given by the fifth Earl of Huntingdon to his son and heir, Ferdinando Hastings, might equally have served to Thomas Grey or any other young country gentleman from his father.

"Endeavour to have a general knowledge in all things; else a country gentleman that can talk of nothing but subsidies, the provision, or petty penal statutes for the punishment of rogues, feeding of oxen or sheep, manuring of land or the change of the seasons, that things are dear or cheap, ploughing of land or inclosure, or what price corn bears, such a one if he be not talking of these things will fall asleep at his meals; unless he hears news from the Court, and then he holds up his hands as if he were at prayers, and, if he hears the king once named, he thinks it high treason".[21]

This advice was voicing an attitude which pervaded a large section of the aristocracy and upper gentry in the early seventeenth century. It was an attitude which was resulting in the renaissance of artistic and literary endeavour both in London and in the provinces. This was the age when English literature reached its zenith - the age of Shakespeare and Raleigh, Jonson and Bacon, Donne and Milton. Education cannot of itself create genius but it does encourage its revelation and extension. This process was in full spate in Leicestershire during Thomas Grey's childhood and if the county did not produce a writer of the very first rank it was not for want of a cultural atmosphere. Unfortunately for the county's status as a literary centre two writers, one of them a major lyrical poet, were of immediate Leicestershire lineage but neither was a Leicestershire figure. Robert Herrick was born in London in 1591, the son of Nicholas Herrick, a Leicestershire emigre, and nephew of Sir William Herrick of Beaumanor. Through Sir William, Robert entered Court life and drifted into the mainstream of so-called 'Cavalier poetry' under the influence of Ben Jonson and John Donne. His poetry, however, owed very little to his conservative puritan family connections and he was very definitely a Court poet. Certainly the sentiments in, for example, 'Gather Ye Rosebuds' savour little of a puritan perspective, but yet may still serve as a poignant reminder of the brevity of our earthly life span in general and of its increased vulnerability in times of strife.

"Gather ye rosebuds while you may, old time is still a-flying:
And that same flower that smiles today, tomorrow will be dying.
The glorious lamp of Heaven, the Sun, the higher he's a-getting:
The sooner will his race be run, and nearer he's to setting.
That age is best which is the first, when youth and blood are warmer:
But being spent, the worse, and worst Times, still succeed the former.
Then be not coy but use your time, and while you may go marry:
For having once but lost your prime, you may for ever tarry".[22]

The second, Sir Kenneth Digby, was a member of an indigenous Leicestershire family who became, among other things, a famous philosopher and scientific writer. Although he held lands in the county, Digby's country seat became Goathurst in Buckinghamshire, which he had inherited from his mother's family.

Not least of the major factors of life which the growing Thomas Grey would learn to be familiar with were the importance of social status and the codes of behaviour expected of the members of the county hierarchy. The English gentry had a strict moral code of public behaviour and carriage. In order to preserve a reputation there were certain things which must be done and others which must not be done. This was all the more so for the self proclaimed 'godly' or Puritan families who claimed to be setting an example to their social and religious contemporaries of lower ascription. The emphasis laid upon 'breeding' did not end merely at lineage, neither did it have much time for mere accumulations of wealth. There was a rigidly defined lifestyle, deviations from which might incur loss of face - a situation much to be avoided in a highly stratified local community. There were times, as we shall see later, when the strain of reconciling the need to maintain one's authority and social position with some of the elements of puritan 'fellowship' amongst the 'saints' proved too much, for the Greys at least. Both Stamford and his heir were very conscious of their hard regained aristocratic status. One can speculate on the influence of the Lady Jane legacy and the psychological impact of the memorial to the first Lord Grey of Groby in the family chapel upon the young Thomas. He spent his early life surrounded by the family memories of former glories and disappointments. As a result he, like his father, was jealous of his status and often proved eager to emphasise it to others. At the same time, and to a greater extent than Stamford, he was later to be prepared to work in co-operation with those from socially inferior origins in the interests of a common cause. Even given the high level of consciousness surrounding social stratification in those days there was in fact, and had been since the Reformation, considerable social mobility over two to three generations. Many of the current nobility had risen through the gentry from the yeoman class by the purchase of lands and titles during the Tudor period. The Spencers of Althorp in Northamptonshire, for example, had risen from Warwickshire yeoman stock by enclosing land and grazing sheep on a large scale. There were many such examples in the Midlands. In addition, the Puritan gentry often saw in similar 'godly' yeomen and burghers the makings of God's fellow 'saints'. The development of a living Puritan faith and way of life among common folk such as John Bunyan paved the way for a social revolution. Oliver Cromwell, who later both sensed and harnessed this new source of spiritual energy in the land, had the advantage that he stood closer in the social order as a member of *"a decaying gentry family"* to the yeomen farmers and tradesmen than did a Lord Grey of Groby, a young aristocrat of considerable wealth and property. Grey, however, most probably shared to some extent his emphasis upon the value of the individual above social position as he matured and as his own career developed at the national level.

In about 1613 the Earl of Huntingdon wrote a number of directions for his son and heir, Ferdinando, some of which have already been referred to. Although the Greys and Hastings were rivals, both aristocratic families were Puritan and the advice to the son might well have been given from Stamford to Thomas - such are the guidelines set out which any sensible and worthy gentleman might follow. Ferdinando was instructed to keep Sunday holy, and that the only proper exercises for that day were *"hearing the Word preached or read abroad or at home, prayer, meditation, conference, the reading of sermons or any books of divinity, visiting the sick, giving unto the poor"*. As far as fellow Puritans were concerned one should *"love them as thou shalt see the graces of God the more to appear in them"*. As for Catholics, *"till the day of judgement the sheep and the goats shall live together"*. Court was a *"glittering misery"* but when there, *"Let thy apparel ..... be neat though not costly, and let not thy speech be loud and gaping for that will show thee to be but a country gentleman"*. Women received short shrift from the old Earl : *"For thy discourse with women, praising of their beauty and talking of their apparel will be subject enough to take up a great deal of time. Care not to compliment for that will but fill thy brain and mouth with superfluous froth"*. On conversation in general the Earl advised that *"if thou enter into any argument, though with thy much inferior, argue patiently ..... In thy speech mumble it not in thy mouth, neither drale out every syllable, as though all the wit in the world were in pronouncing like a schoolboy"*. Ferdinando was exhorted not to accustom *"thyself to drink healths, for that will make thee be thought a debauched person, and if thou seest any of thy friends to swear extremely, tell him of it in private"*. The Earl of Huntingdon concluded that his advice contained *"the true image of me"*.[23] In truth it must be admitted that whilst the above advice was in the true image of the Earl of Huntingdon it was, as will be seen, less so in the case of the Earl of Stamford who evidenced a clear appetite for earthly wealth and pleasures.

Public life was not the only sphere where certain norms of acceptable behaviour existed, and ethics relating to family custom were also important, with transgressions just as poorly regarded; although the dividing line between public and private affairs in a relatively small community is often difficult to draw. Large families, even among the county hierarchy, were common - sometimes as many as twelve to sixteen children. The Earl of

Stamford and his lady with only nine children had a small family by comparison. As inheritance was nearly always by male primogeniture the only way for a younger son to come into possession of the family fortune was through the death of his elder brother(s) and before they had produced offspring of their own. Younger sons often sought other means of livelihood and many became clerics. There were cases though where the eldest son was disinherited by his father whom he had 'disobliged'. Such a threat was a great incentive to filial obedience and family cohesion; at least until the outbreak of the civil war which was to pose so many questions of divided loyalties. Children were used to create bonds of kinship, whether inside or beyond the confines of the county, to strengthen the position and safeguard the posterity of the family dynasty and its property. Marriage portions for daughters were an important part of this linkage and bonding of families. Sometimes economically ailing gentry families might have to swallow their dignity and consider marrying their heir to a wealthy yeoman's daughter. Even the Earl of Huntingdon was bound to include the following words about marriage in his advice to Ferdinando. *"Marry with one of thy own rank, yet be not too curious herein ..... match with one of the gentry where thou mayest have a great portion, for there is satiety in all things, and without means thy honour will look as naked as trees that are cropped"*. Huntingdon had more to say on the choice of a wife which tempers his mercenary, if necessary, outlook on the business. *"Thou shalt have the occasion to err but once ..... Marry not a woman that is deformed ..... Neither think that she is handsome who paints her face ..... Marry not one of a contrary religion, for thou wilt agree no better with her than an ox and an ass that draw together"*. Once married, *"deny thy wife no necessary nor fitting things ..... Nor let her have all things she would"*.[24]

Another outward sign of a private disposition which could translate into a reflection of one's worthy status was the carrying out of good works or provision of bequests. Charity or philanthropy was for some an act of Christian or human kindness, for others an important investment in ultimate salvation and a gesture to one's peers; but few county gentlemen could avoid the obligation completely. Sir Wolstan Dixie of Market Bosworth, for example, founded a grammar school in that market town and his near neighbour, Sir William Roberts, built almshouses next to the church in his village of Sutton Cheney.

These large county families valued the joys of country life. The family would meet together regularly for meals and attend the family chapel or one of the churches in one of their manors for religious services on the Sabbath. Being a member of the local aristocracy or upper gentry also meant having a substantial amount of time available for rest and recreation, even for those like the Earl of Stamford who involved themselves in the onerous tasks of magistracy and local government. Travel, whether abroad or to London, was by no means the only avenue available for a man of substance bored with supervising his tenants and his accounts. Hunting and hawking were sports which set apart the great landowning classes from everyone else. because only they could indulge in them without risking prosecution for trespassing or poaching. Of healthy exercises the Earl of Huntingdon declared, *"Hunting, hawking and riding abroad are the exercises most usual"*.[25] It must have been a grievous loss to the Earl when northbound soldiers killed all the white deer in his park at Ashby in 1640 whilst on their way to the so-called `Bishops Wars' against the Scots. Clearly, hunting was a major pastime. Less vigorous entertainments ranged from gambling at cards and dice and to dining and feasting on a grand scale to attending tilting tournaments and watching lavish musical and dramatic performances such as masques.

This is the sort of life that Thomas, Lord Grey of Groby, would have seen and participated in as he lived and grew up at Bradgate during the 1620s and 1630s. We can perhaps imagine him hunting, hawking, and riding abroad on the extensive family holdings in that attractive part of Leicestershire. He would have covered a large part of the county, even beyond the wide sweep of the strikingly picturesque Charnwood Forest, in supervising work on the estates and tenancies of the Greys that lay further removed from Bradgate Park and its adjoining areas. The separate manors of Groby, Breedon, and Broughton Astley each contained several villages, hamlets, farms and woodlands. Amidst the variety of pursuits, social and economic, legal and family manoeuvrings and law enforcement, country gentlemen like Stamford and Grey of Groby would drink a lot of wine and beer, smoke tobacco, eat heartily of beef, lamb, mutton, veal, capons, turkeys, pigeons, ducks, plovers, larks, woodcocks, curlews, quails, rabbits, lobsters, oysters, and a host of other foods and fruits. They would eat upon pewter or silver dishes brought to them by their servants who lived in the great house with them. They would write letters to their friends and kinsfolk in which news of local and national events bulked large and they would make visits to Leicester and sometimes to London, either on horseback or in their coaches. For people of their station it was a most agreeable life. As the Earl of Huntingdon wrote to another of his sons, Henry Hastings - of whom we shall hear much more shortly - in 1627; *"I can say in my own experience, that I have tasted of all the waters that have issued from honest delights, and that no life for the good of the soul, of the body and estate is answerable to a country life".*[26]

In the same letter the Earl of Huntingdon advised his second son, who was to become an archetypal 'cavalier', against preferring the life of a courtier, against the allure of young women, and ended with an expression

20

of paternal love and affection. *"..... I should be sorry that you should like a court life too well, for it is but 'splendida miseria', and Sir Walter Mildmay, a great courtier and councillor of state in Queen Elizabeth's time, in a little book of his hath this saying 'Know the court, but spend not thy time there' ..... It is true that women are pretty conceited things, pretty especially if they be young, and needs must be full of conceits, for Solomon the wisest of all kings could not dive the depths of this knowledge, the way of a young man with a maid ..... And so, as you crave a blessing from me, I beseech Almighty God to grant you the blessings of Abraham, Issack and Jacob, and to give you a plenitude of all internal, external and eternal happinesses, as he will ever wish and pray for unto his end, that will always be your very loving and affectionate father"*.[27]

Even royalty could appreciate the attractions of the country life. During the summer of 1625 the Parliament was adjourned to Oxford, meeting in the great hall of Christ Church College, to avoid the plague which still raged, not only in London, but also at Windsor in the castle and the town. Charles had been king for less than four months and had been married by proxy to Henrietta Maria, the French princess, in Notre Dame in May. The new young queen, diminutive but vivacious, aged fifteen had arrived in England in mid June. The royal couple were staying at Oatlands, due shortly to move on to Birsham and Woodstock when, in July, it was reported that,

> *"The Queen is much delighted with the River of the Thames and doth love to walk in the meadow and look upon the haymakers, and will sometimes take a rake and a fork and sportingly make hay with them. These are our best country news"*.[28]

Yet even the most ordered of communities contain frictions, and in a community whose well-being rests on landownership, arguments over property and property rights flourish. This was certainly the case here and many of the disputes involved the Greys in clashes with their neighbours. Litigation of itself, however, did not constitute a transgression of the accepted code of gentry morality. Lawsuits instead, indeed the very practice of the law, became a major occupation and emphasised the importance of attendance at the Inns of Court in the education of a major landowning gentleman. Such people were coming increasingly to dominate the Parliament in London; though none had been called to meet between 1629 and 1640.

It may be useful at this stage to give a brief description of Leicestershire and its county town in this period. William Burton, writing in 1662, began his description of his native county as follows :-

> *"Leicestershire, so called from the chief Town Leicester, which stands upon the river Leire or Legre, (as Leyland affirms) now called Sore..... It has the shape of an Heart, broad at the top, and narrower towards the bottom, which shape it truly resembles, and lies almost in the centre of the whole Continent of the kingdom..... It borders on the East, upon Lincoln and Rutland Shires, on the West, upon Warwickshire, separated from it by the great road-way, called Watling Street: on the North upon Nottingham and Derby Shires: on the South, upon Northamptonshire, being divided thence almost all along by the river Welland, and from the residue by the river Avon. This Shire, in the time of King Edward the First, was divided into four Hundreds, viz. Goscote, Guthlakeston, Framland, and Gertre. But in the twentieth year of the reign of King Edward the Third, Guthlakeston was subdivided into Sparkenhoe, and now of later years, Goscote into East and West Goscote."*[29]

From the geographical point of view there is little to add except that Staffordshire also shared a short boundary with Leicestershire in the north west corner between Warwickshire and Derbyshire. The Soar Valley divides the shire into two: to the west lies the Charnwood Forest, a picturesque region of thin soils and rocky granite outcrops which rises to 912 feet at Bardon Hill, and to the east lie the rolling wolds, rising to 690 feet near Skeffington, which gives rise to fertile soils. A further division may be made between the north and south of the county thus cutting it into four portions. Indeed, Burton gives the following quadri-partite description of Leicestershire:-

"South-West	*Rich ground, plentiful in corn and pasture, but wanting wood; forcing the inhabitants to make use of straw, cowshern, & c.*
North-West	*For the most part hard and barren, yielding fruit not without labour and expence, but well stored with wood and pit-coal.*
North-East	*Good soil, apt to bear corn and grass, and sufficiently provided with fuel.*
South East	*Much like the last for fruitfulness, and, of the two, better furnished with fuel.*

However, these quarters, being put together into the body of one shire, competently supply their mutual defects."[30]

Leicestershire's dimensions were set out by Fuller. *"It extendeth from north to south thirty and three miles (measured from the utmost angle); but exceedeth not twenty seven in the breadth thereof."*[31]

In the centre of the county, then as now like the hub in a cartwheel, lay the county town and borough of Leicester. Radiating out in an approximate circle of satellites around it, and acting as the focal points of the hinterlands of the hundreds, were the market towns of which the largest were Ashby-de-la-Zouch and Loughborough (in West Goscote), Queniborough (in East Goscote), Melton Mowbray (in Framland), Lutterworth (in Guthlaxton), Market Harborough (in Gartree), Market Bosworth and Hinckley (in Sparkenhoe).

Some impression may be formed of the appearance of the settlement pattern and landscape of Leicestershire in the mid-seventeenth century from the writing of contemporary travellers, such as Richard Symonds. Writing in 1645 he found that *"The county of Leicester is generally champaigne pasture and erable, little or no waste, and small wood; some quick hedges, and the parishes stand less than one myle distant."*[32]

It may also be useful at this point to note the common practice in seventeenth century England of referring to a county as a country and to every settlement above the size of the smallest hamlet as a town.

Leicestershire at this time was still essentially an agricultural and rural community with marked social stratification amongst its inhabitants. Authority in such a society was a function of social position, which in turn was traditionally linked to landowning. Grazing and farming were the main economic activities. Although coal was mined in the north west of the county at Coleorton and Swannington it was on a very small scale and coal was brought from Derbyshire and Warwickshire as well as from these local workings along trackways through the Leicester Forest. The hosiery industry was not fully established in the county until the second half of the

23

century and it was only in the eighteenth century that improvements in communications brought Leicestershire into relatively easy contact with other parts of England, especially London.

The beginning of the seventeenth century found Leicester itself a small market town of five parishes with a population of approximately 3,500 people. The town still possessed its open fields, its inhabitants still followed largely agricultural pursuits, and what industry and commerce there was in the borough was tied closely to rural activities.

Celia Fiennes writing in the seventeenth century describes how *"Leicester town stands on the Side of a little riseing Ground, tho' at a distance from ye adjacent hills it looks low, but its a good prospect. It has four gates, ye streetes are pretty large and well pitch'd, there are five parishes; the Market place is a Large space very handsome with a good Market Cross and town hall. Ye river Sow* (Soar) *which runs into the river Recke* (Wreake) *and both Empts* (sic) *themselves into ye Trent."* She adds that *"..... their fewell here is but Cowdung or Coale which they are supplied with out of Warwickshire."* [33]

The whole of Leicester's prosperity and economic development appears to have been dependent upon rural or related activities. The town was, in economic terms, a place of craftsmen and small shopkeepers, living by the services given to and received from the surrounding countryside. There were many links between the town and country; together they formed an integrated community.

"The town fields (almost wholly unenclosed) comprised by 1630 some 2,800 acres - an area, that is, about twenty times that of the walled town itself. Two-thirds of this arable, one third pasture. Leicester people also farmed land extensively further out, by payment of rent. Many of them kept dairies, which not only supplied their own households but also provided butter and cheese for the market. As the services of regular carriers developed, a part of this produce may well have found its way to London. There were many graziers in the town. Some of them were dairymen or craftsmen as well; others were also butchers. The largest men of this class were general farmers, growing crops for fodder and brewing, besides much hay and corn. Here was a continuing basis for employment in the town. The farmers required the services of five wage-workers each, on average, without including dairymaids and shepherds. A careful analysis of the evidence provided by wills and inventories suggests that capitalist farmers were the largest employers of labour in Leicester."[34]

24

The poor harvests and diseases which appear to have dominated the period 1625 to 1640 had deep repercussions on the politics of the town and county. These found their expression in Leicester partly in attempts to secure extra privileges for the corporation of the borough, as against the county generally and the leading families, and partly in general opposition to aspects of the economic, social and religious policies of the royal government. At various stages before actual civil way broke out the borough and its magistrates found themselves in opposition to the royal authority. One of the outstanding causes of discontent was the move by Charles I in 1628 to enclose Leicester Forest. This proposal was strenuously resisted by the people of Leicester and the surrounding countryside. The townsfolk had enjoyed the right to cut firewood in the forest since the time of the Beaumont Earls, and the main route by which coal was brought in from the workings in the western part of the county ran through it. The Corporation offered a payment of £500 for the abandonment of the scheme. Unruly persons damaged the ditches that were cut as boundaries. An appeal was addressed to Parliament in the form of "A petition from divers glaziers (sic) of Leicester." It was presented to the House of Commons on 17th February 1629, and referred to the Committee of Grievances.[35] The contents are not recorded in detail but the Journal of the House of Lords contains a reference to grievances including *"the disafforestation of Leicester Forest."*[36] It is almost certain that the `divers glaziers' mentioned as the authors of the petition were in fact graziers. The king was forced to make a compromise and conceded an allocation of forty acres to the townspeople as a whole and other grants were made to those with special claims. The forty acres were let and the income from the rent applied to poor relief. In spite of these concessions the royal action was very unpopular in Leicester. The cash gained by the Crown from the enclosure of the Leicester Forest was outweighed by the ill-will that it created locally. This may have contributed towards the antagonism which the Royal interest encountered later in Leicester; although it should also be observed that with the exception of this issue overt opposition to royal policy was not markedly evidenced before 1640.

As far as the wider county beyond the borough is concerned opinions vary as to the degree of social, economic, and political homogeneity to be found. This question can perhaps best be considered by beginning with an examination of the main layers of social stratification in Leicestershire.

At the top of the county hierarchy were the local members of the aristocracy. In 1640 Leicestershire had eight noble families, the Manners of Belvoir, the Blounts (Earls of Newport) of Allexton, the Brudenells of Cranoe, the Sherards of Stapleford, the Beaumonts of Coleorton, the Greys (of Ruthin and Earls of Kent) of Burbage, the Hastings (Earls of Huntingdon) of Ashby and Castle Donington, and the Greys (Earls of Stamford) of Groby and

Bradgate. These families were of considerable influence and wealth. The annual income of the upper five noble families would be in the 1640s of the order of £4,000. Of these the two leading families of Hastings and Grey of Groby enjoyed considerably higher wealth and income. Back in 1609, for example, the annual expenses alone of the Earl of Huntingdon of Ashby were £2,855. 13s. 4d. and he kept a staff of sixty-one servants plus his four gentlemen.

Below the local aristocracy were the gentry families - those which were armigerous (having the right to a hereditary coat of arms) - and who together with the former constituted the major landowning class of the county. Amongst the ranks of the upper gentry were to be found the following families, Shirley of Staunton Harold, Harpur of Hemington, Herrick of Beaumanor, Brokesby of Birstall, Bainbridge of Lockington, Babington of Rothley, Danvers of Rothley, Wollaston of Shenton, Dixie of Market Bosworth, Roberts of Sutton Cheney, Quarles of Enderby, Faunt of Foston, Staremore of Frolesworth, Cave of Stanford, Halford of Wistow, Bale of Carlton Curlieu, Halford of Welham, Burton of Stockerston, Hesilrige of Noseley, Skipwith of Cotes, Villiers of Brooksby, Smith of Queniborough, Ashby of Quenby, Skeffington of Skeffington, Fountaine of Kirby Bellars, Pate of Sysonby, Lacy of Melton Mowbray, Hartopp of Buckminster, Lister of Thorpe Arnold, Smith of Edmundthorpe, St. John of Cold Overton, and Whatton of the Newarke in Leicester. In addition, there were junior branches of the aristocratic families such as the Beaumonts of Gracedieu, the Beaumonts of Stoughton, the Hastings of Braunstone, the Hastings of Glenfield, the Hartopps of Burton Lazars; and other families not based primarily in Leicestershire but wielding considerable influence through property and marriage connections within the shire. An example would be the Fieldings (Earls of Denbigh) of Newnham Paddox just across the county border in Warwickshire. Taken together these families of the local aristocracy and upper gentry have sometimes been held to constitute a 'county community'. It has been suggested that there were thirty-five ruling caucus families in the county whose members participated in government and administration either as local magistrates or as Members of Parliament.[37]

Below this dominant political community of the county and its aristocratic leaders were the lower gentry - the local squires and landowners of less substance. The average estate in Leicestershire during the reign of Charles I has been reckoned at not more than about 1,000 acres and in many cases extended to less than 700. Alongside this group in terms of wealth, if not of status, were the rising yeoman farmers, merchants and traders. In the towns and villages were the smallholders, landless labourers, journeymen, artisans, and others who were normally excluded from the politically active class before the outbreak of the Civil War put swords into their hands. In Leicester itself, however, the wealthy burgesses who

26

constituted the Corporation - the Mayor, the Twenty-Four [Aldermen], and the Forty-Eight [Councillors of the Common Hall] - which selected itself, was already beginning to assert its position against the traditional hegemony of the dominant county families. A glance at the occupations of the men who held the position of Mayor of Leicester during this period shows a predominance of merchants who made their living from meeting the needs of the town and county; they were chandlers (shopkeepers, grocers, dealers in merchandise, e.g. corn wholesalers), drapers (retailers of cloth), cordwainers (boot and shoemakers), mercers (dealers in textile fabrics and fine cloth), goldsmiths (dealers or manufacturers of gold articles and bankers), graziers (large scale farmers of sheep or cattle), and the like.

A marked political change occurred in Leicestershire during the 1620s and 1630s. The Hastings' domination of the county and the borough began to weaken after the 1621 parliamentary elections. They gained representation in the 1628 elections but it was no longer the monopoly which it had been hitherto. Now the animosities and jealousies of the county gentry towards the resented Hastings hegemony found focus at Bradgate. The year 1628, which saw Henry Grey become Earl of Stamford, also saw the assassination of the king's favourite and Chief Minister George Villiers, Duke of Buckingham, a scion of the Leicestershire Villiers family of Brooksby. The times proved propitious for the marked revival during the 1630s of the influence of the Greys in which the new Earl of Stamford took advantage of the growing discord between members of the Leicester Corporation and the other county magnates, notably the Hastings clan. As the decade progressed the Hastings were increasingly seen as *'a decaying family'*[38] on the defensive everywhere against the reviving power of the Greys of Groby and Bradgate.

In the years before the outbreak of the civil war the Earl of Stamford spent his time mostly at Bradgate living in the manner typical of his class and position in the society of England at that time.

> *"This Earl, having attained from Charles I in 1629, a grant to himself and Daniel Britton, of certain lands in Charnwood Forest, adjoining to his park of Bradgate, continued in this delightful retirement to enjoy the comforts of domestic felicity, till the fatal disturbances that ensued called forth his exertions in far different scenes".*[39]

This is a pleasant sounding account, evocative of pastoral tranquillity, despite the hint at the approach of the storm clouds of strife; but it is not wholly accurate. Stamford was not inactive in this pre-bellum period of the 1630s. Indeed, in the early years of that decade he appears to have enjoyed the royal favour. The only indication at this stage of his future

27

course of action was, as we have noted earlier, that he had attended Cambridge rather than Oxford University.

Leaving aside for a moment his likely political orientations it may be useful to consider what is known of the Earl of Stamford's personality and character. He appears to have had a haughty and irritable disposition and a quick and violent temper which could make him a disagreeable neighbour. There are several accounts of him physically attacking people with whom he disagreed, usually with his walking cane, or employing his servants to carry out such acts.

W. Mercer in 'Angliae Speculum' calls him *"most courteous and right stately Stanford"*, but most accounts of the time belie this image. He also seems to have had something of an avaricious nature although a more charitable interpretation could regard him as ambitious, an entrepreneur, and a man of ideas. His annual income from his estates would be, in the late 1620s, of the order of £4,000. This was at a time when an income of £1,000 betokened very good estates, verging on the wealthy. An income of £1,500 put a man in the class of the very wealthy. The estates of the Earl of Caernarvon, by comparison, yielded an income of £7,000 a year.

Like all the major county families, both the local aristocracy and the upper gentry, Stamford was involved in landowning and land purchase. He was an enclosing landlord and he clashed with the Commissioners for Depopulation when he began enclosing land on his manors at Breedon-on-the-Hill and at Broughton Astley in the years 1629 to 1633.[40] Turning his attention further afield, Stamford set about improving Wildmere Fen in his Lincolnshire holdings in about 1632; and by 1633 he was planning brewhouses in the towns of Leicester and Stamford, as he put it, to provide *"good and wholesome drink at reasonable prices"*.[41] He hoped to secure something of a monopoly in this area of provision. In February 1636 Stamford was proposing a joint scheme with Principal Secretary of State Windebank for patenting the dressing of hemp from which he hoped to make some £4,000 to £5,000 a year profit. As David Fleming in his study on faction and civil war in Leicestershire observes, Stamford must have been overlooked by the historian R. H. Tawney when he declared of the seventeenth century that **"experiment and innovation ..... were all on the side of the enterprising country gentlemen"** and not on that of the peerage.[42]

So, here we have a picture of the Earl of Stamford in the mid 1630s - like Lord Mandeville (later the Earl of Manchester) and several other later leaders of the early Parliamentarian military effort and members of the 'Presbyterian' Puritan political group such as Denzil Holles and Lord Saye and Sele - an enclosing landlord, an aspirant monopolist, and a business associate of high ranking Crown servants. On the face of it this hardly seems a likely profile of a potential rebel. Indeed, in 1634, he received a royal visit; an accolade which marked his rise and the restoration of the Grey family fortunes in the county. King Charles I and his French wife, Queen Henrietta Maria, on their way to Leicester from Nottingham were entertained on the 9th August by the Earl of Stamford at Bradgate, to whom the Corporation of the borough at Leicester had previously made a complimentary present of a hogshead of claret wine and 43 lbs of sugar in order to assist.[43] At the time of this visit Thomas, Lord Grey of Groby would be aged ten or eleven. It is interesting to speculate whether King Charles noticed, or had pointed out to him, the pollarded oak trees in the Park at Bradgate which according to Leicestershire folklore even to this day had been so cut as a sign of mourning after the death of Lady Jane Grey under the executioner's axe - then only some eighty years earlier. Certainly the pollarding of the oaks seems to have been far more severe than would normally be the practice in forestry. By an irony of history, or perhaps later intent, Thomas Grey was to play a significant part in the process which led immediately to the severing of Charles' head from its royal shoulders in 1649.

On 16th May in the following year the king affirmed the original grant by Queen Elizabeth I in 1574/5 of Groby Manor, including Bradgate Park and its other lands, to the Grey family. What, then, may be considered to have turned the Greys against King Charles I? It is likely that it was a combination of frustrations in business aspirations and differences in policy both locally and nationally. The only clear sign, however, was that barometer of seventeenth century politics - religion. The Greys were a Puritan family and had a long tradition of being so. Their local rivals, the Hastings family, by contrast, had a history of fluctuation between Catholicism and various shades of Protestantism. In the 1630s and 1640s even though the main branch of the family at Ashby-de-la-Zouch were Protestants once more the offshoots at Glenfield and Braunstone had remained loyal to the "Old Religion". While the Earl of Huntingdon was recognised as a staunch Puritan there were strong doubts about his second son, the cavalier Henry Hastings, who was openly an Episcopalian Anglican and was suspected by many county Puritans of being a secret Catholic like the Shirleys of Staunton Harold. It was not beyond question to the more suspicious minded Puritans that the Hastings support for royal innovations in matters of religion might lead to another restoration of 'papism' as with their previous support for Mary Tudor. The Greys of Bradgate, however, stood for an unbroken Protestant stance in the county, and a Puritan one at that. Puritan is a blanket term for those who broadly desired simpler forms of church ceremonies and a system of church government without bishops. It covered a multitude of different factions, some inside the national state church (usually referred to as 'Presbyterians') and some either forced out or feeling the need to withdraw to 'separate' or 'gathered' congregations of the godly where they could manage themselves (usually `Independents' or `Baptists'); but all sharing an emphasis on God's Word as revealed in the scriptures rather than through priests and bishops, and all essentially holding to the Calvinistic idea of predestined salvation for the `saints' like themselves. The term `Puritan' also usually implies a certain strictness in attitude towards morality and individual behaviour on the part of the `godly'. This might sometimes extend to elements of outward appearance such as a preference for plainness in dress or, as in the case of a temporary fashion among the London apprentices who supported the King's parliamentary critics in 1640, for short cropped hair which could be used by their enemies to characterise them as `Roundheads'. Whilst there is no evidence that Stamford fitted the second type of description of a Puritan in terms of personal appearance (as a brief look at any of his portraits will testify) or behaviour by any means, he was certainly strongly opposed to the `Arminian' or High-Church tendencies of the Anglican Church under Archbishop Laud. There are references to *"his unreasonable hostility to the Church in early days"*[(44)] and apparently as chairman of the local quarter sessions he missed no opportunity of showing this hostility to the Church and its priests. In 1638 he caught a clergyman hawking on his estate and so jealous was the Earl of his status and his property rights that a scuffle ensued between the pair. The Earl indignantly reported the matter to Sir John Lambe, Secretary to William Laud, Archbishop of Canterbury.

"I desire your favour to acquaint the Archbishop with this relation. About a fortnight since, as I came from hunting, I heard, not far out of my way, certain falconers. It being within my royalty I made the more haste to see who they were, and there I found one parson Smith, of Swithland, and his company; he with a hawk upon his fist and speaking unto his dogs. So I repaired unto him and told him that I wondered much how he durst be so bold to take his pleasure within my royalties, having been often discharged. He answered that the laws of the realm allowed it him, and so long as the King lived he would take his pastimes at his pleasure. I replied that within his own lands and liberties he might do what he pleased, but he had no property in mine, therefore I discharged him absolutely. Besides some other unmannerly speeches, he told me that he would halt there, whereupon I was very much moved at it, and did make offer to catch off his hawk's neck, but he cast off his hawk from his fist and bore at me with his other hand, and so caught hold of my shoulder. I, for my own defence, caught hold of a riband he wore across his body like a gallant, believing he might have pulled me off from my horse, but the riband, not owing any

30

fidelity to its function, brake, and so we parted. I told him that I would complain to his Grace; he replied that he would meet me anywhere. I told him that then he must appear in a canonical garment; for when we met he had none such upon his body. I considered that he was a clergyman, and although I was very much moved and had a good strong hunting pole in my hand, yet, remembering his function, I forbore to strike him, believing that his Grace will consider that there is a distance betwixt so mean a man, both in learning and gravity, as Smith is, and a peer of the realm. I beseech you let me leave this business to your care.

P.S. - Smith keeps greyhounds, crossbows, guns, and, as I am informed, all sorts of engines for destroying game. [45]

It seems that the Church obstructed the Earl of Stamford at all levels in both the social and business aspects of his life.

The break with the king seems to have come around the period 1638 to 1640. Stamford was summoned to join the king in the 1639 campaign against the Scots in the so-called 'Bishops Wars'. In June 1639, whilst in attendance upon the king at Berwick-on-Tweed, he paid an unauthorised visit to the Scottish army in its encampment. He was hospitably entertained and dined by General Alexander Leslie, a fellow Presbyterian, and was asked to represent the Scots' case to the king. They wished to avoid bloodshed and to be loyal to both the king and their national Covenant which pledged them to uphold a Presbyterian form of church government without bishops in Scotland. Upon his return Stamford gave an account of the Scots' loyalty to King Charles who rebuffed him by dryly observing that *"he had done them too much honour to go"*.[46] Stamford further incurred the royal disapproval in connection with this campaign, but this time it was rather nearer to home. It was discovered in 1640 that he had kept at Bradgate six draught horses which had been raised by Leicestershire for the English army's northern expedition. When confronted with the king's displeasure over the matter he protested that he had meant to pay the £24 the horses were worth. Within the same month, on the king's instructions, the horses were sold by Richard Halford, a deputy-lieutenant of the shire and a member of the Hastings faction, for £41.6s.8d.[47]

The Earl of Stamford now moved more openly as a zealous Parliamentarian in the approaching struggle. Nationally he was prominent in the anti-court faction in the House of Lords which gathered when the Short Parliament was called in 1640. Locally he led the opposition to the long established Hastings hegemony in Leicestershire which now, rightly or wrongly, was seen as representing the royal interest and its policies.

Events both locally and nationally now rapidly gathered speed. Life at Bradgate would not return to normal for many years.

An unusual portent of the impending strife in the form of celestial apparitions is revealed in a letter from Henry Hastings to his father, Henry, Earl of Huntingdon.

"1640 Feb. 3. Donington Park.

Nothing being done upon our earth worthy your knowledge, I will presume to acquaint you what was seen in the air and heard from thence to the great admiration of many. About a week since at eight of the clock at night some clouds being dispersed and at a good distance from one another seemed to the beholders to be like men with pikes and muskets, but suddenly the scheme being changed they appeared in two bodies of armed men set in battalia, and then a noise was heard and sudden flashings of light seen and streaks like smoke issuing out of those clouds. I imagine the report of this strange sight hath come to your Lordship before now, but receiving this information from some who are not so apt to be deceived by their fancies is the cause of writing it .....[(48)]

NOTES

1. The Domesday Survey 1086. folio 232 a.b.
2. William Shakespeare *Henry VI - Part III, Act II, Sc.II.*
3. John Leland *The Itinerary of John Leland the Antiquary* Vol IV, Part II, p. 187a.
4. Ibid.
5. Claire Cross *The Puritan Earl - the Life of Henry Hastings, Third Earl of Huntingdon, 1536-1596* (Macmillan), 1966.
6. Ibid. p. 18
7. Ibid. p. 18
8. Ed. W. G. Hoskins & R. A. McKinley *Victoria County History of Leicestershire* (1954) Vol II, p. 102
9. Ibid. p. 105
10. Ibid. p. 107
11. Brydges *Memoirs of English Peers during the reign of King James* pp. 82-84.
12. Records of the Borough of Leicester, Vol. III, p. 386, & pp. 413-415.
13. Historical Manuscripts Commission; Hastings MSS, Vol. IV, p. 199.
14. Historical Manuscripts Commission; MSS of the Duke of Somerset. (Letter from the King to Thomas Wentworth, Earl of Strafford).
15. Historical Manuscripts Commission; Salisbury (Cecil) MSS, Vol. XXII (1612-1668) p. 122 (Extraict de lettres de Heydelberg et du Camp de Boheme d'Egemberg les 21, 22 et 23 Juillet, et de Prague le 27, 1620. Receues le 20 d'Aoust).
16. Ibid.
17. John Leland *The Itinerary of John Leland the Antiquary'* Vol. IV, Part II.
18. Marie Forsyth *The History of Bradgate* (The Bradgate Books, Vol. 3. Published by the Bradgate Park Trust) 1974, pp. 8-17.
19. John Nichols *History and Antiquities of Leicestershire* Vol. III, Part II, p. 681.
20. David Fleming *Some aspects of the gentry in Jacobean and Caroline Leicestershire* (Unpublished MA dissertation, Department of English Local History, Leicester University, 1976).
21. Historical Manuscripts Commission; Hastings MSS; Vol IV, p. 334 (The Earl of Huntingdon's advice to his son, Ferdinando Hastings).
22. Robert Herrick, *Gather Ye Rosebuds* (Poem)
23. Historical Manuscripts Commission; Hastings MSS; Vol IV, pp 329-335
24. Ibid. p. 332.
25. Ibid. p. 331.
26. Historical Manuscripts Commission; Hastings MSS; Vol. II, pp. 70-71. (Letter from the Earl of Huntingdon to his son, Henry Hastings)

27.   Ibid.

28.   Ibid. p. 67. (Letter from Sir John Davys (Kings Sergeant) to Henry, fifth Earl of Huntingdon, at Dunnington Park. From Engelfield, 1625, July 21.

29.   William Burton, *The Description of Leicestershire: Containing Matters of Antiquity, History, Armour and Genealogy* (1777) p. 1.

30.   Ibid. p. 2.

31.   *Fuller's British Worthies* Vol. II., p. 223.

32.   Richard Symonds, *Diary of the Marches of the Royal Army During the Great Civil War* ed. C E Long (Camden Society, Vol. LXXXIV, 1859).

33.   Celia Fiennes, op. cit.

34.   Jack Simmons, *Leicester - The Ancient Borough to 1860* (Alan Sutton, 1983) p. 73.

35.   Journal of the House of Commons (C.J.) Vol.I., p. 930.

36.   Journal of the House of Lords (L.J.) Vol.III., pp. 872, 875, 878.

37.   David Fleming, MA dissertation (unpublished) *Some aspect of the gentry in Jacobean and Caroline Leicestershire* (Leicester University - Department of English Local History, 1976).

38.   Edward Hyde, Earl of Clarendon *History of the Great Rebellion* ed. W D Macray (1888) Vol. III., P. 473.

39.   Brydges *Collins Peerage of England* Vol. III, pp. 353-366.

40.   Calendar of State Papers, Domestic Series, 1629-31, p. 491; & 1631-3, p. 54.

41.   Calendar of State Papers, Domestic Series, 1631-3, p. 559. Historical Manuscripts Commission, MSS of Earl of Cowper, Vol. II, p. 111.

42.   Calendar of State Papers, Domestic Series, 1635-6, p. 203. David Fleming op. cit. with reference to R.H. Tawney, *The Rise of the Gentry*.

43.   W. Kelly *Royal Progresses and Visits to Leicester* (1884) Records of the Borough of Leicester, Vol. IV, 1603-1688 (1923).

44.   Dictionary of National Biography, Vol. XXIII. See Grey, Henry, First Earl of Stamford, p. 187. and Geoffrey H. White *The Complete Peerage* (G.E.C.) (1853 edition), Vol. XII, pp. 217-223.

45.   Calendar of State Papers, Domestic Series, 1638-9, pp. 81-82.

46.   Ibid. 1639, pp. 330-331.

47.   Ibid. 1640, pp. 141, 174, 340.

48.   Historical Manuscripts Commission, MSS; Vol. II, p. 80. (Letter from Henry Hastings to his father, Henry, fifth Earl of Huntingdon).

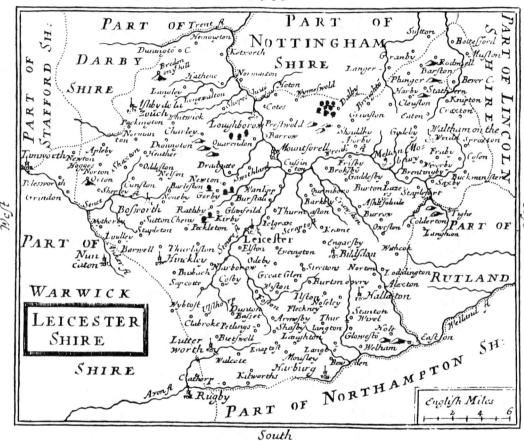

Map of 17th Century Leicestershire

Lady Jane Grey (1537-1554)

Family tomb of the Greys in the Chapel at Bradgate House

Lady Anne Cecil (1603-1676)

Henry Gray Earle of Standford,
Lord Gray of Groby, Bonvile, and
Harington et.

Henry Grey, First Earl of Stamford, Baron Grey of Groby,
Bonvile & Harrington (1599-1673)

Lady Anne Grey (nee Cecil) Countess Stamford (1603-1676)

Henry Grey, Earl of Stamford (1599-1673)

Seventeenth century view of Bradgate

CHAPTER TWO

INTO THE STORM:
FROM YOUNG MP TO EDGEHILL FIELD
(1640 - 1642)

"The young men rose, and from the temples took,
Their arms, now such as a long peace had marred,
And their old bucklers now of leather bared:
Their blunted piles not of a long time used,
And swords with the eatings of black rust abused."
(Thomas May - 'Pharsalia', 1631)

"When civil fury first grew high,
And men fell out they knew not why;
When hard words, jealousies and fears
Set folks together by the ears,
And made them fight like mad or drunk
For Dame Religion as for punk,
Whose honesty they all durst swear for,
Though not a man of them knew wherefore;
When Gospel-trumpeter, surrounded
With long-eared rout, to battle sounded,
And pulpit, drum ecclesiastic,
Was beat with fist instead of stick:
Then did Sir Knight abandon dwelling
And out he rode a Colonelling ...."
(Samuel Butler, 1613 - 1680)

As the dispute between King and Parliament began to gain momentum by 1640 the Earl of Stamford had become a zealous Parliamentarian at the national level and the leading figure amongst their number in Leicestershire. Writs for the first parliamentary elections since March 1629 were issued on 13th April 1640 and in the subsequent contest a considerable victory was achieved locally over the pro-court party as represented by the Earl of Huntingdon, Lord Lieutenant of the county and leader of the Hastings family, and his nominees. Returned to the House of Commons as members for the shire were Sir Arthur Hesilrige of Noseley who was to prove a firm republican, and Lord Grey of Ruthin, a committed Parliamentarian and a member of the Burbage branch of the Grey family, who was to become Earl of Kent in 1643.[1] Returned as members for the Borough of Leicester were a Mr Thomas Cooke, subsequently expelled from the Commons in

43

1645 for having royalist sympathies, and Thomas, Lord Grey of Groby at the ripe young age of seventeen. On the position of the town of Leicester itself in 1640 we read that **"the party that dominated the town's affairs clearly tended to sympathise with the opposition** (to the king); **but did not declare itself imprudently"**.[2]

Thus it was that Thomas Grey came down to London to take his seat at Westminster at a critical time in the history of his country. What sort of place was the London with which this young aristocrat was to become acquainted and where he was to spend much of his future life? After the quiet years spent at Bradgate, Leicester, and the Grey manors in rural Leicestershire it must have been an exciting prospect for a wealthy seventeen year old with many influential connections.

Contemporary prints of seventeenth century London depict an infinitely variegated city set either side of the Thames and encircled by fields, forests, marshes, hills and outlying villages. The river, even at that time, was a vital artery leading to the heart of a great trading nation. Riding at anchor on this river could usually be seen the tall masted sailing ships and along the waterfront on both sides and in both directions were the variety of commercial and residential buildings, which reflected the degree of affluence and the nature of activity in that part of the city. On the north side of the river the spire of St. Paul's Cathedral dwarfed its many rivals. Surrounding the cathedral and the other finer buildings such as churches and palaces were the crowded tall houses of merchants and traders. Many of these houses dated from the medieval period and, given the increase in population, were now old, cramped, and in some cases little better than slums. The huddle of poor tenements at Southwark had by now spread so as to screen the Globe Theatre off from the river. The countryside still almost reached to the medieval walls and gates of the City of London proper, leaving Chelsea, Paddington, St. Pancras, and Islington as villages and giving views beyond of fields, hills, and windmills. The Tower of London was, like St. Paul's, one of the focal points of the city. It was set between neat gabled houses and lawns sloping down to the crowded glitter of the Thames, with its moat, outer walls, triangular courtyards and flagged cupolas. More graceful, whilst still imposing, than most fortresses, less grandiose than neighbouring palaces, it dominated a richly coloured panorama extending from the cold splendour of Westminster to the more romantic elaborations of Greenwich. The Tower of London helped to serve as a symbol of the authority of the Crown and the power of the State. All passing under Tower Bridge or Temple Bar were reminded also, if they looked up at the remains of the impaled and severed heads on display, of the fate of those who had incurred the sovereign's displeasure or imperilled the security of the realm. Then there was London Bridge, that triumph of

44

engineering, with its shops and houses - a sight that must have impressed every visitor or newcomer to the capital. East of the Tower, and downstream from London Bridge, sprawled the wharves, warehouses, and whorehouses of one of the busiest seaports in Europe. On the other side of the city, through the Lud Gate, lay the great houses of the nobility in the Strand. These town residences were conveniently located for the Courts of Law and the Inns of Court. Further on, and following the river, lay the Palace of Whitehall, Westminster Abbey, and the Palace of Westminster. Within the confines of the Palace of Westminster were Westminster Hall and the Parliament House. A little further westwards and on the south bank lay Lambeth Palace, the residence of the Archbishop of Canterbury. This city thus housed within a very short distance the centres of political, ecclesiastical, and economic power in the kingdom.

Away from the comfortable palaces and the stately city residences of the aristocracy, however, the streets of London were dark and narrow. The alleys off the streets were shaded, dark, cool, and they generally stank. Sewage was thrown from the windows into central gutters, if there were any. The stench of decaying refuse and the emptying of chamberpots littered and stained the flagstones and cobblestones of squares and passageways. The Fleet River was an open sewer running into the Thames. In winter the use of coal for fuel instead of wood caused air pollution and fog. Although there was little starvation many died from diseases caused by the lack of sanitation. Only a fraction of children survived their early years and many were still-born. Thieves and murderers lurking in the narrow streets and alleyways were a threat to any late night reveller. Well might the Earl of Huntingdon, in comparison, extol the advantages of a country life!

Yet people were still drawn to London. There was an endless procession of people in the streets; on foot, on horseback, or in carriages. There was a variety of status, dress, and colour to be seen - courtiers and members of the gentry with sword and walking stick wearing plumed felt hats, more soberly dressed merchants and ministers, maids of Court ladies bargaining for goods at market stalls, craftsmen and traders of all kinds, clergymen, burly watermen, cripples, vagabonds, and beggars in rags, sailors frequenting the waterfront taverns, students, apprentices, painted whores, a miscellany of foreigners - and all drawn to London by the prospect of gain of some kind and the desire to be at the centre of things.

The young Lord Grey of Groby was certainly to find himself at the centre of national events very shortly. Living at the family's town house at Grey Court, nr. Devereux Court and Essex Street in the Strand or Exeter House, St. John's, Clerkenwell, part of his mother's Cecil inheritance, he was well placed for access to both the Palace of Westminster and Gray's Inn. Like so many Members of Parliament since he was to find that, although momentous events were unfolding, he had time to engage in other activities. In March 1641 he was admitted, in accordance with family tradition, to Gray's Inn to study law. It was quite common for the students at the Inns of Court to enjoy themselves in their free time in rioting and wantonness, or else content themselves with a smattering of legal knowledge useful for their sole expected destinies as landowners. It is not likely that this aristocratic young Puritan MP indulged himself in the brothels and taverns of the city but he certainly made a number of social connections which were to prove useful later on. Terms at the Inns of Court, as with those of the universities and the sittings of Parliament, still ended in time for a return home to assist with or supervise the hay harvest and the long summer break lasted until the corn had been cut and stored away. Lord Grey's studies were to be rudely curtailed by the outbreak of hostilities the following year, but this was to prove no disadvantage to him. He was to feel that God and his destiny called him to greater things. As 1641 proceeded the dispute between the king and his opposition intensified.

The quarrel between the king and his opponents was a longstanding one; it predated both Charles I and the Long Parliament which had assembled in November 1640. The issues were both deeply rooted and considerably interwoven, making it difficult to set out and separate them briefly.

The story of the gradually deteriorating relations between king and parliament after 1603, the year of James I's accession, was highlighted by a series of major issues and crises. The new dynasty, the Stuarts, were firm believers in the idea of the 'Divine Right of Kings' (i.e. they saw themselves as God's representatives on earth). Their word was law and therefore there was little necessity for a parliament to do anything other than to assist the ruler when he thought fit. Parliament, however, thought differently. For the first time in its history the balance of wealth was shifting from the Lords to the Commons and the latter appears to have been keen to exercise the power which they thought their wealth entitled them to. Conflicts, therefore, arose between Crown and Parliament. Parliament in the late 1620s attempted to invest itself not only with the rights to assess and levy taxes, but also with the right of deciding where the money was spent. James I had ruled for seven years without a parliament in England. Charles I, free, after the death of his father's favourite, the Duke of Buckingham, from costly foreign ventures, dispensed with his parliament for eleven years. He dissolved the parliament in 1629 and provoked the first real crisis by imprisoning its popular leaders in the Tower of London (where one, Sir John Eliot, died three years later) and ruled himself through strong ministers, with unpopular policies in Church and State, Archbishop William Laud and Thomas Wentworth, Earl of Strafford.

46

To increase his slender income Charles I re-introduced, or further developed, several ancient forms of taxation. Thus, for example, he exploited the Court of Wards by which the Crown took charge of the lands of anyone who, under the age of twenty one, had come into possession of estates. This became one of the most unpopular royal courts as the family of the minor were forced into attempting to buy the wardship from the king in order to prevent their estates from becoming an economic ruin or the ward married off by the Crown to the young daughter of a spendthrift courtier. The unpopularity of this system was increased because of the rake-offs taken by the officials who controlled the procedures. It will be recalled that Stamford was aged only fifteen when he became Lord Grey of Groby. When he married at the age of twenty he is referred to as being the ward of his mother, so clearly the family had purchased the wardship back from the Crown by then. The king also extracted loans from nobles and fined people who had extended their estates at the expense of the royal forests. In addition, Charles instituted committees in each shire to investigate the non-payment of distraint of knighthood, the fine paid by those eligible because of their wealth and status to become knights at the coronation of a new monarch but who failed so to do. In Leicestershire the Earl of Huntingdon had been appointed to head the committee. Resistance to such payment was high and the Earl had many occasions to complain to the Mayor of Leicester about the laxity of payment by those eligible.

The most notorious cause of unrest, however, in the 1630s was the collection of Ship Money. This was an old tax levied in coastal counties for the building of naval vessels. Charles extended the collection to the inland counties in order to build up his navy which had suffered under the Duke of Buckingham's unsuccessful foreign enterprises. Resistance to the payment was widespread, the stand of John Hampden in Buckinghamshire becoming of particular importance nationally. In Leicestershire the heavy-handedness of the Earl of Huntingdon's associate, Henry Skipwith of Cotes, resulted in a great deal of reluctance to pay the assessed contribution to the building of a 450 ton ship. By 1638 thirty people in the county had had their goods confiscated to pay their part of the assessment. Huntingdon's involvement in these unpopular activities of the king further alienated him from many of the people of Leicester as well as a concerted body of gentry who allied themselves to the Earl of Stamford.

Archbishop Laud had certainly angered the puritans in England with his Book of Common Prayer in 1635; but it was his attempt to impose it upon the presbyterian Scots which precipitated the second great crisis. The Scots signed the National Covenant to defend their religion and prepared for actual war against King Charles and his advisers. The following letter, dated 12th February 1639, from a Scot, Mr Craig, in Edinburgh to his brother in London conveys the spirit of their resolve and was to prove remarkably prophetic:-

"I am sorry to hear that you ventured yourself in public discourse, disallowing our most just cause and taxing us of so great a folly as to contest without power. I think there be not Scotchmen born more ignorant of our country than you are and I hope that the same God that strengthened the arm of the land of Sweden against Germany will strengthen us against England, at least that part of it that will contest without offence given them for a number of scurvy priests. They may consider that war may well begin here, but like a pestilence it will spread all over this isle. Soldiers will get nothing here but strokes, and many of them, but they will be desirous to fight where they may get plundering without blows. Both the King and England are rending that they will never knit again and it shall be seen hereafter that it is to their great prejudice. Knox, Welch, and your old master Dr Liddell, and many others foretold this storm, and assured us that Christ would again be crucified in this country but joyful and glorious should his resurrection be here, to *the confusion of our opposites".*[3]

Whilst the Scots armies were led by veterans who had served the King of Sweden in the Thirty Years War in Germany, such as Alexander Leslie, the English had few experienced commanders. They even had to refer to the Dutch situation for an idea of the correct rates of pay for the various ranks of officers, there being no standing army and England having been so long at peace. With some difficulty Charles raised an army in England by means of issuing the traditional Commissions of Array to the Sheriffs of the counties. This "First Bishops' War" was to prove humiliating for the king. He had neither the ability nor the money to pursue the war effectively and his army lacked both the commanders and the zeal to match the Scots. The renewal of the conflict in 1639 forced him to recall Parliament, though much against his will. In April 1640 the `Short' Parliament met and proposed to provide Charles with money in return for some political concessions - a bargain that he refused to make. He dismissed that Parliament quickly but by November he was forced to summon another one. This was a crucial step as the new one, known to history as the `Long Parliament', was more radical in its demands. Having secured its own existence by a Triennial Act the Long Parliament promptly launched into a preconceived programme of reforms designed to remove forever the possibility of arbitrary rule by the monarch in England. Under the agreement Leicestershire, like every other county, had to provide soldiers for the war in the north. Henry Hastings, Huntingdon's second son, was a Commissioner of Array, responsible for raising the county militia - the Trained Bands - and leading them north. Parliament might have temporarily bailed the king out of his difficulties in the war with the Scots but in return had taken away some of his power. The Triennial Act of 1641 made it impossible for Parliament to be dissolved without its consent and ensured that it must be summoned at least every three years. The Lords and the Commons had also taken away the king's right to raise tax without their permission and had begun to demand not only a say in foreign policy (to prevent any repeat of the Duke of Buckingham's excesses), but also to demand the right of choosing the king's ministers and even a say in the education and religious upbringing of the royal children. The leaders in Parliament succeeded, before Parliament was prorogued in August 1641, in securing first the impeachment and then the execution of the Earl of Strafford ('Black Tom the Tyrant'), the imprisonment of Archbishop Laud, and the abolition of the Courts of Star Chamber and High Commission, the Council of the North and of the hated Ship Money tax.

The Earl of Stamford and Lord Grey of Groby were not mere spectators in these events. Stamford was a close associate of many of the opposition leaders and in May 1641 he had been proposed by the House of Commons for the strategically important post of Governor of the Isle of Jersey. The appointment was refused by the king who recognised him now as an opponent. In the same month the Earl was sent by Parliament to raise levies for the garrisoning of the key arsenal and port of Hull. In another sign of the times with local implications a Parliamentary Ordinance of 28th August 1641 appointed Thomas, Lord Grey of Groby and Sir Arthur Hesilrige responsible for the disarming of Recusants (Catholics) in Leicestershire. This last summer of peace was spent by the Greys at Bradgate and by the king in Scotland where he presided, none too successfully, over the deliberations of the Estates (the Scottish Parliament).

Charles and the members of his English Parliament returned to London in November 1641. An enormous and wide-ranging attack on the position of the monarchy as a whole and known as the 'The Grand Remonstrance' or 'Petition' had been drawn up by the opposition group in Parliament. It listed every grievance and complaint to which the conduct of Church and State had given rise over the past fifteen years and referred to "Oppressions in Religion, Church Government and Discipline". The consideration by Parliament of the Grand Remonstrance coincided with the arrival of news of a large scale rebellion by the native Irish Catholics in Ulster in the previous month which was said to have involved the horrific massacre of thousands of Protestant settlers from England, Scotland and Wales. This was to constitute the third crisis. The king delayed in condemning this dangerous and bloody rising in the popular perception. Could he be trusted with the control of any army that would have to be raised and sent to Ireland to suppress the revolt? Might not the king or his evil counsellors seize the opportunity to use these forces to reassert his position, avenge Strafford's death, and to crush all his opponents and critics in England? Some of the waverers who had begun to rally back to the king as the demands against him had become more and more extreme hesitated again. In the event the Grand Remonstrance was passed in the House of Commons by eleven votes. Not only did Stamford and his son append their names and seals to the Remonstrance and Petition but Lord Grey of Groby was one of the twelve members of the committee selected to present it to the monarch. Sir Arthur Hesilrige was another member of the committee. Shortly afterwards, in a debate about the troubles in Ulster following the rising there and concerning the losses suffered by his grandmother Elizabeth in that province, Lord Grey of Groby was referred to as *"a lord dear to the House of Commons"*.[4]

In this atmosphere of mutual distrust and growing suspicion both sides looked around for support. In elections to the City of London Corporation the supporters of the Parliamentary party gained power in early January 1642 thus swinging the financial backing of the City behind John Pym and his colleagues. Fearing a coup by Pym with the support of the City militia and the London mob, the king decided upon some resolute action. On 4th January Charles felt strong enough to appear personally in the House of Commons supported by his guards and gentlemen to arrest five of the most radical members for treason. The five were John Pym, John Hampden, William Strode, Denzil Holles, and Sir Arthur Hesilrige, MP for Leicestershire. As the king observed himself, however, the birds had flown. The five members, along with Lord Mandeville (later the Earl of Manchester) also under threat of arrest, were in hiding in the City of London. The king drove back to Whitehall the next day empty-handed through angry crowds shouting out *"Privilege of Parliament!"* One man, following behind the royal coach called out ominously in a loud voice the rebellious words, *"To your tents, O Israel!"*. On 11th January the five members returned to Westminster in triumphant mood and the London Militia, the City Trained Bands, escorted Lord Mandeville back to the Lords with their drums beating and colours flying. Charles had played into the hands of Pym and the opposition leaders. The king left London, never to return as its acknowledged sovereign.

The Journal of the House of Commons records that on 15th February 1642 '*divers gentlemen of Leicestershire*' attending at the door of the House were called in to present a petition to that House, and the copy of a similar petition they were also presenting to the House of Lords, on behalf of the Knights, Gentlemen, and Freeholders of the county. Both petitions supported the Grand Remonstrance, criticised the king's wicked counsellors, registered revulsion and fear at events in Ireland, and pledged support for Parliament. Despite the remoteness of their dwellings from London the petitioners were resolved to *"boldly affirm, that the last drop of our bloods had been freely and speedily hazarded in the defence of your persons, and maintenance of your privileges"*[5] and to *"serve you with our lives as freely as they were given us, and with our estates to the utmost values"*[6]. They were warmly thanked by both Houses of Parliament for the great care and affection they had shown for the public interest. Many messages and responses then passed between the king and parliament but the gulf between them widened rather than narrowed. In particular the question of who should control the local militias or any army raised to quell the Irish rebellion came more and more clearly into focus. Both sides began to seek means of securing weapons, provisions and men for their cause.

Charles' queen, the French Catholic Henrietta Maria, left England for the continent towards the end of February to raise support and arms for her husband's cause abroad. By March 1642 the king had established himself in York with the nucleus of what was to be the Cavalier party. Noblemen and gentlemen came in to join him with horses and servants; amongst them was Henry Hastings. On 12th February Parliament had voted to replace his father as Lord Lieutenant of Leicestershire with the Earl of Stamford. By issuing laws without the royal signature (ordinances) they sought to take control of the local Trained Bands with a Militia Ordinance. Through this device they had by March replaced all the Lords Lieutenants of the counties with men of their own choice. The Earl of Huntingdon considered himself too old to take part in the crisis and sought peace and quiet in his residence at Castle Donington. His heir, Ferdinando Lord Hastings, was content for the time to stay with the Parliament; only Henry Hastings openly upheld the King's cause and was to become its most active representative in the county during the civil war.

Until the queen could return from abroad with arms and money the king, having given up London, had to secure the munitions in the magazine at Hull, a well fortified port convenient for the supply of the army with which Charles and Strafford had intended to teach the Scots a lesson. The time for propaganda and psychological warfare was running out. The Parliament began to raise troops to defend itself against the king. Charles prepared to occupy Hull where he would find not only the magazine for last year's army but also a port ideally suited to receive the arms being bought by the queen in the Netherlands. Hull was commanded by Sir John Hotham, a local East Riding landowner, whose sympathies inclined, though not particularly strongly, to the Parliament. During April the Earl of Stamford and Lord Willoughby of Parham together with a committee of the Commons were dispatched by Parliament to confer with Hotham at

Hull, to stiffen his resolve, and to draw up a report of the proceedings. Moving on afterwards from Hull to York the Earl presented to the king on the 18th April a petition in the name of both Houses of Parliament in response to an earlier royal message informing them of his intention of going to Ireland. There was no reconciliation between the parties. Towards the end of April King Charles appeared before the gates of Hull but Hotham respectfully denied him admittance. The king furiously declared him a traitor and returned to York. (Hotham was to attempt secretly to hedge his bets by keeping in clandestine contact with the king and his advisers. His promise to deliver up Hull to the king in July when the latter made a second appearance at the head of two thousand troops had to be broken, however, because of the loyalty to the Parliament's cause of his subordinate commanders such as Captain Robert Overton of Easington, and because of parliamentary suspicions of his own and his son's unreliability. The result was that the king suffered a second humiliation at his second attempt to summon Hull). For the moment though the pressure mounted on those who wished to take no side or who preferred not to declare their support prematurely. Parliament in London had issued its Militia Ordinances and entrusted their Lords Lieutenants and the local MPs with their enforcement. In response, from York, the king on 27th May issued a proclamation forbidding the raising of any troops whatsoever without his own express command or of those acting under his immediate authority.

"Before the flame of the war broke out in the top of the chimneys, the smoke ascended in every country; the king had sent forth commissions of array, and the parliament had given out commissions for their militia, and sent off their members into all counties to put them in execution. Between these, in many places, there were fierce contests and disputes, almost to blood, even at the first; for in the progress every county had the civil war, more or less, within itself".[7]

Empowered by Parliament to raise the trained bands of the borough and county in Leicestershire in order to assist in *'delivering the king from his evil counsellors'* (for so ran the parliamentarian line) the Earl of Stamford began to encourage popular feeling locally and made preparations to mobilise them in early June. He wrote from Bradgate to the Mayor and the Corporation of the Borough of Leicester informing them of his intention to raise the trained bands of the borough on 8th June. Similar arrangements were to be made to muster the trained bands of the shire in their respective hundreds.

We may well imagine the dilemma that now faced Mayor Thomas Rudyard and the other honest and sober representatives of the burghers of

Leicester. As they met in Common Hall in the medieval Guildhall with its neat enclosed courtyard, seated at the long dark oak tables behind the mullion windows, this collection of mercers, linen drapers, goldsmiths, chandlers, slaters, cordwainers, graziers and the like had a most difficult decision to make. Should they obey the militia ordinance and thus defy the king and be pronounced rebels, perhaps losing life and/or earthly possessions? Or should they have regard to the royal proclamation and incur the displeasure of the Earl of Stamford, the majority of the House of Commons, and their own consciences for the many of them who were puritans? The ambiguous slogan of *'King and Parliament'* would not always serve as sufficient cover. After much deliberation they settled on the following compromise resolution.

> *"That the Lord Stanford's Warrant is to be obaied yf the Kings Proclamacion be not Proclaymed and yf yt be the Proclamacion to be obaied".*[8]

Just what was the nature of this militia which both sides were so eager to secure for their cause? The Trained Bands had evolved from the shire levies of the medieval period. Briefly, this part-time 'home guard' was raised, in both recruits and arms, from people of sufficient affluence graded according to their possessions. The old system which Charles I had tried to improve specified that (in 1621) a man with land worth £10 per annum was to provide a whole 'foot armour' (i.e. breast plate, back plate, tassets or thigh guards, and helmet) and half the cost of him that wore it; if £40 per annum, two foot armours; if £80 per annum, a light horse and foot armour, etc. The assessment of such 'taxes' was a contributory grievance to the civil war. In the general view of the times, however, the trained bands were seen as neither trained nor disciplined. Dryden described them cynically in rhyme as follows:

> *"The country rings around with loud alarms,*
> *And raw in fields the rude militia swarms;*
> *Mouths without hands, maintain'd at vast expense,*
> *In peace a charge, in war a weak defence;*
> *Stout once a month they march, a blustering band,*
> *And ever, but in times of need, at hand."*[9]

Some of these criticisms were well justified. In some counties the so-called 'trained' bands were in such a poor state of readiness that they need not have existed. Some took several days to be mustered, mobilised, and made operational. One critic claimed that even the monthly training and drilling sessions were not taken seriously :-

53

"by the time the arms be all viewed .... it draws towards dinner time, and indeed the officers love their bellies so well that they are loath to take too much pains....."[(10)]

Venn claimed that they worshipped not Mars the god of war but Bacchus the god of wine and strong drink. Another critic wrote that they were *"effeminate in courage and incapable of discipline, because their whole course of life alienated from warlike employment"*.[(11)]

A marked exception to this state of decay were the trained bands of London which in 1642 had been expanded by the Common Council of the City to six regiments containing 40 companies of 200 men each. These were well organised, well drilled and well led and were to prove very useful in the service of Parliament in the early years of the civil war. They were to perform good work in the field at Turnham Green where they halted a royalist advance on the capital and they played a major role in the relief of Gloucester. It was unusual, however, for trained bands to move far from their own locality and when they did they were not at all happy about it. Both sides came to realise very quickly the need to raise new, more mobile, regiments to constitute field armies.

There was another factor at stake in the race to secure control of the local militia. The trained bands were equipped with muskets, pikes, halberds, and other weapons which were often stored centrally along with the slow-match and gunpowder for use with both muskets and cannon - usually at the county magazine or powder store. In county towns all over the land the struggle was on to seize control of the local magazine and its contents on behalf of either *'the King'* or *'the King and Parliament'*. At Hull, for example, Robert Overton had moved swiftly to secure the important arsenal there for Parliament, thus enabling it to send Sir John Hotham to take command with the results that have been noted. In Nottingham John Hutchinson, MP for the town and later parliamentarian Governor, managed temporarily to frustrate the designs of his cousin, Lord Newark, Lord Lieutenant of the county, and Sir John Digby, High Sheriff of the county, who with some 'cavalier' captains tried to seize the weapons and powder stored at the town-hall for the king and carry them off to York. He was supported in this by a crowd of 'honest countryfolk' or yeomen, cursed as a 'roundhead' by those with royalist views, and managed to have the contents of the magazine locked up with two locks - the Mayor of Nottingham having the key to one and the Sheriff of the county the key to the other.[(12)]

On 4th June 1642, the day that the House of Commons enjoined Lord Grey of Groby, Lord Ruthin, and Sir Arthur Hesilrige to return home to assist in the enforcement of the Militia Ordinance, the Earl of Stamford travelled into Leicester from Bradgate. He had earlier instructed the Mayor and Corporation of the borough of Leicester to muster the trained bands of the town on the Horsefair Leas, an open grassy area just outside the town walls near the South Gate, on Wednesday 8th June. Since then he had, as Lord Lieutenant appointed by Parliament, granted warrants to the deputy lieutenants, the deputies to the sheriff, and to the Under-sheriff in the absence of the High-Sheriff, to command the county trained bands from the various hundreds to join in this general rendezvous at Leicester. Upon arriving at the Angel Inn, however, where he intended to stay until the mustering took place he was met by a nobleman sent down by the king from York with a commission under a broad seal to carry out a similar mission. Both noblemen had a number of servants with them, most being armed with swords in the fashion of the time. The Earl of Stamford was accused by the other of seducing the people from their allegiance to the king and ordered to depart at once in the king's name. The Earl became so incensed that he drew his sword, telling the other that he was the one who should leave immediately or else he would make the place *"too hot for him"*. An ugly situation developed when the king's men drew their swords. The Earl of Stamford's men did likewise and a sword fight started which spilled out of the Angel and into the street and became *"a desperate combat"*. It was market day, the town was crowded, and the noise of the melee attracted people to the scene. These were in the main quick to take Stamford's side. The king's representatives, outnumbered and fearing for their lives, were obliged to withdraw and hastily left the town to hisses, cries of '*Popish Lord'*, and other insulting terms ringing in their ears. The Mayor and the Aldermen subsequently came to the Earl of Stamford at the Angel to make an expression of their regret for the unfortunate incident. They presented to him a paper containing a resolution of themselves and the borough to submit to the High Court of Parliament, knowing it to be most expedient both for the king's safety and the kingdom's future security. The Earl duly thanked them, saying he would inform Parliament of their good service; at which the assembled people gave a general shout, crying, *"A Stamford! A Stamford!"* with such joy that apparently *"the good Earl was forced to withdraw, tears of joy standing in his eyes to see his Country's love and obedience"*.[13]

Meanwhile at York, as June progressed, the King realised there was an imminent danger of Parliament raising troops in Leicestershire and other counties despite his prohibitions to the contrary. A more positive and active approach was clearly called for. He therefore issued on 12th June the first Commission of Array, the traditional manner by which an English sovereign mobilised the part-time soldiers, to Henry Hastings. Hastings was sent back to Leicestershire with the Commission and a letter from the king which jointly authorised him, along with his father Huntingdon, the Earl of Devonshire, Sir Richard Halford, Sir Henry Skipwith, and others deemed loyal to the Crown, to raise the local trained bands in the king's name.

Hastings arrived in Leicestershire on 15th June and gathered together his supporters. In the meantime Stamford and Lord Grey of Groby had secured the magazine of the local Trained Bands at the Newarke in Leicester and managed to send the major part of it to Bradgate. They also mustered the town and county Trained Bands at Broughton Astley, Kibworth, Melton Mowbray, Queniborough, Copt Oak and Leicester.

On 18th June Parliament debated the Commission of Array for Leicestershire and declared it illegal, also declaring Henry Hastings a delinquent and summoning him to attend the High Court of Parliament. Hastings ignored this. In the meantime the Earl of Stamford had heard of many threats uttered against him in the locality, hazarding his life and the destruction of his home at Bradgate. Accordingly, on 20th June, he raised a guard of 150 men (120 musketeers and 30 horse), to protect Bradgate House, recruited from servants, tenants, and neighbours and maintained - or so he claimed - at his own cost.

On the morning of 22nd June, Henry Hastings gathered his supporters at Ashby Castle. These included his friends, retainers, tenants and about 100 colliers brought from his father's coalmines in south Derbyshire. From the castle armoury he equipped this force with muskets and pikes. They then marched to Loughborough where they assembled in the market place at 10 am : Hastings himself doubtless striking an imposing martial figure on horseback, armed and wearing the scarlet sash of an officer in the King's Army. (He had, of course, previously raised the local contingents for service in the 'Bishops Wars' against the Scots). The Commission of Array was read out and arms issued to those who volunteered. The force that left Loughborough numbered around three hundred men and included a party of horse in addition to pikemen and musketeers, all armed with an assortment of weapons. They marched south to Leicester with colours flying and drums beating.

Upon their arrival they were confronted on the common known as The Horse Fair Leas by a body of armed footmen led by the pro-Parliamentarian High Sheriff, Archdale Palmer and two Parliamentary Messengers (Chambers and Stanforth). Hastings attempted to have the Commission of Array proclaimed, whilst his rivals cited the recorded votes of both Houses of Parliament concerning the illegality of such commissions and the authority of the Militia Ordinance. Chambers instructed the High Sheriff to arrest the royalist 'delinquents'. Hastings gave orders to his men to fight and a melee ensued. Fortunately, at this point, there was a sudden and most extraordinarily heavy downpour of rain which extinguished the slowmatches and thus prevented the musketeers on both sides from firing.

The parliamentarians, on foot and outnumbered, were chased back into the town where they eventually reached the safety of the 'Heron' Inn and barricaded themselves in and stood guard, exhausted and much alarmed by the afternoon's events. Chambers wrote a letter, though, which was smuggled out of town to the Earl of Stamford and the others at Bradgate, informing them of what had transpired and requesting further instructions. They probably also hoped for rescue and reinforcements. The Royalists in the meantime had entered the town in some jubilation and proceeded to live up to what was to become the simple caricature of their party by getting drunk in the taverns, inns and ale-houses of Leicester.

At about one o'clock the following morning Lord Grey of Groby returned from Bradgate to the Parliamentarians at the 'Heron' with instructions from the Earl of Stamford that he, together with Stanforth and Chambers, the Sheriff, Mayor, and the justices of Leicester, should use their best power and endeavour to surprise the delinquents. A force of about fifty men was gathered at the 'Heron' and at two o'clock a co-ordinated search of the town's ale-houses and taverns began. The royalist 'soldiers' were taken unawares, being either drunken or asleep. When the 'Angel' Inn (known to be used by the chief royalists) was raided, however, it was found that Henry Hastings and his leading confederates had left earlier in the night to rejoin the King at York. Upon his arrival there on 25th June Hastings was appointed by Charles as High Sheriff of Leicestershire, thereby replacing Archdale Palmer. In addition the Earl of Stamford was proclaimed a traitor by the king and orders were issued for his arrest. He was granted in turn an indemnity by Parliament on 23rd July. Thus, after an initial set-back, Leicester and its magazine had been secured for the Parliament.

At the beginning of July, Henry Hastings returned to Leicestershire. He was accompanied by the cavalier captains Lunsford and Digby with other soldiers, match, powder, ammunition, and four field pieces of artillery. Hastings proceeded to issue warrants under his new authority as High Sheriff of the county to the high constables of the county hundreds seeking to raise sufficient forces to seize the magazine at Bradgate by force. He also declared William Reymer, the guardian of the Leicester magazine, a traitor for not delivering it up to him. Reports of his actions were sent to Parliament who resolved that more support be given to the Earl of Stamford for the preservation of the peace of Leicestershire, the suppression of insurrections and the safe keeping of the magazine.

During the next few weeks both the King and the Parliament experienced difficulties in establishing regular and reliable control of trained bands in counties all over the kingdom. Increasingly both sides turned instead to issuing individual major supporters with commissions to raise regiments which could be used as part of national field armies if need be.

Towards the late middle of July the King, having been denied access to Hull by Hotham for the second time, decided both to ascertain and to rally support for his cause by moving around Yorkshire and the Midlands. From Beverley he went to Nottingham on 21st July. The following day, anxious to obtain first-hand knowledge of local feelings, he moved on to Leicester accompanied by his eldest son, Prince Charles, and his nephew Prince Rupert of the Rhineland Palatinate. The royal party received a cool but polite welcome from the new Mayor, Richard Ludlam, and the Corporation at Frog Island, outside the North Gate of the town. They then proceeded to Lord's Place in High Street, the route lined by a crowd estimated at ten thousand people. The Assizes were in progress and the King personally addressed a large assembly at the Castle, desiring that all should assist the royal cause "*with vigour*" and furnish support for his army. If the occasion was to arise he said, "*I know you will bring horses, men, money and hearts worthy of such a cause*". He was offered one hundred and twenty horses and men. The king said that he came "*rather to prevent crimes than to punish them*" but he was asked to receive a petition which regretted his long estrangement from the "*highest and safest council of Parliament*". The Grand Jury for the Assize complained that while the king protected such delinquents as Henry Hastings there could never be peace and they prayed that the Commission of Array be left in the hands of the good Earl of Stamford. (The King had already declared the Earl a traitor. Stamford had left Leicester that very day by a different Gate just as the king had entered the town. He was granted the indemnity by Parliament the following day.) Three later demands for the distribution of the remainder of the magazine among the hundreds of the county were finally met after the king's departure by the mayor and the corporation adopting a compromise approach once more.

As on his previous visit in 1634 the King attended St. Martin's Church (now Leicester Cathedral) on the Sunday accompanied by the robed Mayor and Corporation in walking procession. The route took them from Lord's Place (the Hastings family town residence) up High Street to the High Cross and then left and left again into St. Martin's Lane (now Guildhall Lane), probably entering the church by the west door. A throne had been set up at the instigation of Christiana, the widowed Countess of Devonshire, whose home was at Leicester Abbey. The bill for decorating the church and strewing its floor with flowers, herbs, and six bundles of rushes was met by the Corporation. The royal party could derive little comfort from their visit to Leicester, however, and they departed quietly early the following morning without taking their leave of the mayor and corporation.

Whilst the king was at Leicester he sent for the mayor and sheriffs of Coventry to attend upon him. The message reached them as intended whilst they were out riding on the Sunday morning. They were, however, being closely watched by others from the staunchly pro-Parliamentarian town and were compelled to return to Coventry without meeting the king.

Shortly after the departure of the king from Leicester Henry Hastings made his first and long anticipated attack upon Bradgate.

> *"Information came out of Leicestershire to the Parliament that many of the well-affected in that county, having vigilantly taken care to make the Lord of Stamford's house their magazine, and had conveyed their arms, powder, and ammunition thither, did most valiantly and courageously oppose and withstand Mr. Hastings, the new-made High Sheriff, and a most notorious malignant; and how glad he was to retreat from thence, and fly to York for more aid, which afterwards occassioned much mischief and molestation among them in the county of Leicester, he being a most desperate malignant."*[14]

On 4th August the king empowered Hastings to raise a regiment of dragoons (essentially mounted infantry armed with carbines) and commissioned him as Colonel Hastings.[15] The House of Commons responded on 13th August with a resolution, *"that Henry Hastings, esq. shall be accused of high treason, for actual levying of war against the King and kingdom."*[16]

Both sides were mobilising. The King had by now received supplies purchased by the Queen in Holland and had granted many commissions to his supporters to raise regiments. He made the veteran Earl of Lindsey his General, with Sir Jacob Astley as Major-General of Foot and Prince Rupert in command of the Horse. These generals set about the task of creating an army of cavalry and dragoons, foot regiments and artillery sufficient to defeat any forces that the Parliament could put into the field against them. In mid-July Parliament had voted that an army of ten thousand men should be raised in London and its neighbourhood. By an order of the Committee of Safety set up by both Houses of Parliament dated 6th August 1642 a grant of 17 shillings was made for equipping each man recruited with a coat, shoes, shirt, and cap. Breeches were obviously to be supplied by the individual or by the more affluent and fastidious colonel in chief who favoured a uniform appearance for his regiment! Within a few weeks regiments for the army of the Parliament's Lord General, the Earl of Essex, were being formed and began marching to the appointed rendezvous at Northampton.

On Friday 18th August King Charles with the Prince of Wales and a cavalry escort passed through Leicester again on the road from Nottingham to Stoneleigh Abbey in Warwickshire. From Stoneleigh, where he spent the night, he went to Coventry which refused him entry knowing that he was interested in gaining their supplies of ammunition and that they were notoriously pro-Parliamentarian. Leaving most of his forces outside Coventry to besiege it and for his artillery to bombard the town's walls to no great effect, the king rode with some lords and others from his camp back to Leicester. Here he dined and stayed overnight with the Countess of Devonshire at her Leicester Abbey mansion. He returned again to Leicester a couple of days later when Coventry remained obstinate. On his journey back through Leicester he did not wait to be pressed with politely worded demands for Hastings' arrest and for a reconciliation between himself and his 'loyal' Parliament on the latter's terms. After another dinner and overnight stay at Leicester Abbey he left early the next day for Nottingham.

That same afternoon, 22nd August 1642, the King raised his royal standard amidst strong winds and lightning, on what has since been known as Standard Hill. This was the time honoured signal used to raise royal armies and to declare war. The raising of the standard at Nottingham has often been held to be the act which symbolised the beginning of the English Civil War. In fact, as we have seen, hostilities had already started. It was to become increasingly difficult for people to avoid involvement or commitment to one side or the other from now on.

The social pleasantries of country life had already been strained through the struggles to appropriate resources. On 12th June a Nottinghamshire gentleman of parliamentarian persuasion, Henry Ireton, of whom we shall hear much more later, replied to a letter from Lady Lucy Hastings, wife of Ferdinando, Lord Hastings. Ireton's letter was written on the same day that King Charles in York had issued the very first Commission of Array to her brother-in-law, Henry Hastings.

> *"Nottingham.*
> *"I am sorry to have put your Ladyship to the pains of writing :*
> *I have (notwithstanding Mr. Hastings his undeserving answer)*
> *given order to return your son's grey nag (who is, for present,*
> *an innocent, and (I hope) may prove hereafter a friend and*
> *patron to common right and liberty against unjust*
> *appropriations thereof) and my lord's chestnut mare : th' other*
> *two (which are fit for service) I cannot think secure from being*
> *employed against us, if restored into the hands of my Lord or*
> *your Ladyship, being so much under the power of a brother of*
> *such a will and principles : for all the rest (looking upon them*
> *as my Lord's (the Earl's) and Mr. Hasting's or under their*
> *protection and claiming it) I stick to my former proposition till*
> *Mr. Hastings mend his answer and find some reason (at least)*
> *to wave his presumed principle (that he's i'the right and we in*
> *the wrong) until God or the sword or some more competent*
> *judge than himself have decided it. In the mean time I cannot*
> *but render the duty of deserved honour to your noble Lord and*
> *self, and wish I might be master of the opportunity wherein*

(without neglect or prejudice to the cause I serve in or the friends of it) to evidence how much I am your Ladyship's most humble servant".[17]

At the outset of the conflict in 1642 it was not always easy to see on which side of the dividing line an individual would find him or herself. The real agony of the Civil War was the violation of the dearest and most personal of ties; brother against brother, father against son, and friend against friend.

Before examining, in this and the following chapters, the conduct of Stamford and Grey of Groby during the first civil war (1642-1645) it may be useful to consider some of the underlying factors which may have led to the growing divergence in attitude and policy between them which became more obvious later. Neither religious affiliation nor family connection can be taken as a simple causal factor in determining allegiance during this major period of change and upheaval. Not only were families often divided but individuals could also find themselves on different sides at different stages without consciously altering their own set of priorities. Famous examples of families divided by the war include the Vernays of Claydon in Oxfordshire and the Fieldings (Earls of Denbigh) of Newnham Paddox in Warwickshire. Yet the Cromwell family of Huntingdonshire was also divided - as were, at least nominally, the Hastings and the Greys of Leicestershire. Ferdinando Hastings, heir to the Earl of Huntingdon and elder brother to the active cavalier Henry Hastings, took the field at Edgehill as a Parliamentarian although he excused himself from military service soon afterwards. Anchitel Grey, second son of the Earl of Stamford, was in the Royalist forces in the second civil war and later took part in Booth's rebellion against the Republic. The relatively high incidence of such divided loyalties within families can sometimes prompt the suspicion that it was a convenient device at times for keeping familial property intact, in view of sequestration and compounding, whichever side won. At least that way there would be someone within the family to plead on the other side for leniency, whether for people or property.

During the process of the civil wars and the Commonwealth period the Puritans became dominant on the Parliamentarian side of 'The Good Old Cause of God and Our Country'. The position adopted by any particular Puritan was likely to be the result of circumstances and individual reaction to some of the conflicting influences which informed Puritanism. One of these influences was the clash between, on the one hand, a marked constitutionalism among leading Puritans in Parliament and society who saw royal policies in church and state as dangerous innovations and, on the other hand, the 'revolutionary' aspects of Puritan idealism which called for a godly reformation of the world and an assertion of the rights of the godly in religion and politics. Secondly, there was the separate but related tension between the highly emphasised social stratification of seventeenth century English life with its stress on rank and status on one hand and the Puritan belief in the fellowship of the Saints - all equally God's Elect regardless of social station - especially in the 'gathered churches' of the Independents and the Baptists on the other. Thirdly, there was the pull in one direction of local attachments, to the interests of the family, local community, property and sentiments - especially strong against the perceived centralising power of the Crown to begin with - and in the other direction the idea of building a new national Commonwealth or New Jerusalem of the Saints in England, an idea which in practice necessitated a national view and a more thoroughgoing centralisation of control and taxation under the New Model Army and the Protectorate which would alienate eventually many, if not most, of their own supporters. All of these factors combined to produce a heterogeneous mixture of political and religious stances which included such groups as Presbyterians, Grandees, Independents, Anabaptists, Levellers, Diggers, and Fifth Monarchy Men. An individual could be a member of more than one of these groups at different times (sometimes even at the same time) and each, in a sense, could be termed Puritan in relation to its composition or philosophical roots. One striking example of the confusion that could be produced by the interplay of the influences referred to above was Oliver Cromwell - a radical in religion (Independent), but conservative in many political respects (Grandee) as witnessed by the views he expressed in the Putney Army Debates of 1647.[18] Until his attainment of power as Lord Protector contemporaries seemed never to be sure where he stood on an issue over any length of time; hence the charges of schemer, deceiver, and ambitious dissembler later levelled against him by his enemies. Stamford and his eldest son, both Puritans, were to follow different paths from a similar starting point as a result of their differing reactions to events and these underlying influences.

The patterns and causes of partisan allegiance locally could be equally complicated. Leicestershire, from its central situation, was subject to the ebb and flow of warfare throughout the period of the first civil war, both from the incursions of field armies on either side but also from skirmishes and forays between groups of local 'Cavaliers' and 'Roundheads'. In 1642 Leicester and the surrounding county, as we have seen, aimed initially at neutrality whilst leaning mainly to Parliament in their sympathies. There was, however, as also noted earlier, *"a notable animosity"*[19] between the Grey and the Hastings families. Their deep-rooted and centuries old jealousy and rivalry made Leicestershire *"like a cockpit, one spurring against another"*.[20]

Some commentators, following Clarendon, have maintained that the civil war allegiances of the other major county families who traditionally supported their interests effectively constituted the local Parliamentarian and Royalist causes respectively. Alan Everitt states, for example, that

> **"Behind the Grey family one finds aligned, during the Rebellion, such local families as the Ashbys of Quenby, the Babingtons of Rothley, the Caves of Stanford, the Faunts of Foston, the Hartopps of Buckminster, the Heselriges of Noseley, the Herricks of Beaumanor, the Packes of Prestwold, and the Villierses of Brooksby. Ranged behind the Hastingses, on the other hand, were families like the Shirleys of Staunton Harold, the Turvilles of Aston Flamville, the Turpins of Knaptoft, the Poulteneys of Lubbenham, the Beaumonts of Gracedieu, and the Nevills of Nevill Holt".[21]**

In a later publication Jonathan Wilshere and Susan Green present a similar, but not identical, list.[22] The variations include the Dixies of Market Bosworth, the Palmers of Wanlip, the Pochins of Barkby, and the Smiths of Edmundthorpe as additions to the Parliamentarian list. Added to the Royalist list are the Farnhams of Quorndon, the Skeffingtons of Skeffington, the Skipwiths of Cotes, and the Wrights of Barlestone.

Everitt bases his list of family allegiances during the first civil war primarily on the committee lists for parliamentarian supporters[23] and on the lists of the sequestration of, and compounding for, delinquents' estates for the royalists.[24] Wilshere and Green in turn drew heavily upon the lists and details provided by Everitt's research.

If one examines some of the primary records from the period more closely, however, certain interesting omissions and contradictions appear. The following names appear on the famous (and first) Commission of Array for the county issued by the king at York in June 1642 :-

> **The Earls of Huntingdon and Devonshire; Henry Hastings of Ashby; Henry Barkley, Thomas Burton, and George Villiers - Baronets; Sir Henry Skipwith, Sir John Skeffington, Sir Richard Halford, Sir Wolstan Dixie, Sir Richard Roberts, Sir John Bale, Sir Thomas Hartopp, Sir Erasmus de la Fountaine, and Sir William Jones, Mr Henry Hastings of Humberstone, Mr George Ashby, and Mr John Pate.**

Some of the above, such as Henry Hastings, Sir Richard Halford, Sir John Bale, Mr Henry Hastings of Humberstone, and Mr John Pate we have already noted as active royalist partisans. Others named as Commissioners would, however, have been embarrassed by their inclusion and might have preferred to be regarded as neutral or loyal to both sides. Yet others, it may have been noted, were named as Parliamentarians in the lists given earlier. Sir Thomas Hartopp and George Ashby are such examples. These gentlemen appear on the lists of the local Parliamentarian Committees for February 1642, December 1642, and March 1643. The inclusive list of those named on one or more of these committees for raising men, money, and horses for the Parliamentarian war effort or the later committee for seizing the states of local 'delinquents' is as follows:

Thomas Lord Grey of Groby, Henry Lord Grey of Ruthin, Sir Arthur Heselrige, Sir Edward Hartopp, Sir Thomas Hartopp, William Hewett, John Bembridge, Peter Temple, George Ashby, William Roberts, Richard Bent, Arthur Staveley, William Danvers, John Goodwin, John St John, William Gervase (Jarvis), Thomas Heselrige, John Goodman, Simon Ridgley, William Bembridge, Thomas Brudenell, Thomas Babington, Thomas Merry, Thomas Beaumont, Thomas Cotton, and for the Borough of Leicester the Mayor, Richard Ludlam, and Alderman William Stanley.

Some of the apparent anomalies can be explained by later events. From the chronicled evidence of the period it seems clear, for example, that the Dixies of Market Bosworth and the Villiers of Brooksby (despite Everitt and Wilshere/Green respectively) were Royalists, whilst the Beaumonts were divided and the Manners family of Belvoir were Parliamentarian. The original Sir Wolstan Dixie had been an Elizabethan Lord Mayor of London, a member of the Skinners Company Guild, who had purchased another of the Ulster plantation baronetcies from King James I. The family were keen royalists and though the Sir Wolstan named on the Commission of Array declined to take an active military role for the crown and even at one time served on the local parliamentarian committee for the compounding of delinquents' estates (in order to safeguard his own property) he later served as a royalist Commissioner of the Peace under Charles II. The Villiers family, from whom sprang Charles I's former favourite and chief minister George Villiers, Duke of Buckingham, were active in neighbouring Rutland for the royalist cause along with the Noels (Viscounts Campden) rather than in Leicestershire. The Manners family, Dukes of Rutland, at Belvoir Castle were staunch Protestants and declared for Parliament but the castle was taken by the royalist Sheriff of Lincolnshire early on and was garrisoned for the king by Sir Charles Lucas. The Beaumonts of Gracedieu were royalists whilst their cousin, Lord Beaumont of Coleorton was for the Parliament. The confusion over just who supported which side, particularly during the uncertainty of the early months of the war, is understandable. Switches of support would also occur as time progressed and circumstances changed.

64

Despite these problems it seems that the division of support between the two sides in the county was relatively evenly balanced. This was to have some far reaching consequences. The division in the county tended to be geographical as well as political. Royalist support was strongest north and west of the Fosse Way and in the protrusion towards the Vale of Belvoir in the far north east. Parliamentarian support was found mainly in the central area, the south, and the east of Leicestershire. The reasons for this were partly personal and partly economic - with social and political implications. Hastings property and influence was concentrated in the north of the county; the Greys were stronger in the centre, supported by the majority of the Borough Corporation; other parliamentarian notables such as Sir Arthur Heselrige bulked large in the south.

Altogether it is possible to trace the allegiance of about two hundred and twenty Leicestershire families, or probably about two thirds of the gentry in the shire. According to research undertaken by Alan Everitt the number of gentry families in Leicestershire at the time of the Civil War was about three hundred and fifty. Of these, there were the major aristocratic or 'county' families mentioned earlier together with the lesser landowners. About seventy five of the gentry families had representatives who were at some time or other to become members of the local Parliamentarian County Committee under Lord Grey of Groby. Of these seventy five, the great majority were resident in the south and east of the county. About one hundred and forty members of the local gentry became 'delinquent' from the Parliamentarian viewpoint; and of these more than two thirds (almost exactly a hundred) came from the north and west of the county, from the three hundreds of East Goscote, West Goscote, and Sparkenhoe - all within easy range of Ashby Castle, the war-time operational base of Henry Hastings. As these figures indicate, there appears to have been nearly twice as many nominal 'Royalists' as 'Parliamentarians' amongst the gentry in Leicestershire; but the two parties were evenly balanced because most of the former came from the rather more obscure or minor families.

Whilst it is impossible to recreate with any precise degree of accuracy the intricate matrix of factors which determined the position taken by the members of every gentry family in Leicestershire during the civil war period, broad patterns may still be identified. Political, economic, geographical, religious, familial, and coercive factors all played a part in determining the stance taken by an individual. Families apparently sharing the same values and interests could be, and often were, divided; and people could even change 'sides' over a period of time maintaining quite sincerely that they had remained true to their original principles whilst circumstances had changed around them. The Earl of Stamford was to prove a good example of the latter case.

The political stances later adopted by the Earl of Stamford and Lord Grey of Groby were soon to be reflected by their military conduct in the first civil war.

Within four days of the raising of the royal standard at Nottingham, Bradgate House was attacked by a force of royalist horse. Fortunately for the Parliamentarian cause most of the magazine had by this time been returned to Leicester. The attack was recorded by a Parliamentarian chronicler in the following terms:

"Upon 26th August Prince Rupert together with Master Hastings and many cavaliers, went to my Lord Grey, the Earl of Stamford's house, from whence they took all his arms, and took away and spoiled all his goods, and also the clothes of his chaplain who was fain to flee for his life: And some chief ones asked, `Where are the brats, the young children?' Swearing, `God damn them! they would kill them, that there might be no more of the breed of them'. But God stirred up some friends to succour them. They have also disarmed many of the inhabitants thereabouts; and taken away many of their goods; but no doubt their account is at hand. Amen, Lord!"[25]

The 'brats' referred to here would be Stamford's younger children; Anchitel, John, Leonard, and the five daughters. The chaplain mentioned is most likely to have been Thomas Stirke junior who had succeeded his father to the living of Newtown Linford and to the Grey chaplaincy at Bradgate. The raid had encountered so little resistance this time because the Earl of Stamford had left Bradgate earlier in August and raised a troop of horse and a regiment of foot. The knowledge, however, that their home and property was so vulnerable to enemy attack was to be a major consideration for both Stamford and his heir during the first civil war.

The Earl of Stamford's newly raised regiment of foot had marched during the latter part of August down to the rendezvous set for the army raised by the Parliament at Northampton. The men in the regiment were issued with blue coats, this being the colour of the Grey family's livery as worn by their household retainers. As with most foot regiments of the time there was a double strength Colonel's company of around two hundred men, a Lieutenant Colonel's company of one hundred and sixty men, a Sergeant-Major's (or Major's) company of one hundred and forty men, and seven Captain's companies of a hundred men each. Every company was made up of pikemen and musketeers with two sergeants, three corporals, two drummers, and the junior officers - a lieutenant and an ensign. Whilst Stamford himself was the Colonel he had as his second-in-command and Lieutenant Colonel a certain Edward Massey. His (Sergeant) Major was

66

Constantine Ferrar. Massey, like Stamford, was a presbyterian and was to become famous later as the heroic Parliamentarian defender of Gloucester during its siege in the first civil war. Later still he was to become a royalist, like other presbyterians, in the Worcester campaign of 1651.

The colours carried by the ensigns of each company in the regiment were blue. The Colonel's colour consisted of three lines of writing upon white bands - *'For religion', 'King and Country', 'A MA PUISSANCE'* - on a blue field. The other companies bore versions of this in accordance with the style laid down by prevailing military custom. *"The Colonel's colour in the first place is of a pure and clean colour, without any mixture"*, wrote Captain Venn, a veteran of the English Civil War later. *"The Lieutenant Colonel's only with Saint George's arms in the upper corner next the staff, the Major's the same, but in the lower and outmost corner with a little stream blazant. And every captain with Saint George's arms alone, but with so many spots or several devices as pertain to the dignity of their several places"*. These flags or 'colours' on painted taffeta measured six feet square, and served as rallying points for the soldiers either when in quarters or on the field of battle amongst the confusion of noise and smoke. They also symbolised and enshrined the honour and integrity of the unit. It was a major triumph to capture an enemy colour and a disgrace to lose one. According to the code of the time a unit which had lost its colour in battle could not have another until it had in turn taken one from the enemy.

Most regiments had, in addition to their constituent companies, a regimental staff consisting of a quarter-master, a chaplain, a provost-marshal, a 'chirurgion' or surgeon and his mate, a carriage-master and a drum-major. Each company included both pikemen and musketeers, varying in proportion early in the war from two to one respectively to a later ratio on the parliamentarian side of almost one to one in the New Model Army.

The officers were to be distinguished from the rank and file by the quality of their clothing which they provided themselves as gentlemen and by their personal weapons such as halberds, partisans, expensive swords, etc. This being the time before uniform clothing was adopted for armies it was difficult to tell which side a man was on by his clothing alone. The rank and file of each regiment of foot would wear a coat of the same colour but this could be confusing on the battlefield. Even the flags of opposing regiments could be very similar. For example, both Stamford's and Henry Hastings's regiments of foot wore blue coats and carried blue colours. Blue was the livery colour of both the Grey household at Bradgate and the Hastings household at Ashby-de-la-Zouch and was a popular colour for servants' coats nationally. This confusion was increased in the case of officers wearing their civilian clothing with military additions such as the gorget (metal throat guard and badge of rank), the buffcoat, the sash, and 'bucket top' riding boots. In short, clothing reflected social class rather than allegiance. The usual way to indicate which cause a regiment served was the colour of the sashes or 'scarves' worn by its officers over their shoulders or around their waists. Even this was not without its complications as we shall see. Field-signs such as a piece of paper or coloured ribbons were also worn and field-words, like passwords, used for particular battles or campaigns. Instances of these will occur later.

On 21st August 1642 the Parliamentarians assembled a force of three thousand foot and four hundred horse at Southam, a market town in Warwickshire twenty one miles west of Northampton and ten miles from Warwick Castle. The purpose of the exercise was to relieve the pressure on Coventry which was still being besieged by a royalist force whose artillery had recently succeeded in breaching the town's medieval walls. The regiments involved in the Southam rendezvous were John Hampden's Greencoats, Denzil Holles' Redcoats, Lord Brooke's Purplecoats, Lord Saye and Sele's Bluecoats, Goodwin's Horse, and a small train of six field guns. The letters of Nehemiah Wharton, a puritan sergeant in Holles' Redcoat Regiment, which have survived, give a vivid picture of this campaign in particular and of life in the Parliament Army's foot regiments at this time in general. It appears that Stamford's Bluecoats remained in Northampton at this stage but that Lord Grey of Groby was with the Southam party. A brief skirmish took place at Southam against a royalist force of eight hundred horse and some three thousand foot. The parliamentarians under Colonel John Hampden's command advanced against the royalists, whose foot companies fled after the initial exchange of musket volleys and their cavalry trotted away.

On 26th and 27th August a part of the Southam force marched to the environs of Coventry and skirmished with a party of Cavalier horse who they swiftly put to flight by use of cannon, musketry and superior odds generally. In a series of letters written to his friend George Willingham in London, between 16th August and 7th October, Nehemiah Wharton describes the way in which the soldiers pillaged civilians whom they suspected of supporting the other side - particularly clergymen, wealthy merchants, and members of the nobility. Such behaviour was common on both sides in the early stages of the war but the Parliamentarians appear to have imposed a more effective system of restraint upon their soldiers rather sooner than the Royalists. It is likely that their increasing success in the field and regularity of supply made it less necessary for them to 'live off the land' than their opponents as time went on and that these factors, rather than simply puritan conscience or restraint, explain the later difference in behaviour.

"Thursday, Aug. 26, our soldiers pillaged a malignant fellow's house in this city [Coventry], *and the Lord Brooke immediately proclaimed that whosoever should for the future offend in that kind should have martial law. This day command was given that all soldiers should attend their colours every morn by 6 o'clock to march into the field to practise, which is done accordingly. Friday, several of our soldiers, both horse and foot, sallied out of the city to Lord Dunsmore's park,* [Lord Dunsmore was one of the royalist commanders locally] *and brought from thence great store of venison, which is as good as ever I tasted; and ever since they make it their daily practice, so that venison is almost as common with us as beef is with you. This day our horsemen sallied out, as their daily custom is, and brought in with them two cavaliers, and with them an old base priest, the parson of Sowe near us, and led him ridiculously about the city unto the chief commanders".*[26]

On 31st August the regiments set out on the thirty mile march back to Northampton, pillaging 'papists' and 'malignants' and poaching deer on the way. According to Wharton, in a letter to Willingham, they marched

"over Dunsmore Heath, near 12 miles, without any sustenance, insomuch that many of our soldiers drank stinking water, until we came unto Barby in Northamptonshire, where the country, according to their ability, relieved as many of us as they could. Our soldiers pillaged the parson of this town, and brought him away prisoner, with his surplice and other relics. From hence we marched four miles further into Long Bugby (Long Buckby), *where we had very hard quarter, insomuch that many of our captains could get no lodging, and the soldiers were glad to dispossess the very swine, and as many as could quartered in the church. But here your man Davy, riding before our foot companies, got me both food and lodging. This town has for two Sundays together been so abused by the rebels* (royalists) *that both men, women, and children were glad to leave the town and hide themselves in ditches and cornfields. Friday morning early a message came to our Colonel that in the King's house called Homby* [Holmby or Holdenby House] *, three miles distant, there were 500 musketeers to cut off our straggling soldiers, whereby we prevented them. This morning our soldiers sallied out around the country and returned in state, clothed in surplice, hood, and cap, representing the Bishop of Canterbury. From hence we marched two miles, where Homby House stands very*

69

stately upon a hill, and the Earl of Northampton's house near to it, but we could not restrain our soldiers from entering his park and killing his deer, and had not the Lord Grey and our Sergeant-Major General [Sir John Merrick] *withstood them they had pillaged his house".* [27]

We can note with interest Lord Grey's restraining of the soldiers from pillaging the Earl of Northampton's house within a few days of the raid on Bradgate by Prince Rupert and Henry Hastings. Was he aware of that raid at this time? Was he merely extending the sort of protection to aristocratic property he would have looked for if the situation had been reversed? Landowners, whichever side - if any - their loyalties lay, must have looked with great concern to the security of their estates in these anarchic circumstances.

Wharton concludes this particular letter with the information that

"This day (3rd Sept.) *came Sir Arthur Heslerigg's and other troops into our town* (Northampton). *This day our soldiers brought in such venison and other pillage from the malignants about the country. This evening we feasted all our sergeants, with some other superior officers".* [28]

The pattern of the early civil war period had been set. The horrors of war, and of civil war in particular, for a civilian population and for those either neutral or caught on the 'wrong' side of extremely fluid 'lines' at the mercy of enemy soldiers is graphically presented. Another aspect of the injury caused by the fondness of the soldiers for poaching deer and eating venison in this period is found echoed in one of Andrew Marvell's poems :-

> *"The wanton troopers riding by*
> *Have shot my fawn, and it will die.*
> *Ungentle men! They cannot thrive -*
> *To kill thee! Thou ne'er didst alive*
> *Them any harm : alas, nor could*
> *Thy death yet do them any good .....* [29]

Meanwhile, across the county border in Leicestershire, Prince Rupert had set up his advance cavalry headquarters at Queniborough where there was local royalist support. From here he sent, on 6th September, a letter to the mayor of Leicester demanding the sum of £2,000 *"by ten of the clock in the forenoon"* of the next day, adding that if the mayor refused, he would *"appear before your town in such a posture with horse, foot and cannon, as shall make you know 'tis more safe to obey than 'tis resist His Majesty's command".*(30)

The town appealed to the king, whose reply expressing surprise at Rupert's conduct, discharged the Corporation from its fulfilment. Six dragoons had, however, already been sent with £500 to Rupert. This money was never repaid and Prince Rupert was to return in the summer of 1645 at the head of a field army to teach Leicester the lesson he had threatened.

In the crowded streets of Northampton where the Earl of Essex had concentrated his army, the grumbles and complaints common to most soldiers during periods of inactivity began to break through the earlier feelings of excitement, zeal, and novelty. On 7th September the foot soldiers, especially those from the regiments raised in London, asked for more pay. They wanted an extra five shillings a month per head which they said had been promised to them by the London Committee. The senior officers of the army tried to appease them but Wharton wrote that in his opinion if there were no more money forthcoming there would be trouble. Nobody seems to have had undisputed command over the thousands of soldiers in and around Northampton in the absence of the Earl of Essex, who was in London with the Parliament. John Hampden wrote to the Earl of Essex on behalf of many of the other senior officers advocating martial law in the army in order to restrain the plundering and the 'insolencies' of the soldiers, but also arguing that they did need an increase in pay. The following day he wrote again urging the Lord General to rejoin the army as *"a means to appease these disorders"*.

The Lord General arrived at Northampton shortly afterwards, bringing his own coffin and shroud with him. On Wednesday 14th September he reviewed the army in the fields outside the town. The next day, after the code of martial laws had been read out at the head of every regiment, the army began to march into Warwickshire by way of Rugby.

On 19th September a rendezvous was held on Dunsmore Heath where newly raised units joined the existing army. A force including Holles' Redcoats, Hampden's Greencoats, Stamford's Bluecoats, and two other foot regiments were detached to follow the Lord General to Warwick. From Warwick this army trudged some twenty eight miles westwards through heavy and continuous rain to Worcester. Wharton records *"such foul weather that before I had marched one mile I was wet to the skin"*. The king had by now moved from Nottingham to Chester in order to raise forces in the north-west of England and North Wales. Prince Rupert and his cavaliers had left Queniborough to move forward, however, and course abroad in lightning attacks on 'rebel' forces and property. On 23rd September they inflicted a sharp defeat upon some parliamentarian cavalry at Powick Bridge, within two miles of Worcester on the south side.

71

Nehemiah Wharton regarded the pro-royalist city of Worcester as a contemporary version of Sodom and Gomorrah; he considered it more heathenish than Algiers or Malta. It was at Worcester that the Earl of Stamford was detached from the main Army of the Parliament and therefore missed the campaign and battle of Edgehill. The Earl of Essex sent him with a force which included his own Bluecoat regiment and a commanded party of nine hundred soldiers (one of whom was Nehemiah Wharton) drawn from other regiments to take and occupy Hereford. Stamford entered Hereford unopposed and took up residence as Governor in the Bishop's Palace. It was alleged by royalists later that he had engaged in plunder in order to meet his *'dissolute'* and *'vicious'* habits.[31] Some of the soldiers, including Wharton, attended a Laudian morning service in the cathedral and danced to the organ music in the choir while the *'puppets'* of the choir sang away. When a robed canon prayed for the King a soldier roared out, *"What! Never a bit for the Parliament?"* After this *'human service'* conducted by *'Baalist'* priests, wrote Wharton, the men marched off to a *'divine service'* where they heard a rousing sermon from the chaplain of Holles' Redcoats, the puritan preacher Obadiah Sedgewick. When Wharton and the rest of the commanded party rejoined the main force at Worcester the Earl of Stamford remained as Governor in Hereford with his Bluecoat regiment.

On 12th October the king and his army began to march towards London. When they reached Warwickshire they heard that the Earl of Essex had left Worcester and was closing on them rapidly. After some debate with his chief commanders the king decided to turn and offer the enemy battle at Edgehill near the village of Kineton in Warwickshire on the following day. Owing to a shortage of draught horses the heavier parliamentarian cannon were following some way behind the main force on the road from Stratford-upon-Avon under the guard of Colonel John Hampden and two regiments of foot.

The battle of Edgehill was fought on Sunday, 23rd October 1642. The two armies were about equal in size. The royalist cavalry of some 2,800 horse and 1,000 dragoons slightly outnumbered the estimated 2,150 horse and 720 dragoons of Parliament. On the other hand, the twelve parliamentarian regiments of foot who took part in the battle comprised about 12,000 men compared to the king's infantry forces of some 10,500 pikemen and musketeers. The royalist forces were arranged along the foot of the steep north slopes of Edgehill with their left wing against Radway village. The Earl of Essex drew out his army from the village of Kineton into a great broad field about half a mile away from the enemy and facing them in a broad line. On both sides regiments had been grouped together to form main divisions or brigades. Both generals positioned their foot brigades in the centre of the battle line with clumps of horse on both wings. In order to assist identification in the forthcoming battle officers of horse and foot on both sides, together with cavalry troopers, wore 'scarves' or sashes. The colours of these were mostly red for the Royalists and tawney orange (the livery colour of the Earl of Essex) for the Parliamentarians.

Although the Earl of Stamford's Bluecoat Regiment of Foot was absent, owing to its duties in Hereford, leading Leicestershire families were still represented at Edgehill. Colonel Henry Hastings had command of a foot regiment in the Royalist Army List of 1642; its men wore blue coats and its colours seem to have been blue. At Edgehill, however, Hastings was commanding his cavalry troop who also wore blue coats but whose colour, or cornet, was red and bore the device of a fiery furnace or burning oven within an archway, with the ferocious and intimidating Latin motto, *'Quasi Ignis Conflatoris'* ('That which I light is consumed'). It is likely that he was stationed in the cavalry division of his friend Prince Rupert, on the right flank of the royal army. His elder brother, Ferdinando, Lord Hastings, was on the opposing side at the head of the seventh troop of horse in Essex's army, under the command of Sir William Balfour, the lieutenant-general of the horse. Balfour's division was positioned on the centre left of the parliamentarian front line between Sir Philip Stapleton's Horse on their right and Sir John Meldrum's large brigade of foot on their left.

Also in Balfour's division and in charge of the third troop of cavalry in the Parliamentarian Army List of 1642, after only those of the Lord General's troop and that of Balfour himself, was Thomas, Lord Grey of Groby. This troop had been raised locally in Leicestershire from amongst friends, neighbours, tenants and servants. It had joined the army at the Dunsmore Heath rendezvous and was to see service with Lord Grey in the Midlands in the following years and also to distinguish itself further afield during the civil war. The lieutenant of the troop, under Grey's captaincy, was a Simon Matthews. The cornet, the junior officer who carried the colour of the same title, was listed as a Thomas Barington. This may well have been Thomas Babington of the local Rothley family. The troop's quarter-master was a Daniel Maddox and, to complete the complement in addition to the sixty or so troopers, there were two corporals and a farrier. The members of the troop would have been equipped, like most cavalrymen of the period, with long leather thighboots and buffcoats, back and breastplates, helmet and/or broad brimmed felt hats, a brace of pistols and a basket-hilted cavalry sword. The orange sashes worn in their case would have been either made up by the ladies of the Bradgate estate or, as was quite common, derived from some appropriately coloured drapery 'borrowed' from a local laudian church. Initially, at least, most troopers would have provided their own horse. The cornet, or flag, of the troop was a half blue and half red field fringed in silver and red upon which was set

73

an ermine unicorn on a sun in splendour with the Latin motto *'Per Bellum Ad Pacem'* ('Through War To Peace').

Sir Arthur Hesilrigg's troop was also on the field amongst the parliamentarian horse, but this time with the main body on the left flank under Commissary-General Sir James Ramsay and facing Prince Rupert. This was the forty-third troop in the Parliamentarian Army List and was to be expanded after Edgehill to a whole regiment and to serve in Sir William Waller's campaigns in the south and the west. This troop, and the later regiment, was to become famous as the 'lobsters' because of their complete suits of three-quarter armour. At a time when most cavalry units wore only buffcoats with helmets, back and breast plates Hesilrigg's troopers alone, other than the King's Life Guard of Horse and the Earl of Essex's Life Guard of Horse at Edgehill, wore full armour. Clarendon was to say of them,

"the soldiers of this troop were so prodigiously armed that they were called by the other side the regiment of lobsters because of their bright iron shells".

The king was to observe of Sir Arthur himself during the action at Roundway Down later where he was surrounded by cavaliers,

"if only he had been supplied with food and water he could have withstood a siege"

The colonel's colour of the 'lobsters' was a famous green cornet fringed white and green with a golden anchor (for hope) fixed at the top in silver clouds and in golden letters the motto, *'Only In Heaven'*.

After a preliminary exchange of cannon fire lasting about one hour, the confident cavaliers charged and easily chased away most of the parliamentarian horse on the wings. On the parliamentarian left Prince Rupert swept away twenty-four troops of horse under Ramsay, including the reserve which had been placed on a little hill. On the parliamentarian right wing Lord Wilmot with ten royalist troops of horse scattered both Stapleton's Horse and Lord Fielding's Horse which had been its reserve. The troops in the two regiments commanded by Sir William Balfour mostly stood their ground, however, being partly shielded from Wilmot's charge by the embattled phalanxes of foot regiments in the centre of the field. Some troops, such as that led by Ferdinando Hastings, broke and fled. He is said to have ridden back to London to report that all was lost. This led to his temporary imprisonment and his practical disengagement from the parliamentarian cause which, despite his protestations, he had never supported very zealously.

Grey of Groby's troop under Balfour stood firm and distinguished itself in the action that followed. Whilst the cavaliers on both wings wildly pursued their broken opponents into Kineton and beyond, the royalist infantry in five brigades advanced and engaged the parliamentarian foot, now reduced to two large brigades commanded by Sir John Meldrum and Colonel Thomas Ballard since the breaking and running away of Colonel Essex's brigade. The terrible fight ebbed and flowed with the fury of charge and counter-charge and brief moments of respite. Noise, confusion, and smoke from cannon and massed musketry were everywhere. Balfour's Horse took the royalist left wing foot brigades in front and rear. Grey of Groby's troop assisted in the capture of some enemy cannon. The battle which had first seemed won for the King seemed now to swing to Parliament, largely because the victorious cavaliers had failed to rally and to return to the field to assist their Foot; a failing which was to prove so common and costly to their cause. The royal standard was taken and presented to the Earl of Essex but was recaptured by a clever subterfuge. As the battle raged on some of the cavalier units did drift back and the struggle became more evenly balanced again.

The arrival of Colonel John Hampden with another parliamentarian brigade just as daylight began to fade led to an acknowledgement of a stalemate on both sides. The battle was indecisive with neither side able to gain an outright victory. During the night, however, Essex did withdraw to Kineton leaving the King in possession of the field and preparing to fight the next day.

In propaganda terms this draw favoured the royalists, yet on neither side did the leadership attempt to seize the initiative. The Earl of Essex moved his army back to London whilst the King moved to Oxford and made it his headquarters for the rest of the war. The clamour for a more organised and more vigorous prosecution of the war, particularly on the parliamentarian side, was to grow louder.

NOTES

1.   It is difficult to agree with the following point made by John Morrill, as far as Leicestershire is concerned, when he states that, "No English county except Middlesex returned men to Parliament in 1640 who spoke with one voice in 1642 or later". It rather depends just how much later! The knights of the shire returned for Leicestershire in 1642, Sir Arthur Hesilrige and Lord Grey of Ruthin, were both firm Parliamentarians. See John Morrill *The Revolt of the Provinces - Conservatives and Radicals in the English Civil War, 1630-1650.* (Longman 1980) p. 18

2.   Jack Simmons *Leicester - The Ancient Borough to 1860* (Alan Sutton, 1983) p. 86.

3.   Calendar of State Papers (Domestic Series), 1638-9.

4.   Ibid. 1641-3, p. 359.

5.   Journal of the House of Commons (C.J.), Vol. II, p. 433.

6.   Journal of the House of Lords (L.J.), Vol. IV, p. 590.

7.   Lucy Hutchinson *Memoirs of the Life of Colonel Hutchinson* (Everyman's Library 317, Dent, London 1965), p. 92.

8.   Record of the Borough of Leicester, 1642. (BR./18/22)

9.   John Dryden *Cymon and Iphigenia.*

10. R. Ward *Animadversions of Warre* (London, 1639).

11. J. Corbet *A true and impartiall History of the Militarie Government of the Citie of Glouceste*r (London, 1647) p. 11.

12. Lucy Hutchinson op. cit. pp. 81-87.

13. John Nichols *The History and Antiquities of the County of Leicester* Vol. III, Pt. ii, App. iv. (1804) p. 19. (Source: Horrible News from Leicester!' - a letter from Adam Jones in Leicester to his brother William Jones, Covent Garden, London, dated 6th June 1642)

14. John Vicars *God in the Mount, Or, England's Remembrancer* (London, 1642) p.104.

15. Historical Manuscripts Commission: Hastings Collection. Vol. II. p. 86.

16. C.J. Vol. II. p. 718.

17. HMC : Hastings Collection, Vol II. pp. 83-84. Letter from Henry Ireton to Lucy, Lady Hastings, 12th June, 1642.

18. For the Putney Army Debates see 'The Clarke Papers' ed. C H Firth (Camden Society) Vol. I. pp.226-406, or *Puritanism and Liberty* ed. A S P Woodhouse, Dent, London, 1938. pp.1-124.

19. Edward Hyde, Earl of Clarendon *The History of the Rebellion and Civil Wars in England* ed. W Dunn Macray, 6 Vols., Oxford, 1888. p. 349.

20. J H Plumb *Victoria County History of Leicestershire*, Vol. II, p. 109, quoting *Terrible News from Leicester* (Thomason Tracts, E. 108.16).

21. A M Everitt *The Local Community and the Great Rebellion*, The Historical Association, London, 1969. pp. 15 & 16.

22. J Wilshere & S Green *The Siege of Leicester 1645*, Leicester Research Services, Leicester, 1970. pp. 7 & 8.

23. See the Parliamentarian Committee lists in C H Firth and R S Rait, *Acts and Ordinances of the Interregnum, 1642-1660*, published 1911.

24. Calendar of the Committee for Compounding (Leicestershire cases), State Papers.

25. John Nichols *The History and Antiquities of the County of Leicester*, Vol. III, Part II, AppendixIV, p. 30. citing *Remarkable Passages from Leicester* 1642.

26. Letters of Nehemiah Wharton to his friend George Willingham in London, August - December 1642, contained in Calendar of State Papers (Domestic Series), 1641-43, p. 382.

27. Ibid. p. 334.

28. Ibid. p. 385.

29. Andrew Marvell *The Nymph Complaining for the death of Her Fawn* (Poem).

30. Letter to the Mayor of Leicester from Prince Rupert, 6th September 1642. - Leicester Museum Archives.

31. Calendar of State Papers (Domestic Series), 1641-43, p. 400.

King Charles I

The right Hono.ble Robert Earle of Essex
and Ewe, Viscount Hereford, Lord Fereers of Chartley
Boutcheir, and Lovaine. Lo. Generall of the Army im:
ployed for the defence of the Protestant Religion, the safety
of his Maties Person, and of the Parliament, the preserva
tion of the Lawes, Liberties, and Peace of the Kingdom
and protection of his Ma.ties Subjects from oppression.

Robert Devereux, Earl of Essex

79

The Foote

The Horse

The Artillerie

Civil War Armies

CHAPTER THREE

THE MILITARY COMMANDER (1642-1643)
"A YOUNG MAN OF NO EMINENT PARTS?"

"Who would true Valour see,
Let him come hither,
One here will Constant be,
Come Wind, come Weather,
There's no Discouragement,
Shall make him once Relent,
His first avow'd Intent,
To be a Pilgrim."

John Bunyan,
'The Pilgrim's Progress'

Following the indecisive battle of Edgehill the Royalist army marched to Banbury and entered Oxford in apparent triumph one week after the battle. The Parliamentarian army meanwhile had marched first to Warwick and then to Northampton on their way to London. From Oxford the King sent forces of cavalry to harry the flanks of Essex's army as it moved towards the capital.

On 1st November 1642 Prince Rupert was in Aylesbury whilst his troopers foraged in the surrounding countryside. They were forced to withdraw later that day by six troops of Sir William Balfour's Horse, including Grey of Groby's troop, who had arrived to stiffen the resolve of the local Buckinghamshire militia and fought stoutly against the cavaliers at Holman's Bridge, a half mile north of the town.

Both armies now headed for London with the Parliamentarians, using the Watling Street, arriving first. On 9th November with Prince Rupert besieging Windsor Castle and the main Royalist force at Colnbrook, less than twenty miles from the capital, Parliament gave instructions to the Earl of Essex to take the field again with his army.

On the same day that the Royalist army had marched into Oxford a group of members in both Houses of Parliament who favoured immediate peace negotiations had persuaded the more militant members to agree to send a petition to the king asking for talks. In return the peace group had agreed that more recruits should be found for Essex's army and that a formal message should be sent to the Scots asking them for speedy assistance if it should prove necessary.

Under cover of these 'talks about talks' the Royalists staged a surprise attack on London. On 12th November, as the Earl of Essex spoke in the

House of Lords, the peers heard the sudden thunder of cannon away to the west. Prince Rupert's cavalry, followed by the King with the main Royalist army, had attacked Brentford, taking advantage of a thick early morning mist. Holles' Redcoats and Lord Brooke's Purplecoats bore the brunt of this attack, losing many killed, about five hundred taken prisoner, eleven colours lost, fifteen cannon and much ammunition. The Royalist advance was only halted by the arrival of Col. John Hampden's Greencoats who rallied the remnants of the other two foot regiments until other regiments of Essex's army could come up. The Parliamentarian army had been mustered in Chelsea fields that afternoon fortuitously. Rather than attempt to hold Brentford the King withdrew his forces some distance to the west where they camped for the night.

On the following day the Royalists advanced towards London again but this time they encountered a joint force of some 24,000 men made up of the Army of the Parliament and the Trained Bands of the City of London drawn up in battle order at Turnham Green, just outside Hammersmith. After some opening exchanges of cannon fire and some minor sorties the armies merely faced each other throughout the day. The Earl of Essex had the opportunity to block off the king's retreat but declined to do so. This was to give rise to recriminations between military leaders on the Parliamentarian side later. This was also the nearest the king was to come to his capital during the war before he returned as a prisoner for his trial six years later. Eventually the stalemate was broken when the king, leaving a body of horse to face the enemy, drew his main army back to Kingston-on-Thames and spent the night at Hampton Court. Next day he ordered all his forces to pull back to Reading. Negotiations between the King and the Parliament were now broken off and Parliament ordered the Earl of Essex to march forward with his army to Windsor.

When the king realised that Brentford had both killed the chance of peace negotiations for a time and the likelihood of a successful march into London he left a strong garrison in Reading and withdrew the rest of his army back to Oxford. He turned Oxford into his war-time headquarters and surrounded his new capital with a system of offensive and defensive outposts. The civil war had now begun in earnest and it was clear to all that it would not be over in a short time.

On the Parliamentarian side questions were now being asked about the conduct of the war by the chief commanders and their degree of commitment to securing an outright victory over the King's forces. A certain captain of a troop of horse from East Anglia and Member of the House of Commons, one Oliver Cromwell by name, who was shortly to become better known as a colonel and then as Lieutenant-General of all the Parliamentarian Horse, stressed to his cousin John Hampden MP the need to improve the Army in the following manner, as he later recalled.

"At my first going into this engagement, I saw our men were beaten at every hand. I did indeed; and desired him that he would make some addition to my Lord Essex's army of some new regiments; and I told him that I would be serviceable to him in bringing such men in as I thought had a spirit that would do something in the work. ..... The result was that I raised such men as had the fear of God before them, as made some conscience of what they did."

Later that year the Committee of Safety, created by both Houses of Parliament, began to form local associations of counties for mutual defence. These local groupings of counties in associations provided the necessary financial support for raising new regiments of both horse and foot for the parliamentarian cause.

There was no uniformity of resolve on the Parliamentarian side. Many remained distinctly uneasy about resisting the royal authority and would only do so in so far as it was considered necessary to *"rescue His Majesty from his wicked counsellors"*. From the Royalist point of view it was clearly part of a sovereign's duty to assert his authority by force when required, whether against foreign enemies or rebellious subjects. For the Parliamentarian leaders the question was far more complicated. Except in the case of a national revolt against a foreign oppressor, such as had taken place in the Netherlands against the Spanish, rebellion and revolution had no romantic attraction. The likely consequences of rebellion and civil war in terms of lawlessness and anarchy were sufficiently well known from the recent religious wars in France and the continuing devastation of the Thirty Years War in Germany. The inequality of risk between the two contending parties in the English case was also well understood. Only a few weeks before the war had broken out Bulstrode Whitelocke, a former friend of Clarendon and a pro-parliamentarian, had reminded the House of Commons of the prophetic words, *"He that draws the sword against his Prince must throw away the scabbard"*. For this reason, once the risk of revolt against the monarch had been accepted, it might be thought crucial to secure a quick and irreversible decision. A long and drawn-out war was bound to offer advantages to the Crown as the likelihood of just one vital mistake by the 'rebels' could prove their undoing. As the Earl of Manchester, himself one of the original Parliamentary leaders, was to put it after two years of war,

"If we fight a hundred times and beat him ninety-nine times, he will be King still. But if he beat us but once, or the last time, we shall be hanged, we shall lose our estates, and our posterities be undone."

At this statement and the implication of the sentiments behind it, Oliver Cromwell is reputed to have retorted,

"God's wounds! If that be so then why in God's name did we ever begin this war?"

There are echoes in the above exchange of the differences that were to emerge between Thomas, Lord Grey of Groby and his father; Lord Grey sharing the view of Cromwell, and Stamford that of Manchester. Thomas Grey of Groby was to be one of those who threw away the scabbard once he had drawn his sword against his prince.

Some 'Parliamentarians' had even wavered so much in their resolve as to cease their military involvement against the king altogether after Edgehill, One such, not surprisingly perhaps, was Ferdinando Hastings. He expressed himself as follows in a letter written to the Earl of Essex on 3rd November 1642, excusing his leaving the Army without permission or leave :-

"..... and only profess that my affection to the Parliament cause is still firm, though there are some reasons to withdraw me from continuing my service in the war, but in any particular service to your Lordship I shall be most ready to appear, my Lord, your Excellency's very humble servant."[1a]

Ferdinando, Lord Hastings never again appeared in arms for the Parliament although his younger brother Henry was a most active partisan and promoter of the royalist cause.

In fact, during the winter of 1642/3 the duplicitous Ferdinando was writing an equally sincere sounding letter to Sir Edward Nicholas, Principal Secretary of State to the King, at Oxford from Tutbury Castle.

"..... Sir, I assure you my want of arms makes the service I ought to do the King very difficult, the Rebels lying upon me on every side and within walls that I can attempt nothing against them ..... (they) hath made Ashby often troubled with them ..... the force of Graye and Gell ..... Gray is marched with some troops but whether to Essex ..... I am not certain. You shall hear daily from me that am Yr. affectionate friend & servant - F. Hastings" "Haste, haste. Post haste."[1b]

It is now time to turn from the wider national scene to the development of the civil war in the Leicestershire area, pausing briefly to note the activities of the noble Earl of Stamford, far away from his beloved Bradgate, in the southern Welsh marches and then in the West Country.

Clarendon, in his description of the situation in the Midlands during the opening stages of the civil war, grudgingly admits to some positive qualities in the local Parliamentarian commanders generally.

> *"And it cannot be denied but Sir William Bruerton* (sic - Brereton*), and the other gentlemen of that party, albeit their education and course of life had been very different from their present engagements, and for the most part were very unpromising to matters of courage, and therefore were too much contemned* (sic) *enemies, executed their commands with notable sobriety, and indefatigable industry, (virtues not so well practised in the king's quarters,) insomuch as the best soldiers who encountered with them had no cause to despise them. It is true, they had no other straits and difficulties to contend with, than what proceeded from their enemy; being always supplied with money to pay their soldiers, and with arms to arm them; whereby it was in their power not to grieve and oppress the people. And thereby (besides the spirit of faction that much governed) the common people were more devoted to them, and gave them all intelligence of what might concern them; whereas they who were intrusted* (sic) *to govern the king's affairs had intolerable difficulties to pass through; being to raise men without money, to arm them without weapons, (that is they had no magazine to supply them,) and to keep them together without pay; so that the country was both to feed and clothe the soldiers; which quickly inclined them to remember only the burden, and forget the quarrel.*
>
> *"And the difference in the temper of the common people of both sides was so great, that they who inclined to the parliament left nothing unperformed that might advance the cause; and were incredibly vigilant and industrious to cross and hinder whatever might promote the king's : whereas they who wished well to him thought they had performed their duty in doing so, and that they had done enough for him, in that they had done nothing against him.*
>
> *"..... those counties which lay in the line between Oxford and York were, in the matter, entirely possessed by the enemy. The garrison of Northampton kept that whole county in obedience to the parliament, save that from Banbury the adjacent parishes were forced to bring some contribution thither. In Warwickshire the king had no footing; the castle of Warwick, the city of Coventry, and his own castle of Killingworth* (sic - Kenilworth), *being fortified against him.*

The Lord Grey, son to the Earl of Stamford, had the command of Leicestershire, and had put a garrison into Leicester. Derbyshire, without any visible party in it for the king, was under the power of Sir John Gell, who had fortified Derby. And all those counties, with Staffordshire, were united in an association against the king under the command of the Lord Brook (sic - Brooke)*; who was, by the Earl of Essex, made General of that association; a man cordially disaffected to the government of the church, and upon whom that party had a great dependence. This association received no other interruption from, or for the king, than what Colonel Hastings gave; who being a younger son to the Earl of Huntingdon, had appeared eminently for the king from the beginning; having raised a good troop of horse with the first, and, in the head thereof, charged at Edgehill. After the king was settled at Oxford Colonel Hastings, with his own troop of horse only and some officers which he easily gathered together, went with a commission into Leicestershire as 'Colonel-General of that county', and fixed himself at Ashby-de-la-Zouch, the house of the Earl of Huntingdon, his father, who was then living; which he presently fortified; and, in a very short time, by his interest there, raised so good a party of horse and foot, that he maintained many skirmishes with the Lord Grey: the king's service being the more advanced there, by the notable animosities between the two families of Huntingdon and Stamford; between whom the county was divided passionately enough, without any other quarrel. And now the sons fought the public quarrel, with their private spirit and indignation. But the king had the advantage in his champion, the Lord Grey being a young man of no eminent parts, and only backed with the credit and authority of the parliament: whereas Colonel Hastings, though a younger brother, by his personal reputation, had supported his decaying family; and, by the interest of his family, and the affection that people bore to him, brought no doubt an addition of power to the very cause. Insomuch as he not only defended himself against the forces of the parliament in Leicestershire, but disquieted Sir John Gell in Derbyshire, and fixed some convenient garrisons in Staffordshire.*"[2]

Here, then, we have Clarendon's famous description of Lord Grey of Groby as *"a young man of no eminent parts"* and unfavourably compared to his older adversary Henry Hastings. This assessment will be returned to, and considered fully, in a later chapter. At this point, however, an inaccuracy which occurs a little earlier in this passage, should be noted.

Lord Brooke is referred to by Clarendon as being in command of a Midlands Association of the counties of Northamptonshire, Warwickshire, Leicestershire, Derbyshire, and Staffordshire. In fact Lord Brooke was in command of the parliamentarian forces of Warwickshire and Staffordshire only. He was killed by a royalist sniper stationed in a tower of Lichfield Cathedral on 2nd March 1643 when, having taken the town, he was besieging an enemy force in the Cathedral Close. Indeed, it was the young Lord Grey who, at the age of nineteen or twenty, became one of the first commanders of the forces created by Parliament through its Ordinances of Association. These stipulated that the local parliamentary forces in specified counties,

"..... should associate themselves to protect the counties, raise horse and foot, money and plate, give battle, fight and levy war, put to execution of death, and destroy all who should levy war against the Parliament."[3]

According to Vicars, on 13th December 1642,

"..... the two Houses of Parliament appointed the noble and pious Earl of Stamford to be Lord General of all South Wales, and the four next adjacent counties, viz. Gloucester, Worcester, Hereford, and Cheshire; and gave him power to raise forces in all the said counties, and to appoint officers and commanders over them, to train and exercise them, and to fight with, kill, and slay, all that came against them.
"And upon the confidence and trust which the Parliament had in the fidelity of the noble Lord Grey, son and heir of the said Earl of Stamford, they appointed him also Lord General of the five northern (sic) *counties, Leicester, Nottingham, Derby, Rutland, and Lincoln, giving him the like power as his father ....."*[4]

These commissions were issued by the Earl of Essex as the Lord General of all the forces raised by the Parliament.

Two days later the Journal of the House of Lords records a declaration that an Association of the Counties of Leicester, Derby, Nottingham, Rutland, Northampton, Buckingham, Bedford, and Huntingdon, had been formed for the mutual defence and safety of each other - with Lord Grey of Groby as Major-General.

This new arrangement aroused much initial controversy and criticism. It sharply diminished the military power of the lord lieutenants of the shires in the face of the powers now given to the commanders of the forces of these associated counties. The Earl of Manchester, who was later to exercise more power in this respect (as commander of the more famous Eastern Association to which Huntingdonshire was to be transferred) than any other commander of an association army, is reported to have remarked in the House of Lords that since the power conferred upon Lord Grey of Groby as commander-in-chief of the associated forces of Leicestershire, Nottinghamshire, Derbyshire, and other Midland counties at the end of 1642 *"did interfere with the power of the Lord Leiftenantes* (sic) *for those Counties"*, the latter would be desirous of relinquishing their offices in consequence. As Sir Symonds D'Ewes dryly observed, this seemed clearly to indicate that *"the Lord Leiftenantes for those Counties are not much in love with their Offices"*.[5]

By the end of 1642 local sentiment was already on the way to becoming a nuisance rather than an ally to the Parliamentarian leaders, who were at pains to stress that the central versus local issue was based on a dangerously false dichotomy.

The Earl of Stamford had received his appointment to his lord-generalship just as his position in Hereford had become untenable. At the end of October 1642 he had rather cleverly defeated a Cavalier scheme to take the town by a stratagem and had made some important captures at Presteign without suffering any loss to his own force. In November, however, the parliamentarian garrison left by the Earl of Essex at Worcester had withdrawn back to Gloucester in the face of growing local hostility. Supporters of the Parliament in Worcester had been *'but of the middle rank of people* [artisans and small traders], *and none of any great power and eminence to take their parts'*. This evacuation of Worcester served to isolate Stamford's garrison at Hereford where he was experiencing the same sort of local hostility. In a letter to Parliament he wrote:

> *"..... The county, as well as this vile city, are so base and malignant that although the roguish army of the Welsh Papists and other vagabonds that were beaten in the first battle in Warwickshire"* (an exaggerated reference to Edgehill) *"do plunder, kill, murder, and destroy men and women, take away all their goods and cattle, yet such is their hatred to our condition that they would rather be so used than be rescued by us"*.[6]

This disaffection was to some extent caused by the conduct of Stamford's own men who pillaged *"all that kept faith and allegeance* (sic) *with the King"*, and threatened *"that they would keep them so short that they should eate the very flesh from their arms"*.[7]

It was the attitude of the inhabitants of Hereford towards the Parliamentary cause, together with a serious lack of supplies, that persuaded Stamford to relieve himself of the responsibility of attempting to hold the city. On about 14th December 1642 he marched away with his forces to Gloucester where they knew their welcome would be warmer and their position stronger. Thus the entire counties of Worcester and Hereford, newly included in Stamford's area of command as a lord-general, fell into the King's hands.

As the Parliamentarian commander-in-chief of the forces in the counties of Hereford, Worcester, Gloucester, and Salop (Shropshire), and also General in South Wales in the absence of the Earl of Essex, Stamford had a very large area to try to cover. On 19th December he was in Bristol raising fresh troops from the counties of Somerset, Wiltshire, and Gloucestershire. His main base was at Gloucester where both the county and the town were decisively on the side of the parliamentary party, which established garrisons at Sudeley Castle, taken from the royalists on 29th January 1643, Cirencester and Gloucester itself. The town corporation of Gloucester had ordered that *"two great gilt bowls ..... four old Maces, and one old seal of Mayoralty be sold towards the charge for fortifications of the city"*.[8]

At the beginning of 1643, however, the Earl of Stamford left Gloucester, under the governorship of his original Lieutenant Colonel, Edward Massey, and most of his own Bluecoat Regiment of Foot, and rode with his now two troops of horse to Bristol. From Bristol he was ordered by Parliament to move on into the West Country with his newly raised soldiers from Somerset, Gloucestershire and Wiltshire. His West Country campaign of 1643, after a bright start, was to end rather ignominiously.

He claimed to have won some small successes at Plymouth and Modbury in February 1643. As the spring of 1643 progressed, however, his fortunes turned for the worse. In May 1643, whilst in command of the Parliamentarian forces in Devon and Cornwall he was engaged and beaten on the 16th by Sir Ralph Hopton, the main Royalist commander in the West, at Stratton. According to Clarendon (who we should recall was no impartial commentator), Stamford *"stood at a safe distance all the time of the battle, environed with all the horse ..... (and) as soon as he saw the day lost, and some said sooner, made all imaginable haste to Exeter"*.[9] S. R. Gardiner states that *"from that day the spot on which the wealthy Earl demonstrated his signal incompetence as a leader of men has been known as Stamford Hill"*.[10] Stamford himself argued that he had entrusted the conduct of the battle to Major-General James Chudleigh who was taken prisoner and that he had been betrayed by Chudleigh. The Earl's military career was now virtually at an end.

Stamford's political position is further revealed by events subsequent to the debacle at Stratton. He was besieged in Exeter by Prince Maurice, the brother of Prince Rupert, for three months and nineteen days. In his difficulty he wrote a letter to the King dated 4th August in which he made warm professions of loyalty, but criticised the King's counsellors and asked him to dismiss them. He professed to be holding the city *"for your Majesty, and for the preservation of the peace of this whole Kingdom, as instructed by your Majesty's High Court of Parliament".* [11] He surrendered Exeter to the King on 5th September and the fifth article of capitulation which assured him of a pardon gave great offence to Parliament who thought when they heard of it that a searching inquiry should be made into his whole conduct in their service. His bad generalship brought ridicule now from both sides. The cavaliers lampooned him in song and satire and hinted that he was vicious in his sexual inclinations as well as in other respects. In a published defence to the Parliament he made an awkward attempt to lay the blame for his failures on his officers. He repeated his accusations in the House of Lords. On 30th October 1643 he made a plea to the House of Lords that whilst he had been away commanding in the West Country for eleven months (mostly without any pay for his men) his house at Bradgate had been plundered, his horse and cattle driven away, and his tenants robbed; and that he humbly entreated their lordships that *"some malignant's house that was ready furnished might be allotted unto him for his family".* [12] In 1644 he was awarded the estates of the sequestrated Lord Stanhope of Harrington in Leicestershire and Rutland, his own estate *"being under the enemy's power".* [13] He played no further active military role in the first civil war.

The Earl of Stamford was a monarchist at heart; of the same type as those other early Parliamentarian generals the Earls of Essex and Manchester. He was, as his Colonel's colour proclaimed, a 'King and Country' man. In religion he favoured a state church formed on the model of the Scottish kirk system and he was also a political Presbyterian, allying himself with that group of men very much like himself in terms of status and background who dominated the rebel Parliament in the early period of the Great Rebellion. It seems that, like them, he had entered the war in the hope of limiting rather than abolishing the royal power.

By comparison with his father Thomas, Lord Grey of Groby, was militarily successful during the civil war. Clarendon, as has been noted, referred to him as being in 1642 at the outbreak of the war *" a young man of no eminent parts, and only backed by the credit and the authority of Parliament".* Whether Grey was indeed of no eminent parts' will be considered later. Certainly though he was backed by the authority of Parliament and he was a young man; in 1642 he would have been aged nineteen. We may compare this with the King's nephew, Prince Rupert, who at the same time had been given command of the Royalist Horse and was aged twenty-three. Due to the high mortality rate of the period young men often obtained positions of considerable responsibility very much earlier in their careers than is common today. This was all the more so if they occupied high social position by birth; authority being a function of social position. His main local adversary, Henry Hastings, so praised by Clarendon, was a mature man of around thirty-five at this time.

Thomas, Lord Grey of Groby, had entered the military fray by raising a troop of horse locally in Leicestershire from amongst friends, neighbours, tenants and servants which acquitted itself well at Edgehill. Later he also had a Foot Regiment which was based on Leicester. This had five companies; the first being commanded in Lord Grey's absence by a Colonel Henry Grey. Colonel Grey also acted often as the Governor of Leicester, again in Lord Grey's stead.

Lord Grey had been created Lord General of the Midland Association of Counties by Parliament in December 1642. As noted earlier he received his commission from the Earl of Essex, Lord General of all the forces raised by the Parliament. Essex does seem to have been a particular patron of Lord Grey. Denzil Holles referred to the Lord Grey of Groby *"who had before been zealous for my Lord Essex, as he had good reason for the respects he had received from him"*.[14] Mark Noble mentions *"the many obligations"* and *"a peculiar devoir"*[15] for which Grey owed Essex. It is not clear what these were exactly but the two families of Grey and Devereux were related through the Ferrers connection and the Earls of Essex and Stamford were friends. Essex's family life was unhappy and Lord Grey seems to have been a surrogate son to him in some way. Even though aged only nineteen at this stage Thomas Grey was well enough known to protagonists on both sides through his activities in Parliament. On 15th October 1642 he had chaired a Joint Committee of the two Houses of Parliament.

Robert Devereux, 3rd Earl of Essex, had always been a potential leader of the Parliamentarian cause by virtue of his status and background. And yet, as J. P. Kenyon observes, **"any summary of his career reads like a psychiatric case study"**.[16] Born in 1591, he was only ten when his father was executed for treason by Elizabeth I. His mother was the daughter of Sir Francis Walsingham and widow of Sir Philip Sidney. In 1603 she married Richard Bourke, Earl of Clanricarde, and went off to live in Connaught, leaving her son behind. Already we can note similarities to the Earl of Stamford's early life : the family name tainted through execution for treason, the early death of a father, the remarriage and departure to Ireland of a mother.

James I had been eager to avoid any brooding disaffection that might destabilise his newly acquired southern realm and therefore restored the thirteen year old Robert Devereux to his father's lands and titles in 1604. Shortly afterwards, on January 15th, 1606, he arranged for the boy to be married to Frances Howard, the flighty beauty who was the daughter of the Earl of Suffolk. This attempt to bring about an alliance between two rival families led to disaster in 1613 when Frances gained a nullity of the marriage on the grounds that her husband was physically incapable, not with women in general, but with Frances in particular. As her legal document stated, Essex possessed the *'power and ability of body to deal with other women'* but could *'never carnally know her, nor have that copulation in any sort which the marriage bed alloweth'*. It was known that whilst Essex had been abroad, completing his education, she had begun an affair with the king's young favourite Robert Carr. She was seeking a reason to refuse to have marital relations with her husband because of this; hence the petition for nullity so that she might marry Carr. The king himself presided over the hearing of the case and found in favour of Lady Essex. As may be imagined, it gave the gossips at court much to talk about. Essex's second marriage to Frances Powlett in 1632 provided them with yet more. In 1636 he caught her 'in flagrante' with Sir Thomas Uvedale. When she gave birth to a son many believed Uvedale to be the father. This child was to live for a short period of time and with its last breath died the hopes of perpetuating the patrimony of Essex. All of this was saddening and hurtful, especially for a man as proud and reserved as Robert Devereux.

It is not surprising that the Earl of Essex tried to hide his embarrassment by becoming involved in military affairs. *"I believe verily that the unfortunateness of his marriages had so discountenanced his conversation with ladies, that the court could not be his proper element ....."* claimed 'A' in Hobbes' 'Behemoth'. The early 1620s saw him collecting military experience on the continent in the early stages of the Thirty Years War commanding a company in a regiment which set forth under Sir Horace Vere and accompanied by the Earl of Oxford and the then Henry, second lord Grey of Groby, later the Earl of Stamford. In 1621 he visited the Netherlands and accompanied the Prince of Orange to the field of battle; in 1625 he was offered high command as vice-admiral in a disastrous expedition to Cadiz, but was unable to accept it due to a slight from another royal favourite, this time the Duke of Buckingham, who demoted him to be commander of a foot regiment. As early as Charles I's accession, therefore, Essex had acquired quite an extensive experience of warfare. In 1639 he was appointed Lieutenant-General of the Horse for the campaign against the Scots, although he was slighted again by being quickly replaced by the Earl of Holland.

There was, perhaps, a certain inevitability about the emergence of the Earl of Essex as 'His Excellency, the Lord General of the Army raised by the Parliament' in 1642. *"If the Earl of Essex had refused that command our cause in all likelihood had sunk, we having never a nobleman either willing or capable of it"* noted one contemporary, William Lilly. Clarendon described Essex as *"the most popular man of the kingdom, and a darling of the swordsman"*. It is also not surprising, given his background, that he looked with favour upon his friend and former comrade-in-arms' son, Thomas Grey, as the son and heir he was never to have. In October 1643 the Earl of Essex was paid £500 by the Committee for the Advance of Money on behalf of Parliament, *"for so much advanced by him to pay the regiment of Lord Grey of Groby, to enable them to march".*[17]

Throughout the county of Leicestershire during this early period of the first civil war conditions were anarchic and Henry Hastings appears to have attempted to secure some sort of order by declaring that he would use his utmost endeavour to prevent the plundering of those who had obeyed the ordinance of Parliament for the militia, upon a similar promise from Lord Grey to do likewise for those who had appeared for the king.[18] It is not known whether Lord Grey responded in writing to this request but he must have remembered the attacks upon Bradgate that had already taken place and his subsequent actions speak for themselves.

Lord Grey of Groby had acted swiftly after the battle of Edgehill to secure Leicester for the Parliament. Prudence had led the Corporation, which inclined towards the Parliamentarian cause, to steer a neutral course as far as possible in order to avoid military retribution from either side. Henry Hastings, strongly and menacingly based at Ashby-de-la-Zouch Castle, was not to be lightly ignored. The Corporation's dilemma is well illustrated by this reply dated January 1643 from the Mayor to Henry Hastings in the latter's capacity as (Royalist) High Sheriff of the county.

"Noble Sir,

Had I conceived your letter of the 6th of this instant in any way required an answer, I should have troubled you with the perusal of a few lines; but having nothing at that time worth committing to paper, I thought good to answer your letter by word of mouth. As this day I imparted that letter to certain of the aldermen and those of the most ancient, whereupon having in our town neither arms nor power to resist, we resolved to send tomorrow to the right honourable the Lord Grey, by our town chamberlains, to desire his lordship to forbear bringing any forces to this town, lest otherwise he should be the means to cause our prejudice in this corporation. As for the admitting of forces into the town, I assure you, Sir, I shall be far from it; but if any happen to come I must confess I know not how to prevent them of possessing the towne. Worthy sir, I understand by some speeches given out by your last messenger (tending much to my prejudice, as I conceive) that you are informed that I should send for the Lord Grey the last sabbath day, which I assure you is a false report, and so much troubleth me (knowing my innocency

therein) that I earnestly entreat you would be pleased to vindicate
me in that behalf ..... Thus in haste I take leave, and rest,"
& co.

                                        Richard Ludlam
                                    (Mayor of Leicester) [19]

Interestingly, in view of the reassurances and protestations made towards the end of this letter, Richard Ludlam will be conspicuous shortly as an active partisan and captain of horse in the local parliamentarian forces under Lord Grey's command.

Having subsequently secured Leicester during the winter Lord Grey of Groby based his command of the Midland Association there and set up the local Parliamentary Committees. Garrisons were established throughout the county at Leicester itself, Leicester Abbey, Thurnby, Coleorton, Bagworth, Burleigh (at Loughborough), and Kirby Bellars. He coursed the potentially hostile border areas to the north and west of the county and at an early stage he entered Rutland and secured it for Parliament. There are records of many local skirmishes which took place in Leicestershire between the rival forces of Thomas Grey and Henry Hastings but only a few will be referred to in future pages in order either to identify the main incidents in Lord Grey's military career or because of their specific interest.

The young Lord Grey appears to have survived an early brush with death from one of his own subordinates, according to a royalist newssheet dated January 9th 1643.

"..... The Lord Grey (sonne of the Earle of Stamford) having sent before him from Northampton the last Friday, two Companies of Dragoones, with two pieces of Ordinance, and being resolved to follow after with all speeed (sic) *that might be, was hindred* (sic) *by a mutiny amongst the saylors* (sic) *which were sent to serve him, who made no difference in their plundering and rapines, betwixt their owne party and the Kinges good subjects. For the Lord Grey threatening to strike one of them for some misdemeanour, the fellow with his Pole-axe strooke* (sic) *him in the shoulder, and had not the force of the blowe been taken off by some of the by-standers, it is thought his Lordship had been killed".* [20]

It is not known whether this story is true or not but it does seem to tally with Lord Grey's concern to restrain the excesses of the common soldiery (as in the incident involving the Earl of Northampton's house during the Coventry campaign) and his assertive attitude towards those he considered to be his social inferiors.

He was already being regarded as a factor to be reckoned with by the opposition as the following letter, written on 18th January 1643 from Sir Edward Nicholas, one of the royal aides, to Henry Hastings, illustrates :-

"You will herein receive his Majesty's letters, by which you will perceive his care of you. The Earl of Northampton was the last night at Dayntree (Daventry) *with a very considerable force, and from thence he intends to look further into Northamptonshire. There are more horse to follow him tomorrow as I hear. You shall do very well from time to time to advertise the King and the Earl of Northampton of your proceedings and which way the Lord Grey bends his forces. I have herein sent you the news of these parts.*

Postscript - We hear the rebels have taken Holt and carried my cousin Nevill and his brothers to Northampton. I received your letter dated Sunday last but you therein write not how near the rebels are to you. I believe my Lord of Northampton will divert them".[21]

As the winter of 1642-3 progressed the parliamentarian forces under Lord Grey strengthened their hold on Leicester. Things were much less settled in the county areas, however, and in adjoining shires to the north, east, and west. With the Earl of Stamford engaged in the West Country Lord Grey found himself as commander-in-chief of the eight counties of the Midland Association, but with few soldiers under his command and with several hostile enemy bases to contend with.

His new commitments meant that he was to spend less time in London than had been his practice previously as a member of parliament. On 27th December 1642 he had sent a note to a William Jessop at Sir Gilbert Gerard's City office saying that, as he had to leave town hastily, he could not collect his £174. 13s. personally, but that it should be sent to him via a Mr. Temple whom he had ordered to receive it on his behalf. Mr. Temple is likely to have been Peter Temple, a Leicestershire Committee man and a Captain in the local militia, of whom much more will be heard.

Each of the counties in the Midland Association had a committee appointed to raise men, horses, arms, and money - the costs of which were to be repaid by Parliament with 8% interest. The membership of this Leicestershire Committee *"for the supressing of the present rebellion, stirred up by malignant persons who desire to subvert the happiness of this kingdom"* is recorded in the Journal of the House of Lords as follows:

Thomas, Lord Grey; Sir Edward Hartopp, John St. John, William Roberts, Peter Temple, William Jervase, Richard Bent,

Thomas Hesilrige, William Danvers, Thomas Brudenell, Thomas Babington, Thomas Merry, Thomas Beaumont, Arthur Staveley, Thomas Cotton, William Hewitt, Richard Ludlam, (Mayor of the town), and William Stanley (Alderman).[22]

Many of these committee members also held military rank in the units raised under Lord Grey.

By mid-January the local parliamentary committees were empowered first to assess compulsorily all those who had not yet contributed to the raising of the county forces, and finally to seize the rents, money, horse, plate, and goods of all persons in arms for the king or giving voluntary help to his cause.

The local parliamentarian cause suffered two major reverses during the month of January. The first concerned the royalist base at Ashby-de-la-Zouch. The castle at Ashby was ideally situated from a royalist viewpoint, standing as it did on the edge of a parliamentarian controlled isthmus of territory that stretched from Northamptonshire through Leicestershire, Nottinghamshire, and Derbyshire to Cheshire, thus cutting off Oxford and the royalist west from the royalist north. From its dominant position on a spur, the garrison at Ashby could initiate or support any campaign in the valleys of the Trent and Severn, or the Avon. The line of the river Trent was of great importance. Being a navigable river, supplies could be sent along it from the west to the north or vice versa. Accordingly, Henry Hastings established a series of satellite garrisons at Swarkestone, Kings Mills near Donington, and Wilne Ferry near Shardlow. The nearest parliamentarian commander to these royalist outposts was Sir John Gell, based at Derby, and it fell to him to deal with them. First he attacked the three hundred strong garrison at Swarkestone where, after two days of fighting, he dislodged Hastings' men from the bridge and from the house of Sir John Harper, one of the local royalist commanders. Inspired by this success Gell, along with Sir William Brereton from Cheshire, joined with Lord Grey of Groby in an attack on Ashby-de-la-Zouch castle. Hastings, however, was considered too valuable an asset for the Crown to lose and Prince Rupert was despatched from Oxford with a force of five regiments of foot, horse, and dragoons on 21st January to relieve the castle. The parliamentarian allies had by this time driven the garrison out of the town and into the castle itself. Prince Rupert's arrival at Banbury, en route for Ashby, was communicated to the besiegers by scouts of the Northamptonshire Committee, and Gell's subsequent Council of War decided that each of the three commanders should abandon the siege and return to their home areas in order to safeguard them.

The second reverse, however, was even more serious. The strategically placed castle and town of Newark in Nottinghamshire had been seized at the outbreak of hostilities by local royalist gentry and subsequently reinforced in December by about four thousand horse sent south by the Earl of Newcastle. Commanding the lowest bridge over the Trent and standing on the main road south, it was the funnel through which any invasion of Parliament's territory from the north must pour. Its possession ensured an indispensable link with the king's headquarters in Oxford. It was clearly in the interests of the Midland parliamentarians to remove this dagger from their throats. Equally the royalists were eager to extend their outposts from Newark to Grantham and to Belvoir. Belvoir Castle belonged to the Earl of Rutland who was a supporter of Parliament but was not in residence. Before the end of January Viscount Campden, Colonel Gervase Lucas, and others had secured it for the Crown. Apparently Colonel Lucas, who was gentleman of the horse to the Earl of Rutland, entered the castle on the night of the 28th January with eight men by casting a rope about a balcony up which they then ascended and broke open the castle gates from within. This admitted the Newark forces and the garrison of a hundred men surrendered. During the remainder of the war Belvoir was to prove a major irritant to the local parliamentarians.

From now on the Leicestershire parliamentarians were to be pestered by recurrent raids from Ashby Castle in the north west and from Belvoir Castle in the north east of the county.

In February the king created his own Association of the counties of Leicester, Derby, Nottingham, Lincoln, and Rutland and made Henry Hastings the Colonel-General of all the royalist forces in them.[23]

Parliamentarian reverses affecting Leicestershire continued, although further afield. Earlier it was noted that the Earl of Stamford had left Edward Massey, his original second-in-command, based at Gloucester with satellite outposts at Sudeley Castle and Cirencester. On 2nd February Cirencester, *"a straggling and open towne, neither well fortified nor capable of defence"*[24] was attacked by Prince Rupert with 4,000 horse and foot. In the assault he lost 20 men killed and another 30 were wounded but of the defenders 400 were killed and all their ordnance (six cannon) were taken. According to the pro-parliamentarian commentator, Bulstrode Whitelocke, the royalists put the garrison of the Earl of Stamford's Bluecoat Regiment *"and many others to the sword, took 1,100 prisoners and 3,000 arms"*.[25] The prisoners were taken to Oxford *"tied to one another with cords and match"*[26] (i.e. slowmatch cord, used for igniting the muskets). The victors *"fell to plundering* (Cirencester) *all night, all the next day, and on Saturday ..... to the utter ruin of many hundred families"*, so that *"the inhabitants of the miserable distressed Cyrencester"* were obliged to petition the King that they *"having undergone all the heavy effects of your majesty's justly incensed army ..... acknowledge us inexcusably faulty, but appeale unto your mercy, and beg your pardon"*.[27] Whitelocke records the treatment meted out to the captured parliamentarian soldiers, many of whom had been recruited in Leicestershire.

"These prisoners were led in much triumph to Oxford, where the king and lords looked on them, and too many smiled at their misery, being tied together with cords, almost naked, beaten, and driven along like dogs.

Among them was a proper handsome man, of a very white skin, where it could be seen for the blood of his wounds; he not being able to go, was set naked upon the bare back of an horse, his wounds gaping, and his body smeared with blood; yet he sat upright upon the horse with an undaunted countenance, and when near the king a brawling woman cried out to him, "Ah you traitorly rogue, you are well enough served!" he, with a scornful look towards her, answered, "You base whore!" and instantly dropped off dead from his horse.

And the beginning of such cruelty by Englishmen towards their countrymen was afterwards too too much followed".[28]

Prince Rupert then summoned Massey to surrender Gloucester. This summons was refused, but Massey withdrew his men from Sudeley Castle and other outposts in order to consolidate and prepare for the expected siege of Gloucester.

It was not all reverses, however, for the Leicestershire parliamentarians. Lord Grey of Groby was particularly active in securing the small adjacent county of Rutland for 'The Good Old Cause'. At the beginning of 1643 a detachment of his Leicester forces had marched to Oakham and carried away 22 barrels of gunpowder and other ammunition stored there as the county magazine. In addition, at about the same time as the capture of Belvoir Castle by the royalists the parliamentarians captured the Villiers' (Duke of Buckingham) family seat in Rutland at Burley-on-the-Hill.

The most influential and active of the Rutland royalists seems to have been Edward Noel, Viscount Campden. On the outbreak of the war he received a commission to raise 500 horse, and afterwards another for three regiments of horse and three of foot. He led the royalists in Lincolnshire in 1642 and 1643 when they were called 'Campdeners' by their opponents and he was later with the king's Oxford forces, but died before he had managed to raise all these authorised units. His eldest son, Baptist Noel, succeeded him as a loyal supporter of the king and was in the course of 1643 successively appointed captain of a troop of horse and of a company of foot, colonel of a regiment of horse, and a brigadier of both horse and foot. Lord Grey seems to have waged something of a personal vendetta against this family in his prosecution of the local war effort. The second son of the family, Henry Noel of North Luffenham, seems to have suffered particularly from his attentions. He appears to have collected some of his friends and neighbours together to act as *'a little Guard'* for his home, and

98

he officially informed one of the deputy-lieutenants of Rutland that he had taken this step as a measure of ordinary prudence and without any desire *"to raise any forces to molest the county or meddle with anie of their Armes"*.[(29)] At the end of February Lord Grey joined forces with a Captain Wray from the parliamentarian garrison at Grantham in Lincolnshire with the aim of capturing Lord Campden or his son Baptist. Finding that the father was gone to Oxford and the eldest son to Newark and that the arms and ammunition he was expecting to find at the family seat had been removed shortly before his arrival, he moved his force on to North Luffenham. Here he demanded of Henry Noel the surrender of his person, arms and horses. Though the force under Lord Grey numbered, according to Noel's estimate some 1,300, the latter, whose small garrison had been increased to 200 (of whom 120 were armed with guns and the remainder with pikes and clubs), *"returned answer that he would stand on his defence while he had breath"*.[(30)] In the skirmish which followed, Mr. Catesby, a lieutenant of one of the Lord Grey's captain's troops, was killed by a shot from the house. The next day a parliamentarian common soldier was shot dead and some others hurt but afterwards the house was 'shot through' and the attackers set fire to some hayricks and outhouses in the hall yard. This so alarmed some of Noel's neighbours amongst the defenders that, in order to save further bloodshed amongst those fighting for him, he surrendered on condition that the fire should be extinguished; that all in the house should have liberty to depart; and that none should enter the house but the commanders. Lord Grey, in a letter on this affair sent to Speaker William Lenthall in London, is silent as to these conditions which he seems to have ignored. *"..... the house being shot through, they called for quarter and yielded, and then I entered the house and seized Mr. Noel and his arms and Mr. Skipwith ..... With much difficulty I preserved their lives, but the soldiers were so enraged I could not save their goods"*.[(31)] The Mr. Skipwith mentioned here is Henry Skipwith of Cotes in Leicestershire and although he claims to have been an innocent visitor as friend and near kinsman to Henry Noel, we have already met him in the pre-war period as an active royalist partisan and supporter of Henry Hastings. Both Noel and Skipwith were sent as prisoners to the parliament in London and both petitioned the Commons via the Lords for their discharge, or bail and recompense. Their political sympathies were well known, however, and Henry Noel died in prison the following July, his father having died in March in the King's garrison in Oxford. The title Viscount Campden now passed to Baptist Noel, already noted as another energetic royalist partisan. Complaints continued to be made by the Campden family and on their behalf about *"the unheard of cruelties by the Lord Grey and his soldiers on the person, house, goods and servants of Master Nowell in Rutlandshire"*.[(32)]

Although the acquisition of the goods and property of 'malignants' was to become an increasingly attractive activity for Lord Grey, there was some higher motive behind the attention he devoted to the Noel family. He took a very serious view of the necessity for swift action to counteract the royalist activity in Rutland :-

> *"I found the coals kindle so fast in that country that had I not suddenly quenched them the whole country would have been on a flame. The Malignants flocked so fast, that had I not entered Rutlandshire at that Nick of Time, I am confident in one week the whole Country would have been drawn into a body against the Parliament".*[33]

Hence it is not surprising that he suggested to the Earl of Manchester the seizure of the rents of the young new Lord Campden when the latter was engaged in various operations on behalf of the royalist cause later in the year. Grey's enmity was not directed against all the Noel brothers, however, as he seems to have protected William Noel whom, he was to assure other parliamentarians next year, was 'well-affected'.

On 3rd March Richard Ludlam (Mayor of Leicester), William Stanley (Alderman), and Evers Armyn (a landowner and County Committee member in Rutland), were appointed as members of a new committee for raising money within the town of Leicester for the weekly maintenance of the army.

The spring in 1643 was a period of hectic activity as the rival garrisons and field armies stirred from their winter quarters. Lord Grey, for example, was kept busy in both strengthening his base in Leicester and covering all the parts of his extensive command - all the while with an eye to the security of his patrimony at Bradgate. For example, on 17th March he is reported as coming from Leicester to Northampton to ensure that some ordnance be sent to Lichfield, he having despatched some twelve troops of horse there already.

These local movements often fitted into a larger picture. The Queen, Henrietta Maria, had landed at Bridlington in February with the weapons and ammunition she had purchased in the Netherlands from the proceeds of the sale of the English Crown Jewels. She then moved to York, which was held for the Crown by the Earl of Newcastle, with the intention of gathering an army to enable her to move south. The parliamentarian garrisons of the Midlands were likely to be caught between the Queen's army in the north moving down by way of Newark and the King's forces, probably led by the dashing but vengeful Prince Rupert, moving up from Oxford. Newark and Ashby-de-la-Zouch were likely to be pivotal to the success of the royalist plans and loomed even more threatening to Lord

Grey and his adherents. It is in this context that the manoeuvrings of both sides in the rest of 1643 have to be seen.

Indeed, the horse and cannon sent by Lord Grey to Lichfield were in support of an attempt by Parliament to strengthen its control over Staffordshire, and with it the wedge between the royalist west and north. Lichfield had been captured by the joint forces of Lord Brooke, commander of the West Midland Association, and Sir John Gell, although the former had died in the process. Gell left Lichfield on 19th March intending to attack the county town of Stafford. Before he could rendezvous as planned with Sir William Brereton's Cheshire forces he was attacked on Hopton Heath by the Earl of Northampton and Henry Hastings. The royalists beat both Gell's force and then Brereton's as it arrived on the Heath, capturing all their artillery. The Earl of Northampton died in this encounter. On 21st April Prince Rupert recaptured Lichfield and the parliamentarian attempt to cut off the western channel of royalist communications between Oxford and York had failed.

On 1st April a further committee, this time for the Sequestration of Delinquents' Estates, was set up in Leicester. Sequestration was another means of raising money. It involved the confiscation of the estates of 'notorious delinquents', whom Parliament defined in an ordinance passed on 1st April 1643, as :-

> *"all persons, ecclesiastical or temporal, as have raised or shall raise arms against the Parliament, or have been, are, or shall be in actual war against the same, or have voluntarily contributed or shall voluntarily contribute, not being under any power of any part of the King's army at the time of such Contributing, any money, horses, plate, arms, munitions, or other aid or assistance for or towards the maintenance of any forces raised against the Parliament, or for opposing any force or power raised by the authority of both Houses of Parliament".*[34]

By this act, and on the other side of the King's authority, known royalist or parliamentarian sympathizers residing within the territories controlled by the opposing party forfeited their lands and possessions. The sequestered property was either rented out, or sold, to provide for a further means of realising revenue for the continuance of the war. Both sides appointed special Commissioners of Sequestration who were the sole judges of whether or not a person came within the definition of 'delinquent'.

The administration of sequestrated estates soon became irksome, however, and a system of compounding which was first developed in 1644, was officially introduced by Parliament in the spring of 1645, whereby delinquents could pay a fine in lieu of forfeiting their estates. A composition tariff was laid down, ranging from one half to one tenth of the pre-war value of the estate according to the degree of the owner's delinquency.

Members of the Leicester Committee for the Sequestration of Delinquents' Estates were to be (some familiar names here) :-

Henry, Lord Grey of Ruthin; Thomas, Lord Grey of Groby; Sir Arthur Hesilrige; Sir Edward Hartopp; Sir Thomas Hartopp; William Hewet; John Bainbridge; Peter Temple; George Ashby; William Roberts; Richard Bent; Arthur Staveley; William Danvers; John Goodman (for the county) and Richard Ludlam (Mayor) and William Stanley (Alderman) for the town.

Alderman Robert Billers was added later, as were William Bainbridge and Francis Smalley Jnr.

This was an important committee. Over a period of time some sequestrations were likely to be of personal advantage to particular committee members who might be able to purchase sequestrated property at attractive prices; particularly if as part payment or payment in kind for services rendered to Parliament. It has already been noted how the Earl of Stamford was to plead to the House of Lords in six months time, after his service in the West Country, *"that some malignant's house, that was ready furnished, might be allotted unto him for his family"*.[35]

At the same time yet another local parliamentarian body was created. This was the Commission for Punishing Scandalous Ministers. It was intended to enforce a puritan line amongst the local clergy. The Commissioners were to be :-

Henry, Lord Grey of Ruthin; Thomas, Lord Grey of Groby; Sir Arthur Hesilrige; Sir Wolstan Dixie; Sir Thomas Hartopp; Sir Martin Lister; Sir Roger Smith; George Ashby; Thomas Babington; Thomas Brudenell; Simon Rudgley; Peter Temple; John Bainbridge; Thomas Hesilrige; and William Sherman.

The inclusion of Sir Wolstan Dixie's name in this list is of some interest as he was one of the Commissioners of Array named by the King in the previous year and must have been known to be a royalist by this stage, unless he had managed to perform a very tricky balancing act indeed.

Meanwhile, preparations for the anticipated major military confrontation in the Midlands were gaining pace. The journal of Sir Samuel Luke, at that time Scoutmaster-General to the Earl of Essex's army, records on 6th April 1643 receipt of information that,

> *"..... Colonell Hastings and the Earle of Northampton* (sic) *have drawen their forces to Ashby-de-la-Zouch in Leicestershire, and are about 1,500 strong. That the Lord Grey hearing of his comming sent for some aide out of Leicestershire whoe came in very willingly, and are now fortifying the town of Leicester very strongly ....."*[36]

On 15th April the Committee for the Safety of the Kingdom in London were ordered by the House of Commons,

> *"..... to furnish my Lord Grey at Leicester with six pieces of ordnance, 1,000 muskets, their equipage and furniture, and likewise with ammunition, and to send them away with all speed".*[37]

These provisions may not have been intended for the defence of Leicester itself, however, as Lord Grey was gathering his forces together in preparation for a march southwards.

The peace negotiations between King and Parliament which had been re-opened at Oxford on 1st February had broken down by 14th April. The Earl of Essex, who had been militarily inactive over the winter period, now moved the main army of the Parliament out from Windsor in the general direction of Oxford. It was deemed imprudent to leave the royalists in possession of Reading on the way and on Sunday, 16th April Lord Grey's forces joined Essex's army in surrounding Reading. Sir Edward Nicholas, a royal aide, informed Henry Hastings of these developments in two letters from Oxford delivered at the same time and by the same courier. The first, dated 19th April, had reported that Sir Arthur Aston, the royalist governor of Reading, had not lost a foot of ground but had killed 700 men from *"the two best rebel regiments of bluecoats and redcoats"* and, if royalist reinforcements arrived the whole rebel army might be destroyed. The second letter, dated 21st April, which is a continuation of the first one carries a different tone.

> *"This letter should have been sent by a messenger that neglected to call for it. Since the writing of it we have news that the Lord Grey's forces being joined with the Earl of Essex's, they have begirt Redding so as no man can come forth or go in; that Sir Arthur Aston is dangerously hurt, and that if Prince Rupert*

103

come not instantly Redding wilbe [sic] *lost, wherefor I pray hasten his Highnes with as many dragoons and foot as may be possible* (sic) *spared".*[(38)]

Reading was surrendered on 27th April to the parliamentary forces but the garrison were allowed to march away to Oxford with their colours flying; a settlement which pleased few on either side. The king resented the loss of Reading and many parliamentarians resented the repeated failure of the Earl of Essex as their commander-in-chief to press home his, often hard won, military and strategic advantages. Once more, having this time taken Reading by siege, the Earl of Essex made no move towards Oxford with the main Army of the Parliament.

Lord Grey of Groby returned from Reading with his forces back to Leicester where attempts were made to engage them on the 'northern' front. In Yorkshire Lord Fairfax and his son Thomas had kept up stiff resistance to the Earl of Newcastle's forces but were unable to prevent some royalist incursions into the northern borders of the parliamentarian Eastern Association (made up of the East Anglian counties and the Fenlands) nor from building up their forces at Newark. In order to stop this threat to Lincolnshire and the other eastern counties the Earl of Essex sent orders to Lord Grey of Groby and Sir John Gell to rendezvous at Stamford in Lincolnshire with a certain Colonel Oliver Cromwell of the Eastern Association, prior to a joint offensive against Newark. Gell was willing to co-operate on behalf of the Derbyshire and Nottinghamshire forces but Cromwell was outspoken and bitter in his disgust when Grey failed to keep the rendezvous. He felt that the security of Bradgate and Leicester was Grey's main concern. It is only fair to observe that Cromwell's own property in Huntingdonshire was in no danger at this time or for most of the period of the first civil war. Nonetheless one can understand the strong feelings of frustration he had. It appears to have not been the first time that something like this had transpired. He fully intended to make his feelings on the matter plain to his fellow MP when he next met him. The subordination of private and local aims and interests to the common ends was one of the secrets of Cromwell's success at all stages in his military and political career. He made clear his views in a letter to the parliamentarian Committee at Lincoln on 3rd May thus,

"..... My Lord Grey hath now again failed me of the rendezvous at Stamford, - notwithstanding that both he and I received Letters from his Excellency, commanding us both to meet, and together with Sir John Gell and the Nottingham forces, to join with you. My Lord Grey sent Sir Edward Hartop to me, To let

me know he could not meet me at Stamford according to our agreement; fearing the exposure of Leicester to the forces of Mr. Hastings and some other Troops drawing that way.

"Believe it, it were better, in my poor opinion, Leicester were not, than there should not be found an immediate taking of the field by our forces to achieve the common ends. Wherein I shall deal as freely with him, when I meet him, as you can desire. I perceive Ashby-de-la-Zouch sticks much with him. I have offered him another place of meeting, to come to which I suppose he will not deny me; and that to be tomorrow. If you shall therefore think fit to send one over unto us to be with us at night, - you do not know how far we may prevail with him: To draw speedily to a head, with Sir John Gell and other forces, where we may all meet at a general rendezvous, to the end you know of. ..... If we could unite those forces 'of theirs'; and with them speedily make Grantham the general rendezvous, both of yours and ours, I think it would do well. I shall bend my endeavours that way. .....[39]

It is not known whether Lord Grey attended the meeting on the following day as proposed by Cromwell, but it seems unlikely. In early and mid-May Cromwell was still active in the Sleaford and Grantham areas of Lincolnshire whilst Grey of Groby was making strikes against royalist forces just beyond Leicestershire's borders to the west and to the east.

Sir Samuel Luke notes on 'Sunday, 7th May, 1643' that,

"..... William Richards returned this day from Coventry and saith that on Wednesday last Colonell Hastings' forces which were come to Nuneaton, 8 miles from Coventry, intending to have pillaged the faire which was then kept there and to have driven away the horses and cattle, the Lord Grey hearing of them came with some of his forces, and beat them back, shott and hurt divers of them and tooke 30 prisoners and their horses and arms .....[40]

During May Lord Grey also seized Rockingham Castle which lies just inside Northamptonshire where that county meets Leicestershire and Rutland. He then used Rockingham as a base to increase his control over Rutland. It could also be used 'in extremis' as a refuge if Leicester itself were to be in danger of falling into royalist hands. Sir Lewis Watson, whose home it was and who had surrendered it to Lord Grey, was arrested by Henry Hastings for failing to hold it for the king. Watson protested his loyalty and was eventually released from his imprisonment in Belvoir Castle. He then joined the king at Oxford.

By the late spring of 1643 the parliamentarian garrison of Nottingham, under Colonel John Hutchinson, had become increasingly alarmed at the southwards movement of royalists into Newark and north Lincolnshire. Accordingly, Hutchinson had been sent down to London to give to the House of Commons an account of the danger in which Nottingham stood and an appeal for help. In response the House sent a message to Lord Fairfax in Yorkshire at the end of April asking him to dispatch what aid he could to Nottingham, where the garrison was in *"a weak and languishing condition"*. This proved fruitless as Fairfax himself had his hands full and was on the defensive in Yorkshire at the time. The Earl of Essex, as parliamentarian commander-in-chief, was also urged to take steps for the defence of the town *"in respect of the importance of that place"*.[41]

As a consequence orders were issued that forces from the Eastern Association, Lincolnshire, Leicestershire, and Derbyshire should concentrate at Nottingham under the command of Lord Grey of Groby. The immediate purpose of the rendezvous was to defend the town but an additional objective was to prevent the queen from joining with the king and this might involve a concerted attack on Newark if the circumstances were deemed favourable. Accordingly, in the Whitsun holiday period of 1643 they all mustered together in a force of between 5,000 to 6,000 men. There was Lord Grey from Leicestershire, Lord Willoughby of Parham from Lincolnshire, Sir John Gell from Derbyshire, Colonel Hutchinson with the Nottingham forces, and John Hotham the Younger (son of Sir John Hotham, commander at Hull) who came in with some troops from the East Riding of Yorkshire. In terms of ability and resolution, however, all were outmatched by the Huntingdon colonel who led the detachment from the Eastern Association. Fighting his way north to the aid of the distressed 'Roundheads' in Lincolnshire, Colonel Oliver Cromwell had made his mark in history in a nameless cavalry skirmish which was to anticipate his future military successes and which in S. R. Gardiner's phrase foreshadowed **'the whole fortune of the civil war'**, viz :-

"On the evening of May 13 he found himself with twelve troops of horse, `whereof some so poor and broken that you shall seldom see worse' opposed to double their number, two miles from Grantham on the Newark road. Without counting heads, he gave the word to charge. The spirit of their commander gave force to the followers, and the larger host broke and fled before the smaller, `With this handful', wrote Cromwell, in recounting the event (to the Lincolnshire

Committee), `it pleased God to cast the scale'. **The whole fortune of the civil war was in that nameless skirmish. A body of Puritan horsemen had driven twice their number before them as chaff before the wind, and as armies were then constituted superiority in cavalry was superiority in war".**[(42)]

In this action was seen for the first time that stern spirit and iron discipline, beginning with those first 'Ironsides', which on wider fields was to win the war for the Parliament. In Cromwell's view the offensive was the best form of defence. He had striven early in May, as has been noted, to secure a Stamford rendezvous by all the neighbouring forces for an attack on Newark; but localist feeling had prevented the necessary co-operation. Then came the order to join the Nottingham rendezvous with its real opportunity for pressing forward his strategy.

The original object of the army thus assembled under the command of the young Thomas, Lord Grey of Groby was to defend Nottingham and to hold up the royalist advance from the north. Just as the others were waiting for Gell's arrival on 24th May, however, they received news of a sensational victory won by Sir Thomas Fairfax at Wakefield three days earlier when he had taken 1,400 royalist prisoners. This success, by threatening his rear, compelled the Earl of Newcastle once more to retire to York, and it rekindled the war in the West Riding. For the moment the most pressing danger to Nottingham was thus removed. So the army which had been assembled in Nottingham was now available for potential offensive action. There were two obvious possibilities; it could move to take Newark, or it might march up into Yorkshire to join Fairfax and carry the war into the heart of Newcastle's own territory. The latter course of action might have anticipated Marston Moor in July 1644 and thus have shortened the whole struggle. Cromwell was as eager as ever for vigorous action which might lead to a conclusive decision in the field. He was, however, only one among the five commanders, and it soon became clear that there was little hope, after all, of carrying out either aggressive strategy.

The army was in fact paralysed by the strength of local feeling in its various units, by internal dissensions and treachery, and by the indecision and relative inexperience of its nominal leader. We should remember that Lord Grey of Groby was at this time aged no more than twenty or twenty-one. (John Hutchinson was twenty-six and Oliver Cromwell was forty-four). Blinded by anxiety for local interests to the well-being of the cause as a whole, none of its various divisions, apart from that of Cromwell, was prepared to march as far afield as Yorkshire or leave its native county open to possible attack from neighbouring royalist forces while it was denuded of its own troops. Obstructionism derived from this sentiment was in itself powerful enough to wreck any plan for going to the help of Fairfax. At the end of May Newcastle had sent two regiments of foot to Newark and the presence of these hostile forces was used by the army leaders at Nottingham as an excuse for remaining there and leaving Fairfax to fend for himself. A letter bearing the signatures of the five commanders, amongst which was that of Cromwell - though most likely against his own wishes, was sent to Fairfax to this effect adding that Newcastle's army in Yorkshire had been so weakened that their own presence there was now quite unnecessary. Fairfax in reply told them that they were entirely misinformed and that the *'Popish army'* was strong enough to ruin him, whatever reports might say. His fears were to prove well-founded.

The letter from the Nottingham commanders was in the handwriting of Captain John Hotham who, as the lowest ranking of the allied commanders, was probably acting as secretary for them all. It is also likely that the letter most strongly represented his own views. The general conduct of the younger Hotham added to the aforementioned parochial strategy a further brake upon any decided joint action against the enemy. He was a fiery turbulent individual to whom war excused all licence, and his men, taking their cue from their leader, were rude, undisciplined and unprincipled. In this respect they were like Gell's Greycoats who were originally raised in London, sent to assist the elder Hotham in securing Hull for parliament, and had then been obtained by Sir John Gell to his service in Derbyshire. Sir John, a Derbyshire gentleman, had been before the outbreak of the war the sheriff of that county and a zealous enforcer on behalf of the king of the Ship-Money tax. Lucy Hutchinson suggests that he so feared punishment from parliament for his earlier excesses that to avoid it he put himself into their service and secured the town of Derby for them. She describes his soldiers as *'nimble youths at plunder'* and the following passage gives a fuller picture.

"These were good stout fighting men, but the most licentious ungovernable wretches that belonged to the parliament. As regards himself, no man knew for what reason he chose that side; for he had not understanding enough to judge the equity of the cause, nor piety nor holiness: being a foul adulterer all the time he served the parliament, and so unjust that without any remorse he suffered his men indifferently to plunder both honest men and cavaliers. ..... This man kept the journalists in pension, so that whatever was done in the neighbouring counties against the enemy was attributed to him; and thus he hath indirectly purchased himself a name in story which he never merited. He was a very bad man, to sum up all in that word, yet an instrument of service to the parliament in those parts".[43]

Lucy Hutchinson records how her husband sought to restrain the activities of Gell's men and of Hotham's men, whom she describes as *"some more rude troops out of Yorkshire"*. The behaviour of both groups was causing concern among the local `godly' and could well have alienated neutrals and parliamentarian partisans alike.

> *"Then was Nottingham more sadly distressed by their friends than by their enemies; for Hotham's and Gell's men not only lay upon free quarter, as all the rest did, but made such a havoc and a plunder of friend and foe that it was a sad thing for anyone that had a generous heart to behold it. When the (Nottingham) Committee offered Hotham to assign him quarters for his men, because they were better acquainted with the country, he would tell them he was no stranger in any English ground. He had a great deal of wicked wit and would make sport with the miseries of the poor country; and, having treason in his heart, licensed his soldiers, which were the scum of mankind, to all villainies in the country that might make their party odious. Mr. Hutchinson was much vexed to see the country wasted, and that little part of it which they could only hope to have contribution from eaten up by a company of men who, instead of relieving, devoured them; and Hotham's soldiers having taken away goods from some honest men, he went to him to desire restitution of them, and that he would restrain his soldiers from plunder; whereupon Hotham replied, he fought `for liberty, and expected it in all things'. Replies followed and they grew to high language; Hotham bidding him, if he found himself grieved, to complain to the Parliament".*[44]

Whereas the puritan credentials of Colonel Hutchinson, Colonel Cromwell, and Lord Grey were not in doubt, the latter, as the commander-in-chief, was weakly compliant in his dealings with Hotham and Gell at this stage. It was to be a lesson bitterly learned; and we may compare this with his later attitude to his military subordinates, as for example with Captain Richard Ludlam the following year. Due to his temper, however, Hotham had also strained relations with Cromwell and Grey. When an argument flared up between the colonel and Hotham the latter turned two pieces of ordnance against Cromwell. Again, when Lord Grey of Groby's quartermaster, Daniel Maddox, had been offended by his lordship in a disagreement *'about oats'* Hotham suggested privately to Maddox that they two should draw out their men and make a fight of it with Lord Grey's supporters.

These differences did not go unnoticed by their opponents. In a letter from Oxford dated 21st June, Sir Edward Nicholas informed Henry Hastings that,

109

"..... We are advertised from London and elsewhere that there are so great differences in the rebels' army near Nottingham as that Hotham and Crumwell [sic] *are ready to cut each other's throats. I would write oftener to you, if I had any messengers, but the ways are so dangerous as I cannot meet with any conveyance".*

The postscript to this letter contained news of

"the defeat given to part of the Earl of Essex's forces on Sunday last in which Mr. John Hempden [sic], and Mr. Sheffield, the Earl of Mulgrave's son were dangerously wounded". [i.e. at Chalgrove Field where both sustained mortal injuries].[45]

It was the instability of Hotham's political convictions rather than of his character, however, that was to cause greatest anxiety. Suspicion soon changed to certainty that he, along with his father, was playing the traitor. The elder Hotham had been in secret communication for some time with the Earl of Newcastle to negotiate the best terms for handing over the key stronghold of Hull to the royalists. His son had written to the Earl at the end of March, commenting on the conflicting news of victories and defeats issued by the leaderships of both causes, in a spirit of war-weariness and cynicism, *"..... but I am grown to believe nothing because I thinke our masters of both sides feed us with such meat as they think fittest for us".*[46]

Since April 1643 he had been in secret communication with the Earl of Newcastle and the Queen, and from Nottingham he exchanged frequent messages with the royalists in Newark. This was done through the sending and receiving of trumpeters, the purpose of which he refused to give any account, thus increasing the suspicions of his treachery. As his conduct became more and more insufferable, and the assurance of his infidelity grew beyond doubt, Cromwell and Hutchinson resolved to strike. Taking him at his own suggestion, and without consulting with Lord Grey, Gell, or Willoughby of Parham, they sent up to London a full report of Hotham's behaviour. This they did, according to Lucy Hutchinson, because some of the other commanders (one may speculate about Gell, for example) *"were little less suspected themselves, and others, as my Lord Grey, through credulous good nature, were too great favourers of Hotham".*[47]

The other reason for their lack of consultation with the others was that they also complained about *"the ill management of their forces"* and *"the idle waste of such a considerable force, through the inexperience of the chief commander, and the disobedience and irregularities of the others".*[48]

110

Upon receipt of the message the Earl of Essex issued an order for the arrest of Captain John Hotham. On 18th June he was seized and imprisoned in Nottingham Castle. He managed to escape from a troop of Lord Grey's horse a few days later as they were taking him under guard en route to London. He then made counter allegations to parliament about the *'anabaptist'* nature of Cromwell's troopers. He was recaptured in Hull on 28th June and eventually executed for treason, along with his father, in January 1645.

Essex also appointed Sir John Meldrum, a Scot and a professional soldier who had been trained in the continental wars and had served at Edgehill, to replace Lord Grey as chief commander of the united forces at Nottingham. The news of Grey's replacement on the grounds of his weak and ineffective leadership arrived in Nottingham at the same time as the order for Hotham's arrest.

These internal troubles had effectively prevented any decisive action. For three previous weeks no serious effort had been made to utilise the large number of troops which had been brought together. A feint attack had been made at Newark but by this stage it was too well manned and fortified to be besieged without careful preparation.

At the beginning of June the local Nottinghamshire gentry had goaded Lord Grey into marching out against Wiverton House. This was the fortified country home of the royalist John, Lord Chaworth. The garrison of Wiverton had been disrupting the neighbourhood by its plunderings and an attempt against them by the Nottingham forces in April had been unsuccessful. Lord Grey apparently took with him against this small royalist outpost his whole force of over 5,000 men and quickly drove its defenders from their outworks, back into the house itself. Instead of going on to either storm or besiege the house, however, on the apparently groundless rumour that the Newark forces were marching to its relief he at once fell back on Nottingham, despite the protests of Captain Henry Ireton and other local officers who wanted to stand and fight.

Emboldened by his caution the Newarkers did emerge in force two or three days later and approached within four miles of Nottingham. There they offered to do battle with the Nottingham forces. The parliamentary commanders, though they sent out some troops to scout, declined to take up the challenge on the grounds that the enemy were too strongly placed. Cromwell was present and outwardly at least a consenting party to these timid tactics, but he was in all probability compelled to approve a course which ran counter to what is known of his general disposition by the majority votes of his colleagues, and uncertainty as to how far Hotham's treachery had gone. It should be borne in mind that at this point Hotham had not yet been arrested and Thomas Grey was still commander-in-chief. Lucy Hutchinson claims that though the parliamentarian forces were not inferior in numbers to the royalists they would not be prevailed upon to go out and face them.

The cavaliers of Newark were thus left in undisputed possession of the field and they soon received a formidable reinforcement. On 4th June Queen Henrietta Maria left York with nearly 5,000 men whom the Earl of Newcastle had raised and she had armed. On 16th June she arrived at Newark without interference. This allowed another criticism to be levelled at Lord Grey of Groby. Surely, it was argued, one of the main objectives of the parliamentarian army which had been concentrated at Nottingham, when all idea of co-operation with Fairfax was dropped, was to intercept the queen if she moved south and to stop her from joining up with the king's Oxford forces. As she arrived at Newark only two days before Hotham's arrest and Lord Grey being superseded by Meldrum as overall commander, these circumstances may have crippled the initiative of the parliamentary forces. The entire absence, however, either then or later of any effort to bar the queen's progress was a striking commentary on the helplessness of the host at Nottingham, regardless of whoever was its chief commander. The initiative now lay with the queen. Instead of being attacked she was now the attacker. On 21st June her troops assailed Nottingham. The castle cannon slew some of the attackers but the cavaliers claimed to have killed fifty of the 'roundheads' and to have taken eighty prisoners from those who had sallied out against them. The parliamentarians had been thrown onto the defensive by this attack and the queen's line of march remained unthreatened.

All idea of stopping her progress to Oxford being abandoned by 20th June, when she was still at Newark, Sir John Gell returned with his men to Derby and Lord Grey withdrew to Leicester. The whole episode must have been very embarrassing for Thomas Grey; not to say humiliating. He had learned some valuable lessons from the experience though, as will be seen later. Also, although his first dealings with Oliver Cromwell had not been auspicious the connection now begun between the two was to become of increasing significance. Cromwell himself remained for a while but then seems to have moved back into the territory of the Eastern Association. In July he beat off a raid from Newark upon Peterborough, stormed Burleigh House near Stamford, and with Lord Willoughby raised a royalist siege of Gainsborough. Sir John Meldrum was left alone with Colonel Hutchinson and a small force of only 300 horse and 400 foot at Nottingham. This deliberate disintegration of an army under the eyes of its opponent was a curious episode, and one which is not easy to explain unless we conclude that its commanders, realising that the enemy was too strong to be attacked or checked, felt that their men would be better employed in garrisoning the parliamentarian strongholds of their respective counties. It seems that Sir John Meldrum had no greater success in countering this feeling as commander-in-chief than had Lord Grey of Groby, although the latter admittedly inclined very strongly that way himself. Meldrum as a professional soldier would not have faced the same personal dilemma, and Scotland was a long way off anyway! It was probably all just one more manifestation of that incorrigible localism which wrecked so many campaigns during the first civil war. The queen had, therefore, nothing further to fear. On 3rd July she departed from Newark, leaving behind her 2,000 foot and 20 'companies' (troops?) of horse under Charles Cavendish to hold Nottinghamshire and Lincolnshire in check. Moving through Ashby-de-la-Zouch and Burton-on-Trent she reached Oxford safely on 14th July.

Cromwell had watched the bungling of this campaign with frustration and anger. Had his own force and those of Willoughby, Gell, Hotham, and Grey of Groby been joined to Fairfax there would have been 11,000 men to hold the Earl of Newcastle, and the success of the Grantham skirmish had given him confidence in himself and the quality of his troops. Sir John Meldrum had now let the queen slip through to Oxford. Cromwell wrote to Mr. Speaker Lenthall venting his frustration and complaining about the debilitating effects of localism on the parliamentary war effort. On 4th August the Speaker of the House of Commons informed Colonel Cromwell MP in reply that,

> *"..... nothing is more repugnant to ye opinion and sence* (sic) *of this house and dangerous to ye kingdome than ye vnwillingness* (sic) *of their forces to March out of their severall* (sic) *Countys".*[49]

It was thinking such as this of Cromwell and Lenthall that was to lead to the creation of the New Model Army by the Parliament; a national army and not one based on associations of counties.

An entry by Sir Samuel Luke on Sunday, 25th June 1643 records,

> *"..... That it was reported at Buckingham that the Lord Fairfax tooke yesterday 2,000 of the Queenes forces neare Newarke, and that the Lord Grey had taken 14 of her captaines and commanders of the Queenes army and brought them to Northampton yesterday ..... "*[50]

The actions mentioned above must have taken place whilst the queen was still in Newark and Lord Grey seems to have engaged some of her forces after all, if only in fighting his way back to Leicester, and with some considerable success if the report was accurate.

Despite the success of Lord Fairfax also referred to above, it was to be short-lived. Left isolated by the decision of the commanders of the Nottingham rendezvous Sir Thomas and his father were heavily defeated by the Earl of Newcastle's forces on 30th June at Adwalton Moor near

Bradford. As a consequence the staunchly parliamentarian towns of Leeds and Bradford had to surrender to the royalists. The Fairfaxes fled to Hull, and all of Yorkshire save the south-eastern corner was now in the king's hands.

1643 was proving to be a bad year for the parliamentary war effort. The Earl of Stamford had been defeated at Stratton in May and was to surrender Exeter in September; John Hampden, the parliamentary leader and hero who had been mooted as a probable replacement for the Earl of Essex as Lord General, died in June following wounds received on Chalgrove Field; Sir William Waller was beaten - for the first time - at Roundway Down in July; and Prince Rupert stormed Bristol later that same month. By the middle of 1643, therefore, royalist success had touched high-water mark and the war had assumed the shape that it was to maintain in the years of struggle that were to lie ahead. The Parliament controlled London, the South and East Anglia; the Crown controlled the North and the West with a salient, sharpening its point at Oxford, threatening London. The Midlands, with its divided allegiances and rival outposts of strategic importance, was to be the debateable land of the civil war and the scene of the ebbs and flows of its fortunes over the next two years or so.

Great Seal – King Charles I

NOTES

1.   (a) Historical Manuscripts Commission : Hastings Collection Vol. II p. 87. (b) Ibid. Vol. II letter No. 15. pp. 14 - 15.

2.   Edward Hyde, Earl of Clarendon, *The History of the Rebellion and Civil Wars in England* ed. W. Dunn Macray, 6 vols. (Oxford, 1888) pp. 348 - 349.

3.   John Rushworth, *Historical Collections - abridged and improved*, Vol. V; (London, 1703-08) p. 103.

4.   John Vicars, *God in the Mount, Or, England's Remembrancer* (London, 1642), p. 31.

5.   Harleian Manuscripts : British Museum. 164 folios. 24 (3-3) [b]

6.   J. & T. W. Webb, *Memorials of the Civil War in Herefordshire*, Vol. I., (London, 1879) p. 204.

7.   Ryves, *Mercurius Rusticus* (Royalist newsletter), Part I. pp. 71, 76.

8.   Corbet, *History of the Military Government of Gloucester*, p. 20.

9.   Clarendon, op. cit. Book VII, §89.

10.   S.R. Gardiner, *History of the Great Civil War*, Vol. I. p. 138.

11.   Clarendon State Papers, Vol. II, p. 150.

12.   Journal of the House of Lords (L.J.), Vol. VI, p. 346.

13.   Journal of the House of Commons (C.J.), Vol. III, p. 601 & p. 605.

14.   Denzil Holles, *Memoirs of Denzil Holles* (London edition, 1815) p. 270.

15.   Mark Noble, *Lives of the English Regicides*, (London, 1798) Vol I. pp. 262 - 263.

16.   J. P. Kenyon, *Stuart England* (Pelican, History of England : 6), (Penguin Books, 1978).

17.   Calendar of the Committee for the Advance of Money, Vol. II. Oct. 28, 1643.

18.   Historical Manuscripts Commission: Hastings Collection. Vol. II. pp. 87 & 88.

19.   J. Thompson, *The History of Leicester* (1849) pp. 377 & 378.

20.   *Mercurius Aulicus* - 9/1/1643 - Thomason Tracts. British Museum.

21.   HMC : Hastings Collection, op. cit. Vol. II p. 88.

22.   Journal of the House of Lords (L.J.), Vol V. p. 493.

23.   HMC : Hastings Collection, op. cit. Vol. II. pp. 89-90.

24.   Corbet, op. cit. p. 20.

25.   Bulstrode Whitelocke, *Memorials of the English Affairs*, Vol. I. p. 197.

26.   Nehemiah Wallington, *Historical Notes of Events Occurring Chiefly in The Reign of Charles I* (London, 1869), Vol. II. p. 146.

27. *A Relation of the Taking of Cicester in the County of Gloucester on Thursday, Febru. 2, 1643; Bibliotheca Gloucestrensis*, ed. John Washbourn. (London, 1823/1825), Part I., pp. 183-4, 189.

28. Bulstrode Whitelocke, op. cit. p. 197.

29. Rutland Magazine and County Historical Record. Vol. II., pp. 201-208. - Article based on a petition presented by Henry Noel, Esq., second son of the Lord Viscount Campden to the House of Lords. (L.J. Vol. V. 641).

30. HMC: Portland Manuscripts. Vol. I., p. 99.

31. Ibid. p. 99.

32. *Mercurius Rusticus* Vol. VII., p. 70.

33. Journal of the House of Lords (L.J.), Vol. V., p. 631.

34. A.L. Rait, *Acts and Ordinances of the Interregnum, 1642-1660.* Vol. I. pp. 106-117.

35. L. J. Vol. VI., p. 284.

36. Journal of Sir Samuel Luke; Thursday 6th April, 1643. p. 56.

37. C.J. Vol. III., p. 47.

38. HMC: Hastings Collection, op. cit. Vol. II., p. 98.

39. Thomas Carlyle, *Oliver Cromell's Letters and Speeches*, Vol. I. pp. 127-128. (London, Chapman & Hall, 1888).

40. Journal of Sir Samuel Luke; op. cit. p. 70.

41. Journal of the House of Commons (C.J.), Vol VIII., p. 62.

42. S.R. Gardiner, *History of the Great Civil War*, Vol. I., p. 143.

43. Lucy Hutchinson, *The Life of Colonel Hutchinson*, (Everyman Edition), pp. 101-102.

44. Ibid. p. 120.

45. HMC Hastings MSS Vol. II, pp. 101-102. Letter from Sir Edward Nicholas to Colonel Henry Hastings at Banbury or elsewhere from Oxon. 1643, June 21.

46. Journal of the House of Lords (L. J.), Vol. VI.
    (Hotham's letter to the Earl of Newcastle)

47. Lucy Hutchinson, op. cit. p. 121.

48. Ibid. p. 121.

49. Tanner Manuscript; Bodleian Library. 62, folio 224.

50. Journal of Sir Samuel Luke, op. cit. p. 104.

Oliver Cromwell

117

Colonel John Hutchinson

118

Lucy Hutchinson

Sir John Meldrum

120

CHAPTER FOUR

THE MILITARY COMMANDER (1643)
A HERO OF GLOUCESTER AND NEWBURY

Per Bellum ad Pacem
(Through War to Peace - Motto on the standard of Lord Grey of Groby's cavalry troop)

Upon his return to Leicester Thomas Grey set about reasserting his position. In doing so he managed to upset the House of Lords. The only aristocratic resident who the borough of Leicester could claim was the Countess Dowager of Devonshire. She lived in a large country house built in the grounds of Leicester Abbey from the ruins of the Abbey where Cardinal Wolsey had died. The house lay outside the city walls and covered the northern approach to the town. It may be recalled that King Charles had stayed the night at the Countess's house on the 18th of August the previous year before going on to Nottingham to raise his standard. The lady was well known, therefore, for her royalist affiliations. Grey had placed a garrison in her house and threatened her that, if she did not pay the sum of £150 a week towards the maintenance of this garrison, he would order the house to be pulled down. On 20th July the House of Lords ordered the parliamentarian Committee at Leicester to,

> *"take care that no violence or plundering shall be offered to the said house of the Countess of Devon; but that the said house and goods (nothwithstanding any such order from the Lord Grey) be preserved from spoil and ruin: And the Speaker was directed to write a letter to the Lord General, to acquaint him with their Lordships' order; and to send to the Lord Grey, to preserve the house from violence or plundering".[1]*

Despite this reassurance the Countess Dowager was clearly unhappy at the prospect of possible renewed harassment. Thomas Grey was not the sort of young man to take kindly to this fresh rebuff to his authority by the House of Lords, especially as it followed so quickly on the heels of the rebuff from the Committee of Safety in London when he was replaced as commander-in-chief at the Nottingham rendezvous. On 22nd July permission was granted to the Countess to leave Leicester to go into the county, or further afield to Kent or Surrey. This permission was granted by the House of Lords. The Countess's house in the Abbey grounds was later sacked and burnt down by soldiers in the summer of 1645; but whether this was by royalists some days after the storming of Leicester or by parliamentarians after its recapture following Naseby is unclear.

Later in July 1643 the royalists are reported to have sustained a severe loss in an engagement near Stamford in which Lord Grey's cavalry participated.

On 3rd August Parliament passed an ordinance for raising money in the counties for the maintenance of the army. The county of Leicestershire was rated at the weekly sum of £147 10s. The composition of the committee set up to raise this money in Leicestershire presents few surprises and was as follows :-

> *"Henry, Lord Grey of Ruthin; Thomas, Lord Grey of Groby; Sir Arthur Hesilrige, baronet; Sir Edward Hartopp, and Sir Thomas Hartopp, Sir Martin Lister, knights; William Hewett; John Bainbridge, Peter Temple, George Ashby, Richard Bent, Arthur Staveley, William Danvers, Thomas Hesilrige, John Goodwyn, Thomas Cotton, Francis Hacker, esquire; Richard Ludlam, now mayor of Leicester; William Stanley and William Villers, aldermen there".* [2]

During the latter part of August and through September Henry Hastings was able to gain some advantage from Parliament's straitened circumstances. Lord Grey of Groby having been ordered to join the Earl of Essex in relieving Gloucester, Colonel-General Hastings was left free to course the East Midlands in search of ammunition and food.

Reports of the following skirmishes appear in the journal of Sir Samuel Luke for August 1643. Coming from a parliamentarian source they do, however, tend to give a favourable gloss to the outcomes from a 'roundhead' viewpoint.

> *"Wednesday, 16th August 1643*
> *..... That Colonell Hastings and the forces at Leycester mett on Sonday last at Bagworth heath* [known since locally as Battle Flat] *where there was a short skirmish betwixt them, and that they tooke 30 of them prisoners where one was a lieutenant colonell and some other officers, and brought them to Leycester".* [3]

> *"Friday 18th August 1643,*
> *..... William Sherrwood* [a scout] *returned and saith that on Sonday last some of the Lord Grey's forces coming from Manchester where they had been with ammunition, were intercepted on the way by Colonell Hastings, where after a short*

skirmish they kild 4 of Hastings his men, wounded 30 and brought them prisoners to Leycester whereof 14 were commanders and officers. .....

That the Earle of Manchester was on Wednesday night last at Cambridge, and was expected the last night of Colonell Cromwell at Huntingdon, and is goeing to Peterborough with 1,500 horse to meete the Lord Grey, and so march after the Earl of Newcastle. That Colonell Hastings sent to demand Leycester but upon summoning of the towne and tryall of their afections they found many willing to yeild it upp, all which they presently expeld the towne, whereof 2 were ministers".[4]

Major events were about to unfold far from the confines of Leicestershire but many of the participants were to be drawn from that area.

If he had pushed on hard for London in the first week of August 1643 King Charles might have won the war. The parliamentarian forces had suffered reverses in most parts of the country. Waller's army had been defeated, Prince Rupert had taken Bristol, the Fairfaxes had been driven into Hull, etc. Puritan rule was beginning to irk many ordinary Londoners. Several peers and M.P.'s defected from London to join the king at Oxford. John Hampden had died as a result of the wounds he had received at Chalgrove Field and the other major parliamentary leader, John Pym, was slowly dying of cancer. Although Pym had for some time been negotiating with the presbyterian Scots, they had not yet agreed on a price for crossing the border with their army to attack the Marquis of Newcastle's forces from the rear. Essex's main parliamentarian army lay indolent in and around London. It was royalist high-tide. Surely the king's time had come.

The king's cavalier officers were eager to ride full tilt across the country and lord it again in a plundered London. There they would teach the insolent rebels a lesson they would not forget in a hurry. Yet the king himself was hesitant. The rank and file of his foot regiments were less keen to leave their homes in the north and west of England for any longer than was necessary. Newly enlisted regiments of Welshmen, for example, were reluctant to cross the Severn and join the king at Oxford until Colonel Massey had been driven out of Gloucester from which he could, and did, raid into South Wales.

Prince Rupert was all for taking Gloucester by storm as he had taken Bristol, Cirencester and other places. The fortifications of Gloucester were far inferior to those of Bristol. The twenty-three year old presbyterian Colonel Edward Massey in command of Gloucester's defence had only one regiment of trained and experienced soldiers; these were the remains of the Earl of Stamford's Bluecoats whom he had inherited. But assaulting a fortified town or city always cost lives. The king had been upset by the heavy cavalier losses sustained around the walls of Bristol. *"As gallant gentlemen as ever drew sword"*, he lamented, *"lay upon the ground like rotting sheep"*. London, at that moment, seemed wide open to attack. Had London fallen then the kingdom would again be the king's. Yet he had decided not to leave Gloucester in his rear and now he was determined to take it by a time consuming siege rather than by outright assault.

As a result, by the time Prince Rupert was ready to begin the siege on 10th August, Massey's garrison and the citizens of Gloucester had strengthened the earthworks considerably and were better prepared to withstand a siege. The king called upon the citizens of Gloucester to surrender themselves and the city. In response the governor, Edward Massey, and the mayor, Dennis Wyse, the aldermen and some prominent citizens refused to surrender on behalf of *"the Inhabitants, Magistrates, Officers, and Souldiers within this Garrison of Gloucester .....; and are resolved by God's help to keep this city accordingly"*.[5]

The king was incredulous at the audacity of the inhabitants of Gloucester, the garrison of which numbered a mere 1,500 men, and possessed less than 10 pieces of ordnance. John Corbet, Massey's captain, recorded the king's reaction: *"His Majesty with all mildnesse seemed to receive this answer, onely to wonder at our confidence, and whence we expected succour, adding these words, Waller is extinct, and Essex cannot come"*.[6]

The king was to be proved wrong; and neither for the first nor the last time.

The news of Gloucester's brave defiance, coming after so much bad news, made hearts in London beat faster and caused a miraculous change of mood. Every shop in Cheapside put up its shutters as thousands of apprentices flocked to volunteer for special service. Five new regiments of foot and a thousand horse, nearly all London apprentices, were formed into new Trained Bands or 'Auxiliaries'. The Earl of Essex declared that he would himself undertake the relief of Gloucester and called his former officers and soldiers together. He was anxious to secure the command before it was given to Sir William Waller who was also in London. On 24th August the Earl of Essex reviewed his young volunteers on Hounslow Heath, *'riding with his hat off and bowing to them'*. Gloucester had already lived through twelve days of siege. Would the London forces be sufficient? Would the relieving forces arrive in time?

As Clarendon records :-

> *"At Gloucester the business proceeded very slowly : for though the* (royalist) *army increased wonderfully there, by the access of forces from all quarters, yet the king had neither money nor materials requisite for a siege, and they in the town behaved*

themselves with great courage and resolution, and made many
sharp and bold sallies upon the king's forces, and did more
hurt commonly than they received ; and many officers of name,
besides common soldiers, were slain in the trenches and
approaches; the governor leaving nothing unperformed that
became a vigilant commander".[7]

By the end of August, however, it seemed inevitable that Gloucester would fall. Provisions were running dangerously low and only three barrels of gunpowder remained to the garrison. Added to this Charles had received considerable reinforcements during the siege, including two regiments from Ireland, bringing the total strength of the royal army to 30,000 men, at that time the largest army ever assembled on English soil. An atmosphere of understandable confidence, therefore, permeated the royalist ranks, prompting Prince Rupert to wager £5,000 with his uncle that the city would fall before 6th September. Rupert had brought miners across from the Forest of Dean and they had dug deep trenches, a quarter of a mile beyond the city wall, just beyond the range of the Gloucester musketeers. The miners then dug underground tunnels to the walls, and under the walls the royalists stacked barrels of gunpowder.

On 24th August - the day that the Earl of Essex was reviewing his volunteers on Hounslow Heath - Prince Rupert sent warning to Colonel Massey that, unless he surrendered Gloucester, his fortifications would be blown sky-high. Once more the gallant young governor refused to yield, although he knew the walls were mined. The previous night a secret beacon up on the Cotswold Hills had signalled that help was coming. Fortune was on Massey's side. The weather later that night broke in a heavy storm of rain. Rupert's trenches were flooded and all his stacked gunpowder was ruined. This was confirmation to the 'Godly' inside Gloucester that the Lord favoured their cause.

On 26th August the Earl of Essex with his army of newly-strengthened regiments of horse and foot, together with the new trained band regiments, marched out of London. This time Essex wished to leave nothing to chance. By 29th August he had arrived at Aylesbury where he was joined by Lord Grey of Groby at the head of a large body of forces belonging to the Midland Association of counties and a number of additional volunteers. It is significant that the only other force to join the Earl of Essex at the Aylesbury rendezvous was a party commanded by a Colonel Harvey. Essex was keen to make a success of this campaign following the criticisms of his conduct after Reading the previous year. Lord Grey was equally anxious to reassure his patron after the humiliation of the Nottingham rendezvous in the spring and to repay the Lord General for his past favours. As Mark Noble, a hostile commentator, puts it,

> *"His Lordship was under many obligations to the Earl of Essex,*
> *the parliament generalissimo, who was appointed to go and*
> *relieve Gloucester, then besieged by his majesty in person .....*
> *Lord Grey, to show his respects to his superior commander,*
> *and one to whom he had a peculiar devoir, with Colonel Harvey,*
> *marched to that nobleman's rendezvous at Aylesbury, August*
> *29, 1643 at the head of a large body of forces belonging to the*
> *associated counties, and a number of volunteers; ....."* [8]

It seems that it took the need of his benefactor to get Thomas Grey to leave his home area again as he had done previously to assist 'Old Robin' (as Robert Devereaux, Earl of Essex was known to his own soldiers) in the Reading campaign. For Essex he left Leicestershire once more subject to the coursing of Henry Hastings, although Leicester itself and the major county parliamentarian outposts were left garrisoned. The Gloucester campaign, however, was to be a successful one for Lord Grey of Groby and saw the blossoming of his military career.

Gathering together his forces first at Leicester and then at Northampton he had moved on to Aylesbury. The excitement of the reunion may be imagined as Thomas Grey at the head of his own troop of horse, under his colours of the ermine unicorn in the sun in splendour on its field of blue and red, met his patron. Grey's officers and cavalry troopers would all be wearing their sashes or 'scarves' in Essex's own livery colour - variously described as 'tawny-orange' or 'deep yellow'. This gesture was of great significance. As Bulstrode Whitelocke explains,

> *"The Earl of Essex's colour was a deep yellow ; others setting*
> *up another colour were held malignants and ill-affected to the*
> *parliament's cause. So small a thing is taken notice of in the*
> *jealousies of war".* [9]

This enterprise was a gamble for both Essex and Grey. Their reputations, their fortunes; nay, their very lives, depended upon the success of the venture.

The royalist besiegers did not believe to begin with that Essex seriously intended the relief of Gloucester, but was rather making a move for Oxford to draw the king away from the siege. As Clarendon records,

> *"It would not at first be credited at the leaguer ..... that in truth*
> *he would venture upon so tedious a march, where he must march*
> *over a campaign over one hundred miles in length, where half*
> *the king's body of horse would distress, if not destroy his whole*
> *army, and through a country eaten bare, where he could find*
> *neither provision for men nor horse; and if he should, without*

interruption, be suffered to go into Gloucester, he could neither stay there, nor possibly retire to London, without being destroyed in the rear by the king's army, which should nevertheless not engage itself in the hazard of a battle". [10]

From Aylesbury the combined forces began to skirt to the north of Oxford until they came to a second rendezvous at Brackley. Here they were joined by troops from Bedford and further reinforcements from Leicester with cannon and supplies (referred to by Clarendon as *"the last recruits upon which he* [Essex] *depended".*

By 1st September the Parliamentarian army, now comprising 15,000 men and 40 pieces of artillery had crossed the river Cherwell at Clifton, near Aynho, north of Oxford and close to Banbury. From here progress was rather slower as the king had sent Lord Wilmot with a body of 2,500 horse to Banbury to impede their march. Essex was forced to keep his army in a continual defensive posture but managed to keep the foot and artillery moving whilst his horse, under Lord Grey's command, skirmished daily with Lord Wilmot's force. The king's horse had to continually retire ahead of the column in order to keep within striking range.

This constant harassment did nothing to foster a spirit of tolerance amongst the parliamentarian soldiers towards their opponents. A royalist source claims that as the army passed through Chipping Norton :-

"a woman of that towne (whose zeal for the King and the justice of his cause could not containe itselfe though in the mid'st of mortal enemies) said in the hearing of some of the rebells, "God blesse the Cavaliers" .... This expression of the poore womans affection to the King and his loyal subjects in so innocent a prayer, so highly incensed the rebells, that to punish so hainous a crime, ... they tyed her to the taile of one of their carts, and stripping her to the middle, for two myles marched-whipped her .... They left her a lamentable spectacle of their cruelty ..... and [has] since died of those wounds which she received from them". [11]

The army entered Gloucestershire at Adlestrop and at Stow-on-the-Wold where it encountered a detachment of royalist cavalry under Prince Rupert who were greatly outnumbered and routed by Lord Grey's horse - being pursued for up to seven miles.

Upon hearing of Rupert's failure to check Essex's advance the king sent a trumpeter with some propositions for negotiation. The Essex of the previous year's Reading campaign might have fallen for such stalling tactics but the commander of this campaign had learned from his earlier mistakes and vacillations.

"But Essex, too much acquainted with such small designs to hinder his march, returned a speedy answer, That he had no commission to treat, but to relieve Gloucester, which he was resolved to do, or lose his life there. And his soldiers hearing of a trumpeter come with propositions to treat, they cried out for a long time together with loud acclamations, `No propositions! No propositions! and so the trumpeter was dismissed".[12]

On the clear evening of 5th September the Earl of Essex appeared - *'like a blazing-starr'* [sic]-on the hill above Prestbury. He reined in his charger, lit his long clay pipe, and gazed into the distance at Gloucester's squat but impressive cathedral, crouched inside Colonel Massey's ring of makeshift earthworks, with the raw earth of the royalist trenches farther out, and the gleaming river Severn beyond. Had the relief come in time? Essex ordered a signal gun fired twice. From inside distant Gloucester came a puff of white smoke and then the reverberation of an answering cannon. The city was still holding out, and if the royal army was still down there it would be taken between two hostile fires. That night, under cover of darkness, the king abandoned the siege and the royalist army was marched off.

The king led his forces off to Sudeley Castle, which is about twelve miles north-east of Gloucester, where he positioned them on a line between Worcester and Evesham to await developments. Essex, when he realised that the royal army had withdrawn, made first for Cheltenham. Here, having first driven out a detachment of royalist cavalry, he rested his troops. On 8th September the Earl of Essex's army at last entered Gloucester to the joyful acclamation of its heroic defenders - both garrison and citizens. The relief had come just in time. The defenders were almost out of supplies and ammunition. Thomas Grey and Edward Massey were able to renew their acquaintance and Grey's Leicestershire troops were able to greet some of their friends and neighbours in Stamford's Bluecoat Regiment who they would not have seen for a year.

Essex remained in Gloucester only long enough to re-equip the city with ammunition, money, and other necessities. This took three days. There was a real danger that King Charles, with his larger army still intact, would head for London. There was also the danger that the king would attempt to destroy the parliamentarian army on its way back to the capital. The Trained Bands in particular were anxious to get back to protect their families and their property before the 'cavaliers' could plunder London.

At Sudeley Prince Rupert told the king that despite the lost opportunity at Gloucester there was still a good chance of success. If the royal army could march across England fast enough to get between Essex's army and its London base they could be brought to battle. If the royalists could destroy Essex's army, with the best of the London Trained Bands in it, as

128

they had already done Waller's army at Roundway Down, Parliament would be left with no major field army. The Peace Party in the House of Commons would then triumph and London would open her gates to the king. The king approved of this strategy and the royalist army prepared to march towards the capital on a line that would intercept the 'roundhead' army.

Essex, for his part, attempted a stratagem to throw the royalists off his true intentions. He made a feinted move towards the staunchly royalist city of Worcester by undertaking a forced march to Tewkesbury. He stayed at Tewkesbury until 15th September and then pushed south to Cirencester where his men captured a *'great store of provisions'* that the royalists had placed there for their own army's use. Then the race for London began.

By 17th September the two armies were only ten miles apart. By now they were racing each other for Newbury in Berkshire. Newbury, a Puritan cloth town perched at the end of the chalk downs, commanded the road along the Thames valley to London.

On the evening of 19th September 1643 parliamentarian quartermasters riding ahead of their army were the first to reach Newbury. Food and supplies had been hospitably stocked there by the pro-parliamentary townsfolk in readiness for the arrival of Essex's men. But at this time the army was a dragging column some ten miles long struggling down the road from Hungerford through the rain and wind, several hours' march to the west. The 'roundhead' quartermasters, including Daniel Maddox of Lord Grey's own troop, were riding busily up and down the streets of Newbury. They were in the process of chalking doors to mark welcome dry billets for the officers and men when down the main road came the thundering hooves of Prince Rupert's cavaliers. A few of the quartermasters were captured, others - with Maddox amongst them - got away on horseback under a hail of pistol bullets. These fugitives managed to reach their army in time to give the warning. The Earl of Essex was marching into a trap. The king had got possession of Newbury. The only way to get to London now was to fight.

The battle of Newbury was fought over rolling grassy hillsides intersected by deep lanes. The armies were fairly evenly matched with about 14,000 men and 20 cannon on each side, although the king was stronger in cavalry. The two sides deployed during the night and the battle began at 5 o'clock on the morning of 20th September.

The king placed his army mainly to the north and east of Skinner's Green, but for some inexplicable reason failed to occupy the dominant feature of Round Hill, which was to cause him problems later. The cavalier horse was commanded overall by Prince Rupert with five brigade commanders in addition to himself at operational level. The royalist foot was under Sir Jacob Astley with four brigade commanders. Most of the footsoldiers in the royal army were simple countrymen from Wales and the West Country who by now were becoming restless at being away from home and resentful at not being paid for a long time. The royalists were also rather short of gunpowder, much having been wasted at Gloucester.

The Earl of Essex drew up his forces opposite the royalist lines with the foot above and behind Round Hill and the bulk of the cavalry facing the cavalier horse across Wash Common. There were four brigades of foot, each made up of three regiments, plus the London Trained Bands - probably the best drilled foot on the field - in reserve. There were two brigades of horse; a small one under John Middleton placed amongst the foot units to counter Sir John Byron's and Sir Thomas Aston's royalist horse placed amongst the foot, and a much larger one commanded by Sir Philip Stapleton and divided into three bodies. One of these cavalry bodies was commanded by Lord Grey of Groby.

At the start of the battle Essex sent Philip Skippon, the wise and experienced soldier who had drilled the London Trained Bands, with two field pieces and a brigade of foot to occupy Round Hill. He had the Trained Bands in close support. This dome shaped hill dominated the high ground near Wash Common where the main clash between the two armies was most likely to take place. Its slopes were crisscrossed with the high hedges of small fields and market gardens where footsoldiers would be hard to dislodge even by the best cavalry.

As the battle began and the cavalier horse under Prince Rupert streamed across Wash Common the king's infantry was sent to fight its way up the slopes of Round Hill. The royalist foot were assisted in this difficult task by cavaliers making repeated charges on the flanks of Skippon's mixed bodies of pikemen and musketeers. The royalists were obliged to push up the hill hedge by hedge. Each small field was bristling with roundhead pikes, and behind each hedge were the files, six deep, of the musketeers practising 'rolling fire'. With this tactic, after firing each musketeer would retire to the rear of his file to reload and, after five more shots by the men in the front of him, be ready to fire again. The murderous chatter of this roundhead musketry from behind walls and hedges went on all day long. The royalist musketeers got off only one shot to the roundheads' three and their powder was running low. The initial assault had been made by Sir Nicholas Byron's brigade of foot and Sir John Byron's cavalry. Sir Nicholas called for more cavalry support. While Sir John Byron was calling for a gap in one hedge to be widened his horse was shot from under him. During the delay, as Sir John awaited another mount, the young Lord Falkland galloped through the gap alone and was killed. Byron's regiments assaulted again but the musket fire was too intense and they withdrew in confusion. There were twenty guns in the royalist artillery park. They blasted gaps in the living defence of Round Hill, one cavalier observing *" a whole file of men, six deep, with all their heads struck off by one cannon shot of ours"*. But Skippon's two light field guns on the crest of the hill did damage too.

130

Later in the day an assault by Byron's and Aston's regiments gained the summit of Round Hill briefly, but Skippon then brought up the London Trained Bands and the contest was renewed. The royalist infantry was left to try to hold the hill whilst the battered horse withdrew.

The locus of the fight now switched to the Wash Common area. Rupert charged Stapleton's horse, which was supported by some of the reserve from the Trained Bands, and the charge was repulsed on Enborne Heath. A second royalist charge met with the same result, Rupert being driven back onto the main body of the royalist infantry. A third royalist charge was, however, more successful. Elements of Stapleton's horse routed and the cavaliers pursued them, only to be turned on and shot down in the narrow lanes. It was in this action, as at Edgehill when fighting under Balfour, that Lord Grey of Groby and his troopers distinguished themselves and took several enemy cavalry colours. By this stage in the battle the carnage on both sides was great.

Skippon now stabilised the centre by bringing forward the Trained Bands. He also brought his artillery forward to engage the royalist guns which had been firing on the Trained Bands. This led to probably the most intense artillery duel of the entire civil war. The royalist foot was hotly engaged in the centre and the parliamentarians had the best of the battle there. Yet, as they did not retreat, the royalists might have won the battle for the king if they had maintained their resolve. According to royalist accounts, however, they proved spineless compared to the blind and reckless courage of their own officers and the well drilled determination of the London Trained Bands. As Sir John Byron of Nottinghamshire wrote after the battle, *"Had not our foot played the poltroons extremely that day, we in all probability had set a period to the war".*

This gruelling, grinding battle outside Newbury raged without pause from dawn until ten o'clock at night. Against the implacable resistance of the London lads in the centre the royalist tide ebbed. The cavaliers on Wash Common were contained and prevented from turning the battle. By darkness, when the gunfire had faded, Skippon's Trained Bands held Round Hill.

Late that night, as carts full of the dead and dying rumbled into Newbury, King Charles held a Council of War. Rupert and Byron wanted to continue the battle the following day. Lord Percy, as General of the Royal Artillery, reported that eighty barrels of gunpowder had been used up during the long battle. There were only ten full barrels left for all the cannon, muskets, carbines and pistols. To attack Round Hill the next day, against the rolling fire of the enemy musketeers with little more than courage and cold steel, would condemn the royal army to destruction. The king, cautious as ever, called off the battle and withdrew into Newbury with his army and with the intention of returning to his headquarters at Oxford.

131

The Earl of Essex was amazed at finding the field empty on the following morning, but gladly took advantage of his good fortune and marched on to Reading. He was attacked en route at Aldermaston by a party of cavalier horse under an angry Prince Rupert. The royalists had sprung a skilful ambush which caused considerable panic but few losses in the roundhead ranks before the pikemen of the rearguard fought them off.

What had been technically a draw on the field at Newbury, rather like Edgehill, had become a major parliamentarian triumph because of its implications. Essex's campaign had been a great success. He had relieved heroic Gloucester and at Newbury he had halted the tide of royalist success. The king had lost his best chance and London was now further away than ever from his grasp.

The summer that had begun with so much promise had ended in near disaster for King Charles. Never again would conditions be so favourably disposed to the royalist cause, and never again would the king command an army of such strength. Lord Grey of Groby, through his vital support for the Earl of Essex both on and off the field of battle, had played a major role in this revival of parliamentarian fortune. Recognition of this was soon to come.

Bulstrode Whitelocke records that the Committee of Safety in London sent messengers to the Earl of Essex at Reading to compliment him and congratulate his great successes. They also enquired what supplies were required for his army in order that they might be speedily provided. Messages were sent to the City leaders in London to inform them of the happy success of the army under Lord-General Essex and to negotiate with them about the supplies to be sent to the heroic army. All passes between London and Oxford were stopped to deny the flow of intelligence, money and ammunition to the king.

On 25th September both Houses of Parliament, with 'the assembly of divines' and the Scottish Commissioners met in St. Margaret's Church, Westminster and took the National Solemn League and Covenant. They did this firstly by raising their hands in testimony of their assent as it was read out from the pulpit by a Mr. Nye and then by signing a parchment roll on which the Covenant was written. It was then ordered that the Covenant be taken on the next Lord's Day by all persons in their respective parishes, and the ministers were to exhort all to do so.

The signing of the Covenant was the price paid for Scottish military aid in the civil war against the king in England. In the New Year an army of 21,000 presbyterian Scots under experienced commanders were to cross the border to assist the forces of the English Parliament. In return they were to receive a payment of £30,000 per month and all the English loyal to Parliament were to swear to the Covenant which accepted the strict principles of Calvinism and the reorganisation of the English Church on presbyterian lines.

Most English Puritans would have found the original Scottish form of the Solemn League and Covenant difficult to accept. For the Scots it was a symbol of national self-determination, independence and identity. In the last days of John Pym's life he sent Sir Henry Vane the Younger to negotiate with the Scots a variation in the wording for the Covenant which was to be taken in England. Vane was an 'Independent' rather than a 'Presbyterian' and he managed to achieve a wording to the effect that the promised reformation of the Church in England was now intended to be *according to the word of God*, a much vaguer term than that of the Scots and capable of a much wider interpretation. Most English dissenters, even though they might have inner scruples, could now take the oath and sign the Covenant without too much offence to their consciences. Indeed, to be able to hold military rank, committee membership, or continued religious office under Parliament's authority one had to take the Covenant. Even so, the deadline for taking it had to be extended to March 1644.

The political implications that flowed from this issue were to prove profound. From now on 'Presbyterian' was to be more than ever a party label, and those who wanted a presbyterian organization of England's national church would speak more from political expediency than from religious conviction. Equally it has been suggested that the emergence at Westminster of the 'Independents' as a political group, as distinct from the purely religious Independents, can be dated from this point. From the first they were identified with the "war party" and in the vacuum caused in the parliamentary leadership by the death of John Pym in December their leaders, such as Sir Henry Vane, Oliver Cromwell, Oliver St. John, and Sir Arthur Haselrige were to become both more noticeable and influential.

Meanwhile, on 28th September 1643 the Earl of Essex's victorious army marched into London to the cheers of the crowd. The Trained Bands in particular were welcomed back with fervour - the youngsters marching with pike and musket through their city with the laurel leaves of victory in their hats and helmets. The next day most of them were back behind their shop counters serving customers and most likely regaling them with tales of their brave endeavours at Newbury. The main army moved out, after the celebrations, to its camp at Windsor but the Lord General stayed in the city accompanied by Sir Philip Stapleton, Lord Grey of Groby, and a few other worthies whose names are not recorded.

The hostile commentator, Mark Noble, records the reception of the army and its leaders as follows:-

> *"The parliament and the city were extravagant in their joy upon this occasion; the Scotch covenant was embraced with a kind of holy furor* (sic) *by all ranks of men; from the church they*

removed to the camp, offering the most fulsome addresses to Essex, the vainest of the vain; the mayor and his brethren, with the trained bands, saluted him, as the protector and defender of their lives and fortunes, and of their wives and children".[13]

A more sympathetic chronicler, Bulstrode Whitelocke, comments as follows :-

"The house of commons with their speaker went to Essex-House (the Earl's London residence*), to congratulate the general's safe return to them, and his happy success and valour in the late business at Newbury .....*
"The lord mayor and aldermen of London waited in their scarlet gowns upon the general, ... and the trained bands sent out as he passed by loud acclamations of his praise.
"In human probability the king's army was the more likely to have prevailed, their horse more and better than the parliament's, and their foot near as good, their advantages greater, and their courage higher, and their confidence too much.
"God was pleased to raise the courage of the parliament's forces, and to give them the success; and indeed all success in war, as well as in other matters, is the free gift of the Lord of Hosts.
"Essex and his soldiers acknowledged much gallantry and courage in those of the king's party, and the king's party acknowledged the like of Essex and his soldiers; all were Englishmen, and pity it was that such courage should be spent in the blood of each other".[14]

Whitelocke relates an example of *"the extraordinary mettle and boldness of spirit"* of Sir Philip Stapleton as displayed at Newbury. He, being stationed with other parliamentary commanders (including, one would imagine, Lord Grey) at the head of their bodies of horse, espied a group of royalist commanders opposite in front of their own brigades of horse. Sir Philip rode across to the rival commanders, resplendent in their scarlet sashes and other finery, with his pistol in his hand ready cocked and fitted. Coming to them alone he looked at them in turn until he recognized Prince Rupert and then fired his pistol at the prince's face. Rupert's armour saved him from harm but Sir Philip Stapleton was able to turn his horse around and return to his station unhurt, *"though many pistols were fired at him"*.

Whitelocke also tells of Sir Philip Stapleton's groom, a Yorkshireman, who had his mare shot from under him in a charge. Having returned on foot to safety he remembered that he had left a new saddle and bridle on

134

the dead mare and vowed that *"the cavaliers should not get so much by him"*. Despite the warnings of his friends that the dead horse lay too close to the enemy and the offer of his master to buy him another new saddle and bridle he would not be persuaded. He went back *"and stayed to pull off the saddle and bridle whilst hundreds of bullets flew about his ears, and brought them back with him, and had no hurt at all"*.[15]

Whilst Whitelocke does not detail a similar incident about Lord Grey's actions at Newbury it would seem that he had made a conspicuous contribution to the success of the campaign. There is certainly no doubting the high profile given to Lord Grey of Groby in the celebrations that followed. This much is evidenced by the following contemporary extracts :-

> *"In the thanks which were voted on this occasion by the House of Commons the Lord Grey stands the foremost".*[16]

> *"Those who had contributed to this success were also publicly thanked by the house of commons; amongst them the Lord Grey stood the foremost, for his good service done in the late relief of Gloucester and victory of Newbury; and they ordered that this should be entered in the parliament journals for an honour to them and their posterity".*[17]
> *"The Lord Grey of Groby, Sir Philip Stapleton, and divers other members of the house, and divers officers of the army, received the thanks of the House, for their good service done in the late Gloucester journey, and fight at Newbury, and this to be entered in the parliament journals, for an honour to them and their posterity.*

> *"Amongst the colours taken at Newbury one* (royalist) *cornet was the figure of the parliament house, with two traitors's heads standing on top of it, and by them this word - UT EXTRA, SIC INFRA; but the parliament nevertheless exposed them to public view and censure".*[18]

Noble could not resist the observation that the standard referred to above was most appropriately taken by Lord Grey as it was *"certainly very significant of him, in both senses ..... because he was alike disloyal to his sovereign, both in and out of the House".*[19]

These events seem to have caused the beginnings of a major change in the direction of Thomas, Lord Grey of Groby's life. Hitherto his inclination appears to have been to cautious localism and concern for the security of

Leicester and Bradgate. From this point on the emergence of Lord Grey as a national figure with increasingly wide horizons and political ambitions is discernable.

At this stage his associates, such as the Earls of Essex and Stamford, Sir Philip Stapleton, Sir Samuel Luke, and Edward Massey, are still mainly drawn from the 'Presbyterian' party but his circle is widening. The appeal of life in the backwaters of provincial Leicestershire was to seem dim after the glory, glamour, and popularity of the successful Gloucester/Newbury campaign. The flattery, intrigues and attractions of London seemed to beckon him more and more.

Despite the lure of the capital familial and military obligations required Lord Grey's return home. He had returned by mid-October at the latest as we learn from this extract in a letter from Sir Edward Nicholas (one of the royal secretaries) at Oxford to Colonel Henry Hastings on 14th October 1643:-

"..... Now the Lord Grey is come to Leicester we believe you will have some trouble there".[20]

The local royalist opposition had not been inactive during Lord Grey's absence. Henry Hastings appears to have established a strong garrison at Burleigh House in Loughborough. On 23rd October in recognition of his services to the Crown to date Colonel-General Hastings was by Letters Patent created Henry, Baron Loughborough by King Charles. In December the new Lord Loughborough was to be appointed commander-in-chief of all the royalist forces in Leicestershire and Derbyshire.

In late November the royalists from Belvoir Castle surprised and defeated a strong party of Lord Grey's men at Melton Mowbray. Some three hundred parliamentarian soldiers, including several officers - amongst them Arthur Staveley, Thomas Hesilrige, and Captain Francis Hacker - were taken prisoner. Lord Grey wrote to the House of Commons giving news of this reverse and requesting *'400 arms and 500 pounds in moneys'*. *"Whereupon it was ordered, that it be especially recommended to the Committee for the Safety, to furnish my Lord Grey with the arms and moneys desired; and to take care of the safety of Leicestershire".*[21]

On 16th December it was recorded in the House of Lords journal that Captain William Danvers, a Leicestershire Committee man, had loaned to the Parliament the sum of £1,000 for the purchase of ammunition for the Lord Grey to assist him in *"the present defence of the county"*.[22] By the end of the month it was reported that Lord Grey *("as if to remove the tarnish from his escutcheon")* had attacked the Belvoir royalists and gained some considerable advantages over them.[23]

136

Notes

1. Journal of the House of Lords, Vol. VI., p. 142.
2. Ibid. p. 167.
3. Journal of Sir Samuel Luke; op. cit. p. 136.
4. Ibid. p. 137.
5. Corbet, op. cit. p. 43.
6. Ibid. p. 43.
7. Clarendon, op. cit. Book VII, 1643. p. 426.
8. Mark Noble, op. cit. pp. 262-263.
9. Bulstrode Whitelocke, op. cit. Vol. I p. 180.
10. Clarendon, op. cit. p. 427.
11. Ryves, *Mercurius Rusticus*, Part I., p. 145.
12. Bulstrode Whitelocke, op. cit. Vol. I., p. 211.
13. Mark Noble, op. cit. p. 263.
14. Bulstrode Whitelocke, op. cit. Vol. I., p. 217.
15. Ibid. pp. 217-218.
16. C.J., Vol III., p. 56.
17. Mark Noble, op. cit. pp. 263-264.
18. Bulstrode Whitelocke, op. cit. Vol. I., p. 218.
19. Mark Noble, op. cit. p. 264.
20. HMC : Hastings Collection, op. cit. p.
21. C.J., Vol. III., p. 333.
22. L.J., Vol. VI., p. 341.
23. J. Thompson, *History of Leicestershire to the Seventeenth Century* (1849) p. 379.

ROBERT DEVEREUX EARLE OF ESSEX HIS EXCELLENCY LORD GENERALL OF the Forces raised by the Authority of the Parliament, For the defence of the King and Kingdom &c.

The Earl of Essex – A Hero of Newbury and Gloucester

138

CHAPTER FIVE

THE MILITARY COMMANDER (1644)
"POORE LEICESTERSHIRE !"

"... And in the meane whyle the Lord Grey faced Collonell Hastings ... "
(Thursday, 4th January 1644 - Journal of Sir Samuel Luke, page 229)

1644 was to prove a year of local skirmishes - rather like range war in the American West - between the forces of Grey and Hastings in Leicestershire. It was also to be a period of growing political problems locally for Thomas Grey.

It has been said that it was introspection and concern for local security, together with the even division of initial support, which explains why the struggle for the effective control of Leicestershire was indecisive for so long. Leicestershire people were so fully engaged with mainly local issues that they seem to have had little interest in the concerns of wider importance. Few local families left the county to join the king at Oxford or the parliamentarian field armies under Essex or Fairfax. On the latter side, as has been noted, the Earl of Stamford, Sir Arthur Hesilrige, and then Lord Grey of Groby fought some distance from the county but most of the parliamentarians were fully occupied with their work for the County Committee - even though their frequent disagreements were often to hamper the efficiency of that body. Most of the royalists were either engaged in defending their estates from attack by the parliamentarians, or themselves became members of the predatory Cavalier garrisons at Ashby-de-la-Zouch or Belvoir Castle. Even Henry Hastings, Lord Loughborough, was restricted for most of the war to operating in the north and west of Leicestershire and the fringes of the adjoining counties of Staffordshire, Derbyshire, Nottinghamshire, and Warwickshire.

Every so often the incursion of forces from outside the local area would affect the balance of power. Such was the case when in January 1644 the Marquis of Newcastle established a garrison at Wingfield Manor, only nine miles north of Derby. This made the existing garrisons at Wilne Ferry and King's Mills, established by Hastings, of greater importance as part of a network linking the northern royalist army with that based on Oxford. This point was not lost upon the local parliamentarians and, on 5th February, Sir John Gell attacked and captured the crossing point over the river Trent at King's Mills. There now ensued a war of attrition over this and other strategic outposts in that area.

A Scots army had crossed the border at the start of January, following the understanding that all parliamentarian officers, military and civil, as well as clergy would sign the agreed Solemn League and Covenant by the end of March. The incursion of the Scots put pressure on the Earl of Newcastle's forces and he wished to secure his southern flanks. Hastings must have retaken King's Mills quite quickly because later in February it was reported that the fortified places at King's Mills and Wilne Ferry had been captured by troops from Derby and Leicester; in consequence of which two passes over the Trent fell into the hands of the parliamentarian forces.

Also in February Sir John Gell is reported as having routed a party of the king's horse under Colonel Hastings, taking many prisoners with their arms and 120 horses. Lucy Hutchinson's advice regarding Gell's claims of military success should perhaps be recalled. Often, she alleged, he claimed the credit himself for actions when either he was not present personally or else it was a joint effort. Indeed, he claimed to have taken Wilne Ferry in association with Lord Grey in both February and July of the year - contriving to get the thanks of the Parliament for his services; then similarly taking Wingfield Manor and Shelford Manor in July, although sometime later Gell was besieging Wingfield Manor in conjunction with the Earl of Denbigh, and Shelford Manor was taken more than two years later by Colonel Hutchinson acting under the command of General Poyntz. It is, of course, possible that these outposts had been retaken by the royalists in the intervening periods, but the reputation of Sir John Gell raises doubts.

Meanwhile, Lord Grey experienced some military success of his own near Melton Mowbray. It seems that the enemy had notice of his intention to go to Melton on some business and sent four or five troops of horse to intercept him. He arrived before them and managed to take them by surprise instead :-

> *"They, not knowing that the Lord Grey was there, nor that our forces had so good a strength, did not move at first ; till our men fired so fast upon them, that the rear of them fled, and left two cornets of horse behind, which could not escape ; and those the Lord Grey took, and carried prisoners to Leicester. Unfortunately, we lost a troop of horse, which were surprised near Burley House, and carried away prisoners by the cavaliers ; but our forces have taken another troop of theirs near Somerby in Lincolnshire, which were carried prisoners to Leicester, and will serve to exchange for ours."*[1]

The following comment appeared in the same parliamentarian publication 'Mercurius Veridicus' on 12th March 1644 :-

"Sir John Gell enlarges his quarters southwards, and the Lord Grey's forces northwards, so that the coasts begin to be clear in those parts; Hastings's ruffians annoy them not as they were wont. I could never hear that they appeared so bold since the Lord Grey cudgelled them well near Melton Mowbray".[2]

Another development in 1644, though less favourable for the parliamentarian cause, was the emergence of open differences between Lord Grey and members of his local Committee.

There had been some changes at the turn of the year. William Ward, a mercer, had succeeded Richard Ludlam as Mayor of Leicester and Peter Temple had been appointed High Sheriff of Leicestershire by Parliament. From this point onwards the first rumblings of discontent within the County Committee and between some of its members and Lord Grey of Groby may be discerned. Glimpses of Thomas Grey's attitude to his military subordinates and those he considered to be his social inferiors can also be seen.

The House of Commons Journal for January 1644 records that :-

"It was recommended to the Lord General, to compose the differences between my Lord Grey and the Mayor of Leicester and Captain Ludlam; and that his Excellency [i.e. the Earl of Essex] *be desired to so compose those differences, that, as no affront may be given to the Lord Grey, so that the Committees of that county may not be discouraged".*[3]

The Leicestershire Committee had been formed in the December of 1642. Like its counterparts in other counties it supplied the supportive financial and administrative sinews for the parliamentarian war effort in the locality. The composition of the Committee has already been noted. There was the usual sprinkling of the local nobility and wealthier gentry, led by Lord Grey, but the bulk of the Committee members were local merchants and traders - the backbone of the puritan support. Many of these Committee members held military rank, often as captain of a troop of horse or a company of foot, in the units raised under the Earl of Stamford or Lord Grey.

In the spring of 1644 Richard Ludlam, that active local captain, committee man and recent Mayor of Leicester, was placed under house arrest upon the orders of Lord Grey. He was detained at Burley House. This was either the residence at Loughborough which had been taken from the royalists for a time or else the former Cecil residence of Burley-on-the-hill, near Oakham in Rutland which was also under the control of Lord

141

Grey. The latter seems more likely in the circumstances as for most of this period Burleigh House in Loughborough seems to have been an outpost of Lord Loughborough's Ashby royalists. The detention of Richard Ludlam was :-

"for an affront done to the Lord Grey ; and ..... since his return he hath humbled himself to his lordship; which may prove a good example to others, to refrain themselves from the like offences, and teach them better manners".[4]

The purpose of this action on the part of Lord Grey would seem to have been to remind his social subordinates and inferiors of their place and station in life. The twenty year-old aristocrat might have to accept, unwillingly, 'affronts' to his dignity from such as his patron, the Earl of Essex, or the rapidly rising country squire Oliver Cromwell (made Lieutenant-General of Horse in the Eastern Association under the Earl of Manchester in February 1644) but not from his local tinker, or tailor, or candlestick maker!

Dissent within local committees and between members and their local military commanders were not uncommon. Colonel Robert Overton at Hull, Sir Samuel Luke at Newport Pagnell, and Colonel John Hutchinson at Nottingham, to name but three, were other parliamentarian commanders who had trouble with their committees, or factions on them.

As Lucy Hutchinson, the wife of the Nottingham commander, put it :-

"Almost all the parliament garrisons were infected and disturbed with like factious little people, insomuch as that many worthy gentlemen were wearied out of their commands, and oppressed by a certain mean sort of people, whom to distinguish from the more honourable gentlemen, they called `worsted stocking Men'. Some Governors as violently curbed their committees, as the committees factiously molested them".[5]

When reading this type of observation it should be remembered that in seventeenth century England authority was a function of social position among the nobility and upper gentry. These would normally have worn silk, or of like quality, stockings whereas the middle and lower-middle class tradesmen would have normally worn worsted stockings or the like. The civil war had brought people into positions of authority and put swords into the hands of others who would not normally have been able to challenge their social superiors - whether of royalist or parliamentarian persuasion. Such 'democratic' or 'anarchic' tendencies were, not surprisingly, more advanced on the 'rebel' parliamentarian side who had set the example of resisting the will of their sovereign and God's anointed.

Indeed, it was the view of Clarendon that the Parliament's officers were all *'dirty people of no name'*. While this was clearly untrue it remains the case that at the local level it was the 'worsted stocking' committee men rather than the nobility or gentry who underpinned the parliamentarian war effort. As David Underdown puts it :-

"Though the `vulgar rabble' might be unregenerate, there were enough who were not so, among the `middling sort', to give the servants of Parliament their joyful zest for doing the Lord's work. Yeomen and craftsmen, inspired by the cumulative effects of being for generations a people apart, persecuted yet the Elect of God, charged with the duty of Saints to change for the better a world dominated by the reprobate majority - these were the men who ran Parliament's local administration in the Committees".[6]

Thomas, Lord Grey of Groby was to continue to have problems with such people.

Yet the friction between Lord Grey as local military commander and his fellow Committee men was not confined to the 'worsted stocking men'. There was a rivalry, both personal and familial, with Sir Edward Hartopp of Buckminster. Sir Edward, apart from Sir Arthur Hesilrige MP of Noseley - out of the county with his regiment of 'lobsters' for most of this period, constituted Thomas Grey's most serious social and military rival on the county committee.

Sir Edward Hartopp wrote to Sir J. Coke on 6th March 1644 in the following terms :-

"I know not how long I shall stay at Leicester, because I have received this morning letters from my Lord General to come with my troop to the army; his Excellency being capable of some neglect towards me; the reasons I dare not write; perchance my Lord Grey is pleased to think that I am too considerable to join him, and rather desires creatures of his own making ..... I am afraid he is transported with particular counsels, that aim at their own ends".[7]

It was not only committee members on the parliamentarian side who needed persuading of the correctness of proposed actions. The zealous puritan did what seemed good to his conscience and in the light of the *'Word of the Lord'* as revealed in the scriptures rather than as instructed by priest or prince. This even applied to many of those under military command. As Lucy Hutchinson records:-

> *"the most religious and the best people were so pragmatical,
> that no act, nor scarcely word, could pass without being strictly
> arraigned and judged at the bar of every soldier's discretion,
> and thereafter censured and exclaimed at".*[8]

Indeed, in reference to the horse troopers of the Nottingham garrison she comments that they :-

> *"had the general fault of all the parliament party, that they
> were not very obedient to commands, except they knew and
> approved their employment".*[9]

Given these difficulties it may seem surprising that the parliamentarians ever achieved military success. Yet, rather like the French Revolutionary armies, it was this sense of common purpose and individual commitment to the Cause - by what Oliver Cromwell called *"godly honest men"* of the kind who *"knows what he fights for, and loves what he knows"* - that was to carry them through to victory as at Newbury and at later triumphs.

The parliamentarians had decided quite early in 1644 to both strengthen their hold on Nottingham and to sever the royalist line of communication between the north and south of England on the eastern side by capturing Newark. This town on the river Trent was of great importance as a royalist stronghold. It stood at the juncture of the Great North Road and the Fosse Way, and was the key to the only route from the royalist west to the royalist north since the capture of Wilne Ferry. It was also the route by which the Marquis of Newcastle's army could enter Eastern Association territory. The town had housed the so-called *'flying army'* of Lord Cavendish until its defeat by the Earl of Manchester's army at Winceby and Gainsborough.

Sir John Meldrum was appointed as commander-in-chief of the parliamentarian force of some seven thousand men which began the siege of Newark on 29th February 1644. This force was drawn together from several associated counties and, as with the previous attempt to take Newark a year earlier, the enterprise was to suffer from the jealousies of the chief commanders, much to Meldrum's frustration. Although elements of Lord Grey's Horse and soldiers from the Leicester garrison were present, under the restless Sir Edward Hartopp, it seems as if Lord Grey and his main command were elsewhere.

The following extract from a letter sent from the (Parliamentary) Committee of Both Kingdoms, at Arundel House, London to Sir John Meldrum and dated February 21st seems to bear this out :-

> *"..... The Lord General having acquainted this Committee with
> some letters of yours concerning the design of Newark, they
> have thought fit to recommend the same to the Earl of*

144

Manchester from whom they doubt not but you will speedily hear concerning this business, as also for paying the 700l (pounds) you mention to Lord Fairfax's soldiers. The Lord Willoughby's horse and Sir John Gell's and the Nottingham forces you may depend upon for this service, but for Lord Grey's they are reserved for another important design. ....."[(10)]

At the same time a force was being assembled at Warwick to take supplies to Gloucester *'by horse and not by waggon'.* The supplies included *'50 barrels of gunpowder, two tuns* (sic) *of match, 1,200 coats, pairs of shoes and shirts, 200 firelocks, 400 cwt of brimstone, and 2,200 l* (pounds) *in money'.* The Earl of Denbigh and the Coventry and Warwick forces provided 600 horse for this service, whilst Lord Grey and Northampton furnished some 500 horse. Further supply convoys were assembled at Warwick and sent on to Gloucester during March and Lord Grey's command played a significant part in these operations.

Meanwhile, initial attempts were made by the royalists to raise the siege of Newark. These attempts came from the garrisons of Ashby and Belvoir castles but were unsuccessful. They had the support of the Newark horse who had escaped Meldrum's net and joined the other garrisons to give a combined force of some 2,000 horse. According to Lucy Hutchinson the Newark Horse had slipped out over the Muscam Bridges at Newark through the ineptitude of Sir Edward Hartopp :-

"This day, unexpectedly, came Sir Edward Hartopp, [to Nottingham] *with a thousand horse from Leicester and Derby, to which the governor* [Colonel John Hutchinson], *added between five and six hundred; Sir Edward being appointed to command the party should have gone with them to take Muscam Bridges at Newark, before which place Sir John Meldrum was now come with about seven thousand men, and had laid siege to it. The horse of Newark, as soon as the parliament's forces came, made an escape over Muscam Bridges, which Sir Edward Hartopp, having more mind to drink than to fight, lingering a day at Nottingham, and then marching to no purpose against it, lost his opportunity ....."[(11)]*

Again, according to Lucy Hutchinson, Sir John Meldrum made all preparations for a general assault on Newark :-

" but at a council of war that was called in the field, it was decided that it should not then be .... had they joined in the

145

assault when he then would have made it, they might probably have carried the town: but missing that opportunity, they came off at last with loss and dishonour".[12]

The royalists were not slow to seek to exploit this last opportunity in order to raise the siege. A. J. Thorold, writing from Shrewsbury in March to Robert Sutton in Oxford, reported that :-

"I am now at Shrewsbury where I have desired the Prince's aid for the relief of Newark, which at this time is besieged on both sides of the town. On the south side of the town are all my Lord Willoughby's forces, and their new-made Colonel King's and Meldrom's [sic], with all that they can draw out of their garrisons of Boston, Lincoln, and Gainsborough. My Lord Gray's [sic] forces with all Lester [sic], Melton, Nottingham and Darby [sic] can afford are gone on the north side of the Trent".[13]

Accordingly, Prince Rupert was sent from Chester to raise the siege of Newark. Receiving intelligence of this intention Sir John Meldrum, on 15th March, sent Sir Edward Hartopp with his Leicester, Derby, and Nottingham Horse to intercept the Prince.

Lord Loughborough and Sir Gervase Lucas, the governor of Belvoir Castle, joined forces at Loughborough where they took and fortified Burleigh House. From there they could overlook and seek to control the route from Leicester to Newark by which Lord Grey could support or supply Meldrum. This royalist 'flying army' then made an attack on Leicester in order to distract the garrison. The attack was not pressed home and the royalists retired to Mountsorrel, followed at a distance by Lord Grey.

The following day, Saturday 16th March, the royalist force were surprised in their rear by men from Sir Edward Hartopp's command on their way to prevent Prince Rupert's relief force from reaching Newark. Lord Loughborough's 'army' had been resting in Mountsorrel and engaging in the practice of *"plundering horses from plowmen in the field"*.[14] Hartopp, however, sent only one regiment against the royalists in the initial skirmish. This was the Nottingham Horse under Colonel Thornhaugh. As a result he lost the opportunity to cut them off from their base. The royalists withdrew to the bridges over the river Soar at Cotes Mill on the eastern side of Loughborough.

Here the royalist force under Lord Loughborough fortified themselves on the chain of bridges along a raised causeway that spanned the six channels of the Soar at this point. Hartopp's force faced them from the north side of the river whilst Lord Grey and the Leicester garrison, with two cannon,

146

came up and trapped them from the south side. The skirmish of Cotes Bridges, one of the more notable clashes of the civil war in Leicestershire, then began on 18th March.

Lord Grey's cannon opened the engagement by *"discharging a great piece upon the enemy, which did great execution amongst them, they forced them to retreat, and by that means gained the bridge* (nearest to Loughborough) *which was half a mile in length"*.[15] The royalist foot were then drawn off the causeway into *"a great meadow, and divided into five bodies"*, and there faced their enemies without a blow being exchanged until nightfall. The royalist horse had been thrown into confusion by the initial artillery fire and then put to flight by the Nottingham Horse who had followed up with a charge. They were pursued through Loughborough to Burleigh House. The royalist foot were left stranded in the meadow. Sir Edward Hartopp, however, again refused to follow up his advantage, claiming later that he was not authorised to conduct such an action. Hearing, as nightfall approached, that Prince Rupert with a great force of horse and foot had already reached Ashby, Sir Edward Hartopp withdrew from Cotes back to Newark. The trapped royalist foot were thus allowed to retreat under cover of darkness and Lord Grey retired unsupported back to Leicester to hold it against a possible attack by Rupert.

The small skirmish at Cotes Bridges was of great significance. Such fighting as had taken place had been mostly between cavalry. It had been feared that Leicester, which was unable to withstand any formidable attack, was about to be assailed - firstly by the joint Hastings-Lucas force and then secondly by Prince Rupert. Despite the tactical advantage they had gained initially the outcome was to prove near disastrous for the local parliamentarians. The bad feeling between Lord Grey and Sir Edward Hartopp had added to the latter's over-caution and ineptitude. Further ill-consequences and recriminations followed from it.

The immediate result was that Lord Loughborough's army, virtually undamaged when it might have been destroyed, was able to contribute 2,700 men to the army of 6,500 men with which Rupert was to attack Meldrum and raise the siege of Newark. The united royalist army moved on through Rempstone and Bingham, arriving at 2 a.m. on 21st March at Coddington and taking Beacon Hill, overlooking Newark, without resistance. Rupert had managed to smuggle a cryptic letter into Newark castle, addressed to the Governor, Sir Richard Byron. The message read *"Let the old Drum be beaten early on the morrow morning"*. Byron understood its meaning. Before Meldrum had time to assess the size and nature of the force opposed to him, the prince, with his accustomed impetuosity, charged with his forces down Beacon Hill and, with a shout of *"For God and the King"*, carried all before him. When the town's

147

royalist garrison sallied out and captured Meldrum's fort at Muscam Bridges, part of Meldrum's force mutinied, and he was forced to surrender. The parliamentarians were allowed to retreat to Hull, leaving behind 4,000 muskets, as many pistols, 50 barrels of gunpowder, and 30 pieces of artillery. After three weeks the siege of Newark had been relieved. This was Parliament's most complete defeat of the war locally and Prince Rupert's greatest victory to date.

The effect of the relief of Newark on the morale of local parliamentary supporters was so great that according to Lucy Hutchinson :-

> *"such a blow was given to the parliament interest, in these parts, that ..... even the most zealous were cast down, and gave up all for lost".*[16]

The chronicler for 'Mercurius Veridicus' sounded a characteristically Puritan note :-

> *"..... There was some encounter betwixt the Parliament forces and his* (Prince Rupert's*), wherein the Earl of Manchester's foot* (Eastern Association troops from Lincolnshire) *shewed not that courage and resolution as was expected; there were taken some pieces of ordnance and divers arms; the first charge from Prince Rupert was very violent. The enemy was much stronger than was reported; and it hath pleased God, for our humiliation, to give them the better of us; yet ought we not be discouraged. Victory flies on uncertain wings; and on that side to which it stooped not today; it may please God it may alight on the morrow".*[17]

In the recriminations and attempts to apportion blame that followed the debacle of Cotes Bridges and its consequences there were several allegations of violence of word and physical intimidation of witnesses by Hartopp, Stamford, Grey, and their servants. These are worth examining in some detail in so far as they provide an insight into some aspects of the character of these gentlemen.

Following complaints made by Captain George Palmer, a minister of religion and an officer of the Nottingham Horse, against Sir Edward Hartopp's behaviour the incident became the subject of both a county committee enquiry and then a Parliamentary investigation.

On 4th April 1644 the House of Commons took into consideration *"the managing of the forces sent from Newark and Leicester against the enemy gathered about Loughborough".*[18] The parliamentary enquiry was a bitter

148

one, stirring up local rivalries. The Calendar of State Papers (the Domestic Series) - a collection of official committee diary entries records how those involved were summoned to testify as witnesses to the parliamentary committee. The following entries provide us with a graphic account of the atmosphere surrounding the enquiry.

"April 20th. Ordered
..... 4. That Lord Grey attend this Committee on Monday afternoon, when Sir Arthur Heselrigg be also present.

(Sir Arthur was a member of the Committee. His brother, Thomas, was a member of the local Parliamentary Committee in Leicestershire).

"April 30th
..... 3. That Lord Grey be desired to be at this Committee tomorrow.

"May 9th
..... Information of Jeoffrey Hawkins in the case of Sir Edward Hartopp. Whereas Wm. Swynfen was required to render his testimony concerning the carriage of Sir Edward Hartopp and others near Loughborough, I am ready to depose that this day Lieut. Cotton at Sir Edward's order, meeting at the hall-door with Mr. Swynfen, fell upon him and gave him many ill words and threats.

"May (undated)
..... Petition of Thomas Heselrigg to the Lords and Commons.

Petitioner being one of the Committee for Co. Leicester and employed by them upon the country's affairs to this House, Lord Grey seeing him in Westminster Hall fell upon him with reproachful language in a loud tone, calling him rascal and base fellow, with other threatening language. Petitioner craves a vindication of this Assembly, being a faithful servant to your honours.

"May 10th
..... Petition of George Palmer, Thos. Buckley, Wm. Swynfen, and three others to the House of Commons. Petitioners being commanded to wait at Westminster to give testimony concerning the behaviour of Sir Edward Hartopp and Major Bingley in the

design against the enemy at Loughborough in March last, when coming out of Westminster (hall) *after doing that service* (they) *were repeatedly called a company of rogues by Henry, Earl of Stamford, who particularized Thos. Buckley, calling him a lying rogue and threatening him with his cane-staff. Petitioners pray the House to vindicate their good names from such scandalous and opprobrious speeches.*

"May 10th
..... Ordered by the Commons' House that the above petition of George Palmer, Thos. Buckley, and four others be referred to the Committee for the examination of Sir Edward Hartopp's business.

"May 10th
..... Ordered by the Commons' House that the petition of Thos. Haselrigg and the information of Jeoffrey Hawkins against Lieut. Cotton and the information of Lord Grey against Mr. Haselrigg about the opening of a letter directed to his Lordship be referred to the same Committee. (Written on the same paper as the preceding).

"May 10th
..... Ordered by the Commons' House that it be referred to the same Committee to compose the differences between the gentlemen and commanders in Co Leicester, except in matters concerning the privelege [sic] *of Parliament.*

Endorsed : The business concerning Lord Grey and others of Leicester. (Written on the same paper).

"May 13th
Notes of examinations of witnesses [before the Committee for the examination of Sir Edward Hartopp's business] concerning the petition of George Palmer and other officers, and their connection with the doings of the Earl of Stamford, Lord Grey, and others of Leicester".[19]

The parliamentary enquiry was eventually dropped in order to re-establish unity amongst the local parliamentarians. In this respect it was to fail, as will be seen.

There were some victories, however, for the parliamentarian forces in local skirmishes during the spring and summer of 1644. Following Lord

150

Grey's own success at Melton in February his men scored a notable triumph at Hinckley in March.

Part of the agreement Parliament had made with the Scots entailed the signing of the Solemn League and Covenant by English ministers of religion. In Leicestershire the local clergy and churchwardens were to gather in the county town for a mass swearing-in and signing on 3rd March. In order to prevent this Lord Loughborough dispatched some three hundred cavaliers to round up as many ministers as possible and escort them to Ashby castle. Three accounts of this expedition and its outcome survive, although all are from the parliamentarian perspective.

The cavaliers coursed the countryside as far as Dunton Bassett and Lutterworth, taking prisoner two ministers and thirty countrymen along with some eighty cattle, oxen, and horses for the use of their garrison. Among those taken was one Master Warner, *'a godly minister'* :-

> *"whom they much abused and threatened to hang him. All their prisoners they put into Hinckley Church and in a jeering manner asked them, `Where are the Roundheads your brethren at Leicester? Why come they not to redeem you?'"*[20]

The royalists had assumed that because the Leicester Horse had gone to the siege of Newark they would be safe from attack during this raid. When news of this excursion reached the governor of Leicester, Colonel Henry Grey, his reaction was inspired, however, and resulted in a triumph of improvisation.

> *"..... the intelligence of these things coming to our town of Leicester, all our horse being gone to Newark, we were feign, every private townsman, to spare his own horse, and so sent away 120 of our foot soldiers and some 30 troopers that lie at Bagworth House to keep it from the enemy, under the command of Colonel Grey, whom the Lord Grey hath made governor of Leicester".*[21]

In the action that followed the Leicester forces :-

> *"being upon their march toward Hinckley, so well ordered the matter, that about eight of the clock that night, they fell most valiantly on them in their quarters undiscovered, took the enemy's scouts, and without much resistance took the outworks and a piece of ordnance, and there performed their work also with so good success, that they presently entered the town, killed*

151

one of the enemy's captains named Mainwaring, and four or five more of their soldiers, wounded nine or ten of them very sorely, presently routed them all, took two of their lieutenants, one quarter-master, one ensign, forty-five prisoners, and one hundred and fifty horse, with their arms, released all the countrymen, rescued all the cattle, and restored them to the right owners; and so returned home safe with this victory and booty, the next day being Shrove Tuesday. None of the Leicester men were slain in this defeat; only four wounded, whereof one was casually hurt by Colonel Grey because he forgot their word in the flight, which was `God prosper us!' the enemy's word being `For the King!'! [22]

"Our men went on very courageously; and if they had not been too greedy of prey they had near taken them all; the enemies force were to the number of 300 and ours about 150". [23]

Colonel Grey's own account of the action was recorded in :-

"A letter to the Lord Grey of Groby; wherein is declared a great victory, obtained by the Parliament's forces near Hinckley." [24]

This *'great victory'* was reported to Parliament in another letter from Colonel Grey which also related that, *"divers ministers of the county* [Leicestershire] *refused taking the covenant, whom they have as yet restrained at Leicester till farther orders"*. The ministers were ordered to be brought to London in safe custody, and their estates to be sequestrated. [25]

Throughout April and May Lord Grey's major garrisons at Leicester, Northampton, and Burley in Rutland were active in areas as far apart as Lichfield and Stamford, Newark and Newport Pagnell. This range of activity can be traced by surviving messages between Parliament (and its committees) and the local commanders and county committees. Often the Leicester and Northampton Horse, in particular, were asked to rendezvous with combined forces for operations outside the area of the Midland Association of Counties. Evidence of disharmony between local commanders and their committees began to multiply. So too did reports of the plundering of 'the godly' as well as 'malignants' by parliamentarian troops and requests for the payment of the soldiers, which was often in arrears.

For example, on 9th May the House of Commons received a *"humble petition of the Committee for the county of Leicester"* concerning *"their sufferings under the soldiery there"*. In response it was ordered that *"a*

152

letter be directed to the Committee at Leicester, to raise another fortnight's pay unto the Lord Grey's regiment, to complete that regiment a month's pay and to enable that regiment to march according to the Lord General's direction". It was also *"Ordered, that an ordinance be prepared, and brought in, for the raising of forces for the preservation and settling the county of Leicester; and Sir Arthur Hesilrige is to bring it into the House; and also the letter to the Committee".* [26]

The Commons then received a letter from Colonel Henry Grey, as acting Governor of Leicester, dated 11th May, giving information that the Marquis of Newcastle's forces were marching towards Leicester and that a siege of the town was feared. In the event Lord Goring with 4,000 royalist horse, moving down through Leicestershire, was engaged in skirmishes by troops led by Lord Grey.

On 23rd May it was recorded that the Speaker of the House of Commons, on behalf of Parliament, had authorised a servant of a royalist Colonel Bond to go to the king's headquarters at Oxford in order to negotiate the said colonel's release in exchange for Captain Francis Hacker and Mr. Arthur Staveley who were held prisoner at Belvoir Castle. Captain Hacker was one of Lord Grey's captains of horse and Arthur Staveley was the son of Thomas Staveley esquire of West Langton and a local committee man.

Two days later it was decided by the House of Commons to refer to the Committee of Both Kingdoms a letter from Captain Edward Grey from Leicester *"to consider of the differences between the Committee and the soldiers; and to take some such course as may settle the peace, and provide for the safety of that county".* [27]

In turn the Committee of Both Kingdoms on 25th May recorded *"That Mr. Browne do report to the House* (of Commons) *that the differences between the Committee of Leicester and the soldiers there having been referred to a Committee of that House, it still be left to their consideration".* [28]

On 27th May the House of Commons read an Ordinance to create a Committee of the Militia for Leicestershire *"for raising and maintaining of forces for the defence of the said county".* [29] This was a unification of the local military co-ordinating and fund raising functions. The new arrangement does not, however, seem to have solved the problem of local discord between the leaders of the parliamentarian cause in Leicestershire.

The May 1644 issue of the 'Parliament Scoute' lamented :-

"So sad have been the sufferings of that county [of Leicester], and Rutland, by reason of the disharmony there.

153

..... Poore Leicestershire! not a county more right for the Parliament, and yet no county so tattered and torn as it hath been ..... that a few men in a couple of noblemen's houses, Belvoir and Ashby de la Zouch, should waste a county as they have done".[30]

The raiding carried out by the local royalists was done for economic as well as political reasons. They had garrisons to sustain at Tutbury, Lichfield, and Burleigh House, Loughborough as well as Belvoir and Ashby. As a whole the royalists extracted £97,000 from the county of Leicestershire in 1644.[31], whilst the Belvoir Castle garrison imposed its own levies on the Framland hundred in the north-east of the shire. The unfortunate populace often had to pay the 'tax-collectors' from both sides and sometimes ran the risk of incurring the penalties associated with collaboration with the enemy if insufficient remained to pay the second comer.

Whole areas of Leicestershire, Derbyshire, Nottinghamshire and Warwickshire were subjected to the demands of the Ashby-de-la-Zouch garrison. Here is an example of a demand sent to the parish of Seckington just inside Warwickshire :-

"To the Constables of the Parish of Seckington these - haste, post haste : -
These are to warn you that you, forthwith upon the sight hereof, send in what provisions your parish will afford, to the garrison at Ashby-de-la-Zouch, for the use of His Majesty's army, and, if you fail you must expect to be exposed to the plunder of the hungry soldier".[32]

Foraging raids in the region by the Ashby garrison were commonplace, and tended to disrupt trade; for the royalist troops attacked the carriers who supplied towns with agricultural produce. Carriers from Melton Mowbray, for example, could not trade with London until the power of Hastings' *'flying army'* had begun to decline in the latter half of 1644.[33] At this point in his career Lord Loughborough was known less for his military exploits and more for his raiding and plundering activities. Sometimes he was referred to in parliamentarian publications as *"that notable thief"*, and at others as *"that grand rob-carrier"*.

Allegations of plundering were not directed only, however, against royalist forces. Whilst the parliamentarian forces in the Midlands were rather more regularly supplied than their opponents they were still likely to 'confiscate' property from 'malignants' and to agitate for more regular pay. Lord Grey of Groby was also beginning to show those acquisitive tendencies which so well characterised his father, the Earl of Stamford.

154

The following entry appears in the records of the Committee of Both Kingdoms for May 25th 1644:-

> *"141A.   Notes by Sir John Lamb of a brief against certain persons, including Lord Grey, at Leicester, for depredations and losses sustained by Lambe, between 17th December 1642 and the date of this paper, within the county of Warwick and diocese of Worcester.*
>
> *[Underwritten : -*
> *41A. Weekly tax in England and Wales £33,981. 3s. 0d; inde Northampton £425; Leicester £187. 10s. 0d; Oxford £650. Order against plundering; 22 Nov. 1642]"* [34]

During late June Lord Grey marched one Sunday with a force of 200 foot and 50 horse from Leicester to Stamford and encountered a party of royalists quartered in the vicinity of Belvoir. In the ensuing action *"he killed five or six, took 40 horse, and many gentlemen of quality, one lieutenant, two cornets, and some others"*.[35] A letter dated 1st July was then sent to Parliament by Lord Grey to inform them of this defeat he had given to `Colonel Hastings'. The letter was read to the House of Lords who decided that it should be referred to those members of the House that were of the Associated (Midland) Counties to consider *"what provisions are fit to be made for the enabling of him to keep the field, for the defence of Leicestershire, and the rest of the Association"*.[36]

On 10th July the ordinance creating a Committee of the Militia for the county of Leicester was promulgated by Parliament with the usual membership, headed by Lord Grey of Groby, and authorised to raise forces, appoint officers and levy taxes to support them.[37]

"Poore Leicestershire" was expected to organise and finance its own defence against the royalists. No significant assistance was to be forthcoming from the Parliament in London. Realising this, Thomas, Lord Grey of Groby began to take the initiative.

The tide of fortune in the contest locally between Lords Grey and Loughborough was beginning to turn against the latter as the year 1644 progressed. It was also turning out to be an exceedingly wet summer. Lord Grey, writing from Leicester, lamented on 9th June that *"the ways were never so deep at Christmas in comparison as they are now"*.[38]

On 1st July, the day before the major parliamentarian victory at Marston Moor near York, a party of 120 of Lord Loughborough's men who were out plundering the countryside around Hinckley were attacked by a body of *"80 good horse"*, commanded by Captain Thomas Babington, sent by Lord Grey to intercept them. The action took place on Bosworth Field *"to the very place where King Richard [III] was slain"*. *"At the first charge"*,

155

continues a parliamentarian report of the incident, *"the enemy fled; our men made a hot pursuit for three miles, killed six, wounded many, took 40 prisoners. ..... We lost not one man, captain Babington shot in the hand ..... Three-score horses taken. One hundred cattle, besides sheep and other goods in a very great proportion, rescued and restored to the owners"*.[39]

Following news of the victory at Marston Moor Lord Grey of Groby and Colonel Sir John Gell, anticipating the final demise of the royalist cause, began to attack systematically all the royalist garrisons in their neighbourhoods.

On 6th July there was a raid on Tutbury Castle in Staffordshire, held for Hastings by Sir Andrew Kingston, in which Gell captured 58 horses. At the same time Gell's and Grey's forces mounted a combined attack on the smaller Hastings outpost at Wilne Ferry on the river Trent. This attack was effected by the use of sixty or so cart-loads of hay and similar combustible material. The carts were first hauled to the edge of the royalist outworks, thus providing the parliamentarians with protection against hostile bullets, and then, the wind being favourable, they were ignited. The result was singularly dramatic; within minutes the royalists, blinded and half suffocated by the acrid smoke, and scorched by masses of flying hay, surrendered to a man. This victory provided the parliamentarians with considerable quantities of arms, ammunition and valuable artillery.

The attack on Wilne Ferry was not an end in itself but a preliminary to the successful siege of the more important royalist garrison at Wingfield Manor. Hastings made a futile attempt to relieve this garrison by drawing on troops from several other garrisons in the vicinity, including Ashby, Tutbury and Lichfield, for a concerted attack on the besiegers to be mounted from Burton-upon-Trent. This rendezvous and plan was frustrated by one of Gell's ablest cavalry officers, Major Saunders, who drove Colonel Bagot of Lichfield out of Burton and surprised another royalist regiment under Colonel Eyre which was resting in Boyleston church. From these two engagements Saunders took no less than three hundred prisoners and a considerable quantity of military supplies without any loss to his own force. The siege of Wingfield Manor continued.

Gell and Grey received the thanks of Parliament for taking Wilne Ferry. Subsequent reports on the taking of Kings Mills and Wingfield Manor in Derbyshire and Shelford Manor in Nottinghamshire followed; the latter two claims proving to be premature and the product of Gell's self-publicising machine. Shelford Manor, for example, did not fall until 1646 when it was taken by the more modest and honest Colonel John Hutchinson, Governor of Nottingham.

A letter to Parliament from Derby dated 7th August gave details of the 2,000 horse and foot besieging Wingfield Manor. It also gave a brief report of the situation at Derby and Leicester. In the case of the latter there was a by-now familiar note :-

"..... We hear from Leicester that there hath been some differences there between lieutenant-colonel [Henry] Grey and captain [Richard] Ludlam, who gave either of them a several watchword to the centinel [sic], and had like to have caused some combustions. But, God be thanked, it did not; and the next day, or within a day or two after, Hastings's horse faced Leicester, and gave them an alarm; but stayed not, nor did they or we since hear more of them".[40]

Hastings next attempted to raise the siege of Wingfield by attacking the parliamentary supply line. Hearing that some carriers who lay at Leicester on their way to Derby might be carrying gunpowder and ammunition for the besiegers of Wingfield Manor,

"the Grand Rob Carrier, Generall Hastings, joyning with some other forces from Beaver, came to Belgrave, a small town within a mile of Leicester". They lay there one night and next morning *"they met an honest poor man near Belgrave and asked him whence he came: He answered "From Leicester", and then they asked him where the ammunition was that was brought from London, and who he was for, to which question he answered as well as he could; but, the bloody villains! one of them discharged a pistol against him, and the others cut and hacked him with their swords so that the poor man died there most miserably".* As it happened the man was carrying only *"plums and spice"* which were devoured on the spot by his murderers. ....[41]
".... and when they came to the carriages, they robbed and pillaged all that was worth carrying away in them: But intelligence being brought to the committee of Leicester, they sent a party of horse, which met with them whilst they were eating the plumbs (sic) and spice they had robbed the poor man of; they fell upon them, and, with little loss, rescued the plunder again from them, and returned it to the carriers".[42]

The above report was derived from a letter to Parliament from Derby dated 15th August. A letter to Parliament from Leicester dated 10th August relates an account of a similar incident. In this case:-

"the grand rob-carrier, general Hastings, joining with some other forces from Belvoir on Monday last , came to Belgrave ..... to surprise certain carriers that lay there that night, going

157

from Derby, and accordingly took divers of their horses, and drove them away to Ashby, but dared not stay to plunder their packs ; for the Leicester garrison, having intelligence thereof, with what forces they had in the town, which were not many, their horse being before drawn out by the Lord Grey [to Wingfield one assumes], *marched out against them, and, about the bridge between Leicester and Belgrave, skirmished with the enemy : captain Adkinson, a valiant Scotchman, charged them gallantly, his men playing their parts stoutly, though much overpowered by the enemy. Captain Rowland Hacker, a man whom the enemy set no small esteem of, and in truth the only active man for them in those parts* [and the brother of the parliamentarian Francis Hacker]*was in that encounter dangerously wounded, without hopes of life ; but by the time the other* [parliamentarian] *captains, captain Grey and captain Tapper, came to charge, the enemy retreated, and made haste away; but the Leicester men, wanting horse to pursue them, could not complete their victory, as otherwise they had done".*[43]

To add to Hastings's misfortunes Wingfield Manor finally surrendered on 12th August to Gell's and Grey's forces, who had received valuable assistance from the Earl of Manchester's army returning from Yorkshire via the Midlands to Lincolnshire after the defeat of the royalist armies at Marston Moor. These glad tidings were reported to Parliament in letters to the Earl of Rutland dated Friday, 23rd August.

The above success notwithstanding, on 16th August the House of Commons Journal records that:-

"Mr. Carew presented from the Committee of Both Kingdoms certain information given in by Lord Grey, containing certain passages betwixt him and the Committee for the Militia for the county of Leicester".[44]

This information was referred to a committee of the House of Commons.

It seems from the evidence that Lord Grey had left the Leicestershire area sometime during the summer, probably for London. On 4th September a petition *"of the inhabitants of Leicester"* was presented to the House of Commons *"representing the inconveniences that happened to the country upon the differences that had arisen between the Lord Grey's officers and the Committee"* ; and the petition *"was referred to a committee* [of Parliament] *to see what was fit to be done for the composing of the differences".*[45] It is interesting to note that the differences here are between Lord Grey's military officers and the local Committee for the Militia and that the passage seems to confirm his absence.

158

Meanwhile, Henry Hastings, who had for so long enjoyed the freedom to course and raid Leicestershire and the adjoining counties to his base was increasingly on the defensive. This was so much so that he now felt obliged to withdraw all his men and provisions out of the town of Ashby and into the castle itself. His own exploits, and those of his men, became almost invariably unsuccessful and frequently contained an element of pathos.

Toward the end of September a party of Hastings's men attempted to ambush a parliamentary convoy en route from Leicester to Nottingham, but missed it. Undaunted, they decided to attack the empty wagon train as it passed through the village of Costock in south Nottinghamshire on its return journey :-

> *"..... Hastings's forces placed their ambuscades and lined the hedges on both sides of a lane where the Leicester forces were to pass by, near a town called Costock, within five miles on this side of Nottingham ; and accordingly gave the said convoy an unexpected salute on their return ; but they very gallantly forced their passage through the lane; which done, they wheeled about again upon the enemy, beat them from the hedges, miserably routed and dispersed their whole party, killed eight on the place, whereof one is said to be serjeant-major Whalley, wounded others, took above threescore of them prisoners, the rest that escaped leaving all their arms for haste behind them, and ninety good horse; in which action the Leicester forces lost not one man; only lieutenant Stevens, who deserves much honour for his gallant undertakings in this service, was shot in the back, but not mortally : after which exploit thus gallantly performed by a party of 80 horse against 120 at the least, the convoy returned safe to Leicester the same night with all their prisoners and prize, and were entertained with much joy and triumph".*[46]

This parliamentarian success was also reported in the 'Parliament Scoute' with the summary that *"the Leicester men, though fewer in number, beat the de la Zouchians, killed their captaine, and divers of their men, took many prisoners and horse ....."*[47]

Other exploits carried out by Hastings's men included a raid on the town from which he had taken his title, Loughborough, where :-

> *"..... on the last Lord's day,* [a party of Hastings's horse] *according to their accustomed prophanation of that day, rode into the church at sermon time, and would have taken away the preacher out of the pulpit ; but the women of the town,*

159

expressing more valour than their husbands dared to do at that time, rescued him from them and disappointed their purpose".
The report continues :-

"On the Lord's day before, another party of them came to Rodeley [Rothley], a town near Mountsorrel, and in the same manner entered the church, and took away three men, and carried them to Ashby".[48]

Even though Lord Grey of Groby was absent from Leicester at this time he was still, at least nominally, the commander-in-chief of the Associated (Midland) Counties for Parliament, i.e. Leicestershire, Nottinghamshire, Derbyshire, Rutland, Northamptonshire, and Bedfordshire. It should be remembered that he was aged only twenty-one or twenty-two at the time. He was often called upon to take soldiers, especially cavalry troopers, across or even out of this area to assist the neighbouring parliamentary forces.

During the autumn of 1644 he might have been at times in any of the counties under his authority although in effect Sir John Gell in Derbyshire and Colonel John Hutchinson at Nottingham seemed well able to look after their own areas and might well have resented this young aristrocrat's interference. He seems to have developed a practical respect for both of them by this stage. His own personal authority and patronage seem to have carried more weight, despite problems with some local committee members, in Leicestershire, Northamptonshire, and Rutland. Being apparently based in London during this period he was also cultivating links with the parliamentarian military in Bedfordshire, his southernmost county.

Indeed, during September he sent the following letter, by hand, to Sir Samuel Luke, Governor of Newport Pagnell.

"Daniel Maddock, the bearer, has served under my command ever since my first receiving my commission, first as quartermaster of a troop of horse and since I have made him lieutenant of a troop in my regiment. He has faithfully and honestly demeaned himself but I at present have no employment for him, and he, being desirous to be employed in your service, has petitioned me to testify my knowledge to you and request if you have any employment for him in the like place that he served under me, that you will entertain him".[49]

This testimonial refers to the man who appeared in the original Army List for Grey's own first cavalry troop as *'Daniel Madox - Quartermaster'*. He is the same person whom John Hotham the Younger had offered to help fight Lord Grey over the 'oats' incident at Nottingham in June 1643.

or the last time that a testimonial was used for such a purpose. On the other hand it might just indicate that Lord Grey's own regiment was not particularly active at this point (further 'evidence' that its commander was not in the field?) and that this did not suit Daniel Maddock. At any rate it would seem unlikely that Lord Grey would have recommended anyone about whom he had reservations to Sir Samuel Luke, who was proving to be a valuable ally and friend.

Sir Samuel Luke was the son of a country gentleman, Sir Oliver Luke, of Bedfordshire. Samuel was knighted in 1624 and entered Parliament as MP for Bedford in 1640. When the civil war began he took the side of Parliament and served in the military with courage and ability. *"Great-spirited little Sir Samuel Luke"* said Bulstrode Whitelocke of his performance at the battle of Chalgrove Field, *"so guarded himself with his short sword, that he escaped without hurt, though thrice taken prisoner, yet rescued, and those to whom he was prisoner slain"*. He became scoutmaster-general of the army of the Earl of Essex, and apparently observed the enemy *"so industriously that they can eat, sleep, drink not, whisper not, but he can give us an account of their darkest proceedings"*. He was a presbyterian in his political leanings and when Newport Pagnell became a garrison town in 1644 he had been made its governor. Some influential parliamentary leaders were behind his appointment.

On 17th April 1644 he had written to Lieutenant Colonel Richard Cokayn, from Westminster, to inform him of the appointment in the following terms :-

> *"Through your favours and my friends I am this day elected Governor of Newport [Pagnell] which charge God enable me to undergo and answer their expectations who have engaged themselves for me. I have had many aspersions cast upon me but have cleared myself of them all and should have been glad to have met with any of those that have taxed me but I hear they all went out of the Town the day I came to Town. My Lord Grey and Sir P. [Phillip] Stapleton and Mr. [Denzil] Holles were my very good friends and some others.*
>
> *P. S. Col. Tyrell and Sir Richard Napier and some other of their countrymen have stuck close to me".* [50]

Lord Grey appears to have been looking for some repayment of his support a mere six months later when he wrote from his house in St. John's, Clerkenwell, London to Sir Samuel Luke on 3rd October 1644 :-

"I acknowledge your many favours to me and especially that you were pleased, when my servant waited on you, to make expressions of your affection for me in this public business. For my part I desire to make it appear to all the world that I shall be so far from declining this service that, laying aside all private discontents, I shall content myself with any command to serve the Commonwealth. If you think me worthy, testify the affections of your county [Bedfordshire] *by a petition to Parliament and I believe on your importunity Northampton will join, and if Parliament will think me worthy to be employed, I shall be most willing to serve them. If not, I hope I may challenge the good opinion of all reasonable men, that all my ambition is to be enabled to do my country service and that I never sought my own end. For Derby and Notts. I shall, according to your advice, be content to part with them and shall wholly aim at the other 4 counties"* [viz. Leicestershire, Rutland, Northamptonshire and Bedfordshire].[(51)]

Clearly Thomas Grey was by now engaged in a fight to retain his position, not just against his royalist opponents nor just against some of the Leicestershire Committee members, and was seeking to mobilise his friends and allies from London - the centre of most parliamentarian networks of influence. Here we can see him encouraging the production of a petition of support on his behalf to Parliament from Bedfordshire and possibly one from Northamptonshire. Similar petitions might be expected from Leicestershire and Rutland, his own areas of more immediate control and influence.

In the midst of this manoeuvring Parliament ordered the weekly sum of £31. 5s. to be raised in Leicestershire, *"for the present relief of the British army in Ireland"* by a local committee made up again of the usual membership, viz. *"Lord Grey of Groby, Sir Arthur Hesilrige, Sir Edward Hartopp, Sir Thomas Hartopp, Sir Martin Lister, William Hewitt, John Bainbridge, Peter Temple, George Ashby, Thomas Cotton, William Roberts, Francis Hacker, Richard Bent, Arthur Staveley, William Danvers, John Goodman ; and for the town of Leicester, the Mayor* [William Billars], *Richard Ludlam, William Stanley, and Daniel Morefine"*.[(52)]

The month of October 1644 saw the final battle that Lord Lougborough's *'flying army'* was to fight as a complete unit. This came a month after the fall of Wingfield Manor. A party of royalist horse, having fought its way from the north, became blockaded at Crowland in the Fens. The Ashby *'flying army'* met with the Belvoir and the Newark Horse, near Belvoir

Castle, to set out to rescue the trapped cavaliers. Shortly afterwards, however, they were intercepted by a combined force of parliamentarians including Lord Grey of Groby, Sir John Gell, Colonel Hutchinson from Nottingham, and Sir Thomas Fairfax, and completely defeated on 29th October. News of this great regional victory reached Parliament on 31st October. It took the form of a note, dated 30th October, addressed to the Speaker of the House of Commons, from members of the Leicestershire Committee.

Accompanying the note was a letter from Captain Francis Hacker, by now having escaped from captivity or having been released on a prisoner exchange, giving details of the taking of 600 horse and 400 foot on the 29th October in the Vale of Belvoir. Also delivered was a petition from the Committee at Leicester dated 29th October.

The letter was read in the House :-

> *"from captain Hacker, captain of a horse troop, and one of the committee at Leicester, a gallant spirited gentleman, who was present (and did gallant service with his troop, consisting of above 120 brave horse) at the defeat given to the Newarke forces in Lincoln-shire ....."* It included a reference to *"General Hastings and his crew of rob-carriers in Leicestershire ..... those few men he had, except the standing garrison at Ashby, were all lost in this last defeat in Lincolnshire, ... his garrison at Ashby, it appears, is but weak; a party from Leicester the last week went and faced them to the town side, drove away many of their beasts and cattle, and not a man came out against them, but to requite their courtesy. Two or three days after* [though], *10 or 12 horse from that garrison came to Kilby, within five miles of Leicester, in the night time, and carried away two or three of the lord Grey's commanders, that carelessly staid* [sic] *some days together at a gentleman's house to make merry"* [not the usual behaviour for those characterised as 'roundheads' and 'puritans'!].[53]

At the end of October there were moves to put a stop to Hastings's activities completely. Gell and his Derbyshire forces set up a garrison at Barton Park, opposite Tutbury castle, while detachments from Gells' command and Lord Grey's Leicestershire forces *"being ingrossed into one body ..... advanced to besiege Ashby-de-la-Zouch"* and fortified the *"great house"* of Lord Beaumont at Coleorton, *"..... a very defensible place of itself, which commands one of the chiefest passages ....."* leading to *"that notorious denne* [sic] *of rob-carriers"*.[54]

163

Meanwhile there was the presentation to Parliament on 6th November 1644 of a petition with two thousand signatures subscribed from *"The Knights, Gentlemen, Freeholders, and Best-Affected of Leicestershire"* desiring that the Lord Grey might be sent down to them, he being their commander-in-chief. Whether this was the product of spontaneous and unsolicited concern and support, or as a result of the sort of lobbying already requested of Sir Samuel Luke and a counter to the local Committee's petition of 29th October, is not clear. One can speculate either way.

This new petition was presented to the House of Commons with a speech by Thomas Beaumont from Leicestershire in the following words (addressed in conformity with parliamentary practice to Mr. Speaker) :-

"Sir, The deep expressions the whole kingdom hath received of grace and clemency from this honourable House, hath encouraged us in our great sufferings to make our retreat hither, our country being almost environed with destroying enemies, and ourselves continually exposed to loss and danger; these our miseries (as we humbly apprehend) taking birth especially from two causes. One is, our want of a chief commander; for, whilst the enemy is spoiling our country, the officers of our forces, being under no particular authority, are so long in disputing who shall go out for our defence, that, before they appear, the enemy hath done the mischief, and is retired. The other is, our country's disacquaintance with most of those which sit in the Committee ; which in some averts, in many lessens, a free and lively adhering to them. For the common people, of whom our strength most consists, so only trust and expect an active care from such whose residence with them hath begot affection, and whose estates amongst them give them an apprehension that they are involved in the same danger with them. Our present Committee receive nothing but what they forcibly extort from the country, wherein they make an unprofitable purchase : for, though they get some money, they lose many hearts ; whereas, if men that have estates, and are well known in their country, were joined with them, the people would generally come in, and offer up all they have for the advancement of the public good : for we have men, horses, and money left, good materials to repair our decayed country, if this honourable Parliament (the great architectors of the Commonwealth), will please to depute us good under-builders to prevent a ruin. In these clouds of trouble that darken our whole nation, this parliament is our only sun, that diffuseth

light to the several Committees of every county ; and they, like
stars, should impart their borrowed shine to us ; but, if they be
unknown stars, they do not direct, but distract, the pilot in his
passage. In these our miseries as we have many sharers, so (if
it had been thought necessary) there had been many more
presenters of them to you; but we, in the name of all, do humbly
invocate a gracious and speedy redress, the unhappy distance
of our country prohibiting our frequent addresses to this
honoured place; where, having briefly unbosomed our
grievances, we humbly leave them to the wisdom and
consideration of this honourable Parliament".[55]

In the above speech can be detected shades of Lucy Hutchinson's opinion
of the *'worsted stocking committee men'* given earlier. The petition itself
echoed the two main concerns raised in Thomas Beaumont's speech : Firstly,
the lack of their chief commander (whose return they urgently requested)
and, secondly, the restoration to the local committee of the county's 'great
and good' who claimed to uphold the Cause.

The petition was worded as follows :-

"To the honourable House of Commons assembled in
Parliament.

"The humble Petition of the Gentlemen, Freeholders, and Best-
affected of Leicestershire.
"Sheweth, That whereas, by the gracious care and wisdom of
this honourable house, in appointing gentlemen of judgement
and estates of this country to sit in a Committee for regulating
and equal disposing of all affairs in it; and by sending unto us
the right honourable the Lord Grey of Groby (who first rescued
us out of the hands of malignants, and the town of Leicester,
then ready to be seized on by them, setting therein a garrison,
and gave encouragement and life to the actions of all the well-
affected) with chief command of all the military forces of this
county; the officers of the army, being under the power of one,
were kept from emulation and dissension, and the hearts of the
county so inclined, that they were quickly able to resist, and
almost to suppress the enemy : But we are now (by leaving the
best men of the county out of the Committee in a late Ordinance
for the Militia) fallen under the government of such, whose
defects of number, acquaintance amongst us, and interests in

the county, cannot afford us any probable hopes of preservation, nor the Commonwealth any considerable assistance; and, in the unhappy absence of the lord Grey, most of our horses and arms were sold, our soldiers dispersed, and their headless officers in continual differences for pre-eminence; whilst the enemy's are so much strengthened and increased, that the well-affected are daily exposed to the loss of liberty, their goods to plunder, and their rents sequestered and seized on by the adverse party, that till of late had never the boldness or power to attempt it. In this sad condition we have (under God) no refuge but to this honourable House, the effects and influence of whose great prudence and care the Commonwealth in general, and our county in particular, have so largely and frequently tasted. We do again, therefore, supplicate this honourable and great Council, in ease of our great sufferings, to send again speedily to us the lord Grey, invested with power over the forces of this county, that, under his command, the now dishevelled soldiers being unanimously collected, we may be again able to give limits to the now unbounded enemy; and to command those gentlemen that are appointed to it to sit in the Committee, and do not appear, to repair to the county, and to serve in it; and to add such gentlemen of known integrity and interest in the country, as may so generally draw the affections of this county, that we may the sooner be wholly freed both of these miseries and their authors. And we shall always have cause to pray for the continuance of happy success to this just and honourable Parliament".[56]

The account given of the military situation in Leicestershire in this petition does not entirely square with the picture of unbroken local victories gained at negligible cost as presented in the reports given to Parliament by members of the local committee and some local commanders, such as Francis Hacker.

The petition itself, however, stands as one of the best testimonies to the leadership contribution made by Lord Grey of Groby to the morale and the military efforts of the Leicestershire parliamentarians.

It is not clear in the short term whether the petition succeeded or failed in its prime objective. Lord Grey does not appear to have returned to Leicester on any permanent basis during the winter of 1644/45. The reasons for this are open to speculation. It is possible, with some difficulty, to piece together some evidence of his activities and whereabouts over this period.

During the month of November at least, at the time that the petition was presented and was being considered, Lord Grey was at his London residence - Exeter House, St. John's, Clerkenwell. On the eighth day of that month he wrote to his friend Sir Samuel Luke at Newport Pagnell on behalf of William Noell of the Rutland family of royalists. Sir Samuel had detained some of Noell's cattle and was, reasonably one might think given the reputation of the Noell family in the conflict, suspicious of his affiliations.

Indeed Sir Samuel had written the following letter to his father, Sir Oliver Luke, on 1st November.

"..... There is in this town, one William Noell who professes himself to have £12,000 per annum, a Leicestershire man, and has brought 15 brave oxen into Sir A. Chester's ground. The variety of his stories, together with his carriage, makes us suspect him, so we have presumed to stay both him and his cattle. His brothers we know are all malignants and himself has been malignant enough : Lord Grey and my cousin Purefoy will inform you more particularly of him. Enquire of him as much as you can for I would very fain have these cattle to begin a store for my garrison. His examination receive here inclosed [sic]..... "[(57)]*

Lord Grey's letter of 8th November to Sir Samuel Luke both defended William Noell and linked him to the Leicestershire Petition in support of Grey himself :-

"St. John's.
Being informed by William Noel that you gave order for the staying of his person and cattle on suspicion, I desire that you will take notice of his good affection to Parliament, whereof he gave such a large testimony that his reality is unquestionable. On my first coming to Leicester he did voluntarily lend £500 for the service of the State, besides divers other large sums to buy arms for the garrison of Leicester. He still continues faithful to the State for he attends Parliament and is one of the presenters of the Leics. petition. Excuse him for not waiting on you according to his promise, and in respect that he waits here on public affairs and my occasions, which will hold him here till Wednesday or Thursday, I desire that his cattle may remain in those meadows where they were at his coming up [to London], and that on his repair to you you will deliver them to him.

167

P.S. Mr. Noell hears that the King's forces intend for these parts, Therefore I do, in his behalf, desire you, that in case of danger his cattle may be secured".[58]

Whatever may have happened to William Noell's cattle, something is known of the progress of the Leicestershire Petition. On 28th November it was reported to the House of Commons by Sir Gilbert Gerard on behalf of the Committee of Both Kingdoms,

"That whereas this House formerly referred unto that Committee the consideration of a petition from the county of Leicester; that Committee, in regard of their other great affairs, can have no time for the examining thereof : It is therefore ordered, that the said petition be referred to the examination and consideration of the Committee formerly appointed for Leicestershire, where Mr. Knightly has the chair".[59]

The buck had been passed back to the earlier parliamentary committee set up in the spring of 1644 to examine the differences between the local commanders and the Leicestershire Committee. As is the way with such parliamentary committees it provided a method of delay until larger political developments or events on the field of battle made its further work superfluous.

Back in Leicestershire during the months of November and December the offensive against Ashby-de-le-Zouch was intensified. The following report from Leicester gave news of the latest initiative against the *'den of rob-carriers'* and lost no opportunity to indulge in a detailed piece of parliamentarian propaganda against their local opponents calculated to strengthen the prejudices of the godly reader against the dissolute, immoral, 'papist' cavaliers.

"Lester, Nov.14.
Sir, our forces are gone with the Derby horse towards Ashby; but the enemy are very strong, and their works good; they have vaults under the ground, through which they can go from one fort to another at their pleasure; provisions they have in good store; hung-beef a-plenty round their kitchen within, and have been lately killing and salting of more. There are as debased wicked wretches there as if they had been raked out of hell, as we are informed by some that have come from thence : they have invented a new kind of compliment for a kind of protestation; and if they affirm or deny a thing, it is usual to do

168

it with this saying, "The devil suck my soul through a tobacco-pipe", if such a thing be so, or not so, in their ordinary speech. And this is no wonder, for they have three malignant priests there, such as will drink and roar, and domineer and swear, as well as ever a Cabb of them all; and end and begin one health after another; and swear and domineer, so as it would make one's heart to ache to hear the country people to relate what they heard of them. The Cabb will cozen and cheat one another most wonderfully; steal one another's horses, and ride out and sell them; and sometimes come again, sometimes run away, as if they were even at their wits end. The earl of Huntingdon is in the garrison; but the lord of Loughborough, his brother, is not there; there are also many Irish there, who have lately made a new fort, a very strong work, and it is called the Irish fort; who have been bold upon some clashing between them and those that profess themselves to be Protestants in the Ashby garrison. The Irish rebels have told them to their faces, that they fight for the old true Catholic Religion, which is better than ours, and puts them in a better condition than they that are heretics; and swear that, if ever they be straitened by a siege, that they will burn the town to the ground. But our forces are gone to try what they can do; and I hope in a short time to give you a further account of their actions".[60]

At the outbreak of the civil war additions had been made to the fortifications of Ashby castle. The old medieval walls alone would have been no match for seventeenth century cannon without some form of earth work being thrown up to absorb the shot. It is possible that the whole castle was ringed by some form of protective earthworks. The detached fort, now known as Mount House, was also built at this time. Its purpose would have been firstly to protect the east side of the castle from a direct assault, this being the only side exposed. Any enemy engaged in attacking this section would then have to face a constant threat from the fort in their rear. There was a tunnel (one of the 'vaults under the ground' referred to in the above despatch) from the castle's kitchen tower to the fort which not only was used to supply the fort with food but could be used to convey troops through into the building. Thus there was provision for mounting sallies out to attack any enemy, engaged on the eastern side, in the rear. The common name for this fortification, as is shown by the above parliamentarian report, is the Irish Fort. This does not mean, however, that its inhabitants were necessarily Irish. Parliament, for propaganda purposes, tried to accuse the king of using foreign aid - particularly the Catholic Irish

- and therefore lost no opportunity in labelling any soldier who had served in Ireland during the 1641 rebellion as Irish - even if they were English troops that had been sent over there and had returned. There appears to be no record of Henry Hastings being in receipt of Irish soldiers and none of his officers are listed as Irish. He did, however, have communications with the royalist garrison at Chester and could have received reinforcements from the regiments returned by Ormond, the Lord Lieutenant of Ireland, for the king's service in England via Chester. The fort was a small triangular work ringed by a series of earthworks to give the pattern of something akin to a star fort. Hastings had also fortified some buildings in the town itself as there is reference to his 'outworks' there. It is also likely that the church would have some military presence as its tower overlooked the castle walls and would provide an attacker with a very important vantage point.

The reference in the parliamentarian report to the salting down and hanging up of beef in the castle kitchen and stores indicates the onset of winter and the anticipation by the defenders of their being largely confined to their winter quarters. Although Lord Loughborough was reported to be absent the parliamentarian spies noted the presence of his elder brother Ferdinando. After the death of their father Ferdinando had become the sixth Earl of Huntingdon in November 1643. His lands and house at Donington had then been attacked by the parliamentarians on whose side he had (nominally) taken the field at Edgehill. In order to seek security he fled to the castle at Ashby and lived there for the duration of hostilities.

The characterisation of the Ashby garrison as a bunch of immoral, dissolute, devilish, papist cavaliers was no more or less accurate than the royalist projection of the parliamentarians as dour, narrow minded, psalm-singing republicans. Both myths contained elements of truth but were generalised to cover people in a middle ground that was to shift as time passed.

Name-calling the opposition is a necessary concomitant of war. It can also become a perverse form of tribute - the involuntary homage of the resentful. Henry Hastings is described by Warburton in *Memoirs of Prince Rupert and the Cavaliers* as **"..... the model of a partisan leader. ..... He professed no scruples; he bore a blue banner blazoned with a furnace, and the candid motto, 'Quasi Ignis Conflatoris' ['That which I set alight is consumed'], well suited to his fiery and destructive career; the Parliamentary journals called him 'that notable thief and robber'"**.[61] Martyn Bennett in his research into the career of Lord Loughborough claims to have discovered parliamentarian references to him as *'blind Hastings'*. Whether this relates to an alleged physical impediment or to his 'cavalier' impetuosity, dash and flair is not clear. Bennett also claims to have found royalist references to Lord Grey of Groby as *'the black dwarf'*, a rather unkind but not surprising characterisation judging by his appearance as recorded in portraits. Like his father, the Earl of Stamford, Lord Grey appears to have been short rather than tall in stature, and with long dark hair worn in the fashion of the time for young men of his social class.

These two leading local protagonists and rivals do not appear to have met face to face during this period but they did have occasion to communicate with each other as evidenced by the following letter from Grey to Hastings dated 25th November 1644 concerning a proposed exchange of prisoners :-

> *"We understand that you have given captain Burton and captain West a month's liberty to endeavour an exchange. Your proposition cannot be yielded unto, but if you please to release them for Sir Wingfield Bodenham, now a prisoner in the Tower* (of London), *he shall be set at liberty".*[62]

Captains Burton and West may have been two of the parliamentarian officers taken captive whilst 'making merry' at Kilby a month earlier. The former will be heard of again in January 1647 in connection with Lord Grey's family affairs.

Meanwhile, the parliamentarian pressure on the Ashby garrison continued. The following account, dated 28th November 1644, from 'Perfect Occurrences of Parliament' relates how :-

> *"..... a party from Cole Orton marched to Ashby-de-la-Zouch, which caused the enemy to retreat, and lie close in the castle, so that our forces marched into Ashby; and hearing where Hastings had left his store of provisions (whom, it is reported, is himself gone to the King* [at Oxford], *but for certain he is not in Ashby; but his brother the Earl of Huntingdon is there) but had left some provisions at a house in the town; which our forces hearing of, went into Ashby : And the enemy being retreated into the castle, our forces took carriages, and brought it out into their own quarters at Cole Orton, and sent a summons to the castle, to require it to be surrendered to them for the service of the King and Parliament; but, being denied, go forward with their works at Cole Orton. So that, however, though they do not besiege the castle, yet they will keep them in, and so secure the country from being plundered by them, and procure free trade and free passage in those parts, which will be a great comfort to them".*[63]

A further entry of the same date in the same publication both summarises and emphasises the point:-

"The blocking up of Ashby-de-la-Zouch by the Leicester and Derby forces goes on very well; and the lord Beaumont's house at Cole Orton strongly fortified. There are hopes, if care be taken to prevent the enemy's sending of relief, a good account will be given of that garrison in a short time".[64]

But the following report from 'A Perfect Diurnal' for 31st December 1644 would indicate that the parliamentarian forces were not content with simply blockading Ashby :-

"The Leicester forces at Cole Orton got in very well, and have lately performed a good piece of service against the enemy at Ashby-de-la-Zouch; where entering the town, they beat the enemy into the tower, Hastings's stronghold, took divers papers and many arms".[65]

The Lichfield royalist garrison received similar attention to that afforded to Ashby. The same applied to the royalists at Tutbury Castle after the establishment of a parliamentarian garrison at Burton-upon-Trent. Thus the remaining Hastings forces were separated from each other and bottled up. The only effective royalist garrison of any size in the east midlands was now Newark. In December 1644 combined parliamentarian forces from Nottinghamshire and Derbyshire occupied Southwell *"to block up Newarke, on the North syde Trent"*.[66] The net result of all this was that the local royalist forces were very largely contained and could only wait and hope upon relief from the king's main army in Oxford.

In contrast with the reverses suffered by his forces in Yorkshire and the Midlands during the latter part of 1644 the King had enjoyed an unparalleled run of success in the West of England where he had thwarted the Earl of Essex's attempt to invade Cornwall. With the advent of winter, however, Charles had been forced to return to Oxford, which he had entered with his victorious army on 2nd November.

A move by the royalists at Oxford to relieve their east midlands garrisons was expected by the local parliamentarians. The following letter dated 10th December from the Leicestershire Committee to Sir Samuel Luke expresses such apprehensions and seeks any possible confirmation of their intelligence reports.

"We suppose that your intelligence of the enemy's motions from Banbury to Oxford is more exact than ours. We have been here

172

on some new project for settling garrisons, Col. Rossiter and we of the Committee have a garrison at Coleorton, within reach of a cannonshot of Ashby-de-la-Zouch. We expect that the Oxford party will have an eye to our Midland garrisons which are now in some possibility to be blocked up. Sir T. Fairfax on his march into Notts. with 7 regts of horse, will block up Newark on that side. We have heard from various hands of the enemy's motions, and lately from Northampton, and as it comes to us from your intelligence, that a party of 3,000 horse and foot is marched out from the King's party but which way we know not, nor yet can by any intelligence learn. Communicate such intelligence as you conceive may concern us in these parts, either of Col. Rossiter or ourselves. We are in an honest resolution to join with Nottingham and Derby in one body if we hear of the enemy's march this way. Furnish us with intelligence.

P.S. We desire that your speedy post may bring intelligence to us".[67]

It is interesting to note that the letter from the Committee bears the names of Thomas, Lord Grey of Groby, Thomas Heselrige, Arthur Stavely, Francis Smalley, and William Stanley. This indicates that the commander-in-chief was in Leicester at this particular time, most probably taking charge of the *'new project for settling garrisons'* in conjunction with Colonel Rossiter who was a cavalry commander from Lincolnshire with the Eastern Association's forces.

Further information was later furnished by the 'London Post' of 31st December 1644 which reported that :-

"Prince Rupert is advancing with another party towards Newark, where no doubt but he will be welcomed by the Parliament's forces; for, as we are certainly informed, we have thereabouts already threescore troops of horse, collected out of the garrisons of Derby, Leicester, Lincoln, and Nottingham, besides some others sent by my lord Fairfax to their assistance".[68]

This concentration of parliamentarian power was sufficient for Prince Rupert to abandon his move towards Newark for the time being and the royalist garrisons in the east midlands remained isolated as the year 1645 by our modern calendar dawned.

The king had not abandoned the east midland counties, however, and on 28th December 1644 he issued from Oxford, in the nineteenth year of

173

his reign, in Latin, a new Commission of the Peace for the County of Leicester.

The royalists were not the only ones to issue pronouncements affecting Leicestershire. On 18th January 1645 it was decided in London that the sum of £250 a month be assessed on the county of Leicester to maintain its parliamentarian forces.[69] On 15th February the parliamentary ordinance was passed to put this into effect and a local committee was appointed to ensure compliance. The following list gives a useful roll-call of locally active parliamentarian partisans, at least from the perspective of London. Some names are very familiar :-

"Thomas, Lord Grey of Groby; Theophilus Grey; Sir Edward Hartopp senior; Sir Arthur Hesilrige; Sir George Villers, baronets; Sir Martin Lister; Sir Thomas Hartopp; Sir Roger Smith; William Quarles; John St. John; Thomas Babington; Peter Temple; Arthur Staveley; Henry Smith; Thomas Hesilrige; William Hewett; William Noell; Francis Hacker; Thomas Beaumont; William Danvers; Thomas Cotton; John Stafford; Thomas Pochin; William Sherman; and Thomas Goddard, esquires; John Goodman; John Swinfield, and Francis Smaley, gentlemen; William Stanley, Richard Ludlam, and Edmund Craddock, aldermen".[70]

By another ordinance issued on 20th February 1645 the monthly sum of £273. 15s. 6d. was also to be raised in the county of Leicester, by a similar committee, with almost the same composition, as a contribution towards the maintenance of the Scots' army in England.[71]

During this period Lord Grey of Groby, whether residing either at Leicester, London, or indeed - as seems most likely - spending time between the two, kept himself informed of the important political developments in the capital. A record survives, dated January 7th, 1645, of the issue of a :-

"Pass by Thomas, Lord Grey, for John Littlebury, his personal assistant, who should therefore enjoy all the privileges belonging to servants of Members of Parliament".[72]

Some momentous developments were taking place in London. As 1644 had drawn to a close there were three separate but complicatedly interwoven strands in the political texture of events involving the parliamentarians in the capital.

First there were prolonged negotiations to secure the assent of the House of Lords to the passing of the Self-Denying Ordinance presented to them by the Commons on 19th December. Under this proposal no member of

174

either House of Parliament could hold high office in the Army from forty days after its passing. This had been regarded as both an attempt to avoid a confusion of roles and interests such as had plagued the parliamentarian armies so far in the war and also, in retrospect, a device used by the Independents to sweep aside the mainly irresolute and semi-royalist presbyterian commanders such as the Earl of Essex and the Earl of Manchester. It also, on the face of it, threatened the military commands of MPs such as Oliver Cromwell, a member for Huntingdon, and Lord Grey of Groby, a member for Leicester.

Secondly, there were the continuing moves of the peace party in Parliament to negotiate in some way with the king. Despite the failure of one round of propositions in November the Scots were the principal instigators of a further set of discussions, held at Uxbridge, at the end of January 1645. These talks finally ended in failure in February.

Thirdly, a joint parliamentary committee, of which Oliver Cromwell was a member, was framing the regulations by which a great 'New Model' Army, the future hope of Parliament, was to be created.

With all this Byzantine activity going on it is unlikely that Thomas Grey would have found it possible not to be involved. Indeed, although not a prime mover at this stage, later alliances and developments in his career seem to point strongly in this direction.

As a postscript to this period the execution by a vengeful Parliament of Archbishop Laud (the sometime rector of Ibstock) after a protracted trial is worthy of note. As a fact it is hardly surprising, but it was significant that the House of Commons managed to secure his execution against the reluctance of the House of Lords.

The form of the New Model Army was announced in late January, although it was not instituted until April - when the Self-Denying Ordinance also came into effect - and did not take the field officially until May 1645. The new national army was to consist of ten regiments of horse of six hundred men each, twelve foot regiments of twelve hundred men each, and a regiment of one thousand dragoons. Later another regiment of horse was added to give a total approaching 22,000 men. The army was to be paid for by a levy of £6,000 a month on all the districts under the control of Parliament. It was symbolic of the new feeling for uniformity and discipline that all the infantry were now to be dressed in red coats, with only the facings and cuffs coloured to distinguish the various regiments. Sir Thomas Fairfax was chosen as the commander-in-chief of the New Model Army. Philip Skippon was appointed as Major-General of the Foot. The appointment of the Lieutenant-General of the Horse was left significantly vacant at this stage. In the meantime the other several armies fighting on the side of the Parliament, including those of the Scots and the local militias, continued in existence.

Meanwhile the bottled-up royalist garrisons in the east midlands were becoming less and less successful in their attempts at replenishing their dwindling supplies from an area that had already suffered somewhat at the hands of the parliamentarians themselves. Mr. Noell of Rutland (whose acquaintance we have already made and whose brother William was on the parliamentarian Leicestershire Committee), for instance, had to witness the firing of his own house and those of his neighbours because he refused *"to forfeit his liberty or goods to the justice of Parliament"*.[(73)] Master Andrewes, Rector of Boughton in Northamptonshire, *"had his benefice sequestered, his estate seized, himself three times imprisoned, at last banished from his parish, and then the leads were pulled off his church to be employed* (as Sir Richard Samuel said) *in a better service"*.[(74)]

Mr. Noell and Master Andrewes were clearly not parliamentarian sympathisers but, according to the royalist 'Mercurius Aulicus', the parliamentarians were not *"perfidious only to His Majesties good subjects, but theire owne creatures are practised upon when the plundering spirit possesses them, as is manifest by Colonell Craford* [Crawford] *of Alesbury in his last weekes circule, who hath so pillaged the veryest brethren in and about Northamptonshire that if their prayers take effect heele* [sic] *not dye like a Englishman"*.[(75)]

Another instance of alleged plundering by the parliamentarians in an area from which they normally drew considerable support occurred at Wellingborough where a party of Lord Grey's men ransacked the town and *"What they could not carry away, they spoile, so that the losse sustained by the towne is valued at six thousand pounds"*.[(76)]

Early in February the garrison at Ashby-de-la-Zouch made a sortie to compel the country thereabouts to furnish it with hay. But while the royalists were bringing the provender to their castle they were set upon by a detachment of parliamentarian troops from Coleorton. Bulstrode Whitelocke recorded the incident in the following manner :-

"Feb. 4, 1645 - Colonell Hastings, for the King, sent out warrants for carriages to fetch hay to Ashby. The Parliament's forces sent out their warrants to bring the hay to Cole Orton; but Hastings was too quick, and had compelled the country to load the hay, and with a strong guard was bringing it to his garrison. Captain Temple, the high-sheriff of the county, having notice thereof, with his troops got between them and Ashby in the van; and, three troops of Derby following in the rear, after a little engagement, Hastings's men fled, and were routed and pursued, 40 of them taken prisoners, 60 horse arms, and all their hay".[(77)]

Captain Temple, the high-sheriff referred to here, was Peter Temple - an active captain and committee man. He is described by the chronicler

Heath as *"..... formerly a linen-draper's apprentice in Friday Street* [in Leicester]; *but his elder brother dying, forsook his trade, and was possessed of £400 a year in Leicestershire; was a Recruit-chosen burgess for that county town* [later in 1645], *as colleague to Sir Arthur Hesilrige; made a captain of horse, and a great committee man ....."*[78] Heath is incorrect here in his reference to Hesilrige; the other borough MP was Lord Grey of Groby himself. Temple replaced Thomas Cooke MP in November 1645. Peter Temple certainly seems to have been one of Lord Grey's most active officers in Leicestershire.

On 21st February a party from Ashby tried to raid, *"..... Mr Quarles his house, a place within some two or three miles of Leicester"*. Quarles was a local parliamentarian Committee man from an Enderby family of some standing. This enterprise also ended in disaster for the would-be plunderers who were routed by a force from Leicester and captured to a man. On 26th February, apparently out of desperation, *"a party of the royalists from Ashby attacked Cole Orton, intending to have surprised and plundered the town, but in the attempt lost seventy or eighty of their horse"*.[79]

The royalist garrison at Belvoir Castle, however, was still able to harass the local parliamentarians. During January a party of twelve troopers from the parliamentarian garrison at Burley House in Rutland escorting two sequestrators on an 'excursion' to Oakham were captured by cavaliers and *"carried prisoners to Belvoir Castle, then under the command of Colonel Lucas"*.[80]

In an attempt to stop this kind of activity the Committee of Both Kingdoms ordered the County Committees of Leicester and Rutland *"to garrison Stonely* [probably Stonesby six miles due south of Belvoir, near Waltham on the Wold] *for the better blocking up of Belvoir Castle, which we conceive will be much to the benefit of those parts if it can be effectively straitened"*.[81] But, according to the parliamentary newssheet 'Perfect Occurrences of Parliament', this did not prevent the 'Cavaliers' from robbing *"Harborough in Leicestershire from one end of the town to the other, beginning at the sign of the Ram, and plundering all along to the Crown"*.

In short, the strife and uncertainty continued. In spite of their territorial gains during 1644 the parliamentarians were still unable to effect an outright victory. *"Two Summers past over"*, lamented one parliamentarian commentator, *"and still we are not saved; our victories so gallently gotten, and (which was more pitty) so graciously bestowed, seem to be put into a bag with holes; what we wonne one time, we lost another; the treasure was exhausted, the countries wasted, a Summer victory proved but a Winters story; the game however set up at Winter, was to be new played again the next Spring, and men's hearts failed them with the observation of these things"*.[82]

NOTES

1.   *Mercurius Veridicus*, Feb. 13th, 1644.
2.   Ibid.
3.   Journal of the House of Commons (C. J.); Vol. III, p. 372.
4.   *Military Scribe*, March 1644. Cited in Victoria County History of Leicestershire. Vol. II.
5.   Lucy Hutchinson, *Memoirs of Colonel Hutchinson*. Everyman Edition, p. 22.
6.   David Underdown, *Pride's Purge*. Oxford, 1971. pp. 12 - 13.
7.   Historical Manuscripts Commission (HMC) : MSS of Earl of Cowper. Vol II., p. 331.
8.   Lucy Hutchinson, op. cit. p. 154.
9.   Ibid. p. 162.
10.   Calendar of State Papers (Domestic Series) [CSP(D)]. Letter from Committee of Both Kingdoms (Signed by Northumberland and John, Lord Maitland) from Arundel House to Sir John Meldrum, dated Feb. 21, 1644.
11.   Lucy Hutchinson, op. cit. p. 172.
12.   Ibid. pp. 173 - 174.
13.   HMC Hastings MSS, Vol. II. p. 124.
14.   Testimony of Geofrey Palmer, in E. Hensman's *Mountsorrel*, in Dryden, *Memorials of Ancient Leicestershire*, Leicester. 1911. p. 127.
15.   *Mercurius Veridicus*, March 26, 1644.
16.   Lucy Hutchinson, op. cit. p. 176.
17.   *Mercurius Veridicus*, March 26, 1644.
18.   C. J. Vol III, pp. 447 - 456.
19.   Calendar of State Papers (Domestic Series) 1644. (Extracts from pp. 129, 140,   158 - 159).
20.   *Military Scribe, publishing his true warlike Preparation to the People*, March 22, 1644.
21.   Ibid
22.   John Vicars, *England's Worthies* (Under whom all the Civill and Bloudy Warres since Anno 1642 to Anno 1647, are related). London, 1845. Part III, p. 169.
23.   *Military Scribe*. op. cit.
24.   Printed Pamphlets in the British Museum. A letter to Lord Grey of Groby ..... from Colonel Henry Grey, Leicester, March 6th, 1643 - 4.
25.   C. J. Vol. III, pp. 423, 424.
26.   Ibid. p. 486.
27.   Ibid. p. 506.

28.   Calendar of State Papers (Domestic Series). May 25th 1644. Proceedings of the Committee of Both Kingdoms - Item 8.

29.   C. J. Vol III. p. 507.

30.   *The Parliament Scoute*, No. 61, 1644, cited by R. E. Sherwood in *Civil Strife in the Midlands, 1642 - 1651*, Phillimore 1874, p. 154.

31.   Richard Symonds, *Diary of the Marches of the Royal Army*, p. 178, cited by R. E. Sherwood in *Civil Strife in the Midlands, 1642 - 1651*, Phillimore 1974, p. 174.

32.   W. Scott, *The Story of Ashby-de-la-Zouch*, Ashby-de-la-Zouch, 1907. p. 204.

33.   I am indebted for much of the detailed information concerning Henry Hastings and his activities to Martyn Bennett and his monograph *Henry Hastings and the Royalist Cause in the East Midlands* taken from the unpublished Ph.D thesis on *The Aristocratic Estate - The Hastings in Leicestershire and South Derbyshire* - Dept., of Local History, Loughborough University of Technology, 1980.

34.   Calendar of State Papers (Domestic Series). May 25th 1644.

35.   Diary of Parliamentary Proceedings, 4th July, 1644.

36.   Journal of the House of Lords (L. J.), Vol. III, p. 552.

37.   C. J. Vol. III. p. 557.

38.   Cited in John Kenyon, *The Civil Wars of England*, Weidenfeld & Nicholson, London, 1988. p. 97.

39.   *A true Relation of a Defeat given to Colonel Hastings by the Lord Grey's forces, July 1, 1644, at Bosworth Field, in the very Place where King Richard the Third was slain.* (London, July 6, 1644); cited in John Nichols, *The History and Antiquities of the County Of Leicester* (London, 1795 - 1815), Vol. IV., Part II, p. 558.

40.   Diary of Parliamentary Proceedings, August 9th, 1644.

41.   *A Perfect Diurnal*, No. 54, 1644.
        or Diary of Parliamentary Proceedings, August 20th, 1644.

42.   Ibid, August 20th, 1644.

43.   Ibid, August 10th, 1644.

44.   *A Perfect Diurnal*, August 23rd, 164.

45.   Journal of the House of Commons (C. J.), Vol. III, p. 592.

46.   Ibid, p. 618.

47.   *The Parliament Scoute*, No. 66 (1644), Thomason Tracts, E 12.

48.   *A Perfect Diurnal*, October 7th, 1644.

49.   *The Letter Books of Sir Samuel Luke* (1644 - 45) HMSO. Calendar No. 810.

50.   Ibid, Calendar No. 1237.

51.   Ibid, Calendar No. 830.

52.   Husband's Ordinances, pp. 572 - 573.

53.   *Alsop's Weekly Account*, Nov. 6; *Parliament Scoute*, Nov. 7; *Mercurius Civicus*, Nov. 7; *True Informer*, Nov. 9; *Perfect Diurnal*, Nov. 11.-all cited in Nichols - *The Civil War in Leicestershire'* - *Appendix to the History of Leicestershire*. p. 38.

54.   *A Perfect Diurnal*, No. 69. (1644).

55.   Quarto Pamphlets, in the British Museum, 1644.

56.   Ibid.

57.   Sir Samuel Luke. op. cit., Calendar No. 77.

58.   Ibid, Calendar No. 926.

59.   C. J.; Vol. III, p. 701.

60.   *A Perfect Diurnal*, Saturday Nov. 16th, 1644.

61.   Warburton, *Memoirs of Prince Rupert and the Cavaliers*, ii, p. 97. (See E. Hensman in Dryden's *Memorials of Ancient Leicestershire*, Leicester, 1911).

62.   HMC. Hastings Manuscripts. p. 134. Letter from Thomas, Lord Grey of Groby to Henry Hastings, Lord Loughborough - Nov. 25th, 1644.

63.   *Perfect Occurrences of Parliament*, Nov. 22 - 29, 1644.

64.   Ibid., Nov. 25 - Dec. 2.

65.   *A Perfect Diurnal*, Dec. 31st, 1644.

66.   Shaw, *History and Antiquities of Staffordshire*, Vol. 1., p. 72. (General History).

67.   Sir Samuel Luke, op. cit., Calendar No. 987.

68.   *London Post*, Dec. 31st, 1644.

69.   C. J., op. cit. Vol, IV. p. 24.

70.   L. J., op. cit. Vol. VII. p. 207.

71.   Ibid, p. 224.

72.   C.S.P.(D)., 1625 - 49, p. 672, para. 252.

73.   Ryves, *Mercurius Rusticus*, Part I, p. 66.

74.   *Mercurius Aulicus*, 21 April 1644. Thomason Tracts, E. 47.

75.   Ibid, 8 April 1645.

76.   Ryves, op. cit., Part I, p. 57.

77.   Bulstrode Whitelocke, *Memorials of the English Affairs*, p. 124.

78.   Heath's Chronicle, p. 200. Cited by John Nichols, *The History and Antiquities of the County of Leicester*, (London, 1795 - 1815).

79.   Ibid.

80.   John Nichols; op. cit. Appendix on the Civil War in Leicestershire, p. 40.

81.   C.S.P.(D)., 1644 - 1645, p. 310.

82.   Joshua Spriggs, *Anglia Rediviva*, p. 6. (London, 1647).

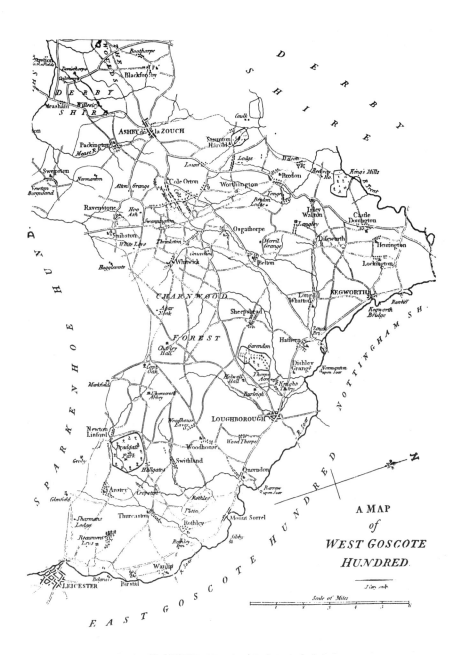

West Goscote Hundred, Leicestershire

181

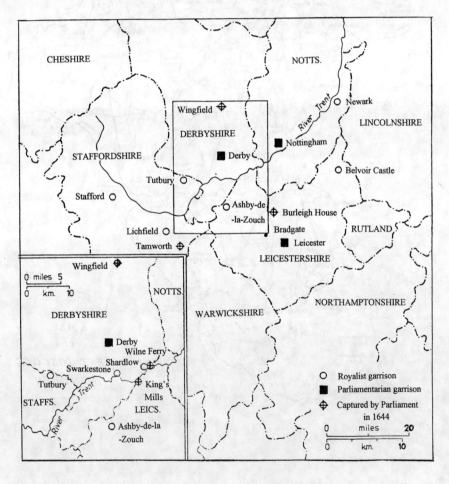

CHESHIRE

NOTTS.

Wingfield ⊕

DERBYSHIRE

■ Derby

River Trent

○ Newark

LINCOLNSHIRE

STAFFORDSHIRE

■ Nottingham

Tutbury ○

○ Belvoir Castle

Stafford ○

Ashby-de ○
-la-Zouch

⊕ Burleigh House

Lichfield ○

Bradgate ●

RUTLAND

Tamworth ⊕

■ Leicester

LEICESTERSHIRE

Wingfield ⊕

NOTTS.

0 miles 5
0 km. 10

DERBYSHIRE

WARWICKSHIRE

NORTHAMPTONSHIRE

■ Derby
Wilne Ferry
Shardlow ⊕
Swarkestone ○
Tutbury ○

STAFFS.

River Trent

⊕ King's
Mills

LEICS.

○ Ashby-de-la
-Zouch

○ Royalist garrison
■ Parliamentarian garrison
⊕ Captured by Parliament
in 1644

0   miles   20
0   km.   10

The civil war in the East Midlands

182

Earl of Stamford

Sir Arthur Heselrige

Lord Grey of Groby

Lord Grey of Groby

Four military colours

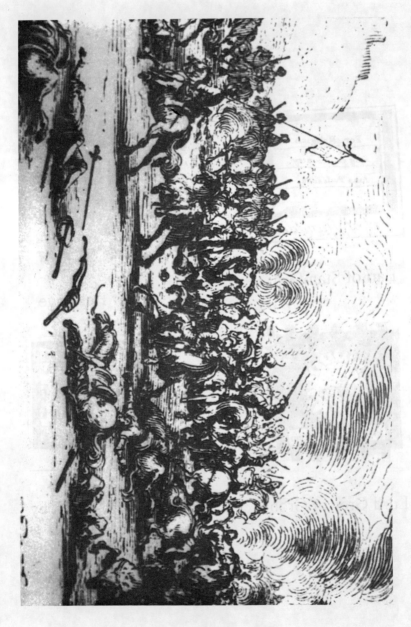

Cavalry Combat

CHAPTER SIX

THE 'SELF-DENYING' MP AND THE KING'S 'LEICESTER MARCH': SIEGE, STORM AND REDEMPTION (1645)

> *"Therefore saith the Lord, the Lord of Hosts, O my people that dwellest in Zion, be not afraid of the Assyrian : Though he smite thee with the rod, and lift his staff against thee, ... for yet a very little while, and his destruction shall be accomplished."*
>
> **(Isaiah. Chapt. 10. vs 24 & 25)**

Just as the parliamentarian victories nationally seemed to fail to deliver their promise, so locally, despite the bottling-up of the local royalist garrisons, there was still a feeling of insecurity. There remained doubts about the ability of Lord Grey of Groby's Leicester garrison to defend the inhabitants of the county from the incursions of royalist forces from beyond Leicestershire's borders.

Even the security of Leicester itself was by no means guaranteed. Unlike either neighbouring Northampton or Nottingham it had never been the base of a large parliamentarian army. Indeed, the last large armed force Leicester had seen was the royal army when it left with the king to march to rebellious Coventry in the autumn of 1642. Clarendon had commented at the time that, *"If the King were loved* (in Leicester) *as he ought to be, the Parliament was more feared than he"*.[1] In fact the reverse was true. The king's cause only received a positive response from the people of Leicester when they were intimidated by armed force - and not even then in the summer of 1645. Yet Parliament had done little to make Leicester a military stronghold despite its clear adherence to their cause. As early as 1643 Henry Hastings had suggested to Prince Rupert that Leicester could easily be taken as it was *"of no considerable strength and full of wealth"*. The town had taken some precautions, but this was wartime and it had already become relatively impoverished. In 1640 reference had been made to *"the small trading we have had of late in our poor Corporation"*. This was attributable in part to a plague epidemic of the previous year. In 1643 the Corporation had decided to sell as much of the town plate as the Mayor and Chamberlains thought necessary to discharge the civic debts. £86 was raised in this manner. As the civil war progressed more private wealth was concentrated in Leicester, however, as those gentry not strongly committed to the King's cause tended to move, with their valuables, into Leicester which seemed more secure than their own undefended homes and had a garrison. Worse than the town's lack of corporate wealth though was its relatively defenceless condition. The river Soar protected it on the west side and toward the north; the low-lying ground being often extensively water-logged. The 600 yard perimeter walls of the Newarke, the old medieval citadel, remained, offering some security to the south side. The four town gates were still in use, but the rest of the medieval stone walls had gone. Mounds and ditches were all that remained of them. The watch had been strengthened, the gates repaired, and some gunpowder bought for the magazine in the Newarke. Lord Grey of Groby had secured the town for the parliamentary cause at an early stage and established its garrison. From that point on it had never seriously been threatened by a strong enemy force.

In late February 1645 there occurred an incident which sent shock waves through the Leicestershire parliamentarians. A large royalist cavalry force, under Sir Marmaduke Langdale, passing through the county were engaged by a smaller force of parliamentarian dragoons. The results of this action are set out below in accounts from both sides. Firstly the parliamentarian Bulstrode Whitelocke relates that,

> *"Between* [Market] *Harborough and Leicester, a skirmish happened betwixt a party of the King's forces, commanded by Sir Marmaduke Langdale, an eminent commander for his Majesty in the North, and a party of the Parliament's forces. The latter lost about 100 men killed , and 250 taken prisoners; beside a considerable number of horses. The victors lay in Leicester that night ..... ".*[2]

The second report comes from a Shropshire royalist officer in Langdale's force who took part in the engagement.

> *"Between Harborough and Leicester, we met with a party of 800 dragoons of the Parliament forces. They found themselves too few to attack; and therefore, to avoid us, had got into a small wood; but, perceiving themselves discovered, came boldly out, and placed themselves at the entrance of a lane, lining both sides of the hedges with their shot. We immediately attacked, and beat them from the hedges into the wood, and out of it, and forced them at last to a downright run-away, on foot, among the inclosures, where we could not follow them, killed about 100, and took 250 prisoners, with all their horses, and came that night to Leicester".*[3]

The fact that this force of some 2,500 royalist horse and their own 800 dragoons could just enter Leicester without further resistance and spend the night billeted in the town reveals the open state of its defences at the time. There is no record of the actions of the royalists during their brief stay, nor of the reactions of the governor, his garrison, and the local committee.

Langdale's force moved on the following day to the relief of Newark which was once more being besieged by parliamentarian forces, probably including most of the Leicester command.

This incident increased the concern of the Leicestershire parliamentarians who realised that, after managing at last to contain the local royalist garrisons which had so plagued them for over two years, the town and county were still wide open to royalist incursions from outside their own boundaries.

Attempts were made to strengthen the local political position. The membership of the parliamentarian county committee was reinforced.

> *"..... the following names were added to the Committee for Leicestershire : Sir Edward Hartopp, Mr. Thomas Beaumont, Mr. William Quarles, Mr. Thomas Goddard, Mr. Thomas Cotton, Mr. William Sherman, Mr. William Danvers".*[4]

On 20th March it was reported to Parliament that a plot to betray the town to the enemy had been foiled.

> *"Letters from Derby certify a plot intended by Hastings against Leicester, in which he wrought with some of the town to have it to be betrayed to him; but (thanks to God!) the plot is discovered, and divers of the complotters are in custody, and like to suffer".*[5]

Although the political resolve of Leicester might have been strengthened by these two developments it was still wanting in terms of physical defence and adequate number of soldiers. Appeals to London for reinforcements appear to have had little effect.

The capital was still hearing of Leicestershire affairs, however, and some related to past events with an unusual ring. On 18th March it was reported in 'Perfect Occurences' that,

> *"Captain Farmer gave testimony against Muckle John, the King's jester (who hath been some time in London), that he saw him in arms with the Queen's soldiers in a skirmish with some of the Leicester forces; and that, after the skirmish, he came after one of Captain Farmer's men, and struck him on the head, and slew him".*[6]

Lord Grey of Groby was also in London, involving himself in the affairs of the Parliament and its committees, and already beginning to profit from his activities on its behalf. On 14th April 1645 he wrote from the family's town residence of Exeter House, St. John's, Clerkenwell to his friend Sir Samuel Luke, Governor of Newport Pagnell.

"..... Parliament [has] conferred on me the keeping of Olney Park, and I have sent the bearer hereof, Mr. Palmer [probably George Palmer], to take charge thereof under Sir Martin Lister. If there shall be occasion of assistance in the removing of Mrs. Willoughby who now lives in the Lodge, send some of your officers to see the directions I gave Mrs. Willoughby observed, which is in a month's time to depart with her goods from the said Lodge".[7]

The Self-Denying Ordinance was passed by the House of Lords on 3rd April 1645 and gradually came into effect. Now all MPs and Lords, at least in theory, had to resign their army commissions. This affected, amongst others, the Earl of Essex, the Earl of Manchester, Sir William Waller, Lord Grey of Groby, Sir Arthur Hesilrige, and Sir Samuel Luke. The only examples of MPs surviving as army commanders were Oliver Cromwell, Sir William Brereton, and Sir Thomas Middleton, partly through universal recognition of their military abilities and partly through political ingenuity. These exceptions were originally granted on 40 day renewable extensions. Sir Thomas Fairfax and the leadership of the New Model Army required Cromwell as their cavalry commander. Once Parliament had agreed to this in June it was to place him in an exceptionally strong position - and one that was to provide the basis for his future rise to power. He had become the key man; the Army's only spokesman in Parliament, and Parliament's only representative in the Army. He was to become a man courted by both parties, and carefully listened to, because he had armed power to back up his arguments. This was to prove critical in the period from 1645 to 1650.

In the meantime any concerns Lord Grey may have felt about the loss of his command over the Midland Association of Counties might have been affected by a letter he received from Colonel George Booth, a Cheshire landowner and his brother-in-law. Booth, later to become Lord Delamere, was a former royalist who had married Grey's eldest sister, Elizabeth. Staying in Leicester on a visit he wrote on 12th April, 1645 from the town to Lord Grey in London, as follows :-

"My Lord; - Being arrived at this place, which, by reason of your public and private interest in it, lays claim to your utmost

188

endeavours for the preservation of it; I shall make bold to present your Lordship with the weak condition it is in, most obvious to the observing eye. By all men's account, there are not above 200 soldiers in the town, and those as peremptory against discipline as their governors are ignorant of it. I am most confident, nay, durst hazard my life and fortune upon it, that 500 resolute well-managed soldiers, at any time might one day make themselves masters of this town, which if lost will take away all commerce from all the North-west of England; and I can assure you, 'tis God's Providence alone in keeping it from the enemy's knowledge, and suppressing their courage, that is this town's defence; but, when we neglect to serve God in his Providence, by the adhibition [sic] of second means, 'tis just with God to leave us to our own strength, which is nothing but weakness. The grand masters, most sensible of danger, and careful of their own security, have all of them houses in a place of this town called the Newarke, where they are fortifying themselves as strong as may be; which will prove, as I fear, of most dangerous consequence; for, I perceive the townsmen much discontented, conceiving themselves deserted by the Committee to the enemy's mercy. I assure you, my Lord, I espy discontent dispersing itself very fast abroad in this town; and if your lordship's care prevent not, I expect very shortly to hear ill news from this place. Pardon my boldness, excuse my haste, and accept of my profession of being, my Lord, your Lordship's most humble servant, 'GEO, BOOTH'"[8]

Upon receipt of this letter Lord Grey of Groby referred it to the Committee of Both Kingdoms at Derby House in the Strand in order to gain the support of its members for the urgent reinforcement of Leicester and its increased security. The Committee at London wrote on 25th April to the Leicester Committee asking for their response and instructing them to immediately improve the garrison and fortifications of the town. The response of the Leicester Committee to the Committee of Both Kingdoms, dated 1st May, 1645, was as follows :-

"Right Honourable; We received your Lordships' letter, on the 25th of April last, about our fortifications; wherein we shall submit to your Lordships' direction. We never had the least thought to desert the town, or any part of it; but have fortified, and still proceed to fortify, all our outworks, and have of late amended them; and never had farther thoughts in fortifying the Newarke, than for a reserve in time of absolute necessity, and as more safety for our magazine, it being a place very easily

*made a very strong place. Our greatest want is of ordnance
and arms; and therefore we humbly desire your Lordships they
may be speedily sent to us by this bearer, Commissary Blunt;
and that he may have your Lordships' warrant to charge carts,
waggons, and horse, for bringing the same hither, giving
reasonable pay for it.*

We take leave, and are, my Lords,

Your Lordships' most humble servants,

Thomas Hesilrige	*Edmund Cradock*
John Brown	*Valentine Goodman*
Francis Smalley	*John Swinfen*
William Stanley"[9]	

Lord Grey of Groby did not wait idly for this exchange of correspondence
to take place. Upon receipt of the letter from his brother-in-law he
immediately set in hand improvements to the defences of Leicester, some
of which are referred to in the Leicester Committee's letter quoted above.

The following order was issued on 19th April 1645 and leaves little doubt
as to his determination as revealed in the postscript. From the signatures it
seems that Peter Temple is acting on his immediate behalf or in his 'stead'
(hence *Vic'*) in this authorisation: Peter Temple, Theophilus Grey and
Francis Hacker representing the military, and John Browne, Francis Smalley,
and John Swinfen the civilian elements of the local Committee. The Grange
Houses referred to were residences which had farm buildings belonging to
them. The reluctance of their owners to demolish them is understandable.

"By the [Committee of] *Leic.r ffor* [sic] *the necessary defense
and safety of the towne and to prevent the enemys approaches
to the ffortifications thereof and the danger thereof It is ordered
that the Grange howses and all building walls thereto belonginge
or adjoyninge lyinge neare the publicke works on the South side
of the towne shalbe taken downe and removed and the ground
there levelled before Wendsday* [sic] *next. And the owners and
inhabitants of the said Granges and premises are ordered and
required to take downe and dispose the same according to this
Order.*

Pe : Temple Vic'	*John Browne*
Theo : Grey	*ffr. Smalley*
ffrancis Hacker	*John Swynfen*

If defalt [sic] *be made herein the soldiers are ordered to putt this order in present operation and Colonell* [Henry] *Grey is desired to see it done.*

Xix April 1645" [(10)]

Meanwhile, in his headquarters at Oxford, the king was keen to begin another campaigning season. He was in a highly optimistic mood. Although considerable territory had been lost to the enemy during 1644, the main field army of the royalists was still intact, and was barely two days' march from London. In addition, the king's Captain-General in Scotland, the gallant Marquis of Montrose, had greatly discomforted Parliament's Covenanter allies during the late winter; and the royal army in the West Country had destroyed Essex's army there during the previous summer in the Lostwithiel campaign.

To King Charles' feeling of confidence was added that of an increased hatred for the enemy. The execution of his old friend and adviser, Archbishop Laud, in January 1645 and the breakdown of the Uxbridge peace negotiations had convinced him that those who adhered to the Parliamentary party *'were arrant rebels, and that their end must be damnation, ruin, and infamy'*. In the past he had often been accused of weakness and hesitation, but now he was resolved to show that he was a man of strength - a true warrior king.

He chose to demonstrate his determination on Wednesday, 7th May, 1645 when he left Oxford with his army at mid-morning. This was to be his third and final march through the midland counties of England. A direct march on London was not the primary objective. The immediate purpose of the march was the relief of Chester, being besieged by Sir William Brereton, through which town the royalists maintained contact with, and reinforcements from, Ireland. After Chester had been relieved the plan was to restore the royalist presence in the north of England which had been so badly damaged by the Marston Moor defeat.

So what was later to be called the king's *'Leicester march'* began in John Milton's *"bounteous May - flowery May, who from her green lap threw the yellow Cowslip and the pale Primrose"*. As they travelled northwards through the west midlands both Rupert and the king drew men out of the surrounding royalist garrisons in order to supplement their army which, at a little under 11,000 men, was the smallest that Charles had yet commanded in the war. The emptied garrisons were then fired to prevent the enemy from taking them.

This army, marching through the heart of England with its brightly coloured war standards streaming in the breezes against the clear blue May skies, was a picturesque and awesome sight; yet it was an unwelcome plague to the countryfolk through whose areas it passed. Both sides tended to live off the land whilst on the march, but with the royalists it was 'free quarter' usually in a less restrained and less ordered manner than with the parliamentarians. In this campaign a series of burning buildings marked the progress of the royal army.

Meanwhile Parliament, hearing of the king's movements, had set in motion its newly reorganised war machine. Intelligence concerning the movements of the royal army poured into Derby House in the Strand in London from whence the Committee of Both Kingdoms conducted military operations. Instructions were sent to Major-General Browne and Lord General Fairfax to move their forces towards Oxford and so prevent the king's return to his base. Another message was sent to Lieutenant-General Cromwell, who had been observing the king's movements since leaving Oxford, to remain in the pivotal area around Warwick if the royal army continued to move northwards.

The royal army then passed through Staffordshire northwards in the direction of Chester, being joined on their way by forces from the garrisons of Hereford, Dudley Castle, and Ludlow. Whilst he was still in Staffordshire the king learned that Sir William Brereton had abandoned the siege of Chester, leaving the royal army free to prosecute its *'northern design'* without hindrance. Following on the news of Chester, however, came the intelligence that Parliament had sent a strong army into the West Country to crush Goring and that Fairfax *"was himself and his army sat down before Oxford"*.[11] Parliament had *"found by experience the three years last past, that the advantage of that place, situate in the heart of the Kingdom, hath enabled the enemy to have ill influences upon the City and Counties adjoining, and to infest all other parts"*. The fall of Oxford was therefore considered essential in the struggle *"to put an end to the continuance of this unnatural war"*.[12]

The king resolved to relieve the pressure on Oxford, and to strike a possibly fatal blow at Fairfax's New Model Army, before proceeding with the plan to reconquer the North. He recalled Lord Goring from the West Country and summoned General Charles Gerard, commander of the royalist army in South Wales, ordering them to rendezvous with him at Leicester. Having issued these instructions he spent a night at Market Drayton and then turned his army eastwards, passing through Stone and Uttoxeter, and thus on into Hastings' territory on the Staffordshire/Derbyshire borders.

Meanwhile, Thomas Grey was pursuing his interests and those of his allies in London. Sir Samuel Luke wrote from Westminster on 10th May to his friend Walter Long concerning *"the establishing of your Lt. Col. in your government at Newport"* [following the Self-Denying Ordinance coming into effect] and *"the testimony Lord Grey and others gave him in the House of Commons"*.[13] A week later Luke wrote to Lt. Col. Richard Cokayn from Westminster,

> *"This day we had part of our hearing but the best part I hope is behind for they are referred till Thursday to prove their charge and in the meantime our witnesses are to be sworn on both sides. They had nothing to charge me with but the business at Swanbourne which I know they will never make good except they can swear unjustly. Lord Grey and Lord North were my very good friends and many others. .....*[14]

Before the king had decided to march on Leicester there had been a separate development which intensified the efforts of the occupants of the town to improve their situation. On 15th May the Leicester Committee had heard the rumour that Lord Hawley, the royalist governor of Bristol, might try to take Leicester. This information had been gained in the following manner. About the 30th April, a Henry Purefoy, who was a Leicestershire man as well as a royalist lieutenant, *"being at Bristol, and coming early in the morning into the governor, the Lord Hawley's chamber, the chamber* [floor] *being matted, and the governor himself in bed and the* [bed] *curtains drawn, he heard the said lord tell* [Bryan] *O'Neale his bedfellow, that he was upon a gallant design the last night for the taking of Leicester, which would be a business of very great consequence; and that the gentry and townsmen invited him thither (or words to that effect); which he marvelled at, the most of the* [royalist] *gentry being either gone to London or in the king's garrison"*.[15] Upon hearing this Purefoy, fearing for the ruin of his home town and county, the following day (being May Day) sent his wife to London to give warning to his parliamentarian relative, Henry Grey, Earl of Kent, and urging that Leicester be put in a posture of defence. Following this, on the 13th May, he took the occasion of the prisoner exchange of a Lieutenant-Colonel Hudson to travel first to Banbury and then to his brother's house at Belgrave. He then sent a message to another of his relatives, Colonel Henry Grey, at Leicester warning him that if the threatened attack came it would be by storming the area near St. Margaret's Church. A party of horse was sent out to Belgrave to escort him into Leicester where he related his story to the local Committee. He was then sent down to London to give evidence to the House of Commons; the House of Lords having already been briefed by the Earl of Kent.

The Leicestershire Committee persuaded the Mayor of Leicester, William Billars, to call a Common Hall (or full meeting) of the Corporation of the Borough at which all members took a solemn oath that they had neither corresponded with the enemy nor assisted him with the supply of arms. Shops were to be closed and an active service list of townsmen aged between sixteen and sixty was prepared. The Newarke fortifications were to be further strengthened and fresh outworks were to be constructed at Grey Friars and Horsefair Leys to protect the quarters of the main defence Guard which covered the London Road to the south. Several houses lying close to the Newarke walls which could be used by the enemy should have been demolished but this was frustrated in some cases by vested interests. Master Wadland, for example, the clerk to the Committee itself, refused to allow a weak point in that part of the Newarke wall abutting on to some of his land to be strengthened as he was unwilling that the ground be cut up. Help was requested from London and from the neighbouring parliamentarian garrison towns such as Coventry, Derby, Nottingham, and Northampton.

At the same time parliament's committee men in the county attempted to carry on their work as normal. The Leicestershire Committee of Sequestrators ordered on 21st May, *"that Mr. Francis Blithe, solicitor of Sequestrations in this county, employ 16 men as agents under him for gathering proposition and sequestration moneys, etc; and they are to receive 13s. 4d weekly each for pay"*.[16] Clearly, it was anticipated that many local royalists were about to be sequestrated. Such royalist families must have received the news of the advance of the king's army towards the county, when it came, with redoubled enthusiasm.

All was not harmonious, however, even among the county parliamentarians. The Earl of Stamford had given up his military career under something of a cloud in 1643. Sir Arthur Hesilrig MP had been forced by the Self-Denying Ordinance to give up his military commands and the governorship of Newcastle-upon-Tyne, which he had found quite profitable. The two families were beginning to clash again over their interests in Leicestershire where Sir Arthur's brother, Thomas, was a member of the group on the local committee frequently at odds with Stamford and Lord Grey.

On 20th May 1645 the noble peer of the realm and two of his servants assaulted the gallant knight of the shire following parliamentary business. The following day it was ordered by the House of Commons :-

"That Sir Arthur Hesilrige be enjoined to keep the peace between the Earl of Stamford and him; and not to receive or send any challenge ; and, that if any challenge be sent, that presently he acquaint Mr. Speaker therewith".[17]

On 23rd May the Commons received a report on *"the business concerning the assault made upon Sir Arthur Hesilrige by Henry, Earl of Stamford. His own relation, in writing was read"*.[18]

The following month, on 28th June, the Commons moved the *"impeachment of Henry, Earl of Stamford, and of Henry Polton and Matthew Patsall, his servants, by the Commons of England, assembled in Parliament, for breach of their privileges; and for an assault upon, and other injuries done unto, a member of their house"*.

The three were charged that they *"upon the 20th day of May 1645, in the common highway, leading from Perpoole-lane to Clerkenwell, in the county of Middlesex, without any injury, offence, or provocation to them given, and for matters and things done in Parliament, did forcibly and unlawfully make an assault upon Sir Arthur Hesilrige, baronet, a member of the said House of Commons, then riding, in a peaceable manner, from the said House of Commons, unto his own dwelling-house in Islington, in the said county; and being then well known by them ..... to be a member of the said House of Commons; and then and there ..... [they] did suddenly and unexpectedly, several times, thrust and strike the said Sir Arthur Hesilrige, with a drawn sword, and other offensive instruments, against the public peace of this kingdom; to the high breach of the privilege of the said House of Commons, and to the great damage of the said Sir Arthur Hesilrige ; For which offences and misdemeanors the said Commons pray that the said Earl, Henry Polton, and Matthew Patsall may be put to their answers; and that such proceedings may be had thereupon, as shall be agreeable to justice"*.[19]

The case was subsequently heard on 30th September but was afterwards dropped in an attempt to restore harmony. There was to be a similar incident later, in 1648, between these two local rivals.

Lord Grey of Groby may have been out of his native county during May 1645 but there is evidence that he was still actively pursuing the Cause. On 25th May, Juliana, Lady Campden wrote a letter from her house at Brooke to Basil Fielding, the Earl of Denbigh and the parliamentarian commander in the West Midlands, seeking his intervention on her behalf. Denbigh was likely to have been concentrating on other matters at that time, but the letter described how Lady Campden :-

'Is prosecuted with much violence and spleen by the Lord Grey, "who upon bare fancies of his owne suggestion, would prove my Lord deceased a delinquent". In her absence and paucity of friends, [she] prays his lordship to own her cause as far as it is just'.[20]

It is not clear whether the Earl of Denbigh felt able to *'own her cause'*. He was a neighbour of Lord Grey, living at Newnham Paddock just inside Warwickshire from the western edge of Leicestershire, and was shortly to become related to him through marriage. Besides, the widow's late husband was Sir Edward Noel, second Viscount Campden, who had died in the King's garrison at Oxford in March 1643. The Noel family of Rutland, with the exception of the younger brother William, a member of the parliamentarian Leicestershire Committee, were known royalists and had already suffered from Lord Grey's attention as noted earlier.

As the royal army moved nearer to the borders of north-west Leicestershire it is not entirely clear where Lord Grey of Groby was or what he was doing. There are some options, however, that may be speculated upon. Since the Self-Denying Ordinance had now taken effect his military responsibilities in the Midlands might be deemed to have ended; whereas as a Member of Parliament active in the prosecution of the war he might reasonably be expected to be in London. In the capital he could engage in the committee work and general 'politiking' to be expected in the atmosphere of the time. Factions were being formed and reformed at Westminster and it was important to observe the first rule of politics - be there! Thomas Grey also had personal matters to attend to in London; including affairs of the heart, as will be seen. One result of his absence from Leicestershire, however, was to perpetuate the limbo caused by the lack of decisive local parliamentarian leadership. The local committee was split into factions which had previously been expressed as either Lord Grey's adherents versus the others; or Stamford and other absentee 'worthies' against the Hesilriges and the 'worsted stockingmen', with the town corporation members (including the mayor) usually supporting the group which best suited their own interests at the time.

There is just a hint that Lord Grey may have been in the area immediately prior to the siege of Leicester. There were many publications issued by some of the participants shortly after the fall of the town, in an attempt to put their own role and conduct in a good light and to cast doubts upon the behaviour of others. In one of these accounts a parliamentarian officer, Major James Innes, refers to how :-

> *"it is well remembered, that captain* [Peter] ***Temple*, ...,** *when the lord Grey began to fortify Leicester, upon intelligence given of the enemy's advance out of Worcestershire towards Ashby, repaired at midnight to the lord Grey's chamber, earnestly persuading him at that instant to remove to Rockingham* [Castle], *with his forces, cannon, and carriages; .....* "[21]

Upon more detailed examination, however, it is clear that the incident referred to above took place not in May 1645 in relation to the fortifications ordered by Lord Grey following Booth's letter in the April and the king's 'Leicester' march from Oxford via Worcestershire, Shropshire and Staffordshire, but on an earlier occasion. Lord Grey had set in hand some fortification of Leicester much earlier and Innes continues his account concerning Peter Temple's conduct :-

> *"and indeed many times since he hath expressed that fearful disposition; for, in times of danger, pretending business, he usually hastens to London; witness the last journey that he made up thither, upon the approach of the King's Army into these parts".*[22]

It is likely that this last reference to the royal army's approach is the one relating to the attack on Leicester, given the conjunction of events and timing of the publication of Innes' pamphlet.

On Whitsunday, 25th May 1645 the royalist army marched to Burton-on-Trent. King Charles dined and spent the night at Tutbury Castle with Lord Loughborough and the governor, Sir Andrew Kingston. The following day, whilst the army rested at Burton-on-Trent, some of Sir John Gell's Derby Horse raided the quarters of Colonel Horatio Cary's Horse Regiment. Gell had also sent messages to the Leicester Committee warning them of the royalist advance. Even at this stage, however, it seems that the Committee thought that the king might be heading for Newark rather than Leicester.

Richard Symonds' 'Diary of the Marches of the Royal Army in 1645' records how on *"Tuesday, May 27, his Majesty marched to Ashby-de-la-Zouch, the head-garrison of the lord Loughborough; the earl of Lichfield to Packington"*.[23] Symonds, who was of a gentleman's family from Great Yeldham in Essex, was a quarter-master in a troop of horse under Lord Bernard Stuart, son of the Duke of Lennox. He adds that *"in this march this day we marched near Shelford, co. Nottingham, a fair seat of the earl of Chesterfield"*.[24] This was probably a morale raising visit by some of the royalist horse to the garrison of Shelford House near Bingham and too far from the main army's line of march unless there was a deliberate feint in the direction of Newark in order to mislead any parliamentarian scouts.

On Wednesday 28th May King Charles led his forces to summon the parliamentarian garrison of 350 horse and foot under Captain Peter Temple at Coleorton to surrender. As members of the Leicester Committee were later to explain, *"..... by which sudden coming of the King we were prevented of the assistance of our forces at Coleorton, ..., they, being not able to bring off their cannon, could not come to us, the garrison standing within cannon-shot of Ashby-de-la-Zouch, for they had shot from Cole Orton into Ashby town. The enemy then summoned Cole Orton garrison; and General Hastings received a preremtory denial to his demand of it; and our horse, issuing out on the rear of the King's army, took and slew 40 of their horse; .....* "[25]

According to Symonds' Diary, *"His Majesty marched with his army into Cole Orton, a garrison of the enemy's; then by the abbey of Gracedieu, where Sir Thomas Beaumont lives. There remains an entire court of cloisters, hall, etc. ..... His Majesty lay this night at Sir Henry Skipwith's house, called Cotes, in the parish of Prestwold. The headquarters* [of the army] *were at Loughborough".*[26] Whilst the royalist army was quartered at Loughborough and in the surrounding villages it was reinforced by Hastings' own Bluecoats (including three troops of horse totalling 100 men) and 1,200 of the Newark Horse under Sir Richard Willys.

Although the arrival of the main royalist field army was a source of great joy and relief to the local beleaguered royalists, both individual and garrisons, it was not welcomed by either its opponents or non-partisans. It was reported that in its progress through Leicestershire the Royal Army did *"very much spoil the country and impoverish it by imprisoning and ransoming the men".*[27] A royalist officer refers to the army in Leicestershire during this march as *"having treated the country but indifferently, as having deserved no better of us, ..."*[28]

Also on Wednesday, 28th May, Sir Marmaduke Langdale arrived with the advance body of royalist horse to surround Leicester. They signalled their arrival by setting fire to three windmills and one watermill. The main body of the royalist army arrived with King Charles himself and Prince Rupert on the following day :-

> *"Thursday, May 29, his Majesty marched and pitched down before Leicester city, a garrison of the rebels, commanded by Theophilus Grey, third brother to the earl of Kent".*[29]

The king based himself at the manor house at Aylestone, belonging to the Earl of Rutland, to the south of Leicester. On the Wednesday the royalist horse had cut off the town, concentrating most of their number on the east side. The river Soar protected most of the west side. The river crossings at St. Sunday's Bridge (north), West Bridge, and the South Bridge at Swan's Mill were all covered, as were the other main exits that lay behind the parliamentarian outworks on the eastern and southern sides. By quartering in neighbouring villages they prevented the delivery of supplies to the town from the countryside. According to Symonds the king encamped most of his army *"In the plains or meadows near Ailstone for two or three days preceding the siege; and the day before it he marched his army and sat down before the garrison of Leicester in St. Mary's field. The day was spent in preparing for the siege, and in parlies and threatenings".*[30]

It was on this day that news reached the king of the capture of Evesham by Colonel Edward Massey. The loss of the strongly garrisoned Evesham, which had occurred on 20th May, was a serious blow to the royalists as it severed their direct line of communication between Oxford, Worcester and South Wales. It may also have strengthened the king's determination to take Leicester and make it an example to others of the price to be paid for resistance to God's anointed sovereign.

According to Symonds' account Charles already had reason enough to choose Leicester as a target:-

"The siege of Leicester had for its object the annoyance of some of the most forward and formidable enemies of kingly government. Men who had brooded over the real and imagined grievances of the state, till their minds grew intoxicated with the wild reveries of reformation, liberty, and equalization; those, too often, flattering dreams of perfection and prosperity. The people of this little province, early in the reign, shewed a spirit of restlessness; even those who professed themselves to be the teachers of the peaceable doctrines of Jesus, hastened with their appeals to the door of the House of Commons, urging the members, by their heated zeal, eventually to war and desolation. The King, on the other hand, unwilling to lose even a shadow of that prerogative which he had received from his royal ancestors, marched with an army of determined friends towards Leicester, to crush the power which had arisen in that place, and was become extremely injurious to his views and interest. There sat the grand Committees of the Midland district; the most formidable then in the kingdom in aid of the schemes of Parliament. Its central situation commanded the most early intelligence of the movements of the little flying armies and scouting parties which everywhere abounded in its vicinity, and from whence Parliament received daily intelligence and advice in the measures about to be undertaken. At this time some of the leading men of the corporation were men of business, intrigue, and discernment; These formed a part of the committee of safety and intelligence, and were members of the committee for the confiscating of the property of the King's friends. .....

199

"The town of Leicester was chiefly governed by a Committee; viz. Mr. Hewett of Dunton, Mr. Hesilrige, Ludlam a chandler there, Mr. Payne of Medbourne, Newton of Houghton, a receiver, sometime high constable, Read of Thirlby, Mr. Lewyn, and Stanley, a mercer there by the West gate".[31]

The above account, and others like it, go a long way to refute the claims of some more modern commentators that it was Leicester's 'neutrality' or 'equivocation' which led to its siege and sacking in 1645. Rather, as contemporary records and events demonstrate, the town's position was clearly pro-parliamentarian and was seen as such by both sides.

Everitt, along with other commentators[32], suggests that **"the infamous and disastrous sack of the town was the price Leicester had to pay for its lack of decision in supporting either party during the previous three years. This is the essential lesson of all the rather confused events of 1642-5 in Leicestershire. If the town had unequivocally supported parliament, its defences would have been more capable of withstanding Rupert's attack".**[33] Against this view it may be argued that it was not lack of commitment to the 'Good Old Cause' but a lack of arms, men, and adequate fortifications that led to the fall of Leicester; and that the latter does not necessarily reflect directly upon the former.

As far as possible, given the situation in the county as outlined in previous chapters, the town had, from the winter of 1642 onwards, made it quite clear that it stood for the Parliamentary Cause. Even prior to this the 1641 Protestation (or Grand Remonstrance) presented to the king, the election of MPs opposed to the royal policies and the Hastings interest, the lack of response to Henry Hastings' attempt to muster the trained bands for the king with the proclamation of the Commission of Array in 1642, in addition to the evidence from the royalist perspective given by Richard Symonds and others; all these make it quite clear where the sympathies of the corporation and most townspeople lay. Despite this, the many requests and pleas to both Houses of Parliament to reinforce the town during 1643, 1644, and particularly in 1645 went unheeded. Indeed, not only had the Earl of Stamford been despatched to the West Country in 1642, but Sir Arthur Hesilrige and Lord Grey of Groby had been increasingly drawn into the national rather than the local military arena and then removed from both by the Self-Denying Ordinance. The effect of this was to reduce further the local political leadership and effective co-ordination of the parliamentary military forces in the Leicester area.

As far as the idea that a more fervent demonstration of opposition to the king being a deterrent to Prince Rupert's attentions is concerned (and Leicester had experience of *'Prince Robber - the Elector of Plunderland'* in 1642 when he had extorted £500 from the Corporation under threat) one only has to look at the bloody fate of the puritan towns of Birmingham in April 1643 and Bolton in June 1644 to see the weakness of that argument. The following words from a song entitled 'The Armourer's Widow' survived in the folklore of the Birmingham area into the middle of the nineteenth century to commemorate the visit of the 'royal cavalier', the hero of so many novels by maiden ladies, to Birmingham :-

"When Rupert came to Byrmingeham
We were in a sorry plyght,
Our blood God's earth y stained by daye,
Our homes in blazing ruins laye,
And stained the skye at night.

With matchlock and with culverin,
With caliver and drake,
He battered down our ancient town;
He shot our sons and fathers down,
And Hell on earth did make.

Our daughters' cries, our widows' prayers,
Ascended with the flame,
And called down God's wrath divine,
Upon that Royal Murtherer's line,
And brought his kin to shame. "[(34)]

Was this the fate that Leicester could now expect?

The Royal Army which surrounded Leicester in the last days of May 1645 consisted of over 5,500 Horse, over 4,000 Foot and an impressive artillery train including at least six siege pieces. To oppose this vast army the defending forces were pitifully small and their fortifications clearly inadequate.

The Committee members in a published defence of their actions written later in 1645 set out the steps they had taken to remedy the deficiencies that had been identified in the middle of May at the meeting of the Common Hall. A request had been made to the Committee of Both Kingdoms for an order to conscript 1,000 men. Another request was for approval being given to a mutual military alliance with neighbouring counties currently being advocated by Mr. Stavely for the Leicestershire Committee and Captain White (much disliked by Lucy Hutchinson) for the Nottingham Committee. A request was also made for more cannon. This latter request was approved, but the town was lost before they were delivered. The Committee also wrote to Lt. General Oliver Cromwell, who had been stationed with a force near Warwick, informing him of their condition. He replied that he had been ordered to join Fairfax in besieging Oxford but that he had left behind a considerable party of horse with whom they should keep in touch. This they did, writing to Colonel Vermuyden, the commander of that party, informing him of the approach of the King's Army and craving his assistance. They also *"wrote to all the Committees round about us for aid, whom we never failed, upon any call, to contribute our assistance unto, viz. Northampton, Coventry, Nottingham, Derby, together with Colonel Rossiter, hoping amongst them to have procured 500 men at least; and we engaged to pay them, but could not prevail for a man"*.[35]

The perimeter line of the outworks, incomplete as they were, was far too long to be defended by the men available against such overwhelming odds. The Committee attempted, in the short time now available to them, to strengthen key points and to reduce the length of the line. *"We also began to cut off some superfluous works at the Horsefair Leys and the Friers, wherein we saved the* [main] *guard of 150 men, and set on labourers to amend the other works where they were in any way defective, causing the townsmen to shut up their shops, and calling in the country; so that, by the continual pains of the townsmen, women and men, they were very well made up in all places. We then debated the strength of the town, and caused the mayor to give us a list of all that were able to bear arms, from the age of 16 to 60; whereof the list contained about 900 townsmen, besides those that were listed under our own captains"*.[36]

They sent out their commissary to London to collect the additional three cannon that Sir Arthur Hesilrige had sent confirmation of approval for, as well as the purchase of 200 new muskets. These were not to arrive in time either, but 70 carbines were received from Sir Arthur. The Committee also distributed into *"trusty and sure hands, in divers parts of the town"* about 100 barrels of gunpowder and match from the magazine. At this point they say they received news of the king's arrival at Ashby. They had been late in drawing in to Leicester the men from their garrisons in the county. These totalled about 560 men, both horse and foot, of whom only 100 cavalry from Kirby Bellars under Captain Francis Hacker seem to have taken part in the defence of Leicester.

By the time the advance party of royalist horse, under Sir Marmaduke Langdale, had arrived on Wednesday 28th May to cut off the town and to check on the weak points of the defensive line on the eastern side, the size of the garrison had been fixed. There were the regular cavalry of the garrison, presumably Lord Grey of Groby's regiment, now numbering 240 men and led by Captain Thomas Babington of Rothley. To these were now added the cavalry from Kirby Bellars, of the same regiment, under Captain Hacker. The regular infantry of the garrison numbered 480 and were placed under the command of Colonel Henry Grey, assisted by

Lieutenant Colonel Whitbroke, an experienced soldier who had seen military service in the Low Countries. These soldiers are likely to have worn blue coats or grey coats. They were supplemented by the 900 townsmen who were issued with arms and 150 recruits from the county, all of whom are likely to have fought in their civilian clothing. The mettle of the conscripts and the recruits was soon to be tested and the Committee were not sure what to expect. *"We had also sent out our warrants into the country to call them in : who came but slowly, being very malignant in most parts of it; many came that meant not to fight: there were not of them above 150 that were willing to take up arms".*[37]

The Committee did, however, have two strokes of fortune to assist them in the forthcoming struggle. Firstly, Sir Robert Pye of Farringdon, an experienced parliamentarian soldier, had been on his way to join his regiment which was with Colonel Vermuyden but had been cut off from his rendezvous by the royalist advance. The Committee invited him to join them and he freely offered his services. To show their gratitude the Committee presented him with 20 gold pieces. Sir Robert appears to have played a major part in the ensuing events and seems to have been regarded by many commentators as the effective military leader of the defending forces, sometimes being mistakenly referred to as the Governor. Secondly, a party of 200 parliamentarian dragoons, under a Major James Innes, heading for Nottingham through Leicestershire, were persuaded to enter Leicester and assist in its defence. With these additions the total number of defenders amounted to just over 2,000 men with which to defend a line of three miles in compass against an army of almost 10,000 royalists.

The leadership of the defence appears to have been shared amongst the members of the Committee and the Corporation, with deference to the professional expertise of Sir Robert Pye and Major Innes once hostilities began. As Major Innes was to explain later, *"It is true that the lord Grey gave a commission to Theophilus Grey, esq. then eldest captain* [senior captain] *of his Lordship's regiment (the superior officers of the garrison being drawn out upon service) to command in Leicester for some days, when there was not danger of an enemy".*[38] Theophilus Grey was the third brother of the Earl of Kent, the head of the senior branch of the Grey family, but he does not appear to have played a leading role in the ensuing military action. He would have been outranked by Colonel Henry Grey and Lieutenant Colonel Whitbroke in `his Lordship's regiment'.

On the Thursday morning, 29th May, the parliamentarians made dispositions of their horse and foot around the defensive line laid out two years previously by Lord Grey of Groby. The County Committee itself was based in a house overlooking the Market Place at the High Cross in the centre of the town. The Town Corporation was located nearby in the Guildhall close to St. Martin's Church. From these buildings the strategic direction of the defence of the town, such as it might be, was to be determined.

When the main body of the Royal Army with King Charles and Prince Rupert arrived from Loughborough they marched down the eastern side of the town and encamped on the south side in St. Mary's fields. Their artillery was then positioned and the horse and foot allocated to their stations. Prince Rupert quickly identified some existing earthworks, known as the Rawdykes, which faced the southern wall of the Newarke as a natural location for most of his siege guns. The town had already been ringed by royalist cavalry and now strong bodies of foot and further horse were stationed facing the town from various positions to the north, east, and south, particularly at St. Sunday's Bridge. The south wall of the Newarke was, not unnaturally, decided upon as the projected chief point of attack.

Throughout that evening and the whole of the night, Rupert supervised construction of an artillery battery on the Rawdykes facing that south wall. At the same time the defenders, both men and women, soldiers and civilians, worked at improving the defences in anticipation of the coming assault.

There is insufficient space here to give a detailed account of the siege and storming of Leicester but some of the key points concerning the nature and implications of the events are included in the following pages.

Failing to receive a response to his summons to surrender by his stipulated deadline on Friday 30th May, Prince Rupert ordered the commencement of a heavy artillery bombardment of the town. This barrage began at 3 o'clock in the afternoon. The garrison's nine cannon fired in response :-

"And now we plied each other both with cannon and musket-shot, as fast as we could charge and discharge; our cannoneers with one shot broke the carriage of one of the battering pieces, and slew the cannoneer; and thus we continued all the day long, and all the night ....." recorded one of the Committee members later.[39]

According to a story handed down over the years, and quoted by Nichols, a Mr. Bent of the Castle Mill in St. Mary's parish, who was a chief gunner in the garrison, during this point in the siege levelled a cannon at the royal tent pitched at the Rawdykes, fired, and struck off the king's hat from his head.[40] Despite incidents such as this the odds were heavily against the defenders and after three to four hours considerable damage had been done to the city walls and outworks, particularly the south wall of the Newarke.

"..... six great pieces from the [royalist] fort on the South side of the town, playing on a stone wall, vulyned [i.e. volleyed], and made ere 6 of the clock a breach of great space, musket and

cannon continually putting us in mind of something done"
reported Symonds in his diary.[41]

The worn and hardpressed defenders were able to throw up a breastwork
five or six yards inside the breach, lining it with woolpacks dragged from
the woolstaplers' yards in the area. The women and children of the town
are recorded as giving the most active and fearless help. For the next six
hours, with shots flying about them and in the face of continued assault,
they repaired the breach :-

> *"..... the women of the town wrought at it, although the cannon
> bullets and some splinters of stones fell amongst them, and hurt
> some of them; yet, to their exceeding commendation, they went
> on, and made it up, to the enemy's admiration".[42]*

The contribution of the women of the town to this and later stages of
the defence of Leicester is widely referred to by commentators, including
royalists, with considerable respect :-

> *"By Friday night, they [the royalist artillery] had made wide
> breaches, which, by the industry of the men and women of the
> town, were some of them made up again with woolpacks and
> other materials; but the enemy pressing hard upon them with
> their numbers, and that round about the town, they were hard
> put to it, the enemy being numerous without, and they but few
> within, and the works very large".[43]*

> *"The night brought on the thunder and lightning of cannon
> and the rattling of cannon-balls on the houses and in the
> streets".[44]*

Orders were sent to the commanding officers of the royalist brigades to
prepare for a co-ordinated general assault at midnight. Sir Bernard Astley
was directed to storm the town from the north side, both across the river
and at a drawbridge facing Leicester Abbey. Sir Henry Bard, from the
neighbourhood of St. Margaret's, was to take the hornwork along the eastern
line, Belgrave Gate, and the East Gate. Colonel John Russell, at the head
of Prince Rupert's Bluecoats, was to engage the Main Guard, the chief
town battery, outside the Horsefair Leas. Colonel George Lisle, with the
largest concentration of royalist infantry, was to storm the breach in the
south wall of the Newarke. A further twenty groups of 100 to 200 men
were to converge on the walls in different places in an attempt to over-run
the town.

205

"All the evening was a general preparation to assault the town, and a little after 12 of the clock in the night this violent storm began, and continued till after one".[45]

The defenders, *"by reason of the smallness of their numbers and the largeness of their works, were enforced to do duty Wednesday, Thursday, and Friday nights together, the enemy keeping them in constant alarm; which did so tire out the townsmen, that they were the more unfit for the resisting the furious enemy; though, to give them their due, they did as much as could be expected, considering the opposition; for, the enemy had about 4,000 foot, who stormed in so many places at once, that the defendants, wanting reserves, were the more easily over-mastered".*[46]

The garrison, subjected to a midnight storming from all sides, had to contend with well over twenty simultaneous attacks. The royalists, whose field-word was *'God and the Prince'*, attacked with bodies of horse behind their infantry to force them on and to prevent retreat or desertion.

The Newarke saw the fiercest assault and the hardest fighting and many brave individual deeds were observed. The defenders had had little sleep for three days since they had been on watch for two nights, and had fought and built or repaired the defences by day. Some contemporary observers considered that their performance in defence of the Newarke ranked as one of the most striking examples of courage throughout the entire Civil War.

Unfortunately for the gallant and hard pressed defenders the enemy attacks were going better elsewhere. On the eastern, northern and southern sides, the royalist foot forced entries and were swiftly followed by the horse regiments, who poured into the areas between the earthworks and the remains of the city walls.

As the royalists streamed in through the outworks and into the town the resistance at the Newarke continued. The king was obliged to send in his own Life Guard of Foot in their red coats and with their distinctive royal company colours to stiffen the shaken and badly mauled soldiers of Lisle's brigade. A royalist officer from Shropshire recorded how :-

"The inhabitants to shew their over-forward zeal to defend the town, fought in the breach; nay, the very women, to the honour of the Leicester Ladies (if they like it), officiously did their parts ..... "[47]

206

Eventually, attacked from behind by royalist horse and foot who had arrived from the northern and eastern parts of the town as well as those pouring in through the breach in the south wall, the parliamentarians were forced to give way. According to Symonds :-

"The garrison were at length driven from the fortifications, at and near the old castle in the Newark, to St. Martin's Church and church-yard, where they made a stand; but were soon after driven thence, from street to street, avenue to avenue, into the market-place ..... "[48]

Heath's Chronicle records this stage of the fighting as follows :-

"The works being seized, there remained a work of greater bloodshed, the Market-Place, where the defendants had drawn up their artillery, and for three hours space maintained their fight at the cross therein".[49]

The royalists now, in ever greater numbers, converged upon the town's defenders at the market place from all directions. The parliamentarians eventually had no option but to throw down their weapons and ask for quarter. At first this was refused; some defenders, soldiers and townsfolk alike, being killed in the heat of the moment. According to the rules of war of that time the garrison of a town that had refused a summons to surrender had no automatic right to be granted quarter. In particular there was one house in Leicester which appeared to have been more strongly defended, and for longer, than most. This was a house where some of the members of the local parliamentarian County Committee had been meeting. It was said that some Scottish soldiers attached to the garrison had retreated into it and fired upon the attackers right up to the last minute. The royalists stormed the house, set it on fire and put all of its inmates to the sword without mercy.

The accounts of the losses suffered in the storming of Leicester and of the nature and extent of the atrocities that followed its surrender vary; and not always strictly according to the allegiance of the commentator.

Bulstrode Whitelock records that :-

"The king's forces, having entered the town, had a hot encounter at the market-place; and many of them were slain by shot out of windows; that they gave no quarter, but hanged some of the committee, and cut others to pieces. Some letters say that the kennels [gutters] *ran down with blood; that Colonel Grey the governor, and captain Hacker, were wounded and taken*

prisoners, and very many of the garrison put to the sword, and the town miserably plundered. The King entered the town on Sunday, June 1; and sent part of his forces into Derbyshire". [50]

The royalist 'Mercurius Rusticus' more matter-of-factly reports that, *"May 30, his Majesty's army sat down before Leicester; and in the morrow morning early took it by storm, and in it the whole Committee, Sir Robert Pye, and many hundred prisoners, many horses, much powder, arms, and ordnance, and great store of wealth".* [51]

Heath's Chronicle tells how :-

"..... the committee-men, with Sir Robert Pye, colonel Hacker, and colonel Grey [were] taken prisoners, and put into custody; only Sir Robert had some more respect shewed him. The town was plundered, and some of the inhabitants for the present secured; the spoil, part of it carried away to the King's adjacent garrisons of Newark, Ashby-de-la-Zouch, and Belvoir". [52]

Whitelock records on 7th June 1645 that :-

"letters from Leicester informed that the Committee men and the Scots there were not killed in cold blood, as was before reported; but that the King's forces killed divers who prayed for quarter, and put divers women to the sword, and other women and children they turned naked into the streets, and many they ravished". [53]

The Leicestershire historian, James Thompson, paints the following graphic picture of the immediate aftermath of the storming of Leicester :-

"At daybreak all the direful and revolting scenes witnessed in a town taken by storm followed the surrender. The women were exposed to the unmeasured brutalities of a licentious soldiery. The shops were broken into and rifled of their contents. Dwelling houses were entered, and the money, valuables and goods of the inhabitants - which had been increased in amount by the large stores brought into the town for security -were taken away by the plunderers. The record room of the borough was invaded, and robbed of its charters. The mace and seals were stolen by the king's soldiers. Every street presented some scene of blood or outrage. Dead and dying men were on the pavement - naked women thrown down in the public streets. The curses

208

and ribald conversation of the drunken cavaliers mingled with the groans of the dying and the screams of the outraged or widowed women. Such were the scenes and such the sounds which greeted the eyes and the ears of men in Leicester, when the morning opened on the last day of May, 1645".[54]

It is said that during the storming of the town King Charles urged the defenders to lay down their arms and to seek quarter. Accounts vary as to just where and when this occurred. One story is that as he watched the storming from the Raw Dykes he repeatedly said (as if to himself), *"Dear and loving subjects, cry quarter : dear and loving subjects, obey!"*[55]

Another version is that he rode through the streets of Leicester towards the High Cross in the closing stages of the fighting crying much the same message out loud to those still resisting. This image contrasts strongly with that attested to by Humphrey Brown, a Rutland farm-labourer, who recalled the king's alleged reference to the brutalising of parliamentarian prisoners, *"I do not care if they cut them more, for they are mine enemies".*[56]

The lack of adherence to the articles of surrender was confirmed even by the royalists themselves. The King's Secretary for War, Sir Edward Walker, admitted that *"the town [was] miserably sackt* (sic) *without regard to church or hospital",*[57] and this was echoed by Clarendon : *"..... the conquerors pursued their advantage with the usual license of rapine and plunder, and miserably sacked the whole town, without any distinction of persons or places, churches, and hospitals as well as other houses* [being] *made a prey to the enraged and greedy soldier".*[58] These atrocities, according to Clarendon, were nevertheless *"to the exceeding regret of the King : who well knew that, how disaffected soever that town was generally, there were yet many who had faithful hearts to him".*[59]

Whatever Charles' role in, and attitudes towards, these excesses it is unlikely that he would have had much influence over the behaviour of his troops anyway, because atrocities in the heat of the action are almost bound to be committed in stormings of this nature where the royalists are said to have *"lost three for one in the assault".*[60]

As to the actual number of those slain at Leicester 'The Moderate Intelligencer', which was usually fairly accurate in its reporting, claimed that the defenders lost 300 men and the royalists some 400.[61] The royalist 'Mercurius Aulicus' refuted this figure for parliamentarian losses and insisted that only 120 'rebels' were slain, *"which may fully stoppe their shameful mouths that offer to talke of cruelty in his Majesties soldiers".*[62] The Leicester Committee in their own report later talked of a total of 719 bodies requiring burial which accords closely with the figures in 'The Moderate Intelligencer'.

209

The king spent the night of the fall of Leicester at the Countess of Devonshire's house at Leicester Abbey. On the following day he levied a fine of £2,000 on the already despoiled and impoverished inhabitants of Leicester. In addition to this official fine Leicester had already been thoroughly sacked and plundered. Some 140 wagon loads of looted goods and property were removed to Newark-on-Trent as well as the personal pilfering which filled the pockets and bags of the royalist soldiers. The ceremonial mace, the town seals, and borough archives were *"taken away by unruly soldiers"*.[63] The archives were later recovered, but the search for the mace and seals was to prove fruitless. A meeting of the Common Hall held later on 22nd August decided *"that a Newe Mace shalbe* [sic] *bought about the size of the old mace as neare to the price as conveniently"* together with new *"silver and gilte bosses"* engraved with the Town Arms. A Corporation Seal, a Seal of Office and a Mayor's Seal were also to be procured in order that civic business could be formally resumed. The cost of the new mace proved to be £24. 6s. 6d.[64]

The royalist cause was very much encouraged by the capture of Leicester. The parliamentarians, on the other hand, were seized by fear and apprehension.

Both Houses of Parliament were now in the utmost consternation. The Earl of Northumberland reported from the Committee of Both Kingdoms on 2nd June :-

> *"That, upon the report of the taking of Leicester, the said Committee do think it fit that Sir Thomas Fairfax with his army before Oxford should rise and take the field"*[65]

The King, in a letter written to the Queen, dated 8th June, used this expression;

> *'I may, without being too sanguine, affirm, that since this rebellion my affairs were never in so hopeful a way!'*[66]

The king appointed Lord Loughborough as his Governor of Leicester on 2nd June, with Sir Matthew Appleyard as his deputy. A garrison of 1,200 men was left to continue the improvement of the town's defences in case of an attempt by the parliamentarians to retake it. Hastings' efforts to increase his garrison had limited success. Some reports say that up to 400 local royalists, aged between 16 and 60, came in from the county to swell his numbers. Of the original defenders of the town a parliamentarian source records that :-

> *"Few of the 800 soldiers, horse and foot, taken prisoners at Leicester, would by any means take up arms for the other party,*

though they were daily solicited both by threats and promises; only one Smith, a lieutenant, who let them in as soon as he could, is since made a captain by colonel Hastings, and he persuaded about 40 foot soldiers to take up arms with him; but some of them have since deserted him, and got to Coventry".[67]

The parliamentarian newssheet 'Mercurius Britannicus' reported, following the fall of Leicester :-

"that snivelling coward Hastings, ... fortifies [Leicester] so earnestly as if he meant to command the whole country, and then woe to the carriers of Derby; for this Goblin of Ashby-de-la-Zouch means to play the Devil at Leicester".[68]

No sooner had the king left Leicester for Oxford than soldiers burned the Countess of Devonshire's house at Leicester Abbey, which had been his residence after the siege. It is ironic that Lord Loughborough could not save his kinswoman's property which had been previously protected from Lord Grey's threats by order of Parliament.

On 7th June it was recorded in London that :-

"the Countess of Devon had a pass to transport herself, with two servants, a coach and four horses, and two saddle nags, beyond the seas".

The same report also recorded that :-

"..... the Lord Grey of Groby was ordered to have the benefit of two assessments for the twentieth part discovered by him to the Committee at Haberdasher's hall".[69]

This was money voted by the House of Commons as part of the arrears owed to him for his service to the Parliament.

Lord Grey was not at Leicester during its siege and storming, but he was losing no time whilst in London in advancing his financial interests through obtaining shares in the assessment of fines and sequestrations laid upon those identified by him as 'malignants'. He was to find this an increasingly lucrative practice.

On 3rd June the Committee of Both Kingdoms wrote to Sir Thomas Fairfax desiring him to send a trumpeter to Leicester in order to determine the number and 'quality' of the prisoners held there, how many wounded, and to think of exchanges. A week later *"One hundred pounds were voted to Major Innes as a gift from the House of Commons. The same sum*

211

was also given to Sir Robert Pye junior, as a gratuity from the Parliament, and in recompense of his losses at Leicester".[70]

After leaving Leicester the Royal Army had passed southwards through Great Glen, where Prince Rupert's cavalry had been quartered, to Market Harborough. Here a review revealed just how much their forces had been weakened by the action at Leicester *"by the loss of those who were killed and wounded in the storm, by the absence of those who were left behind in the garrison, and by the running away of very many with their plunder",*[71] the town of Leicester having been *"full of wealth which the counties had brought in for safety".*[72]

The number of the remaining foot totalled some 4,000 which, as Clarendon observed, *"was not a body sufficient to fight a battle for a crown",*[73] The royalist horse numbered some 3,600. Whilst the army was at Market Harborough the king heard that Fairfax had abandoned his siege of Oxford. From Market Harborough the royal army marched to Daventry, where it stayed for five days. All this time Fairfax and the New Model Army were drawing nearer.

At eleven o'clock on the night of 10th June, Sir Samuel Luke wrote an urgent letter to his father. In this the Parliament's Scoutmaster-General gives the following information :-

"..... I gave Sir T. Fairfax notice of the party drawing out to go to Oxford and also of its retreating back, and yet I cannot see any hope of King-catching or cavalier-catching.

P.S. Acquaint Lord Grey that I hear the King has summoned pioneers to fortify Holmby that he may hunt more securely".[74]

The message for Lord Grey indicates that he was still involved and interested in the activities within the area.

Unknown to the king the two armies were only six miles apart on 12th June. The next day King Charles was hunting deer in Fawsley Park, about three miles south of Daventry, when he learned of the approach of the 14,000 strong parliamentarian army (of whom some 6,000 were cavalry). Fairfax's force was larger than the king had expected and had already reached Northampton. Upon receiving this news Charles pulled his army back some eighteen miles to Market Harborough, intending to return to Leicester where he could receive support from Newark and reinforcements already due from South Wales, under Sir Charles Gerard, and from the west of England, under Lord Goring.

Fairfax moved north from Northampton, however, on 12th June following the king's withdrawal to Market Harborough. By 13th June the

New Model Army had reached Kislingbury where they were joined by Lieutenant-General Oliver Cromwell, with his Ironsides, to lead the parliamentarian horse. This greatly cheered their whole army. On the night of the 13th Fairfax entered Guilsborough. His advance guard under Henry Ireton had gone four miles further north and taken prisoner some twenty members of Langdale's Northern Horse who had been drinking ale and playing quoits at an inn in a small village, located on the Northamptonshire side of the border with Leicestershire, called Naseby. The following day the battle of Naseby, which was to determine the outcome of the first civil war, was fought.

Accounts of the battle of Naseby are generally well known and are not central to this work. Two brief summaries, one from each side, should suffice to give its essence.

The royalist 'Mercurius Rusticus' records how :-

> *"June 14, was that fatal battle at Naseby down in Northamptonshire, where his Majesty's army (till then victorious) was now, by the uncertainty of war, much worsted, his foot, ordnance, and baggage, most lost. ..... The whole number on both sides slain was conceived not to exceed 400; but more wounded. Above all the rebels' cruelty was remarkable, in killing upon cold blood at least 100 women, whereof some of quality, being commanders' wives; and this was done under the pretence that they were Irish women".* [75]

The Scotsman, Robert Baillie, sums up the course of the battle succinctly from the other perspective :-

> *"Rupert, on the King's right wing carried doune the Parliament's left wing, and made the Independent Collonells Pickering and Montague [under Ireton] flee lyke men; but Cromwell, on our right wing, carried doune Prince Maurice; and while Rupert, in his furie, pursues too farr, Cromwell comes on the back of the King's foot, and Fairfax on their face, and quicklie makes them lay doune their armes. Rupert, with difficultie, did charge through our armie. The King, in persone, did rally againe the body of his horse; but they were again put to flight. The victory was entire".* [76]

The cruelties referred to in the royalist account relate to the treatment meted out by the victorious parliamentarian troops to what John Vicars, one of their publicists, called the *"whores and camp sluts that attended that wicked army"*. [77] The Roundhead foot, in the immediate aftermath of the battle, set about plundering the royal baggage park. They found sheltering there a crowd of raggedly dressed women, whom they took for Irish Catholics because they spoke an unfamiliar language, had 'cruel countenances', and tried to defend themselves with kitchen knives. These were almost certainly not Irishwomen, but the Welsh-speaking women of poor Welsh conscripts in the royalist infantry. A hundred of these unfortunate women were put to the sword. Officers' wives and some camp followers who had also taken shelter in the baggage park were, if not killed, deliberately slashed in the face or had their noses slit so as to never again be attractive to men. To these puritan soldiers of the New Model Army in their self-righteous bloodlust, any woman, whether lady or slut, who chose to follow the evil royal army could only represent Sin Incarnate. This great victory, won in the heart of England, was visible proof to the Puritans that God was with their cause. Many of them believed literally that they were fighting God's enemies, just as the Children of Israel had done in the Old Testament. Unfortunately, the parliamentarian triumph at Naseby was stained by such needless atrocity.

In part the violent and cruel actions of the parliamentarian foot at the close of the battle may be attributed to the desire for revenge for the atrocities committed by that very royalist army in Leicester only two weeks earlier, including their treatment of the townswomen there. The 'roundhead' foot also pillaged their 4,500 prisoners and the 1,000 'cavalier' corpses all across Naseby field. They were, in fact, plundering the plunderers, since, as an eye-witness pointed out, *"No royalist prisoner, but had forty shillings on him after Leicester"*. A letter from Sir Samuel Luke to his father, dated 12th June, spoke of captured royalist soldiers being in possession of considerable quantities of plunder and money; one sergeant having £20.

King Charles, with Prince Rupert and the Life Guard of Horse, had fled from the field in the direction of Leicester at about one o'clock in the afternoon, seeing that the battle was lost. Cromwell had sent his cavalry in pursuit having first warned them that any trooper dismounting to plunder would be put to death. The chase was relentless. The first eleven of the fourteen miles to Leicester were littered with 300 cavalier dead, chopped down from behind in their flight. King Charles and Prince Rupert paused briefly at Wistow Hall, Richard Halford's house, to hurriedly exchange their conspicuous royal saddles for plain ones. They passed through Leicester, with Cromwell in hot pursuit, and headed for Ashby Castle. Lord Loughborough was left to hold Leicester as best, and for as long as, he could. By the evening Cromwell had surrounded the town with his cavalry.

The royal evacuation from Leicester was aided by some of the local people including, according to John Throsby the 18th century Leicestershire historian :-

214

"Thomas Throsbie, my great grandfather, who, in his sovereign's distress, went voluntarily to Leicester with his team, when grey in years, accompanied by his son to assist the king's army in their flight from Leicester, after the fatal battle of Naseby. Surely the driving of a baggage-wagon was, in that case, an amiable, if not an honourable service; it was in the aid of the distressed".[78]

After the battle the scattered and confused royalist foot soldiers who had escaped either death or capture were reduced to a starving and desperate condition. An incident is recorded in the north west Leicestershire village of Ravenstone where an exhausted straggler from the defeated army stole a loaf of bread from a farmhouse. He was detected by a stout maid-servant who slew him upon the dunghill in the farmhouse yard with the 'muddle' she was using to stir her washing.

Lord Grey of Groby was not in Leicester at the time of the fall of the town to the royalists; nor does he appear to have been with the avenging army under Sir Thomas Fairfax which was victorious at Naseby. He would, of course, since the coming into effect of the Self-Denying Ordinance, have had no military command role. The former soldiers of his command are likely to have taken part at Naseby or in the recapture of Leicester, unless they were still prisoners in the town. Also, in the absence of their commander, a detachment of Lord Loughborough's Bluecoat Horse fought on the royalist side under Langdale at Naseby, whilst Sir Robert Pye's Regiment of Horse formed part of Cromwell's division in that action.

The speed with which the fortunes of war had been reversed was remarkable. The military victory at Naseby had political spoils attached to it. For example, the victorious parliamentarians discovered in the king's coach after the battle his personal correspondence which revealed, for all the world to see, his dealings with the Irish and the French in an attempt to raise foreign troops to fight for his cause in England. This was a major propaganda coup for the parliamentarians.

The defeat at Naseby, although admittedly suffered against superior odds, had wiped out for the time being the only effective royalist field army in England. The king decided to lead what men were left to him, apart from the garrison of Leicester who would be used to buy time, to Hereford where he hoped to be joined by forces commanded by Gerard from South Wales and Goring from the West of England.

Richard Symonds recorded that :-

"Towards night this dismall Satterday his Majestie, after the wounded were taken care of in Leicester, and that the two princes

were come safe to him, and had taken order with that garrison, had left two regiments of horse there ..... he marched that night to Ashby".[(79)]

From Ashby he moved on through Lichfield, Wolverhampton, Kidderminster, Bewdley, and Bromyard, arriving at Hereford on 19th June, having completed a march of some 120 miles in only five days.

Meanwhile Sir Thomas Fairfax and the main parliamentarian force arrived outside Leicester on 16th June to join Cromwell's cavalry in the second siege of the town in less than three weeks :-

"On Monday the 16th the whole army came before the town, when the general sent a summons to lord Hastings, to deliver it to the use of the Parliament; who very resolutely refused them : And thereupon command was given for a present storm".[(80)]

Lord Loughborough was at first defiant, but after a heavy artillery bombardment, which included the use of the siege guns used formerly by the royalists and captured at Naseby, lasting three hours, a breach was made in the walls on the Newarke side. Even a commander with the single-minded loyalty of 'blind' (for the royal cause) Hastings had to realise that his position was untenable :-

"On the 17th, being Tuesday, great store of ladders were brought against the town of Leicester, a battery raised, and two demi-cannons and a whole culverin taken at Naseby were placed upon an old work against the Newark, being the very same guns which the King, not many days before, had used against the same place. Whereupon the Lord of Loughborough [after the bombardment and the opening of the breach], seeing the resolution of the enemy, sent a trumpeter out that day with letters, desiring a parlay concerning the surrender of the town; which began that evening, and concluded in an agreement ..... "[(81)]

The parliamentarian commissioners who negotiated with Lord Loughborough were Colonel Pickering and Colonel Rainsborough. Under the articles of surrender the garrison marched out on the morning of Wednesday, 18th June, on fair and honourable terms, without arms and with only staves in their hands. Cavalry officers were allowed to retain their arms. Lord Loughborough was allowed to go to Ashby but the other officers and soldiers were to march to royalist-held Lichfield. All prisoners previously taken by the royalists and still held in Leicester were released.

There was considerable rejoicing in the town. The parliamentarian spoils included some 2,000 stand of arms, 500 horses, 14 pieces of cannon, 30 colours, 50 barrels of gunpowder and other ammunition and stores. The following day was a day of public thanksgiving. There were church collections in London for the relief of Leicester.

Despite all this and a substantial grant from Parliament to make good the town's losses, to provide corn for the poor, and to finance traders in giving work to the poor, it was to be many years before the financial health of the town recovered from the events of May and June 1645. Later, during the Preston campaign of 1648 in the second civil war, when troops under Cromwell passed through Leicester the town was unable to meet their needs for footwear. Only when they reached Nottingham were they able to be supplied - with stockings from Coventry and shoes from Northampton. The Corporation of Leicester received an award of £1,500 from Parliament which was raised from the estates of royalist 'delinquents'. The Town Clerk, Master Wadland, and not less than 40 of the 72 members of the Common Hall were removed for supposed royalist sympathies in the recriminations that followed the retaking of Leicester.

Bulstrode Whitelock records how, on 20th June :-

"..... Sir Thomas Fairfax's army, notwithstanding their hard service, marched from Leicester, and sate before Ashby-de-la-Zouch; and on the 24th, Sir Thomas Fairfax prosecuted the King's forces towards Hereford; and left Colonel Needham governor of Leicester".[82]

This John Needham had been before the outbreak of the civil war a close neighbour of Colonel John Hutchinson and Captain Francis Hacker in south Nottinghamshire.

Even though Fairfax's army had followed the king away from Ashby there was continued skirmishing between the members of Hastings's home garrison and the local parliamentarian forces in Leicester and their re-established outpost at Coleorton. The royalists were forced to continue their constant raiding to feed and re-equip themselves whilst the Coleorton garrison sought to contain them with sporadic attacks. A number of parliamentarian letters refer to minor successes achieved over the 'rob-carriers', but they must still have managed to keep themselves supplied.

On 30th August 1645 the Committee at Leicester was authorised *"to compound with such gentlemen of the country as had assisted or countenanced the King or his party; the money to be employed for the service and maintenance of the garrison and forces in the town"*.[83]

The king was soon back in the east midlands. On 25th August it was reported that :-

> *"From Newark the King marched into Lincolnshire, where his army committed many outrages. The next day he again lay at Belvoir castle; and the next day at Stamford".*[84]

While the Scots army now in England was busy besieging Hereford the king had marched as far as Doncaster in Yorkshire. Here he abandoned his journey to Scotland and decided instead to return on a circuitous route through the midlands. On 1st September Lord Leven, the Scottish commander, received intelligence that the king was advancing to the relief of Hereford from the direction of Worcester. The Scots withdrew to Gloucester, where the sight of these ferocious and ill-clad 'foreigners' caused almost as much apprehension among the local population as it had at Hereford. At the arrival of the king it was reported that *"Hereford and the whole country were transported with exaltation and triumph".*[85] This feeling of relief was no doubt short-lived as Wallington records that the Royal Army immediately *"fell to their wonted course of plundering the country, and some of the houses where the Scots quartered they pulled down, others they burnt down, but plundered them all. Honest men, that had never so little showed themselves for the Parliament were fain to fly, and their wives and children turned out all".*[86]

The king spent the following three months in South Wales and the north-east Midlands, during which time he decimated Gerard's army by despatching it to Chester in a vain attempt to relieve the Nottinghamshire royalist Lord Byron who was besieged there. He also attempted to raise recruits and to rekindle the flame of hope in those who by now saw only too clearly that his cause was lost. On 10th July Fairfax and Massey had destroyed Lord Goring's military power by inflicting a demoralising defeat on his western royalist army at Langport. Fairfax had followed this up on 10th September by taking Bristol from Prince Rupert, who had been despatched there by his uncle from Hereford to take command of its defence. Having promised to hold Bristol for the king Rupert was forced to surrender this key city and valuable port after a heavy bombardment and storming.

For failing to hold Bristol the prince was relieved of his command and his regiment cashiered by the king. Charles, now at Newark, sent a curt and angry written order to Rupert and his brother, Prince Maurice, telling them *"to seek your subsistence somewhere beyond the seas, to which end I send you herewith a pass"*. This affront to his honour was too much for Prince Rupert to bear. With a handful of friends he cut his way recklessly through enemy held territory from Oxford, where he had been allowed to retreat with his men and baggage, to meet his ungrateful uncle face-to-face at Newark. He explained that Bristol had proved impossible to hold and that no treachery or disloyalty had been involved in its loss. It was to no

218

avail; the king was implacable. Rupert and Maurice returned to Oxford, shortly to give up the fight and to leave for the continent.

On 5th November the king returned to his winter quarters at Oxford, having finished, as Clarendon relates :-

> *"the most tedious, and grievous march, that ever king was exercised in, having been almost in perpetual motion from the losse of the battle of Naseby to this hour, with such a variety of dismal accidents as must have broken the spirits of any man who had not been the most magnanimous person in the world".*[(87)]

Roy Sherwood sums up the events covered in this chapter fittingly when he states that :-

> *"the net success of Charles' peregrinations around Wales and the Midlands during 1645 was the relief of Hereford. Without doubt this, the last campaign of the ill-starred monarch, was the most disastrous".*[(88)]

Thus ended the so-called *'Leicester march'* of 1645 with its consequences for town, county, and country.

Before the king had retreated to winter quarters once more at Oxford the royalists had managed to reinforce the garrison at Ashby-de-la-Zouch by between 500 and 600 men towards the end of October. This meant that by November offensive raids were being carried out again by Lord Loughborough from Ashby Castle. Indeed, on 16th January 1646 the garrison sallied out and captured a mortar which was being conveyed by the parliamentarians to their forces besieging Newark. Five days later 300 men were sent from Ashby in an attempt to help raise the siege of Chester. It appears that, for all the boasting of the parliamentarian commentators, the force based at Coleorton was not very effective when it came to containing the 'De La Zouchians'.

In Leicester itself the Corporation responded to the wish of Parliament that Thomas Cook (or Coke), the borough MP elected by the burgesses of Leicester to the Long Parliament with Lord Grey of Groby, be replaced because of his suspected royalist sympathies. :-

> *"Whereas Thomas Coke Esquire was lately elected one of the Burgesses for the said Borough of Leicester for the present Parliament begunn at the Cittie of Westminster the third day of November in the sixteenth yeare of the reigne of our Soveraign Lord the King's Majesty that nowe is and being soe chosen and*

219

in due manner retorned into the Lower House for the
Government of the Kingdom of England accordinge to the forme
of the Statute in that case made as amongest the records of the
Parliament aforesaid remaininge in his Majesty's High Court
of Chancery more plainly appeareth and the said Thomas Coke
sithence [sic] *by the judgement of the House of Commons is*
adjudged incapable to sitt any longer there as a member of the
same duringe the present Parliament".[89]

Cook's replacement was chosen in November 1645; the parliamentarians still maintaining the fiction that their actions were being done in the name of the king :-

"An Assemblie of the Mayor, Bayliffes and Burgesses of the
Burrough aforesaid by virtue of a warrantt [sic] *from John*
Stafford Sherriffe of the County of Leicester grounded on his
Majesty's writt to them directed for the choseinge of a Burgesse
of Parliament in the place of Mr. Thomas Cooke late Burgesse
of the Burrough aforesaid and rendered incapable of that service
as by the said writ and warrant may appeare.

Peter Temple Esquire was then freely chosen a Burgesse for
this Burrough of Leicester to serve in the present Parliament
and was then sworn a ffreeman [sic] *of this Burrough and tooke*
the oath of supremacie and allegiance".[90]

This change strengthened Lord Grey's position in Leicester by adding his erstwhile military subordinate (the commander of the Coleorton garrison) and personal supporter to his growing circle of influence at Westminster.

During the winter of 1645/46 the king at Oxford still thought that he might achieve victory. If he could not gain it upon the battlefield outright he schemed that he might achieve it by encouraging a split between the Presbyterian and Independent wings of the parliamentarians. Events, however, were now moving too swiftly for this to be a successful strategy.

The published contents of his cabinet taken at Naseby had revealed that Charles had intended to introduce foreign mercenaries, notably the French and Irish, into the struggle on his side against the English Protestants, and that he was prepared to abolish the anti-papist laws. This caused considerable disquiet among many of his followers who, being aware of the obviously declining fortunes of the king's cause, now began to wonder whether their loyalties had been misplaced. They also began to consider whether a public withdrawal from his cause at this time might protect them from subsequent post-war sequestration, compounding and other forms of retribution or recrimination. The steady stream of royalists compounding for their estates in an attempt to keep them became a flood, and soldiers began to desert from the remaining royalist forces and garrisons by the score, some actually 'turning their coats' and joining the parliamentarian armies.

The king's few remaining strongholds began to capitulate. During the winter royalist garrisons in the midlands fell in quick succession with the parliamentarian chronicler Vicars recording each one with righteous enthusiasm. In November, for example, General Poyntz assaulted the Nottinghamshire garrison of Shelford House, the defenders of which, according to Vicars :-

> *"..... chose rather to die in their obstinance than to aske for quarter, upon which their desperate pertinacy (there being about 180 of them in the house) most of them suffered by the edge of the sword".* [91]

Vicars also records that on 18th December Hereford was *"surprised and taken by a brave stratagem".* [92]

Royalist garrisons continued to fall throughout the winter and into the New Year. On 2nd February 1646 Belvoir Castle surrendered. Vicars records that Belvoir in Leicestershire :-

> *"..... being one of the strongest and fairest buildings in the Kingdome ..... is reduced to the obedience of the Parliament, Sir Jarvis Lucas, the Governor thereof, with all the Commanders, Officers and Souldiers therein, having permission to march away to Lichfield, upon more honourable termes, indeed, then they deserved".* [93]

Chester surrendered the next day. Ashby Castle, cut off from both Lichfield and Tutbury, was now the sole surviving royalist outpost in Leicestershire. Undaunted, the Ashby garrison continued to show defiance. Whitelock records on 1st January that :-

> *"A party of the King's from Ashby took the minister of Morley and of other towns* [in Derbyshire], *and carried them away prisoners; but Sir John Gell rescued them, and took others of the enemy prisoners".* [94]

On 24th January the parliamentarian 'Mercurius Academicus' incorrectly reported Ashby Castle as having been taken. The confusion arose because of a successful raid made upon Ashby by the Leicester forces

221

in late January. In retaliation for this raid the Ashby garrison attacked and beat up the quarters of the enemy at Coleorton.

Such gestures were becoming increasingly futile, however, given the odds, Eventually talks began between Lord Loughborough and Colonel Needham concerning the conditions that might be agreed for the giving up of Ashby Castle to the parliamentarians.

Colonel John Needham, who had been placed as Governor of Leicester in June by Sir Thomas Fairfax, had been confirmed in that office by both Houses of Parliament with Owen Cambridge as his major and deputy. On 28th February 1646 articles of agreement were entered into between 'Colonel-General Hastings' and 'Colonel Needham', concerning the *"rendition and slighting of Ashby-de-la-Zouch"*.

Vicars records the surrender of Ashby Castle in the following terms :-

"Upon the 4th of this instant March, we received certain intelligence and confirmation of the surrender of the strong garrison of Ashby-de-la-Zouch to Leicester forces. The conditions of surrender were, that Hastings, alias the lord of Loughborough, together with his brother [Ferdinando] *the earl of Huntingdon and colonel* [Isham] *Perkins* [the Governor of the castle], *should have their estates unsequestrated, protections for their persons, and passes to go beyond the sea; the rest of the officers to have liberty to compound for their sequestration, and passes (if desired) to go beyond the seas also; and the garrison to be slighted* [to prevent it being used again] *: too good conditions indeed for such a desperate and wicked Rob-carryer as Hastings was, but that the kingdom may be glad to be rid of such wretches. The surrender was made accordingly on Monday the 2nd instant. We took therein five pieces of ordnance, about 300 arms, little ammunition, and no great store of other provisions; a great mercy and mighty preservation of the peace and tranquillity of all those adjacent parts about it, for which let God have all due praise and glory"*.[95]

The fall of first Belvoir Castle and then Ashby Castle saw the end of the first civil war in Leicestershire. Henry Hastings, Lord Loughborough, the chief military antagonist of Lord Grey of Groby during this period now left the area, ostensibly to pass *'beyond the sea'* into exile - at least for the time being.

As another interesting postscript there is a reference in the Harleian Catalogue as a loose paper, which can no longer be traced, to an original pass granted by Colonel John Needham, governor of Leicester for the Parliament, to a Mr. Richard Symonds [whose account of the siege and storming of Leicester from the royalist viewpoint has been noted], his two servants, with their horses and arms, dated at Leicester on the 5th day of March, 1646.

The first civil war was now drawing rapidly to an end. During March Sir Thomas Fairfax had taken Woodstock House, the last of the ring of garrisons that had protected the king's capital, and was laying siege to Oxford itself. This was the final blow as, in February, Lord Byron had surrendered to Brereton in Cheshire, and Lord Hopton, who had replaced Lord Goring as commander of the King's Army in the West, had surrendered a month later.

On 21st March Sir Jacob Astley, now Lord Astley, marching from Worcester with 3,000 men to join the king at Oxford :-

> *"..... being set upon near Stow on the Wolds in Gloucestershire, by Raynsborough, Fleetwood, and Sir William Brereton, was so much overpowered by their conjunct strength; that he with all his men, after a sharp dispute and some loss were made Prisoners; this being the last encounter that the Royallists [sic] were able to make with those insolent Rebels".*[96]

There is a story that Sir Jacob, who had commanded the royalist foot at Edgehill and Naseby, made a shrewd prediction at the time of his capture. Sitting on a drumhead at Stow-on-the-Wold the white haired sixty-seven year old Roman Catholic veteran said gently to his 'Roundhead' captors, *"You have done your work, boys, and now you may go play - unless you will fall out among yourselves".*

It was to prove a prophetic statement.

To add to the king's misfortunes he had failed to secure the sought for and controversial military support from France and elsewhere abroad. His military options had run out. As a result *"his Majesty, observing at Oxford the ill Posture of his Affairs, resolved to betake himself to the Scotch Army before Newarke".*[97] The Stuarts had been Kings of Scotland long before they had reigned in England. Charles calculated that he might expect to obtain better conditions of surrender from his Scottish subjects than from the English rebels. On 5th May he gave himself up to the Scots at the Saracen's Head Inn at Southwell, near Newark in Nottinghamshire. He was soon to regret his decision.

As soon as Newark had fallen to the Scots on 8th May they struck camp and moved with the king up to Newcastle-upon-Tyne whilst negotiations as to who would make the final settlement with Charles were undertaken. The Scottish presbyterian nobles had enriched themselves with church land at the time of the Reformation in Scotland and so had a strong motive for

223

supporting the Kirk system and the Covenant. The king was an Episcopalian; even one who was suspected of favouring Roman Catholics. The men of importance in Scotland therefore needed a Presbyterian king who would guarantee their estates, put down dangerous social and religious opinions like those beginning to spread amongst the Independents in the New Model Army in England, and do his best to see that Scotland was not dominated by England. The Scots proved unable to come to a deal with Charles, however, on the question of the nature of the state religion.

Within nine month of his surrender to the Scots at Newark Charles was handed over by them to the English Parliament on payment of £200,000 deposit and security for a similar sum to be paid at a later date. With their 'thirty pieces of silver' secured the Scots marched back north of the border. The king, now a prisoner of Parliament, was conveyed to Holdenby (or Holmby) House in Northamptonshire.

* * * *

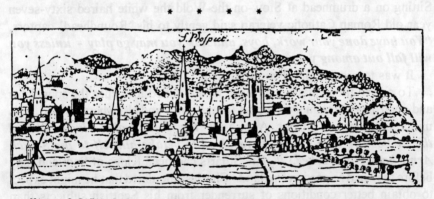

View of C17th Leicester from the south

224

NOTES

1.   Clarendon, *The History of the Rebellion and Civil Wars in England* (published posthumously, 1702 - 1704)
2.   Bulstrode Whitelock, *Memorials of the English Affairs*, p. 130.
3.   From *The History of the Civil Wars in Germany from 1630 to 1635*: also *Genuine Memoirs of the Wars in England in the unhappy Reign of King Charles the First*. Written by a Shropshire Gentleman, who personally served under the King of Sweden in Germany; and on the Royal Side during the unhappy Contests in England. Newark, printed by James Tomlinson, for the Publisher, in 1782. pp. 307 - 310.
   Cited in John Nichols, Appendix to the *History of Leicestershire*, Vol. III; Part II. *The Civil War in Leicestershire*, p. 41.
4.   Journal of the House of Lords (LJ), Vol. VII., p. 276.
5.   *Present Passages of each day's Proceedings in Parliament*, p. 171.
6.   *Present Occurrences*, 12th week, 1645.
7.   *The Letter Books of Sir Samuel Luke* (1644 - 45), HMSO., Calendar No. 1231.
8.   Reproduced in Nichols, op. cit. pp. 41 & 42.
9.   Ibid. p. 42.
10.   Records of the Borough of Leicester, Hall Papers XI, No. 334. - 19 April 1645.
11.   Clarendon, Bk IX, 32.
12.   *Letter from the Speakers of Parliament to the Norwich Committee, 19 May 1645.* (Fairfax Correspondence), *Memorials of the Civil War*, ed. Robert Bell (London, 1849), Vol., pp. 225, 226.
13.   Sir Samuel Luke, op. cit. Calendar No. 1291.
14.   Ibid. Calendar No. 1294.
15.   Nichols, op. cit., p. 46.
16.   Carte's Manuscript concerning the Proceedings of the Leicestershire Committee of Sequestrators, 1645. Cited in Nichols, op. cit. p. 42.
17.   Journal of the House of Commons (CJ), Vol. IV, p. 150.
18.   Ibid. p. 152.
19.   Ibid. p. 188.
20.   HMC. Earl of Denbigh MSS. May 25, 1645, p. 79.
21.   Nichols, op. cit., pp. 50 & 51.
22.   Ibid, p. 51.
23.   *Diary of the Marches of the Royal Army during the great Civil War kept by Richard Symonds*, cited in Nichols, op. cit. p. 44.
24.   Ibid, p. 44.

25.	Nichols, op. cit. p. 47.
26.	Symonds, cited in Nichols, op. cit. p. 44.
27.	C. S. P. (D). 1644-1645, p. 544.
28.	Account by a Shropshire Royalist Officer (see note 3), cited in Nichols, op. cit. p. 46.
29.	Symonds, op. cit. p. 44.
30.	Ibid, p. 45.
31.	Ibid, p. 45.
32.	J. S. Morrill; Jonathan Wilshere & Susan Green, Jack Simmons.
33.	A. M. Everitt, *The Local Community and the Great Rebellion*, Published by the Historical Association, 1969, G.70; pp. 13 - 14.
34.	*The Armourer's Widow* (Song), included in Thomas A. Vaughton's collection of *Tales of Sutton Town and Chase*.
35.	Nichols, op. cit., p. 46.
36.	Ibid, p. 47.
37.	Ibid, p. 47.
38.	Ibid, p. 51.
39.	Ibid, p. 48.
40.	Ibid, p. 42. (footnote)
41.	Symonds, op. cit., p. 44.
42.	Nichols, op. cit., p. 47.
43.	Ibid, p. 52.
44.	Ibid, p. 45.
45.	Ibid, p. 44.
46.	Nichols, op. cit., p. 52.
47.	Ibid, p. 46.
48.	Ibid, p. 45.
49.	Ibid, p. 42.
50.	Whitelock, p. 143.
51.	*Mercurius Rusticus*.
52.	Heath's Chronicle, p. 78.
53.	Whitelock, p. 144.
54.	J. Thompson, *The History of Leicester* (1849), pp. 393 & 394.
55.	Ibid. p. 393.
56.	Nichols, op.cit., p. 42
57.	Walker, *Historical Discourses*, p. 128.
58.	Clarendon, op. cit., Book IX, 33.
59.	Ibid.
60.	Walker, op. cit., p. 128.
61.	*The Moderate Intelligencer*, op. cit.
62.	*Mercurius Aulicus*, 8 June, 1645.
63.	Ibid. [Hall Book, 31 May, 1645]
64.	Ibid. [Hall Book, 22 August, 1645]
65.	L.J., Vol. VII., p. 403.

66. Heath's Chronicle, p. 48.
67. *A Perfect Relation of the Taking of Leicester*, 9th June, 1645. Cited in Nichols, p. 53.
68. *Mercurius Britannicus*, No. 86. June, 1645.
69. C. J., Vol. IV, p. 166.
70. Cited in Nichols, op. cit., p. 54.
71. Clarendon, op. cit., Book IX, 35.
72. *A Perfect Relation of the Taking of Leicester*, 9th June, 1645. Cited in Nichols, p. 53.
73. Clarendon, op. cit., Book IX, 35.
74. Letter Books of Sir Samuel Luke (1644 - 1645), 706.
75. *Mercurius Rusticus*, 1645.
76. The Letters and Journals of Robert Baillie, ed. David Laing, (Edinburgh 1841 - 1842), Vol. II., pp. 286 & 287.
77. John Vicars, *Magnalia Dei Anglicana*, Part IV, p. 164.
78. John Throsby, op. cit. Supplementary Volume to the Leicestershire Views. - *Excursions* - Published 1790. p. 90.
79. Richard Symonds, op. cit., p. 194.
80. Heath's Chronicle, op. cit., p. 80.
81. Ibid.
82. Whitelock, op. cit., p. 147.
83. C. J., Vol. IV., p. 257.
84. Whitelock, op. cit., p. 153.
85. *Military Memoirs of Colonel John Birch* (later Parliamentarian Governor of Hereford) p. 133.
86. Wallington, *Historical Notes of Events*, Vol. II., p. 270.
87. Clarendon, op. cit., Book IX, 132.
88. Roy E. Sherwood, *Civil Strife in the Midlands*, Phillimore & Co., London & Chichester, 1974. p. 206.
89. Records of the Borough of Leicester - Hall Papers XI, No. 421.
90. Ibid ; Hall Papers XI, No. 451 [17 November 1645].
91. John Vicars, *Magnalia Dei Anglicana*, or *England's Parliamentary Chronicle*, (London 1644 - 1646) Part IV, p.177.
92. Ibid ; Part IV, p. 313.
93. Ibid ; Part IV, p. 361.
94. Bulstrode Whitelocke, *Memorials of the English Affairs*, (London, 1682), p. 192.
95. Ibid ; p. 378. [March 4th, 1646].
96. Dugdale, *A Short View of the Late Troubles in England*, pp. 202 - 203.
97. Rushworth, *Historical collections abridged and improved*, Vol. VI, p. 1.

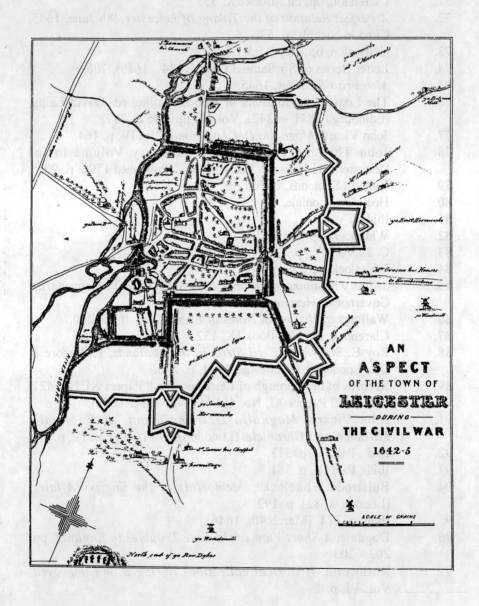

AN
ASPECT
OF THE TOWN OF
LEICESTER
DURING
THE CIVIL WAR
1642-5

An aspect of the town of Leicester during the civil war (1642-5)

Prince Rupert, Count of the Rhineland Palatine

Prince Rupert summoning the garrison of Leicester to surrender 30th May 1645

The Pourtraicture of his Excelleney Sr: Thomas Farfax Generall of all the English forces for the Seruice of ye two houses of Parliament.

Guill: Faithorne Sculp:

Sir Thomas Fairfax

231

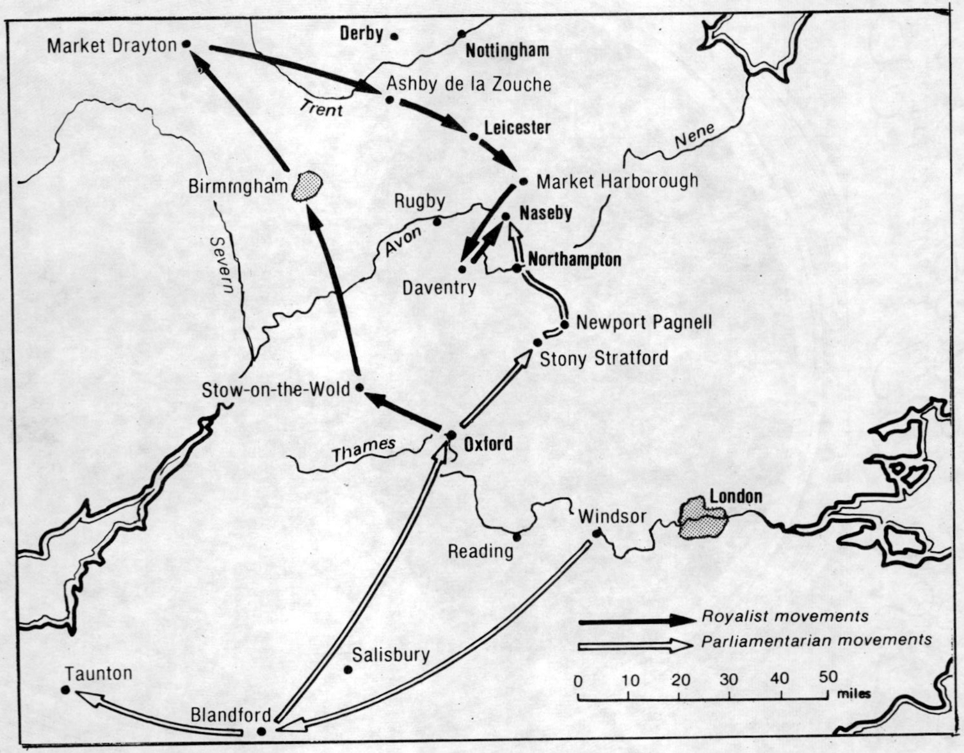

The campaign of the King's 'Leicester March', 1645

CHAPTER SEVEN

THE RISING POLITICIAN (1646 - 1647)
EMERGENCE OF A RADICAL

"Thus saith the Lord to His anointed, ... I will go before thee, and make the crooked places straight .... And I will give thee the treasure of darkness, and hidden riches of secret places."

(Isaiah, Chapter 45. v. 1 - 3)

With the military phase of this titanic constitutional struggle over for the time being the scene shifted to the political context. It is on this stage that Lord Grey of Groby now began to play a role of increasing importance nationally.

It was time first, however, for Lord Grey to turn his mind to family matters and to begin to secure his posterity. Two of his sisters had already become married. Elizabeth had married Colonel George Booth who had sent the warning to Lord Grey about the weakness of Leicester's defences shortly before the royalist attack in the previous year. Then a younger sister, Diana, had married Robert Bruce, Earl of Ailesbury, on 16th February in 1646 at St. Alphege's Church, Cripplegate, in London.

Now it was to be Lord Grey's turn. In the record of marriage licences granted by the Bishop of London in 1646 there is an entry which reads :-

> *"June 4*
> *The Rt. Hon. Thomas, Lord Grey of Grooby, son & heir to the*
> — *Rt. Hon. Henry, Earl of Stamford, Bachelor, 23 (his father's consent), & The Lady Dorothy Bourchier, Spinster, daughter of the Rt. Hon. Edward, late Earl of Bath, deceased (consent of her guardians the Rt. Hon. Oliver, Earl of Bullingbrooke, and Sir Alexander St. John, Knight); at Chelsea or Kensington, Middlesex".*[1]

It is from this entry, stating Lord Grey's age (23) at the time of his marriage, that the year of his birth can be gauged. His bride was one of the co-heirs of the Earl of Bath and there were to be consequent law suits over the question of the Earl's inheritance. She was aged 19 at the time of the marriage. Dorothy's sister, Elizabeth Bourchier, was the third wife of Basil Fielding, Earl of Denbigh. The Denbighs, based at Newnham Paddox in East Warwickshire, were close neighbours, just across the Watling Street old Roman road, from the Greys in West Leicestershire.

Basil Fielding had been the parliamentarian commander-in-chief in the West Midlands during the early stages of the first civil war just as Thomas Grey had been the East Midlands commander-in-chief. Basil's father, the first Earl of Denbigh, was a royalist commander who died of wounds sustained in a battle at Birmingham early in the conflict. The title then passed to his 'roundhead' son. Basil's first wife, whom he had married in 1634, was Lady Ann Weston, daughter of the first Duke of Portland. The match did not last long as she died later that same year in Venice where her husband had been sent as ambassador. He married again a few years later a Barbara Lamb, the *'sole daughter of Sir John Lamb'*. Upon the death of this lady he had then married Elizabeth Bourchier, from whom he had poignant letters of longing and love during his absences fighting in the civil war. Unlike her sister, Dorothy, Elizabeth did not outlive her husband. Upon her death the insatiable Denbigh took as his fourth wife a Dorothie Lane - who, this time, survived him!

The connection, through marriage, between Grey and Denbigh was to prove helpful in some respects but the wrangling over the property inheritance from the Earl of Bath's estate did cause friction between the two noblemen. Documents relating to some of the law suits are to be found in the Warwick Record Office. Lord Grey was represented in these actions by a 'Gamwell Bordman, gentleman'. This is likely to have been Samuel Bordman, one of the two stewards (the other was Randle Cotgrave), appointed to administer Groby Manor in 1636.

Clearly the marriage of Lord Grey was a major landmark in his life and career. Yet little detail of it remains other than the extract recorded above. It seems to have been a love match, although property considerations are likely to have played some part. She was to bear him at least three children, two daughters (Elizabeth and Anne) and a son and heir (also named Thomas). The eldest, Elizabeth, appears to have been conceived before the wedding as scarcely eight months later Dorothy is reported as being *"great with child"* and anxious to be back in London from the country. At the time of Lord Grey's death some ten years later she is reported as being pregnant again but this time no successful birth is recorded. Certainly it seems that whilst he had been away from Leicestershire in late 1644, during 1645, and early 1646, amongst other things he had been courting Dorothy Bourchier and developing new political connections.

Following the wedding Thomas and Dorothy appear to have returned to Leicestershire, probably taking up residence in the manor house at Broughton Astley or with the Earl and Countess Stamford at Bradgate. Of course, parliamentary duties would have meant that Lord Grey visited London regularly.

The second major event to affect Lord Grey's career in 1646 occurred in September when *"about this time the Earl of Essex having overheated*

himself in the chase of a stag in Windsor Forest, departed this life".[2]
The first commander-in-chief of the forces raised by the Parliament had
been a great patron of Thomas Grey and a friend of the Earl of Stamford as
has been noted earlier. He was distantly related to the Greys through the
Ferrers link and also to the Bourchier family. His only child and heir by
his second wife had died in 1637 at the age of five. Lord Grey, aged
fourteen at the time, was taken up by Essex as his friend's son and as a
protege. With two failed and effectively childless marriages behind him
he may well have also played some part in arranging and/or encouraging
the match between Lord Thomas Grey and Lady Dorothy Bourchier. His
unexpected death following the stag hunt was to have political implications
for Lord Grey's future.

Since the cessation of hostilities the energies of the Parliamentarians at
Westminster had been almost exclusively devoted to the struggle for
supremacy between the Presbyterians led by men such as the Earl of Essex,
the Earl of Manchester and Denzil Holles, and the Independents led by Sir
Henry Vane and Oliver Cromwell, and largely backed by the New Model
Army. The death of the Earl of Essex lifted the spirits of the Independents
because it robbed the Presbyterians of an admired figurehead who stood
for much in the popular mind.

A magnificent state funeral was held for the Earl which Lord Grey of
Groby and most of the parliamentarians attended. The funeral cortege
processed from Essex House in the Strand, where he had died on 14th
September, to Westminster Abbey where, after lying in state, he was buried
on 19th September. Parliament paid the full expenses for this which totalled
£5,000. Essex had made his will at the outbreak of the civil war in 1642
and had taken his coffin and winding sheet along to Edgehill just in case he
was killed there. His coffin-plate, exposed at Westminster Abbey in June
1879, is inscribed as follows and details his titles :-

> *"The Right Honourable and Excellent Lord Robert Devereux,*
> *Earl of Essex and Ewe, Viscount Hereford, Lord Ferrars of*
> *Chartley, Bourchier and Lovayne, late Lord Generall of ye*
> *forces raised and imployed* [sic] *by ye Parliament of England,*
> *dyed at Essex House, London, on Monday ye 14th of September.*
> *Anno Domini, 1646, aged 56".*

A wax funeral effigy, dressed in the buff-coat and scarlet breeches which
he had worn at Edgehill was placed in a hearse erected in the south cross of
the Abbey so that people could pay their respects. Unfortunately, during
the night the effigy was hacked and cut, his sword stolen, and his spurs and
achievements torn down. It was a sign of the times that this act of vandalism
was widely thought to have been carried out not by royalists but by
supporters of the anti-presbyterian groups amongst the parliamentarians.

Clarendon, whilst critical of Essex for taking a lead in the revolt against the king, conceded that *"he aimed at no title, office or preferment"*, and admitted that *"he was in his friendships just and constant, and would not have practised foully against his enemies"*.

With the loss of Essex Lord Grey's movement away from the 'Presbyterian' grouping in Parliament seems to have accelerated. He had been friendly with Denzil Holles and Sir Philip Stapleton, the Presbyterian leaders in the House of Commons, in 1643 and 1644. He was also a friend of Sir Samuel Luke, as has been noted, another Presbyterian. Lord Grey began to diverge more openly from their position which was also that of his own father. Father and son were now to find themselves increasingly in different camps.

The Earl of Stamford had been appointed by Parliament in July 1645 as a Commissioner to reside with the Scots army then in England and to which the king had given himself up. His presbyterian allegiance was doubtless an advantage in this. Stamford was sent in December 1646 and January 1647 as a member of the Committee set up by the Parliament to agree articles with the Scots concerning the future of the king and to settle upon relations between the two which suited the 'Presbyterian' interest. In January 1648 he was to go to Scotland again and in the following May was thanked by the House of Lords for his good care and good service in that employment.

How is Lord Grey of Groby's political journey to the Independents and thence to more radical groups to be accounted for? He had always been a zealous puritan but the new circles in which he now began to move and the force of events were to turn him into an active and leading republican.

In 1646 the harvest failed generally in England. This was the first of six deplorable harvests in a row, and the plague also reached London towards the end of that year. The price of bread doubled. A sympathy of opinion and interest grew up in these hard times between London craftsmen, small shopkeepers, wage earners and the radicals in the New Model Army. They were beginning to read pamphlets by writers such as John Lilburne and Richard Overton and to discuss with a new earnestness what should be done about the state of the kingdom now that the long war had been fought and won.

The soldiers of the New Model Army did very little fighting between midsummer 1646 and May Day 1648, but a great deal of arguing and debating took place. The tone and content of their discussions frightened the wealthy landowners in Parliament, particularly those in the presbyterian faction. In England before 1642 the common people did their best to earn a living and to bring up their families. They left politics and government to their social superiors. But now, after their war experiences, the novel idea that they might have civil rights, the right to a say in government - a view supported by the successful challenges to traditionally organised

236

patterns of government in church and state - had begun to germinate amongst soldiers and citizens alike.

It did not go unnoticed in the religious-conscious society of the time that God had favoured those who had resisted temporal and spiritual tyranny in His name. The war had put swords into the hands of those outside the categories of gentry, aristocracy or professional soldiers for the first time.

The Army and the Parliament were now the two powers in the land. The tone of the Army was largely Independent, whilst the dominant party in the Parliament was Presbyterian. King Charles was a prisoner (technically a 'guest' of Parliament), but by clever manoeuvring he did his best to play the two off against each other. He also kept the Scots in mind as a third factor. The king felt, with some justification, that without a monarch at the head of the social pyramid, men of property would never feel secure in their possessions. *"When thieves fall out amongst themselves"*, he is reputed to have told a confidant, *"honest men come into their own"*. He felt that many of the common people would soon tire of the inevitable squabbling between the parliamentarian factions, which he would encourage, and return to their proper allegiance to the crown.

The official agreement between Parliament and the Scots had been signed on 23rd December 1646. The king was then to be conveyed south from Newcastle-upon-Tyne to Holmby House in Northamptonshire. It took until February 1647 to arrange this and in the meantime discussions took place between the king and the parliamentary commissioners. Agreement and reconciliation was hoped for by many. A letter dated 23rd January 1647, referred to earlier, from an Elizabeth Roper to Lady Elizabeth Fielding, Countess Denbigh, gives both national and family news :-

> *"I have to thank your ladyship for the braun, the fine ring (by Captain Lidiate) and now your letter, than which nothing can be more welcome. We are in the country, as many as care for anything but themselves, very sorrowful for the distance betwixt his majesty and the Parliament; it portents ruin I feare* [sic] *to the whole; the Lord in his mercy think upon us for good. ....*
> *Captain Burton lately saw your sister, my Lady Grey, in good health and great with child, but very desirous to be at London ..... "*[(3)]

The Captain Burton referred to here was one of Lord Grey's officers who had been involved in a prisoner exchange in the winter of 1644/45.

En-route to Holmby House the king slept in Leicester at the Angel Inn on the night of 12th February. Holmby was an extravagant mansion in Northamptonshire which had been built for Queen Elizabeth by Sir Christopher Hatton. It had numerous and fantastic embellishments of turrets

237

like chimneys. The king had given it to his wife, Henrietta Maria, for her use and had hunted from here during some of his excursions into this part of the midlands during the first civil war. He was now closely guarded for the Parliament but was not mistreated. Holmby House was a property that was soon to interest Lord Grey of Groby personally.

On 1st March 1647 it was ordered by the House of Commons that Leicester was to be disgarrisoned, and the fortifications were to be slighted. Little seems to have happened in this respect because in July the House of Commons Journal relates the following items :-

> *"July 6, 1647, the petition of Colonel Henry Grey and likewise the officers that formerly served under the Lord Grey at Leicester, was referred to the Committee of that county, for the stating of their accompts* [accounts]*, and paying their arrears".*[4]

> *"July 19, 1647, the garrisons in Leicester were ordered to be disgarrisoned, and the works made sithence* [since] *the troubles dismantled and slighted".*[5]

The above was evidence of a much wider malaise. By the spring of 1647 the men of the New Model Army and the other parliamentarian forces had specific grievances. They had not been paid and the Presbyterian majority in Parliament who feared their political power wanted to disband them. The footsoldiers were owed eighteen weeks' arrears of pay, and the cavalry troopers some forty-three weeks worth. Once they got home cavalry troopers who had laid out their own money for costly equipment would be in desperate need of their back pay to set themselves up again in their workshops or on their farms. Until now soldiers who had lost arms or legs in battle and who owned no property had been put off with a *'licence to beg'*. The soldiers of the New Model Army were no longer prepared to put up with this. They also wanted provision to be made for widows and orphans by what they perceived increasingly as an ungrateful and self-interested Parliament.

The Presbyterians in Parliament decided that they had better get rid of this dangerous fighting force now that it had done their work for them by sending part of it overseas and disbanding the rest of it. When they called for volunteers to go to fight against the 'papists' in Ireland, however, they found that only 167 officers out of some 2,320 and hardly any of the rank and file were prepared to go. They were both alarmed and annoyed at this reaction.

Many of the Puritans both in Parliament and in the City had grown prosperous from victory. For six months after the battle of Naseby, a cavalier was allowed to make his peace by compounding - paying a heavy fine varying from two years' rental of his estate to half its selling price,

238

depending on his rank and importance. In order to pay this fine cavaliers had to borrow at heavy interest rates from City money-lenders or even sell off part of their land so as to save the rest. Other royalist property was sometimes confiscated and given or sold at knock down prices as a reward to influential parliamentarians. Church and Crown lands were also briskly changing hands in the market. So the monied men on Parliament's side - lawyers, merchants, money-lenders and war-contractors - had been able to buy up manors cheaply, and could aspire to become landed gentry. Existing landowners could vastly extend their holdings. Now, if only the Catholic rebels in Ireland could be crushed, there were millions of acres there too, just waiting to be seized.

Even Oliver Cromwell, for all his protestations of being only *"God's poor servant"*, had prospered materially. He had taken up the sword as an impoverished Puritan gentleman who sat in Parliament for Huntingdon but hardly ever spoke, and earned his £300 a year by farming. But after Naseby an official gift was made to him of £2,500 a year in land taken from the confiscated estates of the Marquis of Winchester alone. This income brought Cromwell into the charmed circle of those who had done very well out of the war. Other army leaders who had gone up in the social and material world in this way were nicknamed *`grandees'* by the rank and file. Some members of the Army began to wonder how far they could trust their senior officers in their dealings with the Parliament.

Denzil Holles, who spoke for the rich Presbyterians in Parliament, said of the Army that *"the meanest of men, the basest and vilest of the nation, the lowest of the people have got the power into their hands"*. Baron Holles believed that the Independents were out to *"ruin the King and as many of the nobility and gentry as they could, alter the Government, have no order in the Church nor power in the State over them"*. He thought that any petition from the ranks of the Army was an act of mutiny to be punished by the death penalty. As for payment of arrears to the soldiers, let them wait. This contempt for the wishes and needs of the ordinary soldiers who had won the victories for *`God and Parliament'* was in the end to cost the Presbyterians in Parliament dear.

When the Parliament's commissioners visited Lord General Fairfax's headquarters at Saffron Walden in March 1647 to explain the disbandment proposals and to call for volunteers for the Irish campaign they were struck by the depth of opposition within the Army. A petition was presented to them by soldiers which complained about the treatment of their officers, called for arrears of pay, the need for an indemnity for what had been done during the civil war, freedom from future impressment, and fair treatment for the widows and orphans of soldiers. Such requests in no way transgressed the line drawn by reasonable human expectations and yet such was the clash for many Puritans between the desires for constitutional servatism and godly reformation that even Cromwell felt the soldiers had gone too far in presenting their own petition to Parliament. He regarded it as inconsistent with army discipline. The House of Commons went even further. In a stormy debate on 29th March they gave further proof of how little sympathy the Presbyterian members had for the genuine grievances of the soldiers who had borne the heat and danger of battle for them. They declared their furious dislike of the Army petition and passed a resolution against it. The next day Denzil Holles carried an even more aggressive resolution which declared that all those who continued in their present disobedience should be treated as *'enemies of the State'*. This was deeply resented at Saffron Walden.

A second parliamentary commission to the Army on 15th April had no greater success in either enlisting volunteers for Ireland or in conciliating the troops. Mutiny now began to seem a real possibility. Fairfax had to go to London for medical treatment and his calming influence was removed. To the grievances of the soldiers there were now added the political ideas of such as John Lilburne and the Levellers - seeking greater democracy. Early in May there was talk of going to Holmby to fetch the king. The next stage had been the appointment by the cavalry regiments of *'agitators'* or *'agents'*, to state their grievances. Since Parliament would not listen to these they were addressed to the senior army officers.

The situation was becoming too serious for the House of Commons to ignore. At the beginning of May they sent down a third set of commissioners. This time they included Phillip Skippon, Charles Fleetwood, Oliver Cromwell, and Henry Ireton - now Cromwell's son-in-law. All four were both MPs and senior army officers. The last three were identified as Independents. The commissioners, when they reported back to Parliament the next day that they had found the Army under a deep sense of grievance and much unsettled, must have sympathised in their hearts with the sufferings, if not the unsettlement. Although it seemed for a moment that an understanding had been reached, the Presbyterians were too suspicious of both Cromwell and the army. The London militia was being remodelled on a purely presbyterian basis and secret negotiations took place with the French ambassador and the Scots with a view to reaching an agreement with the king based on a combination of Scots, English Royalists and Presbyterians against the Army and the Independents.

On 25th May the Presbyterians voted in the Commons for a proposal by which the Army was to be disbanded piecemeal, one regiment at a time, in order to avoid united opposition. None of the concessions requested earlier would be guaranteed. They also resolved upon the bringing of the Army's artillery train up from Oxford to London so that it would be under their control. Secretly they were planning to bring the king, the trump card as far as negotiations for a future constitutional settlement were concerned, from Holmby to the capital.

240

The Army at Saffron Walden was stung into revolt by the rumours of these intentions. By 1st June, the date set for the disbandment of the first regiment (the Lord General's), the Army had already taken matters into its own hands. It assembled at a general rendezvous at Newmarket Heath in Suffolk, just across the border from Saffron Walden in Essex. The parliamentary commissioners who had come to order the first disbandment were greeted as enemies and bidden to take their *"two penny pamphlets"* home again. Fairfax, torn between his belief in parliamentary authority and his loyalty to his men, had virtually abdicated his command. The agitators or agents were now in charge. Both Horse and Foot regiments were now represented by them. Cromwell, who had hoped that Parliament would be reasonable, was now forced to a decision. The presbyterian intrigues with the Scots must be crushed; they would mean a second civil war.

It was clear to the Independents that the seizure of the king by the Presbyterians was likely to be the fatal blow to their future. An alliance developed between these MPs, who included Henry Vane, Edmund Ludlow, and Lord Grey of Groby, and the Army. The bridge between them was the small group of senior officers such as Cromwell, Ireton, and Fleetwood who were also Independent MPs.

A certain Cornet George Joyce, originally a tailor, but now high in the Army's confidence, was ordered by the agitators at the Newmarket rendezvous to act in two urgent matters. Joyce had served as a trooper in Cromwell's regiment in the old Eastern Association and then been promoted to Cornet (junior officer and bearer of a troop colour) in the Lord General's Horse Regiment. He had been called to a meeting of a London based group of Army plotters held at Cromwell's house in Drury Lane, London, on 31st May where his instructions were confirmed.

On 1st June he arrived at Oxford with a force of cavalry, hand picked from different New Model Army horse regiments, and secured the artillery train. This had been his first task. He then proceeded with some five hundred horse to Holmby House. His instructions were to prevent the king being carried off to London on the orders of Parliament. This constituted his second task. Whether or not he went on to exceed his orders has been a subject of some debate by historians.

Early on the morning of 4th June the five hundred troopers representing the New Model Army were drawn up in good order on the lawn outside Holmby House. At this point a famous dialogue took place. Joyce had written to Cromwell, or in his absence Sir Arthur Haselrige or Charles Fleetwood, to say that the king had been secured, that his presbyterian guards had fled, and requesting further instructions as a matter of great urgency. He had now decided that he could not afford to wait for a reply

241

and proposed to move the king nearer to the Army rendezvous at Newmarket Heath. King Charles asked to see his commission authorising such action. At this point Joyce could only point to the troopers lined up on their horses behind him. To which gesture Charles made his famous and charmingly ironical reply :-

"It is as fair a commission and as well written as I have seen a commission written in my life - a company of handsome, proper gentlemen".[6]

The king was taken via Hinchingbrooke and Newmarket to a house at Childerley, near Cambridge, for safe keeping.

When the Presbyterians in Parliament heard that soldiers from the Army had taken possession of the artillery train and the king's person they panicked. They quickly voted to expunge Holles' resolution from the parliamentary record and to pay full arrears to the Army. They then planned to arrest Oliver Cromwell, imprison him in the Tower of London, and impeach him. When news of this intention reached him, together with the news of Joyce's action, Cromwell decided to throw in his lot fully with the Army. Taking Hugh Peter, his Army chaplain, with him he rode off at break-neck speed to Newmarket Heath to join the regiments at the general rendezvous. From this point onwards Cromwell emerged publicly as the main spokesman for the Army.

There have been many interpretations of Cromwell's motivations and behaviour during this period and subsequently. Richard Ollard provides what is probably one of the best and fairest summaries of this :-

"Whatever view one takes of Cromwell, short of simplifying him, as many of his contemporaries did, into a hypocrite from first to last, it seems clear that he was a great one for waiting on events. `No man climbs so high as he who does not know where he is going'. His own words spoken on a later occasion come as close to the revelation of his intellectual processes as we are likely to get. His mind was not analytical but it was, perhaps for that reason, all the more easily made up. His practicality and swiftness of decision were never found wanting. What mattered in the spring and early summer of 1647 was to prevent, if at all possible, a breach between Parliament and its army and at all costs between the soldiers and their commanders".[7]

At the Newmarket Heath rendezvous the Army decided to set up an Army Council consisting of senior officers, many of whom were

Independents, but also two junior officers and two members of the rank and file from each regiment. The latter were termed *'agitators'* or *'agents'* and have been referred to earlier. Since their strength lay in keeping the Army together, officers and men alike took a 'Solemn Engagement' on 5th June by which they swore not to disband until their grievances had been remedied.

The Army Council had been set up ostensibly to negotiate on behalf of the army with any other parties, be they Parliament, the King, or the Scots. It also served, however, to curb the independence of the agitators and allow the senior officers (or *'grandees'*) to retain the initiative. As John Lilburne, the Leveller leader, reproached his former comrade Oliver Cromwell, *"You have robbed by your unjust subtilty* (sic) *and shifting tricks the honest and gallant agitators of all their power and authority, and solely placed it in a thing called a council of war, or rather a cabinet junta of seven or eight self-ended fellows, that so you may make your own ends".* Cromwell's intention was to use the army to defeat the intrigues of the presbyterians in Parliament, but also to keep the army under strict military control.

The democratic Leveller movement represented and appealed in the main to the small and medium producers in town and country. They stood for toleration in religious matters, greater representation and involvement in government and politics for the *'free-born Englishman'*, and opposed excessive concentrations of wealth and power. Their main bases of support between 1646 and 1649 were in London and the New Model Army. The appellation of 'Levellers' was given to them by their enemies; they preferred to describe themselves as 'the Moderates'. They are known to history, however, as 'Levellers'. It was the king who had given the nickname of 'Levellers' to those radicals who followed John Lilburne, John Wildman, William Walwyn, Richard Overton and the other pamphleteers. The name of Levellers had first been applied many years before to rebellious villagers who had gone out in armed gangs to level the lord of the manor's hedges and enclosures whenever he tried to annexe the common land. According to the royalist newssheets King Charles had explained that the Levellers *"would make us all even, so that every Jack shall vie with a gentleman, and every gentleman be made a Jack".* The Levellers were England's first political party. They were organised at meetings in London taverns, and had begun to send out their pamphlets, leaflets, and petitions all over England. Local branches began to be established in various parts of the country. The Army Levellers were very active and many of the agitators were amongst their number.

From the spring of 1647, when the cavalry regiments had begun to elect their *'agents'* or *'agitators'* to the crisis of June with the formation of the Army Council, Leveller influence grew rapidly. This was especially so among the cavalry who were almost entirely volunteers and drawn from a more educated and politically aroused strata of society then the infantry. Many of them came from freeholder or citizen families accustomed to political activity. Among them the ideas in the Leveller pamphlets which circulated freely among the troops found a ready response. This was all the more so when these ideas were reinforced by the attempts of the Presbyterian majority in the House of Commons to disband the Army under wholly unacceptable conditions. The problem for the Army Levellers was how to turn this generalised support, when it came to a point of crisis, into a willingness to disobey the commands of the senior officers. Cromwell and Fairfax had built up the Army and led it to victory. It would be difficult for these loyal and highly disciplined soldiers to go against them even in their own, and the democratic, interest when it came to the crunch. This struggle for the leadership of the Army was to prove crucial and Lord Grey was to develop links with both groups.

Meanwhile in London, large numbers of former soldiers from the armies of Essex and Waller, the so-called *'reformadoes'*, poured into the city complaining of their own grievances and threatening to riot. They crowded around the doors of the House of Commons, issuing threats against the members. The Presbyterian MPs realised that this situation could be turned to their advantage. Parliament voted a hasty £10,000 for these *'reformadoes'* and plans were put in hand to turn them into an alternative army under Massey and Waller to oppose the New Model Army.

The New Model Army had moved from Newmarket Heath to Thriplow Heath, seven miles south of Cambridge. Here Cromwell tried to dissuade the Army from its intention of moving on to London. Under persuasion from himself and Fairfax the soldiers agreed to receive a visit from some parliamentary commissioners civilly and silently. The visit ended in failure when the massed ranks of the soldiers cried out *"Justice, Justice!"* The Army moved on again and spent the night of the 10th June at Royston just over the county border in Hertfordshire.

From Royston the Army moved on to St. Albans, which was inside the twenty-five mile limit hopefully proscribed for them by Parliament. In vain the City authorities tried to call out the Trained Bands for their defence and that of Parliament, but the part-time soldiers refused to co-operate. On 15th June the Army issued the "Declaration of the Army", setting out the views of the soldiers on the political situation. The burning question for the soldiers was no longer their arrears of pay, but how the kingdom might best be governed :-

"We are not a mere mercenary army, hired to serve any arbitrary power of a state, but called forth ..... by ..... Parliament to the defence of their own and the people's just rights and liberties".[8]

The Declaration was drafted by Henry Ireton. Its main point was that absolutism must be guarded against at all costs and that a tyrannical government was as dangerous as a tyrannical monarch. It accepted the view of Lilburne that the people were the source of political authority. This delighted Lilburne who was currently imprisoned in the Tower of London by Parliament for a series of offences including a strong verbal attack on the Earl of Manchester. The Leveller leader sent a message of congratulations to his old comrade Lt. General Cromwell for the actions he was now taking for the proper cause. To ensure their accountability to the people, Parliament must be made much more representative and the duration between elections should be shorter. As for the immediate question, the present Parliament should be purged of those who had abused their position of trust, and especially those who had wantonly libelled the Army.

As the members of Parliament began to be more and more concerned about the advance of the Army on London a further broadside of a similar nature entitled the 'Humble Remonstrance' arrived on 24th June. The pace of events was quickening. The Army now specifically charged the eleven most hostile Presbyterian members, including Denzil Holles, Sir William Waller, Edward Massey, Sir Phillip Stapleton, and John Glyn. The House of Commons refused to consider the charges, and the Army moved even closer. It halted at Uxbridge, a very short distance from the capital. On 26th June the eleven members withdrew with the consent of the House.

On 1st July, Fairfax appointed ten of the chief officers of the Army to discuss the 'Humble Remonstrance' with commissioners from the Parliament. The Army then fell back to Reading. Meanwhile the King was brought via Newmarket, Royston and Windsor to Lord Craven's house at Caversham, just across the river from the Army's new position. For a fortnight the three way conversation and negotiations between the King, Parliament and Army were carried on. Charles saw this as an opportunity to play both his adversaries against each other. As Ireton was to exclaim to him, *"Sir, you have an intention to be an arbitrator between the Parliament and us. As we mean it to be us between your Majesty and the Parliament"*. Many of the Army rank and file, particularly the Levellers, were suspicious of a possible alliance between the King and the Parliament against them, or even the Grandees and the King against them. For a while, when negotiations between the king and parliament foundered over the question of the state religion it seemed that an agreement would be reached between the king and the grandees. Charles appeared to have established a surprisingly close relationship with Cromwell and Fairfax. At this point Cromwell is said to have described the king as *"The uprightest and most conscientious man of his three kingdoms"*. Unknown to the army leaders, however, both the king and the Presbyterian leaders in London were engaged in secret talks with the Scots over the price of a re-entry of the Scottish army into England to support their respective causes. As each day brought growing rumours of a Scottish invasion, the Agitators within the English army began to insist that the Army should march on London and settle the whole question by force. This would allow the Independent minority within parliament the chance to seize the initiative and work out a settlement for Church and State more in line with the Army's aims.

It was against this background that a General Council of War was called at Reading on 16th July to consider the Agitators' request. This was a meeting of between fifty and a hundred leading officers and a number of Agitators. It was decided, upon the advice of Cromwell and his son-in-law Ireton, to postpone any march on London whilst the Army's proposals were considered by the Council of War and then put into the form of a manifesto by a committee of twelve officers and twelve Agitators. This manifesto, to be known as the 'Heads of the Army Proposals' would be given to the parliamentary commissioners who would present them to Parliament.

Under the 'Heads of the Army Proposals' Parliament was to have biennial sessions of between 120 and 240 days; there was to be a Council of State with more authority than the old Privy Council; there was to be a better distribution of seats and free elections; MPs were to be allowed to disagree with both King and Lords freely, and the king was not to protect officials from the judgement of Parliament. The king and his family were to be restored to a condition of safety, honour and freedom, without further limits to the future exercise of royal power other than as stated in these proposals. Although the bishops were to be swept away and the Book of Common Prayer no longer legally enforced, neither was the Covenant to be legally enforced and the penal laws against Catholics were to be repealed. A long list of other grievances, ranging from inequalities of taxation to the old forest laws were to be redressed. Control of the city militia in London was to be placed in the hands of Parliament for ten years and the new Council of State would control the regular armed forces and foreign affairs.

The early signs were that these proposals might be acceptable to Parliament, given the circumstances in which it found itself. Before the king could give an official response, however, the situation in London moved to crisis point. As soon as news reached the streets of London that, under pressure, Parliament had agreed to appoint Fairfax to the command of all forces in England, declared against the employment of foreign troops, and put the control of the city's trained bands under army nominees under the cloak of parliamentary control rather than that of the Lord Mayor and the City Council, there was uproar. The London mob, composed largely of city apprentices and *'reformadoes'* and spurred on by the eleven leading

246

presbyterian members who had taken shelter in the City of London, stormed both Houses of Parliament. They demanded repeal of the militias ordinance and the return of the king to the capital. They held down Speaker Lenthall in his chair, forced him to rescind Parliament's control of the militia, and called for the upholding of the presbyterian Covenant and the return of the eleven members.

Alarmed by this and the threat of even worse violence to come the remaining Independents and some from the middle group of parliamentarians decided that the time for flight had come. On 29th June Speaker Lenthall and fifty-seven Members of Parliament, including Ludlow, Haselrigg and Lord Grey of Groby, together with eight peers including even the once hostile Earl of Manchester, fled from London to the safety of the Army. This was now stationed at Bedford, some fifty miles away, pending the outcome of the negotiations. It now began to move closer. This was the sort of development which the Levellers and activists in the Army had been waiting for. It was also the first clear indication of Lord Grey of Groby's future political inclinations.

At about the same time the king had become sufficiently encouraged by the news from Scotland and London to publicly rebut the Army's proposals. He had been assured by the Earl of Lauderdale for the Scots and by others from the City of London that they would support him in opposing the Army to the death. His public rebuttal of the proposals from the Army negotiators had two immediate results. Firstly Cromwell adopted a cooler attitude to the king and secondly Colonel Rainsborough, the most senior Army Leveller, spread the news of the king's reaction among the soldiers.

The fact that the Army, which had now moved to Hounslow Heath on the outskirts of the capital, could count on the two Speakers of Parliament to head its ranks, provided it with the gloss of legality in its urgent desire to march into the heart of London. They could not be held back any longer. They were to escort the godly and true hearted members of parliament back to Westminster and to assert their own rights too. As they threw their hats in the air they cried aloud, with real conviction, *"Lords and Commons and a free Parliament!"*.

In London itself the eleven members returned to the leadership of what remained of Parliament. With more confidence than wisdom they started to prepare for the defence of the capital. But the presbyterians were becoming increasingly isolated as the Army moved nearer. There were fears that the *'reformadoes'*, once armed, might plunder the wealthy City of London. The borough of Southwark even extended an invitation to the New Model Army to enter it. When the presbyterian Lord Mayor of London called out the trained bands to protect the capital from attack, as it had against the King's Army at Turnham Green at the beginning of the civil war, there was a luke-warm response. Only about one man in twelve turned out to the colours. As the unenthusiastic trained bands, with nearly more officers than men, were parading in St. James' Fields, waiting to be inspected by Edward Massey and Sir William Waller, the vanguard of the New Model army reached the outskirts of London.

The vanguard of the Army consisted of regiments led by Col. Rainsborough's Regiment of Foot, many of them New Englanders and with experience of taking towns. They swung round to the south bank of the Thames. On 6th August at about two o'clock in the morning sympathizers in the borough of Southwark opened the gates. As Rainsborough and his men marched in they were given a huge shout of welcome. Southwark was a strong base of Leveller activity. From a vantage point on the south bank of the Thames Rainsborough mounted a battery of guns aimed at the defences of London Bridge. As the dawn broke the sight across the river of these guns and colours of the New Model was decisive. All resistance in the City collapsed.

As the vanguard was moving into Southwark, the main body of the Army marched down from Hampstead Heath, along the Edgware Road, into the heart of London. Soon 18,000 men of the New Model army were marching in triumph through the centre of the capital with sprigs of laurel leaves, the emblems of victory, in their hatbands. The respectable poor were cheering them, whilst some of the richer citizens had sour faces. Cromwell rode his horse at the head of his own regiment of Ironsides which preceded the main body of the cavalry under Fairfax. They were followed by the foot regiments in their red coats with drums beating, flags flying, muskets and pikes shouldered, and the train of artillery guarded by their firelocks. At last the victorious army had come to claim their hard fought for rights.

They marched to Hyde Park where the Lord Mayor and Aldermen met them with hastily prepared speeches of welcome, and at Charing Cross they were greeted by the Common Council of the City of London. They then marched on to Westminster where the Speaker and the fugitive members, including Lord Grey of Groby, were restored to their proper place in Parliament. A day of public thanksgiving was ordered by Parliament, together with a month's pay for the rank and file soldiers. The Commons passed a swift and scarcely sincere resolution that *"This House doth approve of the coming up of the General and the Army for the safe sitting of the Parliament and that Thanks be given to the General and the Army for the same"*. The eleven members had, of course, vanished once more. That night the Ironsides stabled their horses in St. Paul's Cathedral.

The next day the Army marched on through the City to make camp at Croydon. This time Cromwell rode at the head of the cavalry. Fairfax, who was ill, rode in a carriage together with his wife and Mrs. Cromwell. Fairfax was made Constable of the Tower of London. Troops were left to guard both the Tower and Parliament, with a regiment of horse camped in Hyde Park as a visible reminder to the MPs not to ignore the wishes of the Army. The King was brought nearer to London and lodged in his palace at Hampton Court.

Parliament now bore the full brunt of the wrath of the returning Army officers and their Independent allies, prominent amongst whom were Lord Grey and Edmund Ludlow. All ordinances passed in the Speaker's absence by the Presbyterians were to be repealed. In this the Generals were assisted not only by the committed Independents, but by many of the MPs who belonged to the "middle group" as it was termed. This shifting but important group of MPs, whatever their views on military rule, agreed with the Army leaders that there should be no disbandment before a proper settlement; otherwise a vacuum would be created into which a Scottish army could move as agents for either royalists or presbyterians. The majority of MPs, however, were still of the presbyterian tendency and were slow to learn. After a week they had still not passed the 'Null and Void Ordinance'. Only the objection of Fairfax prevented Cromwell from carrying out a drastic purging of the Commons' membership. Cromwell complained angrily to Ludlow that *"These men will never leave till the Army pull them out by the ears"*.[9] On 20th August he rode to Westminster with an escort of soldiers. Although he left them outside, it was at the completion of this gesture that, with the help of his vote and those of the other pro-Army MPs, the bill was finally carried.

The Presbyterians realised that the tide of events was very much against them for the present time. The eleven leading members had already fled abroad. Now others began to leave London. As a result parliamentary attendance declined markedly. Average attendance in the House of Lords was quoted as seven, and that of the House of Commons as little more than one hundred and fifty on even important issues. The locus of political power appeared to have swung from Parliament to the Army Council. An embittered Denzil Holles complained that :-

> *"The Army now did all, the Parliament was but a Cypher, only cry'd Amen to what the Councils of War had determined. They make themselves an absolute Third Estate".*[10]

Despite their support in Parliament for a programme of settlement with the king during most of 1647 Holles and the political Presbyterians had failed to resolve successfully the new problems created by the war. Basically they were conservative, and if not quite so conservative as they liked to imagine by this stage - they did, after all, want to deprive the king of much of his sovereign power - they were nevertheless out-distanced by the more radical groups. All their suspicions and intolerance of the religious ideas of the soldiers, their personal dislike of the Army leaders and the Army's friends in Parliament itself, combined to demonstrate to the Army that they could not be trusted. Their old ideas had nothing to offer in settling the constitutional impasse in the summer of 1647. Their general contempt and arrogance towards those who had served them so well in arms during the civil war deprived them of widespread trust and sympathy.

Various individuals were named as the chief of these *"ambitious, imperious men .....* [who] *'would fain be taken for Gods, and sons of the most high' including the Earl of Manchester, Sir William Erle, and `the proud covetous priests"*. Denzil Holles and Sir Phillip Stapleton, however, were the two leaders most frequently mentioned by their opponents.

Such was the gap which had now developed between the Earl of Stamford and his son. As we have seen, during the revolt of the Army against what it regarded as an ungrateful and untrustworthy Parliament, Lord Grey of Groby had identified with the Independent faction and its links with the Army. Whereas the Earl of Stamford was a member of the 'non-innovatory' wing of the rival Presbyterian faction, Lord Grey was rapidly becoming more and more radical in his politics. John Harris, a pamphleteer who analysed the party situation of 1647 described the Presbyterians as disguised Royalists - under the mask of Presbyterians they were socially conservative and *"royal, not real ones"*. Lord Grey by contrast was following the logic of the revolt against the monarchy and becoming a republican. For him Puritan idealism was more important than constitutional conservatism. His desire to achieve godly reformation was becoming revolutionary. He had been one of the Independent members who fled with the Speaker of the House of Commons to join the Army as it marched on London against the Presbyterian-dominated Parliament. He now became an even closer associate of the Army leaders such as Sir Thomas Fairfax, Oliver Cromwell, and Henry Ireton.

On 7th September 1647 a motion was put to the House of Commons to expel the eleven Presbyterian members who were absent (in theory upon leave), including Denzil Holles. The motion was carried. It was put to the House by Lord Grey of Groby. As a bitter Holles, writing in exile in France in the following year, records it :-

"A little after the Lord Grey of Groby sets on foot the motion concerning those of the eleven members who were beyond the sea".[11]

NOTES

1. Chester, London Marriage Licenses - issued by the Dean and Chapter of Westminster, 4th June 1646, p. 277.
2. *Memoirs of Edmund Ludlow*, ed. C. H. Firth, 2 Vols., 1894.
3. H.M.C. Earl of Denbigh Manuscripts, pp. 80 - 81.
4. House of Commons Journal.
5. Ibid.
6. Rushworth, op. cit., Vol. VII, p. 573.
7. Richard Ollard, *This War without an Enemy*, Atheneum, New York, 1976. p. 161.
8. *Declaration of the Army* or (its full title) *A Declaration of Representation From his Excellency Sir Thomas Fairfax, And the Army under his Command*, 15th June 1647. See *The Leveller Tracts, 1647 - 1653* ed. William Haller & Godfrey Davies. Columbia University Press, 1944; reprinted 1964.
9. Ludlow, op. cit., Vol. I, p. 148.
10. Denzil Holles, *Memoirs of Denzil, Baron Holles* (London edition, 1815), p. 175.
11. Ibid. p. 302.

View of 17th century London

Basil Fielding Earl of Denbigh.

Basil Fielding, Earl of Denbigh

Sir George Booth, Lord Delamere

Elizabeth Booth (nee Grey), Baroness Delamere

CHAPTER EIGHT

THE RISING POLITICIAN (1647 - 1648)
ARMY RADICALS AND THE SECOND CIVIL WAR

"Let God arise, let his enemies be scattered,
Let them also that hate him flee before him.
As smoke is driven away, so drive them away;
As wax melteth before the fire,
So let the wicked perish at the presence of God.
But let the righteous be glad, let them exult before God:
Yes; let them rejoice with gladness".

(Psalm 68 vs. 1-3)

The easy victory they had gained served only to weaken the unity of the anti-presbyterian alliance, however, by increasing the complacency of the Grandees. The demand of the Agitators, endorsed by the Army Council, for a complete purge of the Presbyterians in Parliament was refused. In addition negotiations continued with King Charles, with whom Cromwell and Ireton appeared to many of the soldiers to be on dangerously friendly terms. Cromwell's family, particularly the women, began to attend the court functions which the king maintained even in captivity. This sort of social appeasement alienated the radicals in the rank and file as much as the apparent political appeasement of the *'Man of Blood'*.

On 22nd September the republican MP Henry Marten and the Leveller Colonel Rainsborough, now also an MP, moved in the House of Commons that no more addresses be made to the king (because of his delaying tactics). Cromwell and Ireton both voted with the majority who defeated this motion by 84 votes to 34. This killed the hope that the Heads of Proposals would provide a bridge to peace. Cromwell delivered a three hour speech in the debate which left the rift between the Grandees and the radicals seemingly beyond repair. He defended the institution of monarchy, said that his aim in the civil war had been to strengthen and not destroy it, and pleaded with the Commons to settle with the king without delay.

There was an immediate reaction to this speech which had confirmed growing doubts about the sincerity of the Grandees amongst the Army radicals and the civilian Levellers. They decided to co-operate no longer with the generals or Parliament. Early in October they met at Guildford and produced a new manifesto. This was entitled 'The Case of the Armie Truly Stated'. It was signed by all the Agitators from the regiments of the Army and was heavily influenced by civilian Leveller leaders such as John Wildman, Richard Overton, and John Lilburne. It drew attention to the way the pledges in the previous Army 'Engagement' and the 'Declaration'

255

had been broken or ignored. It went on to outline a programme for political reform which included Parliamentary elections every two years, *"and that all the freeborn at the age of 21 yeares and upwards, be the electors, excepting those that have or shall deprive themselves of that their freedome, either for some yeares, or wholly by delinquency"*.[1]

'The Case of the Armie Truly Stated' was submitted to Fairfax on 18th October, published as a pamphlet about the same date and discussed by the Army Council ten days later. This discussion was brief, for in the interval a new programme document had been prepared which was to serve as a draft discussion document for a new constitution for England. It was entitled 'The Agreement of the People (for a firm and present Peace, upon grounds of Common-right and freedom)'.

Between 28th October and 11th November 1647 the Army Council met to debate this draft constitutional document and the principles contained in it. The venue for this historic gathering was St. Mary's Church, Putney, on the banks of the Thames, just across from Fulham. Here officers and men alike sat around long tables and exchanged views, sometimes very heatedly, for fourteen days. The Putney Army debates were recorded for posterity by William Clarke, then a young man of twenty four. Clarke had been the subordinate to Rushworth, Secretary to Fairfax and the Council of War when the New Model Army had been formed. He had then become Secretary to the Commissioners who had tried to arrange terms between the Army and Parliament in the summer. The notes for the Putney reports, which include references to such anonymous contributors as "Buff Coat" and "Bedfordshire Man", were probably taken down in shorthand by Clarke himself.

The sessions were presided over by Cromwell, Fairfax being officially unwell and staying at Turnham Green. Cromwell had experience of chairing committees as a Member of Parliament and affected a position of neutrality, although at times he appears to have inclined to Ireton's position. On the eve of the 28th October, the Levellers issued a pamphlet entitled 'A Call to All the Soldiers of the Army by the Free People of England' which vigorously attacked both Cromwell and Ireton for their 'hypocrisy' and 'deceit'. Of Cromwell they wrote that he was once loved as *"just, honest, sincere and valiant"*, placing *"the country and the liberties of the people above his life"*, hating the king *"as a man of blood"*; but now, if he did not instantly repent he should *"cease to be the object of your love"*. They said that Ireton by his imperious carriage had made the Army Council *"like unto Star Chambers"*. *"None but flatterers, tale-bearers and turncoats are countenanced by him"*.

For the Radicals in the debates the principal spokesman was Colonel Thomas Rainsborough, supported by Private Edward Sexby and other Agitators and some officers. In addition, two prominent civilian Levellers, John Wildman and Maximilian Petty were there to help them to present their case. On the other side the weight of the argument was carried by Henry Ireton, Cromwell's son-in-law. Cromwell felt obliged to come to Ireton's rescue from time to time when his tactless logic threatened to antagonise the majority of those present. Debating styles varied. Ireton, on the conservative side, was clear cut, legalistic, logical, and superior. Rainsborough was forthright, moving, and with a common touch. Sexby was blunt and belligerent; often unanswerable. Cromwell characteristically sought to explain and excuse, call for patience and prayerful reflection, but left the main partisan debating to Ireton.

The social differences between the *'grandees'* and their opponents was revealed in a long debate on the basis of citizenship. The rank and file, and indeed many officers, supported the Leveller case for manhood suffrage; the generals for a franchise representing property.

The 'Agreement of the People' proposed the dissolution of the existing Parliament and its replacement by a new Parliament of four hundred members chosen every two years, to meet from June to December yearly. This body would then appoint a Council of State, erect and abolish law courts, and generally make laws to which everyone in the realm would be subject. Parliament would take over from the king his control of the armed forces. An Act of Oblivion was to cancel out offences against the law of the land committed during the civil war by royalist and parliamentarian supporters alike, so that all Englishmen could be reconciled. Men should be equal before the law and the practice of the press-gang was to be abolished. As for religion, that was to be reformed *"to the greatest purity in doctrine, worship, and discipline according to the Word of God"* and maintained out of public money with full toleration and freedom of conscience. The new Parliament, moreover, was to be elected by manhood suffrage.

On 30th October, it was agreed that manhood suffrage should be extended to all those who had served the parliament in the civil war, with their services, arms, money, or horses. So the soldiers at least were to be enfranchised.

On 1st November liberty of conscience in religious matters was approved but the original proposal was diluted so that whilst a magistrate could not force a dissenter to attend the state (i.e. now the Presbyterian) church he could prevent other congregations from formally meeting to worship together.

On 2nd November it was agreed to retain the king in office - but deprive him of most of his prerogatives and establish all real power with the House of Commons. The formula was close to that outlined previously by Ireton in the 'Heads of Proposals'.

On 3rd November the meeting demonstrated continuing unease over the subject of the monarchy. Fairfax, in his absence, was accused of wearing *"the King's colours"*; whilst it was reported that some of the soldiers were thought to be suffering a sentimental reaction in favour of the king. In general, however, the tide of the Army Council was running against Cromwell and Ireton despite their attempts to manage its agenda.

On 4th and 5th November two votes hostile to the Grandees were passed. The first stated that :-

> *"..... All soldiers and others, if not servants or beggars, ought to have their voices in electing those which shall represent them in Parliament, although they have not forty shillings per annum in freehold land. (And there were but three voices against this your native freedom)"*.[2]

The second resolution, moved by Rainsborough, agreed that a general Rendezvous of the whole Army should be called to endorse all these decisions, and also that a letter should be sent from the Army Council to Parliament requesting that there should be no more approaches to the king. These were agreed in the absence of Cromwell and in the face of Ireton's adamant opposition. At the next meeting Cromwell, back in the chair, made an outspoken attack upon the Agitators and complained of the letter to the Speaker. He proposed a resolution that the officers and Agitators should immediately return to their regiments to settle the men. The resolution was approved.

The Levellers and Agitators had thought that they had won on 4th and 5th November. They were convinced that at the general Rendezvous the 'Agreement of the People' would be approved by the Army and then in turn accepted by the nation at large. They were, however, already being outmanoeuvred by the Grandees.

On 9th November the Army Council met again, this time with Fairfax presiding. A series of resolutions was passed which had the effect of nullifying those of the earlier meetings. The Army Council was suspended. The Agitators were ordered to return to their regiments although the Council of Officers continued to meet. The Speaker of the House of Commons was informed that the Army was not against further approaches to the king. Most significant of all it was agreed that instead of the one mass Rendezvous of the Army desired by the radicals there should be three separate reviews held in different locations on different dates. It was a classic example of 'divide and rule'. To sweeten the pill, Parliament was asked for more money to pay off a month's arrears of wages. The Putney Army debates were over; as was the brief experiment with democracy within the Army.

At the first of the three regional Rendezvous held at Corkbush Field, Ware, on 15th November 1647 the Grandees demonstrated their ruthlessness. Instead of the 'Agreement of the People' being submitted to the soldiers a 'Remonstrance' was presented to them. In this Fairfax complained of divisions and indiscipline within the Army and threatened to resign. He called on all to resume their obedience and promised that, if they did, he would do his best for them with Parliament. All of this fell far short of what was contained in the 'Agreement of the People' and what had been agreed at Putney. Fairfax had always held himself aloof from political discussions, so the universal respect held for his courage and military leadership provided an untapped reserve of goodwill on which the Grandees were able to draw.

Events also helped the Grandees to gather the unity of the Army behind them. On 11th November the King had escaped from Hampton Court. His motive was to seek his freedom in order to be able to plan co-operation with the Scots in a renewed war for his restoration to power. The effect was to close Army ranks and to rally the men behind their generals.

The soldiers at Corkbush Field who tried to insist upon the 'Agreement' and attempted to resist were accused of mutiny and arrested. Some were court-martialled and one, Private Richard Arnold of Robert Lilburne's Regiment (John Lilburne's brother), was shot at the head of the regiment. He became the first of several Leveller martyrs. The 'Remonstrance' was a defeat for the Agitators and the Levellers.

Then came a development perhaps even more decisive than the king's escape in overcoming disunity in the Army. There were the beginnings of a definite shift in Cromwell's attitude to the king. These were seen in his utterances at a meeting of the Army Council at Windsor Castle on 4th December 1647 when he expressed regret for persevering too long in negotiations with the monarch. He confessed that, *"the glories of the world had so dazzled his eyes, that ..... he was now resolved to humble himself"* and that he desired *"the prayers of the Saints that God would be pleased to forgive him his self-seeking"*.

Cromwell's decisive abandonment of all attempts to negotiate with Charles came shortly afterwards with the speech he made in the House of Commons on 3rd January 1648, supporting a successful motion put by Lord Grey of Groby that no further addresses should be made to the king. In this he described Charles as *"a dissembler and so false a man that he was not to be trusted"*. Lord Grey's role should be noted.

Meanwhile this revision of attitude had been accompanied by reconciliation within the Army. There was, on 21st December, the now customary day of prayer and fasting which brought *"sweet harmony"*, with Cromwell, Ireton and other officers praying *"very fervently and pathetically from nine in the morning to seven at night"*. All the sentences on the mutineers were quashed and they were restored to their posts on undertaking to observe discipline. The Levellers, in turn, expressed their regret for their indiscretions at Ware. At the conclusion of the meeting, General Fairfax invited all the members of the Army Council to dine with him at Windsor Castle, where he congratulated everyone on the unity they had achieved.

In the meantime, however, puritanical strictness was beginning to irritate many ordinary people within the kingdom. Peace, which had been so earnestly desired and striven for, seemed to have brought with it high prices, a bad harvest and unfamiliar rule. The old order of society had been challenged. The country gentry much resented their increasing alienation from the process of government which they had customarily exercised as Justices of the Peace, or leaders of the militia, and which were now controlled from the centre. Not only the gentry but many of the lower orders yearned for a return to pre-war customs and practices. The mobs in London and the provinces began increasingly to turn against the Army and to become pro-royalist. On Christmas Day 1647 there were serious riots in the capital and the soldiers had to be ordered out to quell them. At Canterbury, Kent, on Christmas Day there was a riot when the puritan mayor tried to forbid the annual football match which was traditionally played in the market place. Three thousand men of the trained bands had to be called in to restore order.

New hope had been given to the die-hard Cavaliers, especially in London and the Home Counties, when the king had managed to escape from his captivity at Hampton Court in November 1647. He had taken his opportunity and ridden off to the south coast. On the road he had debated whether to stay in England and plot an insurrection with his friends and supporters or to take a ship to France and join Queen Henrietta Maria. When he reached the Southampton area, however, he discovered that an embargo on all shipping bound for France had forced the decision upon him. He then took the advice of John Ashburton and crossed to the Isle of Wight. Here he called upon Colonel Hammond, Governor of Carisbrooke Castle, expecting to be treated leniently and with respect. Hammond, a distant relative of Cromwell, was torn between sympathy for the king and his duty to Parliament. In the end Charles was imprisoned once more and closely watched. But, now, Charles pictured behind bars and among the seagulls of the Isle of Wight evoked far more affection than the warrior-king who had ranged England with Prince Rupert, Lord Goring and their cavaliers. Thoughts of his losses and disappointments, his fall from high estate, separation from his wife and children, the stories of his gentleness and even piety, easily misled those who had no knowledge of his intrigues and his duplicity.

By the Spring of 1648 Carisbrooke Castle had become the centre of a spider's web of royalist conspiracy. Some threads reached to France where the Queen was pawning her personal jewels to buy further arms. Other threads linked up the many English counties where local cavaliers awaited their second chance. Some threads reached to Scotland where the Duke of Hamilton, and others like him, detested the power and radical opinions of the New Model Army. The Scots, with the secret agreement of many Presbyterians in the English Parliament, were preparing an army to invade England once again. This time a presbyterian system would be enforced there. Presbyterian elements still remaining in the New Model Army were being encouraged to rise in support in parts of England and Wales when the opportunity presented itself.

On 6th April 1648 Cromwell warned Hammond of a plot to rescue the king. Three days later the biggest anti-government riot of all broke out. Playing games on the Sabbath had been forbidden. Some boys broke this rule in Moorfields one Sunday and the Lord Mayor of London ordered soldiers to go and stop them. The London apprentices would not stand by and let this happen. They pelted the soldiers with stones and set London in an uproar. The furious apprentices had for too long been deprived of their holiday fun by the puritanical Lord Mayor and Aldermen for whose cause they had fought in the Civil War. They were angry too because these same rich men were using their new power to ride roughshod over medieval customs that promised them fair wages once they were qualified as journeymen and a chance to set up in business on their own. A mob of 5,000, including many former parliamentarian soldiers, came surging along the Strand. They ran down Whitehall crying, *"Now for King Charles!"* They were going to drive the New Model Army out of Whitehall. Cromwell and Ireton led a cavalry charge against them, killing their leader and wounding others in the process. This episode can be seen as part of a general pattern of violent reaction against the Army and in favour of the absent monarch. Even Parliament voted that the monarchical constitution was not to be altered and temporarily suspended the "Vote of No Addresses" to the king.

With definite news of a Scottish Army preparing to head south at the end of April everything seemed to be flowing in Charles' favour once more. The New Model Army was understandably apprehensive at such developments. Its Army Council met at Windsor to consider the Scottish news and its members displayed an absolute hostility to Charles as the author of their troubles.

On 30th April English Royalists in the North seized both Berwick and Carlisle with the help of the Scots. The following day, May Day, in the midst of the meeting of the Army Council, came the dramatic news that the Adjutant-General in Wales, Fleming, had been killed in a Royalist uprising which coincided with a mutiny of disbanded Parliamentarian soldiers. The whole of South Wales was up in arms. Fleming had been popular in the Army and the news moved the Council to a historic resolution against the person whom they regarded as being responsible for the renewed horrors of war :-

"We were led to a clear agreement amongst ourselves, not any dissenting, that it was the duty of our day, with the forces we had, to go out and fight against those potent enemies, which in that year appeared against us, with an humble confidence, in the name of the Lord only, that we should destroy them. And we were also enabled then, after seriously seeking His face, to come to a very clear joint resolution ..... that it was our duty, if ever the Lord brought us back again in peace, to call Charles Stuart, that man of blood, to an account for the blood he had shed, and mischief he had done to the utmost against the Lord's cause and people in these poor nations".[6]

Fairfax despatched Lambert to the North to encounter the Scottish Army and their English Royalist allies. Cromwell was sent with the largest force to South Wales. Sir Hardress Waller was sent to suppress another rising in Cornwall. Messages were sent out to mobilise local militias under reliable commanders in the counties to support the New Model Army. Lord Grey of Groby's opportunity to return to the military service of the 'Good Old Cause' had come at last. The Second Civil War had begun.

In the twelve months between Spring 1648 and Spring 1649 the government of England was to change fundamentally. Lord Grey of Groby, moreover, was to be a central player in these changes.

In Leicester at the outbreak of the Second Civil War the two Borough MPs, Lord Grey and Peter Temple, stood loyal to *'the Good Old Cause'*.

Lord Grey of Groby was apparently living at his father's home at Bradgate at this time. With Peter Temple and Thomas Wayte (or White), another Leicestershire man and MP for Rutland who was both a friend and client, Lord Grey raised forces within the two counties to crush any likely local royalist risings. He also placed garrisons in local strongpoints such as Ashby Castle. These actions were officially ratified subsequently by the House of Commons on 1st July 1648.[4]

In Leicester itself the Mayor, Thomas Blunt, issued an order to the constables of the wards and parishes on the 5th June in the following terms :-

"Whereas it hath beene made appeare att a Common Hall this present Mundaye by the honorable Committee of this Towne and Countie the eminent danger both this Corporacion and Countie is in, by the greate number of evill affected delinquents assembled together in divers places adjacent; for the speedy suppressinge whereof, and for the preservacion of our selves, and for preventinge the Newarke or any other parte of this Corporacion from Garrisoninge These are to require you

262

ymmediately [sic] upon sight hereof to desire all able and sufficient persons within your warde to appeare tomorrowe morninge by Nine of the clock att ye beate of the drume to their severall Coullers, with such armes as they have, And soe to goe to the Horse faire to a generall Randesvouze [sic] there to shewe theire reddines, for the preservinge both of themselves and frends against the publique enimie".[5]

The banner of the 'Ermine Unicorn' was soon flying again in the East Midlands. Lord Grey's forces won a victory over some royalist horse, led by a Dr Hudson, in a cavalry fight near Stamford. A letter dated 7th June, written by Lord Grey from Leicester, to *"my much honoured friend William Lenthall, esq. Speaker of the honourable House of Commons"*, related the incident and its general context :-

"Sir, being at my father's at Bradgate in this county, upon Sunday the 4th instant, the Committee sent me word that there was a party of cavaliers gathered into a body about Stamford; and desired my present advice and assistance. I immediately repaired to them, and delivered a squadron of horse to Colonel Waite to go into Rutland; and we presently sent warrants to some few towns that we conceived to be the best affected. They coming in freely upon Monday in the evening, being there met, earnestly desired me to take the command upon me and nominated two other gentlemen (Mr. Beaumont and Colonel Hacker) to have command and go along with me. I told them, when my country was in danger, I should be ready to stand in the gap, but I had no authority. But, their desires being earnest, and lest the service should be neglected, I presumed rather to cast myself upon you for your approbation than to let my country be endangered for want of my undertaking the business. I likewise, at the desire of the Committee, desired the Mayor of Leicester to call a Hall; and there acquainted them with the rising of the Cavaliers, and with the danger they were like to be in, if not prevented. They unanimously agreed to draw out the next day; and there appeared six full companies, all ready (if occasion had been) to have ventured their lives, as they unanimously expressed. And likewise there was drawn up of the country to the number of 500 (whereof 300 were horsed and armed), who were all ready to have marched in this business; and expressed that they had hoped the rogues might have no quarter. But Colonel Waite having appeased the business (as I

263

doubt not but he has given you an account thereof before this time) I dismissed them all home this morning; and doubt not they, with many more , will be ready for the defence of the country, if any shall presume to rise upon the like occasion. Having troubled you with a tedious relation, I remain, sire, your most humble servant". [6]

In late June a force of some five hundred cavaliers, led by Sir Philip Monckton, who had broken out of the loosely besieged Pontefract, plundered the Isle of Axholme in north-west Lincolnshire and then took Lincoln itself. This alarmed the parliamentarians in the other East Midland counties. As Colonel Rossiter set out to encounter them with troops drawn from Lincolnshire and Nottinghamshire the raiders, their numbers swollen by local royalists, moved on to Gainsborough. Sir Henry Cholmeley with a force of several hundred parliamentarian horse moved down south from Pontefract to prevent their retreat whilst Rossiter moved to prevent their passage to Newark, the old royalist stronghold. Monckton's royalists paused next at Bingham in Nottinghamshire from whence their aim sees to have been to push south to Kegworth and raise support from the royalists of Leicestershire and Derbyshire. But Lord Grey and his militia had secured the passage over the river Soar at Cotes bridge near Loughborough. With superior enemy forces collecting on all sides every hour, the position of the royalists became more and more critical. On 5th July, they headed on down the old Roman road, the Fosseway, pausing at Owthorpe to plunder Colonel John Hutchinson's house of meat and drink. Somewhere in the neighbourhood of Widmerpool a running skirmish began until the main body of Monckton's force, some 700-800 horse and foot turned at bay in a large bean-field just north of Willoughby Church. Here, after a fierce close-order fight, the weight of Rossiter's reserves told and the royalists broke and fled in complete disorder. Half of them, including Monckton, were taken prisoner. A hundred fell on the spot or in the surrounding cornfields as the victors rode down upon the fugitives. The remainder streamed away in small parties along the Leicestershire lanes to be rounded up later by Lord Grey's men.

Having secured Leicestershire and Rutland Lord Grey was able to turn his attention to assisting the New Model Army in the north of England. Lambert had kept occupied the invading force of Scots and northern English royalists who had crossed the border, whilst Cromwell had put down the risings in South Wales after some initial difficulties.

The Committee of Both Kingdoms sitting at Derby House in London, having been informed by Lord Grey of his preparations and intentions by a letter of 16th August, agreed to write to him expressing their thanks and *"notifying that it is reported to the House that the 500 l. in Colonel*

Needham's hands may be appointed to buy arms for that county (Leicester)".

The reply, which was sent to Lord Grey and the Leicester Committee read as follows :-

> *"By yours of the 16th instant we learn that condition and posture of your forces and their great readiness to serve the public, for which we return your thanks. That part which related to the 500 l. desired by you for providing arms for the forces of your county we have ordered to be reported to the House* [of Commons]*"*.[7]

Fairfax was now besieging the royalist forces under Sir Charles Lucas, Sir George Lisle, and Lord Norwich in Colchester. It was imperative, therefore, that Cromwell with the main English army reach the northern invasion force as soon as possible. Much of the cavalry was sent on in advance whilst Cromwell followed with three thousand foot and twelve hundred horse. Cromwell described his men in a letter as *"so harassed by long marches they seemed rather fit for a hospital than a battle"*. Much of his effort on the way north was spent in trying to get further supplies for his men. In a note to the Derby House Committee in London, written on 24th July from Gloucester, he comments that his *"poor wearied soldiers"* were desperate for shoes and stockings for the long march north. When he reached Leicester he was still waiting for three thousand pairs of each. Such was the after-effect of the siege and sack of Leicester some three years earlier, however, that these could come not from Leicester itself - a traditional boot and shoe and hosiery manufacturing town - but were provided from its neighbours Northampton and Coventry respectively when the army reached Nottingham. Leicester did provide other comforts in the form of wine, biscuits, sugar, beer and tobacco for the Lt. General from the Mayor and Aldermen :-

> *"Item paid for wyne biskets Suger beare and Tobacko when Mr. Maior and the Aldermen went to visit Lord Generall Crumwell att his goeing into the North as apperes by bill. ijli. vjs. iijd"*.[8]

Cromwell was also able to acquire reinforcements from the local forces including *"five or six hundred horse"* from the surrounding counties of Derbyshire and Nottinghamshire as well as Leicestershire. He reported this to the Derby House Committee in a letter written from Nottingham on about 5th August. These reinforcements did not include Lord Grey himself who was to follow on with more reinforcements later.

265

On 12th August the forces of Cromwell and Lambert joined together near Knaresborough in Yorkshire. The combined army totalled eight thousand six hundred men. Against them was a force of some twenty thousand, but it was sprawled across a line of march which extended some fifty miles and was riven by faction and rivalry between the Scots and the English royalists and also amongst the Scots themselves.

The invading force had chosen to take a Lancashire rather than a Yorkshire route to the south on the grounds that royalist support was thought to be stronger in the former area. Cromwell knew that the enemy force would have to cross the bridge over the river Ribble at Preston in its journey southwards. The Parliamentarian army reached Skipton on the night of 14th August. Near Clitheroe Cromwell decided that, rather than follow the course of the Ribble by the south bank thus cutting off the invaders from any further advance into central England, he would take the north bank of the Ribble and thus cut off their retreat :-

"Upon deliberate advice we chose rather to put ourselves between their army and Scotland".[9]

The Duke of Hamilton does not appear to have been aware just how near to him Cromwell was at this point. He made the mistake on 16th August of sending the main body of his cavalry under John Middleton ahead from Preston and south towards Wigan. This meant that the river Ribble now effectively divided his cavalry off from his main force. By early morning on 17th August Cromwell's force, having followed the north bank of the Ribble, were in position to launch their attack.

They first encountered the royalist eastern vanguard of three thousand English cavaliers and some six hundred foot under Sir Marmaduke Langdale. The result was some of the fiercest hand-to-hand fighting of the war at Longridge to the northeast of Preston. Whilst this went on Langdale rode off to warn Hamilton of the attack. The Scottish commander-in-chief was with the main body of his troops on the Preston Moor, just over a mile north of the town and engaged in the complicated process of getting the rest of his army across the Ribble by the Preston Bridge to follow Middleton's advance cavalry. He declined to stand and fight on the Moor but preferred to continue with the crossing whilst ordering Langdale to hold off what was in effect the elite of the New Model Army. One cynical report alleges that when he first heard of the fighting at Longridge he had exclaimed, *"Let them alone. The English dogs are but killing one another".*

By the time Langdale had returned to his men he found them ensconced across the Preston-Skipton road, with the open ground of Ribbleton Moor beyond. Here the royalists fought an obstinate delaying action along a

266

sunken lane leading into Preston. The year 1648 had been the wettest summer in living memory and the mud was deep. Langdale's dour infantry had to be pushed back step by step in bloody frontal charges over four hours before Cromwell's men could break through to Preston. To seize the bridge there cost them another two hours of repeated pike attacks and musketry with *"push of pike"* and *"close firing"*.

In the end Langdale's brave men, outnumbered two to one in the fighting in the sunken lane, were beaten down and retreated into the town in disorder. Sweeping into Preston itself the New Model Army were now able to fall upon Hamilton's crossing party at the bridge. Hamilton sent his rearguard horse back to join the infantry of Sir George Munro who were thought to be advancing from the north as reinforcements. In the event they were chased off the battlefield by elements of Cromwell's cavalry. A fierce fight now raged around the Ribble Bridge whilst Baillie tried to form up the main body of the Scottish Foot on the south bank. The Ribble Bridge was now the key to the battle and the fighting on it and around it was very fierce. But the Scots army was cut in half and demoralised and the original odds greatly reduced. Finally Cromwell's men broke through again at 'push of pike' across the bridge and fighting continued on the south bank. Hamilton only got to his remaining main force on the south bank by swimming across the swollen torrent of the Ribble with some of his officers. Night fell and brought a respite from the fighting.

Under cover of the darkness Hamilton's men headed south to join Middleton's cavalry at Wigan. Unknown to them, however, Middleton had heard of the battle and, hurrying back in the dark by another road missing them, encountered instead Cromwell's cavalry. The battle for Preston now turned into a prolonged and rain-soaked rout rather than a renewed conflict. Cromwell's cavalry rode through the darkness and drenching rain to destroy that part of the invading force south of the river. All that night and the next day his men killed fugitives. Three thousand of the Scots were killed in the pursuit and ten thousand taken prisoner. On Saturday, 19th August, the Scottish Foot under Baillie made its last stand at Winwick, three miles from Warrington. After several hours, with the loss of one thousand dead and two thousand taken prisoner, they were forced to surrender.

The Duke of Hamilton escaped into Cheshire with Langdale and about three thousand of his Horse. Cromwell and his Ironsides were too weary to pursue them. It is hardly surprising. Altogether in nine days they had covered some 140 miles and been involved in sustained fighting for much of that period.

The battle of Preston can be seen as being as crucial to the outcome of the second civil war as Naseby was to the first civil war. The invading force had been completely smashed and its inadequate leadership scattered.

Sir Marmaduke Langdale was captured soon afterwards in a tavern in Nottinghamshire. He was imprisoned at Nottingham Castle but managed to effect an escape. James, Duke of Hamilton, got as far south as Uttoxeter in Staffordshire where, on 24th August, he was taken by parliamentarian forces in highly controversial circumstances featuring Lord Grey of Groby.

Hamilton claimed that he had already surrendered on agreed terms to Lambert when Lord Grey of Groby rode up with his own forces and made him his prisoner. This was the culmination of Lord Grey's role in the second civil war and before the incident is examined in more detail it will be useful to see what Lord Grey had been doing since Cromwell had left Leicester on his way north earlier in August.

During this campaign Lord Grey wrote a wonderfully titled letter to Parliament - *'Old English Blood boyling afresh in Leicestershire Men'*. The letter is addressed directly to Major-General Phillip Skippon for transmission on to Parliament and gives an interesting insight into Grey's religious and political attitudes at this time; attitudes which were becoming increasingly radical in their puritan zeal. The letter, which was written in instalments, appears to have been completed the day before the 'capture' of the Duke of Hamilton :-

"Sir, Because your antient [sic] *and well approved faithfulness speaks itself through the kingdom; I have thought good to communicate the state of our affairs in this County unto you; which is thus. When we understood that our proclaimed enemies (the Scots) were drawing upon us, even to fall upon this Nation when it was weak; (as Esa[u] did on his brother, and this Esa[u] is Edom, red and bloody), or as those brethren in iniquity did upon the Shechamites, when they were sore : We thought all lay at stake ; and the God of our mercies awakened us here, to see what might be done for our safety. We tried what Volunteers would appear; which were not a few, that tendered themselves and their own horses; and those that wanted we horsed upon those that were Dissenters : insomuch that, by the blessing of God, we have mounted a considerable number for so inconsiderable a County, and shall be able to march with a good strength very suddenly. And this course we have and do propound with all earnestness to all our neighbouring Counties; not waiting upon the customary way of pay and quarter, which would retard us, and such a work as this. We had our men so willing to go forth, as if they should find their `wages in their work'; yea, though in the highest of their harvest, and this unseasonable weather : at our meeting, a march being propounded, they cried - ONE AND ALL.*

"Sir, We are prest forwards hereunto by the violent call of necessities surrounding us; nor can we be blamed for neglecting some punctilios, since self-safety, and our present preservation, admit no delay. It would rejoice our hearts to see English blood stirring in the veins of men at this juncture; professing to yourself, that your honourable carriage in order to the good of this poor, shattered Nation, makes us to assure you we can (through God's mercy) readily live and die with you upon your pious and noble principles.

"I have inclosed [sic] *sent you a copy of the last* [communication] *from Lancashire; whereby you may judge of the inhuman temper of the enemy, and the sad condition of our friends.*

"I wish every tribe in Israel had this laid at their doors. Alas! (Sir) did these men [the Scots] *bring to us more holiness, justice, truth, and faithfulness, or rather did they not undermine that Gospel they say they come to settle, we would meet them with open arms and bended knees : but I wish that their inviters hither* [the English Presbyterians] *do not feel to their cost the ill consequences of the bargain.*

"Sir, (with our worthy neighbours in the Eastern Association, or any others like-minded), we resolve, by God's help, rather to die free Englishmen, than to live `hewers of wood', and `drawers of water', to base men whose mercies are cruelties.

"Our horse appearing last Monday at our rendezvous were near 3,000, all of this County, who expressed so much forwardness in this service, ambitiously desiring to be in action, waiting only upon a call, which we daily expect from our friends in the North, and for which we are making ourselves ready upon an hour's warning.

"My request unto yourself, and all honest English hearts, is, that you send us all the help you can through your prayers. And I beseech you to continue to improve your interest in Heaven and Earth, to preserve a Kingdom that must be saved against its will, for which God hath so immediately and even miraculously spoken from Heaven within three or four months last past in curbing the malice of men, appearing in such desperate tumults everywhere : the great monuments whereof remain in these places, viz. London, Norwich, South Wales,

269

Kent, Bury, Willoughby, Kingston, Needs [St. Neots], *Hereford,*
Shropshire, Stafford, Nottingham, Woodcraft, Scarborough,
Yarmouth, Teignmouth, Cumberland, Bristol, Isle of Wight,
Chester, Exeter, North Wales, and Cambridge, & c. [royalist
risings].

"Oh that men would see these wonders! and bow before the
Lord that hath smitten them, and tremble before his footstool!
To whose grace I commend you, and all the faithful with you. I
remain, Sir, yours ready to serve you, THOMAS GREY.

August 24, 1648

"Postscript - Sir, Since I began to write, the Scots are beaten;
12,000 prisoners are taken - their army broken. 3,000 horse of
theirs, where Duke Hambleton [Hamilton] *is, we are this*
morning pursuing with my forces who bend towards the North,
but [the enemy] *are in desperate confusion : we hope to give a*
good account of them.

Yours THOMAS GREY"[10]

Accounts of the capture of the Duke of Hamilton vary in their details,
but examination of a number of them written from different perspectives
allow for enough overlap of shared elements for an essentially clear picture
to emerge.

S. R. Gardiner, the Victorian historian, gives a succinct account which
encompasses all versions in all but the most disputed respect :-

"On the 22nd [August], **with rapidly diminishing numbers,**
Hamilton reached Uttoxeter. There his soldiers mutinied,
refusing to go any further. On the 25th Hamilton offered to
capitulate to the governor of Stafford. Before the terms had
been agreed on, Lambert appeared on the scene.
Commissioners on both sides were appointed and articles of
surrender were agreed on and signed. Then Lord Grey of
Groby rode in with a body of horse from Leicestershire and
seized on Hamilton as his prisoner. Lambert, however,
insisted on the observance of the articles signed. Hamilton
and all those with him were to be prisoners of war, having
`the lives and safety of their persons assured to them'".[11]

Lucy Hutchinson records simply that,

"Hamilton himself, with a good party of horse, fled to Uttoxeter, and was there taken by the Lord Grey". [12]

Another account by a parliamentarian partisan, Edmund Ludlow, gives both more detail and a more favourable construction to Lord Grey's actions.

"..... about Leicestershire, which county the Lord Grey of Grooby [sic] *had raised, and brought together about three thousand horse and foot to preserve the country from plunder, and to take all possible advantages against the enemy : and though a body of horse from the army* [i.e. under Lambert] *was in pursuit of the Scots, yet the Leicestershire party came up first to them at Uttoxeter in Staffordshire, where the body of the enemy's horse was ; and whilst the Scots were treating with the other party from the army, the Lord Grey's men, observing no guards kept, entered upon them before any conditions were made ; whereupon Hamilton surrendered himself to Colonel* [Thomas] *Wayte, an officer of the Leicestershire party, delivering to him his scarf* [i.e. sash], *his george* [i.e. insignia of a Knight of the Garter], *and his sword, which last he desired him to keep carefully, because it had belonged to his ancestors. By the two parties the Scots were all made prisoners, and all their horses seized ; the Duke of Hamilton was carried prisoner to Windsor Castle, and all their standards of horse and foot were taken and sent up to London, where the parliament ordered them to be hung up in Westminster Hall. The House of Lords who had avoided to declare the Scots enemies whilst their army was entire, now after their defeat prevented* [i.e. pre-empted] *the House of Commons, and moved that a day might be appointed to give God thanks for this success".* [13]

Burnett, in 'The Memoirs of the Duke of Hamilton', relates how Lord Grey's men arrived after the terms of surrender had been agreed between the representatives of Hamilton and Lambert but before they had been formally signed. The delay appears to have been caused by Hamilton's reluctance to authorise the delivery of Berwick and Carlisle to the New Model Army. He did not wish,

"..... to do anything [that] *might so far prejudice the King's Service, as the delivery of these towns would do ; whereupon he*

271

dismissed the Colonels [Robert Lilburne, Hezekiah Hayns, and Edward Manwaring] *with some very sad expressions. During this the Lord Grey of Grobie* [sic] *came towards Utoxater* [sic]*, to whom the General* [Hamilton] *sent Colonel Kerr to tell him he was in Treaty with Lambert ; and those who were appointed to treat, agreed on the following Articles.*

"I. That James Duke of Hamilton his Grace, with the rest of the Officers and Souldiers under his command, now at Utoxater, shall render themselves up Prisoners of War, with their Horses, Arms, and all other provisions of war, bag and baggage whatsoever, (except what is mentioned in the ensuing Articles) to Major-General Lambert, or such as he shall appoint, without spoil, concealment, or imbeazelment [sic]*, by four of the Clock this afternoon, upon Utoxater Heath, or some convenient Field near unto it.*

II. That the Duke of Hamilton, with all Officers and Souldiers of the said Scottish forces at Utoxater, shall have their Lives and Safety of their Persons assured to them, and shall not be pillaged or stript of their wearing cloaths, or what they have about them, or otherwise wronged, beaten, or harmed, upon the delivering up of their Arms, or afterwards, and shall have civil usage during the time of their imprisonment.

III. That all Field Officers, and Captains of Horse in command, shall have each of them a horse provided to ride on, to such places as shall be appointed by Major-General Lambert for their stay ; each Colonel in command to have one horse for his servant to ride with him, and each Commission-Officer that is sick or wounded, and not able to go on foot, to have one horse provided for himself to ride on, and that a safe Convoy shall be provided to conduct the prisoners to the places they shall be sent to ; and if any that are sick or wounded do desire it, they may have liberty to stay at Utoxter till further order from Major-General Lambert.

IV. That the said Duke of Hamilton shall have six of his servants, such as he shall choose, allowed to wait on him, and each of them an horse to ride with him, till they come to the place of stay, and have none of their wearing cloaths or what they have about them taken from them.

272

V. That all Treasure and Plate remaining in the Scottish Army at Utoxater, shall be delivered up to such persons as Major-General Lambert shall appoint.

Signed,

Rob. Lilburn	*William Lockhart*
Hezekiah Hayns	*James Foules*
Edward Manwaring	*James Turner*
[Parliamentarians]	[Scots/Royalists]

"Lambert desired them to sign the Articles quickly, and he would go to Utoxater to save the Duke from Grey of Grobie's men : but before he came they had fallen in, not regarding the Treaty nor the Cessation of Arms, and had taken the Duke ; yet Lambert would not look on him as a prisoner until the Articles were signed, which he ratified, and disclaimed Grey of Grobie's taking of him, as done in time of Treaty and Cessation, against the Law of War and Nations : neither was the Lord Grey empowered by the Parliament, so that Lambert having authority from them, they were obliged by his Treaty and Articles. The Articles were also signed, though not sent back, some time before Grey himself came up.

"The Duke was carried to Derby, from that to Loughborough, from that to Leicester, and from that on the 28th of August to Ashby-de-la-Zouch, where he continued prisoner till the beginning of December that he was carried to Windsor".[14]

Nichols refers to an entry in the House of Commons Journal concerning this event and its immediate consequences :-

"A letter from the Lord Grey and Colonel-General Lambert, from Uttoxeter, relating to the taking of Duke Hamilton and 3,500 horse with him, having been read in the House of Commons, August 28 ; thanks were ordered to be returned, and £1,000 bestowed on Mr. Edward Evans, his [Lord Grey's] *secretary; and, the next day, the government of Ashby-de-la-Zouch was entrusted to his* [Lord Grey's] *charge ; with directions "to take care for the securing and safe keeping* [of] *Duke Hamilton, a prisoner there, till further order; to allow him two servants to attend him, and no more; to take care of the safekeeping of the rest of the officers and gentlemen that were prisoners ; and that the other prisoners might be secured".*[15]

The hostile anti-republican Tory vicar and commentator, Mark Noble, records the incident and its aftermath as follows :-

"The Duke of Hamilton having been defeated at Uttoexeter, and having surrendered himself upon articles, Lord Grey came up, and shamefully took him out of the hands of Lambert, to whom his Grace had signed the treaty, and then pretended that he was a prisoner without any stipulation for life, or liberty ; and the parliament, to shew [sic] their sanguinary dispositions, in exact opposite to justice, adjudged the duke a prisoner to Lord Grey, that they might have a pretence to destroy him ; and to affect this the better, they of the house of commons passed a vote of thanks to his lordship, for taking his Grace a prisoner, and dispersing a brigade of his horse ; and though the unfortunate Duke applied to the honour of Grey to save him at his trial, it was to no purpose ; his death had been decreed, as his royal master's, before he came to trial, and he fell a sacrifice to the shameless policy of the times. He [Lord Grey] mocked God by a day of thanksgiving for this victory over the Scots, and feasted one hundred and fifty of his officers for it at Leicester".[16]

In addition to the vote of thanks and the £1,000 in August, Lord Grey was granted £1,500 out of Crown lands by a grateful Parliament in November because he had been *"very zealous in forwarding Parliamentary interests"*.[17]

It had been necessary for Parliament to ratify Lord Grey of Groby's military actions retrospectively because he had been disqualified as an MP from holding military command by the Self-Denying Ordinance. His letter of 24th August to Parliament via Skippon had set out the reasons that had forced him to ignore this restriction.

Parliament's gratitude in respect of the contributions made by its Leicestershire supporters was not limited to Lord Grey of Groby. On 29th August, the day that Lord Grey was awarded the governorship of Ashby Castle, the sum of £200 was awarded to Colonel Thomas Waite out of the sequestered estates of John Pate, Lord Bodenham, and Wingfield Bodenham. The following month, on 25th September, the Leicestershire forces under Colonel Francis Hacker and Colonel Waite, who had been sent to assist in the siege of Pontefract Castle by Cromwell, were ordered £3,000 out of the estates of other local royalist 'delinquents'. They were then directed to march to Cumberland and Westmoreland to assist in the suppression of disorder there.

To celebrate the victories of Preston and Uttoxeter Lord Grey, as noted by Noble above, held a day of thanksgiving to God and a banquet for one hundred and fifty of his officers in Leicester. Other records of the campaign and its costs survive amongst the list of expenses incurred by the Corporation of the Borough of Leicester :-

"Item paid by appoyntment of Mr. Maior and Mr. Cradocke towards the quartering of 140 Scotch prisoners and to prevent their quartering in ye Towne. i. li.

"Item paid Mr. Martin for wood and Cole used att the Guard when Duke Hamilton was prisoner in his house as appeare by his bill. vs.

"Item paid Mr. Henry Hemmings Collector for 4 months tax ymposed [sic] upon freaks land belonging to the Towne for the payment of the county souldiers that went with the Lord Grey to Utceter [sic] as appears by his receipt. iiij li. xiijs. viijd. "[18]

The consequences of the incident at Uttoxeter proved to be fatal for the Duke of Hamilton. The Grandees had hoped to pressure him into testifying that the king had ordered the invasion of England by the Scots. This, Hamilton, who had been the king's Master of the Horse before the first civil war, refused to do. He was then put on trial for his life.

His defence was made under three headings. Firstly, he had acted upon the instructions and authority of the Estates [Parliament] and Kingdom of Scotland - over whom English courts had no jurisdiction. Secondly, he was born in Scotland before his Scottish father had become naturalised in England and therefore considered himself an alien and not triable in England. Thirdly, he had rendered himself prisoner upon capitulation and articles with commissioners who had Major-General Lambert's commission; and that by these he was both a prisoner of war and entitled to his life and the safety of his person as guaranteed to him by the articles which had been signed by commissioners of both sides before he was made a prisoner.

In response he was told that the court regarded him as an Englishman and thus subject to English jurisdiction, partly because of his father's naturalisation (as a courtier of James VI of Scotland when he became also James I of England - despite Hamilton's point that he had been born before this naturalization), and partly because he held the title of Earl of Cambridge in addition to that of Duke of Hamilton. The holder of an English title was deemed to be English and subject to English law and English courts. Consideration then centred upon the nature and conditions of his capture at Uttoxeter.

Lord Grey's evidence was to the effect that :-

".... two several summons, which were sent by him to his Grace to yield upon Mercy, were both answered negatively in respect of the Cessation and Treaty ; That by a letter from Cromwell, dated Warrington August 20th, he was enjoined to pursue the Scottish forces with all vigour ; That he had received letters from the Staffordshire Gentlemen with whom the Cessation begun, intimating that they had condescended to it, on purpose to gain a few days time to strengthen themselves, in regard the Scots were so numerous ; and, that he dispatched away Wayte and Peters that morning in which the Treaty ended to protest against it.

"Peters was next examined, and answered, That going that morning to protest, by order from the Lord Grey, he came accidentally to the Duke, where he found the hostages in his chamber, and asked if he was willing to be the Lord Gray's [sic] prisoner, who answered, he could not, in regard of the Treaty ; but if he were afterwards to be disposed of, he had rather be his Lordship's prisoner than any others, being of his acquaintance ; That he had seen the Summons, and the negative answer to them ; That this was about five in the morning ; and that Wayte and he went a part of the way towards the place of the Treaty, where he heard the Articles were concluded".[19]

Other witnesses included Robert Lilburne, commissioners from both sides and the Duke's servants. Their testimonies were of no avail. Hamilton was sentenced to be beheaded.

When, on 23rd November, the king was brought to Windsor Castle he was met as he entered by the doomed Hamilton who fell to his knees and stammered. *"My dear master"*. Charles raised him to his feet and embraced him. *"I have been so indeed to you,"* he said.

This episode might not appear to show Lord Grey of Groby in a particularly gallant light but John Buchan comments :-

"It is reasonably clear that Hamilton had been captured, and had not surrendered to quarter, and that his execution was therefore not a breach of military justice".[20]

Little mercy was now being shown to the defeated royalists and those who were regarded by the victors as having changed sides. Colchester had fallen on 18th August. Sir Charles Lucas and Sir George Lisle were shot by order of a Council of War presided over by Fairfax. Lords Holland and

276

Capel, like Hamilton, were sentenced to the block. Lord Norwich, the former Lord Goring, was only saved by the casting vote of the Speaker when the fate of those members of the Houses of Parliament who had been involved in the risings were referred to Westminster for sentence.

Towards the close of 1648 orders were issued by Parliament for the disgarrisoning of Leicester and the 'slighting' of Ashby-de-la-Zouch. In December, after the transfer of the Duke of Hamilton to Windsor Castle, William Bainbridge of Lockington, a member of the Leicestershire Committee, was sent to Ashby with one troop of horse to supervise the demolition of the castle and its outer fortifications. A plaque in the 'Bull's Head' Inn records that he resided there whilst this was accomplished. (The 'Bull's Head' was the traditional livery badge of the Hastings family). One may imagine the satisfaction derived from this particular exercise by the latest governor of the castle. The Greys of Bradgate finally seemed to have triumphed over their Leicestershire rivals. Henceforth the family residence of the Hastingses would be at Castle Donington rather than at Ashby-de-la-Zouch. In reality this merely confirmed a trend that had already begun before the original outbreak of hostilities in 1642.

An extract from the pro-royalist Heath's Chronicle may serve as an interesting postscript to the end of the second civil war. It features two exiles, former enemies, who would make common cause in the future and return to Leicestershire with varying degrees of success :-

"The Lord Loughborough, brother to Ferdinando then Earl of Huntingdon, famous for several loyal services, but most maligned by the Parliament for the last effort thereof at Colchester [where he was Commissary-General for the royalist forces], *gave them also the slip from Windsor Castle (where the Colonels Tooke, Hammond, and Francis Heath - newly at liberty upon his parole to find good security - and other royalists were imprisoned), and got cleverly away, and in March (1649) arrived at Rotterdam in Holland, where on the New Bridge he accidentally met with Colonel Massey* [the former parliamentarian hero of Gloucester and the Earl of Stamford's original second-in-command]; *who claiming knowledge from Lidbury fight, where they unhappily encountered each other, his lordship was civilly and nobly pleased (upon the Colonel's protestation of a return and entire obedience to his Majesty's authority) to pass with him in company to the Hague".*[21]

NOTES

1. *The Case of the Armie Truly Stated* (15th October 1647) *Leveller Manifestoes of the Puritan Revolution*, ed. Don M. Wolfe, Nelson, 1944; reprinted 1967.

2. *A letter from Several Agitators to the Regiments.* November 1647. See *Puritanism and Liberty* ed. A. S. P. Woodhouse, (Dent, Second edition, 1950) cited in A. L. Morton, ed., *Freedom in Arms - A Selection of Leveller Writings*, Lawrence & Wishart, London, 1975.

3. *Resolution of the Army*, April 1648, from Adjutant-General Allen's pamphlet (published in 1659) - *Somers Tracts*, Vol. VI. pp. 499 - 501, and in *Letters & Speeches I* pp. 307 - 310. Cited in John Buchan's *Cromwell*, (Sphere Books, London, 1971) p. 267.

4. House of Commons Journal, Vol. V. ; p. 620.

5. Records of the Borough of Leicester. DXX. - Hall Papers XII, No. 162. [5 June 1648].

6. C. J. op. cit. Vol. V. ; p. 620.

7. Calendar of State Papers (Domestic Series), 1648.

8. Records of the Borough of Leicester. DXIL. - Hall Papers XII, Accounts. 1648. p. 378.

9. Thomas Carlyle, *Cromwell's Letters and Speeches*, (ed. Lomas), 3 vols. 1904. Vol. II. p. 215.

10. John Nichols, *History and Antiquities of Leicestershire*, Vol. III., Part II., Appendix to the History of West Goscote. p. 634. Copied from a very scarce Tract, intitled, *Old English Blood boyling afresh in Leicestershire Men; occasioned by the late barbarous Invasion of the Scots; as appears by this Letter from my Lord Grey to Major-Generall Skippon, London; printed for Giles Calvert, at the Black Spread Eagle; at the West End of St. Paul's; 1648.*

11. S. R. Gardiner, *History of the Great Civil War*, 1893. Vol. IV., p. 192.

12. Lucy Hutchinson, *Memoirs of Colonel Hutchinson*, Everyman edition - Dent, London, 1965. p. 255.

13. Edmund Ludlow, *Ludlow's Memorials*, p. 112.

14. Burnett's, *The Memorials of the Dukes of Hamilton*, Lib. VI. pp. 364 - 365.

15. C. J. op. cit., Vol. V. pp. 688 - 692.

16. Rev. Mark Noble, *The Lives of the English Regicides*, etc., London, 1798. Vol. II. pp. 265 - 266.

17. C. J. op. cit., Vol. V. pp. 688 - 692.

18. Records of the Borough of Leicester, op. cit. p. 393.

19. Burnett's, *The Memorials of the Dukes of Hamilton* op. cit. p. 387.

20.   John Buchan, *Cromwell*, Hodder & Stoughton 1934.
       Reprinted Sphere Books 1971. p. 285. Footnote.
21.   *Heath's Chronicle*, p. 227. cited in John Nichols op. cit.,
       Appendix on *The Civil War in Leicestershire*, p. 67.

Henry Ireton

280

Oliver Cromwell

James, Duke of Hamilton

282

CHAPTER NINE

THE ARISTOCRATIC REGICIDE (1648 - 1649)

"Fret not thyself because of evil-doers, Neither be thou envious of them that work unrighteousness, For they shall soon be cut down like the grass, And wither as the green herb."

(Psalm 37 vs. 1 & 2)

As a result of his perceived zeal and activity for the radical parliamentarian cause Lord Grey of Groby now moved into the leading circle of the emerging 'junta' of Army leaders and parliamentary Independents. Insufficient attention has previously been given to his central role in the momentous events of this period which has thus been seriously underestimated.

Early in September 1648 the Army leaders and their parliamentary allies began to discuss the situation now facing them. Colchester had fallen, the second civil war was over; but the openings of negotiations between the king and parliament again were imminent. Many of them recalled their resolution at the Army Council at Windsor earlier that year that

"..... it was our duty, if ever the Lord brought us back again in peace, to call Charles Stuart, that man of blood, to an account for the blood he had shed, and mischief he had done to his utmost against the Lord's cause and people in these poor nations".[1]

If the king and the parliament were to reach a compromise agreement in the forthcoming negotiations then all the sacrifices made would have been for naught and godly justice frustrated.

Edmund Ludlow, one of the leading radical Independents in the House of Commons and an associate of Lord Grey of Groby, went to Colchester sometime before the 6th of September to talk to Fairfax *"by the advice of some friends"*. The Lord General was typically non-committal. Ludlow argued that any negotiations with the king would be likely to *"betray the cause"*, and that it was vital for the Army *"to prevent the ruin of themselves and the nation"*. Fairfax did not argue, but would only say that he would *"use the power he had, to maintain the cause of the public"*. A frustrated and angry Ludlow then went to Henry Ireton. Their ensuing conversation, which he recalled in his memoirs, demonstrates both the agreement of the senior army officers with the parliamentary radicals on aims, and their disagreement over tactics and timing.

"We both agreed that it was necessary for the army to interpose ..... but differed about the time ; he being of opinion that it was best to permit the King and the Parliament to make an agreement, ... whereby the people, becoming sensible of their own danger, would willingly join to oppose them".

Ludlow, on the other hand, thought it vital to act before the Treaty was completed, fearing that a reunited King and Parliament would court popular support by disbanding the army, *"under pretence of lessening their taxes"*, and thus presenting the military opposition as self-interested *"disturbers of the public peace"*.[2]

Ludlow's arguments carried conviction, but without the support of the army the radical MPs could not purge Parliament. Ireton was not yet ready to act. Fairfax preferred not to act ; whilst Cromwell was far away in Scotland.

Before Ireton could be convinced of the need to act the intense feeling on this matter within the army had to be communicated to the more cautious officers and to the country at large. The revolutionary minority in the country also had to be given time to bring pressure on Parliament to break off the treaty negotiations with the King. The Parliament, now dominated by a majority of 'Presbyterians' and 'Moderate Independents' (known as the 'Peace Party'), had repealed the 'Vote of No Addresses' and sent negotiators with a renewed application to the king. The negotiators included Denzil Holles who had returned from his earlier flight. The negotiations were referred to as the potential 'Treaty of Newport' after the town on the Isle of Wight, near to Carisbrooke Castle and the king, where the talks were held. It was necessary, therefore, for the radicals in the army and in parliament to press for these negotiations to be stopped. Hence the petitioning campaign which began in September, and continued throughout the autumn of 1648. Just how much official inspiration and central co-ordination there was for this it is difficult to judge. It is more likely to have been orchestrated and easier to achieve within the Army. Outside the Army there was at least the spontaneous recognition that this was the time to speak out. Ireton felt, therefore, that he could afford to wait in the hope that the petitions from all parts of the country might persuade the Parliament to withdraw from the talks. If this did not happen then at least a climate of opinion favouring a more drastic course of action could be seen to be building up.

The Levellers were amongst the first to participate. On 11th September they presented to Parliament their 'Humble Petition of Thousands of Well-affected Persons'. This called for the implementation of the 'Agreement of the People' and for the abolition of the veto power of the King and the

House of Lords. Two days later, after the House of Commons had ignored the petition, a crowd of Levellers appeared at the door of the House with another petition repeating these demands. There was a disturbance and the demonstrators were heard to say, *"that they knew no use of a King or Lords any longer; and that such distinctions were the devices of men, God having made all alike"*. There were some members in the House who, without accepting the democratic implications of such language, recognised its political value. Some of them came out to encourage the demonstrators. The moderate majority were not deterred, however, seeing, as one of them remarked, that it merely showed *"what we are to look for from such a kind of men ..... if the Treaty should not proceed"*.

On 15th September, amid incessant rain, the parliamentary commissioners arrived in the Isle of Wight to open the negotiations with the king. The very next day the first of the county petitions against the Treaty was adopted in Leicestershire. It had been circulated by the County Committee and the sequestrators and it is thought that it was inspired by Lord Grey of Groby.[3] The petition was presented to the House of Commons on 2nd October, *"in the name of the well-affected ministry, gentry, and other inhabitants of the said county* [of Leicester]; *taking notice of some declarations of the Kirk of Scotland and of this kingdom, and of the votes for no further addresses"*. Some 'divers gentlemen of the county of Leicester' were called in to receive the following answer from the Speaker : -

> *"The House has commanded me to acquaint you, that they have read your petition ; that they are engaged in a treaty with the King ; and do assure you that, in that treaty, they will provide and take care for the preservation and security of the religion, laws, and liberties, of the kingdom : and for the security and maintenance of all those who have adhered unto them".*[4]

Compared with later petitions the Leicestershire petition was relatively restrained. It called for a suspension of the treaty negotiations pending investigation into the king's conduct and his responsibilities for the revival of warfare in the second civil war. The conclusion of the petition was more threatening, however, when it pointed out that since the Lord God had put *"the main principal enemies into your hands ..... impartial and personal justice may be speedily administered"*.[5] This could mean the Duke of Hamilton and the instigators of the second Civil War; it could also include the king.

Similar petitions were soon being prepared : a Leveller one in Oxfordshire, and three more in Newcastle, Yorkshire, and Somerset. Of these the Somerset one was the most radical. The Somerset men rejected the Treaty absolutely as the *'ruin of God's people'*, declared that Charles could not be trusted to keep any engagement and called in plain language for him to be brought to trial in order *"that justice be executed upon all delinquents, from the highest to the lowest, without exception"*.[6]

Though the Army was marking time in September while the petitions were being prepared, this was not the case with supporters of the treaty negotiations in the House of Commons. On 26th September there was a large attendance at Westminster. Correspondence between the commissioners in the Isle of Wight and their friends in Westminster reveals a concerted effort, on the one hand to force the king to make concessions and on the other hand to prevent the more rigid Presbyterians and radical Independents from insisting upon impossible terms. John Crewe, one of the commissioners, wrote to John Swynfen, a middle-group supporter like himself, in these terms,

"We shall use our utmost endeavours here to bring the King nearer the Houses, and you will do good service at London in persuading the House to come nearer the King ..... No man knows what will become of religion and the Parliament if we have not peace".[7]

Although progress at Newport was slow the two sides were moving gradually towards each other. On 9th October the king made a major concession - parliamentary control of the militia for twenty years. With the possible exception of Sir Henry Vane all of the commissioners were united in a strong desire to reach a successful conclusion of the Treaty. The king was urged to accept a Presbyterian religious establishment. This remained a stumbling block. Vane offered the king promises of better terms from the Army, including toleration for Episcopalians and the Common Prayer Book for those who wished to use it. Charles revelled in playing them off against each other.

The negotiations continued through October in much the same manner. Although on 27th October the House of Commons rejected the king's latest counter proposals, the majority of members still hoped for an eventual agreement. It was becoming increasingly clear, however, to the Army Council that little could be expected from King and Parliament except only procrastination from the former and concessions towards the originators of the second civil war from the latter. In these next developments Henry Ireton, in the absence of Cromwell, played a decisive role. Charles indeed had a vested interest in neither accepting nor denying the Treaty of Newport (although called a treaty, the term actually covered the negotiations rather than the resolution). Whilst playing for time and the hope of further external assistance there was also the real prospect of growing disagreement between Parliament and the Army working to his advantage.

Cromwell had left Scotland in the middle of October and joined the forces besieging the royalists still holding out in Pontefract Castle. He seems to have been in a hesitant state of mind as far as non-military matters were concerned. He was, at the same time, exultant, anxious and confused. He had crushed the Scots and Royalist armies in the north of England, and by his arms and diplomacy had removed Scotland as a threat for the time being. He realised, however, that the victories in the field had left some major issues unresolved. His language, like that of Lord Grey of Groby, became more and more that of the puritan zealot. Amongst all the uncertainties he began more clearly to discern the providential hand of the Lord revealing his purposes to the Saints through the evidence and blessing of the many victories granted to them. Equally it was becoming more and more clear that the Lord God had signalled his displeasure with the malignant royalists and those renegades from the Cause who had gone over to them. Most of all King Charles was being seen increasingly as the chief architect of all the misery, death and destruction of the civil wars.

At the end of October an incident occurred which further angered the army radicals, and the Levellers in particular. Four cavaliers from the Pontefract garrison, armed with a forged message from Cromwell, entered the lodgings at Doncaster of Colonel Thomas Rainsborough, that military Leveller leader and veteran of the Putney Army Debates. They attempted to abduct him with the intention of exchanging him for Sir Marmaduke Langdale, believed by them to be languishing in Nottingham Castle, although he had escaped by his own efforts the day before. There was a scuffle in the street as Rainsborough valiantly struggled to break free from his captors. In the melee the hero of the Levellers and the champion of democracy was killed by these members of what Clarendon, in reporting the incident, chose to call *"the gallant party"*. Rainsborough's murder outraged his comrades in the army and the civilian radicals. It also caused a sensation in Parliament where it was generally attributed to Rainsborough's reputation as one of the first advocates of putting the king on trial. Cromwell personally took urgent steps to trace and punish the killers.

Meanwhile, Henry Ireton had become a different man from the patient lawyer of the Putney Army debates of 1647. Then he had been prepared to speculate on the foundations of government with safeguards for property interests. He had been essentially a conservative in the discussions with the Levellers, seeking not a breach with the past but rather organic evolution. He had opposed the republican theorists even though he was an Independent. But the second Civil War and its immediate aftermath had changed his attitude. It was now clear to him that there could be no agreement or trust with such a man as Charles Stuart, since no form of words would be held by the king to bind him. To Ireton, as increasingly to Cromwell also, the Newport negotiations were only *"ruining hypocritical agreements"*. He saw Charles as not only responsible for the recent war but incorrigible, and he believed that unless the army intervened to stop the treaty, the civil and religious liberties that it had fought for would be signed away. In the middle of October Ireton's own regiment produced a petition calling for justice which he endorsed.

Ireton had spent the greater part of October in partial seclusion at Windsor, drawing up the draft of a 'Remonstrance' from the Army to Parliament. The presentation of this document, which denounced the attempts to agree the Newport Treaty and asked for justice on the king, would precipitate the crisis. On 10th November its contents were placed before Fairfax and his Army Council of Officers, with Ireton strongly urging immediate action. Fairfax hung back and was not alone amongst the senior officers in his doubts. The junior officers, the army rank and file, and the radical Independents in Parliament pressed for action. Cromwell continued to hesitate at Pontefract. Lord Grey was kept informed of events by those of his Leicestershire troops who formed part of the besieging forces there.

Ireton resorted to further lobbying and held talks with the leaders of the radicals amongst the army, the parliamentarian Independents, and the chief men of the Levellers. A new version of the 'Remonstrance' was then produced, a mixture of the old "Heads of the Proposals" and the old "Agreement of the People". On 16th November, following another fruitless approach to the king which had been seen to have failed, Ireton placed the revised 'Remonstrance' before Fairfax and the General Council of the Army again. It called for parliament to break off negotiations with the king and to bring him to trial. This time it was accepted by the Army Council. Fairfax was passive and Cromwell, still at Pontefract, apparently now approved of this latest version which seemed to him, as he told Fairfax, to have *"nothing in it but what is honest, and becoming honest men to say and offer"*.

Fairfax signed a covering letter to the Speaker urging him to place the 'Remonstrance of His Excellency, Thomas Lord Fairfax ..... and of the General Council of Officers' before the House of Commons without delay. The lengthy document condemned the king's policy, exposed the folly of attempting to treat with him, summed up the Army's plans for justice, peace and reform, and openly demanded : -

*"that the capital and grand author of our troubles, the person
of the King, by whose commissions, commands or procurements,
and in whose behalf, and for whose interest only, all our wars
and troubles have been, with all the miseries attending them,*

may be speedily brought to justice, for the treason, blood and mischief he's therein guilty of".[8]

The 'Remonstrance' was delivered to Westminster on 20th November by a deputation of officers led by a Colonel Ewer who had distinguished himself in the second civil war by taking Chepstow Castle and killing the governor. With a desperate obstinacy the House of Commons refused to discuss the 'Remonstrance'. The patience of the Army had now been stretched to breaking point. Cromwell too was at last beginning to stir at Pontefract. He wrote to Fairfax that in his heart he concurred with the troops' desire to see justice done upon offenders.

Meanwhile, Ireton was now being troubled on his other flank by the Levellers who had revived and strengthened their influence in the Army in recent months. Rainsborough's murder had heightened their resolve. They stipulated that the Army should do nothing else until it had committed itself to establishing a democratic Commonwealth of England, based on an "Agreement of the People" which every well-affected citizen should be invited to sign. Reluctantly, to avoid dissension in the army's ranks at this critical stage, Ireton agreed that a committee of Levellers, Army Officers, radical MPs, and London Independents - four from each group - should draft a new version of the "Agreement of the People". He hoped for a less radical and more specific version than the one that had been the subject of the Putney Army Debates in the previous year.

Ireton's plan at the end of November was that the army should be used to dissolve the Parliament and recognise those members who opposed the Newport Treaty as a provisional government for as long as it would take to arrange a general election and assemble a new parliament. But these members, including Ludlow and Grey, would not give their consent to a dissolution by military force, even though they wanted the treaty stopped. They insisted that the army should merely exclude those MPs who were obstinately pursuing an agreement with the king and recognise the rest as still constituting a valid parliament. In the meantime, petitions from the 'well-affected in the counties' continued to be received by the Army and the Parliament.

According to Ian Gentles : -

"Lord Grey of Groby visited St. Albans on 23rd November [1648, where there was a meeting of Army commanders], ostensibly **to present a petition from Leicestershire in support of the Remonstrance, but more likely so that he could advise about the list of MPs slated for purging. The capital was alive with fears of the army's advance".**[9]

The House of Commons themselves had to sit through a violent sermon by the radical Independent George Cokayne, calling for justice against those guilty of *'shedding innocent blood, at their now regular monthly Fast Day on 29th November'*.

On 28th November Fairfax, under pressure from Ireton and a decision of the Army Council, agreed to march on London *"for the public interest"* and the safety of the nation. On 30th November a 'Declaration' justifying the march appeared. Protesting at the Parliament's refusal to discuss the 'Humble Remonstrance', the Army appealed over their heads to *"the common judgements of indifferent and uncorrupted men"*. The Army stated that their aim was *"a more orderly and equal judicative of men in a just Representative* [i.e. Parliament]*"*. They would try to preserve as much *"of the present parliamentary authority ..... as can be safe, or will be useful to those ends"*. They gave parliament a last chance to exclude *"corrupt and apostatised members"*. Failing this, the Army called upon the 'upright' members to withdraw (as they had done previously in the summer of 1647); they would be regarded as *"having materially the chief trust of the kingdom remaining in them"*, until *"a more full and formal power in a just Representative "* could be settled. *"For all those ends"*, they concluded, *"we are now drawing up with the Army to London, there to follow Providence as God shall clear our way"*.[10]

David Underdown has demonstrated that at the time the 'Declaration' went to press Ireton's original intention of facilitating the withdrawal of the *'upright'* members and dissolution, rather than a purge, was still the aim. It was believed by him and Fairfax that their friends in the House of Commons would accept this programme. As late as the 30th November a newsletter from Windsor reported that since the Commons had again (on the 17th) refused to debate the 'Remonstrance', *"the members of the House who were for it do intend this day to declare and protest against the rest and come to the Army, and the Army marches tomorrow to the rendezvous on Hounslow Heath and so on to secure those members who declare with the Army"*.[11] The plan was changed, therefore, on 30th November argues Underdown. The reason for the change was that the *'honest members'* such as Grey, Ludlow, and John Hutchinson did not issue their expected declaration of secession. They considered themselves to be legitimately and constitutionally elected and saw no reason why they should be included in any general dissolution. Their obstinacy forced a change of tactics on Ireton and the Army from the path which they had originally favoured. Lord Grey's visit to St. Albans earlier had been part of this lobbying. On Ludlow's evidence, however, it would seem that it was only during the march on London that Ireton gave way to the civilians and accepted the alternative of a purge of Parliament.

Ludlow gives the following account of the evolution of this strategy : -

"This remonstrance they [the Army] *presented to the parliament on the 20th November, 1648. The king and parliament seeing this cloud beginning to gather, endeavoured by all means possible to hasten their treaty to a conclusion. The army also were not wanting to fortify themselves against that shock, sending some of their own number to those members of parliament, whom they esteemed most faithful to the common cause, to invite them down to the army, after they should in a publick* [sic] *manner have expressed their dissatisfaction to the proceedings of those who had betrayed the trust reposed in them by the good people of England; and declared, that finding it impossible to be any further serviceable in parliament, they had resolved to repair to the army, in order to procure their assistance in settling the governance of the nation upon a just foundation. At a meeting of some members of parliament with the said officers from the army, it was resolved, that though the way proposed by them might be taken, in case all other means failed, yet seeing there was more than a sufficient number of members in the parliament to make a house, who were most affectionate to the publick cause, it would be more proper for the army to relieve them from those who rendered them useless to the publick service, thereby preserving the name and place of the parliament, than for the members thereof to quit their stations wherein they were appointed to serve, and to leave the civil authority in the hands of those who would be ready to fall in with any power that would attempt to frustrate what should be agreed on by them and the army. In prosecution of this result, the army drew to Colnbrook, from whence commissary-general Ireton sent me word, that now he hoped they should please me; which I must acknowledge they did by the way which they were taking; not from any particular advantages that I expected from it, except an equal share of security with other men; but that the people of England might be preserved in their just rights, from the oppressions of violent men; the question in dispute between the king's party and us being, as I apprehended, "Whether the king should govern as a God by his will, and the nation be governed by force like beasts : or whether the people should be governed by laws made by themselves, and live under a government derived from their own consent?" Being fully persuaded that an accommodation with the king was unsafe for the people of*

*England, and unjust and wicked in the nature of it. ..... I was
convinced by the express words of God's law; "That blood
defileth the land, and the land cannot be cleansed of the blood
that is shed therein, but by the blood of him that shed it, "Numb.
XXXV. 33. And therefore I could not consent to the counsels of
those who were contented to leave the guilt of so much blood
upon the nation, and thereby to draw down the just vengeance
of God upon us all; when it was most evident that the war had
been occasioned by the invasion of our rights, and open breach
of our laws and constitution, on the king's part".* [12]

Appalled by the threat of military occupation of the capital the Lord
Mayor and City Corporation sat up all night in council and sent a desperate
message to the House of Commons. Here the die-hard Presbyterians still
held out and one of them, the pedantic lawyer William Prynne, urged his
colleagues to declare the Army as rebels. The majority, however, had
enough sense to refrain from offering this needless provocation to an armed
force which they had no power to resist.

As the Army marched through the mist of a grey last day of November
they sent messages to reassure moderate members of the House of their
intentions. On 1st December Parliament made a last minute effort to halt
the Army with an offer of £40,000. But this was the sum that they had
expected to extract from the City anyway and they knew that they could
get more than this. It would take more than a bribe to stop them now.

On the same day the Army had the King moved from the Isle of Wight
to Hurst Castle on the Hampshire coast, replacing the increasingly worried
Colonel Robert Hammond, Cromwell's cousin, with the more determined
Colonel Harrison as the king's gaoler. Fairfax's letter accompanying the
'Declaration' had scarcely been read out to the House of Commons before
word arrived from Hammond that he had been removed from his position.
The members at last addressed themselves to the 'Remonstrance' and
decided, by a vote of 125 to 58, to reject it. Finally, during the evening,
some of the commissioners reached London from Newport. Hearing that
the Army intended to intercept them they had split up into smaller groups
and travelled by night *"along the byways"*.

By now the Army was only a mile away. The main force had
rendezvoused that morning on Hounslow Heath. There were two full
regiments and seventeen troops of horse, five full regiments and ten
companies of foot. Fairfax issued a proclamation ordering the soldiers to
maintain strict discipline. Officers were not to be absent from their
commands without written authorisation. By the evening of 1st December
the rain-soaked force had reached Kensington and was encamped in Hyde
Park. The inhabitants of the capital were left anxious and apprehensive.

292

It rained again throughout the following day. Before the troops moved off two deputations arrived at the camp. The first one was from the Speaker of the House of Commons commanding the Army to halt. Fairfax replied that unfortunately it was too late to countermand the orders given to march. Sir Hardress Waller was sent to explain this to the Commons and to suggest that they reconsider the 'Remonstrance'. But the House was *"intent upon other matters"* and he was not admitted. The second deputation came from the Common Council of the City of London. The citizens were trying to raise the £40,000 of arrears, that the Army had demanded of them. They had been ordered to pay it within two days. They pleaded for the Army not to enter the City and for more time to raise the money. This was not well received and Fairfax told them that he expected the money by Monday, 4th December.

At about noon on Saturday, 2nd December the final advance of the Army to Westminster began. When Fairfax arrived at Whitehall the Army's parliamentary allies were there to welcome him. Underdown states that **"Lord Grey of Groby obsequiously held his stirrup when he alighted, other MPs attended him `bare-headed to his lodging, which he entered with great magnificence'. Fairfax may not have been entirely happy about the policy which he was implementing, but he was obviously enjoying himself"**.[13] The common soldiers had less comfortable quarters. The Foot were allocated accommodation throughout Whitehall, York House, and St. James. The Horse were stationed in the Mews, Durham House and other mansions, some as far away as Southwark.

The next day was a Sunday and there were no major incidents, although conservative presbyterian pastors in City pulpits denounced the Army and its own preachers extolled its righteousness. On Monday, 4th December, Parliament continued its business and for the next two days the House of Commons continued to function, with considerable uneasiness, but unmolested.

The session on Monday, 4th December was a marathon one, lasting until eight o'clock on the Tuesday morning and concluding with a crucial vote on the king's response to the treaty negotiations. Before the main debate began it was officially reported from the Isle of Wight that the king had been removed by the Army to Hurst Castle. This produced a vote that the Army's action was *"without the knowledge or consent of this House"*.[14] They debated the Army's removal of the king for some time but the end result was a mild message of protest to Fairfax. With the king no longer in their power and with the Army at the door, the House of Commons continued to debate the question of the Treaty.

On the previous Friday the most notable speech on this issue had come from Nathaniel Fiennes who echoed the view of his father, Lord Say and

293

Sele, that it was time for a settlement. It was a remarkable statement from the man who, less than a year earlier, had drafted the 'Declaration of No Addresses' (to the king). He now argued that the king's concession over control of the militia and the appointment of the officers of state and the Church were, *"enough to secure religion, laws and liberties"*. Since these were the *"only things which the Parliament had so often declared to be the ground of their quarrel"* nothing further was necessary. The king's agreement to a temporary suspension of episcopacy, and even its permanent suspension unless Parliament ruled otherwise, amounted in effect, he argued, to its abolition[15] This was the case for the so-called 'middle group' of MPs. On the following day it had been the turn of an opponent of the Treaty, in the shape of Sir Henry Vane, to dominate the debates. He began his speech ominously by announcing, *"we shall soon guess who are our friends, and who our enemies"*. Looking back to the *'happy days'* after the 'Vote of No Addresses', when *"the Kingdom had been governed in great peace"*, Vane recalled how that peace had been shattered by the malignant combination between the Scots and the City. The Treaty, he declared, had been a mistake from the very beginning. The king could not be trusted, whatever he might appear to promise. The Commons should therefore *"return to their former resolution of making no more addresses to the King; but proceed to the settling of the government without him, and to the severe punishment of those who had disturbed their peace and quiet"*.[16] They should conciliate the Army and fulfil the programme set out in the 'Remonstrance'. In response William Prynne moved for an adjournment *"till they were a free Parliament"* released from intimidation by the military. The presbyterians and the 'middle group', who formed the majority of the Commons, had clearly wanted such an adjournment in order to play for time. This had been opposed by the radicals but the adjournment until Monday morning had been approved.

On the Monday, having condemned the Army's removal of the king from the Isle of Wight to Hurst Castle, the Commons returned to the main debate. The radical members moved a motion which asked "Whether the King's answers to the Propositions of both Houses be satisfactory?" As only a committed royalist could support this it was defeated as a motion. In its place the 'moderates' proposed the more ambiguously worded proposal "That the answers of the King to the Propositions of both Houses are a ground for the House to proceed upon for the settlement of the peace of the Kingdom".[17] This motion was approved the same day by the House of Lords without a division. Sir Henry Vane's opposition to the Treaty, although not shared by his fellow Commissioners, had been supported by John Hutchinson and Edmund Ludlow. Now came the longest speech of the entire debate from William Prynne. He spoke for over three hours, condemning the actions and views of the Army, giving every possible argument for the Treaty and attacking every argument against it. He also criticised the motives of those who opposed a settlement, particularly those who had picked up Church, Royal, and 'malignant' property at bargain prices. On the Tuesday morning, when attendance had fallen considerably, the motion to put the question was passed by 129 to 83. The subsequent question was passed without further division. This meant that the Commons (and the Lords) had voted that the partial agreement reached at Newport provided a basis for further negotiations. Underdown points out that in effect, by doing this, they had voted for a restoration - but eleven years before it was to be achieved.

Angry scenes followed. Speaker Lenthall is said to have warned the members that this vote would lead to their own destruction. Ludlow, Hutchinson, Lord Grey of Groby, and several other radical members tried to enter a formal protest against the vote but were told that this was not allowed under the rules of the Commons. The members of the House did, somewhat belatedly however, seem to recognise the menace posed by an Army which was likely to have been even further antagonised by their decision. They appointed a deputation to go to see Fairfax for the purpose of *"keeping and preserving a good correspondence between the Parliament and the Army"*.[18] The Lord General received them after an unusually long delay. When he did at last see them he suggested that if they really wanted friendship with the Army, they should give their attention to the neglected 'Remonstrance'. Like the Commons, the Army Council had been meeting in session throughout the previous day and night, *"debating upon high matters"*. As the other senior officers were no longer with him he *"desired them to come tomorrow morning"*.[19] Fairfax's colleagues had other business in mind for the morrow.

All hope of averting the next phase of the effective coup d'état had gone. The last preparations could now be made. As soon as the House of Commons rose at mid-morning on Tuesday, 5th December, Ludlow, Grey of Groby and other leading radical MPs met in conference with Ireton and some leading army officers *"in a chamber near the Long Gallery"* in Whitehall.[20]

There are two accounts of this important meeting. One is by Edmund Ludlow who was present; the other is by John Lilburne who was told about it by one of the participants very soon after it happened. Ludlow relates *"a full and free debate"*, which according to one of Lilburne's informants was very acrimonious. It was characterised by the old disagreement between the Army advocates of dissolution and the MPs who wanted only a purge of the existing Parliament. Ireton insisted that a purged House of Commons would be *"a mock-power, and a mock-parliament"*. In the end, however, he accepted the need for an immediate purge on the understanding that the

House would then dissolve itself and *"procure a new and free Representative"*. Underdown points out that the continuation of this division is important as it demonstrates the army officers' stubborn adherence to a programme of thorough-going parliamentary reform. It also foreshadows the eventual dissolution of the Rump Parliament in 1653 after its repeated failures to 'go to the country' itself.

The conference also addressed the criteria necessary for placing a name on the list of members to be purged from the House of Commons. It was agreed that those members who had supported the crucial motion passed that morning (or more correctly, those who had voted that the motion be put), and/or those who had voted against the August motion declaring those who assisted the Scots invaders as rebels and traitors, should be listed for exclusion.

Finally, a sub-committee of six, consisting of three army officers and three civilian MPs, withdrew into a private room to make the more detailed arrangements for the purge. Who were the members of this key sub-committee which was to trigger a chain of events leading to the establishment of the first and only English Republic? Of the three officers, Henry Ireton was undoubtedly one. Colonel Thomas Harrison was almost certainly another. The third one may have been Colonel Thomas Pride after whom the purge has been traditionally named. He may have been only the instrument who carried it out, however, and if so then the third officer may have been any one of half a dozen New Model Army colonels at that time in London. Of these Sir Hardress Waller and Sir William Constable seem the most likely, according to Underdown. Of the three non-military MPs, Edmund Ludlow was one, by his own statement. Lord Grey of Groby, who was to stand at Colonel Pride's elbow on the following morning to identify members as they approached, was almost certainly another. It is suggested by some hostile commentators that he probably took on either or both roles to gratify his sense of importance. Contemporaries, such as Ludlow however, refer to Grey's undoubted zeal for involvement in the progress of the Cause. For the third parliamentary member Underdown suggests that the most likely candidate is Cornelius Holland, who had been prominent in the discussions at Windsor.

The sub-committee agreed that the Army should be mustered in the morning with guards posted in and around Westminster Hall. Only members *"faithful to the public interest"* should be permitted to enter the Commons chamber. *"To this end"*, recorded Ludlow, *"we went over the names of all the members one by one, giving the truest character we could of their inclinations"*.[21] These decisions having been taken, Ireton went off to give the orders to the regiments and to inform Fairfax what was being done.

296

The decision reached represented the compromise between the wishes of the two groups led by Ireton and Ludlow. Ireton wished to use Parliament to implement the Army's reform programme. Ludlow and his colleagues wished to use the Army to expel their political opponents from Parliament and to keep power in the hands of elected politicians.

The following day, Wednesday, 6th December, was a dry blustery day. It was to be the day of the momentous purge of the Long Parliament, elected in 1640. The army regiments paraded at seven o'clock in the morning. When the Parliament's usual guards, the City Trained Bands, came marching down to Westminster to perform their daily duties they found their way blocked by a thousand men from the army regiments quartered nearby. Whilst the officers on both sides conferred there was an exchange of good-natured greetings with the troopers urging the citizen soldiers to go home to their shops and their wives and to leave their military duties to the Army. Had the latter any doubts about relinquishing their charge, these were laid to rest by their own commander, Major-General Philip Skippon, who had been general of the infantry in the Army and who now threw his influence onto the Army's side and persuaded the Trained Band men to return to the City. By eight o'clock, when the MPs began to assemble, the dispositions around the Parliament House were completed. Colonel Rich's Horse and Colonel Pride's Foot were stationed in Palace Yard, Westminster Hall, the Court of Requests, and on the stairs and in the lobby outside the House of Commons. Soldiers from two other regiments patrolled the surrounding streets.

At the top of the stairs into the Parliament House stood Colonel Thomas Pride, hat in hand, with a list of the members to be purged. It was said that in his youth Pride had been a brewer's drayman, but by 1648 he had become an officer and a gentleman with a good presence and civil manners. He was a stalwart of the Army radical cause and had fought at Naseby and Preston with Cromwell. He knew very few of the members of parliament by sight, however, and was accompanied by Lord Grey of Groby who directed him as to which members were to be admitted, excluded or detained.

According to Antonia Fraser : -

"In this task he [Pride] **was ably assisted by Lord Grey of Groby, a peer** [actually the eldest son of a peer] **ever active in the Roundhead cause, described** [by Lucy Hutchinson and quoted in an earlier chapter] **as having** *"credulous good nature"*, **qualities which no doubt enabled him to take part in this extraordinary ritual. The obstreperous William Prynne was told that Pride's commission was the power of the sword as he** [Grey] **pointed out the members whose faces were unknown**

297

to Pride, a strange echo of Joyce's words to the King a year back. Prynne, however, did not think it a *"fair commission"*. Some members were simply turned away, but those who resisted were locked up together in a chamber, and thirty-nine of these spent the night in a near-by tavern known as "Hell", even the seven older men present, who were offered parole, refusing it for the sake of their outraged honour".[22]

The exact nature of Lord Grey's role in this episode has been open to conjecture, ranging from being a too *"credulous"* tool of others to being the prime mover. The accounts of his contemporaries include the following from Edmund Ludlow and Bulstrode Whitelock.

Ludlow, a close colleague of Grey recounts how : -

> *"Colonel Pride commanded the guard that attended at the parliament doors, having a list of those members who were to be excluded, preventing them from entering into the house, and securing some of the most suspected under a guard provided for that end; in which he was assisted by the lord Grey of Grooby [sic] and others, who knew the members".*[23]

Whitelock describes how : -

> *"Colonel Pride drew up divers of his foot in the court of requests upon the stairs, and in the lobby before the house; and as the members were coming in to go into the house, colonel Pride having a paper of names in his hand, and one of the doorkeepers, and sometimes the lord Grey of Groby standing by him, and informing him who the members were, the colonel seized upon such of them as he was directed by his note, and sent them away with soldiers, some to the queen's court, and court of wards, and other places, by special order from the general and council of the army".*[24]

The later, and very hostile, commentator, the Rev. Mark Noble, ascribes the major role in the purge to Lord Grey, as set out below : -

> *"Lord Grey had always been the foremost for violent measures, fearing, perhaps, that as he had sinned past forgiveness, he would take every occasion to urge on the destruction of the captive monarch and demeaned himself by being, not only secretly in the council of officers, but openly the particular*

instrument to accomplish it : for when it was resolved that they would oblige the house of commons to sanction their unheard-of impious deed, he, with a pride that distinguished itself in wickedness, undertook to perform the dirty office by garbling the house of commons.

"This has been called Colonel Pride's purge, but he was only the inferior instrument, for when that officer's foot were drawn up in the courts of requests, upon the stairs, and in the lobby before the house, just preceding the time the house was to meet, his lordship stood near to direct him in what he was to do, and though Pride had a paper in his hand of the names of such members as were too honest to give any sanction to the murder of their sovereign; yet, as he did not personally know them, this office was performed jointly by his lordship and the door-keeper; and as each obnoxious member came, he was pointed out, secured, and sent away by some soldiers to the queen's court, court of wards, and other place, according to the imperious commands of the general and council of the army. These were men who dared to say that they drew their swords for the protection of the king, the freedom of the parliament, and the liberty of the subject, and could mock the Almighty by pretending that it had his sanction".[25]

Noble having raised the question of Lord Grey's individual motivation, it may be useful to consider David Underdown's general view of the motivation of the 'radicals' who carried out the purge : -

"Religion was not the determining, nor perhaps even the most important, issue in the split in the parliamentarian movement that produced Pride's Purge and the revolution of 1648-9. Yet it cannot be doubted that it was of very great importance indeed. The men who led Parliament into war in 1642, and the overwhelming majority of their committed or reluctant gentry supporters, were moderate reformers in both Church and State. In the end, in 1648, they were pushed aside by a handful of revolutionaries; a small handful in Parliament, though supported by a much larger number of lesser men in the Army and the country at large. Some of the revolutionaries in Parliament, those from whom the main initiative came, and a larger proportion, perhaps most, of their supporters, were motivated not so much by any sharply

distinguished theology as by a Puritan determination to achieve the reformation of society fiercer than that exhibited by the original leadership. For them, at least, Puritan idealism would triumph over constitutional conservatism. For them a reform movement would become a revolutionary one".[26]

Lord Grey of Groby and Colonel Pride were jointly directing on the morning of 6th December 1648 the first scene of a revolution which would lead within a few weeks to the trial and execution of the king, the abolition of the monarchy and the House of Lords and the establishment of a Puritan republic in the form of the Commonwealth of England.

By the end of the day only about 120 members were left in the purged body of the House of Commons or the 'Rump' as it came to be known. Some members, warned of what was happening, had stayed away from the House. Two members - John Birch and Edward Stephens who were both intended victims - had managed somehow to enter the chamber. Messages were sent into them and they were *'pulled out ..... as they looked out of the door'* by Pride's men. Those who were left in the Commons sent out a protest to Fairfax asking for the release of their colleagues and for an end to such high breaches of the privilege of Parliament. This was a formal gesture, however, as the House by definition was now composed only of the allies of the Army. In reply Fairfax and the General Council of Officers issued a declaration that they had liberated the faithful and trustworthy members of Parliament from an oppressive faction and enabled them to carry out their duties to the nation.

The Purge threatened to disrupt other bodies beside the House of Commons. The House of Lords managed to hold an abbreviated session attended by their acting speaker, the Earl of Manchester, and six other peers. After hearing prayers they made one order on a law case, voted six weeks leave of absence for the Earl of Stamford to his home at Bradgate, and then hastily adjourned. Presumably Lord Grey's more conservative father was anxious to get home to Leicestershire and away from such alarming developments.

When Bulstrode Whitelock and his fellow Commissioners of the Great Seal arrived at Westminster Hall to hold their Chancery session they were stopped by two soldiers and allowed to enter only after Whitelock had complained to an officer.

The commissioners were then uncertain whether to sit in session or not, but were persuaded to do so by the ubiquitous Lord Grey. Mark Noble comments, in his usual vein, that : -

"It redounds very little honour upon those tools of the parliament, who continued to sit in his majesty's courts to

300

administer justice, when their sovereign was in the hands of men going to prostitute all laws, human and divine, by solemnly mocking justice, with bringing him to trial, and especially to take the council, and be persuaded to sanction, as it were, the intended deed by Lord Grey, one of the most infamous of men, because they supposed him armed with a little paltry authority ; and yet Whitelocke, who well knew his character, owns, that he, and the other judges sat in the courts whilst preparations were making in Westminster Hall, for the trial of their unhappy king, basely seized by the army".[(27)]

During the evening of 6th December Oliver Cromwell made his belated appearance in Whitehall, after riding down from the north. His late arrival, indeed his whole behaviour during the month before the Purge, suggests that he was reluctant to be identified with it and the movement of which it was a part. On 28th November he had still been with the besieging force at Pontefract. On that same day an urgent summons had been sent to him from Fairfax and the Council of Officers at Windsor ordering him to return to headquarters *"with all convenient speed possible"*. Cromwell certainly did not comply with these orders. He was expected to return to Windsor by 2nd December. Intelligent contemporaries were quick to note that he had deliberately stayed away. Marchamont Nedham observed that he *"never vouchsafed his presence when the Remonstrance was hatching"*. *"..... observe further, that Oliver forbore coming to London, till after the force acted upon the House of Commons"*. Edmund Ludlow records that when Cromwell at last arrived on the evening of 6th December he said *"that he had not been acquainted with this design; yet since it was done, he was glad of it, and would endeavour to maintain it"*.[(28)] Underdown points out that it is possible that Cromwell was unacquainted with the projected purge. Perhaps he shared his son-in-law Ireton's objection to a purge and would have preferred a dissolution of Parliament. **"The most likely solution is that he balked at the use of force against constitutional authority, but could suggest no alternative which would avoid splitting the Army. Not for the last time was Oliver torn between the two conflicting principles of Puritan idealism and constitutional propriety. Like most of his military colleagues he was still following the more decisive leadership of Henry Ireton".**[(29)]

Cromwell's first appearance in the Commons for some time the following morning gave the purged House the opportunity to open proceedings without facing awkward questions about the legality of the previous day's actions and the absence of their imprisoned fellows. He entered arm in arm with Henry Marten, a convinced Republican whose

301

eloquence, wit and ingenuity often influenced the Commons. Marten had not always been on good terms with Cromwell, but their unity of purpose was emphasised when he began the business of the day by moving a vote of thanks to General Cromwell for his services in the field. The House voted their thanks for Cromwell's great services without dissent. They also thanked Skippon, now member for Barnstaple, for his action in turning back the trained band guards for the City, and voted to dispense with the citizens' services in the future.

The number of members now attending the Commons had reduced to eighty or so on this first day following the initial purge. Whilst a debate went on concerning whether further business should continue until the imprisoned or debarred members were released the purge continued outside. This time the work was carried out by the soldiers of Deane's and Hewson's regiments. Altogether about a further fifty members were kept out on the Thursday, many apparently because they had protested and insisted on the privileges of Parliament and the restoration of their fellow members, some imprisoned, on the previous day. Altogether, something approaching 100 members were either arrested or excluded on the first two days of the Purge. In addition many more than 100 effectively removed themselves without waiting for the Army to move against them.

Whilst unpurged members of the Commons were meeting in session on the Thursday the General Council of the Officers considered the matter of the City of London. The Army had occupied Westminster and some of the suburbs, but they had not yet entered the City itself. On the first day of the Purge the officers had received what they regarded as an evasive answer from the City about the £40,000 arrears of pay - the Treasurers at War had assigned all recently collected taxes and assessments to other purposes. On Friday, 8th December Fairfax issued a proclamation justifying the forcible collection of bedding, with quartering of the troops in the City as an alternative. At two o'clock in the afternoon troops under Colonel Deane moved into the City. Artillery was soon conspicuously displayed at Blackfriars, large forces quartered in St. Paul's and St. Martin's Ludgate. Other detachments were distributed around Paternoster Row, Cheapside, Lombard Street and *'all the heart of the City'*. The occupation was complete; but it was money the Army were after now. A force drawn mainly from Colonel Hewson's regiment went to secure the Parliament's main treasuries. That of the Committee for the Advance of Money was at Haberdashers' Hall; one of its sub-committee had its funds deposited at Weavers' Hall; and the Committee for Compounding kept its cash store at Goldsmiths' Hall. Guards were left at Haberdashers' and Goldsmiths' Halls, but at Weavers' Hall the door was battered down, £27,000 seized, loaded onto carts and taken to Whitehall. Fairfax justified all this to the

Lord Mayor as necessary to provide money for quartering allowances until the City paid up its £40,000, and pointed out that there were precedents for the seizure of local treasuries to collect arrears in other places.

The next three weeks - from 7th December onwards - were weeks of manoeuvre and negotiation, in the course of which Cromwell became convinced firstly of the need to put the king on trial and secondly to execute him.

In the House of Commons on 13th December the 'Vote of No Addresses' was reinstated, by revoking its repeal, and the votes in favour of regarding Charles' answers to the Newport Treaty proposals as a basis for negotiation were annulled as being *"highly dishonourable and destructive to the peace of the Kingdom"*. Two days later the Council of Officers voted that the king be moved to Windsor from Hurst Castle, *"in order to the bringing of him speedily to justice"*, in accordance with their Remonstrance of 20th November.

In spite of the efforts of the leaders of the Purge to preserve the appearance of continuity, the House of Commons was not the only branch of government to be disrupted by events. The House of Lords sat even more briefly on Thursday, 7th December than they had the previous day. This time they merely heard prayers and then quickly adjourned until the 12th to await the unfolding of events. The Commissioners of the Great Seal met again on the morning of the 7th, but went home without hearing any cases. According to Whitelocke they met on the following Saturday, at his suggestion, in the seclusion of the Middle Temple. On Monday, 11th December, they sat again, but found little business to deal with. Lord Grey of Groby, in Underdown's view **"obviously enjoying himself as one of the ruling junto"**,[30] tried to persuade them not to sit the next day, because of important business in Parliament for which their attendance was required but the commissioners decided to ignore his advice.

According to Whitelocke : -

> *"Little business in the chancery. The lord Grey of Groby came to the lord Grey* [of Ruthin]*, one of the commissioners, and wished us not to sit tomorrow, because it would be a busy day. It seems he was acquainted with the private councils of the army. We all advised together about this matter, and resolved to meet tomorrow at Westminster, to prevent any failure of justice, and to do as we should see cause, as to the hearing of motions, or other business of the chancery".*[31]

It was safer not to be attending the Commons chamber. By sitting all day on the 12th December the commissioners gained another respite from their parliamentary duties. Indeed, Whitelocke claims that he came home so tired that he had to rest all the next day!

In some ways the Army had done its work too well. It was becoming difficult to find enough members to undertake the constitutional government of the country. Those who had organised Pride's Purge - that mixed group of parliamentarians and Army officers - had intended to keep at least a respectable semblance of a Parliament in being and had acted with the tacit approval of the Speaker, William Lenthall. Had the expulsion of the 'obnoxious' members been engineered from within, however, it would have appeared less nakedly illegal and would not have caused so drastic a reduction of the House. What caused the current emptiness of the House of Commons was not so much the forcible exclusion of the members who had actively favoured the Newport Treaty. After all, pro-royalist MPs had been excluded at various times since the beginning of the first civil war. Thomas Cook, Lord Grey of Groby's fellow MP for Leicester in the elections of 1640, who was later replaced by Peter Temple, was such an example. Rather it was the voluntary absenteeism of many others who were not implacably opposed to the Army's interests but who resented their assault on Parliamentary freedom at the time of the Purge, or who feared that they might subsequently find themselves out of favour. Amongst these even Sir Henry Vane absented himself after the Purge, although until that point he had been in effect a leader of the Army's allies in the Commons. Now the House sometimes had difficulty in raising its quorum of forty members.

On 23rd December the depleted House of Commons appointed a small Committee to consider how the king should be tried. Colonel Harrison was sent to fetch him from Hurst Castle to Windsor. At the first meeting of this Committee Ireton, on behalf of the Army, was present. Perhaps significantly Fairfax was not present and the meeting was chaired by Cromwell. Grey of Groby and Ludlow were amongst the members. Bulstrode Whitelocke and Thomas Widdington, both Commissioners of the Great Seal, went *'down into the country'* by coach, according to Whitelocke's memoirs *' purposely to avoid this business'*. With every passing day the potential support, or even the acquiescence, of the most experienced parliamentarians and lawyers was being withdrawn from the projected trial of the king.

Even the Levellers, who at the outbreak of the second Civil War had been amongst the most vocal advocates of trying the *'Man of Blood'*, had begun to back away. Before the Army had marched from Windsor to Whitehall John Lilburne had been persuaded by Ireton and Harrison that joint meetings of the Army Council and representatives of the Leveller movement would be held to consider a new representative form of government for England. This had been in order to quieten Lilburne and his colleagues at a time when unity was essential amongst the radicals.

After the purge Lilburne had lost no time in organising these joint meetings. Indeed, he had gone further and drawn up a detailed programme of reform for consideration. If he had expected this to be accepted by the Army leaders without further delay he was to be disappointed. It was noticeable that all representation of the rank and file had been dropped by the Army Council for the last thirteen months. It was now simply a Council of Officers. The officers of this Army Council were concerned for religious liberty, but were little interested in, and in some cases actually hostile to, the Leveller demands for a more evenly distributed representation of the people in Parliament, for greater social and civil justice, and such. John Lilburne was quick to see that the 'Grandees' of the Army meant to smother his proposals under a mountain of arguments and then to weaken and/or destroy his programme. The joint discussions were chaired by Lord General Fairfax. The Levellers were allowed to have four representatives but there was no limit on the number of the Grandees who attended. Cromwell was rarely present but those whom Lilburne referred to as his *"creature colonels"* came and spoke frequently. Fairfax made no attempt to treat both parties fairly or equally. On one occasion he allowed Ireton to speak again and again whilst Lilburne and his friends had difficulty in being allowed to put their case at all. There was bitter disagreement about the terms of a revised 'Agreement of the People'. The Levellers realised that they had been used. On 12th December John Lilburne withdrew, declaring that the officers were *"a pack of dissembling, juggling knaves"*, the worst being that *"cunningest of Machiavellians"*, Henry Ireton.[32]

A few days later he presented to Fairfax 'A Plea for Common Right and Freedom' in which he complained of the unfairness of the debates and declared that the future happiness of the country was in the hands of the Army which he hoped would stand for the liberties of the people as they had claimed previously.

Fairfax had little sympathy with Lilburne's ideas. Whatever he might feel about the king's trial he was in sympathy with Cromwell, Ireton, and the other Grandees in thinking that the liberties of the people depended upon the preservation of the social hierarchy and the political rights of the privileged landowning class to which he belonged. He remained unresponsive to Lilburne's appeal. This came as no surprise to Lilburne. He was already coming to the view that the people had merely exchanged one type of tyranny for another. What annoyed him and the other leading Levellers was that they had been duped into assisting the Grandees into power. Before the end of December Lilburne left London for Durham in order to secure some property and income to the value of three thousand pounds that had been awarded to him by Parliament in respect of his sufferings in the time of the royal tyranny. He returned to London only after the king's death and had in the meantime let it be known that he had become opposed to the king's execution. He could see that with the king gone and the Grandees *"fully got up into the throne"* he could do no more to advance the Levellers cause at that point. By stirring up riots in London and mutinies in the ranks of the Army, he might delay the king's trial and create disorder. But this would only assist the royalists. When he cursed the Grandees for being *"juggling knaves"* it was because they had juggled him into a position where he could strike no blow against them without damaging his own cause more than theirs.

While the small committee of the House of Commons set up to manage the trial of the king was drawing up its proposals one last attempt was made to reach a settlement short of his execution. Some commentators believe that Cromwell was behind this initiative. Monday, 25th December, a working day rather than a 'Christmas Day' holiday under puritan rule, saw an obscure approach made to the king at Windsor by Lord Denbigh. Denbigh, with whom we are familiar as Grey of Groby's brother-in-law, had already been employed on various missions to the king. This time he had a ready-made excuse to visit Windsor Castle as the Duke of Hamilton, also imprisoned there, was the widower of Denbigh's sister. It was said, however, that his real purpose was to put some secret proposals to the king from Cromwell. For some reason Charles never saw Denbigh. The king may have been unaware of his true purpose or have reconciled himself to becoming 'the royal martyr'. The king's rejection of Denbigh's mission seems to have finally determined Cromwell that there was no outcome possible other than the king's trial and execution. *"Since the Providence of God hath cast this upon us, I cannot but submit to Providence".*

The committee for the king's trial reported its recommendations to the Commons on 28th December. They advised that a special Court should be appointed for the purpose, to consist of men representing the interests of the nation and empowered to act for a period of one month. The plan was generally acceptable to the purged Commons, but there was a long discussion over terminology and a phrase which described Charles Stuart as being *"entrusted with the government of the kingdom"* was changed to *"Charles Stuart the now King of England".*

To speed up the arrangements the committee was now enlarged to include several more of the members who were also senior Army officers, including Cromwell. Henry Marten, Thomas Scot, and Lord Grey of Groby were amongst the original members of the committee.

On 1st January 1649 Henry Marten, as spokesman for the committee, placed the completed draft of the ordinance for the king's trial before the

306

House of Commons. Generally, the king was accused of having *"traitorously and maliciously"* plotted to enslave the English nation, and he was to be put on trial before a High Court of Justice consisting of about 150 commissioners as a jury, including 6 peers and presided over by the Chief Justices. The ordinance was passed by the Commons without a division. They then added a resolution which declared that it was treason on the part of a king to levy war on his subjects.

Lord Grey of Groby volunteered, or was selected, to present the ordinance to the House of Lords for their concurrence. The Lords, however, much reduced in numbers, had decided to take the New Year's Day as a holiday. The next day when the full twelve peers reassembled, with the Earl of Manchester taking the place of the Lord Chancellor as the Speaker, the Lords refused to co-operate. It was not that they cared particularly for the person of the king. He had brought himself to his present situation by errors of policy in which these remaining peers had all been opposed to him. Nevertheless, some of them now saw it as their duty to uphold the laws of the land against the brute force of the Army and the actions of a radical remnant of the Commons. The Earl of Manchester, who at the outbreak of the first civil war had raised and led the forces of the Eastern Association against Charles Stuart, now opened the debate with the strong statement that the king alone had the power to call or dissolve Parliament, and that it was therefore absurd and illegal to accuse him of treason against a body over which he exercised the ultimate constitutional authority. Then the Earl of Northumberland, who had supported Parliament throughout the war, now doubted whether one in twenty of the people of England was satisfied that the King rather than Parliament had begun the conflict. Unless that point were settled he argued that it was impossible to accuse the king of treason. The Earl of Denbigh, Basil Fielding, who had been a parliamentarian commander in the West Midlands at the outbreak of the first civil war, strongly opposed putting the king on trial. He would rather be torn in pieces, he avowed, than have any part in so infamous a business. Unanimously, therefore, the House of Lords rejected the ordinance. They then adjourned for a week, and most of them departed with all haste to their country estates.

The Chief Justices nominated to preside over the High Court of Justice also refused to take part in the trial of the king. Yet neither the refusal of the House of Lords nor the leaders of the judiciary to participate was likely to deter the radical Rump of the Commons from their intent. It was reported that an angry Lord Grey of Groby, at the news that the Lords had rejected the bill that he had delivered to them, declared that he would himself perform the role of the executioner rather than let the king escape from justice.[33] The House of Commons was now prepared to take the sole responsibility for the king's trial and execution. They declared their right to proceed without further reference to the Lords, revised their proposed list of members of the High Court of Justice, and hurried an amended bill through its first and second readings at a single session on 3rd January.

The new High Court of Justice was to contain only 135 Commissioners who were to act as both judge and jury. Three key resolutions were passed on 4th January. Firstly, *"That the people are, under God, the original of all just power"*; secondly, that *"the Commons of England in Parliament assembled"* had the supreme power in the nation; and finally, that anything enacted by this Commons had the force of law, to be obeyed by the people *"although the consent and concurrence of King or House of Peers be not had thereunto"*. The Commons had taken the supreme power to themselves. But behind them stood the Army. With the passing of the Act on 6th January a new era had begun.

The first meeting of the High Court of Justice was held on 8th January in the Painted Chamber in the Palace of Westminster. This was one in a series of meetings to determine procedural details before the actual trial itself could begin. It again revealed the general reluctance to be involved in the business. Of the 135 individuals nominated as Commissioners only 52 turned up for this first meeting. Fairfax was one of them, but it was his first and last appearance. Half of those nominated refused to serve. One was Sir Henry Vane who had not been seen in the Commons since Pride's Purge. Another was Colonel Algernon Sidney, second son of the Earl of Leicester, who objected to the court on two counts : -

"First, the King can be tried by no court; secondly, no man can be tried by this court".

To this Cromwell is said to have replied without hesitation : -

"I tell you we will cut off his head with the Crown upon it".

Sidney riposted as he left in disgust : -

"You may take your own course, I cannot stop you, but I will keep myself clean from having any hand in the business".[34]

The next morning it was formally proclaimed in Westminster Hall, by the House of Commons Sergeant-at-arms attended by six trumpeters and two troops of horse, that Charles Stuart, King of England, was to be tried and that the Court of Justice for that purpose would be in session from 10th January in the Painted Chamber. Similar proclamations were repeated in Cheapside and at the Old Exchange.

The Commissioners met for the second time on Wednesday, 10th January. Forty-five of them were present. The major business of the day was to choose a lawyer from amongst their number to preside at future meetings and at the king's trial. In his absence a John Bradshaw, who had been a judge of the Sheriff's Court in London for some years and had recently been appointed chief justice of Chester and a judge in Wales, was nominated to take the chair. At the next meeting, on 12th January, he was persuaded to take the chair and accept the title of 'Lord President'. When the trial itself began he wore a long robe concealing armour and a high crowned black hat lined with steel plates as a protection against a possible royalist assassination attempt.

Among the commissioners or judges, in addition to Cromwell and Ireton, were such colonels of the New Model Army as Sir Hardress Waller, Pride, Whalley, Harrison, Ewer, Hewson, and Goffe. Also present on most occasions were Lord Grey of Groby, Edmund Ludlow, Henry Marten, and John Hutchinson who, whilst not serving in that Army, had all held military commands on the side of Parliament. The civilian members who were intended to represent the localities of England were less well known and less conspicuous. There had been an attempt to bring in the landed gentry of as many counties as possible and citizens of the principal towns. The list contained past or current Mayors of York, Newcastle, Hull, Liverpool, Cambridge and Dorchester, and several London Aldermen - two of whom had held the office of Lord Mayor. Reading, Bridport and Great Yarmouth were represented by their Recorders. Norwich, Gloucester, Shrewsbury, Nottingham, Ipswich, Canterbury, Winchester, Leicester and others by their respective members of Parliament. Both the Borough MPs for Leicester, Lord Grey and Peter Temple were members. Another Leicestershire squire, Thomas Waite, MP for Rutland, was also a member although he was to claim later that he had been persuaded to do so by Lord Grey. Sir Arthur Hesilrige was named as a member but rarely attended as his duties kept him in the Newcastle-upon-Tyne area.

Of all the active commissioners the one with the highest social status was none other than Thomas, Lord Grey of Groby - as the son and heir of an English peer. The others with aristocratic connections named on the original list included Lord Fairfax, whose title related to a Scottish rather than an English barony : Lord Mounson, the holder of an Irish title; and Lord Lisle, son of another English peer and Algernon Sidney's brother. All of these failed to participate. Lord Grey of Groby was the only aristocratic regicide.

The commissioners held several sparsely attended meetings to make arrangements before the trial proper began on Saturday, 20th January. On the previous day King Charles was brought from Windsor to the Palace of St. James in a coach guarded by troops of horse.

Meanwhile the Great Hall of Westminster had been prepared as the venue for the trial. At about 2 pm on the 20th January Charles was brought from St. James Palace to Westminster. In order that this be done quietly he was transported firstly in a curtained sedan-chair and then by boat along the Thames to Sir Robert Cotton's house where he was to be lodged during the trial. The commissioners waiting in the Painted Chamber saw him arrive before they had decided upon the authority on which they should found their case. The Painted Chamber, so called because of the splendid gildings, frescos and black lettered scriptural texts on its walls, was where the commissioners were to hold their private sessions. Its windows looked out onto the gardens of Cotton's house. They were well aware of the legal and constitutional weakness behind what they were proposing. Cromwell is reported as asking what they were to say if the king demanded to know by what authority they had brought him to judgement.

"To which none answered presently. Then after a little space Henry Marten rose up and said: 'In the name of the Commons in Parliament assembled, and all the good people of England". [35]

Having decided upon this formula the commissioners, headed by Lord President Bradshaw in his steel-lined hat, processed with their ushers and guard of halberdiers into Westminster Hall.

King Charles was brought in through a side door. He wore a dark suit and over it a cloak that partly hid the great star of the insignia of the Order of the Garter that he wore on his breast. The commissioners sat facing him in their three rows, soberly dressed in dark suits and cloaks, with tall crowned hats and white linen neck bands. Neither Charles nor his adversaries removed their hats as a mark of respect for the authority of the other. When the roll of the judges' names were called out only sixty-eight responded. When the name of Lord Fairfax was called out, Lady Fairfax, in one of the distinguished visitors' galleries shouted that he had too much wit to be there. The charge was read out, accusing : -

"Charles Stuart here present, of high treason and high misdemeanours ..... in the name of the Commons of England ...... " [36]

When he heard this charge of treason the king's stern expression relaxed and he laughed aloud. He tried to interrupt the clerk who had read out the charge by touching him with his walking cane. The silver head ominously fell off the cane and there was an awkward silence as he paused before retrieving it himself. Bradshaw called upon him to plead in response to the charge, using Henry Marten's newly-coined formula which invoked *"the good people of England"*. Again there was an interruption, with a woman's voice crying out from the distinguished visitors' gallery, that it was a lie; that not a half nor a quarter of the people of England was with them, and that the charge was brought by rebels and traitors. It is not quite clear whether this was Lady Fairfax again or Lady De Lille. There was a delay while the gallery was cleared by the guards. Then Charles asked the expected question; by what authority was he being tried? England, he pointed out, had never been an elective kingdom. He was the sovereign monarch not by election but by inheritance, and to acknowledge a usurped authority would be a betrayal of his trust. He refused to plead in answer to the charge or recognise the authority of the court. As he was removed from the court at the end of this first session of the trial the soldiers, by order, shouted out *"Justice! Justice!"*, but many of the spectators cried out *"God save the King!"*

He was next brought before the court on the 22nd January. This time seventy commissioners were present and the proceedings opened with a proclamation that anyone who caused a disturbance would be instantly arrested. Again the king refused to plead and persisted in demanding to know by what authority the court had grounds to proceed. Eventually this second public session of the trial ended without further progress.

In his room at Cotton House the king is said to have asked about the composition of the so-called Court of Justice. His principal attendant, Thomas Herbert, told him that they were a mixed body of members of Parliament, Army officers, and leading citizens from the City and the rest of the country. The king does not seem to have pursued the inquiry, merely stating that he had looked carefully at them all and did not recognise more than eight of their faces. As C. V. Wedgewood observes : -

> **"It was true he would have known Cromwell, Harrison, Ireton and the principal officers; he would have known Henry Marten, whom he detested, and the dwarfish Lord Grey and the one-time courtier John Danvers. But Bradshaw and his two assistants, Lisle and Say, with most of the other Commissioners, were wholly strange to him - men who to his knowledge had played hitherto no noticeable part in the affairs of the nation".** [37]

The reference to Lord Grey of Groby's lack of height is an echo of an earlier description of him used by the same author in respect of his role in the first day of the purge as,

> **" - `that grinning dwarf' as he was unkindly described . He had been himself a member of the House of Commons since it first assembled in 1640 and was a consistent supporter of the Army".** [38]

311

He was a regular attender at the High Court of Justice.

On Tuesday, 23rd January, the session in Westminster Hall began in the early afternoon. Seventy One Commissioners were present, including Lord Grey of Groby, the largest attendance so far, although still only a little over half the total number appointed. A shield bearing the national symbol, the Cross of St. George, had been set up in the centre of the wall above the Commissioners. This was its first appearance and by replacing the royal arms usually displayed on such formal occasions intimated that the creating of a new form of state structure was imminent. The result of the proceedings was the same as for the previous day. The king refused to plead or to acknowledge the authority of the court. Finally Bradshaw instructed one of the clerks, Andrew Broughton, to read out for the last time a formal demand for the king's answer to the charges. Charles again denied the legality of the court in the interests, he said, of the laws and the privileges of the people of England. Bradshaw countered by observing, *"How far you have preserved the privileges of the people, your actions have spoke it, but truly, Sir, men's intentions ought to be known by their actions; you have written your meaning in bloody characters throughout the whole Kingdom"*. Charles attempted to reply but Bradshaw continued, *"Sir, you have heard the pleasure of the Court, and you are (notwithstanding you will not understand it) to find you are before a court of justice"*. The king replied dryly, *"I see I am before a power"*, and he rose to go. As he rose the Crier called out loudly, *"God bless the Kingdom of England!"* This unprecedented shout may well have been prompted by the need to drown, or to disguise, shouts less welcome to the ears of the Commissioners such as *"God save the King"* or *"God bless you, Sir"*, as Charles walked away between his guards.

The king went back to Cotton House but the Commissioners went as a body to the Painted Chamber. Here, in private, they reconsidered the position and their strategy. That evening the final session was postponed and the next morning they appointed a committee to hear witnesses give condemning evidence against the accused in his absence. By this process it was hoped to convince the waverers in their own membership, of whom there were many, and to indicate to the public that they did not lack evidence to support the charges against the king. The thirty-three witnesses were heard by the appointed Committee (of which Cromwell was not a member but Lord Grey of Groby was) on 24th January. On 25th January their depositions were read out at a public session of the High Court in the Painted Chamber. They demonstrated beyond doubt, if any had doubted it, that the king had been seen in arms against the parliament and had invited foreign armies to enter England. They included the evidence of Humphrey Brown, the husbandman from Whissendine, Rutland, that, at the surrender of the

312

Newarke fort during the storming of Leicester, the king had not only permitted the parliamentarian prisoners to be stripped and cut about by his men, but when a Royalist officer had tried to stop this barbarity had said, *"I do not care if they cut them three times more, for they are mine enemies"*, the king being all this while *"on horseback, in bright armour, in the said town of Leicester"*. The depositions of the witnesses put beyond doubt not only his personal participation in the war, but also his intention of continuing it, even during the recent Treaty negotiations. They may have helped a little to strengthen the wavering resolution of the more doubtful Commissioners and to impress any members of the public in the Painted Chamber or who read the newssheets being issued at the time.

After hearing the depositions of the witnesses on 25th January, the forty-six Commissioners present (it was the smallest attendance yet recorded and did not include Lord Grey) resolved that they should now proceed to sentence the king to death. A small sub-committee was appointed to draw up the sentence. Neither Cromwell nor Lord Grey were on this sub-committee which consisted of only seven members - Alderman Thomas Scot, Henry Marten, Henry Ireton, Thomas Harrison, and three lawyers; William Say, John Lisle and Nicholas Love.

Next day, 26th January, when the Commissioners reassembled in the afternoon, sixty two were present (including Lord Grey of Groby) which was an improvement on the very poor attendances of the previous day. The draft sentence was produced, condemning the King as *"a tyrant, traitor, murderer and a public enemy to be put to death by the severing of his head from his body"*. The public were not admitted to the discussions which continued throughout the afternoon. It does not appear that any vote was taken amongst the Commissioners, but if they were unanimous it was only because those of·stronger wills and stronger voices overwhelmed the weaker, less resolute, members. The form of sentence was agreed by nightfall and the king was to be brought to Westminster Hall next day to hear it pronounced.

At ten o'clock on Saturday, 27th January, the Commissioners reassembled. They were sixty eight in number this time, including Lord Grey of Groby. After some initial delay, caused by interruptions from the galleries, Lord President Bradshaw, wearing a scarlet gown for the first time in order to indicate the solemnity of the occasion, announced that the Court, having fully considered the case; the prisoner having consistently refused to plead, could be regarded as having confessed. Furthermore, the things with which he was charged were notorious. They had therefore agreed upon the sentence, but were nonetheless willing to hear him speak in his defence before it was pronounced, provided he did not *"offer any debate"* concerning the jurisdiction of the Court. Charles did not offer any

313

debate, but he took care to repeat his attitude to the Court. He also asked that before sentence was pronounced he be allowed to speak to the members of the House of Lords and the House of Commons in the Painted Chamber. Bradshaw could only reiterate that the king had already delayed justice for many days by refusing to plead, and ought not to be permitted to delay it any further, but as he warmed to his task he became aware of a disturbance amongst the Commissioners on his left. It came from John Downes who felt that, in all fairness, the king should be heard. Despite the remonstrations of those sitting either side of him and Oliver Cromwell, who sat immediately in front of him, he struggled to his feet and in a loud voice declared that he was not satisfied. Bradshaw therefore suddenly announced that the Court would withdraw for further consideration.

Once back in the Painted Chamber unseemly arguments broke out between Downes and one or two other waverers and the hard-line regicides. The chief of the latter was now unequivocally Cromwell who scornfully overruled all protests. Half an hour later the Commissioners, either resolute or ruffled, re-entered Westminster Hall, leaving John Downes to retire in an upset state to the Speaker's room. When the king had been once again brought back to his chair Bradshaw addressed him with renewed resolution. The President of the Court accused the king of attempting to delay judgement, refused to call a meeting of Lords and Commons to hear what he had to say, and announced that the Court would now proceed to the sentence. Charles's attempts at further protest were swept aside and Bradshaw launched into a lengthy oration. He quoted the scriptures and the classics, medieval lawyers, and expounded the idea of the social contract between rulers and the ruled. He was determined now to stop the king from speaking again, concluded his address, declared the king guilty and commanded that the sentence be read. The Clerk read out the formula previously agreed upon, concluding with the sentence, *"that the said Charles Stuart, as a Tyrant, Traitor, Murderer and a public enemy, shall be put to death, by the severing of his head from his body"*. At the conclusion of the reading the Commissioners rose to their feet to signify their agreement. The king, who had listened calmly to the end now asked, *"Will you hear me a word, Sir?"* Bradshaw curtly replied, *"You are not to be heard after the sentence"*, and ordered the guards to take him away. Charles was taken aback by the abruptness of this conclusion and protested as he was surrounded by the soldiers. He found the opportunity for one last protest. *"I am not suffered to speak : expect what justice other people will have"*. As he was removed from the Hall the soldiers, upon a signal from Colonel Axtell, shouted, *"Justice!"* and *"Execution!"* *"Poor souls"*, said the king with a smile, *"for sixpence they would do the same for their own commanders"*. This time he was removed not to Cotton House but to Whitehall in a sedan chair. The Commissioners returned to the Painted

314

Chamber where John Downes, either through curiosity or fear, rejoined them. They appointed some of their number to *"consider of the time and place for the execution of the sentence against the King"*. Five of the military officers were chosen - Sir Hardress Waller, Commissary General Ireton, and Colonels Harrison, Deane and Okey. After that they adjourned until Monday morning, having the intervening Sabbath for their thankful and anxious prayers to the Lord.

As the news of the verdict spread a feeling of shock fell upon London. The death sentence against the king was not the work of the people of England in whose name it had been pronounced. Rather it was carried through by a small, resolute and armed minority in the face of a stunned nation. Yet this minority was convinced that it was doing the Lord God's work on behalf of the people of England. Lucy Hutchinson wrote that : -

> *"The gentlemen that were appointed his judges and divers others, saw in the King a disposition so bent on the ruin of all that opposed him, and of all the righteous and just things they had contended for, that it was upon the conscience of many of them that if they did not execute justice upon him, God would require at their hands all the blood and desolation which should ensue by their suffering him to escape, when God had brought him into their hands"*.[39]

John Hutchinson, according to his wife, had been put in as a commissioner *"very much against his will"*, *"but looking upon himself as called hereunto, durst not refuse it, as holding himself obliged by the covenant of God and the public trust of his country reposed in him, although he was not ignorant of the danger he run as the condition of things then was"*.[40] Oliver Cromwell justified their actions as taken in respect of *"This man against whom the Lord hath witnessed"*.

By Monday, 29th January, the Commissioners responsible for deciding on the place of execution had already made their choice. King Charles was to die outside the royal Banqueting House completed for him by Inigo Jones about twenty years previously. It stood in a relatively small square, overlooked on three sides by the buildings of Whitehall. Whilst the carpenters got to work on erecting the necessary scaffold and railings the Commissioners met once more in the Painted Chamber. Only forty eight-attended this time. They included Lord Grey of Groby. According to the records of the meeting they agreed to the suggested place of execution for the king and that it should take place on the following day. They also ordered that the death warrant be drawn up accordingly. This was quickly done and the document brought back for signatures.

315

That is the account given in the record of John Phelps, the clerk, which was later entered on the parchment that was transmitted into Chancery in December 1650 as a perpetual record. There is other evidence, however, that indicates that these minutes are not an accurate record of how the Death Warrant may have been drawn up and the signatures added. The warrant had certainly been drawn up and partly signed before the meeting in the Painted Chamber on 29th January. The document which was spread out for signing on that day contained a number of erasures and the date, 29th January, had clearly been altered. It seems from these changes that the warrant had been drawn up in advance, probably on the previous Friday, 26th January, the day on which it had been assumed that the sentence would be pronounced. By this date it seems that some of the most determined men amongst the commissioners had already signed and were the first to do so. It is likely that the protest of John Downes and some of the other unexpected developments on that day had delayed matters. Also, some of the commissioners who had already signed might have been considering changing their mind ; which is why the document was amended rather than replaced with a new one.

Out of the sixty-two commissioners who had agreed verbally to the sentence and stood up on the Friday in the Court to signify such, plus the unhappy John Downes, only fifty-nine ultimately signed the warrant itself. A quorum of twenty signatures was required but the more that could be obtained the better it would appear. It is almost certain that Bradshaw, Cromwell, Grey of Groby, Ireton, Whalley, Marten and others who were fully resolved had been, ever since the Friday or Saturday gathering signatures to add to their own and that the document presented in the Painted Chamber on the Monday already had about half the signatures on it. The minutes of John Phelps were intended to indicate that the commissioners signed the warrant on that day and no other. He did not, however, tamper with the roll-call of attendance for that day, and fifteen out of the fifty-nine who signed the warrant are not recorded as present on Friday, 29th January.

The Death Warrant, which still survives, carries the fifty-nine names set out in seven irregular, parallel columns, with matching seals, at the foot of the warrant. Some signatories, as was alleged by those threatened with royalist vengeance in 1660, had been pressured into signing, but at least two thirds had signed willingly. It was natural that those who hoped for mercy at the time of the Restoration should make a great deal of the force and fear which dominated the proceedings, particularly in the shape of Cromwell, in the session in the Painted Chamber on 29th January, 1649. Nevertheless the great majority of commissioners signed their names without persuasion.

This is particularly evident in the case of the first four signatures which appear in the first column. John Bradshaw's name comes first, (*Jo*

Bradshawe) as President of the High Court of Justice. The second signature (*Tho. Grey*) is that of Lord Grey of Groby, in a clear bold hand, taking the precedent due to his rank in the social hierarchy. Next comes that of *O. Cromwell*, written as large as that of Grey. It is followed by that of Colonel Whalley (*Edw. Whalley*). One can speculate on the implications of the prominence and position of Grey's signature alongside that of Cromwell's, remembering that at the time the younger man as an aristocrat was the social superior of the East Anglian country squire turned General. Amongst the other signatories appear Henry Ireton (ninth), John Hutchinson (thirteenth), Thomas Pride (fifteenth), Peter Temple (sixteenth), Thomas Harrison (seventeenth), Edmund Ludlow (thirtieth), Henry Marten (thirty first), and Thomas Waite (fifty sixth).

Amongst those who alleged intimidation by Cromwell was Richard Ingoldsby who claims that the Lieutenant General had held his hand and forced him to sign after dragging him to the table. Ingoldsby's flowing signature on the warrant would not seem to bear this out, but he was helpful to the restored monarchists in 1660 and it suited them to believe his story. Another witness, Colonel Ewer, claimed to have seen Cromwell and Henry Marten inking each others faces with the pen after they had signed their own names. Cromwell's attempts at persuasion seem to have been directed particularly at the wavering members of the House of Commons who were commissioners. At about eleven o'clock in the morning on the day of the official signing he was standing with others at the doors of the Commons chamber to intercept commissioners on their way in. Later, when most of them were in their places, he went into the House to round up any he may have missed, saying, *"Those that are gone in shall set their hands; I will have their hands now".*[41]

Amongst the members likely to have been influenced by such tactics are the hesitant John Downes and Thomas Waite. Downes had made the awkward scene on the 27th January, though he had previously shown no qualms following the Purge. Thomas Waite, the Leicestershire squire and MP for Rutland, made less noise at the trial, although he may have supported Downe's move to adjourn proceedings on the 27th, but his claims in 1660 to have been lukewarm about developments carry some conviction. He claims to have withdrawn from the Commons on 12th or 13th December and to have returned to Leicestershire where he later claimed to have suppressed republican petitions both there and in Rutland. He had returned to London around 25th January. He claimed to have been tricked into attending the Court by a message allegedly from Lord Grey. He had served under Lord Grey previously in the war and, although they had then quarrelled, he and Grey were apparently on good terms again at this time. The forged note, purporting to have come from Lord Grey of Groby calling him to the Court on the 27th January, the fateful day of the verdict, had actually been sent by Cromwell and Ireton. According to his story he only attended on Monday the 29th because he had been assured there would be no execution, but he had been forced to sign the death warrant by Cromwell and Ireton who were collecting signatures at the House of Commons. Waite thus seems to have been deceived twice. Lord Grey's degree of complicity in the deception is not clear but he certainly seems to have had influence over Waite.

Other Leicestershiremen who signed the Death Warrant, in addition to Lord Grey of Groby, Peter Temple, and Thomas Waite were Henry Smith, a relative of Edward Smith of Edmundthorpe, and Thomas Horton, originally a falconer and servant to Sir Arthur Hesilrige. Sir Arthur, although a commissioner of the court, did not sign as his duties kept him at Newcastle-upon-Tyne. Until the signing of the Death Warrant it had been possible to pretend that the trial and sentencing of the king were for show: that they were a means of compelling Charles Stuart to abandon his authority without the shedding of further blood. Those who took part in them might still claim that they had not really intended the king's death. Those who signed the warrant, however, made themselves fully responsible for his execution. The warrant was directed to three officers of the Army. These were Colonel Francis Hacker, the Leicestershireman and protege of Sir Arthur Hesilrige, Colonel Hercules Hunks and Colonel Robert Phayne. It required them to see that Charles Stuart was put to death by the severing of his head from his body between the hours of ten in the morning and five in the afternoon on Tuesday, January 30th.

King Charles walked through the Banqueting Hall of Whitehall, under the painted ceiling he had commissioned from Rubens, and out to the scaffold in the open air accompanied by William Juxon, the Anglican bishop of London. Around the timber scaffold, cavalry troopers had been drawn up on horseback in ranks so deep that the vast crowd of patiently waiting Londoners would be unable to hear the king's voice. Charles therefore repeated to the bishop what he had intended to say to the crowd. These last words, as reported by Bishop Juxon, give the clearest expression to the real difference between King and Parliament, the fundamental disagreement about the way to govern England, which at last had sent him to the scaffold : -

> *"For the people, truly I desire their liberty and freedom as much as anybody whatsoever, but I must tell you that their liberty and freedom consists in having government, those laws by which their lives and their goods may be most their own. It is not their having a share in the government; that is nothing appertaining unto them. A subject and a sovereign are clear different things".*

318

The king's human sympathy had been broadened by his war experiences, but from first to last, his principles had never changed. As Charles saw it, even at that last moment of his life, the responsibility of governing the realm of England had been placed on his shoulders by God, and this Divine Right he would neither yield nor share.

The king knelt at the block in prayer. He then stretched out his hands as a signal to the masked executioner. The glittering axe fell. The masked man stooped to lift up the king's severed head for the waiting crowd to see. At the executioner's traditional cry, *"Behold the head of a traitor!"* a huge groan of horror and anger broke from the watching Londoners. Two troops of cavalry promptly turned their horses' heads outwards and patrolled threateningly up and down Whitehall, hands on sword hilts, to disperse the crowd to their homes.

Lord Grey of Groby did not stay in London to witness the execution of the king. He left, after signing the death warrant, to return to Bradgate. He had played a leading role in the sequence of events from the time before the move of the Army from Windsor to Whitehall, through the Purge, the trial and the sentencing of the king. According to Noble : -

"He sat in the Painted Chamber January the 8th, 15th, 17th, 18th, 20th, 22nd, 23rd, 24th, 26th, 27th and 29th; and he sat every day in Westminster Hall, when his majesty was brought before them, and signed the warrant for execution. His presence probably was absolutely necessary to give some sanction to the infamous proceedings, and to overawe such as might be refractory".[42]

In relation to Cromwell's assumed influence over the other signatories it seems that Lord Grey of Groby's role is likely to have been underrated.

Further information from local Leicestershire sources points to the probability of Lord Grey having signed the Death Warrant before Monday, 29th January 1649 (1648/9 by the calendar then in use). He arrived at Bradgate to break the news of the king's imminent execution himself. It would have taken him at least a day to have travelled by anything other than galloping horse or a relay of horses from Whitehall to Bradgate, even longer by coach. Such momentous news, of the execution having taken place on Tuesday, 30th January, would surely have reached Leicestershire by the time he arrived otherwise.

The Earl of Stamford had been alarmed by the Army Revolt of 1647 and the 1648 purge of the Parliament in which his son had played a major role against the former's friends and allies. It will be remembered that on the first day of the purge the House of Lords had granted him leave of absence to return to Bradgate. The final straw for him was the trial, and subsequent sentencing and execution, of the king. He disassociated himself from his son's involvement in these events and from this time on he was a royalist, like most presbyterians. Perhaps he had been consistently for *'King and Parliament'* or *'King and Covenant'* all along as he maintained.

John Throsby, the eighteenth century Leicestershire historian, recalls how his great-grandfather was at Bradgate Park conversing with *'Lord Grey'* (Stamford) when his son arrived from London immediately after the condemnation of Charles I and received the unwelcome news, like that nobleman, with horror : -

> *"'Well Thomas', says the father to the son, 'King, or no King?'*
> *- 'No King, my lord', replied the son - 'Then no Lord Grey!'*
> *rejoined the father and left him in disgust".*

Throsby adds, *"This nobleman (Stamford) like Fairfax and many others was friendly to the cause of the people, but not to a governing army".*[43]

One can imagine this meeting between Thomas Grey and his father. The former arriving flushed, excited, triumphant, righteous and feeling in the van of great events and the dawn of a new era: the latter feeling saddened, angry, worried, disgusted, regretting what had been lost and apprehensive of what might be. When Stamford issued the retort *"Then no Lord Grey!"* he may have been referring to himself by his original title as he often did. Others did so too, as evidenced in the first part of the Throsby extract given above. This could have meant that the whole social hierarchy, including themselves, was now in danger: no king and no lords. He might also have been referring to Thomas Grey the regicide - the only aristocratic regicide - whom, in that moment of anger and disgust, he refused to acknowledge as his son because of the shame he had brought upon the family name. Throsby also records that a Mrs. Margaret Choyce (Joyce?) of Whittington Grange at Ratby, the village just one mile to the west of Groby and on the Bradgate estate, and who lived to be 106 years old, was present at the time of the incident mentioned above, then aged fifty two years.

> *"..... on the arrival of the news at Bradgate that Charles I was condemned to die she fell on her knees, and wept bitterly, praying fervently to the Almighty to save 'the best of men'".*[44]

The prayers of Margaret Choyce and of countless others proved to be of no avail. The tremendous storm of the Puritan revolution reached its peak with the purge of Parliament in December 1648 and the trial and execution of King Charles in January 1649 : -

> *"The forest bent ; the oaks snapped, the dry leaves were driven before a gale, neither all of winter nor all of spring, but violent and life-giving, pitiless and yet tender, sounding strange notes of yearning and contrition, as of voices wrung from a people dwelling in Meshech, which signifies Prolonging, in Kedar, which signifies Blackness; while amid the blare of trumpets, and the clash of arms, and the rending of the carved work of the Temple, humble to God and haughty to man, the soldier-saints swept over battlefield and scaffold, their garments rolled in blood".*[45]

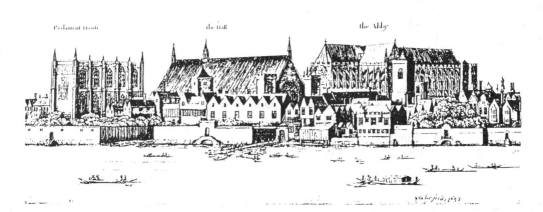

The City of Westminster

NOTES

1. Resolution of the Army, April 1648, from 'Adjutant-General Allen's pamphlet (unpublished in 1659) - *Somers Tracts*, VI., pp. 499-501, and in Letters and Speeches I, pp. 307-310. Cited in John Buchan, *Cromwell*, (Sphere Books, London, 1971). p. 267.

2. Various extracts from Ludlow's Memoirs, Vol. I. 203-205. See Edmund Ludlow *Memorials*, - as listed in Underdown's *Pride's Purge*.

3. See David Underdown, *Pride's Purge*. p. 109.

4. Journal of the House of Commons (C.J.) Vol. VI., p. 41. Quarto Pamphlets, British Museum, p. 389.

5. HMC., Portland, i. 497; Petition of James Smith : HMC., Seventh Report, Appendix. (House of Lords MSS), p. 121.

6. C. J. Vol. VI., p. 49.

7. Calendar of State Papers (Domestic); 1648-9, p. 319.

8. *Old Parliamentary History*, XVIII, pp. 160 - 238.

9. Ian Gentles, *The New Model Army*, Blackwell, Oxford, U.K. p. 278. (derived from *Mercurius Pragmaticus*. 21-28 Nov. 1648. E473/35).

10. The Declaration of His Excellency the Lord General Fairfax (30 November 1948 : British Museum Manuscripts. E. 474, 13).

11. Worcester College, Clarke MS. cxiv, fol. 116.

12. Ludlow's *Memorials*, i. 206.

13. See David Underdown, *Pride's Purge*. p. 135 (Footnotes : The Moderate, no. 21 (28 Nov. - 5 Dec. 1648 : [BM] E. 475,8); Merc. Elen., no. 54 (29 Nov. - 6 Dec. 1648 : [BM] E. 475, 22).

14. C. J. Vol. VI. p. 93.

15. Ibid. p. 92.

16. Ludlow's *Memorials*. op. cit. Vol. I. p. 208.

17. C. J. Vol. VI. p. 93.

18. Ibid. p. 93.

19. Ibid. p. 94.

20. Ludlow's *Memorials*. Vol. I. p. 209.

21. Ibid. pp. 209-10.

22. Antonia Fraser, *Cromwell : Our Chief of Men*. Panther Books, Granada Publishing, 1977. p. 270. Originally published by Weidenfield & Nicholson, 1973.

23. Ludlow's Memorials. op. cit., Vol. I. p. 116.

24. Bulstrode Whitelocke, *Memorials of the English Affairs*. Vol. I. p. 468.

25. Mark Noble, *The Lives of the English Regicides*, London, 1788. Vol. I. pp. 267-268.

26. David Underdown, *Pride's Purge*, op. cit. p. 23.
27. Mark Noble, op. cit. pp. 266-267.
28. Ludlow's *Memorials*. op. cit. Vol. I., 211-212.
29. David Underdown. op. cit. p. 150.
30. Ibid. p. 157.
31. Bulstrode Whitelocke, op. cit. Vol. II. pp. 472-474.
32. John Lilburne, *Legal Fundamental Liberties*. pp. 38-39.
33. *Mercurius Pragmaticus*, De. 26 - Jan. 9.
34. R.W. Blencowe (ed.), Sidney Papers, 1825. p. 237.
35. State Trials, Cobbett's Complete Collection, 1810.
    Mark Noble, *Memoirs of the Protectoral House of Cromwell*, Vol. I., p. 119. Birmingham, 1787.
36. Ibid.
37. C.V. Wedgwood, *The Trial of Charles I*, The Reprint Society, London. (Collins), 1966. p. 141.
38. Ibid. p. 42.
39. Lucy Hutchinson, *Memoirs of Colonel Hutchinson*, Everyman's Library, Dent, London. 1965. p. 266.
40. Ibid. p. 265.
41 State Trials. V. 1129 ff.
42. Noble, op. cit. p. 268.
43. John Throsby, *Select Views in Leicestershire*, 1789. Supplementary Volume to the Leicestershire Views. Vol. II. (Excursions) 1790, p. 90.
44. Ibid. Vol. II. (Excursions) 1790, p. 82.
45. R.H. Tawney, *Religion and the Rise of Capitalism*. Pelican Books, London. 1964. p. 197.

King Charles I in armour

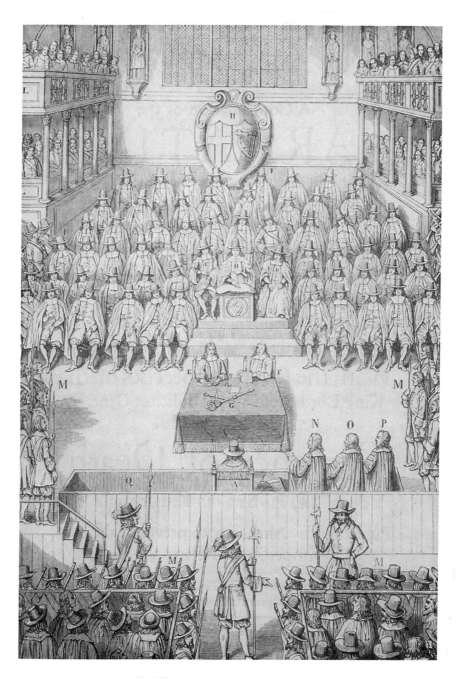

The trial of King Charles I by the High Court of Justice

A Continuation of the

NARRATIVE

BEING

The laſt and final dayes Proceedings

OF THE

High Court of Iuſtice

Sitting in Weſtminſter Hall on Saturday, *Jan.* 27.

Concerning the Tryal of the King;

With the ſeverall Speeches of the
King, Lord Preſident, & Solicitor General.

Together with a Copy of the

Sentence of Death

upon CHARLS STUART King of ngland.

Publiſhed by Authority to prevent falſe and
impertinent Relations.

TO *theſe Proceedings of the Tryall of the King,* I ſay,
Imprimatur, GILBERT MABBOT.

London, Printed for *John Playford,* and are to be ſold at his
ſhop in the *Inner Temple, Jan.* 29. 1648.

An account of the trial of King Charles I

326

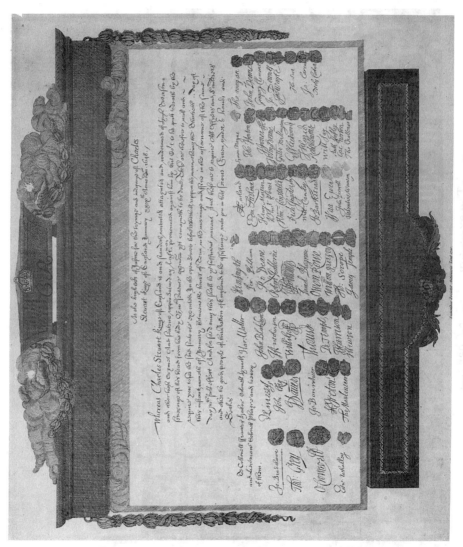

The death warrant of King Charles I

327

The Execution of King Charles I

328

CHAPTER TEN

THE COUNCILLOR OF STATE (1649)

- "In the First Year of Freedom, by God's blessing restored".
(Wording on the new Seal of the Commonwealth)

"Let the saints exult in glory,
Let them sing for joy upon their beds,
Let the high praises of God be in their mouths,
And a two-edged sword in their hands,
To execute vengeance upon the nations,
And punishments upon the peoples".
(Psalm 149 vs. 5 - 7)

Charles I was beheaded on 30th January 1649. This act had been carried out in the name of *"the Commons in Parliament assembled, and all the good people of England"*. What now held the power of government in the country was an oligarchy composed of the remnant of a nine-year-old House of Commons, supported by the Army. They set about recasting the constitution of England.

Oliver Cromwell and Henry Ireton had increasingly taken the lead amongst the army grandees as Fairfax sought to distance himself from the recent momentous events. According to Blair Worden, "[Thomas] **Scot, [Henry] Marten, and [Thomas] Challoner stand out as the major parliamentary figures between the purge and the execution, but other regicides were also well to the fore in these weeks"** notable amongst these being **"Lord Grey of Groby, a Leicestershire magnate still in his twenties during the Rump period".**[1]

Worden also points out that amongst the leading figures of the fifteen 'revolutionaries' drawn from the greater gentry families (of whom fourteen were regicides) and to whom the others tended to turn for leadership during this period were John Hutchinson, John Carew, Gregory Norton, Thomas Scot, Henry Marten, Thomas Challoner, and the aristocratic Thomas, Lord Grey of Groby.

On 1st February 1649 the remaining members of the House of Lords proposed to the House of Commons a joint committee *"to consider the settlement of the government"*. Their message was rejected. On 6th February, after a *"long and smart"* debate lasting for two days, the Commons voted to put an end to the House of Lords altogether. The vote was 44 to 29 with Cromwell voting against. A protesting Bulstrode Whitelocke was instructed to frame the Act of Abolition.

329

On the same day the Earl of Denbigh and the five other remaining peers met for their last session, heard prayers, disposed of a rectory, and then adjourned. They were not to reassemble for another eleven years.

Despite this abolition of the peers' own chamber a few of the nobility were willing enough to accept a republican form of government. During the four years which the Commonwealth lasted the peerage was never without its representatives, both in the now unicameral Parliament and the Council of State. Neither amongst the limited number of men who monopolised political power, nor amongst the electorate in general, was there any hostility to peers as such. According to C. H. Firth, if so few of them held office in the new state, it was because the majority of those who had adhered to the parliamentary cause remained so obstinately aloof from it. Of those who did actively participate Lord Grey of Groby was one of the most thorough-going supporters of the Republic.[2]

The following day the Commons turned to the institution of the monarchy. The proclamation of another king had already been prohibited on pain of treason. Now it was voted *"that the office of a king in this nation, and to have the power thereof in any single person, is unnecessary, burdensome, and dangerous to the liberty, safety, and public interest of the people of this nation; and therefore ought to be abolished"*. The same committee charged with preparing the Act to abolish the House of Lords was directed to prepare another one to abolish the monarchy. The two Acts were passed on 19th March. The kingdom was not formally declared to be transformed into a republic until 19th May. This late date may suggest that republican principles were somewhat lacking in the new regime but, on the other hand, much had to be accomplished during the transitional period. The Act establishing the Republic or Commonwealth, as it was known, stated that *"England should henceforth be governed as a Commonwealth, or a Free State, by the supreme authority of this nation, the representatives of the people in Parliament, and by such as they shall appoint and constitute under them for the good of the people"*.

The word 'Commonwealth' had originally meant the public welfare or general good. By the beginning of the sixteenth century it had come to mean the body politic or the state, particularly one in which the whole people had a voice or interest. By the seventeenth century it was coming to be associated with a republican form of government.

The remaining members of the House of Commons had now, with the support of the Army, to reconstitute the executive and judicial branches of English government and to institute new symbols for the Commonwealth. The Privy Council had gone with the monarchy; there were no more Exchequer and Admiralty departments, no more Star Chamber, Court of Wards, the Courts of the King's Prerogative; no more Lord Chancellor, Chancellor of the Exchequer or Secretaries of State.

The solution was found in the creation of a new and powerful Council of State, set up by Act of Parliament, with wide executive powers. In turn this Council of State would work through a series of committees responsible to it for such matters as foreign affairs, the Army, the Navy, Ireland, and the raising of money. The Council was in part the heir to the old royal Privy Council, but also owed something to the two previous committees set up by Parliament, in effect to govern, since 1642, the Committee of Both Kingdoms and the subsequent Committee of Safety. Parliament put in a regulation limiting the Council of State's life to one year, annually renewable. It began by sitting in Derby House, where the previous committees had met, until in May it moved to Whitehall.

On 7th February a committee of the Commons was set up to consider nominations to the Council of State. The committee consisted of five dedicated 'revolutionaries' : Edmund Ludlow, John Lisle, Cornelius Holland, Luke Robinson, and Thomas Scot. After some discussion in the Commons the final number of members for the Council of State had been fixed at forty-one, although suggestions had ranged as high as one hundred, and nine members were to be required for a quorum. Barely half of the forty-one councillors of state nominated by the committee had demonstrated that they were really committed to the revolution either by signing the king's death warrant or by taking the declaration of dissent to the 5th December motion before his execution.

Ludlow related how the regicides were determined to exclude *"those who were likely to seek to undo what they had done"*, yet they were *"unwilling to lose the assistance of many honest men, who had been in the country during the late transactions"*.[3] The speed with which many members came forward to take the dissent after the execution and were readmitted to the House made it a very different one in composition by the end of February from the one which had pushed zealously forward with the revolution from the purge to the end of January. Amongst those nominated by Ludlow's committee for membership of the Council of State, to give it as broad a base as possible, were such well known moderates as Fairfax, the peers Denbigh, Mulgrave, and Grey of Wark, and the judges Henry Rolle and Oliver St. John. They also included the Earls of Pembroke and Salisbury who were only elected after a division of the House. Bulstrode Whitelocke and Henry Vane, whose opposition to both the purge and the trial had been made clear, were also nominated. It seems that the committee wished to enlist as many moderates as could reasonably be expected to accept the new arrangements. Indeed, the names of Henry Ireton and Thomas Harrison, leading architects of the military coup, were rejected by Parliament without a division. Their places were taken by Cornelius Holland and Luke Robinson. This first selection was made on 14th February and

331

remained largely intact with the exception of Harrison and Ireton, the latter being particularly resented because of his known preference for a dissolution of Parliament.

Whitelocke records the acceptance by Parliament of the final list (in rank order) as follows : -

> *"14. Vote for thirty eight persons to be the council of state, viz.*
> *earls of Denbigh, Mulgrave, Pembroke, Salisbury, lord Grey*
> [of Wark], *Fairfax, general Grey of Groby, lord L'Isle,* [Phillip,
> Viscount Lisle, son of the Earl of Leicester], *Rolles, St. John,*
> *Wilde,* [the three Justices], *Bradshaw, Cromwell, Skippon,*
> *Pickering, Massam, Haselrigge, Harrington, Vane junior,*
> *Danvers, Armine, Mildmay, Constable, Pennington, Wilson,*
> *Whitelocke, Martin, Ludlow, Stapely, Heveningham, Wallop,*
> *Hutchinson, Bond, Al. Popham, Valentine Walton, Scot,*
> *Purefoy, Jones. "*

> *"Their powers were,*
>
> *1. To command and settle the militia of England*
> *and Ireland.*
> *2. To set forth such a navy as they should think fit.*
> *3. To appoint magazines and stores, and to dispose*
> *them, & c.*
> *4. To sit and execute the powers given them for a*
> *year.*
>
> *Instructions passed for altering patents of sheriffs, and their*
> *oath, and a list of all the justices of peace brought into the*
> *house".*[4]

As mentioned earlier, the names of Cornelius Holland and Luke Robinson were added to replace those of Ireton and Harrison which had been rejected by Parliament. There were to be other difficulties, however, in making up the full complement of the Council of State.

The first acting chairman was Oliver Cromwell. He was replaced a month later by John Bradshaw, but in the meantime he performed a useful mediating role over the awkward question of the Engagement or loyalty oath to the Commonwealth. Firstly, of the peers voted to serve, both Lord Grey of Wark and Lord Mulgrave refused to do so. The three remaining peers, Denbigh, Salisbury and Pembroke all had serious reservations, as did Fairfax, Skippon, Sir Gilbert Pickering, Rowland Wilson, Alexander

Popham, Bulstrode Whitelocke and even supposed radicals such as Sir Arthur Haselrigg, Sir James Harrington and Denis Bond, amongst others. The difficulty arose over the initial form of the Engagement, suggested by Henry Ireton, which gave specific retrospective approval and support to the events of the last two months, including endorsement of the proceedings of the High Court of Justice and the execution of the king.

As Whitelocke records it : -

> *"At the council of state they were all demanded to subscribe the test appointed by parliament for approving all that was done concerning the king and kingship, and for taking away the house of lords, and against the Scots invasion, & c.*

> *"All the lords, and divers other members of the council, refused to subscribe this test; the general [Fairfax] desired to be spared for what was past, as to subscribing; but he and the rest of the refusers affirmed, that for the future, if the parliament thought them worthy to be employed, they would join with them, and faithfully serve them.*

> *"Many of the commons refused to sign it as it then was, made divers scruples, some to one part of it, some to another.*

> *"I scrupled that part of approving the proceedings of the high court of justice, because I was not privy to them, nor did know what they were in particular, nor ever heard any report of them made to the house; and not knowing what they were, I could not sign that paper to approve of them : the like was said by divers others".*[5]

Cromwell produced a characteristic compromise by which the councillors were to be allowed to *"approve of what shall be done by the Commons in Parliament, the supreme authority of this nation, but nothing of confirming what was past"*.[6] The Oath of Engagement of 1649 was finally settled upon as follows,

> *"I do declare and promise that I will be true and faithful to the Commonwealth of England as the same is now established, without King or House of Lords".*

Ireton's failure to restrict membership of the new executive body to real revolutionaries through the wording of his proposed Engagement demonstrated the difficulty faced in attempting to overcome the residual constitutional conservatism still to be found in the minds of his parliamentary allies.

Yet he had been supported in his attempt by the ever radical Lord Grey of Groby. This is borne out by an account given by Algernon Sidney. Hesilrige and Vane, both of whom had declined Ireton's oath, seconded Cromwell's attempt at a compromise solution. So did Algernon Sidney who argued that Ireton's text, requiring full approval by councillors of state of the judicial proceedings against the king and the abolition of the House of Lords, *"would prove a snare to many an honest man, but every knave would slip through it"*. Lord Grey of Groby *"took great exception to this"*, claiming that Sidney *"had called all those knaves"* who had taken Ireton's oath; *"upon which"*, Sidney subsequently recalled, *"there was a hot debate, some defending; others blaming what I had said"*.[7] Sidney claimed that he was to suffer from the resentment of Lord Grey of Groby and the other radicals for this personal animosity two years later. Indeed, he records that his wording on that occasion was such *"as to make Cromwell, Bradshawe, Harrison, Lord Grey and others, my enemys* [sic]*, who did from that time continually oppose me"*.[8]

The relationship between Thomas Grey and Algernon Sidney is an interesting one. They were the same age, having been born in 1623, both were the sons of peers, and both were radical republicans and *'commonwealthmen'*. Yet, during the life of the Rump Parliament they seem to have been more often opposed to each other than working together. Whereas Lord Grey always seems to have been confident in the expectation of inheriting his patrimony from the Earl of Stamford, even when they began to diverge in their political views, Algernon Sidney was always conscious that, as the second son of the Earl of Leicester, his eldest brother, Philip Sidney, Lord Lisle, was most likely to inherit the Sidney titles and estates. The family seat of the Sidneys was at Penshurst, near Tonbridge, in Kent; and, despite the father's title, the family had few links with Leicestershire.

Algernon Sidney was a dominating and indomitable personality. He was also a gifted writer, with a formidable contemporary humanist education, which left him with a wide range of historical and political knowledge. This left its mark on his political thought, but was frustrated in practice by his chronic inability to co-operate with or defer to the judgement of others. His contemporaries seem to have agreed that he could not tolerate contradiction. He had a dictatorial temper, but it was combined with great courage and sense of honour. A consequence of this was the continual personal tension generated even against those who might have been thought closest to him in politics and background, such as Thomas

334

Grey. In some respects they were too similar in terms of personality to work well together. Algernon Sidney's personality was crucially characterised by an imperiousness and pride which combined a high opinion of his own abilities with a temperamental and aristocratic refusal to be ruled. This would conflict with a similar aristocratic arrogance which appeared to characterise the young Lord Grey during his early years in public life. The latter had, however, developed an ability to relate to people from other stations and walks of life so that, by this period, he was well regarded by most elements in the Army, the Levellers, and later the Fifth Monarchists. A link between the two men was Henry Neville, another radical republican, who was Sidney's second cousin and a political ally of Grey in the Marten-Challoner faction. Sidney tended to favour the more 'religious' Vane-Hesilrigg faction through his admiration of Henry Vane and his work. Thus Sidney acted as a bridge between the two groups at times, via Neville.

Henry Marten was *'long an enemy of Vane'*, and Rump politics was punctuated by the conflict between Vane's religious radicalism and social conservatism, and Marten's irreligious, at times, social radicalism. Marten was allied with Neville, Challoner, and Lord Grey of Groby whose alleged *'continual opposition'* to him Sidney has already mentioned. Sidney's association with this group, rather than the Vane group, when it did occur is explained only by his association with Henry Neville, and despite the presence of Lord Grey.

Lord Grey was not on bad terms with all of the Sidney family at this time though. Bulstrode Whitelocke recorded in his diary for 21st April 1649 that he and Lord Lisle, Algernon's elder brother, had been *"highly entertained"* by the Countess Dowager of Exeter whom the Lord Grey of Groby, *"her Grandchild"*, brought to her. Both Lisle and Whitelocke were senior law officers in the Commonwealth and it is likely that the Countess was hoping to influence them or win their goodwill, probably in connection with her claims over her Irish property.

The ill-feeling between the two young, and superficially similar, aristocratic republicans continued through the life of the Rump Parliament. In 1651 Sidney helped to push some recommendations from a committee which supervised the finances of the Army, of which he was a member, through Parliament against the opposition of Henry Marten and Lord Grey. In the August of 1652 he headed a committee to draft legislation necessary for the settlement by the Adventurers for lands in Ireland. He was assisted in its passage through the House by Neville against the opposition of Marten and his group. Again, he was closely involved with the sale of Church and Delinquents' lands to raise money for the Navy, allying in this again with Henry Vane and his group against the Marten group. To a large extent the internal politics of the Rump's regime was carried out within the committees of the House, the Council of State, and the Army.

In the Commonwealth the whole executive government system of the monarchy was replaced, under the Council of State, by a system of committees. In the anxious avoidance of individual, rather than collective, responsibility no one man - apart from the cases of command in the army and navy - accepted office other than through membership of committees. The main governing power, the Council of State, was itself virtually - although not nominally - a committee. The other main committees were the Committee for the Advance of Money, the Sequestration Committee, the Committee for Compounding, the Committee for Plundered Ministers, the Committee for Indemnity, and the Committee of Trustees for the Sale of Fee-farms or Crown Lands.

The Committee for the Advance of Money had been established in 1642 and was to last until 1655. Its object was to find means, voluntary or by compulsory assessments on the estates of delinquents, of obtaining money to finance the war effort.

The Sequestration Committee was centralised in London, but with local committees in each county also, whose object was to seize and sequester the estates of 'delinquents', i.e. royalists and papist recusants. On information of delinquency, if considered well-founded, the estate was seized and secured, pending investigation. If proved to the satisfaction of the local committee (as was the outcome in nine tenths of cases) the delinquent was deprived of the whole estate, but one fifth was allowed for the maintenance of the wife and children. A further one fifth of the clear proceeds of the sale of an estate was awarded to the informer against the delinquent. Moreover a half, or sometimes the whole proceeds, were frequently assigned to an officer in the army, or an MP, or a public servant who could not otherwise obtain payment of salary arrears due. In the case of the sequestration of an estate for recusancy up to one third could be allowed to the recusant. Members of the local committee had one shilling in the pound on all monies brought in by this method. During the periods of actual civil war, where the royalists prevailed they used this system too. In areas of strong royalist sentiment it was sometimes difficult to find enough parliamentarian sequestrators. In areas where the parliamentarian interest prevailed the 'delinquents' became a helpless prey to their enemies. Informers were rife, under the incentive and lure of self-interest, and estates were sequestered and let at mere nominal rentals, often to the local committee men and their friends; whilst the one fifth due to the delinquent's family was thus reduced to a mere nothing, and often ill-paid, if at all. Yet, though the losses of the delinquents were enormous, such was the malpractice of the committees that the profits to the state were small by

336

comparison. As a result, eventually, another system was introduced which gave rise to a new and very important committee which in a few years absorbed the Sequestration Committee. This was the Committee for Compounding.

The Committee for Compounding existed from 1644 to 1657. Its three main objectives were to obtain from delinquents firstly, a confession of their delinquency, secondly a pledge of their adherence to the new government (particularly after the establishment of the Republic), and thirdly, a full account of their possessions, both real estate and personal. When these had been secured a legal report was made, and the delinquents were admitted or allowed to compound in proportions, according to their guilt. One half of the estate was exacted from any delinquent MP. One sixth was confiscated from those who had taken part in either the first or later civil wars; this could be raised to one third for those who had supported the royalist cause on all occasions. Those who had been in cities that had surrendered on articles of war compounded according to the terms granted at that time. This was to have considerable significance in some cases and to cause a difference of attitude between the Army and the Parliament. Payments, in the case of compounding, were made not through the local county committees but directly into the Treasury at Goldsmiths Hall in London. This was speedier and more efficient. The numbers of compounders may be gauged from the fact that the original orders and papers relating to them fill more that 250 volumes (large folios) of 1,000 pages each approximately. The total income from the end of 1644 to August 1652 came to £1,304,957. 2s. 1d.; and this excluded the proceeds from the very wealthiest delinquents and those who remained abroad who were not allowed to compound, but whose entire estates were seized by sequestrators.

The Committee for Plundered Ministers existed from 1649 to 1653. Its object was to augment, from the revenues of rectories, tithes, etc. raised from the estates of sequestered delinquents and the livings of scandalous ministers, the income of the neighbouring godly ministers; but always with the condition of their taking first the Covenant and then the Oath of Engagement to the current government.

The Committee for Indemnity existed from 1649 to 1656. Its creation had been one of the demands of the Army. Its object was to indemnify those persons who had seized horses or goods for the service of Parliament, damaged lands, crops, property, etc. in the prosecution of the war effort against the future legal consequences of their actions. It could compel landowners to grant allowance or deduction from rents against amounts paid for free quarter of troops or parliamentarian assessments. It protected the purchasers or leasees of sequestered property against the claims of the original owners. It also guaranteed apprentices, who had taken up arms on the parliamentarian side, against suits of non-fulfilment of indentures by their masters.

The Committee of Trustees for the Sale of Fee-Farms or Crown Lands (and their rents) existed from 1650 until 1660. This was a very significant, lucrative, and influential committee which dealt with the distribution of crown lands and the income derived from them following the abolition of the monarchy.

There were many other committees, of which no other record books still remain but there are collections of papers, more or less numerous which relate to them. These include committees for the Army; the Navy; the Mint; the Revenue; Whitehall; for receiving the Accounts of the kingdom/ commonwealth; for removing obstructions in the sale of delinquents' lands; for relief upon articles of war, i.e. for those who were denied the privileges accorded by the articles of war on which they surrendered; and for the investigation of the law concerning debt.

In addition to the system of executive committees a range of insignia for the new state was created. A splendid new Great Seal was produced for the Commonwealth. It was struck in the name of 'the keepers of the liberties of England by the authority of parliament'. The engraver was Oliver Simon who had struck seals for Charles I, the civil war parliaments, and would do so in future for the Protectorate and the restored monarchy. It was designed with the assistance of Henry Marten and bore on one side the map of England (including Wales) and Ireland, combined with their respective arms (the cross of St. George and the harp); and on the other side a representation of the House of Commons in session with the Speaker in the chair, around which appeared the words *"In the first year of Freedom, by God's blessing restored"*. Bulstrode Whitelocke was confirmed as Lord Commissioner and Keeper of the Great Seal. He was joined by John Lisle and Richard Keeble to replace the reluctant Earl of Kent, Lord Grey of Wark, and Sir Thomas Widdrington. Oliver St. John, Henry Rolle, and John Wilde were appointed as the Chief Justices. A whole range of other new state seals were now produced for the work of the new state, following similar patterns. The old royalist seals, when they could be found, were ceremonially smashed.

A new mace was produced for the now unicameral Parliament. The king's arms gave way to those of England and Ireland, and around the rim of the mace oak trees were inserted for the crosses. The coinage also had to be changed. An order of 13th February provided for a series of coins with variations of a design which included the arms of England and Ireland, a palm and a laurel branch and two inscriptions, *'The Commonwealth of England'* and *'God With Us'*. Some things took a little longer. It was not until February 1650 that orders were given to take down the King's Arms

338

from all public places, and to substitute those of the Commonwealth. This work was to be overseen by JPs and churchwardens. In August 1649, however, Lord Grey of Groby and a group of fellow republicans had introduced a measure with this intention. His colleagues included Henry Marten, Edmund Ludlow, Cornelius Holland, Henry Smyth (of Leicestershire), Augustine Garland, Luke Robinson, and the Chaloners - Neville, Thomas and James.

Lord Grey of Groby now found himself a leading member of the Council of State. On 6th January an order of the House of Commons had added him and Thomas Wayte to the influential and lucrative Committee for Compounding (of Delinquents' Estates) which met at Goldsmiths Hall. He was also appointed to a number of other committees. These included committees to consider *'for providing salt petre* (for gunpowder) *without making it at home'*; *'the propositions given in, from time to time, by the serjeant'*; *'the condition of the relations of Dr. Dorislaus* [the Commonwealth's ambassador to the Netherlands who had been assassinated by royalists], *he being taken from them while in the service of the commonwealth, as also his interment'*; *'the matter concerning the export of gold'*; and *'how the money now come in upon the sale of deans and chapters lands, and lying in bank in the Treasury, may be disposed of to the best advantage'* [i.e. Church lands]. He was also appointed a member of the committee set up to investigate the debt law. All of these positions provided him with opportunities to advance his personal fortune at the same time as advancing the Cause. He was not slow to do either as his critics have recorded.

On 1st February Parliament appointed Lord Grey of Groby, along with Lord Lisle, Lord Mounson, and twenty eight others to *"take note of the dissent of any member from the vote of 5 December* (i.e. grounds for proceeding with a settlement with the king). *No person who has not entered his disapproval is to sit in the House. All those who have not done so by 1 March are to be suspended"*.[9] This was an attempt to increase the number of active MPs but also to continue to exclude those who were perceived to be crypto-royalists. It was followed up on 23rd February by another move by the 'revolutionaries' to secure control of the navy as well as the army.

> *"The Lord Grey made reports from the Council of State to the house of theyre opinion for repeal of the ordinance contributing the Earle of Warwick, Lord High Admiral, and that the Commission under the great Seale making the Earle of Warwick, Lord High Admiral of England be called in ..... "*.[10]

This was agreed.

Of more local interest, on 15th June the Council of State agreed to write to Sir William Armyne and Lord Grey of Groby requesting them to appoint whom they thought suitable to supervise the demolition of Belvoir Castle.

By the end of February and the beginning of March 1649 the apparatus of the new state had been created. With the election of the Council of State there were already signs that many of those who had established the Commonwealth had no intention of allowing the revolution to get out of control. As Underdown puts it : -

"Even stout republicans like Ludlow and Thomas Scot were also politicians who wanted to stay in power and could appreciate the benefits of moderate support. Even more important were the reservations of men like Cromwell, converted to regicide by the dictates of Providence, but never quite allowing Puritan zeal to overcome their ingrained attachment to Common Law and Parliament. They needed moderate allies like Whitelocke, and having acquired them were inevitably restrained by them".[11]

Such moderate allies were needed not only because of the danger of counter-revolution from the royalists and presbyterians but also because of a perceived threat of a social revolution from groups such as the Levellers.

The Parliament and its Commonwealth depended for its very existence upon the Army. Within the ranks of the army, however, were to be found its strongest critics; their thoughts articulated by the Levellers. Parliament could not afford to face a dissolution since that could mean the end of the republic. It had to carry on, whilst attempting to reduce the level of taxation required to maintain the army and the new administration. The rank and file soldiers who had supported their officers against firstly the king, then parliament in 1647, then the royalists again, and the parliament again in the purge were still waiting for their reward. If England was now a free state, the people must be free to govern themselves. In January 1649 the army had drawn up a new form of the 'Agreement of the People'. Under this the present parliament was to dissolve itself in April; a new representative parliament was to be elected every two years and to sit for only six months in the year. There was to be manhood suffrage, apart from paupers, menial servants, and irreconcilable 'delinquents'; equal electoral districts; freedom of conscience and worship, no compulsory recruitment or 'pressing'; and equality before the law. The whole arrangement was to be embodied in a written constitution. Parliament received the 'Agreement' with thanks but did nothing. All this served notice on the Levellers and the more radical republicans that they could not expect much in the way of rapid and far reaching change from this parliament. Hence the determination of the radicals to press for a new assembly elected on a wider franchise. It has often been assumed that this would have led to a royalist majority. That is, however, by no means certain. There is little evidence of support for the 1648 royalist rising amongst the groups who would have been newly enfranchised in 1649. In any case, the Rump was not ready then - or later - to take chances. Having taken power as *"the only visible authority in being"* (Whitelocke), the Rump intended to retain it. Confident that the army grandees associated with its establishment would not desert it the Commonwealth parliament intended to move slowly, if at all, in the direction of basic social and political reform. An army would have to be maintained, but as a disciplined non-political force, led by non-political officers.

The revised 'Agreement of the People' had been presented to the House of Commons on Saturday, 20th January, together with a petition from Lord General Fairfax and the General Council of Officers of the Army. This was the same day that the formal trial of the king had opened and it was now seen as a device merely to secure the support of the Levellers and the army rank and file at that time. The main point made by the Levellers now was that the parliament and the Army grandees were busy betraying the aim of the revolution by not implementing those social and political reforms they had believed implicit in all their agreements.

Under the terms of the 'Agreement of the People' draft which had been indefinitely shelved by parliament there were to be 400 elected representatives, with approximately 1,000 electors to each member. Of these the City of London would have eight members, the Borough of Leicester one (instead of the existing two), the rest of Leicestershire five (instead of the existing two), and the county of Rutland one (instead of the traditional two for the shire). On 22nd February a "humble Representation of the Committee, Gentry, Ministry, and other well-affected persons, in the County of Leicester, in reference to the Agreement of the People tendered to the Kingdom as touching Religion", was presented to Lord General Fairfax and the General Council of Officers of the Army. It was reported that this 'humble Representation' was *"received with noble candour; his Excellency promising to take it into consideration, to communicate it to his general council of officers, and to endeavour the satisfaction of these, and all other well-affected in the nation".*

This was followed up by a petition to parliament from the gentlemen of the county of Leicester who were answered thus:

> *"Gentlemen, you of the county of Leicester; the House has read your petition; and I shall, as near as I can, declare their sense. The House doth take notice of the modesty and discretion of*

the petition, and the petitioners, in the way of delivering it, and the expressions in it. The House doth likewise take notice of some things out of the petition : and that is, concerning your county; whose readiness to the service of the publick the last summer, wherein you did great and acceptable service to the Commonwealth ..... .

And for these and your good affections always to the publick, the House hath commanded me to return you hearty thanks; and I do, in their names return you hearty thanks. For the particulars in the petition, some of them are of great weight and consequence, fit for you to present, and for them to take consideration of : some of which, as taking off free quarters [for troops] and others, are already in a way of settlement : and the whole House is zealous to give you and the whole kingdom satisfaction therein. For the rest of the particulars, they doubt not but you will leave it to them, as the urgent and important affairs of the kingdom will admit, to take the same into consideration; and doubt not but to do it so, as the kingdom may receive satisfaction and safety".[12]

The new Establishment was receiving similar petitions from other counties and was beset on all sides by complainants. By the beginning of March the royalist newsletter 'Mercurius Pragmaticus' claimed to have heard of open dissension between Cromwell and Henry Marten and his *"levelling crew"* in the very Commons chamber itself, in the course of which Cromwell was reported to have drawn his dagger.[13]

On 26th February John Lilburne presented 'England's New Chains Discovered' to Parliament. This was not his first appearance at the bar of the House of Commons; he had stood there as a prisoner to answer for his life previously. On this occasion he stood there as the leader of a party on whose alliance, at least in principle, his hearers depended. The explanation may lie in the fact that the Leveller party had been growing rapidly. The Levellers still cherished the illusion that the Grandees of the Army had been serious when they had adopted the 'Agreement of the People'. Lilburne, therefore, devoted much of his time to an able criticism of the officers' version of this charter. He stressed the danger inherent in the provisions for a biennial Parliament which would sit only for six months whilst the Council of State, armed with very strong powers, would reign supreme and unchecked for the other eighteen months. He also criticised the intolerance of the new Council of State to date in matters of religion, the failure to abolish tithes, the reintroduction of the press-gang and censorship by the new government and the severe limiting by the Grandees of the soldiers' right to petition. These points might have impressed the House more favourably had he not called for the dissolution of the Council of State which it had just elected.

The real purpose of 'England's New Chains Discovered', however, was to awaken civilian concern about the danger posed by the Army. Lilburne dwelt on the power the Grandees possessed, through the selection and promotion of officers, to make it their own personal instrument. By exercising martial law with much cruelty they debased the mens' spirits and made them subservient to their own wills and pleasures. The pamphlet wound up by beseeching the House to consider *"how dangerous it is for one and the same persons to be continued long in the highest commands of a military power ..... which was the original of most regalities and tyrannies in the world"*. Though it named no specific names it was clear that this was a demand for the dismissal of Cromwell and most likely Ireton and Fairfax too.

To ask this of the House that was the product of the Army's purge was expecting a very great deal indeed. The Levellers were not totally without friends in Parliament, however, or even in the Council of State itself. Edmund Ludlow was sympathetic and, according to Brailsford : -

"Two [members of the Council of State] **could be described as Levellers, but they were Colonel Henry Marten, a big landowner, and Lord Grey of Groby".**[15]

Lilburne's challenge to the Army Grandees found an immediate echo from the ranks. On 1st March eight troopers, representing various regiments of the Army, presented a petition to Lord General Fairfax protesting against his order of the day issued on 22nd February restricting petitions. It was 'ghost-written' by Richard Overton, the Leveller author, for the soldiers. It referred back to the heady days of 1647, when the Army was unanimous in claiming for the soldier against the harsh ruling of Holles and Stapleton the basic right to petition Parliament. Once again the troopers proclaimed that they were *"English soldiers engaged for the freedoms of England and not outlandish mercenaries to butcher the people for pay"*. They reminded Fairfax that he had formerly backed them in asserting that *"our being soldiers hath not deprived us of our right as commoners"*. They resented the idea that any petitions could be vetoed by their officers, the officer being nothing without *"the soldier that endureth the heat and burden of the day and performeth that work whereof the officers bear the glory and name"*. They criticised the High Court of Justice and the Council of State, *"entrusted with little less than unlimited power"* and

343

composed of *"the most pernicious interests of our rotten state, lords, lawyers, Star Chamber judges and dissenters from the proceedings against the King"*.[16] They ended by declaring their agreement with John Lilburne's 'England's New Chains Discovered'.

These eight brave troopers were immediately arrested and court-martialled on 3rd March. Three of them apologised, asked for forgiveness and were pardoned. The other five remained resolute. They were told that as their petition was *'tending to breed mutiny in the Army'* they deserved to be punished with death, but *'in mercy'* they were sentenced to be cashiered from the Army after riding *'at the head of their regiments with their faces towards the horses' tails, their faults written upon their breasts and their swords broken over their heads'*. After this degrading punishment had been carried out the five troopers found coaches waiting for them which carried them off to one of the Leveller taverns, where they were entertained to a *'plentiful dinner'* as the party's guests of honour.[17]

The Leveller campaign went beyond the publishing of petitions. There were reports that during March both military and civilian Levellers were active in distributing and posting notices and copies of petitions calling on people to refuse to pay excise, tithes, and other unreasonable taxes in many counties, including Hertfordshire, Berkshire, and Hampshire.

Two new publications were soon in circulation. From Richard Overton on 21st March and from John Lilburne on 24th March came pamphlets which completed their breach with the Cromwellian Independents. Overton's was a defence of the five troopers who had been cashiered for petitioning. It was entitled 'The Hunting of the Foxes from Newmarket and Triploe Heaths to Whitehall, by five small Beagles (late of the Army)'. It showed how the Grandees had run away from all the proud principles to which they had pledged their loyalty at Newmarket in the summer of 1647. To require from soldiers abstention from political activity is a reasonable rule, but only if the same applies to their officers. But the chief officers of the New Model Army were the leading figures in the political life of the Commonwealth. They were particularly active, vocal and conspicuous. That they should expect to exact silent compliance from their men was both hypocritical and an example of class discrimination. It was now all but impossible for a soldier to request redress for any wrong an officer may have done him. Daily honest men were being cashiered for complaining against their officers.

Cromwell's character was particularly criticised and his ambition recognised.

> *"Was there ever* [asks Overton] *a generation of men so apostate, so false and so perjured as these? Did ever men pretend an higher degree of holiness, religion and zeal to God and their*

344

country than these? These preach, these fast, these pray, these
have nothing more frequent than the sentences of sacred
scripture, the name of God and of Christ in their mouths. You
shall scarce speak to Cromwell about anything, but he will lay
his hand on his breast, elevate his eyes and call God to record,
he will weep, howl and repent, even while he doth smite you
under the fifth rib".[18]

Overton went on to predict, as Lilburne also did, that the usurpation of power by the Council of State would end in some form of monarchy - *'a new regality'*. Originally it was thought that the future single ruler might be Fairfax with Cromwell as the real dictator behind him. This was a presentiment of the Cromwellian Protectorate five years before it was actually established.

Lilburne's pamphlet appeared as 'The Second Part of England's New Chains Discovered'. It attacked the ambition of Cromwell and his fellow Grandees. Then it described how they were turning the Army into their subservient tool by dismissing and cashiering godly men who had served the Cause well and replacing them with ex-royalist hirelings. The New Model was evolving under Cromwell's direction into *"a company of bloody and inhuman butchers of men, that had served seven years' apprenticeship to that bloody and wicked trade of cutting men's throats for money and nothing else"*. Lilburne refrained from any direct attack on the House of Commons, but he did say that it had become *"the channel through which is conveyed all the decrees and determinations of a private council of officers"*. He pointed to the return to the days of no press freedom and the intolerable burden of taxation. There were two ways to save England from military dictatorship and he appealed to the Commons to further them both. The first was to adopt the 'Agreement of the People', which would involve the election of a new Parliament. The second was that the Army should have a truly representative Army Council, chosen by the men as well as the officers according to the pattern agreed at Newmarket in 1647. The loyalty of MPs to their trust was appealed to. This pamphlet was seen as the manifesto of the Leveller party. It struck at Cromwell and his control over the Army, the source of his power. He would see it as more than a personal attack. It threatened, from his perspective, the new Commonwealth and its stability.

According to Blair Worden : -

**"Matters were made worse by the behaviour of Henry Marten
and Lord Grey of Groby, who between them had organised
the resistance in parliament to Cromwell's bridge-building
after the king's execution. Both men were achieving
popularity among the lower-ranking officers, some of whom**

345

were said to want Grey as Lord General, and Marten as Lieutenant-General, of the Army. Marten and his regiment seem to have been instrumental in the spring of 1649 in provoking popular disturbances in Hampshire and perhaps elsewhere".[19]

There is evidence that despite the 'Self-Denying Ordinance' of April 1645, Thomas Grey had managed to retain his reputation as a military commander amongst the parliamentarians. Moreover, he had, through his puritan zeal, become accepted as a keen Commonwealthman and a radical republican. The pro-Leveller regicide of 1649 presents a very different image from the socially superior young aristocrat of the days of 1642 and 1643.

On the afternoon of Tuesday, 27th March, 1649 Oliver Cromwell struck back in the House of Commons at the Leveller leaders. Earlier that morning John Lilburne had rejected the bribe of the offer of a well-paid post from one of the Lieutenant General's men. Cromwell now moved a resolution in the House to declare that *"the authors, contrivers and framers of"* `The Second Part of England's New Chains Discovered'*, which "doth contain most false, scandalous and reproachful matter"* and *"tends to division and mutiny in the Army, and the raising of a new war in the Commonwealth, and to hinder the present relief of Ireland and to the continuing of free quarter" ..... "are guilty of high treason and shall be proceeded against as traitors"*.

The debate on this motion lasted for three hours. In favour of the resolution spoke Cromwell and Sir Arthur Hesilrige, a long-standing rival of the Lilburnes in County Durham. There is no record of a division and the motion was passed without one. It is likely that those who spoke against it would have been Lord Grey and Henry Marten or Edmund Ludlow, but they were heavily outnumbered in the chamber.

> *"Ludlow, with Marten and Grey of Groby, consistently endeavoured to protect the Levellers from those Rumpers who were mercilessly keen to crush them, but the months after Charles' execution exposed the disparity between his aims and those of Lilburne".*

Cromwell was seeking to drive a wedge between them. The resolution concluded with the sentence : -

> *"And ..... all persons whatsoever that shall join with and adhere unto and hereafter voluntarily aid or assist the authors, framers,*

346

and contrivers of the aforesaid paper, in the prosecution thereof,
shall be esteemed as traitors to the Commonwealth and be
proceeded against accordingly". [20]

In the early hours of the following day, between four and six in the morning, four detachments of horse and foot numbering each between one and two hundred men, marched to the homes of John Lilburne, William Walwyn, Richard Overton and Thomas Prince, and arrested them. The prisoners appeared one by one that afternoon before the Council of State, at Derby House, for examination with John Bradshaw in the chair. Whilst being kept in an ante-room Lilburne overheard Cromwell banging a table with his fist and saying loudly, *"I tell you, Sir, you have no other way to deal with these men, but to break them in pieces ..... if you do not break them, they will break you ..... ".*

Cromwell's motion was to commit all four prisoners to the Tower.

Ludlow proposed that they should be released on bail. He was defeated, but only by one vote. The prisoners were sent to the Tower of London. Richard Overton wrote shortly afterwards,

"For my part, I had rather die in the just vindication of the
cause of the poor oppressed people of this Commonwealth than
to die in my bed". [21]

By the middle of April several petitions, with thousands of signatures, had been presented to Parliament calling for either the release of the four or their bail and trial before an ordinary court of justice with a jury. The latter was granted but without bail.

In the meantime Leveller unrest in the Army had surfaced again. On 15th March the Council of State had nominated Cromwell to take command of a military expedition to Ireland. (The Irish Royalists under the Earl of Ormonde had concluded an alliance with the native Irish Catholic forces in the Treaty of Kilkenny in January). He gave his reply in an address to his officers at Whitehall on 23rd March. He would only lead an expedition to Ireland if it was fully supported and resourced. At least four regiments of horse, four regiments of foot, and five troops of dragoons would be required. They were to be chosen by lot. The Levellers, however, opposed the project in principle. They saw in the native Irish their fellow men, whose claim to liberty and their birthright was as valid as their own. Also; they reminded the soldiers of their resolutions of 1647 not to disband or go for service abroad until their full arrears of pay and their political rights had been secured. Hence there was no basis for compromise. The Cromwellians had no use for the 'Agreement of the People' and the Levellers did not wish to re-conquer Ireland for the Grandees.

347

On 30th March Cromwell's appointment as commander-in-chief of the army for Ireland was approved by Parliament. There was trouble in the Army, particularly within the regiments selected for Irish service, throughout the spring and summer of 1649.

A campaign to weed out the Levellers from amongst the ranks of those regiments destined for Ireland was considered essential. It sparked an outright mutiny in Whalley's Regiment of Horse who had been ordered to a rendezvous in Essex. They refused to leave London until they received their arrears of pay. Thirty of them seized the colours and only surrendered upon the arrival of Fairfax and Cromwell. At the following court martial on 26th April six troopers were sentenced to death and five to be cashiered after suffering the painful and humiliating punishment of riding the wooden horse.

On Cromwell's intercession those sentenced to death were spared with the exception of the alleged ringleader, a twenty-three year old trooper named Robert Lockier. Lockier had served seven years in the Army and was very popular. Whether he was the actual ringleader may be disputed, but he was a known Leveller and had been the political leader of his troop in 1647. This was his first offence against military discipline. His courtesy and his bravery were widely acknowledged. Even the Cromwellian 'Moderate Intelligencer' described him as *"a pious man, of excellent parts and much beloved"*. A hastily produced Leveller petition and a letter signed by Lilburne and Overton proved futile. Lockier declined a blindfold as he faced the firing squad in front of St. Paul's. Before he was shot dead he told the members of the squad that their obedience to their superiors' orders did not acquit them of murder. On the following Sunday, 29th April, his friends carried his body to a grave in Westminster through silent streets lined with respectful crowds. Even respectable burgesses wore the sea-green ribbons of the Leveller party. First in the funeral procession came six trumpeters sounding the last post, followed by many hundreds of troopers and other soldiers marching in step. Then his horse, draped in black, was led by friends in mourning cloaks, an honour usually reserved for high ranking commanders. On his coffin, borne by six soldiers in mourning, his unsheathed sword lay upon sprigs of rosemary (for remembrance) dipped in his blood. His relatives followed and after them came many hundreds of citizens. At the end of the procession walked a contingent of women. Everyone wore the sea-green ribbons and black ribbons. A great crowd of additional citizens, also wearing these colours, awaited the coffin at the grave side. Thus the first Leveller martyr of the new campaign was laid to rest. A new leaflet had been circulated on the previous day which concluded with an appeal to the soldiers to *"keep every man his place and post and stir not, but immediately choose you out a Council of Agitators once more"*. The call was swiftly obeyed.

348

By early May breaking-point on the subject of the Irish expedition had been reached by various angry regiments. Round about May Day several regiments of horse elected Agitators again. Scroop's, Ireton's, and Harrison's were amongst the first to do so. Now a more extensive mutiny than Lockier's outbreak exploded. The two chief centres were at Salisbury and Banbury. At Salisbury the regiments of Ireton and Scroop declared their intention to remain in England until that nation's liberties should be secured, called for the implementation of the 'Agreement of the People', and issued a tract entitled 'The Soldier's Demand' which ended with this conclusion : -

"What have we to do in Ireland, to fight and murder a people and nation (for indeed they - the Grandees - are set upon cruelty and murdering poor people, which is all they glory in) which have done us no harm .....? We have waded too far in that crimson stream already of innocent and Christian blood".[22]

The Salisbury mutineers had no single leader. It was a basic tenet of Leveller democracy that officers should be elected by the men. They had a Council of Agitators, drawn from the six regiments that had joined the revolt - four of horse (Scroop's, Ireton's, Harrison's and Horton's) and two of foot (Skippon's and Ingoldsby's). Amongst the officers who joined them the most senior was Lieutenant Colonel Eyres who had served in the first troop raised by Cromwell. He had been arrested previously for siding with Leveller troops at Corkbush Field near Ware at the time of that meeting. He had also assisted Henry Marten to raise his regiment in Berkshire; yet the Agitators declined to place him in overall command.

The news of the Leveller mutinies was the signal for panic in London. The Grandees and the City were alarmed. The four Leveller leaders were now closely confined in separate cells and denied visitors. Their erstwhile allies in Parliament and the Council of State saw discretion as the better part of valour for the time being and distanced themselves from their cause. It was decided by the government that both Fairfax and Cromwell would be needed to subdue the Army Levellers who were in arms.

Before setting out for the West the two generals held a review of the forces based in London in Hyde Park. Many of the men even in their own crack regiments of horse came to the rendezvous on 9th May with sea-green ribbons in their hats. Cromwell made a persuasive speech at the head of each regiment whilst Fairfax nodded in support. In the five months since the Army had entered London, it was pointed out, Parliament had performed that great work of justice against the grand delinquents which had cleansed the land from the stain of innocent blood; it had made an end of the monarchy and the House of Lords, raised the navy to its greatest strength in history and revived trade. He then promised that those who resented martial law could lay down their arms and they would receive vouchers for their arrears of pay which would be honoured as swiftly as for those that stayed. He had appropriated £10,000 for the Army which had originally been intended for the Navy. The programme of the officers' version of the 'Agreement of the People' would be carried out, including *"putting a period to this present Parliament"*.

A declaration which repeated the substance of Cromwell's speech, with some additions, was issued over Fairfax's signature and was addressed to the mutineers. It warned them that they were tempting the cavaliers to take advantage of the divisions in the ranks of the godly and to take to their arms again. It told them that they were defying God's will if they disobeyed his call to serve in Ireland if the lot had fallen upon them. Fairfax promised to pardon those who surrendered but to reduce by force those who did not.

The mutineers at Salisbury marched north to Marlborough and thence by way of Wantage to Abingdon where they were joined by the remaining adherents of the Banbury mutiny. They were also joined by two troops of Harrison's regiment. There were now over eight hundred in the Leveller force and all were cavalry, thus providing a serious and mobile threat to the Grandees. Their next aim was to link up with elements of Colonel Horton's horse in and around Gloucester. In the meantime Fairfax and Cromwell had advanced westwards from London to Andover in the north of Hampshire.

Finding that the Salisbury force had moved up into Oxfordshire the generals sent two messengers after them in order to delay their movements either further westwards or towards London. These two messengers or 'commissioners' were Colonel Scroop himself and a Major Francis White. Scroop had no success in persuading either his own men or the others to submit. Major White, however, was one of the few senior officers whom the Levellers respected, since the death of Colonel Rainsborough, and whom they regarded as one of their own. He had boldly taken their part during the Army's revolt of 1647 and his integrity was unlikely to be questioned by them. The instructions he received from Fairfax were that he should try to 'procure a union' with the revolted regiments. According to his own narrative of events Cromwell added, as he rode off : *"Let them know that though we have sent messengers to them, we will not follow with force at their heels"*. These words *"my Lord General confirmed"*. This was an explicit assurance that the generals were prepared to negotiate. White's account is confirmed by correspondence between the two parties. A letter from the Agitators to Scroop's and Ireton's regiments sets out their financial grievances, and their emphasis on the Engagement of June 1647. It asked Fairfax to listen to their case, safeguard their interest, and honour the

Engagement of Newmarket and Triploe Heath. In his reply Fairfax assured the men that they would not be disbanded without sufficient pay, criticised them for their disobedience, stated that Colonel Scroop was authorised to extend his protection, and that he was ready to hear their points regarding the Engagement. A further letter from the men's Council thanked the Lord General for his *'clemency'* but stressed in blunt terms their views of the obligations under the Engagement. *"You kept not covenant with us"*. In conclusion, it told him that if he refused to call a General Council of the Army all the bloodshed which would follow would be his responsibility.

While these exchanges were taking place the Levellers began to suspect that the generals were playing for time and were not to be trusted. They confronted Major White and accused him of being an accomplice in an exercise to betray them. He replied that both the Lord General and the Lieutenant-General had given their words not to engage with them in any hostile manner until answers to proposals had been received and given an assurance that the messengers or commissioners would not be followed with force : -

> *"And being too credulous to the General's words, knowing that he never broke engagement with the Cavaliers in that kind, we gave the more credit to the Major, who seemed extreme forward and hasty to make the composure* [i.e. the agreement]*".* [23]

Major White and the Agitators appeared so fully in sympathy that they entrusted him with drafting a reply to Fairfax. In this they repeated their demand for a General Council and agreed to abide by its decisions. They then moved on from Abingdon. Heading westwards they encountered a party of Colonel Reynolds' horse which fell back to Newbridge and held that crossing over the Thames against them. The Levellers had no scruples about attacking these men who were *"a mercenary, damme crew"* largely recruited from ex-royalist soldiers taken prisoner at Colchester. When Lieutenant-Colonel Eyres was about to lead an attack by a vanguard unit to force a passage Major White intervened and persuaded them to cross the Thames by a less convenient ford further north to avoid shedding blood.

On the evening of 14th May the Leveller force had reached the village of Burford in north Oxfordshire. Their twelve troops of horse were quartered for the night in Burford and two neighbouring villages. Only a very slight guard was posted as they trusted Major White's assurances. He had vowed that if the forces of the generals should fall upon them he would stand between them and the bullets.

During that day, however, Cromwell, to whom Fairfax had given command of the operation, did follow hard with force. He covered some forty-five miles with his cavalry and dragoons by forced marches. At midnight with greatly superior numbers they fell upon Burford in the darkness from both ends of its main street and took the sleeping Levellers by surprise. Some shots were fired in reply from the inn where Lieutenant-Colonel Eyres and some of the troopers were quartered, but there was little other resistance. When the news reached Major White that Fairfax and Cromwell were attacking with two thousand horse and dragoons he sought to keep his word. In an attempt to avoid bloodshed he rushed out in his slippers to try to find the Lord General and in the confusion was taken prisoner. Only one man was killed on either side and three or four wounded, amongst them being Colonel Okey who commanded the dragoons. Three hundred and forty prisoners were taken and placed under guard in Burford Church. A note in the church register records three soldiers shot to death on 17th May 1649, following court-martial, and buried in Burford churchyard. The rest of the mutineers, some five hundred men, escaped but mostly without their horses. These leaderless men never rallied, but made their way, embittered, to their homes. Cromwell's deceitful victory over the Levellers was complete and it was nearly bloodless. Nonetheless the manner in which it was gained increased suspicions of his untrustworthiness amongst both Levellers and his parliamentarian rivals. The epitaph of the too trustful Levellers, including Major White, may be directed at Cromwell as well as Fairfax, *"You kept not covenant with us"*.

The relief with which Parliament and the City of London greeted the news of the defeat of the Army Levellers at Burford reveals the extent of the fears of the major property-owners. The officer who brought the glad tidings to the Commons was rewarded with a gratuity of £150. At Oxford the victorious generals were entertained with great pomp and ceremony. The university convocation conferred the honorary degrees of Doctors of Civil Law on Fairfax and Cromwell, those twin son of Mars - *'alteri Martis gemelli'* as the Public Orator put it - while Harrison, Hewson and Okey received honorary Masters degrees. Finally, Cromwell and Fairfax paraded in their newly acquired scarlet gowns through the streets of Oxford.[24] Later Parliament declared 7th June as a Thanksgiving Day for deliverance from the threat of *'levelling'*.

What had happened at Burford in the Cotswolds in May 1649 settled the allegiance of the New Model Army. For the rest of Cromwell's lifetime it was his to command. The influence of the Army Levellers had been destroyed and with it any prospects of Lord Grey of Groby becoming Lord General rather than Oliver Cromwell.

As for the Leveller leaders in London, they were dismayed and dejected by the news from Burford. None of them were responsible for the course that events had taken. As Brailsford comments : -

"The incompetence of the men's leaders, the readiness of Major White to believe and of Lieutenant-General Cromwell to promise, - no one could have forecast it all. None the less, the fact was that the Levellers had challenged the revolutionary government to a decision by arms and suffered an overwhelming and pitiful defeat. It was to the soldiers that all their arguments had latterly been addressed - over martial law, the right to petition, the Engagement of Triploe Heath, the iniquity and unwisdom of re-conquering Ireland. To make an end of the rule of the sword they had unsheathed their swords. The battle was over : the side with the longer sword and the fewer scruples had won".[25]

One more general lesson had become clear. "When Cromwell feared a man, he struck him down, were he monarch or Leveller".[26] Cromwell was now increasingly seen as the power holder.

Those parliamentarians who had supported the Levellers up to and including March had become increasingly embarrassed by the events of April and May which had led to such an ignominious defeat. More fundamentally, however, the persistent distrust of those in authority by the civilian Leveller leaders placed the radicals in a difficult position as members of the Council of State and the Parliament. As Gentles points out : -

"This unyielding animosity to the leaders of the Republic was to prove a grave blunder on the Levellers' part. It is no accident that about this time several of their friends began to desert them. Major Francis White and Captain (now Colonel) John Reynolds, who had been their prominent advocates in 1647, decided to back the grandees. White remained a critical and independent-minded supporter, who was not afraid to publish several radical letters that he had written to Fairfax and Cromwell in early 1648 and 1649. Having supported the resistance to parliament in 1647, endorsed the Leveller petition in September 1648, and opposed the execution of the king in January 1649, he obviously could not be counted on to back the grandees' every move. Yet he refused to align himself with the plot to overthrow them. In May he would be one of Fairfax's emissaries to the mutineers. Henry Marten, perhaps because of the handsome grant he was voted, perhaps because of the bullying of Oliver Cromwell, would also soon cease speaking and organising on the Levellers' behalf. Lord Grey of Groby and Alexander Rigby too were silent when the

353

grandees decided to eradicate Leveller influence in the army. The draining away of Leveller support was remarkably sudden. In December and January a majority of the officers had compelled the grandees to adopt an `Agreement of the People' very similar to what the Levellers wanted. In April and May the only officer of note to maintain his radical allegiance was Major John Cobbett of Skippon's Regiment". [27]

There are a number of possible explanations for the apparent acquiescence of the radical parliamentarians. These include discretion, impotence, prudence, disagreement over tactics, division through private matters or economic self-interest, and change of attitude. Worden suggests some motivations : -

"The taming of the radicals outside the House was paralleled within it ..... . Among the Rumpers with former Leveller connections, Cornelius Holland, now Cromwell's `present darling', was the most blatant .... More significant was the behaviour of both Marten and Grey of Groby at a critical moment during the Leveller unrest of April 1649, and the Leveller leaders believed that the two men had been bought off. Marten's reputation for integrity in such matters makes this unlikely, but the Rump's generosity doubtless encouraged his growing inclination to work for reform from within".[28]

A contemporary account from Lucy Hutchinson gives another perspective : -

"*A council of state was to be annually chosen for the management of affairs, accountable to the parliament, consisting of forty councillors and a president, twenty were every year to go off by lot, and twenty new ones to be supplied. It is true, that at that time almost every man was fancying a form of government, and angry, when this came forth, that his invention took not place; and amongst these John Lilburne; a turbulent spirited man, who was never quiet in anything, published libels; and the levellers made a disturbance with a kind of insurrection, which Cromwell soon appeased, they indeed being betrayed by their own leaders.*

"*..... Mr Hutchinson [Colonel John Hutchinson] was chosen into the first counil of state, much against his own will ..... [being persuaded by his cousin Henry Ireton that it was his duty to do so]*

*".....   Though he had now an opportunity to have enriched
himself, as it is to be feared some in all times have done, by
accepting rewards for even just assistances, ... he never had
anything in money or presents of any man".*[29]

Others were to display no such inhibitions. Cromwell had succeeded
with great political astuteness in crushing with armed force the last of his
really organised rivals for power, the Levellers; and he had done it by
securing the acquiescence of other grandees and parliamentary leaders. In
many cases material temptations were sufficient to induce the Army's
grandees and leading members of the Rump Parliament to accept, in effect,
an oligarchy backed by a military dictatorship after a war that had been
fought to extend freedom.

On 26th October 1649 the jury in the case of the Leveller leaders found
them not guilty of any of the treasons they stood accused of. The failure of
the new regime to obtain a 'guilty' verdict against Lilburne involved the
release of himself and his colleagues to jubilant popular acclaim. The only
condition was that they take the Oath of Engagement to be faithful to the
Commonwealth. This they had no difficulty in doing; they only required
the grandees to do the same in practice and to implement the reform
programme. Paradoxically the triumph of the Leveller leaders in October
1649 dates the decline of their party's fortunes. By the end of 1649 it had
become obvious to everyone that only the New Model Army stood between
the English people and another invasion by the Scots intent on imposing
on England their Covenant, kirk system of church discipline, and young
king. So alarming was the prospect of invasion that early in 1650 Parliament
decided to recall Cromwell from his campaign in Ireland, although he did
not return until May.

View of the Thames

NOTES

1.   Blair Worden, *The Rump Parliament 1648 - 1653*, Cambridge University Press, 1974. pp. 37, 38, & 55.
2.   C.H. Firth, *The House of Lords during the Civil War*, Longmans, 1910.
3.   Edmund Ludlow, *Memoirs of Edmund Ludlow*, Vol. I. p. 223.
4.   Bulstrode Whitelocke, *Memorials of the English Affairs*, pp. 532-3. (In the Year 1648/9)
5.   Ibid. p. 537.
6.   Calendar of State Papers (Domestic) 1649-50. p. 9.
7.   Cited in Blair Worden, op. cit. p. 181.
8.   Cited in Jonathan Scott, *Algernon Sidney and the English Republic, 1623 - 1677*. Cambridge University Press. 1988. p. 93.
9.   Calendar of State Papers (Domestic), 1649-50. Feb. 1. 1649.
10.   Calendar of State Papers (Domestic), 1649-50. Feb. 23. 1649.
11.   David Underdown, *Pride's Purge*. op. cit. p. 206.
12.   Calendar of State Papers (Domestic), 1649-50. Feb. 1. 1649.
13.   *Mercurius Pragmaticus*, 27 February 1649.
14.   *England's New Chains Discovered*, February 1649.
15.   H.N. Brailsford, *The Levellers and the English Revolution* edited by Christopher Hill. Spokesman University Paperback. No. 14 Spokesman Books 1976. p. 468.
16.   D.M. Wolfe (ed.), *Leveller manifestoes of the Puritan Revolution*. (Nelson, 1944). p. 372.
17.   *The Moderate* (Leveller newsletter) (6-13 March, 1649).
18.   Wolfe, op. cit. pp. 370-1.
19.   Blair Worden, op. cit. p. 187. citing Carte, *Original Letters*, i. 225, 229.
20.   Ibid. p. 199.
21.   Richard Overton, *The Picture of the Council of State*, H & D., p. 225.
22.   *The Soldier's Demand*, 18th May, 1649, Thomason Tracts.
23.   *The Levellers, falsely so-called, Vindicated*, 14th August, 1649, Thomason Tracts.
24.   For much of the content of this chapter which relates to the Levellers during the spring and summer of 1649 I am indebted to H. N. Brailsford's *The Levellers and the English Revolution*.
25.   Francis White, *A true relation of the proceedings in the business of Burford, 1649*.
26.   H.N. Brailsford, op. cit. pp. 520-1.
27.   Ibid. p. 77.

28.   Ian Gentles, *The New Model Army*, Blackwell, Oxford. p. 320.
29.   Blair Worden, op. cit. p. 198.
30.   Lucy Hutchinson, *The Memoirs of Colonel Hutchinson*, Everyman Books. pp. 268-9.

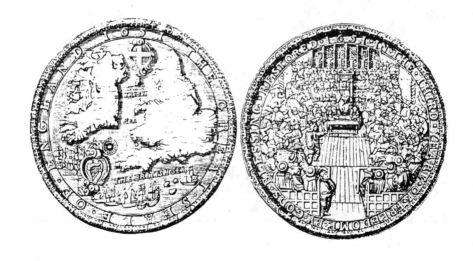

Great Seal of the Commonwealth

357

Sir Arthur Heselrige

358

Henry Marten

Algernon Sidney

CHAPTER ELEVEN

THE COUNCILLOR OF STATE (1649 - 1653)
"IN HIS MERIDIAN GLORY"

"For the Lord loveth judgement,
And forsaketh not his saints;
They are preserved for ever:
But the seed of the wicked shall be cut off.
The righteous shall inherit the land,
And dwell therein for ever."
(Psalm 37. vs. 28 - 29)

Lord Grey of Groby displayed few scruples when it came to accumulating wealth in the form of either monies or property through taking advantage of his public roles. He was a member of the Council of State in 1649, 1650, and 1651 (the first, second, and third Councils), returning in 1653 after a year out (fifth Council). During this period his personal estate and fortune grew markedly. Sometimes this was a result of the generosity of a grateful Parliament rewarding his zealous service as a military commander, MP, or Councillor of State; sometimes through land speculation; and sometimes he took advantage of discomfited royalist families.

He had already received rewards following the first and second civil wars for services to the parliamentarian cause in the form of cash or the property of 'malignants' or 'delinquents' in Leicestershire and the neighbouring counties. Accounts of his awards and acquisitions, together with some unsuccessful attempts on his part, exist in the records of the Calendar of State Papers (Domestic), the Calendar of the Committee for the Advance of Money, the Calendar of the Committee for Compounding, and other official papers. Amongst examples are the following.

In April 1645 he was granted Olney Park in Northamptonshire, the property of a Mrs Willoughby. On 3rd October 1645 he received the sum of £422 forfeited by John Bale for his delinquency by the Committee for Examinations through the authority of Parliament; *"Lord Grey to employ the money for paying his officers"*. On 29th November 1645 a James Martyn, executor to a Lewis Paddy, was summoned before the Committee for Examinations *"at the prosecution of Lord Gray* [sic] *to pay certain legacies pretended to be given by the said testator to some delinquents and St.John's College in Oxford, and that upon the full hearing of the cause two several days he was thence dismissed and freed from the payment thereof upon just reasons, which satisfied that Committee"*.[1]

In March 1647 at the request of Lord Grey a George Staremore of Frolesworth and a George Faunt, both of Leicestershire, were summoned to pay money owing to a Colonel or Sir Francis Wortley, a royalist, and his wife, Frances, the widow of a Faunt. Lord Grey returned to this case in May 1649 in respect of the Wortleys giving *"information that they are delinquents, and that Mr Staresmore, of Leicestershire, owes them 2,000l"*.[2] They needed the money in order to pay him.

On 26th December 1646 he had been awarded the use of Coombe Abbey, near Coventry in Warwickshire, the property of Lord Craven, including the deer in the park. The hostile contemporary presbyterian writer, Clement Walker, includes in his 'The History of Independency', written in 1648 before the purge of Parliament, the following entries amongst others : -

"..... 49. Cromwel [sic]. Lieut. Gen. hath 2,500 l. per an. given him out of the Marquess of Worcesters [Winchester's] Estate, for which 4,000 l. per an. is set out at the rate of 2,500 l. ....

"..... 51. Thomas Waite, Col. Governour [sic] of Burley, where he thrives so well, as he is now buying 500 l.per an. who before was not able to buy 5 l. a year. ....

"..... 80. Henry Martyn, Col. of a Regiment of Horse, and a Regiment of Whores ....
[Marten was regarded as a libertine by the more narrow-minded Puritans because of his private life]

"..... 89. The Lord Gray [sic] of Grooby, (son to the Earl of Stamford) Col. and hath given to him the Queens Manor house, Park, and Lands at Holdenby, and their's a great fall of the Woods. .....

"Besides these Offices, Commands, and Gratuities, every Member of the House of Commons, being in all 516, are by their own Order allowed 4 l. per Week a man; which amounts to 110,000 l. per annum.

"By the Ordinance for sequestering Delinquents (1 April, 1643) it was declared, That their Estates should go for maintenance of the Publick Affairs, and several Ordinances designed Bishops Lands for pay of 200,000 l. Publick debt: Yet by this, and the following Centuries, thou shalt see how both Delinquents Estates and Bishops Lands are by Members of Parliament shared

amongst themselves, whilst the 200,000 l. is unpaid, the publick affairs supported by unsupportable Taxes and that Dutch Devil Excise, that insensibly devours the poor, and will impoverish the rich".[3]

The Queen's Manor House, Park and lands at Holdenby (pronounced Holmby) in Northamptonshire, where the king had been held for Parliament until taken by Cornet Joyce on behalf of the Army, must have been an attractive acquisition for Lord Grey. It would be pleasing to have possession of such a desirable residence as the royal hunting lodge so near to Leicestershire. The further rapid accumulation of wealth by Lord Grey of Groby whilst a member of the Council of State is partially recorded in the House of Commons Journal between 1649 and 1653.

As he had advanced considerable sums for the use of the Cause from his personal resources, and much was owing to him in his military capacity, the disbursements and arrears that he had presented to the House of Commons were taken into consideration in the summer of 1649. On 25th June they were referred to the Committee of the Army to consider how they might be met. On 3rd July a Mr Purefoy reported from the committee the extent of the expenses of *"the lord Grey, disbursed for the state in the late summer service; and the reasons of such expenses"*. These were that, in early 1648 Lord Grey had : -

> *"repaired into the county of Leicester, where he used his endeavour to engage that county to the interest of the Parliament, making it his whole business to go into all parts thereof; to persuade the people to an unanimous resolution of forming themselves into several regiments, for their own, and the defence of their neighbour counties and the whole nation; that this service did occasion a daily charge, public meetings being frequent, wherein he constantly kept a public table, to his very great expense; that he did constantly keep ten horses extraordinary, to promote the services aforesaid; that he kept constant correspondence with the armies and forces, as they stood then divided in the several parts of the Commonwealth; and that he continued upon the said public charge from the 1st of April to the 30th of November 1648".*[4]

After consideration of this information the Committee reported to the House of Commons that they were of the opinion that £1,500 be awarded for his lordship's expenses for the said service for that eight month period. This £1,500 was to be secured out of the king's lands and parks which had been assigned for sale as security for the arrears of the army. Lord Grey of Groby was to be *"admitted a purchaser accordingly"*.

On 2nd November 1649 £750 was paid to Lord Grey *"in part of 1,500 l. assigned him by Parliament"*. On 2nd February 1650 Treasurer Dawson, on behalf of the Committee for the Advance of Money, received an order to pay *"Thomas, Lord Grey of Groby, the money received by him from the Earl of Bedford, Lord Mohun, Sir Francis Vane, and Ralph Snead till 750 l., balance due of 1,500 l. assigned him by Parliament, any order of the committee notwithstanding, Sir Arthur Hesilrigge having consented thereunto"*. Finally, on 31st July 1650 Lord Grey received the balance of the 1,500 l. following an order for £350 dated 21st July 1650. On the basis of these figures Lord Grey managed to receive, over a nine month period, a total up to £1,850 in respect of his award of £1,500.

Earlier, on 21st March 1648, the Committee for Compounding received an order from Parliament that Thomas, Lord Grey of Groby *"receive 5,120 l. from the Earl of Chesterfield's estate, in lieu of all demands as Major-General"*. This was followed on 4th April 1648 by another order from Parliament that *"the Earl's tenants pay him* [Lord Grey] *their rents accordingly till the sum is paid"*. Again, on 31st August, 1649, the Committee for Compounding, of which he was now a member, noted that *"The revenue of the Earl of Chesterfield is received by order of Parliament by Lord Grey"*. This included *"rents and profits to Lord Grey as Major-General, up to the value of 5,120 l."*

On 20th March 1650 he was awarded the custody of Hyde Park in London, including a fine house within its own grounds, during the pleasure of Parliament, the Attorney-General being authorised to prepare a patent for that purpose. Nearer to home he was granted on 28th March the tenancy of Lord Hatton's estate at Moulton Park in Northamptonshire.

On 31st July 1650 an account was presented to Parliament which showed that Lord Grey had received, from the rents of the Earl of Chesterfield's estates in south Nottinghamshire and Derbyshire, a payment of £2,929. 16s. 2d. as the first instalment of the initial sum of £5,120 due to him from the *'publick'*. An order was made for the payment of the remainder.

In April 1650 he had attempted to appropriate money and land belonging to the Duchess of Rutland. He had already gained much land in Rutland, some of it from Lord Campden's estate. The Duchess was Lady Grace Manners. On 29th April the County Committee for Leicester wrote to Thomas, Lord Grey of Groby, on the matter, in terms that must have greatly pleased him : -

"In reference to the enquiries of the Committee for Compounding about Lady Grace, some of the witnesses

examined could prove her delinquency if they were not so biassed [sic], *and the bearer can testify against her. If there be evidence to sequester her, the state will reap much benefit thereby, and she may well spare it, being a miserable, covetous, greedy woman, and of a very great estate, and doth little good with it".*

On 2nd May the Committee for Compounding noted *"Depositers to prove that she ordered her bailiff to pay 200 l. or 500 l. for the Ashby-de-la-Zouch garrison, and many larger sums to Lord Loughborough, and that she is thought sequesterable".* It is further noted on that date that, *"On Lord Grey's presenting these examinations to the Committee for Compounding, Lady Grace was discovered at Haberdasher's Hall* [where the committee sat] *by Colonel* [Peter] *Temple - order she be heard at Haberdasher's Hall tomorrow".* On 14th May it was ordered *"that both the charges against her be put into one, and her estates in counties Rutland, Notts., Derbys; and Middlesex be seized and secured for the State".* On 18th May it was noted that *"the estate in Co. Derbys., and some trunks of writings in Westminster have been seized accordingly".* On 16th September it was noted that her estate in County Rutland had also been seized.

Finally, and surprisingly, on 6th November 1650 it was noted in the record of the Committee for Compounding : -

"Order on hearing her case that she is cleared of delinquency".[5]

One can imagine the frustration of Lord Grey at the outcome of this episode and only speculate about the possible factors which may have brought it about. Lady Grace was clearly still not without influence after all.

On 7th August 1651 a committee of the House of Commons was named to consider the charges expended by Lord Grey *"in his great service done against the Scots when they last came, and services for the publick; and how he might have satisfaction, and some mark of favour and respect from the Parliament".* It was voted on 8th December, *"that Thomas, lord Grey of Groby have settled upon him, and his heirs for ever, lands, tenements, and hereditaments, of the yearly value of £1,000 in full satisfaction of all charges and demands, and as a mark of favour and respect from the Parliament to the said lord Grey, for his great services done to this Commonwealth; and that an act be brought in on that behalf; all which the said Committee humbly leaves to the grave consideration of the Parliament".*[6] This annual pension was approved by Parliament.

On 13th January 1653 the Committee for Compounding recorded that the estate of William, Lord Craven, at Coombe Abbey in the county of Warwickshire had been bought by Thomas, Lord Grey of Groby, who had enjoyed the use of the property since December 1646. This estate was said to be worth at least £3,000 per annum, but Lord Grey as a member of the Committee was able to purchase it at a bargain price. On 5th April the Committee clarified the point that the purchase had included *"the deer in the park, unless specifically exempted from the contract"*. Three days later the Drury House Committee certified payment, and *"begged allowance of the rents thereof to Lord Grey"*.[7]

Lord Grey's father, the Earl of Stamford, had petitioned the House of Commons on 7th May 1651 that the arrears of £1,500 a year, formerly ordered to be paid to him out of the sequestrated estates of Sir Charles Smith of Wooton in Warwickshire, Peter Gifford of Chillington in Staffordshire, and Richard Eyre of Hassop in Derbyshire should be paid. It was agreed that this should be done - but only until the next Lady Day, and then no longer.[8] Lord Grey also received income from the estates in both Warwickshire and Leicestershire of the unfortunate Sir Charles Smith. In 1652 he purchased the forfeited property of a Mr. George Smith, a papist 'recusant' of Queniborough and of a Ralph Allerton of Newbold, both in Leicestershire, at greatly reduced prices.

By these various means Lord Grey had amassed a considerable amount of wealth. With part of this he had bought, as has been noted - at a considerable discount - Coombe Abbey near Coventry where he had already established his main family residence. This was to be the home where he and Lady Dorothy would live with their children whilst not in London or at Bradgate.

The hostile commentator, Mark Noble, drawing on the writings of two of Thomas Grey's virulently antagonistic presbyterian contemporaries, Denzil Holles and Clement Walker, describes this period of Lord Grey of Groby's life in the following terms : -

> *"Lord Grey was now in his meridian glory; he had destroyed the sovereign, and with him monarchy : he rose to be one of the heads of the state; having gratified his ambition, and the lust of rule, he sought also to glut himself with wealth, and this he had by no means been delicate in doing before; for Denzil Lord Hollis says, `he obtained a considerable sum, to be paid out of such discoveries of the royalists' estates, denominated then delinquents, as he should make; whereupon, says his lordship, he and his terriers were long attending the committee of examinations, in the prosecution still of some game or other,*

till his sum was made up". This sum he had got by the army ; and, as one of the chief governors of the nation, he gained far greater sums, and more valuable acquisitions. With part of this money he purchased, at a very easy rate, the largest part of the loyal Lord Craven's estate, particularly Coombe Abbey, worth at least three thousand pounds a year; and he received a grant from his brethren of the queen's manor-house, park, and lands at Holdenby, where he made a great devastation in the woods".[9]

Even allowing for the hostile bias of Noble's observations there seems something particularly apt about the imagine of Lord Grey of Groby *"in his meridian glory"* given his heraldic family crest, as displayed on his cavalry standard, of an ermine unicorn ('armed and unguled or') set upon a `sun in splendour'.

Royalist and Presbyterian critics such as Clarendon, Holles, and Walker made many allegations of fraud and corruption against the members of the new regime. The observation by De Croullé, the agent of Cardinal Mazarin - chief minister of France - , in relation to the members of the Commonwealth's Council of State is capable of more than one interpretation. *"They are economical in their private affairs and prodigal in their devotion to public affairs, for which each man toils as if for his private interest".*

Of course, public affairs and private interest could often coincide. Establishing the real extent of abuses by these 'heads of the state' is not a simple business. As Worden points out, for example : -

"To discuss the charge of corruption in terms of motive may ultimately be fruitless. Corruption could, however, carry the more specific and sinister charge of embezzlement or bribery. It seems likely (although the evidence is not conclusive) that John Dove, John Wylde, Sir William Constable, Lord Grey of Groby, and Thomas Birch, as well as some government officials, trafficked during the Commonwealth in the thriving trade of forged debentures for fee-farm rents".[10] (These were rents from the former crown and church owned lands.)

That the business of the disposition and acquisition of these fee-farm rents was important and affected Lord Grey's home territory can be seen in an entry in the House of Commons Journal on 23rd April 1650. A "humble Petition of the Mayor, Aldermen, and Chamberlain of the Borough of Leicester, Masters of the Hospital of the Holy Trinity in the Newark,

367

near Leicester" was read. It was referred to the Committee for removing obstructions in the sale of fee-farm rents. The Committee was asked to consider the petition and *"how it is fit the petitioners should be paid, and all others of the like nature, whereby the sale of the fee-farm rents is hindered; and to present an Act to the House for the one and the other if they see cause, for the better expediting the sale of the said fee-farm rents"*.[11]

Amongst his other acquisitions Lord Grey seems to have obtained some horses from 'The Tutbury Race', a highly valued establishment of racing stables and stud for race horses in Staffordshire, located near the former royalist stronghold of Tutbury Castle. In July 1649 it had been reported that there were 102 horses present at the Tutbury Race *"being part of the late king's personal estate"* at an estimated total value of £1,982. On December 9th, 1650 the Council of State instructed *"Major Downes at Tutbury to put off the horses and mares at the Race at the best rates he can, and Lord Grey to be furnished with as many as he desires, paying as much as others, provided it be no prejudice to their sale; a letter to be written him to that purpose"*.[12] This love of horseflesh, and the income which accrued from it, he seems to have shared with his father. Back in 1640 the Earl of Stamford had been in trouble with the king for appropriating horses intended for use in the war against the Scots and adding them for far too long to his own collection at Bradgate.

On 20th June 1649 Parliament formally appointed Oliver Cromwell Lord-Lieutenant of Ireland as well as the Commander-in-Chief of the projected army expedition. Lucy Hutchinson's observations about the nature and implications of his growing power, made with regretful hindsight, are apposite : -

> *"..... But now had the poison of ambition so ulcerated Cromwell's heart, that effects of it became more apparent than before; and while as yet Fairfax stood an empty name, he was moulding the army to his mind, weeding out the godly and upright-hearted men, both officers and soldiers, and filling up their rooms with rascally turn-coat cavaliers, and pitiful sottish beasts of his own alliance, and others such as would swallow all things, and make no questions for conscience' sake. Yet this he did not directly nor in tumult, but by such degrees that it was unperceived by all that were not of very penetrating eyes; and those that made the loudest outcries against him lifted up their voices with such apparent envy and malice that, in that mist, they rather hid than discovered his ambitious minings"*.[13]

Cromwell delayed his departure for Ireland for quite a while, lingering in London until the middle of July and then moving slowly via Bristol to Milford Haven. He was awaiting further reinforcements and provisions for the expedition. He was also, as was his way, waiting upon events and seeking signs of God's Providence. Cromwell finally arrived in Ireland on 15th August and was joined by Ireton with heavy reinforcements two days later. The ensuing campaign was to leave a stain on his military career for centuries to come, particularly in respect of the stormings of Drogheda and Wexford.

In his absence the autumn of 1649 saw the emergence of an effectively organised radical party within the Rump Parliament which was characterised by its republicanism. The members of this group were Henry Marten, Edmund Ludlow, Lord Grey of Groby, Cornelius Holland, Henry Smyth, Neville Chaloner, Thomas Chaloner, James Chaloner, Augustine Garland and Luke Robinson. Algernon Sidney was also on the fringe of the group for a while. In August they inspired a measure to remove the royal coat of arms from public places and its replacement by the arms of the Commonwealth. This was implemented throughout the country over the next twelve months.

In October the Oath of Engagement which had previously applied to members of the Council of State, declaring and promising *"that I will be true and faithful to the Commonwealth of England as the same is now established without a King or House of Lords"*, was extended to all sitting or future members of Parliament. This was expected to keep former royalists from having a hand in determining the nation's affairs. Later it was to be extended to all public officials and ministers of religion. Even later it was to be extended to all active citizens.

It must have been a cause of embarrassment, not to mention sadness, for Lord Grey of Groby that his father, the Earl of Stamford, had made his opposition to the events leading to the establishment of the Commonwealth so clear. Not only was the political gulf between them wide but it may well have affected their personal relationship, at least for a time. Consequently, it must have been with some relief and probably as a result of considerable urging, on the part of his son, that the Earl became the first peer to take the Oath of Engagement early in 1650. This information was relayed by Lord Lisle to his father, Philip Sidney, the Earl of Leicester in a letter dated 21st February, 1650 from London : -

".....A letter came lately from Leicester acquainting the Councell [of State], amongst other things, that the Earl of Stamford had signed the Engagement before that committee; he is as yet the only Peere which I heare of in that businesse. I

369

heare that on Tuesday a vote passed in the Parliament that the
subscribing of the engagement should not be pressed upon the
Generall [Fairfax] *in regard that he had signed one very like it*
at the first sitting of the Councell".[14]

On 5th March 1650 Lord Grey of Groby was appointed Colonel of Horse
in the militia for the county of Leicester. This commission, issued in the
absence of Cromwell in Ireland, allowed Grey to both strengthen his position
in the Midlands and to renew his links with the Army. In a contrast of
fortune his former wartime ally Sir John Gell of Derbyshire, who had been
one of the Midlands parliamentarian commanders but now regarded as a
leading presbyterian turned neo-royalist, was tried at the bar of the High
Court of Justice. He was condemned to lose his estate and suffer perpetual
imprisonment.[15]

After a successful but bloodstained campaign in Ireland Cromwell set
sail in return to England on 26th May. Henry Ireton was left behind in
command of the English forces in Ireland. Unfortunately he was to die
there of plague in November 1651. This sad event was perhaps of crucial
significance for the future development of the Commonwealth in general
and for the relationship between Cromwell and Grey of Groby in particular.
Ireton was Cromwell's friend, companion of his early struggles, his son-
in-law, and a considerable influence on him. Some contemporaries believed
Ireton to be Cromwell's *'eminence grise'*. He and Thomas Grey knew
each other well. Ireton, from south Nottinghamshire, was a neighbour of
the Greys of Leicestershire. The two men had grown closer politically as
members of the 'junta' which had planned the purge of Parliament in
December 1649. Events might have turned out very differently if he had
survived to contribute his serious, thoughtful and well considered approach
to the councils and counsels of the Commonwealth.

Cromwell was back in London for only four weeks. It was time enough
for Andrew Marvell to begin his 'An Horatian Ode upon Cromwell's Return
from Ireland', but it was not completed until July when the Republic's
military hero would be on campaign again - this time in Scotland : -

> *"..... And now the Irish are ashamed*
> *To see themselves in one year tamed:*
> *So much one man can do,*
> *That does both act and know.*
> *They can affirm his praises best,*
> *And have, though overcome, confessed*
> *How good he is, how just,*
> *And fit for highest trust:*
> *Nor yet grown stiffer with command,*

370

But still in the Republic's hand:
How fit he is to sway
That can so well obey.
He to the Commons' feet presents
A kingdom, for his first year's rents: .....'[16]

The subjugation of Ireland by Cromwell had put an end to the hopes of Charles II from that quarter. A royalist rising under the gallant Montrose for *'King and no Presbytery'* had failed in Scotland. Montrose had been captured by the Covenanters in May and executed. Charles had reluctantly now aligned himself with them. On 10th June 1650 he sailed for Scotland from the continent and swore an oath to uphold the Covenant whilst he was still on board ship just before he landed. It was in no sense a sincere conversion. Indeed, he was later to observe that the Presbyterian religion might be a very good religion; but it was not the religion of a gentleman. For the time being, however, it was to be *'Presbytery and King'* in Scotland. The one threatened the religious settlement and the other the political settlement of the English Commonwealth. It was only a question of time before their Scottish supporters did so by force.

In June 1650 it was decided that an English military expedition should be sent into Scotland in order to pre-empt any invasion of England by Charles Stuart backed by a Scottish army. Thomas Fairfax, still the theoretical commander-in-chief of the Army of the Commonwealth, declined to take command of such an expedition on the grounds that he saw its offensive nature as an obstacle to justice. Accordingly, Lord Fairfax, who had been a member of the first two Councils of State, resigned his post as commander-in-chief and ceased at the same time to sit in the Council. He pleaded in his letter of resignation *"debilities both in body and mind, occasioned by former actions and businesses"*, but his real motive was his disapproval of the proposed invasion of Scotland. There were already strong suspicions, stemming from the time of Charles I's trial and execution, that he had begun to favour a rapproachment with the presbyterians, and perhaps with the royalists too. He was replaced as Lord General by Oliver Cromwell who was thus to take command of the Army which would invade Scotland.

This was a crucial development because now all military commissions would be issued by Cromwell. As far as the true republicans or commonwealthmen, such as Lord Grey of Groby, Edmund Ludlow, Henry Marten, and John Hutchinson, were concerned : -

"From thence the tide of fortune left their shore,
And ebbed much faster than it flowed before".[17]

371

In Cromwell's absence Major-General Thomas Harrison was to have chief military command in England. Harrison was a military zealot who had millenarian tendencies. The English army under Cromwell's command left London on 28th June and crossed the border into Scotland on 22nd July 1650.

Marvell's Horatian Ode could now confidently conclude.

"The Pict no shelter now shall find
Within his parti-coloured mind,
But from this valour sad
Shrink underneath the plaid:
Happy, if in the tufted brake
The English hunter him mistake,
Nor lay his hounds in near
The Caledonian deer.
But thou, the Wars' and Fortune's son,
March indefatigably on,
And for the last effect
Still keep thy sword erect:
Besides the force it has to fright
The spirits of the shady night,
The same arts that did gain
A power, must it maintain". [18]

Lord Grey of Groby was one of the commanders in the English army in Scotland. The month of August was spent in a series of advances and withdrawals whilst the Scots avoided pitched battles and fell back on strongpoints, harrying the invaders on their flanks. Growing numbers of the English soldiers fell ill. As a consequence of these factors Cromwell kept his forces in the region around Edinburgh and maintained supply links with English navy ships off the Lothian coast. Evidence for Lord Grey's presence comes in a report from Major-General Robert Montgomery, in General Leslie's Scottish forces, to his father Alexander, sixth Earl of Eglinton, dated 22nd August 1650 from Corstorphine. This report informs him that *"the leaders of the Scots army had resolved to draw their forces a mile or two westwards (from Corstorphine) and offer battle to the enemy (under Cromwell) by 'shotting three piece* [sic] *of cannon towards them'. That it was reported that 3,000 men under Lord Grey of Groby were marching to recruit* [i.e. reinforce] *the enemy".* [19]

The end of August saw the English invasion force hemmed in against the sea at Dunbar. Here Cromwell seized victory from the jaws of defeat. On 3rd September 1650 he won against the Scots, under Leslie, the greatest military victory of his career. At the urging of the presbyterian ministers the Scots army, which heavily outnumbered the English, came down off the heights from where they had dominated the topography. Seeing this movement Cromwell had declared, *"God is delivering them into our hands"*. So it had proved. In his report to Parliament after the great victory he described it as *"one of the most signal mercies God hath done for England, His people, this war"*. The occupation and pacification of most of Scotland followed. On 7th September Cromwell entered Edinburgh and in October Glasgow was occupied.

By the end of 1650 the royalist inspiration of Cromwell's Scottish opponents was becoming more marked. On 1st January 1651 Charles Stuart, eldest son of the executed monarch, was officially crowned King of Scotland at Scone. This united a broad range of Scottish support behind him. The English army's campaign in Scotland continued through the months of 1651. By 1st August Cromwell had advanced as far north as Perth and bombarded the fortress of St. Johnston. This move, however, left the way open for the bulk of the Scottish forces under Charles II to invade his *'southern kingdom'*. This they duly did. They had reached Carlisle by 5th August. On the following day *"the dark young man about two yards tall"* was proclaimed King of England. The terms of the proclamation offered a free pardon to all those who would join him, whatever their past actions, with the three exceptions of John Bradshaw, the President of the High Court of Justice, John Cook, the prosecuting counsel, and the *'arch-criminal'* Oliver Cromwell. It seems clear that the *'arch-criminal'* had deliberately tempted Charles to invade England so that the enemy could finally be brought to a conclusive battle.

In the meantime the South and the Midlands of England had not been idle in preparing to meet what the Commonwealth regarded as a Scottish invasion as much as a royal return.

For example, as early as March 10th, 1651 the Council of State requested Lord Grey *"to move Parliament to give an order for making the city of Worcester untenable, for preventing the danger that may come to the Commonwealth thereby"*.[20]

As soon as news of the Scottish invasion reached London the Council of State called in all available members for deliberation and to mobilise the local militias. A letter was issued from Whitehall to Lord Grey of Groby on 10th August : -

> *"Having intelligence that the Scots have entered England, we desire you to repair to the Council* [of State] *forthwith, that they may have your assistance"*.

373

The following day Lord Grey was authorised by the Council *"to repair to Leicester, to do what shall occur to him to be for the prevention of the Scotch army in their march, and for the safety of the commonwealth".*

The Council also instructed its Committee for the Advance of Money *"..... to consider what is fit to be done in order to sending Lord Grey into Leicestershire and Northamptonshire, for the safety of those parts".*[21]

On 12th August 1651 Lord Grey of Groby was appointed as commander-in-chief for the counties of Leicestershire, Rutland, and Northamptonshire. He raised six troops of volunteer horse from these counties. The standard of the ermine unicorn was flying again in the midlands. Lord Grey's own troop also carried a larger colour, depicting the House of Commons in session, which resembled the Seal of the Commonwealth's reverse face. The following day the Council of State issued instructions to the militia commissioners of Leicestershire, Rutland, and Northamptonshire to *"draw the forces of their counties to the several rendezvous, to receive orders from Lord Grey, and to send a month's pay with them ..... Lord Grey to have power to enlist volunteer horse, and to assure them pay so long as they continue in service".*[22]

Lord Grey mustered the forces of the three counties at Daventry and then headed further west, linking up with John Desborough who was Cromwell's brother-in-law. The Council of State sent a letter to Lord Grey from Whitehall on 25th August : -

> *"We understand by yours from Spratton that you have marched up to the rendezvous with Lieut-General Fleetwood, with the troops of cos. Northampton, Leicester and Rutland, and that they are 1,100 horse, which will be a considerable addition to the army. We are very sensible of your great pains, and look upon it as a very acceptable service. As for the pistols desired for some of your men, we have referred it to a committee of this Council to consider what may be done .... We doubt not but you will make bold with any arms or military provisions you find in the hands of any suspicious or disaffected persons, to furnish your recruits".*[23]

Fleetwood's rendezvous was at Banbury; but Lord Grey and Desborough moved on with their combined force of two thousand men to join Cromwell and his northern army who had marched rapidly down from Scotland to another rendezvous at Warwick. From there the main Commonwealth force moved on to Stratford-upon-Avon by 27th August.

Meanwhile, the invading army had reached as far south as Worcester by 22nd August. Here the townspeople, extremely royalist in their sympathies, had driven out the local parliamentarian garrison and welcomed the new king and his sixteen thousand men. While Charles appealed desperately to English and Welsh royalists to join him, with very little success, three English armies under Cromwell, Harrison, and Fleetwood were converging on Worcester. By the night of 27th August they had combined at Evesham, only fifteen miles south-east of Worcester, with a total of twenty-eight thousand men which was still growing with the arrival of more militia forces. By the day of the battle, which was 3rd September and exactly twelve months to the day since the victory of Dunbar, the English army totalled over thirty one thousand men.

The Commonwealth forces were divided into two parts; twelve thousand men under Fleetwood crossed to the west of the Severn whilst the remainder under Cromwell and Lambert stayed on the east side of the river. Lord Grey of Groby and his men served under Fleetwood on the day.

Edmund Ludlow, although personally serving in Ireland at the time, gives the following account of the battle of Worcester in his memoirs : -

> *"Their* [the Cavaliers and Scots] *first attack was made upon lieutenant-general Fleetwood's quarters that were on the other side of the river, who with some forces of the army, and a reinforcement of the militia* [including Lord Grey of Groby's forces], *made a vigorous resistance. The general* [Cromwell], *fearing he might be over-powered, dispatched some troops to his assistance by a bridge laid over the river, commanding major-general Lambert to send another detachment to the same purpose; but he desired to be excused, alleging, that if the enemy should alter their course, and fall upon those on this side, they might probably cut off all that remained : which was not unlikely, for soon after, most of the enemy's strength fell upon that part of the army where the general and the major-general Lambert were. The battle was fought with various success for a considerable time; but at length the Scots army was broken, and, quitting their ground, retreated in great disorder to the town, where they endeavoured to defend themseves. Major-general Harrison, colonel Croxton, and the forces of Cheshire, entered the place at their heels; and being followed by the rest of the army, soon finished the dispute, and totally defeated the enemy. Three English earls, seven Scots lords, and above six hundred officers, besides ten thousand private soldiers, were made prisoners. The king's standard, and a hundred fifty-eight colours, with all their artillery, ammunition and baggage, was also taken. On our side, quarter-master Mosely, and captain Jones, with above a hndred private soldiers, were killed, and captain Howard, with one captain more, and about three*

375

hundred soldiers, wounded. This victory was obtained by the parliament's forces on the 3rd of September, being the same day of the same month that the Scots had been defeated at Dunbar the preceding year".[24]

This was a decisive defeat for the greatly outnumbered royalists. Many of them were to be killed or captured in the rout that followed the actual battle. The Scots were in a hostile country and very far from home. Charles himself managed to escape and to begin the famous journey which would take him, via the 'royal oak tree' and Boscobel, back to the continent. Every other leader of note was taken captive, either on the field or afterwards. Leslie, Lauderdale and Middleton were taken, as were the Earl of Derby, shortly to be executed, and Lanark who had succeeded his executed brother as Duke of Hamilton and who had sustained a mortal wound. Major-General Edward Massey who had tried, without success, to raise his former comrades at Gloucester, for the royal cause this time, managed to get as far away as the east midlands. Cromwell described the victory at Worcester as *'a crowning mercy'.* It was to be the last battle that either he or Lord Grey of Groby were to fight in personally.

A grateful Parliament bestowed upon the victor of Worcester an additional £4,000 a year, raised from the income from the estates of the Dowager Countess of Rutland and those of Burghley and Newhall. They also gave him the use of a royal palace, Hampton Court, for his country home.

Later, in May 1652, John Milton was to praise him and his list of victories in a sonnet too : -

> *"Cromwell, our chief of men, who through a cloud*
> *Not of war only, but detractions rude,*
> *Guided by faith and matchless fortitude,*
> *To peace and truth thy glorious way hast ploughed,*
> *And on the neck of crowned fortune proud*
> *Hast rear'd God trophies, and his work pursued,*
> *While Darwen stream with blood of Scots inbrued,*[Preston]
> *And Dunbar field resounds thy praises loud,*
> *And Worcester's laureat wreath. Yet much remains*
> *To conquer still ..... "*[25]

Much remained indeed.

Four days after Worcester, Edward Massey, who had been wounded before the main battle, surrendered to Lord Grey of Groby at Bradgate. Ludlow records this event and the successful escape of Charles II in the following account : -

376

"Colonel Massey escaped into Leicestershire, but being dangerously wounded, found himself not able to continue his way, and fearing to be knocked on the head by the country, delivered himself to the countess of Stamford, mother to the lord Grey of Groby, who caused his wounds to be carefully dressed, and sent notice of his surrender to the army. Whereupon a party was dispatched with orders to conduct him from thence to London, as soon as he should be fit to travel, which was done, and he committed prisoner to the Tower. The Scots king with the lord Wilmot were concealed by three countrymen, till they could furnish him with a horse; with which he crossed the country to one Mr. Gunter's near Shoreham in Sussex, carrying one Mrs. Lane behind him; from whence in a small bark [barque] *he escaped to France".*[(26)]

The circumstances of Massey's surrender were described by Lord Grey of Groby himself in a letter to the Speaker of the House of Commons : -

"SIR, - My lord general being pleased to dismiss those troops under my command, I came hither last night; and this morning, a servant of my father's, and one that hath been constantly faithful to your interest, did acquaint me that major-general Massey came to his house upon Friday night; and, upon that assurance which the inclosed [sic] *paper doth give an account of, and the grounds therein mentioned, he did receive him, with one major Wood, who had formerly served you under sir William Waller. Upon this first notice given, I sent for a party of horse to take charge of him; and, after evening sermon, went to him, took the inclosed examination : and although much of it may be held to be unimportant, yet, the words being his own, I thought it my duty to present the whole to you : which discovers his temper, and that he is not inclined to make any ingenuous confession as to that which is most considerable, although I examined him as strictly as my weak abilities would give leave : and finding his condition to be such as he represents it, occasioned by his hard riding, and want of a chirurgeon* [surgeon] *to dress his wounds, I did forthwith send for the ablest man we have in these parts to take care of him; that by the means used, if God did see it good, he might be restored to his former health, and thereby made more fit for a public trial, and your justice thereupon. I hope, within two days, to remove him to Leicester, where I intend he shall remain, until I have commands otherwise to dispose of him.*

Sir, The relation of our proceedings at Worcester coming to you from better hands, I shall not trouble you with any; but cannot omit the acknowledgement of God's goodness to us, which indeed was so signal that I never was witness to the like. That the Lord would give us hearts filled with admiration and praise for his great deliverance, for never any nation had the like, and that we may improve it to his glory, for it was he alone that did the work, and that his presence in all your counsels and actings may be continued to you, is the prayer of,

Sir,
Your most humble and obedient servant,
THO. GREY.
Broadgate
Sept. 7, 1651"[(27)]

A letter from Edward Massey to the Countess of Stamford also survives. Massey had been lieutenant-colonel, under the Earl of Stamford, at the beginning of the civil war in 1642 and, as such, would have been well known to the lady : -

"THRICE NOBLE AND THRICE VIRTUOUS LADY, -
These are the humble requests of your poor servant, whom it hath pleased the Lord at present deeply to afflict; and, by his providence, being cast into these parts, and full of anguish and pain, by reason of my wounds and weakness got before the defeat at Worcester, I resolved to cast myself upon the favour of my lord Grey, which, by your ladyship's intercession, and of which I dare presume, knowing your charity to all men, I hope will find his nobleness, that I may have leave, as his prisoner, to stay and repose my sick body, and refresh my wound, either here or where his lordship shall please to command, being unable to ride or travel further at present; but shall be a faithful prisoner, either under or without guard, as his lordship shall please.
Thrice virtuous madam, this is the most humble request of Your ladyship's Most humble and devoted servant,

EDW. MASSEY.
Leics.
Sept. 10, 1651".[(28)]

378

Clarendon, who was able to admire fidelity to one's cause in a friend, but not in an enemy, remarked somewhat unfairly on this incident that *"the lady had only charity to cure his wounds, not courage to conceal his person"*.[29] Massey was imprisoned in the Tower of London, as related earlier in the extract from Ludlow's memoirs, but shortly escaped to the continent once more.

On 9th September the Council of State agreed to pay £10 to the man who had brought the news of the capture of Colonel Massey from Lord Grey. Also, Sir John Taylor was instructed *"to report to the House of Commons the letter from Lord Grey relating the taking of Colonel Massey, as also the examination of him"*.[30]

Sometime later, on 22nd September, a letter was sent from the Council of State to Lord Grey of Groby at Outhorp, near Stamford, giving instructions regarding Edward Massey : -

> *"We received your letter and Massey's examination, and as you have now left the county, we desire you to appoint a convoy to carry him to Warwick Castle, and we enclose a warrant for his reception there"*.[31]

It is tempting to speculate whether Lord Grey had been visiting Colonel John Hutchinson at his country home of Owthorpe Hall in the south east Nottinghamshire part of the Vale of Belvoir to discuss matters of common political, military or business interest. Hutchinson was 'out' of the Council of State during 1651, returning to membership in 1652. The distance between Owthorpe and Stamford is approximately thirty miles, however, so it seems unlikely that this is the Outhorp referred to.

Lord Grey was once more thanked by Parliament for his services at Worcester and in respect of the taking of Massey on 30th September. On 18th December 1651 a Committee of the House of Commons reported in favour of a grant to him of lands worth £1,000 a year for *"his great services to the Commonwealth"*.[32]

From February 1649 to December 1651 Lord Grey of Groby remained an active member of the Council of State and the Parliament. During the twelve months from February 1649 to February 1650 the forty-one members of the Council of State held 319 sittings. The quorum for their sessions was nine and the average number present was between thirteen and fourteen. They would meet at 7 a.m. or 8 p.m. for business with sessions of the House of Commons in between. During this period the House sat on 232 occasions. The average number of attendances by members of the Council in this year was 106. The recorded number of attendances for this period for Oliver Cromwell was eighty-one, for Lord Grey of Groby seventy-six, and John Hutchinson seventy-five. During 1650/51 the total number of sittings was 295 and the average number present was between eighteen and nineteen. This time Cromwell attended on only twenty occasions, military operations in Ireland and Scotland explaining this. Similarly, Lord Grey attended on ninety-nine occasions, because of his period in Scotland, compared to John Hutchinson's 124 attendances. During the 1651 session there were 249 sittings of the Council with an average attendance of between nineteen and twenty members. Colonel Hutchinson was not a member of the Council during this year and military activities in the Scottish and Worcester campaigns reduced the attendances of Lord Grey to eighty-five and Oliver Cromwell to thirty-five. During 1652 Lord Grey *"went out off"* the Council of State, according to its own regulations, to return at the beginning of 1653.

Lord Grey continued to have some dealings with the Council of State throughout 1652, although he concentrated on his parliamentary duties, his newly acquired estates, and his family life. In January 1652 some sort of audit seems to have been carried out into the expenses he had claimed for Leicestershire in respect of the Worcester campaign, for which he had been well recognised and rewarded : -

> *"Captain Blackwell jun. and Capt. Deane to examine and state the account presented to the Council by Lord Grey, of the charges of Leicestershire in raising and sending two regiments of horse for the service of Worcester; to peruse the lists and muster rolls and ascertain whether the accounts are made up at the rate of pay allowed in the establishment on foot at the time when those troops were in service".*[33]

Was Lord Grey suspected of exaggerating, and thus falsifying the account? Unfortunately the outcome of the enquiry is not recorded.

Also; on 13th January the Council of State called upon Lord Grey, Sir William Constable, and a Mr. Gurdon to deliver back to them the reports which they had been asked to make to the House of Commons concerning the Isle of Man, for further consideration. This was followed, on 28th January, by a request from the Council for *"Mr. Corbett to make the report to the House concerning Lieut. Col. Roseworm, which was entrusted to Lord Grey".*[34]

It seems that Lord Grey was otherwise engaged.

Lord Grey of Groby certainly seems to have been *"in his meridian glory"* during the period from 1649 to 1653. His immediate family had grown at this time and they seem to have lived mainly at Coombe Abbey, near Coventry. The Greys already had two daughters, Elizabeth and Anne.

380

Elizabeth, the elder, was probably aged between five and six at the beginning of 1653 as Dorothy had been reported as being 'heavy with child' in January 1647, some seven months after their marriage. Elizabeth was most likely named after either Thomas's grandmother, Lady Elizabeth Bingley, or Dorothy's sister, Lady Elizabeth Fielding, Countess of Denbigh. The younger daughter, Anne, was probably aged around three years old and named after Thomas's mother, Lady Anne Grey (nee Cecil), Countess of Stamford.

Dorothy, Lady Grey, now gave birth to Lord Grey of Groby's son and heir, also named Thomas, at Coombe Abbey in the spring of 1653. There would be, of course, frequent visits to the grandparents, Earl and Countess Stamford at neighbouring Bradgate, across the county border a couple of hours gentle ride away in Leicestershire.

Parliamentary and Council of State business would take Lord Grey, and sometimes the family, to London. Here, instead of Exeter House at St. John's in Clerkenwell, which had come to the Earl of Stamford through the Cecil inheritance, Lord Grey had the use of Hyde Park House and its grounds. Sometimes the use of the latter had to be shared, as is evidenced by the following passage from the records of the Council of State : -

"July 18, [1652],
To write to Lord Grey and James Challoner to permit the Danish
Ambassadors to take their pleasure in the parks under their
command, and to kill what venison they think fit.

Sir Oliver Fleming to acquaint them that Council have given
order to the keepers of Hyde Park and Hampton Court Park to
permit them to take their pleasure there, and to kill venison".[35]

This was probably the happiest period of Lord Grey of Groby's life. Certainly it was the best time of the Greys' relatively short family life together. In particular the hours spent in the midlands countryside or at Coombe Abbey and Bradgate would seem, in retrospect, as idyllic.

The original Coombe Abbey had been founded by Cistercian monks in 1150. After the dissolution of the monasteries Coombe Abbey and its lands passed into the hands of Henry VIII in 1539. The estate then changed hands several times over the next forty years. New owners converted the monastery building into a country mansion and by 1603 the first formal gardens had been created by its nobleman owner, Lord Harington, for his pleasure. In 1622 Coombe Abbey was purchased by the Craven family and remained in their possession for the next 300 years, except for the period when it was occupied by Lord Grey of Groby's family. In 1632

William, first Lord Craven, had been given permission by King Charles I to enclose 600 acres of surrounding land to form a park. The deer were introduced shortly afterwards. This was the imposing residence now purchased by Lord Grey.

Life at Coombe Abbey would have been similar to that at Bradgate. Such household communities in country estates lived a virtually self-sufficient existence. The estate workers would keep horses, cattle, sheep and deer. They would churn milk, ground meal, bake bread and brew beer. They also bred, fed, killed and ate their own beef, sheep, deer, poultry and pigeons. Timber for fuel and construction was produced from trees on the estate. Horses were shod and rough ironwork was forged and mended in the estate's own smithy. In addition to the blacksmith's, other estate buildings around the secularised Abbey itself where the family lived included the slaughter-house, the carpenter's workshop, the malting and brewhouses, the laundry, the dairy, the stables, stalls and barns, the apple and root vegetables store outhouses, together with a sawpit with logs cut for burning in the great fireplaces, and a wood-yard stacked with timber.

Outside activities would include work in the meadows, pastures, woodlands and deer park. In the late summer there would be the haymaking and the harvesting with the traditional activities and ceremonies that they involved for a community that lived off its own land and depended upon the Lord for good weather and His bounty. Even though, as a young bride, Lady Dorothy had expressed a preference for London life, it was possible to enjoy aspects of country life; as the young newly married queen, Henrietta Maria, had enjoyed the haymaking in Oxfordshire in 1625.

Within doors the female members of the household community would be busy with the spinning of wool and flax (an occupation so common that any unmarried woman of any rank became known as 'a spinster'), embroidering and sewing. Cooking, curing meats, and preserving fruits would have gone on incessantly. Lady Dorothy would have been in overall control of all these activities and her children would have been taught to take an interest in the running of such a large household. There would still have been time for her to participate in both the local social scene and also in the capital as the wife of one of the leaders of the Commonwealth. Lady Dorothy would have seen much of her sister, Elizabeth, Lady Denbigh, who also resided in Warwickshire, at her adjoining estate at Newnham Paddox only some five miles away from Coombe Abbey.

Lord Grey's bailiff and stewards would have taken care of most of the other business of the estate whilst he concerned himself with matters of state, both locally and nationally. Lucy Hutchinson describes how her husband, Colonel John Hutchinson, passed his time whilst not serving as a member of the Council of State. From this we may gain some idea of Lord

Grey's activities during 1652, after making some allowance for their different personalities and networks : -

> *"..... Colonel Hutchinson was in the country, where, since his going in his course out of the council of state, he had for about a year's time applied himself, when the parliament could dispense with his absence, to the administration of justice in the country, and to the putting in execution those wholesome laws and statutes of the land provided for the orderly regulation of the people. And it was wonderful how, in a short space, he reformed several abuses and customary neglects in that part of the country where he lived, which being a rich fruitful vale, drew abundance of vagrant people to come and exercise the idle trade of wandering and begging; but he took such courses that there was very suddenly not a beggar left in the country, and all the poor in every town were so maintained and provided for, that they were never so liberally maintained and relieved before or since. He procured unnecessary alehouses to be put down in all the towns, and if any one that he heard of suffered any disorder or debauchery in his house, he would not suffer him to brew any more. He was a little severe against drunkenness, for which the drunkards would sometimes rail at him; but so much were all the children of darkness convinced by his light, that they were more in awe of his virtue than his authority. In this time he had made himself a convenient house, whereof he was the best ornament, and an example of virtue so prevailing, as metamorphosed many evil people, while they were under his roof, into another appearance of sobriety and holiness".*[36]

In addition to discharging their local and national public responsibilities gentlemen like John Hutchinson and Thomas Grey would have found time for contemplation, elegant studies on matters biblical and philosophical, rational converse, virtuous pursuits, useful occupations, conciliating hospitality, leisure time amusements including appreciation of music and drama, riding abroad and hawking.

Indeed, some of the hunting and hawking parties could attract, as followers, interesting characters from amongst the local population. The Leicester Hall Papers in 1652 record that a certain *"Mr. John Norrice hath gone towards Bradgate in a pare [sic] of shoes made of an old Hatte and a pare of Buskens or Corkers, and leaves them at one Foxes house, an alehouse, and there putte on a pare of bootes or shoes and then goes to Bradgate House."* There he *"did the last summer runne on foote with the gentlemen att Bradgate when they were hawking and one of the gentlemen perseving* [sic] *the sayd Mr. Norrice to be weary did take him, the sayd Mr. Norrice, upp behind"*. This Norrice, who was an Alderman of the Borough, was also privileged to be taken by the Grey family to their relatives' estates at Dunham Massey, near Altrincham in Cheshire, where in spite of contemporary Puritanism it is reported that they were *"very merry"*.

Politically and financially Lord Grey of Groby was at the height of his powers and prestige. He had acquired a considerable amount of property and wealth. It is likely that the oil paintings of him that still exist today were commissioned at this time when he was aged around thirty years old. The oil portraits provide a good idea of the physical appearance of Thomas, Lord Grey of Groby. They can be related to the descriptions given by some of his contemporaries. That he was dark haired and wore his hair shoulder length is clear. He was apparently short in stature, as can be seen by comparing his height with the adolescent page in the full length portrait. This would accord with the rather unkind descriptions of his 'dwarfish appearance' and as 'that dark dwarf' or 'that grinning dwarf'. The portraits also seem to present, perhaps intentionally, an aristocratic, even haughty, or arrogant bearing. If this is a true interpretation it would seem to match well with his father's nature and behaviour, as has been commented upon earlier. An assessment of Lord Grey of Groby's character and personality will be made later.

In the immediate period following the establishment of the Commonwealth the MPs in the Council of State had constituted a working majority in the House of Commons which had an average attendance of fifty-seven members. This did not, however, guarantee that the republican 'revolution' would continue. It would be wrong to suppose that there was no impetus to reform within the Rump Parliament itself, but it soon became blunted. Why was this?

Most of the 'revolutionaries' of December 1648 still retained strong vestiges of their constitutional past. They were held back by some of their leaders, such as Oliver Cromwell, who were not revolutionaries by conviction, and therefore repeatedly hesitated and faltered. Furthermore, all but the most thorough-going of them wished to mask the brutal reality that their new regime rested ultimately on the swords of the Army, wished to broaden the base of their support, and to regain some shreds of constitutional legitimacy. As soon, therefore, as the crucial step had been taken and the king was dead, they made it as easy as possible for all those who were not their openly irreconcilable opponents to return to the fold and take their seats in the Rump Parliament and the other institutions of government in the Commonwealth, including the Council of State and its committees. Lord Grey of Groby, Henry Marten and the other more revolutionary republican and pro-Leveller regicides had tried to prevent this but had been outvoted. The moderates having been admitted, the radicals like Grey of Groby, Henry Marten, and Edmund Ludlow were hedged in by them. David Underdown, who has analysed this period of Pride's Purge and its aftermath in some detail, has argued that there was a social distinction between the radicals and the growing number of moderates amongst the politicians of the Rump and its Council of State : -

> **"If the real revolutionaries are isolated ..... it will be found that there were in fact some significant differences between them and the more conservative majority. For one thing, many of them display a fiercer, more intense, Puritan zeal, though not necessarily of the Independent or sectarian variety. But the revolutionaries also seem to have been drawn in a marked degree from families which were insecure ('declining gentry', in a famous phrase), or from outside the traditional political establishment (nouveaux riches, lesser gentry, families of obscure and usually urban origins)".**[37]

If this is true then Thomas, Lord Grey of Groby, the only aristocratic regicide, was a most marked exception as far as social background is concerned; but he did display a fierce and intense puritanical zeal.

The revolutionaries still had their reform programme. This included a church settlement which would incorporate a disestablishment of the state church and the abolition of tithes; a constitutional settlement which would incorporate parliamentary reform, redistribution of seats, extension of the franchise, law reform - all as in the 'Agreement of the People' endorsed by the Levellers. The moderates, however, were able to sidetrack or talk them out, often in collaboration with the Army Grandees. The conservative reaction was in effect engineered by the men of December 1648 themselves by their tactics in the late winter of that year and the following spring. The Grandees completed the reaction during the spring and summer of 1649 when they crushed the Army revolutionaries, leaving the parliamentary radicals without a power base. There were, it is true, still the activities of the radical republican group in Parliament, as mentioned earlier, and the civilian Levellers. These, however, had limited scope for manoeuvre given other factors.

Cromwell's victory at Dunbar in September 1650 did little to relieve the tension. In a civil war situation there is no room for a third party. In a choice between the royalists and presbyterians on the one hand and the leaders of the Commonwealth on the other, even with all their reservations, the Levellers had no choice but to support the latter. John Lilburne actually accompanied his old comrade Oliver Cromwell for part of the Scottish campaign to demonstrate the 'solidarity' of the commonwealth cause. The Leveller party had reached the height of its influence in the autumn of 1649 when it had gathered almost 100,000 signatures to its revolutionary 'Remonstrance', and again in the celebrations that had followed the acquittal of Lilburne and his comrades. Thereafter it faded away as a mass movement although individuals continued the struggle. After Worcester in September 1651 a relieved and grateful English people would not have taken kindly to a revival of the agitation and opposition to Cromwell on the old lines. In 1652 the war with the Dutch broke out. Again, it was no time to divide the English nation. After 1653 the mass of Levellers were merged in the general republican opposition, whilst others joined millenarian groups such as the Fifth Monarchy Men. Fifth Monarchism became a mass movement only after the failure of the Levellers. Other former Levellers, including John Lilburne himself, eventually joined the Society of Friends (Quakers) and sought a spiritual rather than a political Commonwealth.

The Rump Parliament had declared in March 1649 that it would dissolve itself and make way for a newly elected parliament *"so soon as may possibly stand with the safety of the people"*. This turned out to be an empty promise because safety was so slow in coming, given the dangers in Ireland and Scotland, and the threat of royalist invasion and rebellion. It will be recalled that Ireton and the Army Grandees had formerly favoured a dissolution of Parliament and fresh elections rather than a partial purge in December 1648. The Commonwealth parliamentarians feared that new elections in 1649 might result in the return of a majority hostile to the continuation of the Commonwealth itself. When the Army put pressure on the Rump in May 1649 to make way for *'a new representative'* body, it responded with an alternative proposal. This alternative involved the holding of carefully regulated elections to the many seats that had been vacant since Pride's Purge. This would have allowed the active Rump MPs to continue sitting indefinitely. Such a scheme was quite unacceptable to the Army. Cromwell's opposition persuaded the Rump to shelve this proposal, but it was to crop up again over the next three years or so.

For two and a half years the Army, busy fighting in Ireland and Scotland, and then in England, had to swallow its distaste of the Rump's failure either to enact reforms or to make way for a newly elected successor. Only after the battle of Worcester was Cromwell free to resume his seat in Parliament and his role as the army's chief spokesman. By this time the gap between the soldiers and the parliamentarians had widened considerably. The former believed that the work of the Commonwealth should be about a godly reformation. This was why the Lord God had favoured their cause. Such a godly reformation would include the establishment of zealous preaching ministers to propagate the Gospel throughout the land; the restriction of public office holding to honest God-fearing men; the reform of the law to make it fairer, quicker, simpler, cheaper and surer, and for its penalties to be more humane; the better relief of poverty; and improvements in social justice. The Army saw the Rump politicians as worldly oligarchs, contemptuous of 'the cause of God's people', and clinging to power for their own interests and profit.

At the same time the Rump parliamentarians began to view the Army differently. They began to be viewed as pliant tools of an ambitious hypocritical Cromwell and his creatures. As Edmund Ludlow puts it : -

"..... thus the troops of the parliament, which were not raised out of the meanest of the people and without distinction, as other armies had been, but consisted of such as had engaged themselves from a spirit of liberty in the defence of their rights and religion, were corrupted by him [Cromwell], *kept as a standing force against the people, taught to forget their first engagements, and rendered as mercenary as other troops are accustomed to be".*[38]

The parliamentarians were not so generally corrupt as the Army supposed, but enough of them had enriched themselves through their tempting opportunities to make the charge plausible. They had showed some modest reforming activity during 1650, particularly concerning themselves with poor relief, ordering legal proceedings to be held in English, and encouraging the propagation of the gospel throughout the Commonwealth. After that they tended to lapse into the politics of survival more and more. They formed factions and interest groups, combined against proposals they disliked, and opposed any measures that might antagonise the country gentry. The group of republican radicals that had formerly been most active for social reform, in which Henry Marten, Thomas Chaloner, and Lord Grey of Groby had been prominent, now interested itself mainly in promoting trade, national power and prestige. It is significant that the Navigation Act, aimed to boost English shipping and commerce in the face of Dutch rivalry, was the main legislative achievement in 1651. The Rump's chief preoccupation in 1652 was the commercially motivated Dutch war.

As soon as Cromwell returned from the battlefield in the autumn of 1651 he pressed Parliament to declare when it would make way for the *'new representative'*. It tried at first to revive the scheme for holding elections only to the vacant seats. When that was proved to be unacceptable Parliament voted, albeit reluctantly and after a lengthy debate, that it would dissolve itself no later than 3rd November 1654. That was a full three years ahead and nearly six years after Pride's Purge. It would have been fourteen years after the previous general election. The Army was, not surprisingly, very annoyed by this decision and its discontent accelerated. By the summer of 1652 its patience had shown signs of reaching breaking point, but from June the Dutch war forced reform proposals once more into the background.

The Dutch war was supported enthusiastically by the dominant faction in the House led by Sir Arthur Hesilrigge and Thomas Scot, who jealously guarded the Rump's monopoly of political authority, especially against the Army, but also against the Marten-Challoner group. The split between this dominant group in the Parliament and the Army began to widen even more. The Rump had already sold off the lands of the crown and the church (the 'fee farm rents'). Now, in order to make ends meet, it sought to confiscate and offer for sale the estates of over seven hundred royalist gentlemen and former officers in addition to those who had lost their lands earlier. This deeply offended the Army, not only because it deepened old divisions which Cromwell for one wished to see healed, but because some of the victims had surrendered upon terms that guaranteed them their landed property. If these terms were now violated the Army's honour would be besmirched. The Army requested its 'friends' in the House to oppose this proposal. They proposed the establishment of a Commission to investigate the issue and moved for a division in Parliament in May 1652 on a bill to give protection to royalists who, in the army's view, were exempt from further punishment by virtue of articles of war. Colonel Pride was nominated as a Commissioner in this respect. In the division that followed on Colonel Pride's nomination the tellers in his favour were Phillip Skippon and Lord Grey of Groby. The tellers against Colonel Pride's nomination were Henry Neville and Denis Bond. Pride's nomination was defeated and the Army rebuffed again. The vote is interesting because it reveals that Lord Grey was still well disposed towards the Army at this point.

In August 1652 a petition was presented by the Council of Officers to the Rump urging the dissolution of Parliament. The Rump responded by instructing a committee to prepare a *'bill for a new representative'*. Throughout October there was a series of meetings initiated by Cromwell between MPs and officers to discuss the Parliamentary options. The parliamentary committee allowed the bill to lie until the army officers began to renew their agitation at the turn of the year. As winter approached criticisms of the Rump increased again. These concerned their perpetuation of their own powers, their continued delays, their scandalous private lives, their self-enrichment, injustice and partiality.

The turn of the year into 1653 brought no apparent solution to the problems of a new Parliament, while the demands of the Army for dissolution became even stronger. In January the Army itself formed a committee to put forward its own demands, which included successive Parliaments, reform of the law and some liberty of conscience. Under this

388

pressure, and with Cromwell acting as a broker between the two parties, the Rump revived their earlier bill. Thinking to placate the Army it put the parliamentary committee under Major-General Thomas Harrison. It was probably unaware that Harrison had become one of the leaders of the Fifth Monarchy Men, who had lost faith in elected parliaments and aimed instead to put power into the hands of godly saints. The army officers continued with their meetings and their pressure until the bill for a new representative was given its first reading on 23rd February 1653. `

The MP who introduced the bill was, however, not Thomas Harrison but Sir Arthur Hesilrigg. This was significant as Hesilrigg was clearly seen as a leader of the anti-Army party and this implies that the bill would not have contained that which the Army expected. What was actually contained in the bill, in detail, is not known for certain as it did not survive. All the signs are that the army officers did not accept it as a satisfactory response to their sustained pressure for a new elected parliament. Cromwell himself stayed away from the House from mid-March to mid-April, thus boycotting several of the weekly debates on it. It was on this issue that the Commonwealth was to founder in the spring of 1653.

In the meantime Lord Grey of Groby had returned to membership of the Council of State. On 24th November 1652 he had been nominated as a member of the Council for the ensuing year, and on 21st December he had taken the oath to rejoin it. Lord Grey returned to the Committee for Compounding and on 28th January 1653 he was added to the Mint Committee. On the surface things were still progressing well for him, but much was about to change.

Between May and June 1650 Andrew Marvell had written the following prophetic words : -

> *"..... So restless Cromwell could not cease*
> *In the inglorious arts of peace,*
> *But through adventurous war*
> *Urged his active star*
> *And, like the three-forked lightning, first*
> *Breaking the clouds where it was nursed,*
> *Did through his own side*
> *His fiery way divide.*
> *For 'tis all one to courage high*
> *The emulous or enemy :*
> *And with such to inclose*
> *Is more than to oppose".*[39]

In the spring of 1653 *"restless Cromwell"* did indeed begin to *"through his own side his fiery way divide"*.

Notes

1.   Calendar of State Papers (Domestic), 1625 - 1649 Addenda; Vol DXI. (58) Nov. 29; 1645.

2.   Calendar of the Committee for the Advance of Money. Vol. II. p. 796.

3.   Clement Walker, *The History of Independency*, 1648.

4.   House of Commons Journal, Vol. VI., p. 248.

5.   Calendar of the Committee for Compounding, 1650.

6.   House of Commons Journal, Vol. VII., p. 53.

7.   Calendar of the Committee for Compounding, 1653.

8.   House of Commons Journal, Vol. VI., p. 571.

9.   Mark Noble, *The Lives of the English Regicides*, Vol. I., London, 1798. pp. 628-9.

10.   Blair Worden, op. cit. pp. 94-5.

11.   House of Commons Journal, Vol. VI., p. 402.

12.   Calendar of State Papers (Domestic), 1649-50, p. 250., 1650, Vol. XI. (19).

13.   Lucy Hutchinson, *The Memoirs of Colonel Hutchinson*, Everyman Books, p. 272.

14.   Historical Manuscripts Commission, (HMC) De L'Isle & Dudley MSS. p. 474. Letter from Lord Lisle to the Earl of Leicester. 1649/50 Feb. 21. London.

15.   Heath's Chronicle, p. 270.

16.   Andrew Marvell, *An Horatian Ode upon Cromwell's Return from Ireland*.
      Written May to July 1650.

17.   Lucy Hutchinson, op. cit. p. 274.
      Footnote by Rev. Julius Hutchinson, 1806.

18.   Andrew Marvell, op. cit.

19.   Historical Manuscripts Commission MSS of the Earl of Eglinton. (162), p. 57. Letter from Major-General Robert Montgomery to the Earl of Eglinton, - 22nd August 1650.

20.   Calendar of State Papers (Domestic Series), Vol. XVI, 1651.

21.   Ibid.

22.   Ibid.

23.   Ibid.

24.   Edmund Ludlow, op. cit. p. 156.

25.   John Milton, *To the Lord General Cromwell*.

26.   Edmund Ludlow, op. cit. p. 156.

27.   Henry Cary, *Memorials of the Great Civil War*, - letter from Lord Grey to the Speaker - Sept. 7. 1651. pp. 376-7.

28. Henry Cary, Ibid. - letter from Major-General Massey to the Countess of Stamford - Sept. 10, 1651. pp. 381-2.
29. Clarendon, op. cit. Vol. VI. pp. 576-7.
30. Calendar of State Papers (Domestic Series), Vol. XVI., 1651.
31. Ibid.
32. Journal of the House of Commons (C.J.), Vol. VII., p. 52.
33. Calendar of State Papers (Domestic Series), Vol. XXIII., January 12, 1652. (17).
34. Ibid.
35. Calendar of State Papers (Domestic Series), Vol. XXIV., July 28, 1652. (20).
36. Lucy Hutchinson, op. cit. pp. 289-291.
37. David Underdown, pp. 4 & 5.
38. Edmund Ludlow, op. cit. Vol. III, p. 21.
39. Andrew Marvell, op. cit.

Arms of the Commonwealth

Edward Massey

392

Thomas, Lord Grey of Groby, with page

Anchitel Grey

Unknown subject – probably John Grey

Hon:^ble Leonard Grey

Leonard Grey

Diana Bruce (nee Grey) Countess Ailesbury

Mary Grey

CHAPTER TWELVE

DECLINE AND FALL (1653 - 1657)

"Troubled on every side, yet not distressed ....
perplexed, but not in despair;
persecuted, but not forsaken;
cast down, but not destroyed.
2 Corinthians, Chapter 4, verses 8 - 9

The 20th day of April 1653 was a crucial date in the history of the English Republic. On that day the Parliament was due to consider the bill for the new representative assembly at last. It seems that this bill provided for the Rump Parliament's final dissolution and the meeting of a new parliament in November 1653. This would be elected with seats redistributed on lines similar to those the army officers had agreed in the amended 'Agreement of the People' in 1649.

On the previous evening, however, Oliver Cromwell called a meeting between some twenty leading MPs and some senior Army officers and put a proposal to them. In order to save the Commonwealth from its current divisions he seems to have suggested that the Rump should instead hand over the supreme authority for a while to about forty *"persons of honour and integrity that were well known, men well affected to religion and the interest of the nation"*, nominated by itself, and should then dissolve itself. This interim Council or government would hold the reins of power, with enough authority to initiate certain long overdue reforms, until the nation was judged settled enough to elect a new parliament of representatives. At the end of this meeting Cromwell seems to have thought that sufficient of the MPs had agreed that the bill would not be proceeded with any further until his alternative scheme had been fully considered by the House of Commons.

The next morning he stayed at his lodgings in Whitehall with a general conference of army officers to consider some of the details of how the interim government council might work. He would not at first believe it when a messenger brought word from the House of Commons that the chamber was packed, with at least a hundred members present, and that the bill regarding the new representative was to be discussed immediately. Since nothing had been decided definitely concerning the interim council the resultant bill would deal with merely an adjournment of the present Parliament rather than a dissolution. This news seems to have been a total surprise to Cromwell who was apparently outraged by the betrayal of what he had thought was accepted on the previous evening. He sent messengers down to the House to check on what was happening. Back came Colonel Ingoldsby with confirmation that the Rump was indeed discussing the bill. What was more they intended to pass it that morning and it would be done through an Act that would occasion the Rump to meet again, thus prolonging its own existence. Then a third messenger came back to report that the House was drawing towards the close of the debate prior to taking a vote on the bill.

Cromwell sprang into action; his blood was up at what he regarded as a breach of faith by self-serving politicians. Pausing only to order up a party of musketeers he hastened with them through Whitehall to the House of Commons chamber. The informality of his clothing showed that he had been taken by surprise by events. He was wearing, according to contemporary witnesses, a plain black coat, with grey worsted stockings and shoes, rather than the usual grandee attire and riding boots. The sight of the Lord General dressed as a *'worsted stocking man'* must have given some of his fellow MPs cause for alarm even though he left the musketeers outside the chamber at first. For a short time he sat slumped in his place listening to the closing stages of the debate. Then, standing up, he began to speak evenly at first but with increasing passion as his anger mounted. Soon his feelings of outrage spilled out. He criticised them in what Whitelocke called *"a furious manner"* and as Ludlow described it, *"with so much passion and discomposure of mind as if he had been distracted ....."*, walking up and down like a madman, kicking the ground with his feet and shouting. He strode about, pointing at various members, calling them by such names as whoremasters, drunkards, corrupt and unjust men, and some scandalous to the profession of the Gospel :-

> *"Perhaps you think this is not parliamentary language,"* he shouted.
> *"I confess it is not, neither are you to expect any such from me ..... It is not fit that you should sit as a Parliament any longer. You have sat long enough unless you had done more good. In the name of God, go!"*[1]

He then turned to Thomas Harrison who was sitting on the other side of the House and shouted, *"Call them in!"*. In rushed five or six files of musketeers, between twenty and thirty soldiers, from Cromwell's own regiment under a Lieutenant-Colonel Worsley. Cromwell pointed to the Speaker and instructed them to *"fetch him down"*. This being done, Sir Henry Vane called out, *"This is not honest, yea it is against morality and common honesty. We did cut off a king's head for such as this!"* Cromwell turned on him abruptly and cried out, as if to heaven, *"O Sir Henry Vane,*

Sir Henry Vane, the Lord deliver me from Sir Henry Vane!". Algernon Sidney, who was sitting next to the Speaker and refused to leave was forced to go after threats of physical ejection from Harrison and Worsley. Cromwell turned then to the mace, the symbol of the Speaker's authority, lying on the table in front of the Speaker's chair. Pointing to it he asked contemptuously, *"What shall we do with this bauble? Take it away"*. Within a few more minutes all members of parliament had been cleared from the chamber.

Cromwell himself picked up the paper containing the Bill of Dissolution which was lying on the table waiting to be passed. He stuffed it under his coat and took it away with him. Its exact contents remain a mystery as it disappeared from history following this episode. Cromwell never let it be seen again and changed his opinions about it in subsequent speeches. It may have been that it did not, after all, contain provisions for the Rump to perpetuate its own existence. If so, Cromwell's pretext for abolishing the Rump Parliament would have been unfounded and only carried out following a sudden loss of temper brought on by an assumed slight. Nonetheless, any fresh elections were likely to involve a risk, especially if the transition from an old to a new parliament was not carefully supervised to ensure that the Commonwealth's new rulers could be trusted to keep their Engagement oaths to be true and faithful to it. Whoever were to scrutinise the election returns, the army's co-operation would be needed to ensure that cavaliers and others who were seriously disaffected to the Commonwealth were kept out.

The risk was acceptable and the achievement of a new parliament desirable so long as the Rump and the Army could watch over the transfer of authority in mutual trust and harmony, but the worsening state of relations between the two pillars of the Commonwealth in spring 1653 had probably made the risk too great.

The Rump had probably tried to rush its bill through because it feared a military coup or another purge. The Army, for its part, was suspicious that Sir Arthur Hesilrigg's new dominant faction was still trying to trick it. The Rump Parliament only existed because the Army had done its bidding in December .1648 through Pride's Purge. The Army officers probably asked themselves why they should be denied any participation, therefore, in the long delayed transmission of power to a new parliament. Also, there were rumours abroad that the Rump intended to remove Cromwell from the Lord Generalship and restructure the army command to reduce its independence. Whether these rumours had any foundation or not, it is likely that they were given some credence.

Having dissolved the Rump Parliament, quite illegally, Cromwell returned to the meeting of the officers in Whitehall and informed those

401

who were not MPs of what he had done. In the afternoon he went to the Council of State, telling them that in future they could only meet together as private persons, since the Parliament of which they were the servants had been put to an end. John Bradshaw replied to him bravely, *"Sir, we have heard what you did at the House in the morning and before many hours all England will hear of it; but, Sir, you are mistaken to think that the Parliament is dissolved; for no power under heaven can dissolve them but themselves; therefore take you notice of that"*.[2] Of the Councillors of State present Hesilrigg, Love, and Scot are recorded as making similar statements to the same effect but all eventually departed.

Cromwell had finally decided in favour of the Army, that he had largely remodelled and could control, rather than the Parliament which regarded him as just one of their number and their servant. The Army produced a 'Declaration' on 22nd April which set out the reasons for the abolition of the Rump. On 29th April a new executive body was set up consisting of Cromwell, Desborough, Thomas Harrison and a number of officials. On 30th April an announcement was signed by Cromwell, and eventually printed on 6th May, which made it clear that there would be a new representative assembly (the word Parliament was not used) consisting of *"persons of approved fidelity and honesty"* from all quarters of the Commonwealth. This would be a nominated assembly. By expelling the Rump Cromwell had effectively closed the option of calling a newly elected parliament for some time to come. Not only had he no legal right to summon one, but even if he tried the men most likely to be chosen would have been either presbyterians of the type excluded by Pride's Purge, or crypto-royalists. To these could now be added another group likely to be hostile to Cromwell, his army and its aspirations. These were republican sympathisers with the Rump, or Commonwealthmen as they would term themselves.

Lucy Hutchinson gives an account of the abolition of the Rump Parliament from the perspective of the Commonwealthmen such as her husband John, Edmund Ludlow, and Lord Grey of Groby. It accords with the accounts of Whitelocke and Ludlow :-

"Cromwell ..... and ..... Lambert ..... took to them Major-general Harrison, who had a great interest both in the army and the church; and these, pretending to be piously troubled that there were such delays in the administration of justice, and such perverting of right, endeavouring to bring all good men into dislike of the parliament, pretending that they would perpetuate themselves in their honours and offices, and had no care to bring in those glorious things for which they had so many years

contended in blood and toil. The parliament, on the other side, had now, by the blessing of God, restored the commonwealth to such a happy, rich, and plentiful condition, that it was not so flourishing before the war, and although the taxes that were paid were great, yet the people were rich and able to pay them : they (the parliament) were in a way of paying all the soldiers' arrears, had some hundred thousand pounds in their purses, and were free from enemies in arms within and without, except the Dutch, whom they had beaten and brought to seek peace upon terms honourable to the English : and now they thought it was time to sweeten the people, and deliver them from their burdens. This could not be but by disbanding the unnecessary officers and soldiers, and when things were thus settled, they had prepared a bill to put a period to their own sitting, and provide for new successors. But when the great officers understood that they were to resign their honours, and no more triumph in the burdens of the people, they easily induced the inferior officers and soldiers to set up for themselves with them; and while these things were passing, Cromwell with an armed force, assisted by Lambert and Harrison, came into the House and dissolved the parliament, pulling out the members, foaming and raging, and calling them undeserved and base names; and when the Speaker refused to come out of his chair, Harrison plucked him out. These gentlemen having done this, took to themselves the administration of all things; a few slaves of the House consulted with them and would have truckled under them, but not many. Meanwhile they and their soldiers could no way palliate their rebellion, but by making false criminations of the parliament-men, as that they meant to perpetuate themselves in honour and office, that they had gotten vast estates, and prevented justice for gain, and were imposing upon men for conscience, and a thousand such like things, which time manifested to be false, and truth retorted all upon themselves that they had injuriously cast at the others".[3]

Lucy Hutchinson also relates how her husband and many of his fellow MPs reacted to the dissolution of the Rump Parliament :-

"He was going up to attend the business of his country above, when news met him upon the road, near London, that Cromwell had broken the parliament. Notwithstanding, he went on and found divers of the members there, resolved to submit to this

403

providence of God, and to wait till he should clear their integrity, and to disprove those people who had taxed them of ambition, by sitting still, when they had friends enough in the army, city, and country, to have disputed the matter, and probably to have vanquished these usurpers. They thought that if they should vex the land by war among themselves, the late subdued enemies, royalists and presbyterians, would have an opportunity to prevail on their dissensions, to the ruin of both : if these should govern well, and righteously, and moderately, they would enjoy the benefit of their good government, and not envy them the honourable toil; if they did otherwise, they should be ready to assist and vindicate their oppressed country, when the ungrateful people were made sensible of their true champions and protectors".[4]

Amongst those groups who supported Cromwell's actions, however, were the Fifth Monarchy Men. These were a rapidly growing group of millenarians who had found a leader and champion in Major-General Thomas Harrison. Harrison was the son of a Newcastle-under-Lyme butcher. He had risen to the highest levels of the New Model Army through his excessive zeal for the *'Good Old Cause'*. The Fifth Monarchists were imbibers of a peculiar kind of apocalyptic thought and vision that thrives during times of acute social crisis, which are seen as a sign of Christ's second coming. To the Fifth Monarchists the four monarchies of Babylon, Persia, Greece and Rome had all passed into history, and the fifth monarchy - as prophesied in the Book of Daniel - the monarchy of King Jesus, was now imminent. Their conviction had grown stronger as the fortunes of war had gone against the king, and when, in 1649, the monarchy was finally overthrown and the worldly king executed, they saw it as a positive, divinely-inspired presage of the second advent of Christ, and the establishment of His thousand years' rule upon earth. During the period of preparation for this outstanding event the Millenarians believed that England should be ruled by an interim government of saintly men chosen by the godly churches and exercising the minimum of direct political power. A system of free elections was rejected for it was considered that this might produce a Parliament of malignants, delinquents, and sinners who might hinder the Millennium and the return of King Jesus.

The proposals which Cromwell had put forward to the joint meeting of some MPs and army officers on the evening of 19th April had borne some similarity to this scenario and his language - coloured by puritanical reliance on the Providence of the Lord of Hosts - led the leaders of the Fifth Monarchists to give him their support. For example, Robert Overton, the governor of Hull and one of the leaders of the successful military campaign in Scotland, who was deeply imbued with the views of the Fifth Monarchy Men, and dissatisfied with the slow progress of the work of reformation under the Rump Parliament, hailed with enthusiasm Cromwell's forcible dissolution of that body. He wrote at once to Cromwell approving the act, and promising his support and that of his garrison in 'More Hearts and Hands appearing for the work ..... being two Letters ..... from Colonel Robert Overton, Governor of Hull ..... and the Officers of the said Garrison, 1653'.

Cromwell's alliance with the Fifth Monarchists was to be a brief one. Later in the year they were to say of him that in the field - on campaign or in battle - the Lord General was *"the graciousest and most gallant man in the world, but out of the field and when he came home again to government, the worst"*.

His other allies during the period of the abolition of the Rump Parliament were clever young ambitious generals such as Major-General John Lambert and Charles Fleetwood, now Cromwell's son-in-law having married the widow of the late Henry Ireton. They did not share the millenarian dreams of the Fifth Monarchists but felt the distrust, and perhaps a degree of contempt, often found in successful military leaders for prevaricating, self-serving politicians. From late April 1653 onwards civil affairs were put in the care of a small provisional Council of State under Lambert's presidency.

It is not clear exactly what Lord Grey of Groby's reaction to the dissolution of the Rump Parliament and its Council of State was, but it is almost certain that he would have been opposed to it. At a stroke he had lost his public positions and, with them, some of his possessions. This would have affected him materially; but there is no doubt too that he was committed to the Commonwealth as established in 1649. Like many of his colleagues he now turned against Cromwell. Again, like many of his colleagues, he would be increasingly viewed with suspicion by Cromwell and the new ruling clique.

On 11th June it was noted that *"the lodgings* [in Whitehall] *formerly Lord Grey's to be reserved by the Committee, and not disposed of until further notice"*.[5] It is likely that he had also lost the use of the house and the parkland at Hyde Park.

On 4th July Oliver Cromwell opened the first session of the new nominated assembly. Its members were chosen by the Council of Officers, sometimes based upon nominations received from borough corporations and *'godly'* churches. But the officers observed an important restraint, probably on Cromwell's advice and against Harrison's inclinations: they did not nominate themselves or each other, with the exception of Admiral Blake, General Monck and a few garrison commanders. This

405

unrepresentative gathering is known to history as the 'Assembly of the Saints' or the 'Barebones Parliament'. The latter term became contemptuously attached to it through the membership of a city merchant of some substance, a puritan named Praise-God Barebone.

The members nominated to the 'Barebones Parliament' for the borough and county of Leicester were, according to the borough records, Henry Danvers, Edward Smith, and John Pratt. The last two named are noted as being *"for the godly learned ministry and universities"*. That John Pratt was a serving MP is confirmed by the record of a letter to him in that capacity at London on 22nd November, 1653 regarding the removal of a Mr. Lee, the Master of Wyggeston Hospital in Leicester.

By the summer of 1653 Lord Grey of Groby was already becoming more and more conscious of his now private rather than public status. He was summoned from the midlands to give evidence before a committee of the new 'parliament'. On 27th July it was ordered, on the presentation of a petition *"of the inhabitants of several parishes having right of common in the forest of Whittlewood, co. Northampton, that Col. Norton, Mr. Williams, Mr. St. Nicholas, and Mr. Courtenay be a Committee to hear the petition, examine witnesses if they see cause, hear what Lord Grey has to say in answer, and report back"*.[6]

The 'Assembly of the Saints', however, soon fell foul of factionalism, largely between the zealots (especially the Fifth Monarchists) and the moderates. On Monday 12th December during the morning session the Speaker and the moderates walked out of the House of Commons chamber, where the 'Barebones Parliament' had sat, and processed to Whitehall Palace where they resigned their authority back into Cromwell's hands. Within hours a clear majority of members had signed a brief document of abdication. Cromwell then officially dissolved the Assembly. Many suspected that he and Lambert had orchestrated this development.

Four days later, on 16th December, 1653, Oliver Cromwell was announced to be head of state with the title of Lord Protector. John Lambert had earlier drawn up a new constitution entitled the 'Instrument of Government'. Originally Lambert and his supporters had hoped to persuade Cromwell to accept the title of king, but he had refused. The creation of the Protectorate, whilst falling short of restoring a monarchy under a different dynasty, did antagonise all the republicans, commonwealthmen, and the Fifth Monarchists who held that the only sole ruler could be King Jesus. The new Protectoral constitution contained a Protector, Council, and Parliament. Executive authority was vested in the Lord Protector advised by the Council. There was to be a separation of powers between the executive and the legislature. The Protector was obliged, under the Instrument of Government, to call parliament at least every three years and to keep it sitting for at least five months. Parliament itself was reformed in the way that the army had been demanding since 1647. The precise distribution of seats was as the Rump's bill for a new representative had defined it, except that thirty members were added for each of Scotland and Ireland. Many small boroughs lost their seats, and the proportion of county representatives was raised from less than a fifth in 1640 to about two thirds. The franchise also followed the Rump's bill and gave the vote to all adult males who owned real estate or personal property worth £200. This did not have to be freehold property, as previously, or even landed property at all. Meanwhile, the Instrument gave Cromwell and his council the authority to make ordinances until the first Protectoral Parliament met in September 1654. He used this power to advance the causes he believed in, namely, propagating the gospel, liberty of conscience, a *'reformation of manners'* (in the sense of raising standards of moral conduct), the reform of the law and the improvement of social justice.

Despite his avowed intention of founding a system of *'government by consent'* Cromwell found it difficult to reconcile the divisions in the nation that had now grown so many and so deep. During the Protectorate he was to win over a few royalists and rather more of the old political presbyterians, but most remained hostile. He never reconciled the parliamentary republicans such as Hesilrigg, Bradshaw, Vane, Marten, Grey of Groby, Hutchinson and Ludlow. There were 'commonwealthmen' too in the army, and he had to cashier a number of his old comrades who publicly challenged his authority as Lord Protector or worked to undermine it. Thomas Harrison also had to go when he, and other militant Fifth Monarchists, incited their brethren to resort to armed resistance. When Harrison and his colleague, John Carew, were summoned before the Protectoral Council to answer for their activities Carew told Cromwell to his face that when he had taken over authority from the 'Assembly of the Saints' he had *"took the crown off from the head of Christ and put it upon his own"*. The Levellers too, although broken as an organised movement by now, had left a residue of frustrated democratic aspirations. These erupted again in large demonstrations of sympathy when John Lilburne returned to England to challenge his banishment and stood his last trial in August 1653. In a nation so torn by so many recent divisions it was to be expected that plots and speculations about plots would thrive.

Lucy Hutchinson gives the following account of the period following the dissolution of the Rump Parliament and the establishment of the Protectorate :-

"In the interim Cromwell and his army grew wanton with their power, and invented a thousand tricks of government, which,

when nobody opposed, they themselves fell to dislike and vary every day. First he calls a parliament out of his own pocket, himself naming a sort of godly men for every county, who meeting and not agreeing, a part of them, in the name of the people, gave up the sovereignty to him. Shortly after he makes up several sorts of mock parliaments, but not finding one of them absolutely to his turn, turned them off again. He soon quitted himself of his triumvirs, and first thrust out Harrison, then took away Lambert's commission, and would have been king but for fear of quitting his generalship. He weeded out, in a few months' time, above a hundred and fifty godly officers out of the army, with whom many of the religious soldiers went off, and in their room abundance of the king's dissolute soldiers were entertained; and the army was almost changed from that godly religious army, whose valour God had crowned with triumph, into the dissolute army they had beaten, bearing yet a better name. His wife and children were setting up for principality, which suited no better with any of them than scarlet on the ape; only, to speak the truth of himself he had much natural greatness, and well became the place he had usurped".[7]

Whilst people like Lucy Hutchinson and her husband could only lament the usurpation of power by Cromwell they could find some advantages in concentrating on their own affairs at home in the country rather than matters of state :-

"Colonel Hutchinson, in his own particular, was very glad of this release from that employment [Parliament and the Council of State], *which he managed with fidelity and uprightness, but not only without delight, but with a great deal of trouble and expense, in the contest for truth and righteousness upon all occasions. ..... As for the public business of the country, he would not act in any office under the protector's power, and therefore confined himself to his own, which the whole country* [i.e. county] *about him were grieved at, and would rather come to him for counsel as a private neighbour than to any of the men in power for greater help. He being now reduced into an absolutely private condition, was very much courted and visited by those of all parties, and while the grand quarrel slept, and both the victors and the vanquished were equal slaves under the new usurpers, there was a very kind correspondence between him and all his countrymen."*[8]

There remains a poem written by Lucy Hutchinson, probably at the time of her husband's retirement from public business to their country home of Owthorp Hall in south Nottinghamshire. It extols both the virtues of country life and the pursuit of the private rather than the public life :-

"All sorts of men through various labours press
To the same end, contented quietness;
Great princes vex their labouring thoughts to be
Possessed of an unbounded sovereignty;
The hardy soldier doth all toils sustain
That he may conquer first, and after reign;
Th' industrious merchant ploughs the angry seas
That he may bring home wealth, and live at ease.
These none of them attain : for sweet repose
But seldom to the splendid palace goes;
A troop of restless passions wander there,
And only private lives are free from care.
Sleep to the cottage bringeth happy nights,
But to the court hung round with flaring lights,
Which th' office of the vanished day supply,
His image only comes to close the eye,
But gives the troubled mind no ease of care,
While country slumbers undisturbed are;
Where, if the active fancy dreams present,
They bring no horrors to the innocent.
Ambition doth incessantly aspire,
And each advance leads on to new desire;
Nor yet can riches av'rice satisfy,
For want and wealth together multiply:
Nor can voluptuous men more fulness find
For enjoyed pleasures leave their stings behind.
He's only rich who knows no want; he reigns
Whose will no severe tyranny constrains;
And he alone possesseth true delight
Whose spotless soul no guilty fears affright.

This freedom in the country life is found,
Where innocence and safe delights abound.
Here man's a prince; his subjects ne'er repine
When on his back their wealthy fleeces shine:
If for his appetite the fattest die,
Those who survive will raise no mutiny:

409

His table is with home-got dainties crowned,
With friends, not flatterers, encompassed round;
No spies nor traitors on his trencher wait,
Nor is his mirth confined to rules of state;
An armed guard he neither hath nor needs,
Nor fears a poisoned morsel when he feeds;
Bright constellations hang above his head,
Beneath his feet are flow'ry carpets spread;
The merry birds delight him with their songs,
And healthful air his happy life prolongs;
At harvest merrily his flocks he shears,
And in cold weather their warm fleeces wears;
Unto his ease he fashions all his clothes;
His cup with uninfected liquor flows:
The vulgar breath doth not his thoughts elate,
Nor can he be o'erwhelmed by their hate.
Yet, if ambitiously he seeks for fame,
One village feast shall gain a greater name
Than his who wears the imperial diadem,
Whom the rude multitude do still condemn.
Sweet peace and joy his blest companions are;
Fear, sorrow, envy, lust, revenge, and care,
And all that troop which breeds the world's offence,
With pomp and majesty, are banish'd thence.
What court then can such liberty afford?
Or where is man so uncontrol'd a lord?"[9]

Such a life-style, albeit rather romanticised and idealised in this presentation, might have satisfied John Hutchinson; it could not satisfy, however, a restless Thomas Grey, Baron Groby. Coombe Abbey and Bradgate were both far grander residences than Owthorp but the active Lord Grey of Groby did not take well to *"being reduced into an absolutely private condition"*.

Lord Grey was wealthy, aristocratic, centrally placed with influence in London and the Midlands, ambitious, and had been well thought of in the Army, by the republicans in the various parliaments, had links with the Levellers and, more recently, the Fifth Monarchists. His relationship with Oliver Cromwell had been increasingly strained by a succession of events which had first weakened and then destroyed the Commonwealth; such as the crushing of the Levellers in the Army at Burford by duplicity and force in 1649, the abolition of the Rump Parliament in April 1653, and finally the dissolution of the 'Assembly of the Saints' and the establishment of the Protectorate in December 1653.

410

In turn, the Lord Protector would have noted Lord Grey of Groby as one of the major figures likely to be implacably opposed to the new regime of which he was the head. Lord Grey's fortunes had changed dramatically during 1653, largely as a result of the abolition of the Rump Parliament. The hostile commentator, Mark Noble, records this change in the following terms-:

> *"So far he had been trusted, courted, applauded, and gratified, chiefly by Cromwell; but as that great man saw that Grey was as ambitious as himself, or at least that he could no brook a superior, he began to treat him with less confidence, and at length to watch him as a dangerous person; as inimical to those great designs he was meditating.*

> *"They probably most cordially hated each other; he feared Oliver, and regarded him as a revolter from the common interest; and the other knew the wickedness of his heart, and that a man who had been so untrue to his lawful sovereign could not be expected to be loyal to one whom he viewed as inferior to himself.*
> *"Outwardly, however, they behaved with seeming attention to each other, whilst each was watching for the favourable moment to ruin his enemy. Oliver durst not trust him in London, the seat of government; he therefore kept him in his station in Leicester: but that being the central situation of the kingdom, and, in case of a revolt, a very dangerous one for a person of Lord Grey's consequence and turn of mind, he kept constant spies upon him; .....*[10]

Elections to the first parliament of the Protectorate were held in August 1654. They were keenly contested, even in Scotland and Ireland as well as in England and Wales. In spite of the changes in seat distribution and the franchise most of the men returned were of a moderate and conservative inclination - probably being best described politically as Presbyterians. In many areas the only national issue raised was: should the radical reforming schemes announced in the Assembly of the Saints be confirmed and continued? The reply was an emphatic 'No'. Over a hundred members of this new parliament had sat in the Long Parliament, not only republicans and members of the Rump Parliament such as Haselrigg, Bradshaw, and Scot, but others who had been excluded at Pride's Purge or even earlier. From the West Country came some who were crypto-royalists. All of these potentially unmanageable elected members were allowed initially to take their seats.

Some candidates were, however, banned from being elected by a Council committee charged in August with identifying men not of known integrity and likely to be disturbers of law and peace or Levellers and kindred *'dangerous spirits'*. Numbered among the latter was Lord Grey of Groby.

On 3rd September 1654, the fourth anniversary of Dunbar and the third of Worcester, 300 members of the new Parliament assembled for the first time. In the afternoon the Lord Protector addressed them, standing on a pedestal in the Painted Chamber. In his speech, according to Ludlow :-

> *"he endeavoured to make it appear, that things were brought to this pass, not by his contrivance, but by the over-ruling hand of God; assuring them, that he was much rejoiced to see so free an assembly of the people met together, and that he resolved to submit himself to their judgement. But notwithstanding these specious pretences, he caused the lord Grey of Grooby, Mr John Wildman, Mr.* [Samuel] *Highland, and others, who had always manifested a constant affection to the commonwealth, to be excluded from the house. And though many undue methods had been used at the elections, to procure those to be chosen who were enemies, and to keep out many who were known friends to the common cause .... yet they appeared in a few days not to be for his purpose, but resolved, at the least, to lay a claim to their liberties."*[11]

On 21st August a petition had been received by the Protectoral Council from "gentlemen, ministers, and freeholders, co. Leicester", to the effect that,

> *"Mr. Prettiman, high sherrif, had returned Henry, Earl of Stamford and Thos. Beaumont, who were not only unduly elected, but are not qualified according to the Instrument. We beg an examination and summons for both parties, and witnesses".*

It was also alleged that the Earl of Stamford *"had assisted the late King of Scots"* [Charles II] *and is not of good conversation".*[12] Someone who was `not of good conversation' (that is, who criticised the regime openly) could be excluded from the elections.

Once the new parliament established itself, however, Haselrigg, Bradshaw, Scot, and others of the republican group set out to take the lead in restoring their parliamentary sovereignty. They began to win over some of the new members so that, as Ludlow put it, *"the commonwealth party increased daily, and that of the sword lost ground"*. The parliament's committee of privilege, with Haselrigg as its chairman, reasserted the Commons' claim to judge its own election returns and promptly allowed two members, previously rejected by the Council, to come in and take their seats. Accordingly, Lord Grey of Groby was returned as member for Leicester and the Earl of Stamford was confirmed as member for the shire. As S. R. Gardiner puts it, **"the claim of the Council ..... to regulate the admission of members by certificates of qualification was set at defiance by an order that the Earl of Stamford and his son should take their seats"**.[13]

On 7th September the Instrument of Government was forthrightly impugned by a proposition that the government should be in a single person, perhaps, but one limited and restrained as the Commons should think fit. In the debate that sprang up, kept on heat by the republicans, a member declared bluntly that the Protector's right to rule could *'be measured out no otherwise than by the length of his sword'*. The court party tried to prevent an immediate resolution but the matter was passed by a small majority to a committee. Parliament was already registering its distaste for the lowly place assigned to it in the new constitution. Cromwell was extremely annoyed by these developments and from this point Lord Grey of Groby was a marked man.

After only eight days of its first session Cromwell intervened in the business of the wayward Protectoral Parliament and pointed out that a formal acknowledgement of the new constitution under the Instrument of Government had been written into every member's election return. He claimed that both electors and those elected were bound by it. The members were not allowed to resume their seats unless they signed a promise that they would not attempt *"to alter the government, as it is settled in one single person and a parliament"*. This move got rid of the more doctrinaire republicans from the House including Lord Grey of Groby, but those who signed still wanted to know why a few army officers should lay down the laws of the constitution rather than themselves, the people's elected representatives. So, rather than meekly approving the proposals of the Protector and his Council, they continued to attempt to alter the constitution into a form nearer to their own preferences. Tiring of such confrontations a frustrated Cromwell dissolved the first parliament of the Protectorate on 22nd January 1655, before it had passed a single bill or voted a single penny in tax. Their continued presence, he said, was no longer for *"the profits of these nations, nor for the common and public good"*.

The winter of 1654 and the spring of 1655 were characterised by rumours of plots and counter espionage activity co-ordinated by John Thurloe, Cromwell's Spymaster-General :-

413

"In January there would be meetings of the disaffected at various places, such as Marston Moor and Salisbury Plain. Though the conspirators could not count with certainty on Haslerigg, they expected to be supported by Lord Grey of Groby, one of those who had refused to sign the Recognition, as well as by Saunders and Okey".[14]

At times football matches and race meetings were banned in order to prevent large assemblies of men that could have served as cover for a rendezvous prior to a rising. England in the spring of 1655 has been described by Antonia Fraser as appearing to lie in a clamp, and **"it was difficult indeed to see how the Royalists - or for that matter the Levellers, still less the Fifth Monarchists - would be able to free it"**.[15]

The Cromwellians feared in particular a rising by an 'unholy' alliance of the various groups hostile to the Protectoral regime. The Levellers had never ceased their opposition to any governmental moves that departed from the principles of the original 'Agreement of the People' of 1647. The real danger of the Levellers lay now, not in their principles as such, but in the alliances they might make and the converts they might win as opposition to Cromwell's personal rule spread. A Leveller-Royalist alliance, strange though it might sound, could present a serious challenge to the regime. John Lilburne had moved steadily to a position of being prepared to accept a 'balanced' or 'constitutional' monarchy if accompanied by a much extended franchise and freedom of conscience in religion. John Wildman and Edward Sexby, both formerly active in the Leveller cause were active again amongst dissident groups. There was even the suggestion by the Cromwellians that a Leveller-Royalist axis was being financed by Spanish gold. Then there were the disaffected republicans such as Sir Arthur Hesilrigg, John Bradshaw, and Lord Grey of Groby who might well be in a mood to join them, particularly after this latest dissolution of a parliament which had once again deprived them of a forum. Like their fellow Commonwealthman Edmund Ludlow, still at this time in Ireland, they saw *"things running every day more and more into confusion, the cavaliers being enraged to see the throne usurped, and those who had hazarded all for their country finding themselves cheated, custom and excise raised without authority of parliament, and taxes imposed to no other end than to support the pride and insolence of a single person"*.[16] Then there was the possibility of enlisting the support of those zealous and committed soldiers of King Jesus, the Fifth Monarchy Men.

There was evidence that some of these groups at least were working together. A petition was drawn up in November 1654 by certain of Cromwell's former close comrades, Colonels Okey, Allured and Saunders referring to the unsatisfactory nature of the present government. What made this development more menacing than its face value was that the petition had been drafted by John Wildman, the long standing Leveller author and leader. It called into question the basis of Cromwell's power and demanded *"a full and free Parliament"* to reconsider those freedoms originally requested by the `Agreement of the People'. The plan was to secure a large number of Army signatures to the petition (an old Leveller tactic), and to distribute it as widely as possible in all three kingdoms. But the petition was rapidly seized and the three colonels court-martialled. They were subsequently cleared of charges of treason.

In Scotland, where a real conspiracy appears to have developed at this time, General Monck, the former royalist officer now turned Cromwellian, acted with great speed and imprisoned Colonel Robert Overton who was held to be the leader of the plot in that country. Overton, who had supported Cromwell's dissolution of the Rump Parliament as a Fifth Monarchy Man, had been filled with doubts and suspicion about Cromwell following the latter's dissolution of the 'Assembly of the Saints' and the establishment of the post of Lord Protector. He had declared his dissatisfaction directly to Cromwell, telling him that if he saw that he designed to set up himself and not the good of the nation, he would not set one foot before another to serve him. *"Thou wert a knave if thou wouldst"*, Cromwell had answered. Overton had thereupon retained his commission on the promise to deliver it up when he could no longer conscientiously serve any longer. In September 1654 he had returned to his command in Scotland, but in December was arrested by Monck and sent as a prisoner to England on the charge of intending to head a military revolt against the government. His own rather indiscreet conduct in approving meetings of the disaffected officers under his command certainly gave grounds for suspicion. The enemies of the government regarded him as a probable leader and used his name freely in their plans. Charles II actually wrote to him promising to pardon his past disloyalty, and to give him rewards for service in assisting in the restoration of the monarchy on `balanced' terms. The Levellers had expected that he would seize Monck instead, take command of the army in Scotland, and march into England to restore the Commonwealth. An examination of the evidence seems to show that he was in fact innocent of the charges, but it is not surprising that the regime thought him guilty. Cromwell regarded him as deliberately faithless to his earlier promise and treated him with great severity. His supposed accomplices in Scotland were court-martialled and cashiered. Robert Overton was never formally tried. After about two years of close imprisonment in the Tower of London he was transported to Jersey, in order that - like John Lilburne - he could not be released under the issue of a writ of Habeas Corpus in the jurisdiction of the English law courts. He was confined in Elizabeth Castle, Jersey until March 1658. In 1654 he had written :-

"If I be called to seal the cause of God and my country with my blood, by suffering death, or by bearing any testimony to the interest of my nation and the despised truths of these times, He is able to support and save me, as the sun to shine upon me ..... If I can but keep faith and a good conscience, I shall assuredly finish my course with joy".[17]

In England Cromwell and his agents struck in the new year with quick and decisive ruthlessness. As S.R. Gardiner puts it :-

"Consequently the Government resolved to do its best to arrest the leaders of that party, of which Wildman and Sexby were the leading political agents, whilst Lord Grey of Groby was expected to stand forth as its military head".[18]

Of the three, Wildman was arrested by Major Boteler (or Butler), Lord Grey by Colonel Hacker, and Sexby managed to escape to the continent.

On 10th February 1655 John Wildman was seized in the very act, it was alleged, of writing - with the ink still wet - a rousing pamphlet against *"the tyrant Oliver Cromwell"*. The Leveller conspiracy was finished. But the hunt for their allies began.

Two days later Lord Grey of Groby was arrested at Bradgate by Colonel Francis Hacker on the Lord Protector's orders for his opposition to the Protectorate, his sympathy with the Levellers, and his adherence to the principle of the Commonwealth. This event was reported, in its context, the following month by Lorenzo Paulucci, the Venetian Secretary in England, to his colleague Giovanni Sagredo, the Venetian Ambassador in France :-

"To make absolutely certain of quiet at home and to establish his own arbitrary power the more securely, some leading men, who had retired some time since to live in the country and who are suspected of a share in this last conspiracy, have been suddenly arrested by order of the Protector. Chief amongst these is the eldest son of the Earl of Stamford, a man of noble birth, considerable following and high spirit, but very apt to stir up disorder and restlessness. To help himself and to dissipate evil humours he [the Lord Protector] recently had Maj. Gen. Harrison and other prisoners of account brought before him and examined about their objects and the charges against them.

They all repeated their denials and refused to give a fresh oath or pledge themselves to keep the peace. They were accordingly removed from the prisons here and sent separately under a strong escort of horse to distant places of great strength".[19]

The French writer, Guizot, noted that following the arrest of Robert Overton and then John Wildman :-

"Several other leaders of the Anabaptists and Levellers - Harrison, Carew, and Lord Grey of Groby - before they had engaged in any hostile undertaking, were arrested, dispersed and confined in various prisons, but no prosecution was initiated against them. When he had to deal with men of his old party, Cromwell's aim was to forestall and stifle their plans; to render them powerless, not to make them public victims".[20]

Colonel Francis Hacker, who appears to have had little compunction about acting against his fellow Leicestershireman and former commander, reported his arrest of Lord Grey to Cromwell in a letter dated 12th February :-

"May it please your Highness,

According to your command, I have seized the lord Grey and captain Bodell. I have alsoe [sic] *according to order seised* [sic] *3 horses and 5 case of pistols, being all the armes I could find, and those unfixed. My lord did informe mee, that 3 of his best horses was not yett come from Stamford, where a race was lately; but he expected them this night, and if I would send for them, they will bee forthcoming. The lord Grey is much distempered with the gout and was desirous to knowe, whither hee was to goe, which I concealed from him, and hee perceiving mee not willing to declare, said hee was willing to submitt to goe whither I pleased; but desires to come to London. I have not acquainted him, whither hee is to goe, but have presumed upon the advice and consent of those with mee, in regard of his indisposition of health, to let him rest at Leicester, where will bee three troopes for his guard, untill further order from your highness. I shall be carefull to gett what intelligence I can; but yet see noe appearance of danger, except by those called quakers, who will not bee persuaded to returne home, but sayes they stand in the counsell of the Lord, and not in the will of man. My lord, there is a chirurgeon in my lord Lambert's regiment, who writ to one*

417

Smith, who lives in Newarke, who had beene his mate, that the under officers of the army had a designe in hand; and if it tooke place, wee should see glorious tymes. And this man is a great favourer of the quakers, if not one. The truth of this will bee testified by honest men, who have seene the letter. I am,

Your highnes most humble servant,
FRANCIS HACKER"[21]

This letter is interesting in several respects. Not only does it reveal how the early Quakers were viewed as turbulent dissidents but shows that Captain Bodell, one of Lord Grey's longer serving captains, had stayed loyal to him, unlike Francis Hacker. It also gives the first indication of Lord Grey's ill health. Gout seems to have been a fairly common complaint; both the Earl of Stamford and Oliver Cromwell suffered from it too. It was a very painful condition, somewhat akin to arthritis, characterised by severe inflammation of the joints and a swelling of the toes, knees and fingers. It was a disease of which the physician Sir Theodore Mayerne was to quote the saying of his former master King Henry IV of France : *"Sometimes he had the gout and sometimes the gout had him"*. It was a condition which tended to become worse with advancing age and it is something of a surprise that at the comparatively young age of thirty two Thomas Grey was so `distempered with the gout' that Hacker was persuaded to allow him to stay at Leicester under guard until further orders were received from the Lord Protector.

According to the unsympathetic commentator Mark Noble :-

"The protector, however, did not chuse [sic] *to permit a man to remain a prisoner where he had been a governor; and therefore, notwithstanding the ill state of his health, ordered him to be brought up to Windsor Castle, where he came the 27th of the same month* [February]*; and we may suppose he entered it with different sentiments than he left it, after he had contrived the agreement of the people previous to the king's trial. How long he remained in prison, I have not seen; .....".*[22]

Thurloe and his agents claimed to have amassed evidence linking various conspirators to Wildman's plot. According to their notes the first meeting of the plotters had been held at the house of a Mr. Allen, a merchant in Birchen Lane, London in early September 1654. Those present included Wildman, Okey, Allured, Saunders, Lawson, and Hacker; the latter probably acting as a spy or agent-provocateur. The Petition had then been drawn up

418

by Wildman in November 1654 and passed to a Captain Bishop who had shown it to ex-Lord President John Bradshaw. Further meetings were held at the Blue Boar's Head Inn in King Street, at Wildman's own house, the Dolphin tavern in Tower Street, and even at Derby House in the Strand, the former base of the Committee of Both Kingdoms. Those alleged to have attended were *"Henry Marten, Lord Grey, Captain Bishop, Alexander Popham once, Anthony Peirson some tymes. The men they built upon was* [sic] *Sir G. Booth, Bradshaw, Haselrigg, G. Finwicke, Birch, Mosley, Wilmer, Pynne, Scott, F. Allen; and Peirson went with Haselrigg"*.[23]

At the same time it was claimed that a petition was devised for the City of London upon the advice of Bradshaw and that several met at his house, including Scot, Sir Arthur Haselrigg, Colonel Sankey, Ayers, and Weaver to agree how it should be circulated and used. Colonel Sankey was often at Bradshaw's house where he met Captain Bishop.

Robert Overton and John Wildman had allegedly spoken together *"before notice given of their dislike of things, but noe design laid therein concerning the situation of the English army in Scotland." "But after they were, he writt letters to lett them know that there was a party which would stand right for a commonwealth"*.[24] Following this it was claimed that Bradshaw had sent messages to them and that a meeting of army officers who were trusted was held. The regiments that were relied upon by the conspirators were Riche's, Tomlinson's, Okey's, Pride's, Allured's, Overton's, the garrison of Stirling Castle, and elements of *'the generall's regiments'*.

The plan was alleged to have been that the army in Scotland would mutiny and seize Edinburgh Castle. Overton would be obliged to take command. They also expected to take Berwick Castle at Berwick-on-Tweed. Amongst other areas where they expected support were Hull, through Overton's influence and support amongst the townsmen; *"Leicestershire, Grey and Captain Baliard"*; Bedfordshire through Okey and Whitehead, *"and great depending on Hacker"* [again]; Taunton, Bristol, Portsmouth, Hereford. In addition it was claimed that other participants included *"Harrison, Cary, King, Roberts, of the junto for the 5th monarchy"*.[25]

Evidence was taken from a Samuel Dyer, formerly a servant to Colonel Edward Sexby, later in February 1657 which related to the events of the 1655 plot. Dyer had fought in the English army in the Dunbar campaign. In 1653 he had entered into the service of Colonel Sexby with whom he went to France on state business for the Commonwealth. They had returned in August to a new political situation :-

"Colonel Sexby, upon return into England, not finding things answering his expectations, took party with Wildman and the

lord Gray of Grooby [sic], *and Saunders, and promised the said Samuel Dyer, if he would be faithful and secret, he would give him 500 l. (Sexby about 20 months ago, Sam. Dyer asking why he would be more for the Spaniard than for the English nation, he suspected him and flung him into prison* [in Ghent Castle in the Spanish Netherlands on 5th July 1656]*). At that time there was a design on foot to destroy his highness* [Lord Protector Cromwell]*, and to bring all into blood and confusion".*[(26)]

In his written deposition Dyer gave even more detailed information regarding Lord Grey of Groby's alleged involvement in the plot :-

"Soon after his highness was declared lord protector, there were divers meetings between the said colonel Sexby, major Wildman, capt. George Bishop, mr. Cockayne a minister, and capt. Lawson; as also lieut. Braham; and somewhat after that colonel Sexby sent down to Hartlerow a hamper of arms, together with several boxes of declarations, and papers subscribed by colonel Saunders, col. Allured and col. Okey : and this informant remembreth, and he said, Braham being sent for by colonel Sexby, took with him some quantities of the said declarations and petitions into Scotland, and capt. Bishop sent divers boxes of the said declarations and petitions to the Bristol carrier, to be sent into the [West] *country. That colonel Sexby went with this informant, and one William Randall (who was also his servant) to Hartlerow, to an inn, ... and there had a meeting with the said Braham, who carried divers of the said declarations and papers with him, and the rest colonel Sexby took with him into Warwickshire, and there at Warwick did distribute divers of those declarations and papers among many countrymen, who had a meeting there with him and a major and a cornet of the said company, belonging, as this informant was told, to colonel Saunders. From thence the said colonel Sexby went to Coventry, and from thence to the house of the Lord Gray of Grooby, with whom the said Sexby, Wildman, and divers others had formerly had divers meetings before at the said lord Gray's house* [Coombe Abbey]*; and by the lord Gray's direction, he delivered to the lord Gray's butler a great number of the said declarations and papers, which the said butler, together with colonel Sexby, carried into the county of Leicester, and there dispersed about 5,000 of them. Two days after they returned to the lord Gray's house, and from thence colonel Sexby came to Coventry, and*

from thence into Berkshire to the house of major Wildman's mother-in-law, where they sent his informant to the lord Gray's, with a packet of letters, which this informant delivered to the said lord Gray; who told this informant, that he should acquaint colonel Sexby, that what he the said lord Gray desired him he should be sure he would perform, for that the said lord Gray's Somersetshire friends would not fail him; and said these words, `I hope to have more than five thousand' [Anchitel Grey was active in the Taunton area]*: and that colonel Sexby told this informant, that the said lord Gray was to be head of this party. And further saith, that before the lord Gray gave this answer, colonel Sexby had been with Sir Arthur Haselrigg at Woodstock-lodge, and did communicate this answer to him; who made at first slight of the answer, but told him in the close, that he was loth to begin the business; but as soon as he saw the candle lighted, the bishopric of Durham and Newcastle* [where Haselrigg was a major figure] *should set it up.*[27]

Dyer recounted how, from Major Wildman's mother-in-law's in Berkshire, Colonel Sexby and his two servants went on to visit Bristol. Staying at a place ten miles outside the city Dyer was then sent into Bristol by Sexby to Captain Bishop's house. Bishop being absent, Dyer delivered letters - as per instruction - to a Major Clarke. Clarke then met with Sexby that evening. Next Sexby and his servants went to the house of a Lieutenant Braham at Alton in Hampshire. From here he sent Dyer to a Colonel Bishop to arrange a meeting with Major Wildman. From Alton they moved on to Mead in Sussex and met Wildman. Next they were at Deal meeting with Captain Lawson and others from the navy. Following this they returned to London where several people, some known to Dyer and some unknown, *"had meetings with the said major Wildman and colonel Sexby, from whom this informant carried several letters to capt. Lawson to his house at Tower hill, who was also present at several meetings with the said persons"* :-

"And there were several meetings had by the said Sexby and Wildman, and many other persons, at the house of one mr. Howe, a merchant in London, whither a gentleman, who waited on the lord Grey in his chambers, came often from the said Grey with letters to Sexby and Wildman. From thence colonel Sexby went to Brentford with major Wildman, having sent their horses thither before; and there this informant heard the said major Wildman say, `Shall such a tyrant live? (meaning the

lord protector): No, if there be (or might be) two Feltons [the assassin of the Duke of Buckingham] *to be found'. Thence the said Sexby and Wildman went into the country to major Wildman's mother-in-law's house, and sent this informant to London".*[28]

Shortly after this Wildman and Lord Grey had been arrested, Sexby had gone into hiding and then managed to escape to the continent.

Whilst Lord Grey of Groby was imprisoned at Windsor Castle there were no moves to bring him to trial. Whatever the truth of the 'evidence' provided by Thurloe's informants there is no doubt that Lord Grey was opposed in principle to the Protectoral regime. For him, as for many of his republican colleagues from the disbanded Rump Parliament, opposition to Cromwell had become something of a personal creed and crusade.

What Burnett says of Algernon Sidney is equally true of Lord Grey of Groby :-

"..... he was stiff to all republican principles, and such an enemy to every thing that looked like monarchy, that he set himself in high opposition against Cromwell when he was made Protector".[29]

Similarly as with John Wildman :-

"he was a great commonwealthman, and both Sidney and he had appeared very resolutely against Cromwell when he began to set up for himself".[30]

Lord Grey of Groby wrote from his confinement in Windsor Castle to Cromwell during the summer of 1655 :-

"A letter from Lord Grey of Groby, dated Windsor Castle, July 7th, to his Highness, read".[31]

It is not clear what the letter contained but it evidently had some effect as 'Mercurius Politicus' reported in its news from Whitehall on July 26th that :-

"It was certified from Windsor, that the Lord Grey of Groby, upon application made to his Highness, hath been set at liberty from the Castle. His Highness this afternoon retired to Hampton Court".[32]

Though he had regained his liberty after just six months in detention Lord Grey still found it difficult to accept his reduced political role. His support continued to be sought by radical groups opposed to the Protectorate, such as the Levellers and the Fifth Monarchy Men.

The royalists in exile on the continent took a close interest in these radical plots, hoping to harness them to their own ends, perhaps backed by Spanish gold. At about the time of Lord Grey's release from Windsor Castle Father Peter Talbot, a Jesuit and brother of the royalist Colonel Talbot, was acting as an interpreter for the Prince of Condé and the Count of Fuenseldagna in their negotiations with Colonel Sexby in Brussels. On 28th July Father Talbot wrote to Charles II at the royal court in exile to report on the level of support in England for Sexby and his connections :-

"After a little time he received many letters from friends in England, remitting themselves to all that he might agree on; among others, Lord Grey of Grooby, Wildman, Allen and some Anabaptists are sure to him, above fifteen colonels, a great part of the navy and some sea-ports; he does not trust Harrison".[33]

There was no direct connection between the politics of Sexby, the erstwhile Leveller, and Thomas Harrison, the Fifth Monarchist, and they distrusted each other, having differing aims. They were united only in their opposition to Cromwell. Lord Grey of Groby was a common link between them as were also John Bradshaw, Sir Arthur Hesilrigg, Algernon Sidney, Henry Marten and Edmund Ludlow - all republican Commonwealthmen. Before the start of the first civil war, according to Ludlow, Henry Marten had informed Edward Hyde, later the Earl of Clarendon, that *"I do not think one man wise enough to govern us all"*. What had applied to Charles Stuart in 1642 applied also to Oliver Cromwell in 1655 and 1656.

Although Lord Grey of Groby's family may have preferred him to devote his attention to them and his estates it is by no means clear that this was a real option for him. He was subject to close scrutiny by Cromwell's security agents who seem to have been eager to find another pretext for moving against him. Abstention from any form of political activity was no guarantee of safety, as the case of John Hutchinson illustrates.

Colonel Hutchinson had retired to country life in south Nottinghamshire at Owthorp and refused invitations by Cromwell to participate in the government of the Protectorate :-

"But", *says he* [Cromwell], *"dear colonel, why will you not come in and act among us?" The colonel told him plainly, because*

423

he liked not any of his ways since he broke up the parliament,
being those which would lead to certain and unavoidable
destruction, not only of themselves, but of the whole parliament
party and cause; ..... "[34]

He was about to be arrested on Cromwell's orders when he was saved by the Protector's death in September 1658 :-

"..... he [Hutchinson] was informed, that notwithstanding all
these fair shows, the Protector, finding him too constant to be
wrought upon to serve his tyranny, had resolved to secure his
person, lest he should lead the people, who now grew weary of
his bondage. But though it was certainly confirmed to the
colonel how much he was afraid of his honesty and freedom,
and that he was resolved not to let him be any longer at liberty,
yet before his guards apprehended the colonel, death imprisoned
himself, and confined all his vast ambition and all his cruel
designs into the narrow compass of a grave".[35]

To his republican opponents during the Protectorate Cromwell seemed a hypocrite whose *"cloak is so threadbare that he has nothing left to cover his knavery"* and that *"the king lost his head for raising a little ship-money, but now things are ten times worse".*

In January 1656 a committee of the Protectoral Council of State which had been established to consider several petitions for exemption from delinquency penalties was asked to examine a declaration of what Lord Grey of Groby had *"acted upon Henry Neville to make him a delinquent, and to report"*.[36] Henry Neville was another Commonwealthman and an associate of Algernon Sidney.

It is more likely that Sidney rather than Grey of Groby influenced Neville's attitudes. As recently as 1653 Algernon Sidney had still not split with his brother Lord Lisle, despite the latter's loyalty to the new regime. By 1656, however, the breach was overt. During this year Algernon Sidney appeared in a performance of 'Julius Caesar' at his country house at Penshurst in Kent. He played the part of the good republican Brutus. It was clear that Caesar was meant to be Cromwell. This performance received much publicity of which Lord Lisle complained to their father the Earl of Leicester.[37] What makes the suggestion of such a miming of tyrannicide at this time more interesting is the political context of 1656. This year saw a renewed republican campaign against Cromwell's government. Amongst other examples Sexby and Titus published 'Killing Noe Murder' in which tyrannicide was recommended. These works shared associations of personnel amongst ex-Rumpers such as Henry Vane, Henry Neville, and Lord Grey of Groby, and linked radicals and republicans in, or attached to the army, like Colonel Edward Sexby, Major John Wildman, and Captain Titus.

Many of these republicans, such as Lord Grey of Groby, Algernon Sidney, and Edmund Ludlow had refused to give an assurance that they would abstain from actions against the Protectorate. The latter had been summoned back from Ireland in 1654 and forced to give up his command there. Despite a period of detention in North Wales he remained true to his convictions. A royalist officer, writing on the continent in a letter dated 10th January 1656 related :-

> *"I hear from England that ..... Ludlow, after his close imprisonment at Beaumaris, was brought before Council on the charge of not acknowledging the present power; he refuses to give bond to be faithful to it, yet he is set at liberty, and has leave to go around the country, to ensnare him (as is believed). When Cromwell, lest he should disturb him during his absence in Scotland,* [had] *made him his Lieutenant-General of the Irish Horse* [in 1650] *, a friend called to congratulate him, when his reply was that `he must needs go when the devil drives'; so you see the jealousy between them".*[38]

In the spring of 1656 Lord Grey of Groby was implicated in a conspiracy with the Fifth Monarchists against Cromwell which was known as the Shoreditch Plot. Guizot gives the following account of 'Venner's Rising' which was a manifestation of the Shoreditch Plot :-

> *"On the 9th of April, a score of them* [Fifth Monarchists], *under the command of Thomas Venner, a wine cooper, met at Shoreditch, `booted and spurred', ... to proceed from thence to a general place of rendezvous; but a squadron of cavalry occupied the ground before them, and took them all prisoners. In a field near the place appointed for the general meeting, the soldiers found a large supply of arms, a quantity of pamphlets intended for distribution, and a standard bearing a red lion couchant, with this motto, `Who shall rouse him up?"* [the ensign of the conquering lion of the tribe of Judah].

> *Some men of greater importance, such as Vice-Admiral Lawson* [recently promoted from Captain], *Colonels Okey and Danvers, Major-General Harrison, Colonel Rich* [and Lord Grey of

Groby] *who had been recently liberated from imprisonment, were compromised, either by their own acts, or by the words of these sectaries, and were also arrested.*

Two days later Thurloe, by Cromwell's command, gave an account to Parliament of the plot, giving full details of the secret organisation of these sectaries, and their relations with all the disaffected politicians of the day". [39]

There seems little evidence that Lord Grey was directly involved in the details of the failed coup, or that he was himself a Fifth Monarchist, but had rather been envisaged as an acceptable figurehead of the new order until the actual arrival of King Jesus. The connection, however tenuous, was convenient for Cromwell and Lord Grey of Groby was imprisoned once more at Windsor Castle. This time his freedom was only to be obtained by the payment of a large sum of money paid as an alternative to his guarantee of future political acquiescence :-

"[Colonel] Sexby, who had become the most active of levelling conspirators, was pursued, but made his escape to France. Lord Grey of Groby, son of the Earl of Stamford, but an extreme democrat, was imprisoned at Windsor until he made his submission". [40]

Edmund Ludlow, who appears to have had a high regard for Lord Grey's principles and conduct, attributes his arrest more to an alleged association with the distribution of leaflets and pamphlets rather than to his intending to head an armed insurrection. He also respects Thomas Grey's preference, like himself, to forfeit a monetary fine rather than to parole his honour by accepting the Protectorate :-

"It having being discovered that the lord Grey of Grooby had given to a person a copy of the momento which I [Ludlow] *had before dispersed in Ireland, he was sent for to London, and committed prisoner to Windsor-castle for the same. The next term he sued for a habeas corpus, which the chief justice, according to the law, granted him, but the governor of Windsor castle refused to give obedience to the order of the court, and so rendered it ineffectual to him, insomuch that he could not obtain his liberty till he had given a pecuniary security not to act against the government, which he chose to do rather than to engage his parole, thereby hazarding only the loss of so much money, and preserving his honour and integrity.*

426

Colonel Sexby was also suspected to have had a hand in the dispersion of the petitions and momentos before-mentioned; and thereupon was sent for in order to be secured, which he having notice of, fled, but was pursued so close, that his man was taken with his portmanteau. ..... "[41]

The virulently hostile Mark Noble recounts his version of this period in Lord Grey of Groby's life in typically exaggerated and censorious manner :-

"..... he obtained his liberty [after the first period of imprisonment at Windsor Castle], *yet sunk into the most wretched state of contempt.*

"As a proof of this, it is sufficient to remark, that all parties, but the most despicable, viewed him with scorn; and his reputation was at so low an ebb, that he could not get the confidence of any but those wretched fanatics, the fifth monarchy-men, at the head of whom was Major-General Harrison. So fallen was this haughty, turbulent, and traitorous man, becoming the derision and contempt of all sober and rational people. The projects of these despicable persons were long carried on, and, as they weakly imagined, with the utmost secrecy; the scheme was to destroy the protector, seize Monck in Scotland, and erect the kingdom of Christ. Grey was to be at the head; Colonel Sexby, as less suspected, they supposed, than Harrison, was made the active mover of the plot. Their chief cabal was held in a house near Shoreditch, where they had agreed to print vast numbers of declarations against the protector's government; five thousand of them were to be sent into Leicestershire, where his lordship's chief interest lay; and Heselrigge, and other disaffected persons of various religious principles, were invited to join them. What raised their consequence, and made them more dangerous was, that the Spanish court was persuaded, that money lent to these fifth monarchy-men would be better employed than if advanced to the cavaliers, as more desperate, and better calculated to the temper of those who hated Oliver's person and government.

"Thurloe, to whom as secretary nothing was unknown, soon came to the information, which detected all these schemes which Grey was carrying on with his despicable associates; but he did

not interrupt them until the very evening preceding the day they meant to declare themselves; when, sending a party of soldiers, they seized the chiefs, Lord Grey, Venner, Gowler, Hopkins, Ashton, and others with all their apparatus ready prepared. Amongst these, the principle object that arrested their notice was a standard with a lion depicted upon it, in a couchant posture, as of the tribe of Judah, with this motto : `Who shall rouse him up?' There were numberless copies of these printed declarations, beginning with `The principle of the remanent', & c. suitable to the wild visionary ideas of these expectants of seating Christ in the temporal as well as spiritual government of these nations. None can think that Grey had the least opinion of the possibility of establishing such a monarchy; he only guided a silly multitude to perform what he alone believed he should obtain the advantage of - wealth and power.

"He was sent to his former apartments at Windsor. Ludlow affects to suppose that his imprisonment was solely owing to a copy of the `Momento' he had dispersed in Ireland; but Thurloe's State Papers give us better information. By the same mode of reasoning, the former gentleman imagines that Sexby's disgrace was from the same cause; he, however, escaped a prison by a timely retreat; and that so hastily, that his servant, who was conveying away his portmantua [sic], was seized. The protector, pretending to pass over the misconduct of Sexby, sent him as an agent to Bourdeaux [sic], in France; but took care to dispatch a messenger to that government, to say how much he wished him secured. Sexby, suspicious, obtained information of his intention, and, effecting his escape over the city gate in the night, left that kingdom and no more trusted to Oliver's insidious protestations".[(42)]

So Thomas, Lord Grey of Groby found himself imprisoned at Windsor Castle for a second time. He was accompanied by his servants Humphrey Mawson and Richard Massey. Again he managed to secure his release by the summer of the year. According to Noble's polemical account :-

"Lord Grey determined, if possible, to regain his liberty: to accomplish this most desirable event, he sued for a [writ of] habeas corpus, which the lord chief justice granted; but the governor of Windsor Castle refused to give obedience to it; nor did he obtain his freedom until he had given security, in the

428

penalty of a large sum of money, if he ever again acted against the government; 'which he chose', says Mr. Ludlow, 'to do, rather than engage his parole, thereby hazarding only the loss of so much money, and preserving his honour and integrity', but as perhaps Oliver thought he had neither of those valuable properties, he took what was much better, a pecuniary security; the loss of wealth being, he was convinced, the greatest evil that Grey thought he could suffer.

"The other conspirators [i.e. Venner and the Fifth Monarchists] *were sent prisoners to the Gate-house, where they lay long in a miserable sitution ..... "*[(43)]

Lord Grey's release and return home to his family was celebrated by the conception of a fourth child, Dorothy's pregnancy being remarked upon early in the following year. Yet he had still not lost interest in politics. The need for the calling of a second Protectoral Parliament began to be discussed in the summer of 1656.

In January 1655 Cromwell had dismissed his 1654 Parliament after informing them that their presence was no longer for *"the profit of these nations, nor for the common and public good"*. October of that year had seen the introduction of administration through ten - later eleven -districts in England and Wales by Major-Generals. Major General Whalley was in charge of a district that covered Leicestershire, Nottinghamshire, Warwickshire, Staffordshire and Lincolnshire. These were primarily military and taxing regimes and were consequently very unpopular. Lucy Hutchinson described the Major-Generals as *"silly mean fellows"*. The population at large, who were just beginning to appreciate the stability afforded by the Protectorate, strongly resented the change to restrictive military dominated rule in the localities. By the summer of 1656 the system of Major-Generals had come to represent an experimental attempt to rule the country without Parliament that had not only proved extremely unpopular but had left Cromwell in a situation where he now had to resort to a Parliament in order to raise more money - a situation not dissimilar to Charles I in 1640 and 1642.

Writs were issued on 20th August for elections to a Parliament to meet on 17th September 1656. It was expected that the Major-Generals would ensure that a suitably meek Parliament would be returned which would, this time, meet the Lord Protector's expectations. Overall the Major-Generals did not succeed in maintaining a successful electoral stranglehold. In general the results reflected growing local resistance to the increased centralisation of government and showed the returning power of the great country magnates. Only eight of the returned members had taken part in the 'Barebones' Parliament; two hundred and thirty had sat in the 1654 Parliament; and one hundred and eighty had never before sat in any Parliament.

Lord Grey of Groby stood again as a candidate for MP for the Borough of Leicester. In this *"free and open choice of Burgesses to serve in Parliament for this Burrough ..... made according to the Constitucions of this Commonwealth of England by vertue of a certaine Precept in that behalfe in manner and forme"* (i.e. not a secret ballot) the fifty-nine voting burgesses each cast two votes for their preferred two candidates. It was made known by Major-General Whalley that the Lord Protector did not favour the Lord Grey's candidature. The results were as follows: Sir Arthur Hesilrigg 53 votes; William Stanley 42 votes; Lord Grey of Groby 22 votes; and James Winstanley [a relative newcomer from Lancashire] 1 vote. Lord Grey was, therefore, not elected.

It may seem perverse that, whilst the radical Lord Grey was not acceptable to the regime, the equally republican politician Sir Arthur Hesilrigg was allowed to top the poll. This was not the full story, however, as will shortly be seen.

The mixture of successful parliamentary candidates was not considered sufficiently satisfactory by the Council of the Protectorate until they had exercised the right given to them by the 'Instrument of Government' to approve the choice of members. As a result tickets were prepared by the Clerk of the Commonwealth in Chancery, after the indentures had been scrutinized for each member. Any member lacking *"a certain ticket"* to present at the door of the House of Commons was *"kept out by the soldiers"*. In this manner it seems that about one hundred and twenty elected members were excluded. The Second Parliament of the Protectorate had not got off to a very promising start.

William Stanley, one of the newly elected MPs for the Borough of Leicester, wrote back to his electors and fellow burgesses on 23rd September, 1656 as follows :-

> *"Sirs; I suppose it is not unknowne to you that many worthy members returned from severall places were stopt from entering into the house, they having noe Ticketts appointed them, by the Counsell, of which Number our Noble Burgess, and friend, Sir Arthur Hessilrigg were one, hee goeing forth of the Towne this daye, injoyned mee to present his service and thancks to you, and the Corporacion, for there [sic] great love towards him".*[44]

Lord Grey of Groby's health seems to have deteriorated rapidly between the autumn of 1656 and the spring of 1657. He was sufficiently concerned to have a will drawn up and signed on 4th April 1657. In this he made provision for Dorothy, who was with child, and his children Thomas, Elizabeth and Anne.

During the period of his acute illness momentous events were taking place at Westminster and Whitehall. On 26th March the Protectoral Parliament had offered to Oliver Cromwell by a majority vote (124 to 62) a petition *"requesting the Protector to exercise the name, style, and office of King of England, Scotland, and Ireland"*. Cromwell took a long time over deciding whether to accept the crown and title of king. Finally, on Friday, 8th May, the Protector met the representatives of Parliament in the Painted Chamber, where he and Lord Grey and others of the Commissioners of the High Court had met during the king's trial in 1649, to give his answer. It was, in short, *"I say I am persuaded to return this answer to you, that I cannot undertake this Government with that title of King. And that's my answer to this great weighty business"*.[45]

On that same day, 8th May, 1657, Lord Thomas Grey of Groby's will was produced at London before the Judges for Probate of Wills. He had died some days earlier, very probably of the gout, aged thirty four years :-

> *"I have fought a good fight,*
> *I have finished my course,*
> *I have kept the faith".*
> **(2 Timothy, Chapt. 4 v. 7)**

NOTES

1. S.R. Gardiner, *History of the Commonwealth and Protectorate*. Vol. II. p. 264 n.I., 1903.
2. Edmund Ludlow, *Memorials of Edmund Ludlow*, ed. C. H. Firth. Vol. I. p. 357, 1894.
3. Lucy Hutchinson, *Memoirs of Colonel Hutchinson*, pp. 287-8.
4. Ibid. p. 291.
5. Calendar of State Papers (Domestic), Vol. XXXVII. (18).
6. Ibid. Vol. XXXVIII. p. 53 (4).
7. Lucy Hutchinson, op. cit. pp. 293-4.
8. Ibid. pp. 291-3.
9. Ibid. pp. 385-6.
10. Mark Noble, *The Lives of the English Regicides*. pp. 269-270.
11. Edmund Ludlow, op. cit. p. 211.
12. Calendar of State Papers (Domestic), Vol. LXXIV; p. 316. (100).
13. S.R. Gardiner, *History of the Commonwealth and Protectorate*, Vol. III, 1654-1656 Longmans, Green & Co., London. 1901. p. 20.
14. Ibid. p. 70.
15. Antonia Fraser, *Cromwell: Our Chief of Men*. Granada Publishing 1977. p. 518.
16. Edmund Ludlow, op. cit. p. 223.
17. Thurloe Papers, iii, 47.
18. S.R. Gardiner, op. cit. p. 118.
19. Calendar of State Papers (Venetian), 1655-56, p. 31. Letter dated March 15th 1655 from Lorenzo Paulucci, Venetian Secretary in England to Giovanni Sagredo, the Venetian Ambassador in France. S42.
20. Guizot, *Cromwell and the English Commonwealth*. Vol. II. 2nd Edition, Richard Bentley, London. 1854. p. 129.
21. Letter from Colonel Francis Hacker to the Lord Protector, Oliver Cromwell - February 12th, 1655. Thurloe State Papers.
22. Mark Noble, op. cit. p. 271.
23. *"Thurloe State Papers"*. pp. 147, 148. - `Notes of Major Wildman's plot by Secretary Thurloe.*
24. Ibid.
25. Ibid.
26. Thurloe State Papers. p. 832. - *The Examination of Mr. S. Dyer*.
27. Thurloe State Papers. p. 829. - *The information of Samuel Dyer, late servant to colonel Edward Sexby, taken this 27th of February 1657.*

28. Ibid. p. 830.
29. G. Burnett, *History of My Own Time* (1823), Vol. II. p. 341. cited in Jonathan Scott, *Algernon Sidney and the English Republic*, Cambridge University Press, 1988. p. 113.
30. Ibid.
31. Calendar of State Papers (Domestic), 1655. (52). p. 241.
32. *Mercurius Politicus*, 1655. p. 5514. (Cornmarket Press edition. 1871. - The English Revolution III, Newsbooks 5. Vol. II.)
33. Calendar of the Clarendon State Papers in the Bodleian Library, Oxford. Vol. III, 1955-57. W. Dunn Macray. Oxford. p. 51. (144) Bussein, July 28. [1655].
34. Lucy Hutchinson, op. cit. p. 298.
35. Ibid. p. 299.
36. Calendar of State Papers (Domestic), 1656. Council. (25) 8 Jan.
37. HMC De Lisle MSS. Vol. VI. 17 June 1656. p. 400.
    Letter from Lord Lisle to the Earl of Leicester.
38. Calendar of State Papers (Domestic), 1655-56 Preface.
39. Guizot, op. cit. p. 307.
40. F.C. Montague, *The Political History of England, 1603-1660*, Longmans, Green & Co. (London), 1907. p. 428.
41. Edmund Ludlow, op. cit. p. 224.
42. Mark Noble, op. cit. pp. 271-274.
43. Ibid. p. 274.
44. Record of the Borough of Leicester. Hall Papers XIV, No. 213. Sept. 23, 1656.
45. Mercurius Politicus, 7th May 1657, Abbot, IV, p. 512

Arms of the Cromwellian Protectorate, which resembled the heraldic achievement of a Tudor monarch.

Cromwell's dissolution of the Rump of the Long Parliament,
20th April 1653

OLIVARIVS PRIMVS

Lord Protector Oliver I

435

Edmund Ludlow

436

CHAPTER THIRTEEN

EPILOGUE (1657 - 1667)

"So he passed over, and the trumpets sounded for him on the other side".
(John Bunyan, 'Pilgrim's Progress' - of Mr. Valiant-for-Truth)

The unsympathetic Mark Noble refers to Lord Grey of Groby's passing from this world in the following vitriolic manner :-

"Happily for Lord Grey, and for the noble family from whence he derived his descent, he fell a victim to his own defeated wickedness, which, with the gout, brought to a vast height by the violence of his passions, put a period to his existence in this world, just preceding the restoration [of the Stuart monarchy], *or he would have been held up to the infamy he seemed desirous of aspiring to, by so many, and such atrocious crimes : it is not possible to draw from history a more infamous, or a more detestable character. I have consulted all our best peerages, to find the exact time of Lord Grey's death, and the place of his interment, but they are all silent respecting these circumstances".*[1]

Lord Grey's will, which was presented for probate on the 8th May contained the following terms :-

"Will of Thomas, Lord Grey of Grooby
Made out on 4th day of April [1657]

"viz. IN THE NAME OF GOD AMEN: -
this fourth day of April in the year of our Lord God one thousand six hundred, fifty and seven.

Thomas, Lord Grey of Grooby being not hale in body but in perfect memorie (praised be Almighty God) for the sharing and disposing of the estate which it hath pleased God to bestowe upon me do I make this my last will and testament - etc.
"[Incls]
[To be sold] thro' the Executors and Overseers of this my Will my Mannor of Broughton Astley (and all the lands thereunto,

437

Broughton Astley, Sutton, Elmsthorpe, and Bromkinsthorpe and any of them) in the County of Leicester the profit and interest from the sale to be used thus. The sale of lands and goods thereof for the raising of [marriage] portions for my daughters. And my will is that the money so raised shall be equally divided share and share alike among my daughters towards their portions and to be paid to them at their several days of marriage or age of one and twentieth year which shall first happen (if one or more shall die before this happens it shall go to the survivor(s)).

"And if it shall please God that the child which my dear wife is big withall be a daughter, then my will is that she shall have an equal share and a portion in the moneys to be raised by the sale, etc. of the said Mannor, with the other sisters.

"From the profits of all and singular other mannors, lands, etc. of which I am this day seized for during the life of my dear wife - two annual payments at Michaelmas and Lady Day by equal portions - the sum of one thousand pounds of lawful money of England in full satisfaction of her portion and dowry.
"This my will is that if my said dear wife shall depart this life before my sonne and heir shall accomplish the age of one and twenty years that my executors shall oversee my estate and may take this will as authority for this. A profile of all and singular my Mannors and lands shall be kept and be given to him and for him. Saving only the payments to my dear wife and my daughters.

"And my will is that when my said sonne and heir shall accomplish the age of one and twenty years my steward and the executors shall be answerable to him for all the income from my estate and the surplus (if any shall be).
"My will further is that if it please God that the child with which my dear wife is big with child be a sonne then my will is - and I do hereby give to the said sonne and his sustenance - for a boy Five Hundred Pounds per annum in lands.

"My said sonne (& heir) to be able to dispose of the mannors and lands as he sees fit upon his inheritance.

"To my dear wife I give a full third part of all my household stuffs and a third of all proceeds after sale.

438

"My Executor is to take sufficient whatsoever for and towards the payment of my debts and legacies and satisfy my funeral expenses. And that after my debts and legacies are paid to satisfaction the residue of the money made from my personal estate shall be put towards the raising of the four thousand pounds a year for my daughters.

"To my servants Humphrey Mawson and Richard Massey Twenty Pounds a year apiece for their faithful service to me when I was in prison at Windsor Castle.

"[unclear] pounds a year to my steward for his employment in this business. I do ordain and appoint my well beloved friend and cousin Henry Grey of Enfield [Enville] in the county of Stafford, Esquire and Thomas Wayte of Market Overton in the County of Rutland, Esquire as executors and guardians until my children shall accomplish the age of one and twenty years (and the guardians and executors shall have £200 p. a. each). They shall make an account in writing of this and all that they do.

Signed.
Tho. Grey
Lord Grey of Grooby

Witnesses Signed. Hen. Grey. Tho. Wayte. "[2]

As Noble observed there is no surviving record of the exact time of Lord Grey's death or the place of his interment. The former is likely to have been during the first days of May and at either Coombe Abbey or Bradgate.[3] The place of his interment is likely to have been in the family vault at the chapel at Bradgate or, if he had died in London, in the cemetery favoured by radical puritans at Bunhill Fields Burial Ground off the City Road. There were good political reasons, especially after the restoration of the Stuart monarchy just three years later, for not publicising the last resting place of a leading regicide.

Lady Dorothy Grey, who was aged thirty at the time of her husband's death, seems to have lost the child she was carrying at the time the will was written. There is no record of any addition to Lord Grey's progeny. The young widow was left with three children, Thomas, Elizabeth, and Anne to care for. Her eldest daughter was aged ten and her son was aged approximately four. Losing both her husband and her fourth child must have been very distressing for her.

She was not alone for long, however, as she swiftly married for a second time. Her new husband was Gustavus Mackworth of Normanton Park in Rutland by whom she had two children within two years. The first child was a son, Bourchier Mackworth, and the second child was a daughter, Mary Mackworth. Gustavus Mackworth was the nephew of Sir George Booth, her first husband's brother-in-law.

Whilst Lady Dorothy was re-establishing her position the head of state was doing a similar thing at national level. Oliver Cromwell had declined the title of king on 8th May 1657. When he did so he pronounced against the title and also the House of Stuart. *"I would not seek to set up that that providence hath destroyed and laid in the dust ..... and I would not build Jericho again"*. Despite his refusal of the royal title, however, parliament decided by a narrow majority to accept the proposed new constitution in which it would have fitted, but without changing his title. Accordingly, he was solemnly reinstalled as Lord Protector on 26th June 1657.

The new constitution included a second chamber to assist the Lord Protector in keeping the House of Commons in check. When the latter reassembled in January 1658 the formerly excluded republicans and radicals returned in strength and attacked the new other House where many of Cromwell's ablest supporters now sat. The Lord Protector hastily dissolved the parliament after only a fortnight. The regime had some successes domestically and on the continent in both military and diplomatic terms. Cromwell's health began to fail, however, and on 3rd September, the anniversary of his victories at Dunbar and Worcester, he died.

He was succeeded at first by his eldest surviving son, Richard Cromwell, as the new Lord Protector. Richard did not have the same qualities as his father, however, and he lacked standing with the army. He was basically an ordinary, decent country squire. The nature of his government antagonised the army and the more radical Independents. These differences were smoothed over until a new parliament met in January 1659. The republicans reappeared in some strength. They could no longer be excluded as MPs had re-established the principle and practice that only a majority vote of the Commons could bar the entry of elected members. The republicans now attempted to mobilise opposition to the whole Protectoral constitution. For the time being they failed. The majority of the country gentry who constituted the bulk of the membership of the House of Commons still supported Richard Cromwell as Lord Protector and the Other House as an integral part of parliament; indeed the Commons now wanted to make the latter more like the House of Lords by bringing back the former parliamentarian peers.

Having been repeatedly defeated in divisions of the House of Commons the republicans turned to sowing discontent in the army and the radical

440

sects. From the winter through to the spring a campaign of pamphlets and sermons spread the message that 'the Good Old Cause' was being betrayed. This rather vague notion of 'the Good Old Cause' evoked a powerful nostalgia for a largely mythical time when all elements of the parliamentarian side in the first Civil War had been united in their purpose. Many in the army felt that the high hopes and ideals of the period had not been realised and that a gulf had opened up between themselves and the military grandees who sat on the Protectoral Council and in the Other House. The Protectorate was portrayed as a betrayal, under which the country would be led back into the old monarchical tyranny. It was a view with which Thomas, Lord Grey of Groby would have identified. The republicans appealed to all radical puritans by claiming that the Lord God had withdrawn his blessing from England since her leaders had taken to pursuing power rather than godly reformation. To the millenarians, such as the Fifth Monarchy Men in particular the current regime was seen as an embodiment of the Beast from the Book of Revelations blocking the road to the earthly kingdom of Christ.

The rift in the Protectoral Council widened as senior army leaders such as Fleetwood and Desborough showed some sympathy with the attitude of the junior and middle ranking officers. Consequently Richard Cromwell looked more and more to his civilian advisers and relatives for advice. Amongst these were Lord Broghill, Lord Fauconberg, William Pierrepont, and Oliver St. John - the latter being also Dorothy's uncle. The military grandees resented the decline in their political influence at the Protectoral Court and began to develop links with the leading republicans such as Sir Arthur Hesilrigg and Sir Henry Vane who, with the former grandee John Lambert as their ally, were attacking the Protectorate in parliament.

The army leaders forced Richard Cromwell into letting them revive the General Council of Officers. Once it was re-established it came into conflict with the Protectoral parliament. When the latter attempted to dissolve the General Council of Officers Fleetwood and Desborough carried out a military coup d'état which forced the Lord Protector to dissolve the parliament instead on 22nd April. They had intended to keep him as a puppet Protector with themselves pulling the strings. The majority of their own officers, especially the junior ones, had developed such a strong objection to the Protectorate, however, particularly since the death of Oliver Cromwell, that they wanted it abolished and the Rump Parliament re-established. The propagandists had succeeded in identifying 'the Good Old Cause' with the good old parliament. The Rump Parliament resumed the supreme authority of the state on 7th May 1659.

The leaders of the Rump Parliament had never recognized the authority of the Protectorate and accordingly Richard Cromwell resigned the title of

Lord Protector. He fled to the continent whilst his family moved to the estate of his wife's parents at Hursley, near Winchester in Hampshire. Here 'Tumbledown Dick', as he was rather unfairly called, was to spend the last years of his life, as a country squire, peacefully abstaining from participation in national politics.

The 'good old parliament' refused to grant any significant concessions to the army that had restored it, abolishing the Other House, and even whittling away the authority it had originally and rather grudgingly conceded to Fleetwood as the commander-in-chief of the army. It was only the threat of another imminent royalist rising in the summer of 1659 that kept the restored Rump Parliament and the army from quarrelling openly.

John Hutchinson was one of the returned members and, as his wife records :-

"Now the parliament were sat and were no sooner assembled but they were invaded by several enemies. The presbyterians had long since espoused the royal interest, and forsaken God and the people's cause, when they could not obtain the reins of government in their own hands, and exercise dominion over all their brethren. It was treason, by the law of those men in power, to talk of restoring the king; therefore the presbyterians must face the design, and accordingly all the members ejected in 1648, now came to claim their seats in the house, whom Colonel Pride, that then guarded the parliament, turned back, and thereupon there was some heat in the lobby between them and the other members. Particularly Sir George Booth uttered some threats, and immediately they went into their several counties, and had laid a design all over England, wherein all the royalists were engaged, and many of the old parliament officers; and this was so dexterously, secretly, and unanimously carried on, that before the parliament had the least intimation of it, the flame was everywhere kindled, and small parties attempting insurrections in all places; but their main strength was with Sir George Booth in Cheshire, who there appeared the chief head of the rebellion".[4]

This rising was known as Booth's Rebellion. It will be recalled that Sir George Booth was the husband of Lord Grey of Groby's sister, Elizabeth, and was the man who had written to his brother-in-law in April 1645 to warn him of the weak and exposed state of Leicester's defences to potential royalist attack. After the restoration of the Stuart monarchy in less than a year's time he would be created Lord Delamere.

The rising was timed for 1st August, but caution amongst the cavaliers, given the failure of previous attempts, combined with good counter-intelligence by the Commonwealth's forces, confined the main activity to the area of Cheshire and south Lancashire. Here Sir George Booth managed to muster a few thousand men under arms. Smaller risings occurred elsewhere, particularly in the Midlands. Lambert was appointed by the parliament to lead their forces north against the rebels :-

> *"..... Lambert went forth, and through the cowardice of the enemy obtained a very cheap victory, and returned".*[5]

Booth's followers were routed and the local population helped to round up the fugitives. Although a real attempt had been made to ally royalists and political presbyterians, such as Sir George Booth, in the enterprise the support for it was meagre and half-hearted. Amongst those slain was Gustavus Mackworth who had joined Booth's rising and was killed near Northwich in Cheshire.

In the Midlands there were some outbreaks in support of Booth. A Colonel White from Nottingham seized control of Derby for a short time, but the Derbyshire cavaliers were surprised by White's appearance and did little to help even though Booth had already been in arms for nearly a fortnight. On 12th August one of Lambert's officers, Colonel Mitchell, rode into Derby to warn the rebels of the consequences of *"their base ingratitude to the Parliament, under whom they had such opportunities of gaining estates"*. Mitchell then withdrew to Uttoxeter, and on the following Sunday, assisted by parties of horse from Leicester and Nottingham, entered Derby. There was no resistance and Mitchell's men were feasted by the magistrates who joined in proclaiming Booth and his adherents as traitors to the state. White and his followers found themselves stranded on the losing side.

Lord Byron had raised the Nottinghamshire cavaliers. Some of these had followed White to Derby but others had gone south into Leicestershire where there were two minor incidents which are worthy of mention. Firstly, there was a rumour that Belvoir Castle had been taken by the royalists. Parliamentary troops hurried to the rescue from various directions and, near Melton Mowbray, some of them collided in the darkness. Mistaking each other for cavaliers they blazed away at each other with their pistols and carbines for a few hectic minutes.

The other incident is related as follows by David Underdown in 'Royalist Conspiracy' :-

> **"A detachment collecting horses for the militia called at Bradgate, the house of the Presbyterian Earl of Stamford,**

who happens to have been Booth's father-in-law and whose
son, Anchitel Grey, later a notable parliamentary reporter,
had been involved in the business at Derby. The house was
full of arms, and there were about thirty horses in the stables;
armed men were also conspicuous - some of them, it was
believed, fugitives from Nottingham. One of Ingoldsby's
officers, Major Thomas Babington, invited the Rump officers
to desert to Stamford's side. To make his meaning clearer,
the Earl drank Charles II's health and produced first a
blunderbuss and then a banner with the legend *"King and
Covenant"*. Stamford's behaviour suggests that in August
1659 some even of the Presbyterian grandees would have been
willing to commit themselves if encouraged by an early
victory. The day after the Bradgate incident, however, the
situation began to look less favourable. Stamford's party
dispersed and the Earl came to Leicester to submit to the
county commissioners. He had plentiful excuses : it was only
a gathering of tenants come to present their grievances, and
so on; he was arrested all the same and sent to London for
examination".[6]

The Earl of Stamford was committed to the Sergeant-at-Arms on a charge
of high treason on 3rd September and subsequently imprisoned in the Tower
of London. Bradgate House was searched and stores of pikes, halberds
and muskets were found concealed in the large fireplaces in the Great Hall.
If he had known about the actions of his father, his brother, and his wife's
second husband against his beloved Commonwealth, Lord Grey of Groby
surely would have turned in his grave.

Not everyone in Leicestershire had turned against the Commonwealth,
however, as the following entry in the House of Commons Journal records
for 9th September 1659 :-

*"The House being informed that divers Ministers of the County
of Leicester were at the door; they were called in; and being at
the bar, Mr. Yaxley* [a former parliamentarian cavalry captain
and now the minister at Kibworth and very active in opposing
enclosures], *after a short preamble, spoke to this effect:*
*"That the petitioners, all Ministers of the Gospel in the county
of Leicester, faithful servants to the Parliament, and embarked
in the same bottom with yourselves; some of us marched along
with your forces to suppress the late rebellion of Sir George
Booth and others : We well knowing how much it concerns us,*

444

with all the true Godly of the Lord, are desired by many of our brethren, ministers of the Gospel in the county of Leicester to tender this their humble representation; which as well on their behalf, as on our own, we do humbly present in their and our own names and desire it may be communicated to the House". Which (after the petitioners were withdrawn) was read; and was intitled, [sic] 'The humble representation of divers well affected ministers of the Gospel in the county of Leicester, whose names are hereunto subscribed'.

The petitioners were again called in and Mr. Speaker gave them this answer :-

"Gentlemen, the House have read your petition; and upon due consideration thereof, they find in it a Gospel-spirit of meekness, sincerity, and holiness : And they have also considered the seasonableness of it, and that it expresseth not only an outward letter, but an inward spirit : They likewise find your dislike of the late insurrection, in suppressing which some of you have adventured your persons to hazard; and we and you have cause to give the Lord the glory of this deliverance of us and you. The Parliament, who have always owned and encouraged a godly ministry; have commanded me to let you know that they accept of this petition : and have also commanded me to give you the thanks of this House : And in their names I do give you hearty thanks".[7]

Following the death of Gustavus Mackworth, Lady Dorothy now found herself a widow of just under thirty three years of age with five young children. Her wealthy father-in-law, the Earl of Stamford, was now imprisoned and worse was to follow. On 27th November 1659 she petitioned the Committee for Compounding *"that since the death of her husband, Lord Grey of Groby, she married Gustavus Mackworth, who was engaged with Sir George Booth, and slain, since which many of the goods left her by her former husband have been unduly seized by the Salop Commissioners, though the propriety was never altered, so that by law they ought not to be meddled with. She begs leave to make good her claim".* It was noted as referred to counsel and the petition itself was sent to the Shropshire (Salop) County Commissioners.[8]

On 17th January 1660 it was recorded that the Salop Commissioners replied *"that they seized the goods as Mackworth's, and that nothing as yet appears to the contrary"*.[9]

445

This property was forfeited as the property of a malignant or his widow. There was an element of irony in this as Lord Grey had gained much of his property through the same mechanism.

The defeat of Booth's Rising removed the one serious check on the growing tensions between the members of the Rump Parliament and the army grandees - that is, the threat from the common royalist and presbyterian enemy. Eventually the army interrupted the Rump again on 13th October. As Lucy Hutchinson reports :-

"Lambert being one of them, came in a hostile manner and plucked the members out of the House; Fleetwood, whom they trusted to guard them, having confederated with Lambert and betrayed them. After that, setting up their army court at Wallingford House, they began their arbitrary reign, to the joy of all the vanquished enemies of the parliament, and to the amazement and terror of all men that had any honest interest ....."[10]

The Army grandees then set up a provisional government which called itself the Committee of Safety. Towards the end of 1659 this system was challenged by discontent within England and a threat by General Monck, in charge of the army in Scotland, to march south to the support of the disbanded Rump. Lambert hastened north once more with a force to oppose Monck, and a fresh civil war seemed a serious danger. Major-General Robert Overton had been released by the restored Rump Parliament after some four years imprisonment in Scotland, England, and latterly in the Isle of Jersey. His imprisonment had been voted - unjust and illegal *"because donn by the warrant of a Single person and the cause therein not declared"*. He was restored to his regiment and his other commands. His reputation with the republicans, the strength of Hull, and the importance of its magazine made his adherence of great value to either of the contending parties in the army. He and his officers refused to sign the address to parliament which Fleetwood and the English army circulated, nor would they return a definite answer to Monck's appeals to them to co-operate with the Scottish army. Overton sought to mediate, and published an exhortation to both parties to unite in maintaining the Lord's cause. The ambiguity of his conduct, his preparations for a siege at Hull, and the letters which he circulated among the troops in Yorkshire, caused Monck embarrassment and annoyance. On 4th March 1660 the Council of State tersely ordered Overton to observe whatever orders he received from Monck, whom they believed to be acting for them. Six days later Overton was ordered to come to London at once. He had clearly intended to make a last stand for the Republic, and to frustrate Monck's suspected real intention of bringing back Charles II. The divisions within the garrison at

446

Hull, however, and disaffection in the town obliged him to give up his post to a Colonel Fairfax and obey the orders of the Council. The rest of Robert Overton's life was spent mostly in prison. Meanwhile, as Lambert moved north his men deserted him. Soon Monck was marching southwards with the army from Scotland, pretending to restore and confirm the Rump Parliament.

By 26th December Fleetwood in London sought flight, as had Lambert, and the Rump Parliament reconvened itself again. This was what Monck had claimed to be seeking but he still continued his march down through England. All along the way he received petitions for a full and free parliament, which were barely concealed calls for the restoration of the monarchy. Whether he himself had already made his mind up at this stage to declare for Charles II cannot be known for certain, but he was a former royalist officer, a great opportunist, and a convincing liar. In reality he probably kept more than one option open until the last moment.

A great petition was submitted from the City of London to the restored Rump Parliament in the closing days of December 1659 in favour of 'the Good Old Cause'. It was presented by Mr. 'Praise God Barebone' and several others. At the bar of the House Mr Barebone, addressing the Speaker, said that they were come as lovers of *'the Good Old Cause'* such as are lovers of justice, righteousness and freedom. *"There were many subscriptions, he might say thousands"*. The petitioners described themselves as representing the good old cause of civil and religious liberty against oppression and persecution, and prayed that no one should hold office under the Commonwealth without abjuring solemnly the pretended title of Charles Stewart. The House returned thanks for their good intentions; but Monck wrote to Parliament forthwith, upon hearing of it, expostulating with them for giving too much countenance to *"that furious zealot and his adherents"*. Only five years previously Monck and Barebone had been fellow members of Oliver Cromwell's assembly of *"known persons, fearing God"*.

As General Monck moved down through the Midlands the Corporation of Leicester wrote to him on 18th January 1660 expressing concern about the likely effect of any free quartering of his troops upon them :-

"..... I have (by the advise of my brethren) taken upon mee the boldness to acquaint you with the present condicion of the Inhabitants of this place, which notwithstanding their constant affection to the Parliament and Commonwealth have of late suffered and still doe suffer very much by free quarter whereby all sorte of provision both for horse and men are exhausted and wee of this place made incapable to accomadate [sic] an Army soe greate and of soe high a merritt as that which nowe marcheth under your Excellencys command ....."[(11)]

447

Monck replied the following day from Nottingham reassuring them that only a small part of his force would be billeted at Leicester and that *"those that Quarter shall bee noe burthen to you being they shall pay for what they have ....."*[12]

When the Sheriff of the county, George Faunt, presented an address to Monck at St. Albans giving the support of the county to his endeavours on 30th January the Borough cautiously refused to join in.

Upon arrival in London, after some initial hesitation, Monck declared for a *'free parliament'*. He readmitted the secluded members who had been debarred from sitting since Pride's Purge. Sir Arthur Hesilrigge and other republicans did not fully trust Monck but were outmanoeuvred by him and by their own rigidity. As Lucy Hutchinson records, *"the secluded members whom Monck brought in were, many of them, so brought over to a commonwealth that if Sir Ar. Haslerig and his party had not forsaken their places because they would not sit with them, they would have made the strongest party in the house, but which by reason of their going off were afterwards outvoted in all things"*.[13]

From this point on the Restoration of the monarchy became a certainty. The Rump Parliament and the Army had become too unpopular and the surviving 'Rumpers' had become outnumbered in Parliament. The returned majority of excluded and secluded members had never wanted to depose Charles I and were in favour of restoring Charles II. Soon bells were ringing in every steeple in the City of London and bonfires lit up the sky in anticipation of a return to the old order.

Austin Woolrych summarises the end of the Commonwealth period as follows :-

> **"The rest belongs to the story of the Restoration : the final self-dissolution of the Long Parliament on 15th March, the gathering tide of royalism in the elections to the Convention Parliament [later to be known as the `Cavalier' Parliament and which began to sit on 25th April 1660], the declaration of Breda [which promised, or at least intimated, liberty of conscience, remission of all offences, enjoyment of liberties and estates, as condition for the return of the monarchy], and the proclamation of King Charles II on 8th May. Monarchism was triumphant, yet when the Protectorate had perished a year earlier it had fallen not to the royalists, but to its own radical opponents : the commonwealthmen, the disaffected elements in the army and the sectarian extremists. The Rump, whose agents had exploited their discontents, had been quite**

unable (and largely unwilling) to satisfy their aspirations, and had proved even more politically bankrupt and nationally unpopular than in 1653. The fast rising flood of enthusiasm for the monarchy and the ancient constitution expressed a hankering for security and the rule of law. Both had suddenly become fragile, indeed had almost perished, in the autumn and winter of 1659-60. The Restoration was necessary to fill a political vacuum, for the Commonwealth had collapsed inwards, destroyed by its own internal strife".[14]

Old Sir Jacob Astley's prediction, made whilst sitting on a drum at Stow-on-the-Wold in March 1646 at the end of the first civil war, had been proved correct at last.

In the elections to the Convention Parliament held on 13th April a John Gray of London [no relation to the Bradgate family] and a Thomas Armstrong of Burbage were returned as burgesses for the Borough of Leicester. Returned for Nottingham were Arthur Stanhope and Colonel John Hutchinson, the latter's integrity being generally recognized. Following the proclamation of Charles II in London on 8th May *"with great acclamation of Joy"* he was proclaimed king in Leicester on 12th May. Two days later the Mayor wrote to John Gray MP to assure him that the king had been proclaimed three times in *"the most publique and convenient places of the said Burrough"* and that the proclamations had been received *"with greate solemnity and acclamations of the people than any of the like nature that hath in this place preceded them with as greate Joy and unanimity as it hath beene performed in any place of his Maiesties* [sic] *Dominions whatsoever. It is not the least of our Joyes to heare that the house have sent Commissioners to waite upon his Maiesty in order to his returne* [with a vote of £50,000 to be sent to him] *and wee hope that you (before the receipt hereof) have had the happiness to kisse his Maiesties hand, and that we nowe are under the protection of our most gracious Soveraigne Lord Charles, whom God grant longe to live and happily to governe in these his Dominions. Sir this short Accompt* [i.e. account] *I by thadvice* [sic] *of my Brethren thought fitt to give you for your satisfaccion* [sic] *and for the prevencion* [sic] *of any Calumnyes that may be cast on this Burrough which have soe cordially and sincerely declared themselves for his Maiestye, which is all that I shall trouble you withall at present .....*[15]

The true cordiality and sincerity of this previously staunchly parliamentary corporation can be imagined; but times had changed. As Lucy Hutchinson recounts :-

449

"And almost all the gentry of all parties went, some to fetch him [Charles II] over, some to meet him at the sea side, some to fetch him into London, into which he entered on the 29th day of May, with a universal joy and triumph, even to his own amazement; who, when he saw all the nobility and the gentry of the land flowing in to him, asked where were his enemies. For he saw nothing but prostrates, expressing all the love that could make a prince happy. Indeed it was a wonder in that day to see the mutability of some, and the hypocrisy of others, and the servile flattery of all. Monck, like his better genius, conducted him, and was adored like one that had brought all the glory and felicity of mankind home with this prince.

"The officers of the army had made themselves as fine as the courtiers, and all hoped in this change to change their condition, and disowned all things they had before advised. Every ballad singer sang up and down the streets ribald rhymes, made in reproach of the late commonwealth, and of all those worthies that therein endeavoured the people's freedom and happiness.

"The presbyterians were now the white boys, and according to their nature fell a thirsting, and then hunting after blood, urging that God's blessing could not be upon the land, till justice had cleansed it from the late king's blood. First the fact was disowned, then all the acts made after it rendered void, then an inquisition made after those that were guilty thereof, but only seven were nominated of those that sat in judgement on that prince, for exemplary justice, and a proclamation sent for the rest to come in, upon penalty of losing their estates".[16]

It was now the time for the settling of scores. The 'Cavalier' Parliament began to consider the Act of Oblivion in mid-May 1660. This would wipe out and excuse all offences committed under the Commonwealth unless the 'crimes' and the individuals had been specifically excepted.

In a letter dated 15th May a Mr. Ayloffe informs a Mr. John Langley of proceedings in this matter:-

"..... The Act of Oblivion is the thing they are now vigorously upon; wherein their indulgence to except but seven persons (which 'tis said the General [Monck] was the occasion of) is much wondered at; though the numbers be resolved, yet I do not hear that the persons are yet established, which perhaps may be kept secret till as many as can be found [i.e. of the

regicides] may be secured, and that 'tis thought has made many hide themselves, for there is a stop upon all posts; but 'tis said there are about 20 secured here and fetching up; 'twas moved that the executioner [of Charles I] *might be enquired out, and the Speaker said that would be known in due time .....*

"..... This day 'twas moved to name the seven, to put the others out of terror, but took not; they have ordered bills of Attainder against the late Protector, Bradshaw, Ireton, and Pride for the confiscation of their estates; 'twas moved the Lo. Gray of Groby might ha' been another, but was not. One thought the seven too few, he would have had of all professions, some soldiers, lawyers, courtiers, clergy, but 'twas not seconded; 'tis said divers are run away, as Mildmay, Ludlow, Lo. Mounson, Lisle, and Martin; but they have a plentiful world of these delinquents, enough to hang, enough to confiscate, enough to banish, enough to imprison, and enough to run away. They have secured Thurlow [Thurloe]*; some think rather to squeeze some discovery out of him, than for anything capital".*[17]

Fortunately for the Greys of Groby and Bradgate the Earl of Stamford had been freed from his imprisonment in the Tower of London as a consequence of the Restoration and was able to use his influence to prevent the exhumation and posthumous 'execution' and mutilation of Lord Grey of Groby's body, as happened to the corpses of Cromwell, Ireton, Bradshaw, and some other deceased regicides who had been involved in Charles I's execution. He also managed to save most of his late son and heir's estate from being exempted from the Act of Oblivion.

The Earl was unable to prevent some restitution, however, from taking place where his son had profited from the confiscation of royalist property. William, Lord Craven had the Craven estates, including Coombe Abbey, restored to him in 1660 causing much financial distress to the widow of Lord Grey of Groby. Lady Dorothy must have been attractive as well as resourceful though as, despite being left with five young children from her marriages to Thomas Grey and Gustavus Mackworth, she wed for a third time. This time she married a Charles Howden. Her eldest daughter, Elizabeth, was later to marry a Henry Benson of Charlton in Northamptonshire. Anne, her second daughter by Lord Grey, married James Grove, a sergeant-at-arms, with whom she had offspring. One of their sons, James-Grey Grove became MP for Bewdley in 1714.

Bulstrode Whitelocke incorrectly recorded in his diary on 9th June 1660 that :-

451

> **"Collonell Hutchinson discharged** [from Parliament] **& made uncapable of any office, the like the L** [ord] **Grey & S**[i]**r Gilbert Pickering, the like for many others".**[18]

Colonel John Hutchinson, who was respected by all parties, was persuaded in the interests of his family to profess repentance for his part, as a regicide, in the king's death. He thus purchased his liberty, albeit with a very troubled conscience when he saw what happened to many of his ex-comrades, but was arrested in 1662 on spurious claims of suspicion of complicity in plots against the restored monarchy. He remained in prison, untried, finally dying as a result of the conditions in which he was confined at Sandown Castle in Kent in 1664. He was a fine, proud man, of great integrity who would have won much sympathy from spectators in a public trial.

Sir Gilbert Pickering had been one of the king's judges but had only attended the court twice. He was discharged from sitting in the new parliament on account of his collaboration with the Cromwell regime but was pardoned from any other penalty, however, through the intervention of his brother-in-law, Edward Montagu, Earl of Sandwich.

Whitelocke's information about Lord Grey of Groby is clearly incorrect as he had died in 1657. His son and heir, Thomas, also styled Lord Grey of Groby, was aged about seven years old at the time of the Restoration and would have to wait until his grandfather's death in 1673 to become the second Earl of Stamford at the age of twenty four.

The House of Commons actually resolved on 9th June 1660 :-

> **"That the Lord Grey of Grooby be not excepted out of the Act of General Pardon and Oblivion as to his Estate".**[19]

The House was probably lenient because the heir's stepfather, Gustavus Mackworth, had died supporting his uncle's (Sir George Booth) rising on behalf of the King in August 1659, while his grandfather, the first Earl of Stamford, had also declared for the King and had been arrested and imprisoned for high treason early in the following month. Despite the record of his own father, therefore, the young Thomas Grey found that his family had now acquired acceptable royalist credentials. What would have happened had Lord Grey, the aristocratic regicide, still been alive is a different matter. Some bizarre rumours were in circulation concerning his actual role in the matter of the king's death. Some argued that he, rather than Oliver Cromwell, was the prime mover in securing it and the signatures on the Death Warrant. Some went even further.

On 4th June a Dr. Thomas Smith wrote concerning the Restoration that :-

> *"Our Speaker made a speech to the King in the Banqueting Room and he replied that he would preserve the laws and liberties of his people, with the Protestant religion. He was in a plain stuff suit with a plume of red feathers, the Duke of York with a white one, the Duke of Gloucester green. They are all very pleasing, and humble with majesty. Bonfires are being built in every street, three or four stories high, the Protector's effigy and the States' arms being placed on the top, to be burned.*
>
> *"[News] From H* [umphrey] *R* [obinson] *thus - They have one in hold who affirms that Lord Grey of Groby was the executioner of the late King".*[20]

There is little evidence to support this last allegation and it does not seem to have been taken any further. It is true that on New Year's Day 1649 Lord Grey of Groby had been active in carrying the ordinance for the king's trial from the House of Commons up to the House of Lords. More significantly, it was alleged that when the Lords rejected the ordinance he had proclaimed that he would himself perform the executioner's office rather than let the King escape from justice. On the day of the king's execution the executioner and his assistant had been not only masked, as was usual, but disguised beyond recognition in thick close-fitting frieze-coats with hair and beards that were evidently not their own. Descriptions of the two executioners differed considerably. An account written at the time describes them in seamen's clothes. One of the witnesses in 1660 said that they wore woollen habits like butchers. There is agreement about the grey hair and beard of the executioner but his assistant is variously described as flaxen and black-bearded. The diminutive stature of Lord Grey is likely to have given him away if he had indeed acted in one of these offices. It is more likely that this allegation merely added to the demonic and fanatical image of him created by his enemies.

Reprisals against the Parliamentarians, especially the regicides, began in earnest within six months of the Restoration. In addition to the exceptions to the Act of Oblivion, which in the event numbered far more than the original seven, in November 1660 commissions were appointed *'to inquire of and seize'* the estates of traitors and a list was attached in the case of each of twenty four counties in England and Wales.

There had been in total sixty-nine regicides - the sixty-seven who *'stood up'* at the sentencing of the king, and two others, Thomas Challoner and Richard Ingoldsby, who were not present then, but who later signed the Death Warrant. Of the fifty-nine who had signed the warrant eighteen had already died. On 30th January 1661 the corpses of Cromwell, Ireton, and

453

Bradshaw were exposed all day on the gallows at Tyburn in a grisly spectacle. At sunset the bodies were taken down and buried in a common pit below the gibbet. The heads were cut off and exposed on spikes on the top of Westminster Hall.

Most of those who had been concerned with the death of Charles I were still alive in 1660. Of the forty-one survivors fifteen fled the country. Three of these, John Dixwell, Edward Whalley, and William Goffe found sanctuary amongst the puritans of New England. Whalley, who was a cousin of Oliver Cromwell, had been appointed Major-General for the East Midlands district in 1655. He died in Massachusetts in or about 1675. William Cawley, Edmund Ludlow, John Lisle, and the two former clerks of the Court, John Phelps and Andrew Broughton fled to Switzerland. Lisle was stabbed and killed by an Irish Royalist one Sunday in Lausanne. The other four, with Ludlow surviving the longest, lived out their lives in Vevey and were buried there. Five others, Michael Livesey, William Say, Daniel Blagrave, Thomas Challoner and John Hewson took refuge in Germany and the Low Countries. Three others, John Okey, John Barkstead and Miles Corbet escaped to Holland only to be tracked down and betrayed by a former colleague, Cromwell's Scoutmaster George Downing (after whom Downing Street is named) who was working his way into the favour of the new regime.

Many of the surviving regicides surrendered, hoping for the mercy promised by the king to all but those excepted from the Act of Oblivion who came in within forty days of his return. They mostly made a poor showing at their trial. Richard Ingoldsby's story that Cromwell had forced him to sign the death warrant was accepted because he was useful to the new regime. (He had arrested Lambert on behalf of Monck in the crucial period of early 1660). For his services at the Restoration he was made a Knight of the Bath. No other regicide was so fortunate or so astute in changing sides at the right time. Others, such as John Downes, Edward Harvey and Thomas Wayte (or White), pleaded that they had done all they could to save the king; whilst others, such as Robert Tichborne, Vincent Potter, Simon Mayne, and Henry Smith of Rutland, claimed that they had been ignorant, weak and misled. Smith, originally a Leicestershire lawyer, was spared execution and, like the others, was imprisoned in the Tower of London. He was released before his death in or about 1668. The overwhelming reaction in favour of the monarchy made the regicides scapegoats for the crimes of the nation. Some simply waited to be arrested. Amongst these were the Fifth Monarchist leaders Thomas Harrison and John Carew who put their trust in King Jesus.

When found guilty, the death sentence on the lesser men was usually remitted to life imprisonment. In some cases this included an annual humiliating appearance, on the anniversary of the king's execution, when they were drawn through the streets on hurdles to Tyburn and back. Amongst those who were to remain in prison until they died were John Hutchinson at Sandown Castle, Henry Marten at Chepstow Castle, and Sir Arthur Hesilrigg in the Tower of London. The latter died in 1661 and his epitaph reads that *"He was a Lover of Liberty & Faithful to his Country. He delighted in sober company."* Peter Temple, the former linen-draper, Leicester Committee man, Captain of Horse in the militia, M.P. for Leicester, and long time supporter of Lord Grey of Groby, also suffered this fate. Under the Commonwealth he had been a member of the Council of State and High Sheriff of Leicestershire. After the Restoration his estate at Sibson, near Market Bosworth in West Leicestershire, was confiscated by Charles II for his brother, James, Duke of York. Temple died in the Tower of London in 1663. Another, who was kept in prison in a Jersey castle like John Lilburne and Robert Overton, was Thomas Wayte of Rutland, Lord Grey's colleague and one of the joint executors of his estate. Wayte, or Waite (sometimes even White), was claimed by hostile royalist authors to have been the son of an ale-house keeper at Market Overton in Rutland, but was more likely to have been the son of Henry Waite of Wymondham in east Leicestershire. He had been the Governor of the Burley-on-the-Hill garrison during the civil war and M.P. for Rutland. He died in his island captivity in or about 1668.

In the end only nine of the regicides suffered the hideous death designed by the law for traitors. This was not the dignified decapitation they had given to Charles Stuart but the following grim and vengeful ritual sequence - drawing on a hurdle or cart to the place of execution, half hanging by the neck, cutting down whilst still alive, castration, disembowelling with the entrails being burnt before the victim's eyes, quartering whilst still alive, and finally decapitation. The first six dealt with in this way in October 1660 were Cromwell's brother-in-law Colonel John Jones, Adrian Scroope, Gregory Clement, Thomas Harrison, John Carew, and Thomas Scot who had escaped to Brussels but gave himself up to face his trial and death resolutely. After their capture through Downing's duplicity two years later John Okey, John Barkstead and Miles Corbet suffered the same fate. In addition four men who had not signed the death warrant were also executed in this barbaric manner. They were John Cook who had presented the case against Charles Stuart at the trial, Hugh Peter the most famous preacher in the New Model Army, Daniel Axtell, and the ubiquitous Francis Hacker who had commanded the soldiers of the guard on that fateful day. The last two had been incriminated by their fellow officers of that guard who in exchange had been pardoned; these were Matthew Tomlinson, Robert Phayne, and the inaptly named Hercules Hunks. During the Commonwealth period Colonel Francis Hacker had kept the death warrant at his home, Stathern Hall, in Leicestershire. After his grisly execution at Tyburn his remains are believed to have been buried in Stathern churchyard.

Most of the condemned suffered their dreadful fate with brave resolution. Shortly before he died John Cook wrote to his wife :-

> *"We are not traitors, nor murderers, nor fanatics, but true Christians and good Commonwealth men, fixed and constant to the principles of sanctity, truth, justice and mercy, which the Parliament and Army declared and engaged for; and to that noble principle of preferring the universality, before a particularity, that we sought the public good and would have enfranchised the people, and secured the welfare of the whole groaning creation, if the nation had not more delighted in servitude than in freedom".*[21]

As Solicitor-General at the time of the trial of King Charles I Cook, from Husbands Bosworth in Leicestershire, had prepared the charge and conducted the prosecution. He later said of it, *"I went cheerfully about it, as to a wedding"*. Cromwell had made him Chief Justice of Munster in Ireland, where he is reported as being an efficient reformer. Now he conducted his own defence at another political show trial, before bravely facing his own horrible end.

Thomas Scot declared, as he prepared to die, *"I bless His name that He hath engaged me in a cause not to be repented of. I say, in a cause not to be repented of".*[22] Of all the regicides it was the Fifth Monarchist Thomas Harrison who made the deepest impression at his trial and death :-

> *"I do not come to be denying anything"*, he said to his judges, *"but rather to be bringing it forth to the light ..... It was not a thing done in a corner. I believe the sound of it hath been in most nations. I believe the hearts of some have felt the terrors of that presence of God that was with his servants in those days ..... I followed not my own judgement; I did what I did, as out of conscience to the Lord ..... Maybe I might be a little mistaken, but I did it all according to the best of my understanding, desiring to take the revealed will of God in his Holy Scriptures as a guide to me".*[23]

He went to his death at Charing Cross on 13th October 1660, the first of the regicides to suffer. The crowd was hostile and derisive. *"Where is your 'Good Old Cause' now?"* they jeered. *"Here it is in my bosom"*, declared Harrison, *"and I shall seal it with my blood"*. His courage astonished and impressed the onlookers.[24]

Lord Grey of Groby was fortunate indeed to die before the Restoration; fortunate to be spared the horrible 'live' execution suffered by these regicides or the imprisonment until death of others such as the gallant Independent colonels John Hutchinson and Robert Overton; fortunate not to have his body - wherever it was carefully buried away - exhumed and mutilated like those of Cromwell, Bradshaw and Ireton.

The Restoration reinstituted royal absolution in many respects. A statute of 1661 defined treason so broadly that, with ingenuity, one could be condemned for almost anything. In 1668, for instance, four London apprentices were hung, drawn and quartered for attacking a brothel, Lord Chief Justice Kelyng being of the opinion that it was *'High Treason'* for *'a company of people'* to *'go about any public reformation'*.[25] Sixteen years later only a royal pardon saved a nonconformist preacher, Thomas Rosewell, from suffering a similar fate for questioning the king's power of healing. Sir Henry Vane was executed in 1662, not for regicide - he was not even a member of the Court - but for *'defiant republicanism'*.

There was a last desperate throw of the dice by the sectarian wing of the republican movement. In an attempt to prevent the coronation of Charles II in April 1661 Thomas Venner and the remnant of the Fifth Monarchy Men in London staged an armed rising. As Mark Noble relates :-

> *"..... sallying out into the streets of London, proclaiming `King Jesus', they were surrounded as it were* [by troopers]*; but though they were only a few ill-armed persons, supposing themselves invulnerable, they could not be prevailed upon to submit, until they were fatally convinced to the contrary. The survivors expiated their crimes at Tyburn"*.[26]

The Restoration also brought with it a new church settlement, and the return to Anglican orthodoxy. When the monarchy and the House of Lords were restored in 1660 the bishops returned with the king. This occasioned many changes in Leicestershire as elsewhere. Now the tables were turned. Some of the deprived clergy regained their benefices and the intruders were expelled. In cases where the former incumbent had died his successor was usually left unmolested. There were many incumbents in 1660 who had been intruded by Parliament or appointed during the Commonwealth period. Many of these were now ejected. Some who survived initially were later removed by the 'Bartholomew Act' of 1662. All ministers were required to sign a declaration condemning armed resistance to the king and renouncing the Covenant against episcopacy. If they had not done so

457

by St. Bartholomew's Day, 24th August 1662, they would be ejected, and if they preached thereafter they were liable to imprisonment.

There was strife at the village church once more in Kibworth in 1660. Ex-captain John Yaxley, who had forcibly ejected his pro-royalist Episcopalian predecessor, was one of Lord Grey of Groby's militia officers, had fought under him at Worcester, and was the presenter of the petition to the House of Commons in the previous year, realised what the Restoration meant for 'saints' such as himself and proclaimed from the pulpit, *"Hell is broke loose; the devil and his instruments are coming in to persecute the saints and the godly party!"* He had predicted correctly. He was, in turn, ejected by force in August 1660, being dragged out of his bed by armed men. His wife was said to have been injured in the face by a pistol shot. Later the Yaxleys settled in London. There John became a licensed non-conformist preacher in 1672 and died peacefully in 1687 just one year before the Glorious Revolution.[27]

John Yaxley would have identified with the spirit in which John Milton, the great puritan writer, could entitle his famous work from this period 'Paradise Lost'. Nor was the Restoration fully welcomed in the Borough of Leicester itself in 1660. The town had purchased the Castle Mills, as Crown property, during the Commonwealth period and other Crown property as fee-farm rents. They had now to be surrendered and the Corporation set about raising £300 to secure forgiveness and the re-conveyance of the Mills from the new government. There was still some spirit of resistance though. In May 1660 information was laid against William Dawes, the son of Hugh Dawes who had been the Borough's Sergeant of the Mace during the Commonwealth. It was alleged that, on 27th May *"betweene 11 and 12 of ye clocke in ye fore noon"* William Dawes, upon seeing the King's Arms in paper fixed against the informant Christopher Norris' house end, *"did throwe a stone or clott against the said Armes"*. This was not all. Another informant, William Allsopp, claimed that he had mentioned to William Dawes and his mother, Jane Dawes, that there was a painter in the church *"setting upp the Kings armes and it would doe her good to see them when they were done; whereunto the said William Dawes answered and said that it would doe the Devill good to see them"*.[28]

In a similar spirit the Corporation, which at this time still included such former parliamentarian stalwarts as Arthur Staveley, Richard Ludlam, and Archdale Palmer, had to welcome back to Leicester Lord Loughborough (Henry Hastings) and the former Town Clerk, Edward Palmer, who they had dismissed for his royalist sympathies. The message was underlined in a letter dated 22nd June 1660 to the Mayor and Aldermen from William Staples MP :-

"..... this morning the Lorde of Loughborrow [sic] and Edward Palmer your Towne clarke were with mee making greate Complaints that albeit hee bee returned and restored to his place of Towne Clarke yett hee doth not receive the fruits and profitts thereof and that many things are kept and detyned from him which belongs to his place. And therefore my Lord of Loughborrowe desired mee to write to you and informe you that what Edward Palmer did (for which he was turned out of his place) was by his Comand [sic], And hee willed mee to informe you, and gave me notice thereof as I was your Recorder, that if hee doe not enjoy his place and all the profitts beloneing [sic] to it as fully as hee had it when he was putt out, he would make the King acquainted with it, and with those that were the putters of him out. And that hee would when you came to renewe your Charter move the King to stopp your desires".[(29)]

Despite the Borough's outward show of loyalty to the new dispensation and the lack of any obvious immediate reprisals, changes were soon to be made. The towns had been generally strongholds of the parliamentary cause and the restored monarchy did not leave them undisturbed for long. A Committee for regulating Corporations was set up and it got to work in Leicester in the autumn of 1662. The two Companies (i.e. the twenty-four and the forty-eight) were so drastically remodelled that, out of the total of seventy-two members in November 1660, forty were struck off the rolls. Of these forty, fifteen were Aldermen. The leading men who had governed the town during the civil war years were thus forced into retirement. These included William Stanley, Richard Ludlam, Edmund Craddock, William Ward, Thomas Henshaw, and Samuel Robinson. The constitution of the Corporation was further remodelled in 1684 when the franchise was extended to all freemen of the borough.

With the Restoration Henry Hastings, Lord Loughborough, had been created Lord Lieutenant of Leicestershire. He died in 1666, having spent the last years of his life principally at his London mansion called Loughborough House, in Lambeth, and was buried in the Collegiate Church at Windsor.

Matters at Bradgate following the Restoration, however, were in a far better state than in Leicester. King Charles II treated the Earl of Stamford with favour. On the Earl's petition the king reconveyed to him in 1666 Armtree Manor and Wildmere Fen in Lincolnshire, which had been presented by him to the crown in 1637 for the purpose of effecting some abortive improvements through land drainage.

Young Thomas Grey had become Lord Grey of Groby, after his father's death in 1657, at the age of four. As the heir to the family estates he spent much time at Bradgate, particularly after the Restoration, his grandfather's release from imprisonment in 1660, and his mother's third marriage. He was educated at Christ Church College, Oxford, and was created a Master of Arts on 23rd June in 1668. He was later to succeed his grandfather, Henry Grey, as the second Earl of Stamford on 21st August 1673. The first Earl, aged 73 years at the time of his death, was buried alongside his wife, Anne, with his ancestors in the family chapel at Bradgate. Six years earlier, however, he had celebrated his sixty seventh birthday in style in a manner recounted in a letter to his son-in-law, the Earl of Ailesbury.

> *"January 9th, 1666/7.*
> *Broadgate.*
>
> *I have heard of all your jollities in your house of Austria upon the new year, I pray God to send you many as merry. Friday last was the day of three score and seven pies, and truly in the great hall of Broadgate we dined all our friends and neighbours with a lusty company of Leicester Corporation, but, in truth, ale was our drink and so our venison was seasoned accordingly".*[30]

The old Earl of Stamford does not seem to have been so much of a puritan now; but this was the time of the 'Merrie Monarch'! One wonders what his son, the aristocratic regicide, would have made of this and other changes.

NOTES

1. Mark Noble, *The Lives of the English Regicides*. p. 275.
2. Will of Thomas, Lord Grey of Groby. Canterbury Prerogative Court, Year 1657, Folio. 151/1657 PRO. Ref. PROB. 11/263. British Museum Library, London. The will was also cited in full in *Minutes of Evidence; Dymant, Fitzwaryn & Martin Peerage Claims.* (1915), pp. 259-261.
3. John Hollings, writing in 1840, makes a somewhat puzzling reference to how "Lord Grey of Groby, of whom mention is so often made in connection with the Civil War in Leicestershire, ended his restless and turbulent career in 1657, at his seat at Wirthorp, in Northamptonshire". This is the only reference to the place of Lord Grey's death, but it is not a place name familiar to his biography. The statement is without corroboration. Also, neither this author nor the Northamptonshire County Record Office have been able to identify any such place as 'Wirthorp' in that county. The statement is thus best discounted.
   John F. Hollings, *The History of Leicester during the Great Civil War*, Printed by Combe and Crossley, Leicester. Published 1840. p.68. (First given as a lecture to the Mechanics Institute, Leicester. 1839.)
4. Lucy Hutchinson, *Memoirs of Colonel Hutchinson*. pp. 302-303.
5. Ibid, p. 304.
6. David Underdown, *Royalist Conspiracy in England*, New Haven, Yale University Press. 1960. p. 279.
7. Journal of the House of Commons (C.J.), Vol. VII. p. 776.
8. Calendar of the Committee for Compounding, 27th Nov. 1659.
9. Ibid., 17th January 1660.
10. Lucy Hutchinson, op. cit. p. 308.
11. Records of the Borough of Leicester. DCLXXX Letter to General Monck. Original Letters, No. 78. 18th Jan. 1660.
12. Ibid. DCLXXXI. Letter from General Monck. Original Letters, No. 79. 19th Jan. 1660.
13. Lucy Hutchinson, op. cit. p. 313.
14. Austin Woolrych, *England without a King*, Lancaster Pamphlets, Methuen, London & New York. 1983. p. 46.
15. Records of the Borough of Leicester. DCXCIII. Letter from the Mayor to John Gray, MP. Original Letters, No. 81. 14th May 1660.
16. Lucy Hutchinson, op. cit. pp. 319-320.
17. HMC, Appendix to 5th Report, Folio 72. 1660. May 15., p. 184. Letter from Mr. Ayloffe to Mr John Langley.

18. Ruth Spalding, *The Diary of Bulstrode Whitelocke, 1605-1675*. Records of Social and Economic History. New Series XIII. The British Academy, 1990. Oxford University Press.

19. Journal of the House of Commons (C.J.). Vol. VIII, 61., 9th June 1660.

20. HMC. MSS. of S.H. Le Fleming of Rydal Hall. (385) June 4, 1660. (Cockermouth) p. 25.

21. T.B. Howell, ed. *A Complete Collection of State Trials*, (London, 1809-26), Vol. V. p. 1265.

22. Ibid. p. 1277.

23. Ibid. pp. 1190 ff.

24. Ibid.

25. Ibid. Vol. VI., p. 884.

26. Mark Noble, *Lives of the English Regicides*, p. 275.

27. Cited in *Fifty Years - Thirteen Centuries* - a booklet by Philip Lloyd and Terence Y. Cocks produced in 1976 - A History of the Church and some Churchmen in Leicestershire to mark the Golden Jubilee of the Refounding of the Diocese of Leicester. 1926 - 1976.

28. Records of the Borough of Leicester. DCXCV.
    Hall Papers. XIV, No. 926. 28th May 1660.

29. Ibid. DCXCVIII.
    Hall Papers. XIV, No. 940. 22nd June 1660.

30. HMC, MSS of the Duke of Somerset (Manuscripts of the Marquis of Ailesbury) Letter from the Earl of Stamford to the Earl of Ailesbury. p. 175.

Charles II arriving at Dover

COL.ᵗ FRANCIS HACKER.

(Executed at Tyburn, 1660)

Colonel Francis Hacker

PETER TEMPLE

Died a Prisoner.

Peter Temple

464

Henry Grey, Earl of Stamford (1599-1673)

Robert Bruce, Earl of Ailesbury

CHAPTER FOURTEEN

ASSESSMENT: THOMAS, LORD GREY OF GROBY

"a man of noble birth, considerable following
and high spirit, but very apt to stir up disorder and
restlessness". **(Lorenzo Paulucci, Venetian Secretary in**
England, to Giovanni Sagredo, the Venetian Ambassador in
France - March 15th, 1655, Venetian State Papers)

Hitherto historians and commentators, when they have mentioned him at all, have given obscure glimpses of Thomas, Lord Grey of Groby. These have been partial images usually coloured by their own, or their predecessors', prejudices. The aim of this book has been to produce as full and rounded a portrait of him as possible within the context of the constitutional and political crises of the mid-seventeenth century.

It is often said, with some justification, that the winners write the history books. One of the problems in trying to assess the reputations and actions of the leading parliamentarians of the Great Rebellion era - especially the radical ones like Lord Grey of Groby - is that having won the war they lost the peace; thus forfeiting both the romance which often attaches to 'gallant' losers, for example the Civil War Cavaliers or the American Confederates, and the rehabilitation and self-justification that comes with ultimate victory.

The monarchy was restored in 1660 without much thought for the liberties of the people, such as the parliamentarian radicals and their supporters had fought for. Indeed, the franchise was scarcely extended in practice even during the Commonwealth and Protectorate periods. It was much talked about and debated during these years, especially during 1647, but had to await the constitutional developments of 1688 and the early nineteenth century. In addition, those who had brought about the revolution of 1649 and established the English Republic were subsequently impeached and held up to public infamy in official histories, in the press, on the stage, and in romantic novels. Their former antagonists meanwhile acquired a glamorous reputation which was quite unjustified.

The following example of an assessment of Lord Grey from the Restoration period comes from 'The Loyall Martyrology' by a William Winstanley. This work takes as its subtext the theme that 'Rebellion is as the Sin of Witchcraft'. Included in 'The Character of the Regicides' is :-

"X. Thomas, Lord Grey of Grooby, Son to the Earle of Stamford,
who becoming a Colonel in the Army, grew infected with their
Destructive Principles, and contrary to Honour, Acted with them

in their odious Designs, having his hand in the Murther [sic] of the King, the Fountain and Source of all Honour, from whence others are derived. In regard of the Honour of his Family, he escapes a Mention or Condemnation for this Crime, as well as for some others : He dyed before his Majesties Happy Restauration [sic]".[1]

To some extent this legacy of reactionary partisan prejudice has been mitigated in some cases by the commentaries of more favourably disposed Victorian Liberal historians who saw their philosophical and political antecedents in the Civil War Parliamentarians, if not always in the more radical groups such as the Levellers. Some of these works, however, can bring historiographical problems of their own, a number of which were considered in the Introduction.

Many of the later commentators perpetuate the bias or misinterpretation of earlier chroniclers. This is particularly the case in hostile accounts of Lord Grey of Groby. For example, Clarendon's description of him at the outbreak of hostilities in 1642 as *"a young man of no eminent parts"* is often cited by later writers. This observation requires closer examination in order to determine whether it is justified as an epitaph on his life and career. At the time, it will be recalled, Lord Grey was aged nineteen and was being compared unfavourably by Clarendon with Henry Hastings who, at thirty five, was an experienced military campaigner :-

"But the King had the advantage in his champion, the Lord Grey being a young man of no eminent parts, and only backed by credit and authority of Parliament; whereas Colonel Hastings, though a younger brother, by personal reputation had supported his family, and by the interest of it and the affection the people bore him, brought no doubt an addition of power to the King's cause".[2]

It has to be admitted that in reference to the period from August 1642 to the summer of 1643 this was an accurate observation. Lord Grey had the advantage of the backing of the Parliament's material superiority over their opponents. He also had the important personal support of the Earl of Essex, to whom he owed his original wide ranging regional command. In other respects he was both inexperienced and overly cautious in comparison with Hastings. There can be little doubt that Clarendon's judgement at the time referred to (when he was Sir Edward Hyde), and when taken in its context, was correct. It should be remembered, however, that he was writing with the aim of showing the anarchic consequences of revolt against the

468

established order in both church and state. He had no interest in praising the agents of rebellion, particularly those drawn from the ranks of society's 'natural' leaders. In any case the remarkable fact that Lord Grey of Groby was almost certainly the youngest General of the Civil War period seems to be generally ignored.

This unfavourable, though essentially accurate, description of Lord Grey at the outbreak of hostilities is too often referred to by later authorities to devalue his role generally, particularly ignoring his key role later at national level. The author of the Victoria County History edition for Leicestershire, for example, says that **"Grey had little ability"**[3], but then goes on to cite the Clarendon passage given above in justification. Even when confining one's consideration to the local level, those who have investigated events more thoroughly and over a longer period have often produced a different judgement. For example, John Hollings, writing in 1840 considers Clarendon's comments on Lord Grey to constitute **"a somewhat harsh judgement"**.[4] Again, Alan Everitt in `The Local Community and the Great Rebellion, published in 1969, says of Clarendon's assessment of Lord Grey of Groby that **"this view does not entirely square with his activities in Leicestershire"**.[5]

E. W. Hensman, a local historian of the Victorian period is another critical commentator who draws on Clarendon's work but he also draws on other sources in comparing Lord Grey unfavourably with Henry Hastings. In 'Henry Hastings, Lord Loughborough and the Great Civil War', produced as part of a book by Alice Dryden on 'Memorials of Old Leicestershire' he describes Hastings as :-

> **"a Royalist of the first water. He was the local hero of the war, or rather, if we adopt the attitude of the Roundheads towards him, the villain of the Leicestershire drama. Hardly a skirmish, siege, or battle took place in this or the neighbouring counties in which he did not bear a hand"**.[6]

Clearly Hensman was an admirer of Henry Hastings whom he refers to elsewhere as **"the very model of a cavalier and a partisan leader"**.
By contrast Hensman says of Lord Grey :-

> **"Very soon after the commencement of hostilities Grey was made Lord General of the Midland Association, and he might have been expected to do great things, but he was too impatient of control, too local in his patriotism, and too narrow in his outlook to rise to the height of his opportunities. His fears for the safety of his paternal property in the neighbourhood**

of Leicester forbade him to join his forces with those of the Eastern Association at a critical moment of the campaign against the Earl of Newcastle, and brought him the stern rebuke of Cromwell who never seems to have trusted him again".[7]

Again, as with the Clarendon passage, this seems a reasonable judgement upon the young and inexperienced Lord Grey of Groby during the earliest stages of the first civil war. It is, however, unsustainable as a general comment on his political and military career. Even when Hensman grudgingly admits to Lord Grey's successes both locally and nationally his bias is clear and the derivation from other hostile seventeenth century sources can be discerned :-

"It is true that he met with some local success and that he did good service under Essex in relieving Gloucester in September 1643 [Newbury is not mentioned], but history records no other military exploit sufficiently notable to add lustre to his name. In politics and religion he was an extreme fanatic. As Cromwell's tool, he took part in purging Parliament of the moderates, and when Pride carried out his famous `coup', it was Grey who stood by him with the list of obnoxious members in his hand, and pointed out those who were to be refused admission to the House of Commons. His name is between Bradshaw's and Cromwell's on the King's death warrant, ... Had he lived till the Restoration he would almost certainly have been executed as a regicide, but he died in 1657, and thus a second time escaped a traitor's fate".[8]

Whilst it is true that Oliver Cromwell was clearly frustrated and offended by Lord Grey's failure to support him against the Earl of Newcastle's forces in 1643 and by the general debacle of the Nottingham Rendezvous there is no evidence to suggest that he **"never seems to have trusted him again"**. In the event Lord Grey's fears were shown to have been justified by the cavalier attacks on Bradgate in the early stages of the war and by the later siege and sacking of Leicester in 1645. Lucy Hutchinson referred at the time to the *"credulous good nature"* and the *"lack of experience of the* [young] *chief commander"* of the 1643 rendezvous. It is likely that Oliver Cromwell, who does not seem to be one who harboured grudges, would have taken these factors into account. Lord Grey was certainly a part of the circle of pro-Army `Independent' MP colleagues in the crucial period between 1647 and 1650, as well as a key member of the 'junta' which was

470

responsible for the 'revolution' of 1648-9. There is, moreover, no evidence to support the view that Lord Grey (and others), acted as the tool of Cromwell during the process now known as Pride's Purge. This episode was fully explored in Chapter Nine of this book. Hensman's closing reference to Lord Grey escaping a traitor's fate **'a second time'** is borrowed from Mark Noble and relates to rebellious acts against either the monarchy or the protectorate, or both - demonstrating, on the contrary, his constant loyalty to the principles of the republican Commonwealth.

One of the most vitriolic and biased hostile accounts of the life of Thomas, Lord Grey of Groby comes from the pen of Mark Noble and has been cited extensively earlier in this book. Noble was a Tory 'Church and King' vicar who wrote his 'Lives of the English Regicides' in 1789 at the time of the French Revolution as a warning to potential French regicides. This work draws exclusively on hostile critics of Grey such as Edward Hyde (Clarendon), Denzil Holles, and Clement Walker. In turn later commentators such as Hensman, Nichols for large sections of his work, J. H. Plumb in the Victoria County History of Leicestershire, and Miss E. T. Bradley in the Dictionary of National Biography have tended to draw on this source and its derivatives, often using it word for word, passage by passage, and reiterating opinion as objective judgement.

A flavour of Noble's account of Lord Grey is given in the following extract :-

> *"His Lordship, from his birth, his expectations, the gratitude his family owed to the royal house of Stuart, and particularly to his majesty* [Charles I], *might have been supposed the last to have risen up against his sovereign; and that if he had been led away by the heat of passion from his duty, would, when he saw the adverse party take decided means to destroy the monarch, and abolish the kingly office, have retraced, with the swiftness of an eagle, and the fury of a lion, his devious steps; but, like a rebel against his royal master, and an enemy to that order which he was born to inherit, or bequeath to his posterity at least, he was foremost in throwing down every thing that he, in a peculiar manner, was bound to have upheld and supported, and painful as it is, I am obliged to deliver him down to posterity with an ignominy that has scarce ever been paralleled in the Christian world.*
>
> *"This nobleman having been returned a member in the ever-memorable long parliament, immediately distinguished himself by going into the most violent courses that the worst enemies of the court adopted; he signed the Protestation and sought every*

means to make the wound between the sovereign and his people so deep, that nothing short of ruin could ensue.

"The moment, to him wished-for moment, came that the war was decreed : he signalised himself by collecting his men, and joining the standard of revolt. The parliament, proud of a young nobleman to assist in their cause, gave him every confidence they could, little suspecting that in the end he would prove as faithless to them as he had done to the king; round whom was collected the sons of most of the enobled families in the kingdom. The few on the parliament side, especially in the commencement of the war, made him more conspicuous, and gave him a consequence that was extremely flattering to his pride : he lost sight of all decency and moderation. However, situated as he was, he might have been excused entering in the war on the parliament side, when so large a proportion of the nation at first were so inflamed against the court, and the Earl of Stamford took that side of the cause, and even became a general of their army in the West, though he never made any distinguished figure in the field, that was reserved to this, his son [a back handed compliment to Lord Grey's military prowess].

"The earl was contaminated by every crime; his son seemed ambitious to excel him as much in profligacy as in arms".[9]

....

"It is not possible to draw from history a more infamous, or more detestable character".[10]

....

"..... the Marquis of Stamford [at the time of Noble's writing], *the possessor of so many virtues, is not, I am happy to say, the descendant of Thomas, Lord Grey, who so eminently disgraced his name and title".*[11]

The reliance of later historians on this polemical work and its antecedents has led to several distortions, not all of them overtly political. This highlights a more general historiographical problem. There is always the danger of mistaken interpretations being passed on from one chronicler to a succession of later ones and thus becoming an erroneous 'fact' which can mislead the unwary reader. The example given earlier was when Mark Noble refers to Lord Grey of Groby gaining possession of the Queen's property at Holdenby *"where he made a great devastation in the woods".*[12] This comment made at the close of the eighteenth century is picked up by the Victorian chronicler Miss E. T. Bradley in her entry in the Dictionary of National Biography for Lord Grey. She also refers back to one of Grey's contemporaries, another hostile Presbyterian, Clement Walker, who chronicles - she says - **"a great fall in the woods"**.[13] But Clement Walker actually writes *"there's a great fall in the woods"*.[14]; (i.e. "there's a windfall!") - and is referring to the granting of the valuable manor house, park and lands to Lord Grey of Groby.

It is time to come to an overall assessment of Thomas, Lord Grey of Groby. I shall begin with a summary of his personality and the factors which shaped his political philosophy and stance. Finally, I shall consider his role in the establishment of, and the struggle to maintain, the English Commonwealth.

Thomas, Lord Grey of Groby was a self-proclaimed opponent of tyranny and a passionate supporter of a republican Commonwealth. Amongst his personal characteristics were included a fierce pride in his aristocratic lineage and a determination to oppose autocratic authority, whether of the Stuart or Cromwellian variety, in the name of the *'Good Old Cause'* of liberty, Parliament, and godly reformed religion.

His portraits seem to present, perhaps intentionally, an aristocratic, even haughty or arrogant bearing. If this is a true interpretation it would seem to accord well with his father's nature and behaviour. There are examples of Lord Thomas Grey himself being somewhat overbearing, over zealous and impetuous or hot-tempered. At an early stage of the first civil war there was the incident when he was attacked by a 'saylor' with a pole-axe, whom he had reprimanded for some misdemeanour. That he was highly conscious of his social status was seen when he had Richard Ludlam, Captain of Horse as well as past and future Mayor of Leicester, detained at Burleigh House, Loughborough in 1644 *"for an affront done to the Lord Grey; and ..... since his return he hath humbled himself to his lordship; which may prove a good example to others, to refrain themselves from the like offences, and teach them better manners"*.

He was a committed republican and a seemingly eager regicide, judging by the accounts of his words and deeds. One cannot be sure of how far his political views were formed and affected by the ideas of classical Roman republicanism that he would have studied or by the influence of contemporary writers such as Harrington, Vane and Sidney as part of a wider European debate over the nature and justification of sovereignty.

There has to be a suspicion, however, of a private interest sometimes lying behind the rhetoric of the public principle. His acquisitive tendencies, like those of the Earl of Stamford, have already been remarked upon. The accumulation of wealth and property may have been regarded as a form of divine reward for civic and religious virtue and effort on behalf of the Commonwealth. There was also, especially in the mid-1640s, the suspicion

473

that the Cause was being used to buttress his own patrician assumptions. For him the 'Good Old Cause' may have stood for 'Liberty', but perhaps it was only that liberty which, for the aristocrat, meant never having to say you were sorry.

If it was all just a gloss to justify self-interest, however, it is difficult to account for the gambles he made in his transition from his father's political presbyterian camp to that of the radical republican wing of the Independents. What sort of tactical considerations underlay these decisions if they were not based on principle? And how far can his popularity within the Army, with the Levellers, and latterly with the Fifth Monarchists be otherwise accounted for?

Lord Grey of Groby was evidently popular with middle-ranking and junior officers in the New Model Army in the period 1648-1650; so much so that he was seriously considered as a strong candidate to replace Fairfax as Lord General rather than Oliver Cromwell, until the crushing of the Army Radicals changed the situation irrevocably. He was also well regarded by the Levellers, both civilian and military, and respected by his fellow republicans in Parliament such as Edmund Ludlow and Henry Marten. As such he could not have presented such an unpleasant or officious personality to his colleagues after all. When Lucy Hutchinson referred to his *"credulous good nature"* in 1643 he was aged twenty. Even without making allowance for his age and lack of experience at this point it might have been said of him in his defence, as Lucy said of her own husband John Hutchinson, that *"His own integrity made him credulous of other men's, till reason and experience convinced him otherwise"*.[15]

After some initial doubts about his ability, at such a young age at the outbreak of hostilities in 1642 and through most of 1643, to deal with the very considerable responsibilities placed upon him he seems to have become by the early 1650s a well respected colleague and leader. Despite Clarendon and Hensman, Geoffrey White in 'The Complete Peerage' comments that he appears to have been a successful commander in the field. In a catalogue of portraits he is referred to as **"this celebrated Parliamentary General"**. John Nichols, the Leicestershire historian, writing in 1804 refers to *"Thomas, Lord Grey of Groby, who made so conspicuous a figure in the Civil War"*.[16] Even the hostile Noble, as has been noted, grudgingly admits to his military achievements.

Lord Grey of Groby presents at first examination something of a paradox. He was the only aristocratic regicide and yet despite his clear sense of his inheritance and social status he was regarded from around 1648 by the Army radicals, the Levellers, and later by the Fifth Monarchists as an ally and potential leader. He is described by some commentators as **"an extreme democrat"** and is referred to, along with Henry Marten, as a leading

Leveller sympathiser in Parliament. His political attitude was never in doubt after the momentous events of 1648 and 1649 in which he played such a key part. C. H. Firth described him as **"one of the most loyal and thorough-going supporters of the Republic".**[17] Edmund Ludlow, his contemporary and comrade-in-arms, refers in his `Memorials' to *"Lord Grey of Groby, who has always manifested a constant affection to the Commonwealth".*[18]

It is interesting to compare and contrast Thomas Grey and Algernon Sidney. They had so much in common in terms of social background and political philosophy; yet seem to have co-operated, if at all, with great difficulty. Both were born in 1623 as sons of peers of the realm and both were to become leading republican protagonists of the Commonwealth. They disagreed over the legality of King Charles' execution, however, and almost came to blows over the wording of the Oath of Engagement to the Commonwealth in February 1649. Sidney was more of an intellectual and philosophical republican; Grey was more of a radical republican in practice.

Sidney seems to have felt the need to justify everything he did to an audience, whether seen or unseen; Grey felt no such compunction. The former's political writings are the work of someone with a severely moral and religious aristocratic background thrown into revolutionary politics and later into a penniless exile. No existence of similar discourses by Lord Grey, if he wrote any, remain. Our understanding of his political attitudes comes from his letters, his actions, and the reports of his contemporaries.

Both Algernon Sidney and Henry Neville (with whom Lord Grey of Groby was accused under the Protectorate of having too much influence) wrote after the Restoration political discourses which outlined their republicanism. The genesis of their thoughts in this respect seem to lie in the further development of classical republican ideas at the time of the need to legitimise the founding of the English Republic in 1649. This was also evidenced by John Milton and Marchamont Needham. It continued through the republican opposition to the Cromwellian Protectorate up to 1658 in the works of Harrington, Needham, Neville and Sidney.

Sidney and Neville were second cousins. Both were parliamentary colleagues of Lord Grey and were classical republicans. Classical republicanism described a body of thought which drew principally on Greek, Roman, and Italian Renaissance sources, combining Aristotelian political forms with their idea of 'balance', and the republicanism of Machiavelli's 'Discourses'. Attached to this tradition were a selection of particular republics, each a model for different values. These included Israel before King Saul (a divine institution); Sparta in Ancient Greece (for discipline and longevity); Rome (for vigour and conquest); and Venice (for stability and longevity).

475

Sidney was later to explain during his continental exile after 1660 that :-

"the design of the English [republicans] *had been, to make a Republic on the model of that of the Hebrews, before they had their Kings, and on that of Sparta, of Rome, and of Venise* [sic]*, taking from each what was best, to make a perfect composition".*[19]

To this classical republicanism were added 'puritan' Christian ideas and 'platonist' natural law theories. Algernon Sidney's close political friendship with Sir Henry Vane led him to a form of aristocratic republicanism which tended to clash in the Commonwealth Parliament with the more 'down-to-earth' republicanism of the Marten-Challoner-Grey grouping of which Henry Neville was sometimes a member.

It was the combination by Sidney in his writings of a high moral tone with a ruthless Machiaevellianism that gave his work its force. This was unlikely to pose a problem for Lord Grey of Groby in itself. It was rather the combination demonstrated in Sidney's writings of a high opinion of his own abilities with a temperamental and aristocratic refusal to be over-ruled which provoked the sparks between them. Sidney's personality was crucially characterised by aristocratic arrogance, imperiousness and pride. This would naturally conflict with the similar aristocratic arrogance which, as has been indicated, sometimes characterised that 'extreme democrat', Thomas, Lord Grey of Groby. To the rather less philosophically sophisticated but more practically active Grey, Sidney is likely to have seemed contradictory, hesitant, frustrating, 'all talk and no action' and 'too clever by half'. Their disagreements arose not over similar philosophical or political perspectives, but rather over too similar personalities and the nature of the action which should be taken.

Yet there was a profound difference between the two men which must have affected the relationship between them. When Thomas Grey had put his convictions into practice as a regicide, even being the second person to sign the king's death warrant, Algernon Sidney had refused to serve on the High Commission of Justice and declared it as having no authority despite his fine republican writings. He had then provoked Lord Grey over the wording of the Oath of Engagement to the Commonwealth in a quarrel over, in effect, who were to be the guardians and inheritors of the Republic. This was to prove a critical issue. According to David Underdown the resultant compromise effectively ended the dominance of the radicals of 1648-1649, such as Henry Ireton and Lord Grey of Groby, in the government of the new republican Commonwealth. The failure to ensure adherence to the rightness of the act of the execution of the king meant that the eventual

476

restoration of the monarchy sometime after the death of Oliver Cromwell became inevitable. It is little wonder that the two men continued to be at odds for so long afterwards. Both claimed the moral superiority. Lord Grey must have been very frustrated by Sidney's behaviour and attitude.

Neither of these republicans, having helped to depose their prince, could prevent the rise of the new Caesar in the form of the Lord Protector. They did, however, continue to oppose the usurpation of the Commonwealth by the Cromwellian regime. Indeed, it is from this period that we have the description by Lorenzo Paulucci of Lord Grey of Groby as *"a man of noble birth, considerable following and high spirit, but very apt to stir up disorder and restlessness"*.[20] This is as good a general description of him as any.

Lord Grey of Groby was committed to the cause of the Commonwealth and it was true of him, as John Adair concluded of John Hampden who died in 1643 early in the first civil war, in reference to Bulstrode Whitelocke's pre-war words to Edward Hyde, **"without question, when he first drew the sword he threw away the scabbard"**.[21]

One can speculate upon what might have happened if Lord Grey had outlived Oliver Cromwell. Would he have rallied the forces of the Commonwealth to prevent Richard Cromwell's succession, or later against Booth's Rebellion, or even later (and more crucially) have prevented Monck's march south that prefigured the Restoration? This would, however, only be speculation.

The most significant element that has been overlooked hitherto, however, is Lord Grey of Groby's crucial role in the revolutionary 'Junta' that planned and carried out the purge of Parliament, the trial and execution of King Charles, and managed the earliest days in the establishment of the republican Commonwealth. If it had not been for the failure to prevent the change of wording to the Oath of Engagement to the Commonwealth and the premature death of Henry Ireton, with whom he had a good working political relationship, Lord Grey might have prevented the rise of the Cromwellian Protectorate and ensured the long term survival of the Republic, thus precluding the restoration of the English Monarchy.

It is time that the role played by Thomas, Lord Grey of Groby in the momentous events of the Great Rebellion and interregnum era was rescued from obscurity and drawn to the attention of a wider public. England in general, and Leicestershire in particular, should be made more aware of one of its most neglected sons who stood firmly for that *'Good Old Cause'* of the Commonwealth, described by the poet Andrew Marvell as the *"darling of Heaven, and of Men the care"*.[22]

NOTES

1.   William Winstanley, *The Loyall Martyrology*. (Published approx. 1660). Vol. II. Obituary, p. 110.

2.   Clarendon, *History of the Great Rebellion*. (Published posthumously, 1702-4).

3.   Victoria County History of Leicestershire, Vol. II., (1954) pp. 109-118. The author is Professor J.H. Plumb.

4.   John Hollings, *The History of Leicester during the Great Civil War*. (Published 1840).

5.   Alan Everitt, *The Local Community and the Great Rebellion*. (Published by the Historical Association, London 1969). p. 28.

6.   E.W. Hensman, *Henry Hastings and the Great Civil War*, included in Dryden's *Memorials of Old Leicestershire*, p. 203.

7.   Ibid. pp. 202-203.

8.   Ibid. p. 203.

9.   Mark Noble, *The Lives of the English Regicides*, Vol. I. (Published in London, 1798). pp. 261-262.

10. Ibid. p. 275.

11. Ibid. p. 276.

12. Ibid. p. 269.

13. Dictionary of National Biography, Vol. XXIII., p. 206.

14. Clement Walker, *The History of Independency*, Part II, p. 173.

15. Lucy Hutchinson, *Memoirs of Colonel Hutchinson*, Everyman Edition. p. 22.

16. John Nichols, *The History and Antiquities of the County of Leicester*, Vol. III, Part II, app. IV. (1804) (Bradgate; West Goscote, p. 677).

17. C.H. Firth, *The House of Lords During the Civil War*, p. 229.

18. Edmund Ludlow, *Memoirs* (Early edition) p. 211.

19. Cited in Jonathan Scott's *Algernon Sidney and the English Republic, 1623 - 1677*.

20. Venetian State Papers, March 15th, 1655.

21. John Adair, *A Life of John Hampden, The Patriot*. (Published by MacDonald & Jane's, London, 1976) p. 252.

22. Andrew Marvell, *The Character of Holland* (Probably written shortly after 20 February 1653, and first published in 1665).

478

Thomas, Lord Grey of Groby (1623-1657)
'The Ermine Unicorn'

Unknown Lady of the Bourchier family

480

POSTSCRIPT

"The glories of our blood and state
Are shadows, not substantial things;
There is no armour against fate;
Death lays his icy hand on kings:
Sceptre and Crown
Must tumble down,
And in the dust be equal made
With the poor crooked scythe and spade.

Some men with swords may reap the field,
And plant fresh laurels where they kill;
But their strong nerves at last must yield;
They tame but one another still:
Early or late
They stoop to fate,
And must give up their murmuring breath
When they, pale captives, creep to death.
The garlands wither on your brow;
Then boast no more your mighty deeds;
Upon Death's purple altar now
See where the victor-victim bleeds:
Your heads must come
To the cold tomb;
Only the actions of the just
Smell sweet, and blossom in their dust."

JAMES SHIRLEY
(1596 - 1666)
('Death the Leveller')

The younger Thomas Grey became the fourth Lord Grey of Groby at the age of around four years upon the death of his father in 1657. He was brought up by his grandfather, the Earl of Stamford, as the heir to his titles and estates at Bradgate. He matriculated at Christ's College, Oxford University on 1st July 1667, aged thirteen, and was awarded his MA in the following June.

When the Earl of Stamford died in 1673, and was buried with his wife in the family vault in the chapel at Bradgate, Thomas became the second Earl of Stamford. He took his seat in the House of Lords on 13th April 1675 at the age of twenty two.

481

He seems to have been faithful to his father's radical views and also his talent for getting involved in political intrigue and conspiracy. Under the Restoration monarchs Bradgate appears to have been regarded as a possible centre of suspicious activity, he *"being a strenuous opposer of Popery and arbitrary power"* (Nichols). Along with others, including Anthony Ashley Cooper, the first Earl of Shaftesbury, and Lord William Russell, son of the first Duke of Bedford, who opposed the succession to the throne of James, Duke of York, he formed the Whig Party. The name of Whig came from 'Whiggamore' a nickname for rebel Scottish Covenanters (Presbyterians). It came to be applied by supporters of the Stuart monarchy to those who wished to exclude the future James II from the crown because he was a Roman Catholic. Shaftesbury had replaced Clarendon as Lord Chancellor under Charles II in 1672, but in the following year he went into opposition and began to organise the Whig Party. Shaftesbury's London supporters formed a Green Ribbon Club, echoing the earlier Leveller use of that colour as a radical symbol.

The day he first took his seat in the House of Lords the new Earl of Stamford gave notice of his political stance by voting against the King's Speech. During 1679 the Whig group secured the passing of the Habeas Corpus Act as a safeguard against arbitrary imprisonment. On 2nd May 1679 both Stamford and Shaftesbury were amongst the signatories to a protest against a bill *'for the better discovery of papists'* on the grounds that it might be used against the protestant dissenters. During the next few years Stamford joined with Shaftesbury, Forde Grey - Lord Grey of Wark (later Earl of Tankerville) - and others in a number of protests of a similar nature. In January 1682 he was one of the lords who petitioned the king against summoning a parliament to meet at Oxford. During the session at Oxford he opposed the Lords' rejection of the impeachment of Fitzharris on 26th March that year. In the same year Shaftesbury was accused of treason and fled to Holland.

In 1683, after an attempt on the life of Charles II, a warrant was issued against Thomas, Earl of Stamford and his house at Bradgate was searched for arms by Lords Beaumont and Sherard in July. These arms, which were not found, were said later to have been hidden in a passage between two great ovens in the servants' wing of the house near the kitchens. This was the time of the Rye House Plot to murder the king and his brother. Lord William Russell was accused of involvement in this and, on dubious evidence, was convicted and executed. Stamford was suspected of complicity but managed to survive this episode.

In 1685 Charles II died, becoming a member of the Roman Catholic Church just before he passed away. He was succeeded by the Duke of York as James II. In the first parliament of the new monarch the Earl of Stamford was one of those who protested on 22nd May against reversing the order for the impeachment of three peers then held in the Tower of London for alleged involvement in the Popish Plot fabricated earlier in the 1678 to 1680 period by Titus Oates. On 5th June he also voted against reversing the attainder on William, Viscount Stafford, who was beheaded for his alleged role in the same plot. This action almost certainly increased the new monarch's hostility toward the Earl of Stamford.

The situation deteriorated further with the defeat of the rising in the West Country led by James Scott, Duke of Monmouth, an illegitimate son of Charles II. Many dissenters had joined the rebellion which was crushed at the battle of Sedgemoor in Somerset. Monmouth was executed along with 320 of his followers, who had marched under a sea-green banner reminiscent of the Levellers' colours. Thousands more, mostly innocent, suffered afterwards in the 'Bloody Azzizes' presided over by Judge Jeffreys.

Amongst those executed in 1685 was Colonel Richard Rumbold, a one-time Agitator and Lieutenant of Horse under Cromwell. He had been tried and sentenced for his implication in the Rye House Plot two years earlier. On the scaffold he proclaimed a magnificent Leveller sentiment:-

"I am sure there was no man marked of God above another; for none comes into this world with a saddle on his back, neither any booted and spurred to ride him".

This was a real cavalryman's metaphor and the spirit of forty years earlier was in these words. The political creed of the civilian and army radicals from amongst the ranks of the parliamentarians of the first civil war period could not have been better expressed.

The Earl of Stamford was suspected, almost certainly with justification, of intention to join in Monmouth's rebellion. He was arrested at Bradgate on a charge of *"High Treason, in conspiring the Death of the late King"*, relating to the Rye House Plot. He was committed to the Tower of London together with his cousin, Lord Delamere, and Lord Brandon on 24th July. He petitioned for the right to be heard by his peers and was brought before the House of Lords on 17th November. His trial was fixed for 1st December 1685. It was to be held in Westminster Hall where Charles I had been tried and Lord Grey of Groby had sat as one of his judges. Fortunately for Lord Grey's son, Parliament was prorogued on 20th November and the proceedings against him lapsed. He was released on bail on 9th February 1686 and received a pardon in the April. This was part of a general pardon issued by the king on 10th March. During the short remainder of the reign of James II, the Earl of Stamford stayed at Bradgate, in peaceful retirement, supervising the estate and acting as a Justice of the Peace.

Back in 1672, just before his grandfather's death, he had become engaged to Elizabeth Harvey, eldest daughter of Sir Daniel Harvey of Combe Nevill in Kingston, Surrey who had been appointed ranger of Richmond Park at the Restoration of Charles II, later becoming Ambassador to Constantinople. Elizabeth was apparently a great beauty and brought with her a dowry of £10,000. They married sometime between August 1673 and April 1675 when he was aged about 21 years and she was aged about 17 years. Some time after the marriage he brought her to Bradgate for the first time. Among the attractions of the new Countess was the fact that her father had just died, leaving her a fortune rumoured to be worth £100,000. Nichols records that *"This lady, as appears by a print of her, engraved by Thompson from a painting by Lely, was a remarkably handsome woman"*. She was also tall. In 'The Ladies March', a satire in verse written in February 1682, she is referred to as follows :-

"Stamford's Countess led the van,
Tallest of the caravan,
She who nere wants white or red,
Nor just pretence to keep her bed.

During her first period at Bradgate her sister wrote to her enquiring how she liked the place. She wrote back saying that *"the house was tolerable, the country was a forest, and the inhabitants all brutes"*. Whereupon the sister wrote again advising her to set fire to the house and run away by the light of the blaze. Shortly afterwards there was indeed a fire. Oral tradition has it that it was started deliberately by the Countess. It began in the north-west tower where the Earl and his family slept. Nichols records that the ends of the burnt beams were still to be seen in his day. The Countess, with her infant daughter, Lady Diana, narrowly escaped with their lives. Fortunately the fire was restricted to a small area of the house and the damage was limited. Thomas and Elizabeth appear to have separated for a time after December 1675, but they must have come together again as two further children were born of the marriage and references to her in July and December 1685 when he was a prisoner in the Tower of London imply a normal relationship. Sadly, she died in 1687 aged only 30 years and none of the children of their union survived. A son had died soon after birth; another, named Thomas, died as an infant; and the daughter Diana also died young.

In 1688 the Earl of Stamford was present as a sympathetic spectator in Westminster Hall to witness the trial and acquittal of the Seven Bishops who had been charged with *'having written or published in the county of Middlesex a false, malicious, and seditious libel'*. The Archbishop of Canterbury and six fellow bishops had presented to the king a petition declaring their loyalty to the crown but declining, for conscience sake, to instruct clergy to read out a declaration from James II from all Anglican

484

pulpits annulling the penal laws against Roman Catholics and Protestant Dissenters. The news of the acquittal was greeted in Westminster Hall and throughout the country with almost universal thanksgiving and celebration. Thomas Grey would have joined in the rejoicing. The puritan dissenters preferred rather to endure the penal laws than to give their support to the rule of an autocratic Catholic Stuart monarch.

At the time of the 'Glorious Revolution' later in 1688 the Earl of Stamford was one of the first to take up arms. Upon the landing of William, Prince of Orange at Torbay in November he raised men in Leicestershire and Nottinghamshire. Together with his cousin, Lord Delamere, he is reported as joining the Prince's forces at Hungerford on 7th December with a force of 400 horse under his father's standard of the ermine unicorn. An account by Sir Thomas Fotherley, however, claims that *"they were not above half that number; that they were very shabby fellows, pitifully mounted, and worse armed"*. They had arrived at Gloucester from the Midlands before 1st December when they heard that the Prince was moving rapidly eastwards. Their messenger reached the Prince of Orange at Hindon in Wiltshire. One hundred of the midlanders stayed at Gloucester as a rearguard whilst the remainder linked up with him at Hungerford in western Berkshire.

The Revolution of 1688 transformed the Earl of Stamford's fortunes. On 8th April 1689 he was rewarded for being *'a zealous promoter of the Revolution'* by being made High Steward of the Honour and Lordship of Leicester. About the same time he was amongst those signatories of protests in the House of Lords through May and July against the penalties inflicted by the previous regime on Titus Oates. On the basis of Oates' (largely false) evidence many innocent Catholics had suffered execution and/or imprisonment. When the Roman Catholic James II had succeeded to the throne Oates was flogged, pilloried and imprisoned for perjury. After the Glorious Revolution, however, he was pardoned and granted a pension as a Protestant hero. Oates had been born in 1649 at Oakham in Rutland, the son of a Baptist preacher and teacher. Stamford may have felt a particular obligation to support him. In November 1689 the Earl was one of the so-called 'murder committee' appointed by the House of Lords to inquire into the executions by the previous regime of Algernon Sidney (his father's former colleague and rival) and Lord William Russell for their alleged involvement in the Rye House Plot.

The Earl married again, shortly before 12th March 1691. His bride was a Mary Maynard, the daughter of a Joseph Maynard of Ealing. He was now thirty eight years old and she was twenty years of age.

In November 1691 he was talked of for the lord-lieutenancy of Middlesex, and in April 1694 he was named as a likely candidate to become one of the Lords of the Treasury.

On 3rd May 1694 he was made a member of King William III's Privy Council. His other appointments included a Commissioner of Greenwich Hospital (August 1695), a Commissioner of Trade and Foreign Plantations (December 1695), and on 24th April 1696 Lord Lieutenant of Devon (though Nichols records it as 'Lord Lieutenant and custos rotulorum of Derbyshire').

In the summer of 1696 the Earl and the Countess were honoured by a visit to Bradgate by William III. Local tradition relates that a new bridge was constructed over Anstey brook, by-passing what is now referred to as the 'pack-horse bridge', to allow the royal coach easier passage on the road from Leicester to Bradgate through the village of Anstey. No expense was spared in order to impress the king. A great new window was added to the house and larger stables were erected. The king stayed for only one night but Stamford appears to have benefited from the visit by being appointed to further lucrative and prestigious offices of state. In December 1696 he was made 'custos rotulorum' for Leicestershire. On 23rd April 1697 he was appointed Chancellor of the Duchy of Lancaster. Through this office he became involved in a quarrel with the Duke of Devonshire over his rights to hunt in Needham Forest. On 9th June 1699 he became President of the Board of Trade and Foreign Plantations. A son was born to Countess Mary and the Earl in 1696, but he died in infancy.

Upon the accession of Queen Anne to the throne in 1702 the Earl of Stamford was dismissed from all his offices of state as she initially favoured the Tories. He visited the Elector of Hanover (who was to become King George I of Great Britain in 1714) and his wife Sophia at Hanover and Zell in 1702. Stamford must have been an earnest and rather tiring guest for the Elector who spoke no English. According to an entry in the Portland Manuscripts it appears that Lord Stamford *"was very constant both at dinner and supper with the Elector till his Electoral Highness took his journey towards the mines, which - some people say - was at least hastened if not purely occasioned for the decent avoiding* [of] *his Lordship"*.

Slowly but surely Stamford re-established himself in the government of Great Britain. On 25th April 1707 he was again made President of the Board of Trade, retaining this office until June 1711. He was also reappointed as a privy councillor.

During the early eighteenth century he led the Whig aristocracy in Leicestershire politics against the local Tory gentry. At national level he remained a leader of the Whig party which dominated British government after the accession to the throne in 1714 of George I, who spent most of his time in Hanover, never having learned to speak English.

The second Earl of Stamford lived through a variety of regimes and reigns stretching from the days of the English Republic to the Hanoverian period. He was a child under the Protectorate and the briefly restored Commonwealth; he survived the reigns of Charles II and James II; he was

486

a member of the Privy Council in the reigns of William and Mary, Anne, and George I.

It may be reasonably assumed that, politically, his father - Lord Grey of Groby - would have been proud of him. He continued that radical political tradition, defence of liberty and resistance to arbitrary authority in government and religion associated with the *'Good Old Cause'*. He was interested in learning and progress, becoming a Fellow of the Royal Society on 12th May 1708. He seems to have been an honest and principled man.

Macky says of him in 1703, when he turned fifty, that *"He doth not want sense; but by reason of a defect in his speech, wants elocution"*.

Dean Swift comments that, *"He look'd and talk'd like a very weak man, but it was said he spoke well at* [Privy] *Council"*.

Some regarded him as rather narrow-minded because of his adherence to his and his father's political principles. Macky comments that he *"is a very honest man himself, but very suspicious of everybody that is not of his party"*. Perhaps we can see here elements of the father in the son.

Unfortunately in terms of family posterity and prosperity he was less successful. His public life led him to neglect his private affairs. According to Macky *"..... from a good estate he is become very poor, and much in debt"*.

The Earl of Ailesbury (Aylesbury) seems to confirm this by recording that :-

> *"That poor headed Earl had a reasonable paternal estate, but entailed, so he cut down all the vast fine woods,* [now there is a <u>real</u> fall in the woods!] *ruined the mansion house, and took money by advance on this Estate and spent it ..... his maternal estate, upwards of three thousand pounds per annum, he ate up absolutely and all sold"*.

He appears not to have inherited the acquisitive tendencies of his father and grandfather.

Thomas Grey, second Earl of Stamford, died on 31st January 1720 aged 67 years. Sadly, all four of his children by his two marriages had died shortly after birth or in infancy. His widow, Mary, died on 9th November 1722 at her house in Great Russell Street, Bloomsbury, London aged 51 years. They were buried together in the family chapel at Bradgate along with his ancestors. In a vault in the middle of the chapel, built to contain only three coffins, are the earthly remains of Lady Diana Grey, daughter of Thomas, Earl of Stamford, by his first wife Elizabeth; Mary, Countess Dowager of Stamford, and Thomas, Earl of Stamford; for whom there is the following epitaph on a blue slate slab on the floor :-

"D. G.
THE RIGHT HONOURABLE THOMAS GREY,
BARON OF GROOBY, VISCOUNT
WOODVIL, AND EARL
OF STAMFORD, LATE LORD-LIEUTENANT
OF DEVONSHIRE AND
SOMERSETSHIRE, DIED JANUARY
THE 31ST, 1719,[*] AGED 67 YEARS.
THE RIGHT HONOURABLE
MARY, COUNTESS DOWAGER
OF STAMFORD, DIED
NOV. 10, 1722
AGED 51 YEARS. "

As the son of the aristocratic regicide left no surviving children the succession to the titles of Earl of Stamford, Lord Grey of Groby, etc. and the family estates passed on his death to a cousin, Harry Grey, who lived at Enville in Staffordshire. The family connection with Leicestershire immediately became more tenuous. The park at Bradgate continued to be used for hunting expeditions. A pack of foxhounds and a stud of hunters were kept in the park. Bradgate House, however, was deserted and gradually began to fall into ruins. It was just over two hundred years since it had been completed by that earlier Thomas Grey, the ambitious Marquis of Dorset.

[*] According to the old calendar.

Lady Diana Grey (miniature) by Peter Cross:

Inscribed: '*Lady diana graye/Erle Stanfords dafter*'circa. 1680

488

The Countess of Stamford

P. Lely Pinxit.   R. Tompson exudit.

Elizabeth, Countess Stamford (nee Harvey)

Thomas Grey, Second Earl of Stamford (1653-1720)

Mary, Countess Stamford (nee Maynard)

Ruins of Bradgate House – past and present

DETAILS OF ILLUSTRATIONS

1. THOMAS GREY, BARON GROBY (1623-1657) + signature
   "In his meridian glory" (Mark Noble), probably circa 1653. Lord Grey would have been aged around thirty at the time. The artist is thought to be Robert Walker. This portrait is reproduced from The Collection at Althorp by permission of the Spencer Estate, Althorp, Northamptonshire and courtesy of the National Portrait Gallery, London.

2. FAMILY TREE - THE GREYS OF BRADGATE AND GROBY

3. MAP OF C17th LEICESTERSHIRE
   This map of Leicestershire by Seller in 1695, despite the misspellings of 'Dradgate' for Bradgate and 'Gorby' for Groby, amongst others, gives a good representation of the settlement pattern of the county in the seventeenth century.

4. LADY JANE GREY (1537-1554) - 'The Nine Days Queen' + signature
   The tragic fate of the young Lady Jane and the ambitions of her family were to have ironic consequences in the following century.
   Here she is shown, aged sixteen, as 'Lady Jane Dudley' following her marriage to Guildford Dudley; with her signature as 'Quene' and with a greeting to her father. This portrait is by an unknown artist and is reproduced by courtesy of the National Portrait Gallery, London.

5. FAMILY TOMB OF THE GREYS IN THE CHAPEL AT BRADGATE HOUSE
   The effigy of Henry, first Lord Grey of Groby and his wife Anne, both of whom died in 1614. The tomb and the chapel remain intact in the ruins of Bradgate House in Bradgate Park, some six miles north west of Leicester. This display of the importance of the family lineage would have impressed the young Thomas Grey as he grew up at Bradgate. The crest of the ermine unicorn, within a sun in splendour, was to become the emblem on his personal cavalry cornet or standard in the civil wars. This print is reproduced from John Nichols' *History and Antiquities of Leicestershire*, Vol.III, Part II. (West Goscote) page 681. Circa 1790.

6. LADY ANNE CECIL (1603-1676)
   Lady Anne Cecil was the younger daughter of the Earl and Countess of Exeter. She married Henry Grey, then 2nd Baron Grey of Groby, in July 1620 when she was about seventeen years of age. This portrait, attributed to Daniel Mytens on the frame, is thought to have been painted by William Larkin, along with matching portraits of her sister

Diana (later Countess of Oxford) and her sister Elizabeth (later Countess of Berkshire) on the occasion of the latter's marriage to Sir Thomas Howard. The portrait is reproduced by courtesy of the National Portrait Gallery, London.

HENRY GREY, FIRST EARL OF STAMFORD, BARON GREY OF GROBY, BONVILE, & HARINGTON (1599-1673) + signature
This drawing of Lord Grey's father was based on a portrait by Wenceslaus Hollar. A version of it appears in John Vicars' *England's Worthies*. Although described by W. Mercer in *Anglia Speculum* as *"most courteous and right stately Stanford* [sic]*"* he appears to have been hot-tempered, haughty and arrogant on many occasions.

AND THE STAMFORD INSIGNIA
The horizontal stripes in the predominant top left hand side of the shield are white/silver and blue with the three red spheres and constitute the original Grey family coat of arms (Barry of six, Argent and Azure, in chief three torteauxes Gules, and a label of three points Ermine). The other seven elements displayed in the shield represent the other illustrious families with which the Greys were linked through marriage, including their local rivals - the Hastingses, top left of centre.

LADY ANNE CECIL, COUNTESS OF STAMFORD (1603-1676)
This portrait was painted in 1618 by an unknown artist. A copy of a similar portrait of her sister Elizabeth exists which was done by the so-called 'Comet Master' (because a comet appears in the background). This, however, shows no comet. The title 'Countess Stamford' was added to the portrait after 1628. The Countess bore the Earl of Stamford five daughters and four sons, including Thomas, Lord Grey of Groby. The portrait is reproduced by courtesy of the National Portrait Gallery, London.

HENRY GREY, EARL OF STAMFORD (1599-1673)
This portrait of the Earl of Stamford from the period around 1640 is by Cornelius Jonson and is reproduced by courtesy of Dunham Massey, The Stamford Collection (The National Trust): photograph Courtauld Institute of Art.

SEVENTEENTH CENTURY VIEW OF BRADGATE
The drawing by Knyff of *'Broadgate in Leicestershire Being the Seate of ye Rt. Hon: the Earle of Stamford'* and its surrounding deer park has been produced in more than one version. The one showing the wider panorama of the house, parkland, and surrounding countryside (also featured on the cover) dates from circa 1700, and is printed by Hulsbergh. A version which focuses more on the house and the hinterland from the northeast, printed by Malcolm in 1794 appears

494

in John Nichols' *History and Antiquities of Leicestershire*, Vol. III, Part II. (West Goscote), page 680.

11. KING CHARLES I

This portrait of Charles I was painted by Daniel Mytens before the outbreak of the civil wars. It emphasises the king's belief in the majesty and power of the monarchy. The portrait is reproduced by courtesy of the National Portrait Gallery.

12. ROBERT DEVEREUX, EARL OF ESSEX

The Earl of Essex, first Lord General of the Army raised by the Parliament in the first civil war, was a patron of Lord Grey of Groby and issued his commission as General for the (East) Midland Association of Counties. This print appeared in John Vicars' *England's Worthies - under whom all the Civill and Bloudy Warres since Anno 1642, to Anno 1647, are related.*

13. CIVIL WAR ARMIES

Civil War armies were composed of three main elements:
1) Foot - Pike and Musket;
2) Horse - Cavalry and Dragoons (mounted infantry);
3) Artillery - Cannon and their crew.

14. OLIVER CROMWELL

This drawing of Oliver Cromwell is from John Vicars' *England's Worthies* and is from the time when he was General of the Horse in the New Model Army under Sir Thomas Fairfax. His first impressions of Lord Grey whilst Cromwell was a colonel were not particularly favourable. They were to become much closer politically by 1648-1650, before their rift in 1653.

15. COLONEL JOHN HUTCHINSON

John Hutchinson, Parliamentarian Governor of Nottingham and a fellow regicide with Lord Grey, was a man of widely recognised integrity. He was committed to the Commonwealth and opposed to the Protectorate. Shortly after the Restoration [of the monarchy] he was imprisoned and he died in Sandown Castle, Kent, in 1663. He was then aged 49 years. The portrait is by Robert Walker and is reproduced by courtesy of the National Portrait Gallery, London.

16. LUCY HUTCHINSON

Lucy, the wife of Colonel John Hutchinson, was a firm puritan and an observant commentator on John's contemporaries. She was critical of Lord Grey of Groby initially because of "his too credulous good nature" and his inexperience as a chief commander. The child is thought to be her son. This portrait is also by Robert Walker and is reproduced by courtesy of the National Portrait Gallery, London.

17. SIR JOHN MELDRUM

Sir John Meldrum was an experienced professional soldier. A captain by 1611, at the age of twenty-six, he was knighted for his services in the Low Countries. He had fought at La Rochelle and served as a colonel under the Protestant Swedish king, Gustavus Adolphus, in the Thirty Years War in Germany. He successfully commanded a brigade of parliamentarian foot at Edgehill. Although he was appointed to replace Lord Grey of Groby as the overall commander of the forces at the Nottingham rendezvous in the summer of 1643, he was also later in charge of the parliamentarian army besieging Newark which was compelled to surrender ignominiously to Prince Rupert's relieving forces in the spring of 1644. This engraving of Meldrum is from J. Leycester's *The Civill Warres of England* (1649), reprinted 1818.

18. THE EARL OF ESSEX - A HERO OF NEWBURY AND GLOUCESTER

Lord Grey of Groby contributed to, and shared in the glory following, the victories at Newbury and Gloucester won nominally by his patron. His own military reputation now began to grow. This engraving, by Wenceslaus Hollar, is reproduced © The British Museum,

19. MAP : WEST GOSCOTE HUNDRED IN LEICESTERSHIRE

In the early years of the civil war much of the fighting between Lord Grey of Groby's parliamentarian forces and the royalist soldiers under Henry Hastings, Lord Loughborough, took place in West Goscote Hundred, which lies to the north-north-west of Leicester. This area includes Bradgate, (Groby was close by in neighbouring Sparkenhoe Hundred to the west), Cole Orton, Ashby-de-la-Zouch, Castle Donington, Birstall, Belgrave, Rothley, Burleigh, Loughborough, and many other places mentioned in this book. This map is reproduced from John Nichol's *The History and Antiquities of the County of Leicester*.

20. MAP : THE CIVIL WAR IN THE EAST MIDLANDS

This map shows the area particularly in contention between the forces of Lord Grey of Groby and those of Henry Hastings, Lord Loughborough, who was based at Ashby-de-la-Zouch castle, between 1642 and 1645. I am obliged to Martyn Bennett for the use of this map.

21. FOUR MILITARY COLOURS - all of Leicestershire Parliamentarians

Top Left : The Colonel's colour of the Earl of Stamford's Regiment of Foot. The field of the colour is blue. The family motto *'A Ma Puissance'* is included.

Top Right : The cavalry cornet of Sir Arthur Heselrigg's own troop of Horse (the so-called 'Lobsters'). The field of the colour is green. Our *'Hope'* or *'Anchor'* is *'Only In Heaven'*.

Lower Left : The cavalry cornet of Lord Grey of Groby's own troop of Horse - the famous 'Ermine Unicorn'. The left side of the field is blue and the right side is red.

Lower Right : Another colour said to belong to Lord Grey of Groby. It features a body of armed men beside a Parliament House with the legend *'Per Bellum ad Pacem'* (*'By War to Peace'*).

Another recorded colour of Lord Grey is of a circle of hands holding daggers or short swords, surrounded by the same legend and on a field of half (left) blue and half (right) red.

Sources - various.

22.   CAVALRY COMBAT

Apart from the fact that most of the participants are wearing full cuirassier armour, this is a good representation of the type of fight or skirmish between two bodies of horse that took place in the East Midlands between the parliamentarian forces of Thomas, Lord Grey of Groby and the royalist 'cavaliers' of Henry Hastings, Lord Loughborough during the first civil war. This engraving by Jacques Callot is from *'Miseres et Malheures de Guerre'* (1633).

23.   AN ASPECT OF THE TOWN OF LEICESTER DURING THE CIVIL WAR, 1642-5

This map of Leicester as it would have looked in 1642-45 was published in James Thompson's book *'A History of Leicester from the time of the Romans to the end of the seventeenth century' (1849)*. The outworks and hornworks constructed for the defence of Leicester during the civil war may be noted. The royalist artillery was mounted on the north end of the Raw Dykes, pictured at the bottom left corner, during the siege and storming of the town at the end of May 1645.

24.   PRINCE RUPERT, COUNT OF THE RHINELAND PALATINE

Rupert was the third son of Frederick, the Elector Palatine, and Elizabeth of Bohemia ('The Winter Queen'), sister of Charles I. As a young man he fought for the Prince of Orange in the Thirty Years War, and at the outbreak of the English Civil War this favourite nephew of the king was given command of the Royalist cavalry at the age of twenty-three. With his tireless gallantry, devotion, dash, and a degree of irresponsibility he initially won a number of brilliant victories. These were followed by the defeats of Marston Moor (1644), and Naseby (1645); and after the surrender of Bristol to Fairfax in 1645 he was summarily dismissed by the king. In December of the same year he went to Oxford and was reconciled to him, but his commissions were not restored.

This portrait by Van Honthorst is reproduced by courtesy of the National Portrait Gallery, London.

25. PRINCE RUPERT SUMMONING THE GARRISON OF LEICESTER TO SURRENDER, 30 MAY 1645

This print is reproduced from John Throsby's *The History and Antiquities of the Ancient Town of Leicester* Vol. III. Appendix. Page 45. 1791.

26. SIR THOMAS FAIRFAX

Sir Thomas Fairfax was Lord General of the New Model Army. He declined to participate in the trial and execution of the king.

This portrait is by William Fairthorne and is reproduced by kind permission of the National Portrait Gallery, London.

27. MAP : THE CAMPAIGN OF THE KING'S 'LEICESTER MARCH' - 1645

This map shows the movement of both the main royalist and parliamentarian 'New Model' army during the spring and summer of the king's so-called 'Leicester March' which included the siege and storming of Leicester and culminated in the crucial battle at Naseby.

28. BASIL FIELDING, EARL OF DENBIGH

Basil Fielding, Earl of Denbigh, was the Parliamentarian commander in the West Midlands following the death of Lord Brooke early in the civil war. He was also Lord Grey of Groby's brother-in-law and a rival co-heir over the Earl of Bath's inheritance.

This print is reproduced from John Vicars' *England's Worthies*.

29. SIR GEORGE BOOTH, LATER LORD DELAMERE (1618-1680)

Sir George Booth began the first civil war as a royalist. He had married, as his second wife, Elizabeth Grey, a sister of Thomas, Lord Grey of Groby before he wrote to warn him of the poor state of Leicester's defences in April 1645. Imprisoned for his part in the abortive royalist rising (based mainly in his home area of Cheshire) named after him in 1659, he was released in 1660 upon the Restoration and was created first Baron Delamere by Charles II in 1661. This portrait by J.M. Wright is reproduced by courtesy of Dunham Massey, The Stamford Collection (The National Trust): photograph Courtauld Institute of Art.

30. LADY ELIZABETH BOOTH (nee GREY), LATER BARONESS DELAMERE

She was the eldest sister of Thomas, Lord Grey of Groby. It has been observed that this portrait, by Peter Lely, shows her as having the same 'Rossetti-like hair' as her brothers; especially Anchitel, Leonard and John. This portrait is reproduced by courtesy of Dunham Massey, The Stamford Collection (The National Trust) : photograph Courtauld Institute of Art.

31.   HENRY IRETON

This Nottinghamshire parliamentarian became Cromwell's son-in-law and was a close colleague of Lord Grey of Groby in the 'revolutionary junta' of 1648-1649. He exercised a degree of influence over Cromwell and were it not for his untimely death of plague in Ireland in November 1651 events might have turned out differently. The portrait miniature is attributed to Samuel Cooper and is reproduced by courtesy of the Fitzwilliam Museum, Cambridge.

32.   OLIVER CROMWELL

This portrait miniature of Cromwell is attributed to Samuel Cooper. It shows Cromwell as he looked in the 1648/49 period and is reproduced by permission of the National Portrait Gallery, London.

33.   JAMES, DUKE OF HAMILTON

The Royalist Duke of Hamilton invaded England with a Scots Army in July 1648, but his incompetent generalship allowed Cromwell to win the Second Civil War. Hamilton was captured at Uttoxeter by Lord Grey of Groby in controversial circumstances.

This portrait, which was painted in the style of Van Dyke by an unknown artist, is reproduced by courtesy of the Scottish National Portrait Gallery.

34.   KING CHARLES I IN ARMOUR

This contemporary engraving of Charles I in armour may give some idea of how he looked *"on horseback, in bright armour, in the said town of Leicester"* following its storming in 1645.

35.   THE TRIAL OF KING CHARLES I BY THE HIGH COURT OF JUSTICE

The trial of King Charles I from a contemporary print. It is thought that Lord Grey of Groby sat on the front row of the Councillors or Judges who faced the solitary figure of the king. John Bradshaw presides and the arms of the soon to be declared 'Commonwealth' are displayed at the back of the court. This print is reproduced by courtesy of the Mary Evans Picture Library.

36.   AN ACCOUNT OF THE TRIAL OF KING CHARLES I

This is the third instalment of Mabbot's licensed contemporary account of the trial. The title page is reproduced by courtesy of the British Library, London.

37.   THE DEATH WARRANT OF KING CHARLES I

Thomas, Lord Grey of Groby, was one of the first and the principal signatories of the death warrant of Charles I. His signature appears as the second one, between those of Lord President John Bradshaw and Oliver Cromwell.

This print is reproduced by courtesy of the National Portrait Gallery, London.

38. THE EXECUTION OF KING CHARLES I

This contemporary Dutch print of the execution of the king on the afternoon of 30th January 1649, on the black draped scaffold outside his splendid Banqueting House was very popular. Unfortunately it contains several inaccuracies , including the height of the block which was lower than depicted here. This print is reproduced by courtesy of the Ashmolean Museum, Oxford.

39. SIR ARTHUR HESELRIGE

Although a Member of Parliament for Leicestershire, and active Parliamentarian partisan, Republican and Commonwealthman, Sir Arthur and his family were local rivals of the Greys in the Leicester area. He had a fiery temper, but also displayed a sense of humour at times. After being Sir William Waller's Lt. General of the Horse early in the first civil war Sir Arthur established himself in the Newcastle-upon-Tyne area where he also became a local rival of 'Free-born' John Lilburne, one of the leading Levellers. His surname is found spelt in a bewildering variety of ways! His brother, Thomas, was a member of the local parliamentarian Leicester Committee. He was a patron of Francis Hacker. Sir Arthur was imprisoned in the Tower of London at the Restoration, where he died in 1661. This portrait by Robert Walker is reproduced by permission of the National Portrait Gallery, London.

40. HENRY MARTEN

Henry Marten was a wit and a leading republican Commonwealthman. His free-living private life (it was said that he had both a Regiment of Horse and a Regiment of Whores) was a cause of great scandal to many Puritans. He was, nonetheless, a close political ally of Lord Grey of Groby and at one time they were favoured by significant elements within the New Model Army to replace Fairfax and Cromwell as its chief commanders. After the Restoration he was imprisoned at Chepstow Castle until he died. The portrait, by Sir Peter Lely, is reproduced by courtesy of the National Portrait Gallery, London.

41. ALGERNON SIDNEY

Despite the similarities of age, aristocratic social background, and a shared aggressive republican political outlook Algernon Sidney, a younger son of the Earl of Leicester, and Lord Grey of Groby seem to have disliked each other deeply at a personal level. He was executed

500

some considerable time after the Restoration for alleged involvement in the Rye House Plot shortly before the death of Charles II in 1685. The portrait is by an unknown artist, dated around 1663, and is reproduced by courtesy of the National Portrait Gallery, London.

42. EDWARD MASSEY

From being the Earl of Stamford's second in command and the parliamentarian hero of the siege of Gloucester in the first civil war Edward Massey became a royalist and surrendered to Lord Grey of Groby at Bradgate following defeat at Worcester in 1651 in the third civil war. The artist is unknown but this contemporary engraving, showing Massey from the time of the first civil war, appears in Josiah Ricraft's 'A Survey of England's Champions'.

43. THOMAS, LORD GREY OF GROBY, WITH PAGE

This portrait of 'this celebrated Parliamentary General', accompanied by a page, gives an impression of both his relatively short stature and his aristocratic bearing. It was probably painted between 1646 and 1653. The artist is unknown. It was later copied by T. Athow in a watercolour version from the original oil painting which was at Fawsley House in Northamptonshire at the time. The Athow version shows clearly a body of cavalry in the landscape to the left of the two figures. The portrait is reproduced by kind permission of Sotheby's and by courtesy of the National Portrait Gallery, London.

44. ANCHITEL GREY (1624-1702)

Anchitel Grey was the second of Henry Grey, first Earl of Stamford's four sons. Unlike his elder brother, Thomas, he appears to have been pro-royalist, being active in that cause in the West Country. Together with his father he took part in Booth's Rebellion (named after his brother-in-law). Later he became a noted parliamentary reporter. He was the author of Grey's Debates (published in 1763), detailing House of Commons debates from 1667 to 1694. He was married to Anne Willoughby, daughter of Sir Henry Willoughby, and the widow of Sir Thomas Aston. The portrait, from the studio of Peter Lely, is reproduced by courtesy of Dunham Massey, The Stamford Collection (The National Trust) : photograph Courtauld Institute of Art.

45. UNKNOWN SUBJECT - PROBABLY JOHN GREY

The subject of this portrait, from the late 1650s, was previously thought to be Sir George Booth and it was regarded as a companion picture for that of his wife, Lady Elizabeth Booth (nee Grey) - see earlier portrait. It is now thought that it is of one of her brothers, most likely John Grey, as he differs from the other three in their own clearly identified portraits. Certainly Elizabeth, Mary, Anchitel, Leonard, and John seem to have shared the same 'Rossetti -like'

501

hair. After his nephew, the second Earl of Stamford, died without surviving heirs the title was inherited by John's son, Harry, who lived at Enville in Staffordshire. The portrait, by Peter Lely, is reproduced by courtesy of Dunham Massey, The Stamford Collection (The National Trust) : photograph Courtauld Institute of Art.

46. LEONARD GREY

Leonard Grey was the fourth and youngest son of the Earl and Countess of Stamford. Like his eldest brother, Thomas, Lord Grey of Groby, Leonard was a supporter of the parliamentarian cause. This portrait, by Peter Lely whose monogram (PL) appears, is reproduced by courtesy of the National Portrait Gallery, London.

47. DIANA BRUCE (nee GREY), LATER COUNTESS OF AILESBURY

Diana Grey, the second eldest of Lord Grey of Groby's sisters, married Robert Bruce in February 1646. Bruce inherited the title of second Earl of Elgin and, following the Restoration, in 1663 was created first Earl of Ailesbury. The Earl of Stamford appears to have been on very friendly terms with him. Despite Peter Lely's rather less than flattering portrait, (compared to those of her siblings also depicted in this book) Diana and her husband enjoyed a fruitful union, producing no less than eight sons and nine daughters! This portrait is reproduced by courtesy of the National Portrait Gallery, London.

48. MARY GREY

This attractive portrait is of Lord Grey of Groby's youngest (despite the inscription) sister, Mary, who married a William Sulyarde Esq. Painted in the style of Caspar Netscher, this portrait is reproduced by courtesy of the owner (Private Collection) : photograph Courtauld Institute of Art.

49. CROMWELL'S DISSOLUTION OF THE RUMP OF THE LONG PARLIAMENT, 20th APRIL 1653

This is the act that almost certainly turned Lord Grey of Groby, and other supporters of the Republic or the Commonwealth, against Oliver Cromwell. According to contemporary accounts Cromwell was not as smartly dressed on the day as he is portrayed here.

This imaginative nineteenth century painting of the incident by Benjamin West (1738-1820) is reproduced by courtesy of the Mary Evans Picture Library.

50. LORD PROTECTOR OLIVER I

This portrait of Lord Protector Oliver Cromwell by William Fairthorne appeared in a publication in 1656. Together with the Arms of the Cromwellian Protectorate with their strong monarchical connotations, also featured here, it illustrates just what Commonwealthmen like Lord Grey of Groby, Henry Marten, Edmund Ludlow,

Algernon Sidney, and John Hutchinson objected to.
This portrait is reproduced by courtesy of Cambridge University Library.

51. EDMUND LUDLOW

Starting the civil war as a member of the Earl of Essex's Lifeguard of Horse this lawyer and MP rose to become a parliamentarian cavalry commander. Involved in the 'coup' and the revolutionary junta which included Ireton and Grey in the 1648/49 period, he was a republican and regicide and a firm supporter of the Commonwealth. He was sent to Ireland by Cromwell and kept there to remove him from domestic politics. He seems to have been a colleague and admirer of Lord Grey of Groby. At the Restoration he escaped to Switzerland where he eventually died peacefully and in freedom. This engraving by an unknown artist is reproduced by permission of the National Portrait Gallery, London.

52. COLONEL FRANCIS HACKER

Originally from a Nottinghamshire royalist family, (his brother Rowland was with Henry Hastings), Francis Hacker moved to Leicestershire where he became a captain in Lord Grey of Groby's Regiment of Horse. He commanded the garrison at Kirby Bellars and distinguished himself in the defence of Leicester during its siege and storming in 1645. One of the three officers to whom Charles I's Death Warrant was addressed, he guarded the king and supervised his execution. During the Commonwealth, the Warrant was kept at Hacker's home, Stathern Hall in Leicestershire. He was a protégé of Sir Arthur Hesilrige rather than Lord Grey of Groby, however, and under the Protectorate he arrested Lord Grey on Cromwell's orders. With the Restoration his major involvement in the death of Charles I led to his imprisonment in the Tower of London. He was hanged at Tyburn in 1660 and his remains are believed to lie in Stathern churchyard. This Restoration period engraving from 'Rebels no Saints' portrays in its borders the grisly fate of the regicides.

53. PETER TEMPLE

Originally a linen draper and a Leicester Committee man, Peter Temple served as a captain in Lord Grey of Groby's Regiment of Horse, commanding the Coleorton garrison in particular. In 1645 he was chosen by the burgesses of Leicester to replace Thomas Coke as Leicester's other M.P. alongside Lord Grey, whose trusted supporter he seems to have been. He was one of the king's judges, signing the Death Warrant, and became a member of the Commonwealth Council of State. Locally he became a landowner and High Sheriff of Leicestershire. After the Restoration he was imprisoned in the Tower of London for life. His estate at Sibson, near Market Bosworth in west Leicestershire, was confiscated by Charles II for his brother, the Duke of York. Peter Temple died in the Tower in 1663. Again, this contemporary engraving from *'Rebels no Saints'* displays in its borders the vengeance meted out to the regicides.

54. **HENRY GREY, EARL OF STAMFORD (1599-1673)**
This portrait of the Earl of Stamford was painted after the Restoration and shows him later in life. It is dated 1673, the same year as his death, and is attributed to J. B. Gaspars. The portrait is reproduced by courtesy of Dunham Massey, The Stamford Collection (The National Trust) : photograph Courtauld Institute of Art.

55. **ROBERT BRUCE, EARL OF AILESBURY**
Robert Bruce married Diana Grey in February 1646 and thus became Thomas, Lord Grey of Groby's brother-in-law. He first inherited the title of second Earl of Elgin and was later created first Earl of Ailesbury by King Charles II after the Restoration. The Earl of Stamford seems to have been on particularly cordial terms with him. This portrait, by J.M. Wright, is in the Savernake Collection and is reproduced by courtesy of the National Portrait Gallery, London.

56. **THOMAS, LORD GREY OF GROBY (1623-1657)**
'THE ERMINE UNICORN'
This fine portrait of Lord Grey of Groby is by J. M. Wright. It shows him as a military commander. In the landscape area to his left a castle is under heavy attack beyond a long bridge. The portrait is reproduced by courtesy of Dunham Massey, The Stamford Collection (The National Trust) : photograph Courtauld Institute of Art.

57. **UNKNOWN LADY OF THE BOURCHIER FAMILY**
Unfortunately there does not appear to be any surviving portrait of Lady Dorothy Grey (nee Bourchier), the wife of Thomas, Lord Grey of Groby, and the mother of his three children, Thomas, Elizabeth and Anne. After Lord Grey's death Dorothy was married twice more and produced additional children. This portrait of a female member of the Bourchier family, painted circa 1650, may give some idea of her appearance. It is by an unknown artist and is from over the door in Lady Chesterfield's Room at Beninbrough Hall, North Yorkshire. It is reproduced by courtesy of the National Trust Photographic Library.

58. **ELIZABETH, COUNTESS STAMFORD (nee HARVEY).**
This mezzotint copy by R. Tompson of a portrait by Peter Lely depicts Elizabeth Grey, the first wife of Thomas, Second Earl of Stamford. She was apparently a great beauty and, in reference to this print, John Nichols describes her as 'a remarkably handsome woman'.

Unfortunately the marriage did not prove to be a success. The print is reproduced from the Sutherland Collection by courtesy of the Ashmolean Museum, Oxford.

59. THOMAS GREY, SECOND EARL OF STAMFORD (1653-1720)
Thomas, Lord Grey of Groby's son and heir, also named Thomas, survived his father and numerous political regimes, becoming the second Earl of Stamford on his grandfather's death in 1673. Unfortunately none of his children lived to maturity. This magnificent portrait of him in his peer's ermine robes is by Jonathan Richardson and is reproduced by courtesy of Dunham Massey, The Stamford Collection (The National Trust): photograph Courtauld Institute of Art.

60. MARY, COUNTESS STAMFORD (nee MAYNARD)
Mary Maynard became the second wife of Thomas Grey, second Earl of Stamford, in March 1691. She died two years after him, in 1722. None of their children survived to maturity. This portrait, by Michael Dahl, is reproduced by courtesy of Dunham Massey (The Stamford Collection) : National Trust; photograph Courtauld Institute of Art.

61. RUINS OF BRADGATE HOUSE - PAST AND PRESENT
1) This view of Bradgate House, taken of the south-western aspect, was produced in 1793 after it had fallen into disuse and ruin following the death of the second Earl of Stamford without surviving heir in 1720. This print is reproduced from John Nichol's *History and Antiquities of Leicestershire*, Vol. III, Part II. (West Goscote), page 680.

2) This modern photograph shows the current view from almost the same angle, illustrating that most of the ruin and decay took place soon after the Grey family seat passed from Bradgate to Enville in Staffordshire. (It later moved to Dunham Massey, near Altrincham in Cheshire and the title of the Greys became that of Earls of Stamford and Warrington. The title became extinct during the twentieth century). In 1928 Charles Bennion purchased Bradgate Park from the seventh Earl of Stamford's niece. He then presented it to the City and County of Leicester, in an act of outstanding generosity, to be administered by trustees so "that for all time it might be preserved for the quiet enjoyment of the people of Leicestershire". It is now a fine Country Park, containing the ruins of the old mansion and a new Visitor Centre in a strikingly picturesque setting, which provides free access for both local people and visitors to Leicestershire.

THE ILLUSTRATIONS ON THE PAGES NUMBERED BELOW
ARE REPRODUCED BY KIND PERMISSION
OF THE FOLLOWING :-

The National Portrait Gallery, London.	xvii,36,38,40,78,118, 119,229,231,281,327, 358,359,360,393,396, 397,436,466
The British Museum, London.	138
The British Library, London.	326
The Scottish National Portrait Gallery, Edinburgh.	282
The Collection at Althorp.	Front cover & xvii
Cambridge University.	435
Fitzwilliam College, Cambridge.	280
The Dunham Massey Collection (The National Trust) : photography by the Courtauld Institute of Art.	41,253,254,394,395, 465,479,490,491
The Ashmolean Museum, Oxford.	328, 489
The Mary Evans Picture Library.	325, 434
Private Collection : photography by the Courtauld Institute of Art.	398
The Beninbrough Hall Collection (The National Trust)	480
Leicester and Leicestershire Libraries, Museums and Records Services	Various.

BIBLIOGRAPHY

A.   Manuscript Sources

Last Will and Testament of Thomas, Lord Grey of Groby.
Canterbury Prerogative Court, Year 1657, Folio 151/1657 PRO.
Ref. PROB. 11.263.
British Museum Library, London.

The will was also cited in full in *Minutes of Evidence*; Dymant,
Fitzwaryn, & Martin Peerage Claims'. (1915), pp. 259 - 261.

The case between the Earl of Denbigh and the co-heirs of the Earl
of Bath.
Correspondence regarding legal action in relation to the late Earl
of Bath's Will and legacy.
CR   2017/L2/32 - March 1645
CR   2017/L2/27 - September 1646
Warwick Record Office.

B.   Contemporary Pamphlets and Newspapers

Answer to the Nineteen Propositions - written by Culpepper and
Falkland, 18th June 1642.
Borough of Leicester - see Records of the Borough of Leicester
British Museum Manuscripts - various
Carte's Manuscript concerning the Proceedings of the
Leicestershire Committee of Sequestrators, 1645.
England's New Chains Discovered - Leveller Tract, 1649.
Leicester Museum Archives
Leicester Reference Library Sources
London Post (Parliamentarian newsletter)
Mercurius Academicus (Parliamentarian newsletter)
Mercurius Aulicus (Royalist newsletter)
Mercurius Britannicus (Parliamentarian newsletter)
Mercurius Politicus (Parliamentarian newsletter)
Mercurius Pragmaticus (Parliamentarian newsletter)
Mercurius Rusticus (Royalist newsletter)
Mercurius Veridicus (Parliamentarian newsletter)
Military Scribe (Parliamentarian newsletter)
The Moderate (Leveller newsletter)
The Moderate Intelligencer (Parliamentarian newsletter)
[All *Mercuries* : Cornmarket Press edition, 1871 - The English
Revolution, Newsbooks & Thomason Tracts]

The Parliamente Scoute (Parliamentarian newsletter)
(*Diary of*) *Parliamentary Proceedings* (Parliamentarian newsletter)
A Perfect Diurnal (Parliamentarian newsletter)
Perfect Occurrences of Parliament (Parliamentarian newsletter)
Present Passages of each day's Proceedings in Parliament (Parliamentarian newsletter)
Present Occurrences (Parliamentarian newsletter)
Records of the Borough of Leicester
The Parliament's Post (Parliamentarian newsletter)
Tanner Manuscript; Bodleian Library, Oxford
Thomason Tracts - British Museum, London (various)
The Mystery of the Good Old Cause (Royalist pamphlet) - published 1660
Letter dated Birmingham, February 22 1643, from Jonathan Langley to jointly Sir Francis Otley, Royalist Governor of Shrewsbury, and Henry Bromley, Parliamentarian High Sheriff of Shropshire.

C.   Other Contemporary Printed Matter

John Bunyan, *A Pilgrim's Song* from *The Pilgrim's Progress*, (first published in full in 1684)
Clarendon (Earl of) - see Edward Hyde
John Corbet, *A true and impartial History of the Militarie Government of the Citie of Gloucester*, (London 1645)
Robert Herrick, *Gather Ye Rosebuds*, (Poem, 1648)
Denzil Holles, *Memoirs of Denzil, Lord Holles*, (London, 1699)
Edward Hyde, Earl of Clarendon - see section D
Edward Husband, *Husband's Ordinances*, (London, 1647)
Lucy Hutchinson, Untitled Pastoral Poem, (circa 1653 - 1663)
John Lilburne, *Legal Fundamental Liberties of the People of England*, (London, 1649)
Andrew Marvell, *The Nymph Complaining for the death of Her Fawn*, (Poem) (1640's)
Andrew Marvell, *An Horation Ode upon Cromwell's Return from Ireland*, (Poem) (1650)
Andrew Marvell, *The Character of Holland*, (Poem) (1653) (Published in part in 1665)
John Milton, *To the Lord General Cromwell*, (Poem) (1694)
Richard Overton, *The Picture of the Council of State*, (Leveller Tract) (London, 1649)
B Ryves, *Mercurius Rusticus* (Royalist newsletter), (Oxford, 1646)
James Shirley, *Death the Leveller*, (Poem, circa 1646 - 1650)

Joshua Sprigge, *Anglia Rediviva; England's Recovery* (Parliamentarian publication), (London, 1647)

John Vicars, *God in the Mount, Or, England's Remembrancer*, (London, 1642)

John Vicars, *England's Worthies (Under whom all the Civill and Bloudy Warres since Anno 1642 to Anno 1647, are related)*, (London, 1649)

John Vicars, *Magnalia, Dei Anglicana, Or, England's Parliamentary Chronicle*, (London, 1644 - 1646)

Clement Walker, *The Compleat History of Independency, 1640 - 1660*, (London, 1660 - 1661)

Sir Edmund Walker, *Historical Discourses upon Several Occasions*, (London, 1705)

Nehemiah Wallington, *Historical Notes of Events Occurring Chiefly in the Reign of Charles I*, (Republished London, 1869)

R.Ward, *Animadversions of Warre*, (London, 1639)

Francis White, *A true relation of the proceedings in the business of Burford*, (1649)

Bulstrode Whitelocke, *Memorials of the English Affairs*, (London, 1682)

William Winstanley, *The Loyall Martyrology*, (Published approximately 1660)

D. **Later Publication of Contemporary Diaries, Correspondence, Histories, Memoirs, Official Documents, Records and other works**

W C Abbott, *Writings and Speeches of Oliver Cromwell*, (Cambridge, Massachusetts, 1937 - 1947)

Marquis of Ailesbury (Aylesbury) MSS

Army Lists of the Roundheads and Cavaliers (1642) - edited by Edward Peacock, (1863)

Richard Atkyns, *The Vindication of, Military Memoirs of the Civil War*, ed. P. Young and N. Tucker, (London, 1967)

Brydges, *Collins Peerage of England*

Brydges, *Memoirs of English Peers during the reign of King James*

Robert Baillie, *The Letters and Journals of*, ed. David Laing (Edinburgh, 1841 - 1842)

Robert Bell (ed.), *Fairfax Correspondence - Memorials of the Civil War*, (London, 1849)

John Birch, *Military Memoirs of*, ed. J & T W Webb, (Camden Society, 1873)

Calendar of State Papers (Domestic Series)

Calendar of State Papers (Venetian Series)

Calendar of the Committee for Compounding (State Papers)

Calendar of the Committee for the Advance of Money (State Papers)

Calendar of Clarendon State Papers in the Bodleian Library, Oxford

Thomas Carlyle, *Oliver Cromwell's Letters and Speeches*, (Chapman & Hall, London, 1888)

Chester, *London Marriage Licenses - issued by the Dean and Chapter of Westminster*, (1646)

The Clarke Papers, ed. C H Firth (Camden Society, 1891 - 1901)

Commons Journal (C J) - See Journal of the House of Commons

(Earl of) Cowper MSS. (HMC)

(Earl of) Denbigh MSS. (HMC)

De Lisle MSS. (HMC)

De L'Isle & Dudley MSS. (HMC)

Diary of Parliamentary Proceedings

The Domesday Survey, 1086. folio 232 a.b.

John Dryden, *Cyman and Iphigenia*

Sir William Dugdale, *A Short View of the Late Troubles in England*, (Oxford, 1681)

(Earl of) Eglinton MSS. (HMC)

John Evelyn, *Diary of John Evelyn, 1654*, ed. H B Wheatley, (London, Bickers & Son, 1906)

Fairfax Correspondence - Memorials of the Civil War, ed. Robert Bell (London, 1849)

Celia Fiennes, *Diary of Celia Fiennes*, (Field & Tuer, Leadenhall Press)

C H Firth (ed.), *The Clarke Papers*, (Camden Society, 1891 - 1901)

C H Firth (ed.), *Memoirs of Edmund Ludlow*, (Published 1894)

C H Firth & R S Rait (ed.), *Acts and Ordinances of the Interregnum, 1642 - 1660*, (published 1911)

William Haller & Godfrey Davies, *The Leveller Tracts, 1647 - 1653*, (Columbia University Press, 1944)

Harleian Manuscripts : British Museum. 164 folios

Hastings MSS (HMC)

Heath's Chronicle - James Heath, *A brief Chronicle of the late Intestine Warr*, (1663)

Historical Manuscripts Commission (HMC)

- see also under individual Manuscript Collections, e.g.

      Hastings MSS

      MSS of the Duke of Somerset

      MSS of the Marquis of Ailesbury

      Salisbury (Cecil) MSS

MSS of the Earl of Cowper
Portland MSS
Harleian MSS
Denbigh MSS
De Lisle & Dudley MSS
MSS of the Earl of Eglinton
MSS of S H Le Fleming of Rydal Hall

Denzil Holles, *Memoirs of Denzil, Baron Holles*, (London edition, 1815)

T B Howell (ed.), *A Complete Collection of State Trials*, (London, 1809 - 1826)

Lucy Hutchinson, *Memoirs of the Life of Colonel Hutchinson*, (Everyman's Library 317, Dent, London, 1965)

Edward Hyde, Earl of Clarendon, *History of the Great Rebellion and Civil Wars in England*, ed. W Dunn Macray, 6 Volumes, (Oxford, 1888)

Journal of the House of Commons (C J)

Journal of the House of Lords (L J)

David Laing (ed.), *The Letters and Journals of Robert Baillie*, (Edinburgh, 1841 - 1842)

John Leland, *The Itinerary of John Leland the Antiquary, in or about the years 1535 - 1543*, ed. Lucy Toulmin Smith. (London, 1907 - 1910)

The Leveller Tracts, 1647 - 1653, ed. William Haller & Godfrey Davies. (Columbia University Press, 1944)

Leveller Manifestoes of the Puritan Revolution, ed. Don M Wolfe. (Nelson, 1944)

Freedom in Arms - A Selection of Leveller Writings, ed. A L Morton. (London, 1975)

Lisle MSS (HMC)

De L'Isle & Dudley MSS (HMC)

S H Le Fleming of Rydal Hall MSS (HMC)

Lords Journal (L J) - See Journal of the House of Lords

Edmund Ludlow, *The Memoirs of Edmund Ludlow, 1625 - 1672*, (ed. C H Firth, 1894)

Journal of Sir Samuel Luke, ed. I G Philip, (Oxfordshire Record Society, 1947)

The Letter Books of Sir Samuel Luke 1644 - 1645, (HMC, HMSO, London, 1963)

All *Mercuries*: Commonmarket Press edition, 1871- The English Revolution, Newsbooks

Military Memoirs of Colonel John Birch, ed. J & T W Webb, (Camden Society, 1873)

511

John Milton, *To the Lord General Cromwell* in *The Prose Works of John Milton*, ed. J A St John. (London, 1848)

A L Morton (ed.), *Freedom in Arms - A Selection of Leveller Writings*, (Lawrence & Wishart, London, 1975)

Portland MSS (HMC)

Records of the Borough of Leicester - Hall Papers, 1603 - 1688, ed. Helen Stocks (Cambridge, 1923)

John Rushworth, *Historical Collections - abridged and improved*, (London, 1703 - 1708)

Salisbury (Cecil) MSS (HMC)

(Duke of) Somerset MSS (HMC)

Somers Tracts VI ; (1748 - 1751)

Sidney Papers, ed. R W Blencowe, (1825)

Ruth Spalding, *The Diary of Bulstrode Whitelocke, 1605 - 1675*, (The British Academy, 1990. Oxford University Press)

Richard Symonds, *Diary of the Marches of the Royal Army During the Great Civil War*, ed. C E Long. (Camden Society, Vol. LXXXIV, 1859)

Thurloe State Papers - A Collection of the State Papers of John Thurloe, (ed. Thomas Birch, 7 Volumes, 1792)

J & T W Webb, ed. *Military Memoirs of Colonel John Birch*, (Camden Society, 1873)

John Washbourn, ed. *A Relation of the Taking of Cirencester in the County of Gloucester on Thursday, February 2, 1643*, Bibliotheca Gloucestrensis. (London, 1823, 1825)

Don M Wolfe, ed. *Leveller Manifestoes of the Puritan Revolution*, (Nelson, 1944)

A S P Woodhouse, ed. *Puritanism and Liberty*. (Dent, Second edition, 1950)

E   **Secondary and General Sources**

John Adair, *A Life of John Hampden - The Patriot (1594 - 1643)*. (Macdonald and Jane's, London, 1976)

Martyn Bennett, *Henry Hastings and the Royalist Cause in the East Midlands* taken from unpublished Ph.D. thesis on *The Aristocratic Estate - The Hastings in Leicestershire and South Derbyshire*, Dept of Local History, Loughborough University of Technology, 1980

H N Brailsford, *The Levellers and the English Revolution*, (Spokesman University Paperback No. 14, Spokesman Books, 1976)

John Buchan, *Cromwell*, (Hodder & Stoughton, 1934; reprinted Sphere Books, London, 1971)

Gilbert Burnett, *The Memorials of the Dukes of Hamilton*, (Oxford, 1852)

William Burton, *The Description of Leicestershire: Containing Matters of Antiquity, History, Armour and Genealogy*, (1777)

Henry Grey, *Memorials of the Great Civil War*

Claire Cross, *The Puritan Earl - the Life of Henry Hastings Third Earl of Huntingdon, 1536 - 1596*, (Macmillan, London, 1966)

Dictionary of National Biography, entries for

- Henry Grey, First Earl of Stamford
- Thomas Grey, Baron Grey of Groby
- Thomas Grey, Second Earl of Stamford

Alice Dryden, ed. *Memorials of Ancient Leicestershire*, (Leicester, 1911)

Alan Everitt, *The Local Community and the Great Rebellion*, (Historical Association, London, 1969)

Alan Everitt, *The Community of Kent and the Great Rebellion 1640 - 1660*, (Leicester University Press, 1973)

David Fleming, MA dissertation (unpublished) *Some aspects of the gentry in Jacobean and Caroline Leicestershire* (Leicester University - Department of Local History, 1976)

C H Firth, *The House of Lords during the Civil War*, (Longmans, London, 1910)

Marie Forsyth, *The History of Bradgate*, (The Bradgate Books, Vol. 3. Published by the Bradgate Park Trust, 1974)

Antonia Fraser, *Cromwell : Our Chief of Men*, (Panther Books, Granada Publishing, 1977)

Fuller's British Worthies, Vol II

S R Gardiner, *History of the Great Civil War, 1742 - 1649*, (Longmans, London, 1893)

S R Gardiner, *History of the Commonwealth and Protectorate*, (Longmans, London, 1901)

Ian Gentles, *The New Model Army*, (Blackwell, Oxford)

M Guizot, *Cromwell and the English Commonwealth*, (2nd edition, Richard Bentley, London, 1854)

E W Hensman, *Henry Hastings and the Great Civil War*, included in Dryden's, *Memorials of Old Leicestershire*, (1911)

John Hollings, *The History of Leicester during the Great Civil War*, (1840)

History Today (Magazine/Journal) - November 1984 issue, Vol. 34. pp. 46-49, article by Robert Lockyer

W G Hoskins & R A McKinley, ed. *Victoria County History of Leicestershire*, Vol. II, (1954)

W G Hoskins, *The Heritage of Leicestershire*. (1950)

W Kelly, *Royal Progresses and Visits to Leicester.* (1884)

J P Kenyon, *Stuart England*, Pelican History of England : 6, (Penguin Books, 1978)

J P Kenyon, *The Civil Wars of England*, (Weidenfeld & Nicholson, London, 1988)

Philip Lloyd & Terence Y Cocks, *Fifty Years - Thirteen Centuries*, (Leicester, 1976)

Robert Lockyer, article in *History Today*, - Vol 34, (November 1984)

F C Montagne, *The Political History of England, 1603 - 1660*, (Longmans, London, 1907)

John Morrill, *The Revolt in the Provinces - Conservatives and Radicals in the English Civil War, 1630 - 1650*, (Longmans, London, 1980)

John Nichols, *The History and Antiquities of the County of Leicester*, (London, 1795 - 1815)

Mark Noble, *Lives of the English Regicides*, Vol. I & II. (London, 1798)

Mark Noble, *Memoirs of the Protectoral House of Cromwell*, (Birmingham, 1787)

Richard Ollard, *This War Without An Enemy*, (Atheneum, New York, 1976)

J D Paul, *Bradgate House and the Greys of Groby*, (1899)

J D Plumb, *Victoria County History of Leicestershire*, Vol. II. (1954 edition)

A L Rait, *Acts and Ordinances of the Interregnum, 1642 - 1660*

Ivan Roots, *The Great Rebellion, 1642 - 1660*, (1966)

Rutland Magazine and County Historical Record

Jonathan Scott, *Algernon Sidney and the English Republic, 1623 - 1677*, (Cambridge University Press, 1988)

W Scott, *The Story of Ashby-de-la-Zouch*, (Ashby-de-la-Zouch, 1907)

Stebbing Shaw, *History and Antiquities of Staffordshire*, (London, 1798, 1801)

Roy E Sherwood, *Civil Strife in the Midlands, 1642 - 1651*, (Phillimore, London & Chichester, 1974)

Jack Simmons, *Leicester - The Ancient Borough to 1860*, (Alan Sutton, 1983)

State Trials, Cobbett's Complete Collection, (1810)

Joan Stevenson, *The Greys of Bradgate*, (The Bradgate Books, Vol. 2. Published by the Bradgate Park Trust, 1974)

Sutherland Collection, Ashmolean Museum, Fairclough Portraits

R H Tawney, *The Rise of the Gentry*

R H Tawney, *Religion and the Rise of Capitalism*, (Pelican Books, London, 1964)

John Thompson, *The History of Leicester*, (1849)

John Thompson, *History of Leicestershire to the Seventeenth Century*, (1849)

John Throsby, *Select Views of Leicestershire* - from original drawings - containing seats of the nobility and gentry, town views and Ruins, accompanied with descriptive and historical relations, (Published 1789)

John Throsby, *Supplementary Volume to the Leicestershire Views - Excursions*, (Published, 1790)

David Underdown, *Pride's Purge*, (Oxford, 1971)

David Underdown, *Royalist Conspiracy in England*, (New Haven, Yale University Press, 1960)

Thomas A Vaughton, *Tales of Sutton Town and Chase*, (Birmingham, 1904)

Victoria County History of Leicestershire, Vol. II. (1954) Vol. IV. (1958) ed. W G Hoskins & R A McKinley. Key chapter by J H Plumb

E G B Warburton, *Memoirs of Prince Rupert and the Cavaliers*, 3 vols. (1849)

J & T W Webb, *Memorials of the Civil War in Herefordshire*, (London, 1879)

C V Wedgwood, *The Historian and the World*, (1942) republished in *History and Hope* - C V Wedgwood's collected essays, (Fontana, 1989)

C V Wedgwood, *The Trial of Charles I*, (The Reprint Society, Collins, London, 1966)

James Weinstock, *England during the Interregnum*

Geoffrey H White, *The Complete Peerage* (GEC) (Vol. XII; 1853 edition)

J Wilshere & S Green, *The Siege of Leicester, 1645*, Leicester Research Services (Leicester 1970)

A S P Woodhouse, ed. *Puritanism and Liberty*, (Dent, London, 1938)

Austin Woolrych, *England without a King*, (Lancaster pamphlets, Methuen, London, 1983)

A C Wood, *Nottinghamshire in the Civil War*, (Oxford, 1937)

Blair Worden, *The Rump Parliament, 1648 - 1653*, (Cambridge University Press, 1974)

G Yule, *The Independents in the English Civil War*, (Cambridge)

INDEX OF PEOPLE

A

Abergavenny, Lord Edward Nevill 8
Adkinson, Captain 158
Ailesbury, Countess of – see Diana Bruce (nee Grey) 196
Ailesbury, Earl of – see Robert Bruce
Allerton, Ralph 366
Allsopp, William 458
Allured, Colonel 414, 418, 420
Anne, Queen 486
Appleyard, Sir Matthew 210
Armstrong, Thomas 449
Armyn, Evers 100
Armyne, Sir William 340
Arnold, Richard 259
Ashburton, John 260
Ashby, George 63, 64, 102, 122, 162
Ashby, of Quenby 26
Astley, Sir Bernard 205
Astley, Sir Jacob 59, 129, 223
Aston, Sir Arthur 103, 501
Axtell, Colonel 314, 455
Ayloffe, Mr. 450, 461

B

Babington of Rothley 26
Babington, Thomas 64, 73, 96, 102, 156, 174, 222, 444
Bacon, Francis 16
Bagot, Colonel 156
Baillie, Robert 213, 227, 267, 511
Bainbridge, John 102, 122, 162
Bainbridge, of Lockington 26
Bainbridge, William 102, 277
Bale of Carlton Curlieu 26
Bale, Sir John 63, 361
Balfour, Sir William 73, 74, 75, 81, 131
Ballard, Col. Thomas 75
Barebone, 'Praise-God' 406, 447
Bard, Sir Henry 205
Barkley, Henry 63
Beaumont, Lord of Coleorton 25, 64, 163, 165, 172,
Beaumont, Mr. 263

Beaumont of Gracedieu 26, 63, 64
Beaumont, Sir Thomas 64, 96, 164, 165, 174, 187, 198, 412, 482
Beaumonts, Earls of Leicester 2, 25
Beaumonts, of Stoughton 26, 64
Bedford, Earl of 364
Bembridge, John 64
Bembridge, William 64
Bennion, Charles 505
Bent, Mr.of Castle Mill 204
Bent, Richard 64, 95, 102, 122, 162
Billers, Robert 102
Bingley, Dame Elizabeth 8
Bingley, Lady Elizabeth 381
Bingley, Major 149
Bingley, Sir John 8
Birch, Col. John 227, 300, 419, 509, 511, 513
Birch, Thomas 367, 513
Bishop, Capt. George 419, 420, 421
Bishop, Col. 421
Blackwell, jnr., Capt. 380
Blunt, Thomas (Commissary & later Mayor of Leicester) 190, 262
Blount of Allexton (Earls of Newport) 25
Blithe, Francis 194
Bodell, Captain 417, 418
Bodenham, Sir Wingfield 171, 274
Bodenham, Lord 274
Booth, (nee Grey) Elizabeth – later Lady Delamere
Booth, Sir George – later Lord Delamere 10, 61, 188, 197, 233, 419,
440, 443, 444, 445, 446, 452, 477, 483, 485, 498, 501
Bond, Denis 332, 333, 388
Bond, Colonel (Royalist) 153
Bordman, Samuel 234
Borough of Leicester 15, 33, 34, 43, 52, 64, 76, 219, 225, 236,
283, 286, 287, 345, 372, 439, 440, 441, 453, 467, 470, 471, 513,
514, 515
Boteler, Major (Butler) 416
Bourchier, Dorothy – see also Grey, Dorothy 233, 234, 235, 504
Bourchier Elizabeth – see Countess of Denbigh 233, 234
Bourchier family 235
Bourke, Richard – Earl of Clanricarde 91
Bradshaw, John 309, 311, 312, 313, 314, 316, 332, 347, 373, 402, 407,
411, 412, 414, 419, 423, 451, 454, 457, 499, 500,
Braham, Lt. 420, 421
Brandon, Charles – Duke of Suffolk 4

518

Brandon, Lord 483
Brereton, Sir William 85, 96, 101, 188, 191, 192, 223
Britton, Daniel 27
Broghill, Lord 441
Brokesby of Birstall 26
Brooke, Lord 68, 69, 82, 86, 87, 101, 498
Broughton, Andrew 312, 454
Brown, Humphrey 209, 312
Browne, John 190
Browne, Maj.Gen 152
Browne, Mr. 153
Bruce, (nee Grey) Diana – Countess of Ailesbury 233
Bruce, Robert – Earl of Ailesbury 233, 460, 462, 487, 502, 504
Brudenell, Thomas 64, 96, 102
Brudenell of Cranoe 25
Brydges 33, 34, 509
Buckingham, Duke of 27, 46, 64, 92, 98, 422
Buckley, Thomas 149, 150
Bunyan, John 17, 81, 437, 508
Burton, Captain 171, 237
Burtons of Stockerston 26
Burton, Thomas 63
Burton, William 22, 34, 513
Butler, Samuel 43
Byron, Sir John 130, 131, 218, 223, 433
Byron, Sir Richard 147

C

Caernarvon, Earl of 28
Cambridge, Owen 222
Campden, Henry 99
Campden, Lady Juliana 195, 196
Campden, Viscounts (see Henry and Noel) 64
Carew, John 158, 329, 407, 416, 417, 454, 455
Carr, Robert 92
Cary, Col.Horatio 197, 419
Catesby, Lt. 99
Cave of Stanford · 26
Cavendish, Charles 113
Cavendish, Lord 144
Cawley, William 454
Cecil, Ann 8, 45
Cecil, William (Earl of Exeter) 8

Chaloner, James 339, 369, 388
Chaloner, Neville 335, 339, 388
Chaloner, Thomas 339, 369, 386, 388
Chambers, Parliamentary Messenger 56, 57
Charles I, 8, 21, 25, 26, 27, 29, 31, 46, 47, 48, 49, 50, 51, 52, 53,
57, 58, 59, 60, 64, 92, 115, 121, 123, 125, 128, 131, 132, 136, 172,
191, 192, 193, 197, 198, 199, 200, 204, 206, 208, 209, 210, 211,
212, 213, 214, 215, 217, 218, 219, 220, 223, 224, 236, 237, 238,
240, 241, 242, 243, 245, 246, 247, 249, 250, 255, 256, 257, 258,
259, 260, 261, 262, 275, 276, 283, 284, 286, 287, 288, 289, 292,
293, 294, 303, 304, 305, 306, 307, 308, 309, 310, 311, 312, 313,
314, 315, 316, 318, 319, 320, 321, 323, 324, 325, 326, 327, 328,
329, 382, 448, 450, 451, 452, 453, 454, 455, 456, 468, 471, 475,
483, 495, 499, 500
Charles II, – also Prince of Wales & 'King of Scots' 64, 355, 371,
373, 375, 376, 412, 415, 423, 444, 446, 447, 448, 449, 450, 453,
455, 457, 458, 459, 482, 484, 486
Chesterfield, Earl of 197, 364
Cholmeley, Sir Henry 264
Choyce, (Joyce) Margaret 320
Christiana, Countess of Devonshire 58, 60
Chudleigh, Maj.Gen.James 89
Clarke, Major 421
Clarke, William 256
Cobbett, Maj. John 354
Cockayne, Lt.Col.Richard 420
Cokayne, George 290
Coke, Thomas – see Thomas Cook or Cooke
Condé, Prince of 423
Cook, John 455, 456
Cooke, Thomas 219, 220, 304,
Cooper, Anthony Ashley (Earl of Shaftesbury) 482
Cooper, Samuel 499
Corbet, John 76, 115, 124, 137, 508
Corbet, Miles 454, 455
Cotgrave, Randle 234
Cotton, Lt. 149, 150
Cotton, Thomas 64, 96, 122, 164, 174, 187,
Craven, Lord William 362, 366, 381, 451
Craven family 381
Crewe, John 286
Cromwell, Mrs.Elizabeth 257
Cromwell, Oliver 17, 61, 62, 82, 84, 104, 105, 106, 107, 108,

109, 110, 111, 112, 113, 123, 133, 142, 144, 148, 175, 179, 188, 192, 196, 201, 213, 214, 215, 216, 217, 235, 239, 240, 241, 242, 243, 245, 246, 247, 248, 249, 250, 255, 256, 257, 258, 259, 261, 262, 264, 265, 266, 267, 278, 279, 281, 284, 286, 287, 288, 289, 290, 292, 301, 302, 303, 304, 305, 306, 308, 309, 310, 311, 313, 314, 315, 316, 317, 318, 319, 322, 327, 329, 332, 333, 334, 340, 341, 342, 343, 344, 345, 346, 347, 348, 349, 350, 351, 352, 354, 355, 362, 368, 369, 370, 371, 372, 373, 374, 375, 376, 379, 380, 385, 386, 387, 388, 389, 390, 399, 400, 401, 402, 403, 404, 405, 406, 407, 408, 410, 411, 412, 413, 414, 415, 416, 417, 418, 421, 422, 423, 424, 425, 426, 427, 429, 430, 431, 432, 434, 435, 440, 441, 451, 453, 454, 456, 470. 471, 474, 477, 483, 495, 499, 502
Cromwell, Richard 440, 441, 442

D

Danvers, Henry 406
Danvers, John 31, 332
Danvers, of Rothley 26
Danvers, Capt. William 64, 96, 102, 122, 136, 162, 174, 187, 425
Dawes, Hugh 458
Dawes, Jane 458
Dawes, William 458
Dawson, Treasurer 365
de Ferrers, Henry 3
de Ferrers, William (see Groby, Lord Ferrers) 2, 3
de Grentesmainell, Hugo (Baron of Hinckley & High Steward of England) 2
De Grey, Anchitel 1
de la Fountaine, Sir Erasmus 63
De Lille, Lady 311
de Quincy, Roger 2
Deane, Captain 320
Deane, Colonel 302, 315
Delamere, Lady (see Elizabeth Booth nee Grey) 188, 498
Delamere, Lord (see George Booth) 188
Denbigh, Countess 237, 336
Denbigh, Earl of 26, 61, 140, 145, 195, 196, 225, 233, 251, 291, 306, 307, 330, 331, 332, 498, 507, 510, 511
Desborough, John 374, 402, 441
Devereux, Robert (3rd Earl of Essex) see Essex, Earl of
Devonshire, Countess Dowager 121, 210, 211
Devonshire, Duke of 56, 63, 486
D'Ewes, Sir Symonds 88

Digby, Sir John 54, 57
Digby, Sir Kenneth 17
Dixie of Market Bosworth 26
Dixie, Sir Wolstan 19, 26, 63, 64, 102
Dixwell, John 454
Donne, John 16
Dorislaus, Dr. 339
Dorset, 1st Marquis of (Sir Thomas Grey) 3, 4, 11
Dorset, 2nd Marquis of (Thomas Grey) 4, 5, 9, 488
Dorset, 3rd Marquis of (Henry Grey) 4, 5, 11
Dove, John 367
Downes, John 323, 329, 330, 331, 332
Downes, Major 368
Downing, George 454
Dryden, Alice 469
Dryden, John 53, 76, 178, 510
Dudley, John (Duke of Northumberland) 5
Dudley, Lord Guilford 5, 6
Duke of Suffolk 4, 5
Dyer, Samuel 419, 420, 421, 432

E

Edward I, King 22
Edward III, King 22
Edward IV, King 3
Edward V, Prince 3
Edward VI, King 4, 5
Eglinton, Alexander Earl of 372, 390
Eliot, Sir John 46
Elizabeth, Queen of Bohemia 9
Elizabeth I, Queen 6, 7, 21, 29
Elizabeth of York 4
Erle, Sir William 250
Essex Col. 75
Essex, Earl of 7, 9, 59, 71, 72, 73, 74, 75, 81, 82, 83, 84, 86, 87,
88, 89, 90, 91, 92, 93, 103, 104, 106, 110, 111, 114, 122, 123, 124,
125, 126, 127, 128, 129, 130, 132, 133, 134, 136, 139, 141, 142,
161, 172, 175, 188, 191, 234, 236, 244, 235, 468, 470, 495
Evans, Edward 273
Everitt, Alan 63, 64, 65, 77, 200, 226, 469, 478, 513
Ewer, Colonel 289, 309, 317
Eyre, Richard 366
Eyres, Lt.Col. 156, 349, 351, 352

F

Fairfax, Lady 310, 311
Fairfax, Lord (Sir Thomas) 104, 106,
Fairfax, Sir Thomas 104, 106, 107, 108, 112, 113, 139, 163, 173, 175, 188, 192, 202, 210, 211, 212, 213, 215, 216, 217, 218, 222, 223, 225, 240, 241, 244, 245, 246, 248, 249, 250, 251, 256, 257, 258, 259, 260, 262, 265, 274, 280, 283, 284, 285, 286, 287, 288, 290, 291, 293, 294, 297, 299, 306, 307, 310, 311, 313, 314, 315, 316, 327, 328, 329, 380, 397, 412, 414, 416, 424, 425
Farmer, Captain 187
Farnham of Quorndon 63
Faunt of Foston 26, 63
Ferrar, Constantine 67
Ferrars, Lord of Groby 2, 3, 5
Ferrers, Elizabeth 3
Ferrers of Chartley (Staffordshire) 2, 235
Fielding, Anne 336
Fielding, Basil, Earl of Denbigh – see also Denbigh Earl of 74, 195, 233, 291, 414
Fielding, Lady Elizabeth (Countess of Denbigh) 237, 336, 381
Fielding of Newnham Paddox (Earls of Denbigh) 26, 61
Fiennes, Celia 24, 34, 510
Fiennes, Nathanial 293
Fifth Monarchy Men 62, 386, 389, 404, 405, 414, 423, 441, 457
Fleetwood, Charles 223, 240, 241, 374, 375, 405, 441, 442, 446, 447
Fleming, Adjutant-General 261
Fleming, David 28, 33, 34, 513
Fleming, Sir Oliver 381
Fountaine of Kirby Bellars 26

G

Gardiner, S.R 89, 115, 116, 270, 278, 413, 416, 432, 513
Garland, Augustine 339, 369
Gell, Sir John 84, 86, 96, 101, 104, 105, 106, 107, 108, 109, 110, 112, 113, 139, 140, 141, 145, 156, 158, 160, 163, 197, 221, 370
George I, King 486, 487
Gerard, Gen. Sir Charles 192, 212, 215, 218
Gerard, Sir Gilbert 95, 168
Gloucester, (Richard) Duke of 3
Gerard, John 64, 102, 162, 174
Gerard, Valentine 190
Gifford, Peter 366
Glyn, John 245

Goffe, Col. William 309, 454
Goodwin, John 64
Goring, John (Lord Norwich) 153, 192, 214, 218, 223, 260, 265, 277
Grandees 62, 239, 243, 245, 255, 257, 258, 259, 275, 305, 306, 329,
341, 342, 343, 345, 347, 349, 350, 353, 354, 355, 385, 386, 390, 441,
444, 446,
Gray, John 449, 461
Green, Susan 63, 64, 77, 226, 430
Grey, Anchitel son of Henry 2nd Lord Grey of Groby 13, 378
Grey, Anne daughter of Henry 2nd Lord Grey of Groby 13
Grey of Burbage (Earls of Ruthin) 25
Grey of Groby and Bradgate 1, 13, 27, 383
Grey, Earls of Stamford 25
Grey, Captain Edward 133
Grey, Colonel Henry 78, 132, 133, 165, 171, 179, 205
Grey, Diana (infant daughter of Thomas Grey, 2nd Earl of Stamford) 419
Grey, Diana (later Diana Bruce) daughter of Henry 2nd Lord Grey of Groby
13, 233, 405, 406, 417
Grey, Dorothy (nee Bourchier) 233, 234, 235, 376, 419
Grey, Elizabeth daughter of Henry 2nd Lord Grey of Groby 8
Grey, Elizabeth – later Elizabeth Booth – Lady Delamere 196
Grey, Forde - Lord Grey of Wark (later Earl of Tankerville) 332, 482
Grey, Frances 4
Grey, Henry (Duke of Suffolk) 4, 54, 7, 11, 13, 14, 15, 27, 91, 151,
153, 178, 193, 202, 203, 238, 376, 386, 411, 416, 419, 427
Grey, Henry, 1st Lord Grey of Groby 7, 8, 11, 17
Grey, Henry, 2nd Lord Grey of Groby – see also Stamford, 1st Earl of
8, 9, 13, 14, 15
Grey, Henry (of Enville, Staffs) 439, 488, 502
Grey, Henry, Lord of Ruthin (Earl of Kent) 43, 64, 76, 102, 193, 203,
308
Grey, Jane daughter of Henry 2nd Lord Grey of Groby 13
Grey, John son of Henry 2nd Lord Grey of Groby 13
Grey, Lady Ann 11
Grey, Lady Anne (nee Cecil) Countess of Stamford 13, 336
Grey, Lady Elizabeth Woodville 3, 4
Grey, Lady Jane 4, 5, 6, 7, 9, 17, 29
Grey, Leonard son of Henry 2nd Lord Grey of Groby 13
Grey, Mary – see Sulyarde Mary – daughter of Henry 2nd Lord Grey of Groby
13
Grey, Lady (nee Elizabeth Woodville) 3
Grey, Sir Edward 3
Grey Sir John 3, 5, 7, 8

Grey, Sir John of Pirgo 7
Grey, Sir Richard 3
Grey, Theophilus – (3rd Brother to the Earl of Kent) 142, 152, 155, 159
Grey, Thomas, 3rd Lord Grey of Groby xi, xii, xiii, xiv, xvii, xxiii, xxiv, 1, 13, 14, 15, 16, 17, 18, 20, 29, 44, 45, 46, 49, 50, 54, 56, 57, 61, 62, 64, 65, 66, 68, 70, 73, 74, 75, 81, 84, 86, 87, 88, 90, 91, 93, 94, 95, 96, 98, 99, 100, 101, 102, 103, 104, 105, 106, 107, 109, 110, 111, 112, 113, 121, 122, 123, 125, 126, 127, 128, 129, 130, 131, 132, 133, 134, 135, 136, 139, 140, 141, 142, 143, 144, 145, 146, 147, 148, 149, 150, 151, 152, 153, 154, 155, 156, 158, 160, 161, 162, 163, 164, 165, 166, 167, 168, 170, 171, 173, 174, 175, 176, 177, 178, 179, 180, 185, 186, 188, 189, 190, 192, 193, 194, 195, 196, 197, 200, 202, 203, 211, 212, 215, 219, 220, 222, 233, 234, 235, 236, 237, 238, 241, 244, 247, 248, 249, 250, 259, 262, 263, 264, 265, 268, 269, 270, 271, 272, 273, 274, 275, 276, 277, 278, 283, 285, 287, 288, 289, 290, 293, 295, 296, 297, 298, 299, 300, 301, 303, 304, 306, 307, 309, 311, 312, 313, 315, 316, 317, 318, 319, 320, 327, 329, 330, 332, 334, 335, 339, 340, 343, 345, 346, 353, 354, 361, 362, 363, 364, 365, 366, 367, 368, 369, 370, 371, 372, 373, 374, 375, 376, 377, 378, 379, 380, 381, 382, 383, 384, 385, 387, 388, 389, 390, 393, 402, 405, 406, 407, 410, 411, 412, 413, 414, 416, 417, 418, 419, 420, 421, 422, 423, 424, 425, 426, 427, 428, 429, 430, 431, 437, 438, 439, 441, 442, 444, 445, 446, 451, 452, 453, 455, 457, 458, 460, 461, 467, 468, 469, 470, 471, 472, 473, 474, 475, 476, 477, 479, 481, 482, 483, 485, 487, 488, 493, 496, 497, 498, 499, 500, 501, 502, 503, 504, 505, 507
Grey, Thomas son of Thomas 3rd Lord Grey of Groby – later 4th Lord Grey of Groby & 2nd Earl of Stamford – see Stamford, 2nd Earl
Groby, Lord Ferrers of 2, 3
Groby, Lord Grey of (Title) 7
Gurdon, Mr. 380

H

Hacker, Francis 122, 136, 153, 158, 162, 163, 166, 174, 190, 202, 207, 208, 217, 262, 274, 318, 416, 417, 418, 419, 432, 455, 456, 500, 503
Hacker, Rowland 158
Halford of Welham 26
Halford of Wistow 26
Halford, Sir Richard 31, 56, 63, 214
Hamilton, James (Duke of Hamilton) 261, 266, 267, 268, 270, 271, 272, 273, 274, 275, 276, 277, 278, 285, 306
Hammond, Col. Robert 260, 261, 277, 292

Hampden, John 47, 50, 68, 71, 72, 75, 82, 114, 123, 477, 478, 512
Harper, Sir John 96
Harpur of Hemington 26
Harrington, Lord Stanhope of 90
Harrington, Sir James 11, 13, 332, 333, 473, 475
Harris, John 250
Harrison, Thomas 292, 296, 304, 309, 311, 313, 317, 331, 332, 334, 352, 372, 375, 389, 400, 401, 402, 403, 404, 407, 408, 416, 417, 419, 423, 425, 427, 454, 455, 456, 457
Hartopp of Buckminster 14, 26, 63
Hartopp, Sir Edward 64, 95, 102, 122, 143, 144, 145, 146, 147, 148, 149, 162, 174, 187
Hartopp, Sir Thomas 63, 64, 102, 122, 162, 174
Hartopp of Burton Lazars 26
Harvey, Colonel 125, 126
Harvey, Edward 454
Harvey, Elizabeth – later Elizabeth Grey, 2nd Countess of Stamford 483
Harvey, Sir Daniel 483
Hastings, Family (Earls of Huntingdon), 5, 6, 7, 8, 9, 11, 18, 25, 26, 27, 29, 31, 43, 58, 61, 62, 65, 67, 139, 179, 200, 274
Hastings, Edward of Loughborough 6
Hastings, Ferdinando (Lord Hastings, 6th Earl of Huntingdon) 15, 18, 19, 33, 51, 60, 61, 66, 73, 74, 82, 83, 84, 90, 169, 170, 171, 216, 222, 277
Hastings, Henry (*The Puritan Earl*, 3rd Earl of Huntingdon) 6
Hastings, Henry – later Lord Loughborough xxi, 20, 21, 29, 32, 33, 34, 49, 51, 55, 57, 58, 59, 60, 61, 63, 65, 67, 70, 73, 84, 86, 93, 94, 95, 96, 97, 99, 101, 103, 105, 106, 109, 116, 122, 123, 136, 140, 141, 142, 146, 147, 151, 154, 155, 156, 157, 158, 159, 162, 163, 169, 170, 171, 172, 176, 179, 180, 185, 197, 198, 200, 210, 211, 214, 215, 216, 217, 219, 222, 277, 365, 458, 459, 468, 469
Hastings, Henry, (5th Earl of Huntingdon) – see also Huntingdon 5th Earl
Hastings, Lady Lucy 60, 76
Hastings, Lord (medieval - Wars of the Roses) 3
Hastings, of Braunstone 26
Hastings, of Glenfield 26
Hatton, Sir Christopher 237
Hawkins, Jeoffrey 149, 150
Hawley, Lord 193
Hayns, Col. Hezekiah 272, 273
Henrietta Maria, Queen 21, 29, 51, 100, 112, 238, 260, 382
Henry VII, King 4
Henry VIII, King 4, 6

526

Herbert, Thomas 311
Herrick, Nicholas 16
Herrick, of Beaumanor 26, 63
Herrick, Robert 16, 33, 508
Herrick, Sir William of Beaumanor 16
Hesilrige, of Noseley 26. 63
Hesilrige, Sir Arthur 43, 49, 50, 54, 76, 102, 122, 139, 143, 153, 162, 174, 177, 188, 194, 195, 200, 202, 309, 318, 334, 346, 503
Hesilrigge, – see Hesilrige, Sir Arthur
Hessilrigg, – see Hesilrige, Sir Arthur
Hesilrige, Thomas 96, 102, 122, 136, 174, 190
Hewet, William of Dunton 64, 96, 102. 122, 162, 174, 200
Hewson, Col. John 309, 352, 454
Highland, Samuel 412
Holland, Cornelius 296, 331, 332, 336, 339, 356, 370
Holland, Earl of 92, 290
Holles, Baron Denzil 28, 50, 91, 115, 235, 236, 239, 240, 245, 249, 250, 251, 284, 341, 366, 367, 470, 471, 508, 511
Hopton, Sir Ralph 89, 223
Horton, Thomas 318
Hoskins, W.G. 33, 513, 518
Hotham, John 51, 52, 54, 58, 106, 108, 109, 110, 111, 113, 160
Hotham, Sir John 51, 52, 54, 58 106, 108
Howard, Capt. 375
Howard, Frances 91
Howard, Thomas 494
Howden, Charles 451
Howe, Mr. 421
Hudson, Dr. 263
Hudson, Lt.Colonel 193
Hunks, Col. Hercules 318, 455
Huntingdon, 3rd Earl of 6
Huntingdon, 4th Earl of 5
Huntingdon, 5th Earl of 5, 6, 8, 15, 18, 19, 20, 26, 29, 32, 33, 34, 43, 45, 47, 51, 61, 86, 169, 170, 274, 427
Huntingdon, 6th Earl of – see Hastings, Ferdinando
Hutchinson, John 54, 106, 107, 109, 110, 112, 140, 142, 145, 156, 160, 163, 217, 290, 292, 295, 308, 315, 317, 329, 332, 354, 371, 379, 380, 382, 383, 407, 408, 410, 423, 442, 449, 452, 455, 457, 474, 495, 503
Hutchinson, Lucy 76, 108, 109, 111, 116, 142, 143, 145, 148, 178, 201, 270, 278, 297, 315, 323, 354, 357, 387 390, 391, 402, 403, 406, 408, 409, 429, 432, 433, 446, 448, 449, 461, 470, 474, 478, 495, 508, 511

Hyde, Edward (Earl of Clarendon) 14, 34, 63, 74, 76, 83, 85, 87, 89, 90, 91, 92, 115, 124, 126, 127, 137, 143, 185, 209, 212, 219, 225, 226, 227, 236, 287, 367, 379, 391, 423, 433, 468, 469, 470, 471, 474, 477, 478, 482, 508, 510, 511

I

Independents 62, 133, 175, 224, 235, 236, 239, 240, 241, 243, 247, 249, 283, 286, 288, 289, 344, 440, 474
Ingoldsby, Col. Richard 317, 400, 453
Innes, Major James 196, 197, 203, 211
Ireton, Henry 60, 76, 111, 213, 240, 241, 245, 246, 250, 255, 256, 257, 258, 259, 261, 283, 284, 285, 286, 287, 288, 289, 290, 291, 295, 296, 297, 301, 304, 305, 309, 311, 313, 315, 316, 317, 318 329, 331, 332, 333, 334, 349, 354, 369, 370, 405, 451, 453, 457, 476, 477, 503

J

James I, King (see also James VI) 5, 7, 8, 11, 46, 64, 91, 275
James II, King 482
James VI, King of Scotland (see also James I) 7, 275
Jeffreys, Judge 483
Jervase, William 95
Jessop, William 95
John, Muckle 187
Jones, Adam 76
Jones, Capt. 375
Jones, Col John 385
Jones, Inigo 315
Jones, Sir William 63, 77
Jones, William 76
Jonson, Dr. Ben 16
Joyce, George Cornet 241, 242, 363
Juliana, Lady Campden 195
Juxon, Bishop William 318

K

Kelyng, Lord Chief Justice 457
Kenyon, John 91, 115, 179, 514
Kerr, Colonel 272
King of Bohemia, Frederick 9
King of Sweden 48, 225
Kingston, Sir Andrew 156, 197
Knox, John 48

L

Lacy of Melton Mowbray 26
Lambe, Sir John 30, 155
Lambert, John 262, 264, 266, 268, 270, 271, 272, 273, 274, 375, 402, 403, 405, 406, 441, 443, 446, 447, 454
Langdale, Sir Marmaduke 186, 198, 202, 215, 266, 267, 268, 287
Langley, John 450, 468
Langley, Jonathan 508
Laud, William (Archbishop of Canterbury) 14, 30, 46, 47, 49, 175, 191
Lauderdale, Earl of 247, 376
Lawson, Captain – later Vice-Admiral 418, 420, 421, 425
Le Fleming, S.H. 462, 511
Leicester Corporation 7, 27, 460
Leicester, Earl of – see Sidney, Philip
Leicester, High Sheriff of 6
Leicester, Steward of the Honor of 6
Leland, John 4, 5, 9
Lenthall, William 99, 113, 247, 295, 304
Leslie, General Alexander 31, 48, 372, 376
Levellers 62, 240, 243, 244, 245, 247, 255, 258, 259, 284, 285, 287, 288, 289, 304, 305, 306, 335, 340, 341, 342, 343, 344, 346, 347, 348, 349, 350, 351, 352, 353, 354, 355, 356, 385, 386, 407, 410, 412, 414, 415, 416, 417, 423, 468, 474, 500, 512
Liddell, Dr. 48
Lilburne, John 236, 240, 243, 245, 295, 304, 305, 323, 342, 343, 344, 345, 346, 347, 348, 354, 355, 385, 386, 407, 414, 415, 455, 500, 508, 515
Lilburne, Robert 272, 276
Lilly, William 92
Lindsey, Earl of 59
Lisle, Col. George 205, 265, 276
Lisle, Commissioner 312
Lisle, John 313, 331, 338, 454
Lisle, Lord 311, 390, 424, 433, 451
Lister of Thorpe Arnold 26
Lister, Sir Martin 102, 122, 162, 174, 188
Littlebury, John 174
Lockier, Robert 348, 349
London apprentices 30, 124, 261, 457
London Committee 71
London Militia 50, 240
Long, Walter 192

Lord Ferrers 2, 3
Lord Ferrers of Groby 2, 3
Love, Nicholas 313, 402
Lucas, Col.Gervase 97, 146, 147, 176
Lucas, Sir Charles 64, 265
Lucas, Sir Jarvis 221
Ludlam, Richard 58, 64, 94, 96, 100, 102, 109, 122, 141, 142, 157, 162, 174, 200, 458, 459, 473
Ludlow, Edmund 214, 247, 249, 251, 271, 278, 283, 284, 289, 290, 291, 294, 295, 296, 297, 298, 301, 304, 309, 317, 322, 331, 332, 339, 340, 343, 346, 347, 356, 369, 371, 375, 376, 385, 387, 390, 391, 400, 402, 407, 412, 414, 423, 425, 426, 428, 429, 432, 433, 451, 454, 474, 475, 478, 503, 510, 511
Luke, Sir Oliver 161, 167
Luke, Sir Samuel 102, 105, 113, 116, 122, 136, 137, 139, 142, 160, 161, 164, 167, 172, 179, 180, 188, 192, 193, 212, 214, 225, 227, 236, 511
Lunsford, Capt. 57

M

Mackworth, Gustavus 440, 443, 445, 451, 452
Mackworth, Mary 440
Mackworth, Bourchier 440
Macky 487
Maddox, Daniel 73, 109, 129
Mainwaring, Captain 152
Manchester, Earl of – see Mandeville, Lord
Mandeville, Lord – Earl of Manchester 28, 50, 83, 84, 87, 100, 123, 142, 144, 175, 188, 235, 245, 247, 250, 290, 291
Manners of Belvoir 25
Manners family, (Dukes of Rutland) 64
Manners, Lady Grace 364
Manwaring, Col. Edward 272, 273
Marquis of Dorset 406
Marquis of Dorset (Henry Grey) 4
Marquis of Dorset (Thomas Grey) 3, 4, 7, 9, 11
Marten, Henry 301, 303, 306, 309, 310, 311, 313, 316, 317, 329, 335, 338, 339, 342, 343, 345, 346, 349, 353, 354, 362, 369, 371, 384, 385, 387, 407, 419, 423, 455, 474, 476, 500, 503
Martyn, James 361
Marvell, Andrew 77, 370, 389, 390, 391, 477, 478, 508
Mary, Princess 4
Mary, Queen 5, 6

Massey, Edward 89, 96, 98, 123, 124, 125, 128, 136, 199, 218, 244, 245, 248, 277, 376, 377, 378, 379, 391, 501
Massey, Richard 428, 439
Matthews, Simon 73
Maurice, Prince 89, 213, 218, 219
Mawson, Humphrey 428, 439
May, Thomas 43
Maynard, Joseph 485
Maynard, Mary – later Mary Grey 3rd Countess of Stamford 485, 505
Mazarin, Cardinal 367
McKinley, R.A. 33, 513, 515
Meldrum, Sir John 73, 75, 111, 112, 113, 144, 145, 146, 147, 148, 178, 496
Mercer, W 28
Merrick, Sir John 70
Merry, Thomas 64, 96
Mildmay, Sir Walter 21, 332, 451
Middleton, John 130, 266, 267, 376
Middleton, Sir Thomas 188
Milton, John 14, 16
Monck, George 405, 415, 427, 446, 447, 448, 450, 454, 461
Monckton, Sir Philip 264
Monmouth, Duke of 483
Montague, Col. Edward 213
Montagu, Edward – Earl of Sandwich 452
Montgomery, Maj.Gen. Robert 372, 390
Morrill, John 76, 226, 514
Mounson, Lord 309, 339, 451
Munro, Sir George 267

N

Needham, Col. John 217, 222
Neville, Henry 335, 339, 369, 388, 424, 475, 476
Nevills of Nevill Holt 63
Newcastle Earl of 97, 100, 107, 108, 110, 112, 113, 116, 123, 139, 140, 144, 153, 470
Nicholas, Mr. St. 406
Nicholas, Sir Edward 84, 95, 103, 109, 116, 136
Nichols, John 12, 33, 76, 77, 179, 180, 204, 225, 226, 227, 273, 278, 279, 471, 474, 478, 482, 484, 486, 505, 514
Noble, Mark 91, 115, 125, 133, 135, 137, 274, 278, 298, 300, 319, 322, 323, 366, 390, 411, 418, 427, 432, 433, 437, 439, 457, 461, 462, 471, 472, 474, 478, 493, 514

Noel, Baptist (Viscount Campden) 98, 99
Noel, Sir Edward (Viscount Campden) 98
Noel, Henry of North Luffenham 98
Noel, Viscount Campden 97, 99, 100, 116, 196
Noel, William 100, 167
Noel's of Rutland 100, 196
Norrice, John 383, 384
Norris, Christopher 458
Northampton Earl of 70, 94, 95, 101, 103, 145
Northumberland, Duke of 5, 178, 210, 307
Norwich, Lord – see John Goring

O

Oates, Titus 483, 485
Okey, Col. John 314, 352, 414, 418, 419, 420, 425, 454, 455
Ollard, Richard 242, 514
Overton, Richard 236, 243, 254, 255, 343, 344, 345, 347, 348, 356, 508
Overton, Robert 52, 54, 142, 404, 405, 415, 417, 419, 446, 447, 455, 457
Oxford, Earl of 9

P

Packes of Prestwold 63
Paddy, Lewis 361
Palmer, Archdale 56, 57, 458
Palmer, Capt.George 148, 149, 150, 188
Palmer, Edward 458, 459
Palmer, Geoffrey 178
Palmers of Wanlip 63
Pate, John 63, 274
Pate of Sysonby 26
Patsall, Matthew 195
Paulucci, Lorenzo 416, 432, 467, 477
Peirson, Anthony 419
Perkins, Isham 222
Peter, Hugh 242, 455
Petty, Maximilian 256
Phayne, Col. Robert 318, 455
Phelps, John 316, 454
Pickering, Col. Thomas 213, 216, 332
Pickering, Sir Gilbert 452
Pierrepont, William 441
Plumb, J.H 77, 471, 478, 514, 515
Pole, Cardinal 6

Popham, Alexander 332, 419
Poulteneys of Lubbenham 63
Powlett, Frances 92
Poyntz, General 140, 221
Pratt, John 406
Presbyterians 62, 67, 235, 238, 239, 240, 241, 242, 243, 247, 249, 250, 255,
261, 269, 286, 292, 294, 320, 340, 371, 385, 404, 407, 411, 442, 443,
450, 482
Pride, Col. Thomas 296, 297, 298, 299, 300, 309, 317, 388, 442, 451, 470
Prince Charles 58
Prince of Wales 59
Prince, Thomas 347
Prynne, William 292, 294, 297, 298
Purefoy, Henry 167, 193, 332, 363
Pye, Sir Robert (of Farringdon) 203, 208, 211, 215
Pym, John 50, 123, 133

Q

Quarles of Enderby 26

R

Rainsborough, Col. Thomas 216, 247, 248, 255, 256, 257, 258, 287, 350
Raleigh, Sir Walter 12, 16
Ramsay, Gen. Sir James 74
Randall, William 420
Reymer, William 57
Rich, Colonel 425
Richard III, King 4
Richards, William 105
Ridgley, Simon 64
Roberts of Sutton Cheney 26
Roberts, Sir Richard 63
Roberts, Sir William 19, 26, 64, 95, 102, 162, 419
Roper, Elizabeth 237
Roseworm, Lieut. Col. 380
Rossiter, Colonel 172, 173, 202, 264
Rudgley, Simon 102
Rudyard, Thomas 53
Rufus, William 2
Rumbold, Colonel Richard 483
Rupert Prince 58, 59, 66, 70, 71, 73, 74, 77, 81, 82, 89, 90, 96,
97, 98, 100, 101, 103, 114, 123, 124, 125, 127, 128, 129, 130, 131,
132, 134, 146, 147, 148, 170, 173, 180, 185, 191, 198, 200, 201,
204, 205, 212, 213, 214, 218, 219, 260, 496, 497, 498, 515
Russell, Col. John 205

Russell, Lord William 482, 485
Ruthin, Lord 54
Rutland, Earl of 8

S

Sagredo, Giovanni 416, 432, 467
St. John, John 95, 174
St. John, Oliver 133, 331, 332, 338, 441
St. John, Sir Alexander 233
St.John of Cold Overton 26
Sankey, Colonel 419
Saunders, Major – later Colonel 156, 414, 418, 420
Say, William 293, 311, 313, 454
Saye, Lord 28
Saye and Sele Lord 28
Scroop, Colonel 349, 350, 351
Scot, Thomas 306, 313, 329, 331, 332, 340, 388, 402, 411, 412, 419, 455, 456
Sedgewick., Obadiah 72
Sexby, Edward 256, 257, 414, 416, 419, 420, 421, 422, 423, 424, 425, 426, 427, 428, 432
Shaftesbury, Earl of – see Anthony Ashley Cooper
Shakespeare, William 3, 16, 33
Sherard, Lord 482
Sherards of Stapleford 25
Sherman, William 102, 174, 187
Shirley, James 508
Shirleys of Staunton Harold 29, 63
Sherrwood, William 122
Sidney, Algernon 308, 334, 335, 356, 369, 401, 422, 423, 424, 425, 433, 473, 475, 478, 485, 500, 503, 512, 514
Sidney, Philip (Earl of Leicester) 308, 328
Sidney, Sir Philip 91
Simmons, Jack 34, 76, 226, 514
Skeffington of Skeffington 26
Skeffington Sir John 63
Skippon, Sir Phillip 130, 131, 175, 240, 268, 274, 278, 297, 302, 332, 388
Skipwith, Sir Henry of Cotes 26, 47, 56, 63, 99
Smalley, Francis 173, 190
Smalley Jnr. Francis 102
Smith of Cold Overton 26

Smith, Edward of Edmundthorpe 318, 406
Smith, Dr. Thomas 452
Smith, George 366
Smith, Henry of Rutland 174, 318, 334, 454
Smith, James 322
Smith, John 95, 174
Smith, Lt. 211
Smith, Lucy Toulmin 510
Smith, of Edmundthorpe 26
Smith, of Queniborough 26
Smith, of Swithland 30, 31
Smith, Oliver 133, 306, 308, 377
Smith, Sir Alexander 233
Smith, Sir Charles 366
Smith, Sir Charles of Wooton 326
Smith, Sir Roger 102, 174
Smith, St. John 307
Smyth, Henry of Leicestershire 339, 369
Snead, Ralph 364
Stafford, John 174, 220
Stamford, Earls of 25
Stamford Earl of, Henry Grey (2nd Lord Grey of Groby) 13, 15, 18, 19, 27, 28, 29, 31, 34, 43, 47, 49, 51, 52, 53, 54, 55, 56, 57, 58, 61, 66, 72, 73, 84, 86, 87, 88, 89, 90, 91, 92, 95, 97, 102, 114, 123, 139, 141, 150, 154, 171, 194, 195, 200, 233, 235, 236, 250, 274, 290, 296, 308, 324, 326, 327, 328, 334, 336, 356, 358, 360, 365, 378, 379, 383, 384, 386, 387, 389, 397, 402, 403, 405, 411, 413, 416, 417, 419, 420, 427
Stanforth, Parliamentary Messenger 56, 57
Stanhope, Arthur 449
Stanhope, Lord of Harrington 90
Stanley, William 64, 96, 100, 102, 122, 162, 173, 174, 190, 200, 430, 459
Staples, William 458
Stapleton, Sir Philip 73, 74, 130, 131, 133, 134, 135, 136, 161, 236, 245, 250, 343
Staremore, George 362
Staremore of Frolesworth 26
Staveley, Arthur 64, 96, 102, 122, 136, 153, 162, 174, 201, 458
Staveley, Thomas 153
Stephens, Edward 300
Stevens, Lt. 159
Stirke, Revd. Thomas 13

Stirke, Thomas Jnr. 66
Strafford, Earl of (Thomas Wentworth) 8, 9
Strode, William 50
Suffolk, (Frances), Duchess of 5
Sulyarde, (nee Grey) Mary 502
Sulyarde, William 502
Swift, Dean 487
Swynfen, John 190, 286
Swynfen, William 149
Symonds, Richard 23, 34, 179, 197, 198, 199, 200, 205, 207, 215, 222, 225, 226, 227, 512

T

Talbot, Colonel 423
Talbot, Father Peter 423
Tawney, R.H 28
Temple, Peter 64, 95, 102, 122, 141, 162, 174, 176, 177, 190, 196, 197, 220, 262, 304, 309, 317, 318, 365, 455, 502, 504
Throsbie, Thomas 215
Throsby, John 214, 227, 320, 323, 515
Thurloe, John 413, 418, 426, 427, 432, 451, 512
Trained Bands 49, 50, 51, 52, 53, 54, 55, 56, 57, 82, 124, 128, 130, 131, 133, 134, 200, 244, 246, 247, 248, 260, 297
Tudor, Henry 4
Turpins of Knaptoft 63
Turvilles of Aston Flamville 63

U

Ulf, 1
Uvedale, Sir Thomas 92

V

Vane, Sir Henry 133, 235, 241, 286, 294, 304, 308, 331, 334, 335, 400, 401, 407, 424, 441, 457, 473, 476
Vane, Sir Francis 364
Venn, Captain 54, 67
Venner, Thomas 425, 428, 429, 457
Vere, Sir Horace 9, 92
Vermuyden, Colonel 202, 203
Vernays of Claydon 61
Vicars, John 76, 87, 115, 178, 213, 221, 222, 227, 494, 495, 498, 509
Villiers, George (Duke of Buckingham) 27
Villiers of Brooksby 26, 27, 63

W

Wadland, Master 194, 217

Walker, Clement 362, 366, 367, 390, 471, 473, 478, 509

Walker, Robert 493, 495, 500

Walker, Sir Edmund 509

Walker, Sir Edward 7, 209

Waller, Sir Hardress 262, 286, 287, 293, 296, 315

Waller, Sir William 74, 114, 123, 124, 129, 188, 244, 245, 248, 377, 500

Walsingham, Sir Francis 91

Walwyn, William 243, 347

Waite, Col. Thomas 263, 274, 309, 317, 318, 362, 455

Waite, Henry 455

Wayte, Thomas – see Thomas Waite

Ward, R. 76, 509

Ward, William 141, 459

Wark, Lord Grey of 331, 332, 338, 482

Warner, Master 151

Warwick the Kingmaker 3

Welch, Dr. 48

Wentworth, Col. 9

Wentworth, Thomas (Earl of Strafford) 8, 9, 33, 46

West, Capt. 171

Whalley, Edward 159, 309, 316, 317, 429, 430, 454

Whalley, Sgt. Major (Royalist) 159

Wharton, Nehemiah 68, 69, 70, 71, 72, 77

Whatton of Newarke, Leicester 26

Whitbroke, Lieutenant Colonel 203

White, Captain 201

White, Geofrey 34, 474, 515

White, Maj. Francis 350, 351, 352, 353

White, Thomas – see Thomas Waite

Whitelocke, Bulstrode 83, 97, 115, 116, 126, 132, 134, 137, 161, 176, 180, 186, 207, 217, 225, 227, 298, 300, 304, 322, 329, 331, 332, 335, 338, 356, 451, 462, 477, 509, 512

Widdrington, Sir Thomas 338

Wildman, John 243, 256, 412, 414, 415, 416, 417, 418, 419, 420, 421, 422, 423, 425

Willoughby, Anne 501

Willoughby, Lord of Parham 51, 110, 112, 113

Willoughby, Mrs 188, 361

Willoughby, Sir Henry 501

William, Prince of Orange 92, 485, 497

William the Conqueror 1
Willys, Sir Richard 198
Willis, Sir Richard – see also Willys
Wilmot, Lord 74, 127, 377
Wilshere, Jonathan 63, 64, 77, 226
Winchester, Marquis of 239
Windebank, Principal Secretary of State 28
Windsor, Lord of Bradenham 11
Wollaston of Shenton 26
Wood, Major 377
Worsley, Lieutenant-Colonel 498, 504
Wortley, Col. or Sir Francis 362
Wray, Capt. 99
Wright, J.M. 414, 419
Wrights of Barlestone 63
Wylde, John 367

Y

Yaxley, John 444, 458

538

Index of Places

A

Adwalton Moor – Yorkshire 113
Alton – Hampshire 421
Anstey – Leicestershire 486
Ashby Castle – Leicestershire 56, 65, 97, 214, 219, 221, 222, 262, 274
Ashby-de-la-Zouch – Leicestershire 1, 3, 6, 9, 23, 29, 67, 86, 96, 98, 99, 104, 106, 108, 122, 143, 163, 173, 193, 194, 195, 198, 201, 215, 231, 241, 246, 248, 250, 251, 300, 301, 303, 304, 388, 515
Aylesbury – Buckinghamshire 81, 125, 126, 127, 487, 509
Aylestone – Leicestershire 198

B

Bagworth – Leicestershire 94, 122, 151
Bagworth House – Leicestershire 151
Banbury– Oxfordshire 81, 85, 96, 116, 127, 172, 193, 349, 350, 374
Bedford 87, 127, 161, 247, 364, 482
Belgrave – Leicestershire 157, 158, 193, 205, 496
Belvoir Castle – Leicestershire 64, 97, 98, 106, 136, 139, 146, 153, 154, 162, 177, 221, 222, 340, 446
Berwick-upon-Tweed 31, 261, 271, 419
Bingham – Nottinghamshire 147, 197, 264
Birmingham 201, 234, 323, 508, 514, 515
Bolton 201
Bosworth Field – Leicestershire 4, 155, 179
Boyleston – Derbyshire 156
Brackley – Northamptonshire 127
Bradgate – Leicestershire 1, 2, 3, 4, 5, 6, 7, 8, 9, 10, 11, 12, 13, 14, 20, 26, 27, 29, 31, 32, 33, 44, 49, 52, 55, 56, 57, 59, 66, 67, 70, 73, 84, 90, 93, 100, 104, 136, 234, 262, 263, 277, 300, 319, 320, 366, 368, 376, 381, 384, 410, 416, 439, 443, 444, 449, 451, 460, 470, 478, 482, 484, 486, 487, 488, 493, 496, 501, 505, 513, 514
Bradgate House – Leicestershire 8, 9, 12, 56, 66, 383, 444, 488, 493, 505, 514
Braunstone – Leicestershire 26, 29
Breedon-on-the-Hill – Leicestershire 28

Brentford – Middlesex 82, 421

Bridlington – Yorkshire 100

Bristol 89, 114, 123, 124, 193, 218, 270, 369, 419, 420, 421, 497

Broadgate – Leicestershire – see Bradgate 2, 9, 378, 460, 494

Broughton Astley – Leicestershire 7, 20, 28, 56, 234, 437

Bunhill Fields – London 439

Burbage – Leicestershire 14, 25, 43, 449

Burford – Oxfordshire 351, 352, 356, 410, 509

Burleigh House – Leicestershire 136, 142, 146, 147, 154, 473

Burleigh House, Stamford – Lincolnshire 112

Burley-on-the-Hill – Rutland 98, 455

Burton-upon-Trent – Staffordshire 1, 156, 172

C

Cambridge 8, 14, 15, 28, 123, 222, 242, 244, 270, 275, 309, 356, 433, 499, 503, 506, 509, 512, 514, 515

Cambridge University 356, 433, 503, 506, 514, 515

Canterbury 30, 45, 70, 260, 309, 461, 484, 507

Carisbrooke Castle – Isle of Wight 260, 284

Carlisle 261, 271, 373

Castle Donington – Leicestershire 6, 25, 51, 277

Caversham – Berkshire 245

Chalgrove Field – Oxfordshire 110, 114, 123, 161

Charnwood Forest – Leicestershire 1, 20, 22, 27

Cheltenham – Gloucestershire 128

Chepstow Castle 289, 455, 500

Chester 71, 146, 170, 191, 192, 218, 219, 221, 251, 270, 309, 510

Cirencester 89, 97, 123, 129, 512

City of London 44, 50, 82, 247, 248, 293, 302, 341, 352, 419, 447, 448

Coddington – Nottinghamshire 147

Colchester – Essex 265, 276, 277, 283, 351

Coleorton – Leicestershire 23, 25, 64, 94, 163, 173, 176, 197, 217, 219, 220, 222, 503

Connaught – Ireland 91

Coombe Abbey – Warwickshire 362, 366, 367, 380, 381, 382, 410, 420, 439, 451

Copt Oak – Leicestershire 56

Corkbush Field, Ware – Hertfordshire 258, 259, 349

Costock – Nottinghamshire 159

Cotes – Leicestershire 26, 47, 63, 99, 147, 198
Cotes Bridges – Leicestershire 147, 148, 264
Coventry 58, 59, 60, 68, 69, 85, 94, 105, 145, 185, 194, 202, 211, 217, 265, 362, 366, 380, 420
Crowland Fens – Lincolnshire 162
Croydon – Surrey 248

D

Daventry – Northamptonshire 95, 212, 374
Derby 22, 86, 87, 96, 97, 108, 112, 139, 140, 145, 146, 156, 157, 158, 162, 168, 172, 173, 176, 187, 189, 192, 194, 197, 202, 211, 264, 265, 273, 331, 347, 376, 419, 443, 444
Doncaster – Yorkshire 218, 287
Drogheda – Ireland 369
Dunbar, battle of 372, 375, 376, 385, 412, 419, 440
Dunham Massey – Cheshire 384, 498, 499, 501, 502, 504, 505, 506
Dunsmore Heath – Warwickshire 69, 71, 73
Dunton Bassett – Leicestershire 151

E

East Goscote Hundred – Leicestershire 23, 65
Edgehill, battle of 43, 61, 72, 73, 74, 81, 84, 86, 88, 91, 93, 111, 131, 132, 170, 223, 235, 496
Edinburgh 48, 227, 372, 373, 419, 506, 509, 511
Enderby – Leicestershire 26, 177
Enville – Staffordshire 439, 488, 502, 505
Evesham – Worcestershire 128, 199, 375
Exeter – Devon 8, 45, 89, 90, 114, 167, 188, 270, 335, 381, 493

F

Fawsley Park – Northamptonshire 212
Framland Hundred – Leicestershire 22, 23, 154
France 3, 4, 83, 223, 250, 260, 367, 377, 416, 418, 419, 426, 428, 432, 467

G

Gainsborough – Lincolnshire 112, 144, 146, 264
Gartree Hundred – Leicestershire 23
Glasgow 373
Glenfield – Leicestershire 26, 29
Gloucester 54, 67, 76, 87, 88, 89, 97, 98, 115, 116, 121, 122, 123,

124, 125, 126, 127, 128, 130, 132, 135, 136, 145, 218, 265, 277, 309, 350, 376, 470, 485, 496, 501, 508, 512

Grantham – Lincolnshire 97, 99, 105, 106, 113

Gray's Inn – London 15, 45, 46

Grobi – Leicestershire 1

Groby – Leicestershire 1, 2, 3, 4, 5

Groubi – Leicestershire – see Groby 2

Guildford – Surrey 255

Guilsborough – Northamptonshire 213

Guthlaxton Hundred – Leicestershire 23

H

Hampstead Heath 248

Hampton Court 82, 249, 259, 260, 376, 381, 422

Hanover – Germany 486

Hereford 72, 73, 87, 88, 89, 192, 215, 216, 217, 218, 219, 221, 227, 235, 270, 419

Hinckley – Leicestershire 2, 23, 151, 152, 155

Hindon – Wiltshire 485

Holdenby House – see Holmby House 69

Holmby House – Northamptonshire 237, 238, 241

Hopton Heath 101

Horse Fair Leas – Leicester 56

Hounslow Heath 124, 125, 247, 290, 292

House of Commons 9, 15, 25, 34, 43, 49, 50, 53, 54, 59, 76, 82, 83, 103, 106, 113, 115, 116, 129, 135, 136, 141, 148, 149, 152, 153, 158, 163, 164, 165, 168, 175, 178, 179, 193, 194, 195, 199, 211, 220, 225, 236, 238, 240, 244, 245, 249, 250, 251, 255, 257, 258, 259, 262, 263, 271, 273, 278, 283, 285, 286, 288, 289, 290, 292, 293, 295, 296, 297, 300, 301, 303, 304, 306, 307, 308, 311, 314, 317, 318, 322, 329, 330, 338, 339, 341, 342, 345, 346, 362, 363, 365, 366, 367, 374, 377, 379, 380, 384, 390, 391, 399, 400, 406, 430, 440, 444, 452, 453, 461, 462, 470, 510, 511

House of Lords 13, 25, 31, 34, 50, 76, 82, 87, 88, 90, 95, 102, 115, 116, 121, 136, 137, 155, 174, 175, 179, 188, 193, 225, 236, 249, 271, 285, 294, 300, 303, 307, 314, 319, 322, 329, 330, 333, 334, 350, 356, 369, 440, 453, 457, 478, 481. 482, 483, 485, 511, 513

Hull, Kingston-upon, Yorkshire 49, 51, 52, 54, 58, 106, 108, 110, 111, 114, 123, 142, 148, 309, 405, 419, 446, 447

Hungerford – Berkshire 129, 485

Huntingdon 5, 6, 7, 8, 15, 18, 19, 20, 25, 26, 29, 32, 33, 34, 43, 45, 47, 51, 56, 61, 63, 86, 87, 106, 123, 169, 170, 171, 175, 222, 239, 277, 513
Hursley – Hampshire 442
Hurst Castle – Hampshire 292, 293, 294, 303, 304
Husbands Bosworth – Leicestershire 456
Hyde Park – London 248, 249, 292, 349, 364, 381, 405

I

Ibstock – Leicestershire 14, 175
Inns of Court – London 14, 15, 22, 45, 46
Isle of Axholme – Lincolnshire 264

K

Kegworth – Leicestershire 264
Kibworth – Leicestershire 56, 444, 458
Kilby – Leicestershire 163, 171
Kineton, (Warwicks.) – see Edgehill 72, 75
Kings Mills – Derbyshire 96, 156
Kirby Bellars – Leicestershire 26, 94, 202, 503
Kirby Muxloe – Leicestershire 3
Kislingbury – Northamptonshire 212

L

Lausanne – Switzerland 454
Leicester 1, 2, 6, 7, 14, 15, 20, 22, 23, 24, 25, 26, 27, 28, 29, 33, 34, 43, 44, 47, 52, 53, 55, 56, 57, 58, 59, 60, 62, 64, 66, 71, 76, 77, 86, 87, 91, 93, 94, 95, 97, 98, 100, 101, 102, 103, 104, 105, 112, 113, 115, 121, 122, 126, 127, 136, 140, 141, 143, 144, 145, 146, 147, 148, 149, 150, 151, 152, 155, 157, 158, 159, 160, 162, 163, 165, 166, 167, 168, 172, 173, 174, 175, 177, 178, 179, 180, 185, 188, 189, 190, 191, 192, 193, 196, 197, 198, 199, 200, 202, 203, 204, 205, 206, 207, 208, 209, 210, 211, 214, 215, 216, 219, 220, 221, 223, 225, 226, 227, 237, 262, 263, 265, 268, 273, 274, 275, 277, 278, 285, 304, 308, 309, 313, 332, 334, 341, 363, 364, 367, 369, 374, 377, 383, 390, 406, 411, 412, 417, 418, 420, 424, 430, 433, 438, 443, 444, 447, 449, 455, 458, 459, 460, 461, 462, 470, 473, 478, 485, 493, 496, 497, 498, 499, 500, 503, 505, 506, 507, 508, 512, 513, 514
Leicester – siege and storming of 56, 57, 58, 59, 60, 62, 66, 71, 91, 93, 94, 95, 97, 98

Leicester Abbey 58, 60, 94, 121, 205, 209, 211
Leicester Forest 23, 25
Lichfield – Staffordshire 87, 100, 101, 152, 154, 156, 172, 197, 216, 221
Lincoln 22, 87, 97, 104, 146, 163, 173, 264
London 3, 4, 5, 9, 14, 15, 16, 20, 21, 22, 24, 30, 44, 45, 46, 48, 49, 50, 51, 52, 54, 59, 64, 68, 71, 72, 74, 75, 76, 77, 81, 82, 95, 99, 103, 106, 108, 110, 111, 114, 115, 116, 121, 123, 124, 125, 127, 128, 129, 130, 131, 132, 133, 134, 136, 144, 152, 154, 155, 157, 158, 160, 161, 162, 167, 171, 173, 174, 178, 179, 180, 187, 188, 189, 191, 192, 193, 194, 196, 197, 202, 211, 217, 225, 227, 233, 234, 235, 236, 237, 240, 241, 242, 243, 244, 245, 246, 247, 248, 249, 250, 251, 260, 261, 264, 265, 269, 271, 278, 286, 292, 293, 295, 299, 304, 305, 308, 311, 312, 317, 320, 322, 323, 330, 331, 338, 340, 344, 349, 350, 352, 353, 355, 356, 367, 369, 371, 372, 373, 375, 376, 380, 381, 384, 385, 401, 402, 407, 410, 414, 415, 420, 421, 423, 426, 427, 431, 440, 441, 443, 448, 451, 452, 453, 454, 455, 459, 462, 463, 466, 467, 469, 470, 471, 485, 486, 487, 493, 497, 498, 499, 500, 502, 503, 504, 505, 506, 507, 508, 509, 510, 513, 514, 515
London Bridge 44, 45, 248
Lutterworth – Leicestershire 23, 151

M

Market Bosworth – Leicestershire 19, 23, 26, 63, 64, 455, 504
Market Harborough – Leicestershire 23, 212
Markfield – Leicestershire 2
Marston Moor, battle of 107, 155, 156, 158, 191, 414, 497
Massachusetts – New England, USA 454
Melton Mowbray – Leicestershire 23, 26, 56, 136, 140, 141, 154, 443
Milford Haven – Wales 369
Moorfields – London 261
Morley – Derbyshire 221
Moulton Park – Northamptonshire 364
Mountsorrel – Leicestershire 146, 160, 178
Munster – Ireland 8, 456
Muscam Bridges – Nottinghamshire 145, 148

N

Naseby, battle of 122, 213, 214, 215, 216, 219, 220, 223, 238, 239, 267, 297, 497, 498
Netherlands 51, 83, 92, 100, 339, 420

Newark-on-Trent – Nottinghamshire 54, 96, 97, 99, 100, 104, 106, 107, 108, 110, 111, 112, 113, 144, 145, 146, 147, 148, 151, 152, 162, 172, 173, 187, 197, 198, 207, 208, 210, 212, 216, 218, 219, 223, 224, 225, 264, 367, 496
Newbury – Berkshire 121, 131, 132, 133, 134, 135, 136, 144, 470, 496
Newbury, battle of 129
Newmarket Heath – Suffolk 241, 242, 244
Newnham Paddox – Warwickshire 26, 61, 233, 382
Newtown Linford – Leicestershire 5, 13, 66
Normanton Park – Rutland 440
North Luffenham – Rutland 98, 99
Northampton 59, 66, 68, 69, 70, 71, 81, 85, 87, 94, 95, 100, 101, 103, 113, 126, 145, 152, 155, 162, 173, 185, 194, 202, 212, 217, 374, 406
Noseley – Leicestershire 26, 43, 63, 143
Nottingham 22, 29, 54, 58, 59, 60, 66, 71, 87, 97, 104, 106, 107, 108, 109, 110, 111, 112, 113, 121, 125, 142, 144, 145, 146, 147, 148, 156, 159, 160, 163, 173, 185, 194, 197, 201, 202, 203, 217, 265, 268, 270, 287, 309, 443, 444, 448, 449, 470, 495, 496
Nuneaton – Warwickshire 105

O

Olney Park – Northamptonshire 188, 361
Owthorpe – Nottinghamshire 264, 379
Oxford 9, 14, 15, 21, 28, 75, 76, 81, 82, 84, 85, 86, 92, 96, 97, 98, 99, 100, 101, 103, 104, 106, 109, 112, 113, 114, 115, 123, 126, 127, 131, 132, 136, 139, 146, 153, 155, 171, 172, 173, 178, 191, 192, 196, 197, 199, 202, 210, 211, 212, 218, 219, 220, 223, 240, 241, 322, 352, 357, 361, 433, 460, 462, 481, 482, 494, 498, 500, 505, 506, 508, 510, 511, 512, 513, 515
Oxford University 28, 462, 481, 512

P

Penshurst – Kent 334, 424
Perth – Scotland 373
Peterborough 112, 123
Pirgo – Essex 5, 7
Plymouth 89
Pontefract – Yorkshire 264, 274, 287, 288, 289, 301
Prague – Bohemia 8, 33
Preston – Lancashire 217, 266, 267, 274, 297, 376

Preston, battle of 217, 266, 267, 274, 297, 376
Preston Moor 266
Putney (St. Marys Church) – Surrey 62, 76, 256, 258, 259, 287, 289

Q

Queniborough – Leicestershire 23, 26, 56, 70, 71, 366

R

Ratby – Leicestershire 1, 2, 3, 320
Ravenstone – Leicestershire 215
Reading 82, 103, 104, 125, 126, 127, 132, 245, 246, 309
Rempstone – Nottinghamshire 147
Ribble Bridges – Lancashire 266, 267
Ribbleton Moor – Lancashire 266
Rockingham Castle – Northamptonshire 105
Rodeley – see Rothley – Leicestershire 160
Rotebi – Leicestershire 1, 2
Rothley – Leicestershire 26, 63, 73, 160, 202, 496
Roundway Down – Wiltshire 74, 114, 129
Royston – Hertfordshire 244, 245

S

Saffron Walden – Essex 239, 240, 241
Salisbury – Wiltshire 33, 331, 332, 349, 350, 414, 510, 512
Scotland 7, 31, 49, 50, 113, 191, 218, 223, 224, 236, 247, 261,
266, 275, 284, 285, 287, 370, 371, 372, 373, 374, 380, 386, 405,
407, 411, 415, 419, 420, 425, 427, 431, 446, 447
Shardlow – Derbyshire 96
Shelford Manor – Nottinghamshire 140, 156
Shrewsbury 146, 309, 508
Sibson – Leicestershire 455, 504
Sleaford – Lincolnshire 105
Southam – Warwickshire 68
Southampton 260
Sparkenhoe Hundred – Leicestershire 22, 23, 65, 496
St. Albans – Hertfordshire 3, 244, 289, 290, 448
St. Johnston – Scotland 373
Stafford 101, 174, 220, 270, 439, 483
Stathern – Leicestershire 456, 503
Staunton Harold – Leicestershire 26, 29, 63
Stow-on-the-Wold – Gloucestershire 127, 223, 449

546

Stratton – Cornwall 89, 114
Sudeley Castle – Gloucestershire 89, 97, 98, 128
Sutton Cheney – Leicestershire 19, 26
Swannington – Leicestershire 23
Swarkestone – Derbyshire 96
Swithland – Leicestershire 30

T

Taunton – Somerset 419, 421
The Newarke – Leicester 194, 206
Thriplow Heath – Cambridgeshire 244
Torbay – Devon 485
Tower of London 4, 5, 9, 44, 46, 242, 245, 347, 379, 428, 444, 451, 454, 455, 483, 484, 500, 503
Turnham Green – Middlesex 54, 82, 247, 256
Tutbury – Staffordshire 154, 156, 221, 368
Tutbury Castle 84, 156, 163, 172, 197, 368
Tutbury Race – Staffordshire 368

U

Ulster – 7, 8, 49, 50, 64
Uttoxeter – Staffordshire 192, 268, 270, 271, 273, 274, 275, 443, 499
Uxbridge – Middlesex 175, 191, 245

V

Vale of Belvoir 65, 163, 379
Vevey – Switzerland 454

W

Wakefield – Yorkshire 107
Wales 50, 59, 71, 87, 89, 123, 129, 155, 192, 199, 212, 215, 218, 219, 261, 262, 264, 269, 270, 309, 338, 411, 425, 429, 453
Warwick 3, 68, 71, 81, 85, 145, 155, 192, 201, 234, 339, 374, 379, 420, 507
Warwick Castle 68, 379
Wellingborough – Northamptonshire 176
West Goscote Hundred – Leicestershire 22, 23, 65, 278, 478, 493, 496, 505
Westminster 8, 44, 45, 50, 132, 133, 149, 150, 161, 192, 193, 196, 219, 220, 235, 247, 248, 249, 251, 271, 277, 286, 289, 293, 296, 297, 300, 301, 302, 303, 308, 310, 312, 313, 314, 319, 348, 365, 431, 454, 483, 484, 485, 510

Wexford – Ireland 369
Whissendine – Rutland 312
Whittington Grange – Leicestershire 2, 320
Widmerpool – Nottinghamshire 264
Willoughby-on-the-Wold – Nottinghamshire 264, 270
Wilne Ferry – Derbyshire 96, 139, 140, 144, 156
Windsor Castle 81, 259, 260, 271, 276, 277, 306, 418, 422, 423,
426, 427, 428, 439
Wingfield Manor – Derbyshire 139, 140, 156, 157, 158, 162
Wiverton House – Nottinghamshire 111
Worcester 67, 71, 72, 87, 88, 89, 128, 129, 155, 199, 218, 223,
322, 373, 374, 375, 376, 378, 379, 380, 386, 412, 440, 458, 501
Worcester, battle of 375, 386
Wymondham – Leicestershire 455

Y

York 4, 51, 52, 54, 55, 57, 59, 60, 63, 85, 100, 101, 107, 112,
155, 251, 293, 309, 453, 455, 461, 482, 504, 514